Career Management for Life

Career Management for Life provides students and employees with an integrative approach to managing their careers on an ongoing basis to achieve a satisfying balance between their work and their family responsibilities, community involvement, and personal interests. The career management model guides individuals through the different phases of their career from figuring out what their first job should be right to navigating the road to retirement.

Expert authors Greenhaus, Callanan, and Godshalk bring their wealth of research experience to the book and demonstrate the individual and organizational sides of career management, allowing an appreciation of both. This material is well balanced by a set of practical tools, including self-assessments, case studies, and recommended interviews. The new edition also includes:

- An emphasis on attaining work–life balance, a topic that is of growing concern to workers at all stages of their careers.
- An updated focus on today's career contexts and stages.
- Material on technology and social media, now integrated throughout the book, to reflect the growing importance of these tools in career management and development.
- A chapter on international careers, helping individuals face a globalized world.
- Greater emphasis on alternative career paths, reflecting the newest trends and helping individuals understand all the different career options available to them.

This rich and engaging book will help individuals understand themselves better, which in turn allows them to understand what they really want out of their career. Those taking (or offering) classes in career management or career development will come to rely on this book for years to follow.

Jeffrey H. Greenhaus is Professor Emeritus in the Department of Management at Drexel University's LeBow College of Business, Philadelphia, PA, USA. He has published extensively in the areas of career management and the work–life interface, and, along with Gerry Callanan, co-edited the *Encyclopedia of Career Development*.

Gerard A. Callanan is Professor of Management in the School of Business at West Chester University, West Chester, PA, USA. His research on a variety of management topics has appeared in a number of scholarly publications. He is co-editor (with Jeff Greenhaus) of the *Encyclopedia of Career Development*.

Veronica M. Godshalk is Professor of Management at the Pennsylvania State University in Media, PA, USA. Her research and publications focus on careers, mentoring and plateauing, as well as pedagogically-oriented topics. Dr. Godshalk is Program Coordinator for Penn State's online BS in Business program.

"*Career Management for Life* is one of those rare books that builds from the latest academic research but is written in a clear and lively manner which will engage students and working professionals alike. It provides a comprehensive discussion of established and emerging career theories, concepts, and organizational practices. Each chapter concludes with a realistic case study and active learning assignment designed to encourage readers to reflect upon their own career experiences, values, or goals. It is a powerful resource for helping students to understand and successfully manage their careers in today's turbulent work environment."

Sherry E. Sullivan, *Bowling Green State University, USA*

Career Management for Life

Jeffrey H. Greenhaus, Gerard A. Callanan, and
Veronica M. Godshalk

Routledge
Taylor & Francis Group
NEW YORK AND LONDON

First published 2019
by Routledge
711 Third Avenue, New York, NY 10017

and by Routledge
2 Park Square, Milton Park, Abingdon, Oxon, OX14 4RN

Routledge is an imprint of the Taylor & Francis Group, an informa business

Library of Congress Cataloging-in-Publication Data
Names: Greenhaus, Jeffrey H., author. | Callanan, Gerard A., author. | Godshalk, Veronica M., author.
Title: Career management for life / Jeffrey H. Greenhaus, Gerard A. Callanan, Veronica M. Godshalk.
Description: 5 Edition. | New York : Routledge, 2018. | Revised edition of the authors' Career management, c2010. | Includes bibliographical references and index.
Identifiers: LCCN 2017061081| ISBN 9781138636446 (hardback) | ISBN 9781138636460 (pbk.) | ISBN 9781315205991 (ebook)
Subjects: LCSH: Manpower planning. | Vocational guidance.
Classification: LCC HF5549.5.M3 G734 2018 | DDC 650.14—dc23
LC record available at https://lccn.loc.gov/2017061081

ISBN: 978-1-138-63644-6 (hbk)
ISBN: 978-1-138-63646-0 (pbk)
ISBN: 978-1-315-20599-1 (ebk)

Typeset in Sabon
by Apex CoVantage, LLC

Visit the companion website: www.routledge.com/cw/Greenhaus

To our families, friends, and colleagues who have helped us manage our work and life throughout our careers

Contents

List of Tables and Exhibits

Tables

Exhibits

Preface

For most individuals, work is a defining aspect of life. Indeed, our happiness and fulfillment can hinge on how well we are able to control the course of our work lives, and manage the effects of our work on our family and personal life. Yet many people enter their careers with a lack of insight and purpose, drifting to and from jobs, or lamenting unwise career choices. For others, the task of career management, because of the risks of not making personally sound decisions, is frightening and full of anxiety. We believe that individuals at any age need to approach career management with care and attention, and must have an appropriate decision-making framework in order to achieve personal success and satisfaction over the course of their lives.

These beliefs are especially relevant in the 21st century. Realities in the world of work—increased job insecurity, corporate downsizings and outsourcing, an overall lack of permanence in jobs, new technology, and the globalization of business, to mention a few—have dramatic effects on careers. Unlike earlier generations, people can no longer expect to spend 20 or 30 years in one company or in one industry. And employers are less likely to take an active role in helping their employees manage their careers. In today's world, the relationship between employer and employee has a short-term focus, often with low levels of commitment and loyalty between the two parties. Further, the rapid global expansion by all businesses means that many (or most) of today's younger workers—especially managers and professionals—can expect to be deployed on international assignments during their careers. Therefore, because of all of these changes, it is up to the individual to be proactive in taking responsibility for his or her career management.

In this fifth edition of *Career Management*, we have changed the title to *Career Management for Life*. The "for life" designation emphasizes how our career is interwoven with all other aspects of our life, and that we should manage our career with an understanding of how our career affects—and is affected by—our participation in family, community, self-development, and leisure activities. The "for life" designation also recognizes that career management is an ongoing process that should be conducted for life, not just when selecting a career field or a job. Indeed, career management is a vehicle for individuals to direct their careers successfully over their entire life course. We hope this book is integral to your successful career management and all its attendant rewards.

Structure and Contents

In this fifth edition, we continue to focus on four essential views of careers and career management. *First*, career management is a process by which individuals can guide, direct, and influence the course of their careers. The model of career management presented in this book—an active, problem-solving approach to work and life—specifies how people can collect information, gain insight into themselves and their environment, develop appropriate goals and strategies, and obtain useful feedback regarding their efforts. The career management model is presented and examined in Part I (Chapters 1–6) of the book. Chapter 1 introduces the notion of career management as an ongoing problem-solving process. Chapter 2 discusses traditional and contemporary views of careers and career management, including how a career develops and evolves throughout a person's life. Keeping with the theme of successfully managing our career across the lifespan, Chapter 3 considers the relationship between our work and nonwork lives, and highlights how we can strive to achieve greater balance in life. In Chapter 4, we present the model of career management that forms the foundation for the remainder of the text. Chapters 5 and 6 apply the career management model to individual career decision-making, covering such career management skills as career exploration, career goal-setting, career strategy development, and career appraisal.

Second, it is useful to view a career in light of different career and life stages. Each stage presents unique tasks and issues, ranging from a young adult's preoccupation with choosing an initial occupation, to a middle-aged adult's concern about a career plateau or a devastating job loss, to an older employee's need to remain productive and to prepare for retirement. Despite these differences, the role of career management is fundamentally the same at each stage of career development: to make sound decisions based on insight and to implement the decisions effectively. Part II (Chapters 7–9) of *Career Management for Life* discusses the different stages of career development and emphasizes the role and the propriety of active career management at each stage. Chapter 7 traces the processes by which people choose occupations and enter organizations. Chapter 8 deals with the tasks facing employees in their early career, and Chapter 9 concentrates on issues relevant to seasoned employees who are in the middle and later phases of their careers.

Third, career management must take into account a number of additional factors, including reacting constructively to job stress, thriving in a culturally diverse workplace, and potentially embarking on an entrepreneurial career or an international career. Part III (Chapters 10–13) of *Career Management for Life* is devoted to these issues. In Chapter 10, we examine the effect of work stress on the individual's career management and overall quality of life. Chapter 11 discusses career management in the context of cultural diversity, with specific attention to the careers of women and men in contemporary organizations, the careers of minority employees, and the career challenges and opportunities faced by employees and employers in culturally diverse settings. In Chapter 12, which discusses the choice of an entrepreneurial career, we profile the entrepreneur; review different forms of social, educational, and emotional support; address issues facing female and minority entrepreneurs; and describe the unique demands of entrepreneurial career management. We hope this chapter will help individuals decide whether an entrepreneurial career and lifestyle are right for them. Chapter 13 is an important addition to the fifth edition that focuses on international careers. This chapter discusses how the globalization of business activity over the latter part of the 20th century and into the 21st has reshaped career patterns and influenced individual approaches to career management. In discussing various aspects of career management related to international careers, this chapter shows how international careers can take several different forms and how these different categories of international careers can have positive and negative consequences for the individual in terms of career management and in relation to the intersection of international work with other parts of life.

Fourth, individual career management can be assisted through a number of organizationally sponsored programs. In Part IV (Chapters 14 and 15), we discuss a variety of career management practices available to organizations and we offer specific examples of these practices as used by companies. Chapter 14 offers an overview of the broader spectrum of human resource activities, with special emphasis on how human resource systems can support employee career management. We illustrate how human resource and career management systems must be integrated to maximize individual and organizational well-being, and we encourage the development of career-oriented human resource support systems. Throughout this chapter, we describe and illustrate career management practices in organizations. This information should be useful to human resource specialists in organizations as well as students and employees assessing employers' or prospective employers' support of career management. Moreover, an understanding of the organization's role in career management can help individuals become more effective managers of people over the course of their careers. Chapter 15 provides our closing thoughts on career management and reinforces our belief that individuals can—and must—take the initiative to manage their own careers.

Career Management for Life is intended for several different audiences. First, it is ideal for all individuals who wish to learn more about career dynamics and how to manage their careers, whether they are students, employees, or simply intellectually curious. *Career Management for Life* was written to provide an understanding of career development and a framework in which career management can be pursued. Indeed, the fifth edition contains updated and comprehensive information on different forms of self-assessment—the ways in which individuals can learn more about themselves, their values, interests, talents, personality, and lifestyle preferences. *Career Management for Life* can be used as a primary or supplementary text for undergraduate and graduate courses in careers, human resource management, organizational behavior, psychology, and education. And it can also be utilized in organizations as a resource for employees seeking guidance in the management of their careers.

Our second audience, human resource professionals, can certainly profit from the material in the fifth edition. It is impossible to develop effective career management programs in organizations without a full appreciation of the kinds of decisions and dilemmas individuals face in their careers. The material on the career management process, the emerging contexts of career management and development, work–life balance, job stress, and the management of diversity set the stage for Chapter 14, which deals explicitly with strategic human resource and career management initiatives.

Finally, this edition of the book was written for our peers, researchers in career management and decision-making. As with the prior editions, we hope the fifth edition helps pull together the most recent research and theory on careers and stimulates additional research in this area.

Learning-Oriented Features

To meet the needs of these audiences, the fifth edition contains the following learning-oriented features.

A Balance of Theory and Application

The material in *Career Management for Life* is theory- and research-based because individuals, whether they are students or employees, must appreciate the concepts that underlie career management principles and techniques. In addition, every chapter offers pragmatic applications of the concepts. It is hoped that readers of this text will emerge with a framework and a set of guidelines that can serve as a career management "map" throughout their work lives.

Mixture of Individual and Organizational Actions

Although career management is viewed as an individual problem-solving and decision-making process, work organizations can play an integral part in stimulating and fostering effective career management. Therefore, most chapters include examples of actions or programs that organizations can provide to promote employee career management, and Chapter 14 provides a number of examples of organizational career management programs that are tied into the overall process of human resource management and development.

Learning Exercises to Help Readers Practice Career Management Skills

The exercises offer an opportunity for the reader to engage in career exploration, career goal-setting, and career strategy development, key ingredients in the career management process. Although the conceptual material can be grasped independently of the learning exercises, the experiential learning derived from the exercises can provide extremely valuable insight into one's career. There are three issues to consider regarding the use of the learning exercises. First is the question of timing. Learning Exercises 1–4 appear at the end of Chapter 5. It is suggested that individuals read Chapter 5 fully before beginning these exercises. Learning Exercises 5 and 6 are provided at the end of Chapter 6, and Learning Exercises 7 and 8 at the end of Chapter 7. Again, it is suggested that the relevant chapters be read before the exercises are begun.

Second is the issue of where readers should enter their responses to the learning exercises. We recommend that you create a separate notebook or computer file in which to write your responses to these exercises. A separate career management notebook or file provides flexibility to add more information to an exercise at a later point.

Third, the learning exercises can be—at an instructor's discretion—converted into group or team assignments. Although the learning exercises should initially be completed by individuals working alone, some instructors have found it helpful for groups of students to share their responses to the learning exercises so that they can provide feedback and guidance to each other in a supportive environment.

Cases to Examine Individual and Organizational Career Management

With the exception of the final chapter, the fifth edition includes at least one case at the end of each chapter that serves to highlight the career management issues covered in that chapter. The cases are a great learning tool because they offer competing perspectives on various career management issues and contain real-life complexities that individuals face in making career decisions. Each case is accompanied by questions that facilitate analysis and group discussions. In addition to the end-of-chapter cases, there are a number of short vignettes interspersed throughout the book as a means to give real-life examples and meaning to particular career management topics. We believe that a major strength of the fifth edition is that it allows students to relate sometimes abstract concepts to the everyday realities and demands of work life and career management.

Implications and Summaries

Each chapter includes a "Work–Life Implications Box" that provides a brief set of the career management "*for life*" implications and key takeaways from the work–life issues embodied in that chapter. In addition, each chapter includes a summary of the material contained in the chapter. The summaries reiterate main themes and give a useful synopsis of important concepts.

Assignments and Discussion Questions

At the end of each chapter, the reader is asked to complete one or more assignments that link the material in the chapter with real-life experience. Further, with the exception of the closing chapter, every chapter is supplemented with a series of relevant questions that are useful in guiding discussion of the important material presented in the chapter.

Ancillaries

Instructor Resources

Instructors can access password-protected resources at www.routledge.com/cw/greenhaus. These include guidelines for all in-text discussion questions and assignments, PowerPoint slides for each chapter, and a test bank containing chapter-related questions. Qualified instructors can visit the website to request access.

Student Resources

An open-access student study site includes electronic versions of the in-text exercises.

Acknowledgments

A number of people have provided stimulation, advice, and support and have directly or indirectly contributed to this edition of the book. First, we are indebted to the many other scholars whose research has influenced our thinking about careers and whose works are cited extensively in this book. We hope our interpretation of others' research does justice to their contributions.

We also thank our students for their enthusiasm in discussing their views of career management and their willingness to share many personal career experiences. Our thanks go to the late Professor Saroj Parasuraman of Drexel University's Department of Management, who provided critical and constructive reviews of selected chapters in the original and revised editions of the book. We are also grateful to faculty colleagues and administrators at our respective universities—their help and support have made the process of creating the fifth edition much easier.

We are also grateful to seven anonymous reviewers for their helpful reactions to the proposal for the fifth edition of *Career Management for Life*. We especially thank Sharon Golan, former Acquisitions Editor and Meredith Norwich, Senior Editor at the Routledge / Taylor & Francis Group, for their assistance and support throughout the process of taking the fifth edition from conception to publication. We are also grateful for the expertise, dedication, and care provided by Erin Arata and Alston Slatton, Editorial Assistants at the Routledge / Taylor & Francis Group, Victoria Chow, our copy editor, and Luke Allen, Production Editor.

On a more personal level, we are forever grateful for the love, guidance, and support of our parents—Marjorie and Sam Greenhaus, Loretta and Augustine Callanan, and Catherine and Lawrence Brooks—whose influence extends far beyond this book. Our nuclear families deserve our deepest heartfelt thanks: Adele Greenhaus, Joanne Noble, and Michele and Jeff Levine; Laura, Michael, Timothy, and Ryan Callanan; and Robert, Timothy, and Lauren Godshalk. Their love and support made this edition of the book possible. We are forever grateful for the love you have given and the sacrifices you have made.

Jeffrey H. Greenhaus
Gerard A. Callanan
Veronica M. Godshalk
Philadelphia, Pennsylvania
December, 2017

Part I

The Career Management Process for Life

Theory and Application

1 Introduction to the Study of Careers

We begin Chapter 1 by recognizing a fundamental quality about career management: Career decisions have their roots not only in past experiences but also in a vision of the future. Encounters with the world can teach people about themselves—what they enjoy doing, what they are good at, and what really matters in work, at home, and in life. In most cases, career decisions are based on the belief that the future in a particular occupation, job, or organization can provide experiences, opportunities, and rewards that are meaningful and satisfying. But careers can be highly unpredictable—especially in today's world. It is often difficult and sometimes impossible to foresee the roadblocks and detours that can arise as we progress through the many facets of our lives. How well we cope with the twists and turns in our career is what distinguishes effective from ineffective career management.

Career Management for Life has two major aims. First, it is intended to help the reader understand the principles of effective career management and to provide opportunities to develop and practice skills in career management. In this regard, we underscore the importance of career management *for life*, which actually has dual meanings as we elaborate throughout the book. It means that individuals should manage their career with an eye toward other parts of their life; that is, with an understanding of the impact of their career on their family, community, and personal interests, as well as the effects of these other parts of life on their career. It also means that individuals should manage their career on an ongoing basis throughout their entire life, not just when selecting an initial career field or a job, because people change, the world changes, and jobs change. Second, this book is designed to help managers and future managers respond constructively to their subordinates' career needs, and to assist human resource specialists develop effective career management systems within their organizations.

A major premise of *Career Management for Life* is that individuals can exert considerable—although not total—control over their careers. Effective career management requires not only keen insight into oneself and the world of work but also sound decision-making skills that can be developed and improved. As we will discuss in Chapter 4, career management is essentially a problem-solving process in which information is gathered, insight is acquired, goals are set, and strategies are developed to attain those goals. If practiced properly, it can lead to a career that is sustainable over the course of one's work life, wherein the person can, hopefully, achieve economic security, stay true to important values, adapt to evolving interests, maintain a high level of motivation for work, and attain personal and family well-being.[1]

The study of careers is a popular area of interest and inquiry. There are a number of career planning and other self-help books on the market, and the Internet provides many avenues for self-discovery and also serves to facilitate career exploration and networking opportunities. In addition, there are a number of career planning activities provided by corporations, libraries, social or professional organizations, and adult education programs. Research on careers also has a prominent place in the fields of human resource management and organizational behavior. The Academy of Management, a highly prestigious professional organization for management scholars,[2] has a division devoted to the study of careers. The American Management Association, an organization dedicated to professional development, has hundreds of links to career planning and decision-making resources.[3] In addition, professional journals have published a wide range of articles on career-related issues for more than a century.[4] The primary reason for this popular interest lies in the belief that the concept of career, like no other, can help one to understand the fundamental relationship between people and work, a relationship that has intrigued scholars, mystified organizations, and frustrated people in all sorts of occupations. Consider the following situations:

- An engineer, 20 years out of college, has recently been laid off in a corporate downsizing move. She is beginning to question her competence and drive to succeed.
- A young physician realizes that he chose a career in medicine to please his parents and dreads spending the next 40 years pursuing someone else's dream.
- A regional sales manager in a small city with many recreational opportunities refuses a promotion to corporate headquarters in a large urbanized city. He enjoys the outdoor life, and his wife is committed to her successful career. He wonders about his future in the company.
- A 35-year-old financial analyst whose employer has just been acquired by an international conglomerate watches nervously as her colleagues are laid-off one after another. Will she be next?
- A recent college graduate has been unable to find employment in his chosen field and has taken on two part-time jobs. He has no idea about what career options to pursue.
- A harried mother in a dual-earner relationship is frustrated in her career because she receives little support from her husband, children, or company.
- A 39-year-old manager feels unfulfilled by a stalled career with no promotions in sight and little job security.

All of these situations require the individual to actively manage his or her career. They provide an opportunity for the person to make an effective career decision or, by default, to allow someone else to make the decision. This book provides a framework for individuals to manage their career more effectively and for organizations to develop policies and practices to help their employees with the task of career management.

Before we provide a more formal definition of a career, we set the stage by describing changes in the world of work and in the broader environment that have occurred or evolved over the past few decades. After all, it is in this new reality—amid a great deal of uncertainty and turbulence—that our careers will unfold and our efforts to manage our work and nonwork lives will take place.

The Changing Landscape of Work and Careers

During the first two decades of the 21st century, a host of environmental factors have dramatically transformed employment relationships and upended longstanding approaches to career management for workers throughout the world. These changes—economic, global, political, technological, and cultural—have profound effects on the world of work. Accompanying these changes is a level of uncertainty that can play havoc with people's careers and lives. Intense competition in all industries has been fueled by increased international business activity and an uncertain world economy. This fierce competition has produced numerous mergers and acquisitions, internal reorganizations, a restructuring of jobs, and the pursuit of outsourcing as a means to contain costs. In addition, the push to a globalized and integrated business world, rapid advancements in technology, an increasingly diverse workforce, and greater work–life demands all make career management a more tenuous activity.

Changes in the Nature of Work, Employment Relationships, and Psychological Contracts

Perhaps the most significant change in social structures that has occurred over the past quarter-century is the rapid decline in job security felt by workers in the United States and around the industrialized world. In this contemporary work environment, a consistently high level of job insecurity and job loss has become the "new normal."[5] The desire of modern organizations to remain flexible as a way to enhance competitiveness through increased cost-cutting and flexibility has produced changes in the psychological contract between employers and employees.[6] When applied in the context of an employment relationship, a psychological contract is an implicit, unwritten understanding that specifies the contributions an employee is expected to make to the organization and the rewards the employee believes the organization will provide in exchange for his or her contributions.[7]

Up until the 1980s, a traditional or "relational" contract was prevalent whereby the employee received job security in exchange for satisfactory performance and loyalty to the organization.[8] A relational contract is normally longer-term and involves a high degree of commitment to the relationship on the part of the employee and support of the well-being and employment interests of the employee on the part of the employer.[9] A transactional contract is usually shorter-term and involves performance-based pay, lower levels of commitment by both parties, and an allowance for easy exit from the implicit agreement.[10] Instead of exchanging performance and loyalty for job security, employees are expected to be flexible in accepting new work assignments and be willing to develop new skills in response to the organization's needs. In return, the organization does not offer promises of future employment but rather "employability" (with the current employer or some other organization) by providing opportunities for continued professional growth and development. As we will discuss in Chapter 2, this shift in the psychological contract from relational to transactional—from employment to employability—has major implications for employees' careers.

The movement toward transactional psychological contracts can have negative effects on a number of employee work outcomes. Statistics collected by the U.S. government and independent research point to the presence of job insecurity and job loss over the past three decades. These statistics include incidents of mass job loss, the numbers of jobs individuals hold in a work career, the degrees of unemployment and underemployment, the level of long-term unemployment, and the low degree of employment participation.[11]

Further, changes in employment patterns and the near death of the relational psychological contract have ushered in new terminology reflective of the temporary and uncertain nature of jobs and careers. These new terms include gig employment, precarious work, independent contract work, temporary service personnel, permatemps, freelancers, and on-demand workers.[12] It is estimated that between the years 2005 and 2015, employees engaged in these "alternative work arrangements" in the U.S. grew by approximately 9.5 million, moving from about 10 percent of the total workforce to nearly 16 percent. Further, this increase in the number of employees in alternative work arrangements accounted for all of the net job growth in the U.S. economy from 2005 through 2015.[13] Within the the European Union, the push toward alternative work arrangements has occurred in a similar fashion, where roughly half of all employees who had taken jobs in the post-Great Recession era did so on temporary contracts.[14]

Regardless of the terminology, the common theme in all of these descriptions is a lack of permanence in the relationship between the employee and the employer. The career management consequences of the mass shift to non-permanent work arrangements are significant and far-reaching.[15] First, when individuals repeatedly move into and out of jobs (or "gigs") it means that they are in a state of constant career decision-making. Each alternative work arrangement carries with it a choice of whether to accept or not accept the position, with a real or implied recognition of the attendant opportunity costs of continuing to pursue a short-term and possibly part-time arrangement instead of seeking longer-term and possibly full-time employment. Second, the individual needs to always be prepared to make an impromptu career decision irrespective of whether that decision represents a fit with the individual's interests, values, talents, and personality. In this sense, a career becomes nothing more than a series of economically necessary jobs without regard to whether they collectively fulfill longer-term career aspirations. Third, freelance and involuntary part-time work lacks predictability, which prevents or makes difficult the ability to make long-term life choices concerning marriage, family, homeownership, and retirement. In this sense, a nomadic workforce and populace develop, with long-term negative economic and sociological consequences. Finally, people in alternative work arrangements often give up the "social insurance" that results from permanent and longer-term employment relationships.[16] Programs such as pensions, health insurance, workers' compensation, medical leave, and unemployment insurance that would normally be available to permanent full-time workers would not typically be available to temporary part-time workers and those in other alternative work arrangements.[17]

It is abundantly clear that the prospect of a continuous, lifetime career with one employer (or even within one industry) has faded. As a consequence, job security, defined as the stability and continuance of one's employment,[18] has declined significantly over the past three decades. Individuals who are just beginning their careers can expect to work for anywhere from seven to twelve different employers during their lifetimes.[19] The decline in job security has major implications for career management as individuals all over the world must be on constant alert for abrupt changes in their jobs and career direction.[20]

Economic Turmoil and Disruptions

The Great Recession of 2008 (and into 2009) had a severe and harmful impact on employment on a global scale. Specifically, employment in the U.S. and throughout the rest of the industrialized world took a devastating hit,[21] with far-ranging and long-term negative implications that are being felt more than a decade after the Great Recession's beginning. These outcomes include: an acceleration in the decline of the labor force participation rate;[22] substantial underemployment and underutilization of the workforce, especially among younger workers;[23] a surge in the number of people stuck in involuntary part-time employment;[24] and a consistently high level of chronic, long-term unemployment, especially among older workers.[25]

In all of these outcomes, the individual is confronted with challenges that require active career management responses because they all reflect a sub-optimal utilization of individual skills and human capital.[26] For example, the rapid decline of the labor force participation rate (the ratio of people actively engaged in the labor market to the population aged 16 and older) to levels not seen in the U.S. since the late 1970s reflects the presence of a workforce willing and able to work but too discouraged to seek regular employment. Similarly, the post-recession level of labor underutilization, which has been stuck at or above

10 percent,[27] means that millions of workers either are not working or are in jobs that do not correspond to their abilities and would not likely fit in with longer-term career goals.

The Changing Structure of Organizations and the Design of Work

To meet the challenges of a highly competitive global marketplace, many organizations have made significant changes in their internal structure. Organizations have become "flatter" and more decentralized than the bureaucratic forms of organizational design that existed through the second half of the 20th century.[28] Customer-driven "horizontal" organizational structures contain fewer levels of management and use cross-functional autonomous work teams to manage virtually every process from manufacturing to marketing.[29] Consequently, as we discussed previously, modern organizations employ a relatively small number of employees to handle core business functions, but use outsourcing and a large cadre of temporary or contingent workers to deal with secondary and back office activities.

In addition, contemporary organizations use network structures to form partnerships or networks with other organizations and individuals outside their formal boundaries. Not unlike a computer network, network organizations link a variety of firms together to provide the expertise, knowledge, and resources necessary to complete particular projects, manufacture specific products, or establish strategic alliances.[30] Some scholars have used the term "boundaryless" to describe the characteristics of these organizations because the organization typically accomplishes its goals through collaboration with many resource providers that lie outside its boundaries.[31] In sum, although bureaucratic organizations, with their emphasis on stability and predictability, will undoubtedly continue into the future, most organizations have opted for greater flexibility by utilizing a smaller permanent workforce with an extensive reliance on contingent, part-time, and contract workers and by creating a flatter hierarchy with fewer levels of management.

Another noticeable change in organizational management is the widespread adoption of team-based structures as a mechanism for task accomplishment, decision-making, problem-solving, and organizational design.[32] The move to collaborative teams as a preferred means of organization has happened at all levels within corporate hierarchies, from the executive suite to the shop floor. Team-based structures involve the "structural empowerment" of workers, meaning that employees and teams of employees are given decision-making responsibility for an entire job or project and for knowing how that job or project fits within the organizational purpose and mission.[33] The move to team-based collaborative structures and the use of empowerment have significant implications for the type of work performed by managers and professionals. Managers and non-managers must be effective members and leaders of cross-functional and intra-organizational teams, and attain power and influence as they gain greater information and visibility through their participation in these groups. In addition, it is more difficult for managers in flatter, team-based organizations to supervise their people in a traditional manner and to monitor their performance closely.[34] Indeed, there are fewer managers in the organization to supervise anyone. And the managers who do remain derive their power from their expertise and the respect they have earned rather than from their position in the organizational hierarchy. Further, in order to advance, employees must be accomplished in self-management as the locus of responsibility shifts downward in the organization. These critical requirements include the flexibility to move skillfully from one project to another, the ability to interact with people from a variety of different functional areas, and the utilization of a more collaborative and participative interpersonal style.

Beyond structural changes, over the past several decades the nature of work has shifted in a number of ways, both in the type of work that is performed and in the way that work is designed and managed. For much of the industrialized world, labor-intensive and production-oriented work has been supplanted by knowledge-based and service-oriented occupations. Consequently, cognitive capability and technological and digital fluency become the skills that are most demanded by the majority of modern organizations.[35] As will be discussed more thoroughly in Chapters 2 and 5, employees in today's work environment need to make ongoing investments in themselves to ensure that their knowledge base and skill sets match those demanded by work organizations. By making these investments, individuals increase their employability over the course of their careers.[36]

Globalization and the Rise of World-Based Organizations

The worldwide fall of communism in the early 1990s combined with the emergence of various free trade agreements and economic cooperation zones has led to the rapid, inexorable shift to a globalized business world. The emergence of new world markets, foreign competition, and political realignments has forced both large and small organizations to adopt more global business strategies as a means to optimize competitiveness. The presence of a global perspective has radically changed the face of business and, as a result, how careers develop within these multinational organizations.[37]

The emergence of the multinational corporation (MNC), with extensive sales revenues coming from operations outside the company's home country, has transformed managerial careers immensely.[38] In many such firms, the route to the top now includes significant exposure to the management of international operations.[39] These international experiences can include expatriation, wherein the employee who is a citizen of the country in which the parent MNC is located works in a foreign country at a branch or a subsidiary of the parent company.[40] In a reverse of this process, international careers can include repatriation where the expatriate is brought back to work in the home country. Both expatriation and repatriation hold career management challenges for individuals as they navigate differences between the home and host countries in terms of language, culture, business practices, and local customs. In addition, in order to achieve successful expatriation assignments and further the development of international personnel, organizations must properly support those employees undertaking international assignments.[41] The management of international careers is discussed extensively in Chapter 13.

Advancements in Technology and the Churning of Jobs

Advances in production and communication technology have changed the career and employment landscape forever. Many careers have been altered profoundly while others have disappeared completely. Newly introduced technology is not simply a substitute for old technology; it is transformative in nature, changing core occupations.[42] Jobs with traditionally low barriers to entry have already disappeared and many more will follow. Examples of occupations supplanted to some extent by technology include first-level customer service personnel, toll booth operators, bank tellers, grocery store clerks, and parking lot attendants. Other previously vital intermediaries, such as travel agents, insurance agents, and sales personnel, have increasingly diminished career opportunities.[43] In addition, technology, in concert with shifting demands for products and services, will continue to create new occupations. The creation of new and more technologically advanced jobs combined with the elimination of old "lower-tech" occupations has been referred to as the churning of jobs.[44] As a technology-driven process, the churning of jobs produces new—but unpredictable—options, thereby making career management even more crucial in the years ahead.

As with other environmental factors, technological changes need to be forecast and then taken into account in career planning, goal-setting, and decision-making. Obviously, technological change is a double-edged sword because it simultaneously destroys industries and jobs while creating new ventures and career paths. What is required is a career management style that is flexible and attuned to the many technological changes that lie ahead in the world of work.

Changes in Workforce Diversity and Demographics

A more culturally diverse workforce has produced changes in the way organizations function. The labor force in the industrialized world has become older, more female, and more diverse. The increasing proportion of women, racial minorities, and immigrants in the workforce has put pressure on organizations to manage this gender, racial, and ethnic diversity effectively. But it has also challenged employees to understand different cultures, and to work cooperatively with others who might hold different values and perspectives. Career success in many organizations can often depend on an employee's ability to thrive in a multicultural environment.

Of particular note, the aging and ultimate retirement of the baby boom generation represents a major demographic and sociological phenomenon that has far-reaching implications for individual career management and for organizational human resource management systems.[45] The baby boom generation consists of the roughly 78 million people born in the United States during the 20-year period after World War II. For individuals who are part of this generation, career management is fraught with concerns and challenges, including dealing with the possibility of a plateaued career, maintaining a skill set that is desired by employers, and ultimately deciding on the timing of, and the financial planning for, retirement. At the same time, organizations must also recognize the needs of those younger individuals who were born after the baby boom. The potential exists for the ongoing presence of baby boom workers, who might be reluctant or financially unable to leave the workforce, to block the advancement of a younger and more upwardly mobile cohort of employees.

Work and Family Life

The management of work and family lives has posed a substantial challenge to employee and employer alike. The neat separation of work and family, where neither role interferes with the other, is now a distant memory. As of 2015, among married-couple families with children within the United States, 97 percent had at least one employed parent, and both parents worked in 61 percent of married-couple families.[46] In 2015, 70 percent of married women in the United States with children under the age of 18 were participating in the workforce compared to just 45 percent in 1975 and 30 percent in 1960.[47] In addition, 64 percent of married women with children younger than age six were in the workforce in 2015, compared to only 37 percent in 1975 and only 19 percent in 1960.[48] The employment participation rate for married women with children aged 6–17 was 74 percent in 2015, almost 50 percent higher than the rate in 1975 (52 percent) and nearly double the rate (39 percent) of 1960.[49]

The burgeoning employment of women and men with children present in the household has created new challenges of juggling work and family commitments. Moreover, the divorce rate and a higher degree of out-of-wedlock births have substantially increased the number of single-parent households—the vast majority headed by women—with particularly intense work and family pressures.[50] Indeed, as of 2015, roughly 24 percent of all households in the United States with children under the age of 18 were single-parent households, and of these, 85 percent were headed by the mother.[51] Dual-earner couples and single parents must learn to balance their careers with extensive family responsibilities, often including the care of elderly parents or other relatives. The 21st century is providing even more challenges to women and men pursuing demanding careers and active family and personal lives.

Work and family roles have also been altered by technological advances, which have blurred the demarcation between these two spheres of life. Widespread advances in communications technology have moved work activities from the office to the dining room or study, and even the most remote location can function as an office. These changes provide opportunities for achieving greater work–life balance but also require considerable support from spouses, children, and employers. Chapter 3 provides an extensive discussion of the overarching work–life challenges for employees.

Definitions of Career Concepts

Now that we have summarized the changing landscape of the world of work, we will discuss what constitutes a career, first presenting its historical meaning and then presenting a definition of a career that more closely fits today's world. We will also introduce the career management process and examine the concept of career development.

What Is a Career?

In Chapter 2 we will discuss in detail a number of different perspectives on careers and career management. In broad terms, however, there are two primary ways to view a career. One approach sees a career as a structural property of an *occupation* or an *organization*. For example, one could think of a career in law as a sequence of positions held by a typical or "ideal" practitioner of the occupation: law student, law clerk, junior member of a law firm, senior member of a law firm, judge, and ultimately retirement. A career could also be seen as a mobility path within a single organization or multiple employers,[52] as the following functional path in marketing illustrates: sales representative, product manager, district marketing manager, regional marketing manager, and divisional vice-president of marketing, with several staff assignments interspersed among these positions.

The other primary approach views a career as a property of an *individual* rather than an occupation or an organization. Since almost everyone accumulates a unique series of jobs, positions, and experiences, this view acknowledges that each person, in effect, pursues a unique career. Even within this individual perspective, however, a number of different definitions of career have appeared over the years, each reflecting a certain theme embodied in its meaning.[53]

Taking these varied perspectives into account, in *Career Management for Life*, we define a career as *the pattern of work-related experiences that span the course of a person's life*. In our definition, work-related experiences are broadly construed to include: (a) objective events or situations such as job positions, job duties or activities, and work-related decisions; and (b) subjective interpretations of work-related events such as work aspirations, expectations, values, needs, and feelings about particular work experiences. Exhibit 1.1 portrays some significant elements of a person's hypothetical career. Notice that an examination of the objective experiences by themselves would not provide a full understanding of a person's career. Similarly, an exclusive focus on subjective experiences would not do justice to the complexity of a career. Both objective and subjective components are necessary. As we will see in subsequent chapters, one can manage a career by changing the objective environment (for example, switching jobs) or by modifying one's subjective perception of a situation (for example, changing expectations). Similarly, the unfolding or development of a career frequently involves systematic changes in objective events (as when a person's opportunity for future

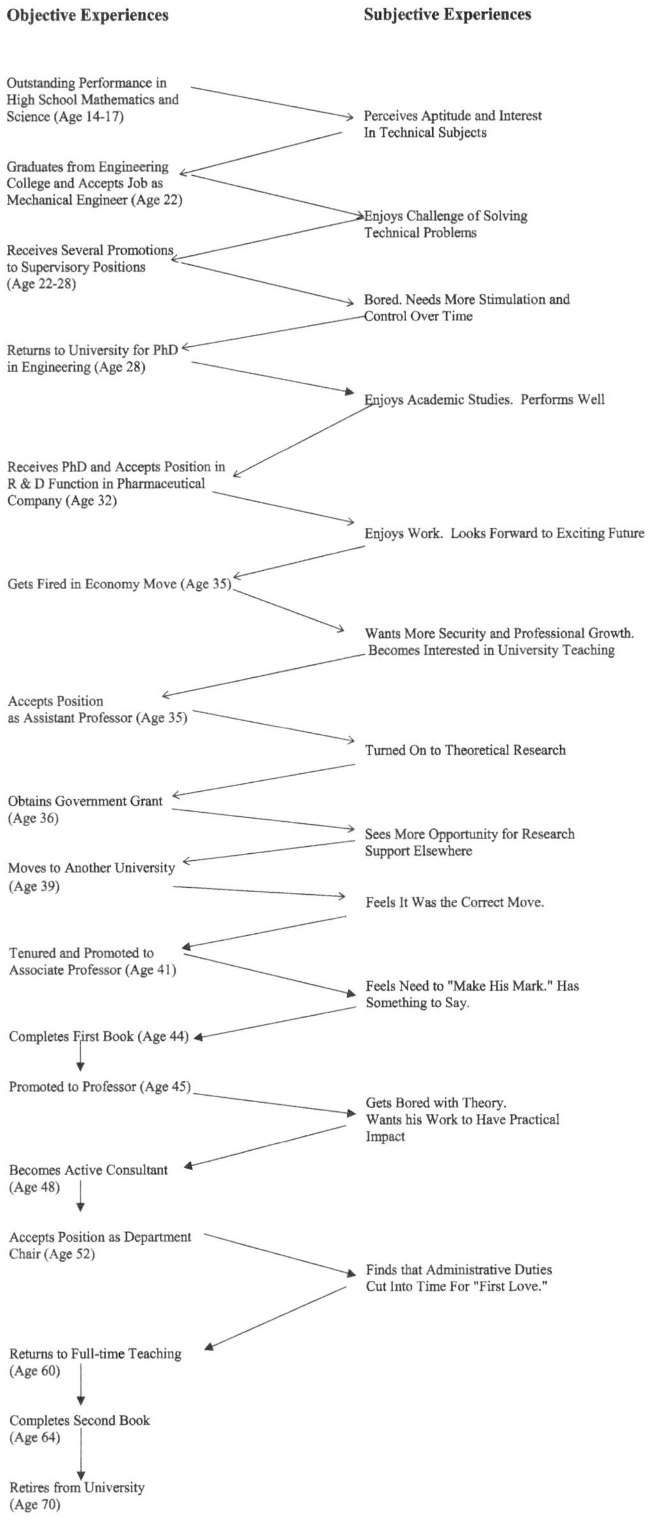

Exhibit 1.1 Objective and Subjective Elements of a Hypothetical Career

promotions becomes limited) as well as changes in subjective reactions to events (such as changes in values or interests or family life).

Our definition of a career does not require that a person's work roles be professional in nature, be stable within a single occupation or organization, or be characterized by upward mobility. Indeed, anyone engaging in work-related activities is, in effect, pursuing a career. This broad definition fits nicely with the changes in the work world discussed earlier in the chapter. For example, the definition's omission of advancement in the corporate hierarchy as a defining characteristic of a career meshes well with the reduced vertical mobility opportunities within today's flat organizations. Similarly, to require that a career provide stability within one organization—or even one career path—is unrealistic in today's world of downsizing, contingent employment, and constantly changing jobs. As we will see throughout this book, individuals need to take responsibility for understanding the type of career they wish to pursue and making career decisions that are consistent with these preferences.

Career Management

Like the concept of the career itself, career management has been defined in a number of ways. We view career management as *a process by which individuals develop, implement, and monitor career goals and strategies.*[54] Because the process of career management is central to this book, subsequent chapters are devoted to the explanation and application of our model of career management. For the time being, career management can be briefly described as an ongoing process in which an individual:

1. Gathers relevant information about himself or herself and the world of work;
2. Develops an accurate picture of his or her talents, interests, values, and preferred lifestyle as well as alternative occupations, jobs, and organizations;
3. Develops realistic career goals based on this information;
4. Develops and implements a strategy (or strategies) designed to achieve the goals;
5. Obtains feedback on the effectiveness of the strategy and the relevance of the goals.

Notice that career management is an individual—not an organizational—activity. Indeed, as we will show in Chapter 4 when we discuss the model in more detail, it is the individual's responsibility to manage his or her career. Many organizations have relinquished an activist role in their employees' careers and are laying the responsibility for career management squarely on the shoulders of the individual. Moreover, individuals will need to develop a set of career competencies that enable them to develop insight into themselves and their environment so they can navigate their increasingly unpredictable and "chaotic" careers. The specific steps in the career management process—and the qualities necessary to carry them out—will be discussed extensively in Chapters 4, 5, and 6.

Career Development

As we will discuss in Chapter 2, people face a number of developmental tasks and challenges as they progress through their careers. The traditional view of career development holds that individuals go through relatively predictable phases in their careers, with each career stage being characterized by a somewhat distinctive set of themes or tasks that need to be confronted.[55] Although the economic and career uncertainty discussed earlier in this chapter can certainly disrupt one's progress through a career, it is still true that as people age they will likely confront a changing set of requirements and demands. For example, a 25-year-old trainee is likely to be preoccupied with gaining competence, acceptance, and credibility in his or her early career. The same person at midcareer (age 50, for example) might be wrestling with gnawing self-doubts about the sacrifices his or her career has required. At age 60, that person might be faced with the task of remaining productive in later career years, switching career fields entirely, or planning for retirement.

We define career development as *an ongoing process by which individuals progress through a series of stages, each of which is characterized by a relatively unique set of issues, themes, and tasks.*

One primary goal of this book is to demonstrate the interplay among career management, career development, and a person's total life. If individuals understand the developmental tasks as they progress through their career and if they appreciate the relationship between their work and nonwork lives, they can formulate goals and strategies that are most appropriate for that particular time in their career and life. In doing so, not only can they achieve a career that fits their lifestyle, but also create positive emotions toward their work and total life.[56] Moreover, organizations attuned to the unfolding of careers can design career management and developmental programs most relevant to an employee's career stage.

The Need to Understand Career Management

An understanding of career management is important in two respects. First, it can help individuals manage their careers more effectively. Second, organizations can benefit from understanding the career decisions and dilemmas that confront their employees. In this section, we will consider the importance of career management both from an individual employee's perspective and from an organization's viewpoint.

The Individual Perspective

From an individual's point of view, effective career management is particularly important in light of the turbulent economic, technological, and global environments discussed earlier in the chapter. In rapidly changing and uncertain times, career success and satisfaction will most likely be achieved by individuals who understand themselves, know how to detect changes in the environment, create opportunities for themselves, and learn from their mistakes—all elements of effective career management. In an era of downsizing, outsourcing, and changing corporate structures, individuals who have insights into themselves and their options should be better able to overcome obstacles to their career growth and maintain ongoing employability.

The environmental changes discussed previously not only create a higher degree of uncertainty for individuals but also demand that career decisions be made more rapidly, and in many cases, spontaneously. The rise of the gig economy, lingering economic insecurity, ongoing technological changes, globalization, work–life pressures, and other factors all carry with them challenges to individual career management. Moreover, careers have become less structured, less automatic, and more unpredictable. More innovative and idiosyncratic routes to success are replacing established career paths. As organizations become more responsive to changing business priorities, greater flexibility will be required on the part of the employee. Flexibility, adaptability, and employability are hallmarks of effective career management.[57] In addition, understanding all of the technology-based approaches to employment or reemployment is important for ongoing individual career management.[58] At a minimum, tech-based career management has two elements—job posting boards that identify employment opportunities, and networking sites that create a forum for social connections and support, advice-sharing, and getting one's name and credentials known to the outside world.

Another pressure for effective career management is the very nature of contemporary employees, who are active and assertive and who demand a high degree of control over their careers and their lives. Behavioral scientists have observed the following significant changes in the workforce in recent years.

High Expectations

The desire for interesting and meaningful work has been matched by the belief that the attainment of these outcomes is likely. To want something from life is one thing; to expect it is another matter. Newer and younger employees often hold inflated, unrealistic expectations about work. High expectations can produce anger, disappointment, and dissatisfaction if work experiences do not live up to values and expectations. Effective career management can play a particularly significant role in the attempt to secure a match between expectations and experiences.

Autonomy

One of the most significant values held by the contemporary employee is the achievement of freedom, independence, and discretion in the workplace.[59] Having substantial freedom to select work projects, to decide how a job gets accomplished, and to set work schedules is crucial to a large number of employees in today's world. Indeed, for many employees, attaining high-quality job performance on challenging, autonomous projects can be more important than receiving a promotion. One positive outcome of non-permanent gig employment relationships is that they allow for high levels of flexibility in deciding when, where, and for whom to work.

Weakening of Sex-Role Boundaries

The arbitrary divisions of labor between men's and women's participation in work roles have become progressively less rigid over the past few decades. As occupational gender-typing continues to weaken, women and men will perceive a much wider range of career options and will need to choose from these options wisely, therefore increasing the need for effective career management.

A Concern for Total Lifestyle

The quest for meaningful and challenging work has been accompanied by an intense concern for a satisfying family and/or personal life. The unwavering pursuit of promotions and a higher salary has potential costs—less time or energy for family, community service, recreation, and self-development, and might even lead to a compromising of one's ethical and moral beliefs.[60] From an opposite perspective, refused promotions or relocations and an unwillingness to work 14-hour days reflect a belief among many employees that the trade-offs associated with the pursuit of the tangible outcomes of career success can be excessive.

A desire for a more balanced lifestyle can produce ambivalent feelings in many employees. On one hand, money, advancement, challenge, responsibility, and interesting work are sought and valued. On the other hand, family, community, leisure, and self-development are also seen as legitimate and important activities that, at times, take precedence over work. In a sense, then, many employees seem to be seeking a bounded involvement with work. That is, they are placing boundaries around their work involvement so that work does not incessantly intrude into other parts of their lives. As we will discuss in detail in Chapter 3 and will reference in all chapters, career decisions must take into account the satisfaction of work, family, and personal needs. Whether the blurring of work and non-work lives has positive or negative consequences (and it probably has elements of both), career management as we move forward in the 21st century requires new insights and strategies to manage not only one's career but one's overall life as well.

Diversity of Career Orientations

Our discussion of the contemporary workforce does not imply that all employees hold the same values and pursue the same type of careers. In fact, there is considerable diversity among employees' career orientations and work values.[61] While some of us value advancement or freedom above all else, others primarily value the intrinsic excitement of work, and still others place the most significance on security and balance in their lives.[62] Although we will examine career orientations more extensively in later chapters of the book, we should realize at this point that active career management is essential if we are to satisfy our unique career values, whatever they might be.

The Organizational Perspective

As indicated in the preceding section, individuals who define career success in broad terms and who feel the need to combine different parts of their lives into a satisfying lifestyle have a real need to understand the nature of careers and to manage their careers actively. Organizations also have incentives for understanding careers. In fact, an organization's ability to manage its human resources effectively depends on how well it understands its employees' work and nonwork needs and helps them engage in effective career management.[63]

Selection of Human Resources

Successful human resource management begins with the effective recruitment, selection, and socialization of new employees. An organization needs to be concerned with identifying a pool of talented applicants, selecting those applicants with the greatest likelihood of success, and bringing the new recruits on board in a way that increases their contribution to the organization. In order to accomplish these tasks, an organization must understand the type of careers and paths it provides and the career programs that it believes are most conducive to success and satisfaction in the organization.

Moreover, an organization must understand the ways applicants approach the job search process so it can present itself to these applicants in the most favorable way. Yet an organization must also avoid overselling itself to the point where new recruits hold unrealistic and unattainable expectations.[64] Finally, an organization must orient new employees to their work roles and positions by helping them understand their jobs, appreciate the organization's culture, and learn required tasks. An organization is more likely to succeed in these activities if it understands the needs, values, and expectations of its job applicants and new employees, a topic we will treat in depth in Chapter 7.

Development and Utilization of Human Resources

Many organizations contend that their employees are their most valued assets. However, employees who are placed in inappropriate jobs and who are frustrated with their opportunities for growth and development can ultimately turn into liabilities, either through poor performance or through voluntary termination. Therefore, it is in the best interest of the organization to help its employees plan and manage their careers. Career planning workshops, job posting, supportive performance appraisal systems, career counseling and mentoring, and job redesign are but a few of the career-related programs that organizations have used to facilitate effective career management.

Further, to enhance the performance and development of its employees, an organization should understand the critical tasks faced by people at different times in their careers. Programs designed to help employees in their early careers, such as a challenging initial job assignment, are likely to be different to some extent from developmental activities most relevant to someone in midcareer (for example, learning to become a mentor) or in late career (pre-retirement counseling). Moreover, the demise of the relational psychological contract combined with an expanded usage of a non-permanent workforce means that organizations will be challenged to keep their employees, especially younger ones, engaged in and committed to their work. Career planning programs could be useful in helping employees improve or maintain employability and enhance interest in their work regardless of the nature of their employment relationship with the company.

In addition, to ensure a steady movement of human resources to key positions, an organization needs to understand the basis upon which employees make their career decisions. It is no longer practical for an organization to assume that employees will automatically accept promotions or other job assignments offered to them. Personal career interests, family considerations, and lifestyle choices can upset a company's best-laid plans. Therefore, the organization needs to understand the dynamics of career decision-making and be aware of its employees' career concerns to avoid miscalculation of its human resource requirements. This recognition of employee desires is especially important given the expansion in global business and the associated growth in international careers. An organization with worldwide operations should understand the personal and family needs of employees before, during, and after international assignments.[65]

Management of the Career Plateau

There is an additional problem experienced by companies that are either not expanding rapidly or are contracting in size. In these firms, there are fewer advancement opportunities for managers and other employees because the number of employees ready for a position may greatly exceed the number of openings. This problem is exacerbated by the aging baby boom generation that is now in middle age and older, where advancement of younger workers is blocked by a massive pool of employees who are not ready or are unable to fully retire.[66] Employees can become plateaued relatively early in their careers, stuck in jobs with little likelihood of promotion or with few opportunities for increased responsibility. Many of these employees may experience a diminished level of work motivation or, as discussed in Chapter 12, may leave their employers to establish an entrepreneurial career. Organizations need to keep plateaued employees performing effectively. To a considerable extent, success in meeting this challenge depends on an understanding of the principles of career management.

The Management of Cultural Diversity

The movement toward equal employment opportunity—fueled by the passage of the Civil Rights Act of 1964 and reinforced by judicial decisions and the Civil Rights Act of 1991—has had a profound effect on organizations' management of their human resources.[67] The focus on equitable career opportunities within organizations requires companies to develop fair assessment techniques so candidates for promotions or other job assignments will be judged on their competence, not on their gender, race, ethnicity, age, or sexual orientation. Beyond that, however, employers need to leverage the perspectives of different cultural groups to create a more effective workforce. As Chapter 11 will demonstrate, an understanding of career management is essential to accomplish this goal.

Work–Life Responsiveness

Organizations recognize that they stand to lose the services of valuable human resources—women and men—if they fail to help their employees resolve difficulties in achieving balance between work and family or personal life. Work–life-responsive organizations increasingly provide more flexible work schedules, part-time employment, opportunities for job sharing, telecommuting, and childcare and eldercare arrangements in an attempt to retain employees who are experiencing extensive work–life conflicts. Moreover, employers may well need to reconsider the level of commitment and involvement they can reasonably expect from employees who are experiencing extensive work–life pressures. As we will discuss in Chapter 3, an understanding of the work and nonwork demands facing employees at different stages of their career development will be required to attract, motivate, and retain an effective workforce.

Summary of the Contemporary Workplace

Modern organizations are staffed by an increasingly diverse group of employees. In general, employees want to derive more meaning from work than simply money and security, and are paying considerable attention to balancing their work, family, and personal lives. As part of a more general trend, employees are more assertive and vocal about their needs and are willing to leave organizations that fail to provide opportunities to meet these needs.

In addition, work organizations face pressures from multiple sources. International competition, technological advances, demanding investors, and the constant focus on efficiency and productivity present a variety of problems in managing human resources. Lean and mean may be a corporate rallying cry, but it can violate employees' expectations for job security and rapid advancement and thereby frustrate the attainment of previously reasonable career goals. Changing technologies can eliminate jobs and career paths in favor of other career routes. Work and nonwork lives are increasingly intertwined as individuals and families attempt to achieve balance in their lives. The adoption of a global perspective and increasing prevalence of a multicultural work environment require new insights into the cultural underpinnings of behavior. This turbulence exists in an era of employee rights and insistence on social justice on one hand, and the need for greater organizational efficiency on the other. Although an understanding of careers will not by itself solve these problems, a failure to understand and apply principles of career management could have unfortunate consequences for employees and their employers.

Summary

A career is defined as the pattern of work-related experiences that span the course of a person's life. All careers have objective and subjective elements that together form the basis of an individual's career. Career management is seen as an ongoing problem-solving process in which information is gathered, awareness of oneself and the environment is increased, career goals and strategies are developed, and feedback is obtained. This process can help individuals deal with the tasks and issues they face in various stages of their career and in their total life.

It is essential that employees and organizations develop an understanding of career management in today's turbulent world. Contemporary employees tend to be assertive and vocal about their needs, and they desire control over their professional and private lives. Organizations concerned with the productive utilization of their human resources can also benefit from understanding the many dilemmas and challenges faced by employees, as they attempt to help them plan and manage their careers.

Career Management *for Life*: Work–Life Implications from Chapter 1

- Individuals should manage their career "for life" with an understanding of the impact of their career on their family, community, and personal interests as well as the effects of these other parts of life on their career.
- Individuals should manage their career "for life" on an ongoing basis because people change, the world changes, and jobs change.
- Many individuals—married or single, parents or childfree—seek a satisfying family and/or personal life *in addition to* meaningful and challenging work.
- Career decisions must take into account the satisfaction of work, family, and personal needs.
- Organizations stand to lose the services of valuable human resources—women and men—if they fail to help their employees resolve difficulties in achieving balance between work and family or personal life.

Assignment

Interview a friend, family member, or co-worker to review the key events in his or her career. Remember to examine objective and subjective factors. Sketch a diagram of the person's career as in Exhibit 1.1.

Discussion Questions

1. Broadly speaking, what are the effects of recent changes in the business and social environment on individuals' careers? Consider the consequences of such factors as intense competition among organizations, changes in the nature of work, globalization, technology, work–life issues, and cultural diversity on career management.
2. Does the characterization of the contemporary workforce described in this chapter (high expectations, a need for autonomy, the weakening sex-role stereotypes, and concern for total lifestyle) fit your picture of yourself, your friends, or your family members? Could there be age, social class, cultural, or gender differences in how people view work and life?
3. Why should people be concerned about managing their careers? What can happen if people do not actively plan and manage their careers?
4. What are the incentives for an organization to help its employees manage their careers? How can the organization stand to gain from offering career management assistance to its employees? Are there any risks in providing these programs?

Chapter 1 Case: Richard the Information Systems Executive

Why was Richard's decision to leave his employer of 14 years such a shock? Maybe it was the outstanding reputation of the company he had decided to leave—a company known for innovative computer technology and progressive human resource practices. Perhaps it was his steady advancement in title, responsibilities, and salary, or his obvious enthusiasm for his work and for the company that had treated him so well. Or possibly it was the fact that Richard had started with this paternalistic company right out of college and it was rare for any employee to leave with such a high level of job security.

Richard had made a significant career decision that, in retrospect, should not have been so surprising. At 38 years of age he yearned for more—more money and a more prestigious title—but, most significantly, he wanted more responsibility and an opportunity to make a meaningful contribution to the destiny of his employer. This opportunity may have come eventually with his current company, but it would have taken a while, and Richard was growing impatient. Richard was in the phase of his career where he needed to have a greater degree of authority and independence, to be listened to seriously, and to make a name for himself. With a stay-at-home spouse and a young daughter, Richard was also concerned about increasing his compensation to provide a more comfortable lifestyle for himself and his family, now and in the future. Aware of his needs and the opportunities at his current company, Richard, with the support of his spouse, decided to risk security in a safe, known environment and pursue his goals. This decision shaped the course of his career and life in profound ways.

Richard left his former employer with goodwill and enormous optimism. He accepted a position as director of customer support with a rapidly growing technology firm. In this new position, he and his staff were in charge of providing technical support for all of the company's clients. Richard approached his new job with the enthusiasm and energy that had produced success in earlier years. He upgraded his employer's back office information system, and built a management structure within his division that was sorely needed. His accomplishments were substantial and were recognized by his superiors, peers, and subordinates alike. It looked like his decision had paid off!

Unfortunately, Richard did not count on, nor did he anticipate, the corporate changes in strategy that were about to take place. Not that he was particularly naïve, but how could he have known that the senior management of the company was planning on "offshoring" all of its customer support to Asia? Facing intense competition and resultant pressures to cut costs, the company's senior management team, with the blessing of the board of directors, decided to reduce labor costs by 40 percent by outsourcing Richard's entire department. After just a few months on what he thought was going to be his dream job, Richard was facing a great deal of uncertainty about his future. It is one thing to know intellectually that a change in corporate strategy can outweigh job performance in the real world; it's quite another to be the victim of a major corporate cost-cutting move. Richard was worried. He had a family to support, a child to eventually put through college, and a heavy mortgage to pay each month.

At the age of 40, Richard found himself unemployed for the first time since high school. Finding a new position became a full-time job, and he approached this task with alacrity and extensive planning. After what seemed like an eternity, he found a position with a brokerage firm, heading up its information systems group. Burned once, he comforted himself that this new company was less likely than his previous employer to make a major change in strategy. But after two years of outstanding contributions, this firm is now undergoing a major reorganization and a reshuffling of personnel. Richard's future? Although he was recently promoted to vice-president, he's not so sure of himself any more. When a friend asked whether he had any regrets about his decision to leave his initial employer, Richard gave an emphatic "maybe."

Case Questions

1. What do Richard's experiences indicate about the process of career management?
2. What environmental factors have affected Richard's career?
3. When Richard decided to leave his initial employer, what career "trade-offs," either consciously or subconsciously, did he make? Do you believe that Richard has done a good job of managing his career? Why or why not?
4. If Richard sought your help, what advice would give him in terms of the future management of his career?

Notes

1 De Hauw, S. & Greenhaus, J. H. (2015). Building a sustainable career: The role of work–home balance in career decision making. In De Vos, A. & Van der Heijden, B. I. J. M. (Eds.), *Handbook of research on sustainable careers* (pp. 223–238). Cheltenham, UK: Elgar Publishing; Greenhaus, J. H. & Kossek, E. E. (2014). The contemporary career: A work–home perspective. *Annual Review of Organizational Psychology and Organizational Behavior*, *1*, 361–388; Hall, D. T., Lee, M. D., Kossek, E. E. & Heras, M. L. (2012). Pursuing career success while sustaining personal and family well-being: A study of reduced-load professionals over time. *Journal of Social Issues*, *68*, 741–766; Newman, K. L. (2011). Sustainable careers: Lifecycle engagement in work. *Organizational Dynamics*, *40*, 136–134.

2 As provided on its website (www.aom.org), the Academy of Management is the preeminent professional association for management and organization scholars. The Academy's central mission is to enhance the profession of management by advancing the scholarship through collaborative opportunities, and enriching the professional development of its members. Founded in 1936, the Academy of Management is the oldest and largest scholarly management association in the world with 19,000 members from 120 nations.

3 See the American Management Association's website for linkages to career planning resources: www.amanet.org.

4 Along with a number of other professional journals devoted to career management, counseling, and decision-making, the journal *Career Development Quarterly* has been published, in one form or another, for more than 100 years. For a description, see Savickas, M. L., Pope, M. & Niles, S. G. (2011). *The Career Development Quarterly*: A centennial retrospective. *Career Development Quarterly*, *59*, 528–538.

5 Callanan, G. A., Perri, D. F. & Tomkowicz, S. M. (2017). Career management in uncertain times: Challenges and opportunities. *Career Development Quarterly*, *65*, 353–365.

6 Cappelli, P. & Keller, J. (2013). A study of the extent and potential causes of alternative employment arrangements. *ILR Review*, *66*, 874–901.
7 Rousseau, D. M. (2010). The individual–organization relationship: The psychological contract. In Zedeck, S. (Ed.), *Handbook of industrial/organizational psychology, Vol. 3: Maintaining, expanding, and contracting the organization* (pp. 191–220). Washington, DC: American Psychological Association; Coyle-Shapiro, J. A. M. (2006). Psychological contract. In Greenhaus, J. H. & Callanan, G. A. (Eds.), *Encyclopedia of career development* (pp. 652–659). Thousand Oaks, CA: Sage.
8 Ibid.
9 Jepsen, D. M. & Rodwell, J. J. (2012). Lack of symmetry in employees' perceptions of the psychological contract. *Psychological Reports*, *110*, 820–838.
10 Ibid.
11 Katz, L. F. & Krueger, A. B. (2016). The rise and nature of alternative work arrangements in the United States, 1995–2015. *National Bureau of Economic Research*, 1–19; United States Department of Labor, Bureau of Labor Statistics. News Release dated March 31, 2015 (and reissued on April 1, 2015): "Number of jobs held, labor market activity, and earnings growth among the youngest baby boomers: results from a longitudinal survey." Available at www.bls.gov/news.release/pdf/nlsoy.pdf; Monge-Naranjo, A. & Sohail, F. (2015). Age and gender differences in long-term unemployment: Before and after the Great Recession. *Federal Reserve Bank of St. Louis Economic Synopses, 26*, 1–2; Bullard, J. (2014). The rise and fall of the labor force participation rate in the United States. *Federal Reserve Bank of St. Louis Review*, *96*, 1–12; Kroft, K., Lange, F., Notowidigdo, M. J. & Katz, L. F. (2014). Long-term unemployment and the Great Recession: The role of composition, duration dependence, and non-participation. *National Bureau of Economic Research, Working Paper 20271*, June; Kalleberg, A. L. (2009). Precarious work, insecure workers: Employment relations in transition. *American Sociological Review*, *74*, 1–22.
12 For a thorough explanation and classification scheme for the various alternative employment arrangements see Cappelli, P. H. & Keller, J. (2013). Classifying work in the new economy. *Academy of Management Review*, *38*, 575–596. See also Irwin, N. (2016). With "gigs" instead of jobs, workers bear new burdens. *The New York Times*, March 31; Kalleberg (2009).
13 Katz & Krueger (2016).
14 Eurofound (2015). *Recent developments in temporary employment: Employment growth, wages and transitions*. Luxembourg: Publications Office of the European Union.
15 Callanan et al. (2017).
16 Irwin (2016).
17 Ibid.
18 Probst, T. M. (2006). Job security. In Greenhaus, J. H. & Callanan, G. A. (Eds.), *Encyclopedia of career development* (pp. 442–446). Thousand Oaks, CA: Sage.
19 United States Department of Labor, Bureau of Labor Statistics (2015).
20 Debus, M. E., Probst, T. M., König C. J. & Kleinmann, M. (2012). Catch me if I fall! Enacted uncertainty avoidance and the social safety net as country-level moderators in the job insecurity–job attitudes link. *Journal of Applied Psychology*, *97*, 690–698.
21 BLS Spotlight on Statistics (2012). The recession of 2007–2009. *U.S. Bureau of Labor Statistics*, April, 1–18.
22 Bullard (2014).
23 Abel, J. R., Deitz, R. & Yaqin, S. (2014). Are recent college graduates finding good jobs? *Federal Reserve Bank of New York Current Issues*, *20*, 1–8.
24 Cajner, T., Mawhirter, D., Nekarda, C. & Ratner, D. (2014). Why is involuntary part-time work elevated? *FEDS Notes*, April 14; Valletta, R. & van der List, C. (2015). Involuntary part-time work: Here to stay? *FRBSF Economic Letter*, June 8, 1–5.
25 Kroft et al. (2014).
26 Callanan et al. (2017).
27 United States Department of Labor, Bureau of Labor Statistics (2016). Economic News Table: A-15. Alternative measures of labor underutilization. Release dated July 8, 2016, Available at www.bls.gov/news.release/empsit.t15.htm.
28 Balogun, J. & Johnson, G. (2004). Organizational restructuring and middle manager sensemaking. *Academy of Management Journal*, *47*, 523–549; Schilling, M. A. & Steensma, H. K. (2001). The use of modular organizational forms: An industry-level analysis. *Academy of Management Journal*, *44*, 1149–1168.
29 Offermann, L. R. (2006). Team-based work. In Greenhaus, J. H. & Callanan, G. A. (Eds.), *Encyclopedia of career development* (pp. 795–796). Thousand Oaks, CA: Sage.

30 Phelps, C., Heidl, R. & Wadhwa, A. (2012). Knowledge, networks, and knowledge networks: A review and research agenda. *Journal of Management*, *38*, 1115–1166; Zaheer, A. & Bell, G. G. (2005). Benefiting from network position: Firm capabilities, structural holes, and performance. *Strategic Management Journal*, *26*, 809–825.
31 Ashkenas, R., Ulrich, D., Jick, T. & Kerr, S. (2002). *The boundaryless organization*. San Francisco, CA: Jossey-Bass.
32 For a thorough discourse on the use of work groups and teams in organizations, see Kozlowski, S. W. J. & Bell, B. S. (2012). Work groups and teams in organizations. In Wiener, I., Schmitt, N. W. & Highhouse, S. (Eds.), *Comprehensive handbook of psychology, volume 12: Industrial and organizational psychology*, 2nd ed. (pp. 412–469). Hoboken, NJ: Wiley. See also Callanan, G. A. (2004). What would Machiavelli think? An overview of the leadership challenges in team-based structures. *Team Performance Management Journal*, *41*, 77–83; Offermann (2006).
33 Lorinkova, N. M., Pearsall, M. J. & Sims, H. P. (2013). Examining the differential longitudinal performance of directive versus empowering leadership in teams. *Academy of Management Journal*, *56*, 573–596; Maynard, M. T., Gilson, L. L. & Mathieu, J. E. (2012). Empowerment—fad or fab? A multilevel review of the past two decades of research. *Journal of Management*, *38*, 1231–1281; Amar, A. D., Hentrich, C., Bastani, B. & Hlupic, V. (2012). How managers succeed by letting employees lead. *Organizational Dynamics*, *41*, 62–71; Mills, P. K. (2006). Empowerment. In Greenhaus, J. H. & Callanan, G. A. (Eds.), *Encyclopedia of career development* (pp. 280–284). Thousand Oaks, CA: Sage.
34 Callanan (2004).
35 Colbert, A., Yee, N. & George, G. (2016). The digital workforce and the workplace of the future. *Academy of Management Journal*, *59*, 731–739. Cappelli, P. H. (2015). Skill gaps, skill shortages, and skill mismatches: Evidence and arguments for the United States. *ILR Review*, *68*, 251–290.
36 DiRenzo, M. S. & Greenhaus, J. H. (2011). Job search and voluntary turnover in a boundaryless world: A control theory perspective. *Academy of Management Review*, *36*, 567–589; van der Heijde, C. M. (2014). Employability and self-regulation in contemporary careers. In Coetzee, M. (Ed.), *Psycho-social career meta-capacities* (pp. 7–17). London, UK: Springer.
37 Baruch, Y., Altman, Y. & Tung, R. L. (2016). Career mobility in a global era: Advances in managing expatriation and repatriation. *Academy of Management Annals*, *10*, 841–889.
38 Ibid. See also Herr, E. L. (2006). Globalization and careers. In Greenhaus, J. H. & Callanan, G. A. (Eds.), *Encyclopedia of career development* (pp. 337–342). Thousand Oaks, CA: Sage; Tharenou, P. (2006). International careers. In Greenhaus, J. H. & Callanan, G. A. (Eds.), *Encyclopedia of career development* (pp. 398–404). Thousand Oaks, CA: Sage.
39 Kraimer, M. L., Shaffer, M. A. & Bolino, M. C. (2009). The influence of expatriate and repatriate experiences on career advancement and repatriate retention. *Human Resource Management*, *48*, 27–47.
40 Selmer, J. (2006). Expatriate experience. In Greenhaus, J. H. & Callanan, G. A. (Eds.), *Encyclopedia of career development* (pp. 306–307). Thousand Oaks, CA: Sage.
41 Collings, D. G., Doherty, N., Luethy, M. & Osborn, D. (2011). Understanding and supporting the career implications of international assignments. *Journal of Vocational Behavior*, *78*, 361–371.
42 Washbon, J. L. (2012). Learning and the new workplace: Impacts of technology change on post-secondary career and technical education. *New Directions for Colleges*, *157*, 43–52.
43 Abram, S. (2010). What you aren't seeing anymore: Has technology changed our learners' futures forever? *Multimedia & Internet*, *17*, 20–22.
44 Cappelli, P. (2006). Churning of jobs. In Greenhaus, J. H. & Callanan, G. A. (Eds.), *Encyclopedia of career development* (pp. 165–167). Thousand Oaks, CA: Sage.
45 Callanan, G. A. & Greenhaus, J. H. (2008). The baby boom generation and career management: A call to action. *Advances in Developing Human Resources*, *10*, 70–85.
46 Statistics available at the United States Department of Labor, Bureau of Labor Statistics at www.bls.gov (www.bls.gov/news.release/pdf/famee.pdf) under the menu item "Employment Characteristics of Families—2015," released on April 22, 2016.
47 Ibid.
48 Ibid.
49 Ibid.
50 Raskin, P. M. (2006). Single parents and careers. In Greenhaus, J. H. & Callanan, G. A. (Eds.), *Encyclopedia of career development* (pp. 741–742). Thousand Oaks, CA: Sage.

51 Statistics available from the United States Census Bureau at their website at www.census.gov. Statistics are listed in Table C2 under the heading "Household Relationship and Living Arrangements of Children Under 18 Years, by Age and Sex: 2015."
52 Greenhaus, J. H. & Callanan, G. A. (2012). Career dynamics. In Wiener, I., Schmitt, N. W. & Highhouse, S. (Eds.), *Comprehensive handbook of psychology, volume 12: Industrial and organizational psychology*, 2nd ed. (pp. 593–614). Hoboken, NJ: Wiley; Ng, T. (2006). Career mobility. In Greenhaus, J. H. & Callanan, G. A. (Eds.), *Encyclopedia of career development* (pp. 127–130). Thousand Oaks, CA: Sage.
53 Collin, A. (2006). Career. In Greenhaus, J. H. & Callanan, G. A. (Eds.), *Encyclopedia of career development* (pp. 60–63). Thousand Oaks, CA: Sage.
54 Our definition of career management is similar to that provided by Gutteridge, T. G. (1986). Organizational career development systems: The state of the practice. In Hall, D. T. & Associates (Eds.), *Career development in organizations* (pp. 50–94). San Francisco: Jossey-Bass.
55 Greenhaus & Callanan (2012).
56 Kopelman, S., Feldman, E. R., McDaniel, D. M. & Hall, D. T. (2012). Mindfully negotiating a career with a heart. *Organizational Dynamics*, *41*, 163–171.
57 DiRenzo & Greenhaus (2011).
58 Stone, D., Deadrick, D., Lukaszewski, K. & Johnson, R. (2015). The influence of technology on the future of human resource management. *Human Resource Management Review*, *25*, 216–231; Colbert et al. (2016).
59 Van den Broeck, A., Ferris, D. L., Chang, C. & Rosen, C. C. (2016). A review of self-determination theory's basic psychological needs at work. *Journal of Management*, *42*, 1195–1229; Zytowski, D. G. (2006). Work values. In Greenhaus, J. H. & Callanan, G. A. (Eds.), *Encyclopedia of career development* (pp. 863–865). Thousand Oaks, CA: Sage.
60 Greenhaus & Kossek (2014).
61 Rodrigues, R., Guest, D., Oliveira, T. & Alfes, K. (2015). Who benefits from independent careers? Employees, organizations, or both? *Journal of Vocational Behavior*, *91*, 23–34; Biemann, T., Zacher, H. & Feldman, D. C. (2012). Career patterns: A twenty-year panel study. *Journal of Vocational Behavior*, *81*, 159–170.
62 Schein, E. H. (2006). Career anchors. In Greenhaus, J. H. & Callanan, G. A. (Eds.), *Encyclopedia of career development* (pp. 63–69). Thousand Oaks, CA: Sage.
63 Baruch, Y. (2006). Organizational career management. In Greenhaus, J. H. & Callanan, G. A. (Eds.), *Encyclopedia of career development* (pp. 573–580). Thousand Oaks, CA: Sage.
64 Morse, B. J. & Popovich, P. M. (2009). Realistic recruitment practices in organizations: The potential benefits of generalized expectancy calibration. *Human Resource Management Review*, *19*, 1–8; Wanous, J. P. (2006). Realistic recruitment. In Greenhaus, J. H. & Callanan, G. A. (Eds.), *Encyclopedia of career development* (pp. 672–675). Thousand Oaks, CA: Sage.
65 Collings et al. (2011).
66 Callanan & Greenhaus (2008).
67 Noble, J. G. (2006). Civil Rights Act of 1964. In Greenhaus, J. H. & Callanan, G. A. (Eds.), *Encyclopedia of career development* (pp. 169–170). Thousand Oaks, CA: Sage; Noble, J. G. (2006). Civil Rights Act of 1991. In Greenhaus, J. H. & Callanan, G. A. (Eds.), *Encyclopedia of career development* (pp. 170–172). Thousand Oaks, CA: Sage.

2 Career Contexts and Stages

In Chapter 1 we defined a career as the pattern of work-related experiences that span the course of a person's life. While this definition is straightforward, there are many different perspectives and themes from which a career can be seen and analyzed.[1] As we move through the first decades of the 21st century, the concept of a career continues to evolve.[2] Accordingly, in this chapter we present a number of ways in which a career and career-related topics can be viewed. We start by looking at the more traditional perspectives on careers, namely the *advancement/stability* theme, the *professional* view of careers, and the career as a *calling* concept. We then provide a discussion of more contemporary perspectives, including the *protean* and *boundaryless* themes, *kaleidoscope* and *customized* careers, the effects of *social influences* on careers, and the differing meanings of *career success*. We conclude this chapter by discussing the *developmental* perspective on careers.

Chapter 3 then provides an overview of the ways in which work and nonwork roles affect each other during the course of a career, with an emphasis on the individual's responsibility in making effective work–life decisions *over the life course*. In Chapter 4 we present a model of career management that is designed to help individuals respond to the many challenges posed by these various perspectives and navigate their careers to help ensure success and satisfaction over the lifespan. Chapters 5 and 6 build on Chapter 4 by providing specific guidelines on how to engage in effective career management.

The Traditional Perspectives on Careers

The traditional view of a career crystallized during the era of prosperity in the decades following the end of World War II. As the industrialized world experienced unprecedented economic growth, demand for human capital soared, and individuals had an abundance of job opportunities.[3] Working under a relational psychological contract, wherein there was a presumption of mutual loyalty between the employer and employee, a career in the latter half of the 20th century was viewed as a relatively stable and consistent undertaking. Put simplistically, you took a job with a solid, respected employer, kept your "nose to the grindstone" and your mouth shut, enjoyed regular promotions that allowed for linear, upward advancement within the organization, and retired with a nice pension when you reached the age of 65. This idealized vision of a traditional "organizational career," in which one expected *advancement and stability* within one's career, became an anachronism in the 1980s as large-scale corporations began shedding human resources in mass numbers as a means to increase competitiveness in a global economy. Beginning in the 1980s and accelerating in succeeding decades, career paths within organizations became more unstructured and unpredictable because of the increasing likelihood that jobs would be eliminated, outsourced, or substantially changed to ensure that organizations could move in different strategic directions if necessary.[4]

Even with the uncertainty in employment and careers over the past four decades, the theme of *advancement and stability* remains a central theme within many definitions of a career.[5] Such definitions are limiting because they imply that a person is pursuing a career only if he or she exhibits steady or rapid advancement in status, money, and the like, essentially with just one or two employers or within a particular industry. In addition, another aspect of this theme revolves around the career as a source of stability within a single occupational field or closely connected fields. In this context, we often hear of the "career accountant" or "career police officer," or we hear of a career "lifer" with a particular organization. Similarly, a person's pursuit of closely connected jobs (teacher, guidance counselor, dean of students) is often thought to represent a career, whereas a sequence of apparently unrelated jobs (novelist, politician, advertising copywriter) violates a neat consistency of job content and would not necessarily constitute a career. Incorporating stability into the meaning of a career is also limiting, especially in today's world in which organizational and occupational mobility are likely to be the norm rather than the exception.

Another traditional theme places an emphasis on the career as a *profession*. A profession is typically distinguished from an "ordinary" occupation based on the belief that a profession represents a more desirable career choice and involves work that is of high economic status, allows for a substantial degree of autonomy, and can provide an enhanced level of compensation.[6] As examples, professionals such as doctors and lawyers are thought to have careers, whereas clerks and machinists typically are not. This traditional emphasis on the career as a profession is also restrictive, because it suggests that one must achieve a certain occupational or social status for one's work activities to constitute a career.

A career can also be seen as a *calling*, whereby one primarily works for the fulfillment that the job or profession brings into one's life.[7] In this sense, a person is "called" to a career based on a strong attraction to (and passion for) particular work, such that the nature of the work fulfills personal values and satisfies the person's "prosocial" need to make the world a better place.[8] Occupations typically associated with a calling are those where there is a helping or nurturing component to the work, although any type of a profession or job could be seen as based on a calling. Nevertheless, it would be a mistake to think that all careers are based on a calling because people have many different motives for entering a career field, as we will see in Chapter 7.

Contemporary Perspectives on Careers: The Protean and Boundaryless Themes

The combined effects over the past few decades of the mass downsizings of numbers of workers, the resultant loss of job security, and the well-documented decline in loyalty between employers and employees have wreaked havoc on traditional organizational careers where the expectation of job stability, security, and advancement had been the norm. In addition, ongoing market pressures for organizations to be flexible in the deployment of human resources in order to stay competitive creates an environment where the psychological contract between employers and employees will remain primarily transactional, where a long-term linear career within a single organization will continue to be the exception rather than the rule, and where many workers are employed in nonpermanent, short-term alternative work arrangements. In organizations that adopt dominant transactional orientations and pursue a workforce based on alternative and contractual employment relationships, their employees are presented with opportunities to remain employable, but they must develop new, more portable skills that hopefully allow for continued professional development.

In reaction to this new world of work, the nature of careers has changed, resulting in new and nontraditional ways of looking at careers and career management.[9] These new conceptualizations recognize the need for individuals to be proactive in managing their career, to view their career in broader terms than their current organization, and to be adaptable as they navigate the uncertainties that exist not only in the general business environment but within particular companies as well.[10] The two most widely recognized contemporary perspectives on careers are the *protean* and the *boundaryless* career concepts.

Protean Career

In his book *Careers in Organizations*, Douglas T. Hall described the protean career as managed by the individual rather than the organization, and guided by the search for self-fulfillment.[11] Named after the mythological Proteus, the Greek god who could change his shape at will, the protean career has been characterized as self-directed, flexible, adaptable, versatile, and initiated by the individual to achieve psychological success; that is, success in reaching goals that are personally meaningful to the individual. Hall and his colleagues have elaborated on the protean career and explored the implications of protean careers for individuals and organizations.[12]

Most of the recent research has focused on a protean career orientation (PCO), which is an employee's disposition or preference to enact a protean career; that is, a career designed to achieve subjectively defined success through autonomous career management.[13] An employee's PCO is an attitude or preference that guides the employee's behavior in two respects. First, employees who adopt a PCO prefer to *self-direct* their career rather than depend on others to direct their career for them. Individuals with a strong PCO take responsibility for managing their career and take the initiative in exploring career options and making career decisions. Second, employees who adopt a PCO are *values-driven* in that they make career decisions to meet their personally meaningful values and goals, in contrast to striving to achieve values and goals imposed upon them by other people, organizations, or society.

Moreover, the personal values and goals that protean-oriented careerists often attempt to achieve are not exclusively tied to their job but rather are relevant to the individual's "whole life space" or "life's work," what we refer to in Chapter 3 as a "whole-life perspective" in which a career decision is made with an awareness of the impact of the decision on other parts of life.[14] In short, a protean perspective on careers emphasizes the active role of employees in defining what is personally meaningful to them in their career and life, and in taking the initiative to manage their career to achieve these important values.

Boundaryless Career

Michael Arthur and his colleagues introduced the boundaryless career concept in the 1990s.[15] Unlike a traditional organizational career, a boundaryless career, or more accurately a boundary-crossing career,[16] is detached from a single employment setting and is not bound by traditional organizational career paths and expectations. In other words, employees who pursue boundaryless careers go beyond the boundaries of their current organization for employment opportunities, social contacts, indeed their very identity. And if they stay in their current employment setting for a period of time, their actions may depart from the organization's traditional norms and expectations.

A boundaryless career is thought to have six different elements or meanings, each of which, in its own way, involves "nontraditional" boundary-crossing.[17]

1. Moving frequently between employers is the most prevalent way of characterizing a boundaryless career because the boundary-crossing (from one organization to another) is an obvious departure from the "traditional" practice of staying with a single employer for an extended period of time.
2. Drawing validation from outside the organization is another form of nontraditional boundary-crossing because employees derive their identity primarily from their profession (e.g., IT, marketing, consulting) rather than from their current employer.
3. Sustaining the career through external networks of relationships involves nontraditional boundary-crossing in the sense that individuals rely on social relationships outside the organization (in their profession, other employers, neighbors, and friends) rather than relying exclusively on networks or sources of information in their current organization, such as their manager or mentor.
4. Departing from traditional mobility expectations in one's current organization, such as opting for a lateral move (nontraditional boundary-crossing) rather than a promotion.
5. Rejecting career opportunities for family or personal reasons, a form of nontraditional boundary-crossing because family or personal considerations cross boundaries to influence a career-related decision.
6. Perceiving that one's career is without boundaries and is independent of traditional organizational career arrangements.[18]

The emergence of boundaryless careers is due to changes in the worldwide economy (increased global competition and advances in technology) that have produced significant alterations in organizational practices, such as acquisitions, reorganizations, reductions in force, and the widespread establishment of alternative work arrangements, all within the context of an increasingly transactional psychological contract with employees.[19] If these forces increase the likelihood that employees move from one organization to another (voluntarily or involuntarily), it is understandable why many employees derive their work identity from their profession or occupation rather than from their current organization, and why they develop networks of relationships that extend beyond the border of their current employer.

Arthur and his colleagues also propose that pursuing a boundaryless career requires the development of three *career competencies* or strategies that are different from those used in a traditional career in that they necessitate looking outside the organization. *Knowing-why* competencies relate to self-awareness of motives and goals and the development of a work identity (often associated with a profession not a particular organization, as noted above) that guide career decisions. *Knowing-how* competencies reflect the human capital skills, knowledge, and experiences employees accumulate that are portable in the sense that they can be transferred from one employment setting to another. *Knowing-whom* competencies are the networks of personal relationships (often outside the current organization) that provide information, guidance, and support in navigating one's career.[20] With these career competencies, the individual psychologically or physically crosses the boundary from one organization to another by pursuing job contacts or leads, expanding knowledge and skills, and establishing connections with a wide network of influential people outside the employing organization.

Protean and Boundaryless Career Conceptualizations: Similarities and Differences

Although the boundaryless and protean career concepts are occasionally linked together, it is more likely that while they overlap one another they are still unique concepts.[21] Nevertheless, the distinctions between the two concepts are somewhat elusive and depend upon how broadly one defines a boundaryless career. Symptomatic of the confusion is that both the boundaryless career and the protean career have been contrasted to a traditional organizational career.[22] If both of these career forms are thought to be the opposite of the traditional organizational career, how are they different from one another? The answer to this question is to view the protean career as an attitude or orientation to a career rather than an actual structure of a career; hence the PCO concept.[23] Indeed, research shows that the PCO is *not* strongly related to extensive inter-organizational mobility preferences and behaviors.[24] Thus, while the PCO reflects a psychological preference for a self-directed and values-driven career, the boundaryless career generally involves boundary-crossing behaviors[25] that are produced by a series of external (e.g., job loss) and internal (goals and values) forces.

Regardless of these fine distinctions in their meanings, it is clear that the protean and boundaryless career conceptualizations reflect not only a fundamental shift in the way individuals view their careers, but also elucidate the behaviors and decisions that are required to manage a career successfully in the 21st century.[26] Indeed, maintaining employability is at the heart of the protean and boundaryless views of career management, both of which stress adaptability and the development of a transportable set of job skills.[27] In this sense, the adoption of protean and boundaryless orientations is especially useful in helping direct an individual's overall career management process in turbulent and uncertain times. With these newer career views, individuals are encouraged to be agents of their own career destinies, taking a longer view of successful career management, with less emphasis on the shorter-term movements from job to job. Further, these orientations should result in more extensive career-planning activities, the accumulation of human, social, and psychological capital, and a resultant higher level of employability.[28]

In addition to the protean and boundaryless views, other recent career models have been developed that build upon these concepts. As one example, the *kaleidoscope* view sees a career as consisting of three elements—*authenticity*, where career choices reflect staying true to one's internal values and interests; *balance*, where career choices allow for a dual commitment and attention given to work and nonwork roles; and *challenge*, where the individual seeks out stimulating work and the opportunity for advancement.[29] The kaleidoscope view of careers follows closely the protean and boundaryless perspectives in that it stresses a values-driven approach to career management and a high degree of self-focus in making career decisions.

Another contemporary perspective is the *customized career*. Monique Valcour and her colleagues conceptualized a customized career as a nontraditional career path that employees pursue in response to their family or personal needs.[30] A customized career can involve one or more of the following departures from a traditional, organizational linear career: (1) a reduced workload through part-time employment or job sharing; (2) a noncontinuous employment pattern characterized by interruptions to attend to personal or family needs; and (3) a nontraditional relationship with an employer that involves temporary rather than permanent status or a contractor/consultant position rather than a core organizational employee.[31]

In sum, there is probably no single career pattern that dominates the current employment scene. As we will discuss in Chapter 4 when we present the career management model, it is up to each individual to be proactive in taking charge of his or her career and in making career decisions that are personally appropriate and are necessary for successful career management; in effect, to claim "ownership" of the career.[32]

Social Influences on Careers

Although the selection, pursuit, and management of a career are seen, at least in Western cultures, as inherently individually based activities, there are many social institutions, structures, and networks that influence our careers.[33] Indeed, the social learning theory of careers posits that occupational choices result, in part, from planned and unplanned learning experiences that occur as we move through various social events and activities during our lifetimes.[34] At the most basic level, family interactions and background can have a pervasive influence on the long-term psychosocial development of the individual that, in turn, affects a wide range of factors associated with career choices and aspirations.[35] These factors can include individual characteristics such as personality, interests, values, abilities, and interpersonal skills, as well as attitudes and expectancies concerning particular occupations.[36] Interpersonal and group experiences within other social organizations such as schools, community groups, sports clubs, and religious institutions can all have an influence on the career attitudes that develop during one's formative years.

Beyond the family, various social networks begin to exert an influence on career decisions as a person ages. For example, college groups and associations can create lifelong affiliations that can assist in networking, employment, and career advancement. Once a person starts working, professional organizations and industry groups can provide useful career support. In addition, organizations that one joins in the community, such as a golf or tennis club, can offer the opportunity to connect with influential members of the business community. Friendships that one develops with current or former co-workers can provide job leads and employment advice. Finally, the vast array of Internet-based social networking sites, such as Facebook and LinkedIn, can allow the establishment of personal and professional connections that foster important career connections.[37]

What each of these examples has in common is that they require the individual to "network" with other people to create interpersonal relationships that could positively influence the individual's career, either at present or in the future.[38] Networking refers to the activities that establish and maintain relationships, both inside and outside the employing organization, which can potentially provide information, influence, guidance, and support to individuals in their careers.[39] Engaging in networks of relationships enables individuals to develop social capital,[40] which are valued resources available to an individual through relationships that exist within a social network.[41] One form of social capital is established internally within a person's work organization where social ties are built with supervisors, more senior officers, mentors, and other associates within the company.[42] In contrast, external social capital results from social connections with individuals outside the organization such as former colleagues or professional contemporaries.[43] The importance of building social capital through external sources has intensified in recent years as increased job insecurity and job loss and the growth of alternative work arrangements has lessened or obviated the chances of building social capital through the more traditional internal sources.[44]

In essence, social capital provides access to people of influence, both within and outside the organization, who can assist the individual in a number of career-related tasks, such as getting information on job openings with a particular company, obtaining an interview for a job that was not advertised, or receiving advice on career paths to pursue or avoid. In addition, as we discussed earlier, the use of networks and the building of social capital are identified as essential (*knowing-whom*) strategies to achieve success in a boundaryless career environment. We will discuss networking and the use of social capital in more detail in Chapter 6 when we review an extensive variety of career strategies that individuals could deploy.

The Different Meanings of Career Success

The changing nature of careers in the 21st century—along with evolving social structures—brings with it new ways of looking at career success. Career success is defined as the positive material and psychological outcomes resulting from one's work activities and experiences.[45] From a more traditional perspective, career success has been viewed primarily in objective terms, which include such factors as total compensation, number of promotions, and other tangible trappings of accomplishment. Although these objective indicators of career success are certainly relevant, because of greater economic uncertainty, career disruptions, the loss of job security, and the shift toward nonpermanent work arrangements, the traditional, objective view is not the only or primary way to gauge an individual's career success.[46] Indeed, these environmental factors along with the pursuit of protean and boundaryless career orientations combine to have individuals place a greater emphasis on understanding career success from a subjective perspective.

From this subjective side, career success is viewed as a function of individuals' perception of satisfaction with different facets of their career. In this sense, the individual uses internal psychological and self-generated guides, such as personal growth and continuous learning, as well as more traditional indicators such as money or status, in interpreting and defining career success.[47] In addition, research has shown that such elements as time for self, job challenge, job security, social and developmental relationships, and a balance between one's career and family life are viewed as important indicators that a person's career and their "whole lives" are successful.[48] These subjective dimensions get at the individual's perception of psychological success that goes beyond such external indicators of success as prestige, power, money, and advancement.[49]

From a career management standpoint, employees often see career success strictly in objective terms, especially when they are early in their careers.[50] In this case, the speed of progression up the corporate ladder can become an obsession. This narrower view of success can lead to career goals and actions that are inconsistent with personal values and beliefs. Further, highly successful managers and executives may experience feelings of personal failure, reflecting regret over having sacrificed family relationships and other affiliations in the ambitious pursuit of the objective form of career success. In contrast, when career success is seen in subjective or personal terms, the focus is on individual satisfaction with the career and how well it has met goals and expectations. The subjective view of career success can also be expanded to include such dimensions as the balance between one's work and family/personal lives or the ability to establish close interpersonal relationships.[51] Adopting a broader meaning of career success can take some of the pressure off upwardly striving middle managers and executives, because the focus of career goals and strategies is no longer exclusively on money and advancement, but encompasses various aspects of personal fulfillment.

Looking to the future, if individuals adopt protean and boundaryless philosophies toward their careers and if they accept a broader view of the meaning of career success, they have a much better chance of managing their careers so that they are able to stay true to their beliefs and values.[52] In addition, organizations can foster greater feelings of career success and an enhanced degree of long-term commitment among their employees by making developmental investments in their workers.[53]

The Developmental Perspective on Careers

It has long been recognized that children pass through a series of rather predictable periods or stages that shape their personality, intelligence, and sense of morality as they mature.[54] In a similar sense, many researchers believe that adulthood also unfolds or develops in a relatively predictable manner, with the premise that each phase of adulthood has its own particular developmental tasks and life and career concerns that need to be addressed.[55]

Do contemporary careers in the 21st century really unfold in orderly stages of development? The answer to this question is uncertain. On the one hand, the answer could be no, given the changes in the business world over the past few decades as described in Chapter 1. These economic, sociological, demographic, and global changes have all affected the orderliness of the ideal progression through distinct life and career phases as we age. Downsizings cause job loss resulting in career disruptions. The proliferation of alternative work arrangements creates a lack of permanence, which makes long-term life and career planning difficult or impossible. Women and men in the workforce might wish to pause their careers to raise children. Many employees return to school to gain new skills to pursue alternative career paths. When individuals step out of the workforce, either voluntarily or involuntarily, gaps are created in their employment histories. It is no surprise that discontinuities in employment can have a negative impact on future income and advancement. Undoubtedly, all of these factors have immediate and long-term effects on many individuals' movement through career and life stages, which might make the seamless progression between career stages an obsolete concept.

On the other hand, the answer to the above question could be yes. The experiences, needs, values, and preferences of all individuals change over time as they age, which could make it appropriate to view a career as a series of relatively unique phases.[56] The career concerns and expectations of a 25-year-old management trainee are different from those of a 45-year-old manager or a 65-year-old executive. Individuals face a variety of career tasks and developmental issues at different life stages. Further, changes in the nature of personal values, interests, and career motivations are likely to occur over the course of an employee's life. An understanding of the tasks and developmental implications of different career stages can help individuals manage their careers more effectively and can help organizations manage and develop their human resources.

On balance, we believe that it is still important to understand the concept of career stages, aging, and generational differences as a way to examine how career development fits within the larger context of adult life development. In this section, we first consider different views of adult life development, providing brief descriptions of the pioneering works of Erik Erikson and Daniel Levinson and his colleagues. We then discuss how chronological age and generational differences can provide insight into career development. We conclude by briefly discussing our view of career development and preview the subsequent chapters that explore specific stages of career development.

Adult Life Development

There is a commonly held stereotype that adulthood, especially old age, is synonymous with decline.[57] In a youth-oriented culture, it is not surprising that adulthood is often viewed (and feared) as a period of deterioration of physical, intellectual, and emotional functioning. Although various aspects of biological functioning undoubtedly decline during adulthood, the decline is generally quite gradual until very late adulthood.[58] In addition, research on the psychological and physical functioning of individuals as they age demonstrates that stereotypes that inspire age discrimination are without merit; indeed, the majority of older workers are able to perform their work roles far beyond the typical age of retirement and well into later years in life.[59] In addition, research findings refute the assumptions that age changes precipitate declines in work performance or lead to an increase in workplace accidents or absenteeism.[60] In fact, older workers tend to be more loyal, have lower rates of absenteeism, and are generally more reliable than younger workers.[61]

But there is more to the study of adulthood than simply cataloging physical, intellectual, and psychological functioning over time. There is a much broader question of concern: "Is there an underlying order in the progression of our lives over the adult years, as there is in childhood and adolescence?" Historically, the most influential models of career development have proposed a series of stages that are closely linked to age. For example, Donald Super identified five stages—growth, exploration, establishment, maintenance, and decline—that were thought to capture individuals' work-related experiences from the years of childhood to retirement.[62] In addition, these models generally assume that individuals pursue a continuous linear career within one occupational type, perhaps one or two organizations, and without major disruptions or redirections. As we will discuss shortly, the movement over the past four decades away from stable, traditional careers can make it difficult to apply somewhat rigid age-based stages to modern careers that are subject to increased uncertainty and disruption.

Erikson's Approach to Life Development

One of the earliest and most influential writers on life development, Erik Erikson, proposed that people progress through eight stages of psychosocial development (Table 2.1).[63] Each stage poses a crisis of sorts and, depending on the outcome of the stage, provides the setting for either growth or arrested development.[64] For example, at the first stage of development, the helpless infant is totally dependent on others for its nurturance and survival. Under favorable circumstances, the infant will develop a sense of trust in parents and other people. With unfavorable conditions, the child will emerge with a basic mistrust of the world that may be difficult to reverse throughout life. At

Table 2.1 Erikson's Eight Stages of Development

Stage of Development	*Age*
1. Basic trust versus mistrust	Infancy
2. Autonomy versus shame and doubt	Ages 1 to 3
3. Initiative versus guilt	Ages 4 to 5
4. Industry versus inferiority	Ages 6 to 11
5. Identity versus role confusion	Puberty and adolescence
6. Intimacy versus isolation	Young adulthood
7. Generativity versus stagnation	Middle adulthood
8. Ego integrity versus despair	Maturity (late adulthood)

Note: Based on material from the following: Erikson, E. H. (1963). *Chilhood and society.* New York: W. W. Norton & Company; Adams, G. R. (2006). Erikson's Theory of Development. In Greenhaus, J. H. & Callanan, G. A. (Eds.), *Encyclopedia of career development* (pp. 295–298). Thousand Oaks, CA: Sage.

each stage of development, the ratio of positive and negative experiences determines the nature of the outcome.

The last three stages of Erikson's model are most relevant to adulthood and careers. The major task of early adulthood is the development of intimacy, a deep commitment to other people and groups. Failure to develop and maintain intimate relationships can bring a sense of isolation to the young adult and impair his or her ability to love. As a person approaches middle adulthood, the development of generativity (literally guiding the next generation) becomes particularly important and can be accomplished through such actions as parenting and, in a work context, serving as a mentor to a younger colleague. Failure in this task can bring a feeling of stagnation in which no contribution or legacy is left to future generations. During late adulthood, people need to understand and accept the ultimate meaningfulness and limitations of their lives or risk ending life with despair.

Erik Erikson's major contributions to the study of life and career development are twofold. First, he proposed an underlying order in which certain key issues present themselves at critical parts of our lives. Although "success" at each stage does not guarantee permanent resolution of a conflict, "failure at an early stage jeopardizes full development at a later stage."[65] Second, he identified three key developmental tasks of adulthood—intimacy, generativity, and ego integrity—that are particularly relevant to an understanding of careers.

Levinson's Approach to Adult Life Development

The seminal work of Daniel Levinson and his colleagues plays a particularly significant role in the overall understanding of adult life development and in the delineation of career and life stages.[66] In the 1970s, Levinson's research team conducted interviews with 40 American-born men between the ages of 35 and 45. Each man in the sample (ten business executives, ten university biologists, ten novelists, and ten industrial workers) was seen between five and ten times, and the interview transcripts generated an average of 300 pages of text per man.[67] These biographical interviews attempted to reconstruct the story of each man's life from childhood to the present. After this initial study, Levinson conducted interviews with 45 women, also ranging in age from 35 to 45.[68] Fifteen women were stay-at-home parents, 15 were pursuing corporate careers in finance, and 15 were pursuing academic careers. Levinson conducted interviews similar to those of his male sample, generating reconstructions of the stages of the women's lives.

Levinson proposed that there are four eras of the human life cycle: pre-adulthood, early adulthood, middle adulthood, and late adulthood (see Table 2.2). Each era consists of alternating stable and transitional periods. In stable periods, which usually last six or seven years, people pursue goals to accomplish their significant life values. Stable periods are not necessarily tranquil, but they are stable in the sense that people attempt to create a desired lifestyle. Because no life structure remains appropriate forever, transitional periods, normally of four or five years in duration, are necessary to question and reappraise the established life structure and to consider making changes in various parts of one's life.

According to Levinson, early adulthood normally begins in the late teens and culminates in the mid-40s with the termination of the midlife transition. In the very beginning period of adulthood, people emerge from adolescence and try to create a niche for themselves in adult society. Young adults need to begin the process of separation from their parents, often leaving home and becoming less financially and emotionally dependent on their

Table 2.2 Levinson's Eras of Development

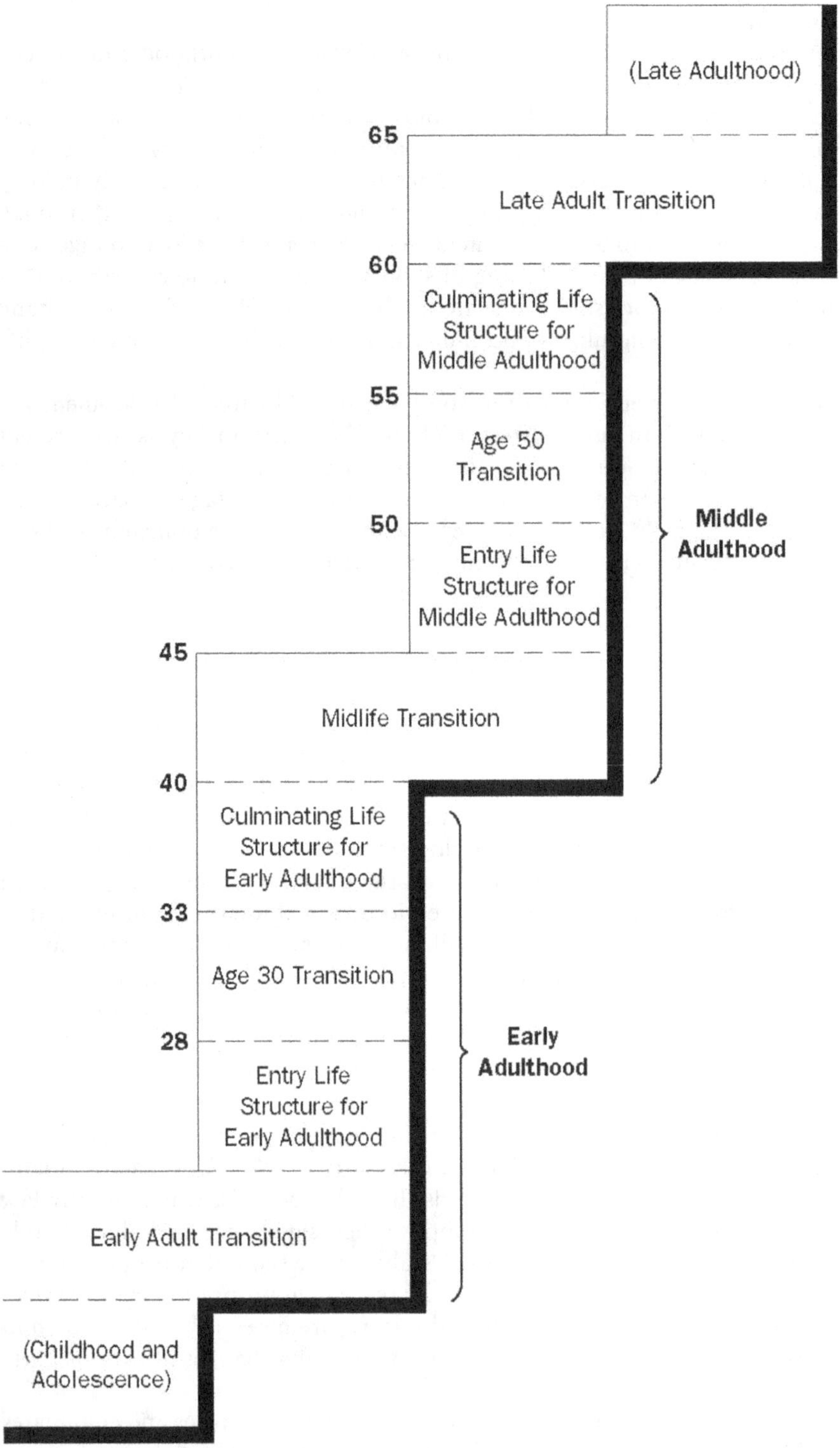

Source: Based on a diagram originally included in *The seasons of a man's life,* by Daniel J. Levinson et al. (1978). Updated to be consistent with terminology in Levinson's "A Conception of Adult Development," *American Psychologist 41* (1986: 3–13).

parents. They also need to take some tentative steps into early adulthood by imagining or even trying out an adult role in some manner.

Levinson considers the mid-20s to be a stable period in which the young person enters into the adult world, but faces two potentially conflicting tasks: (1) to explore adulthood by trying out different roles (for example, jobs, relationships) while keeping one's options open; and (2) to settle down and create a stable life. Whereas some people emphasize the exploratory task and form no real commitments to people or organizations, others form relationships that are expected to endure well into the future. Whatever decisions are made in this period, there are bound to be flaws. People who emphasized options and exploration may begin to wonder whether they are capable of developing and maintaining meaningful relationships. People who emphasize stability and commitments to an occupation, a company, or another person may wonder whether these commitments were premature and overly constraining.

In Levinson's model, the late 20s and early 30s represent a transitional period that stimulates a reappraisal of one's current life. These first three periods comprise the novice phase of early adulthood in which one is struggling to become a "real" adult. A major task of this novice phase is to form, refine, and pursue a "Dream," a powerful view of how one wants to live his or her life. The Dream frequently has occupational goals (for example, becoming a rich and famous financier or becoming a world-renowned scientist), but it can extend beyond work to one's role in family, community, or the larger society. During the mid-30s, the person has two major tasks: (1) to establish a niche in adult society in areas of life (work, family, leisure) that are central to the person; and (2) to "make it"—that is, to advance along some timetable in an effort to build a better life. This period is primarily devoted to the pursuit of one's Dream and becoming a full-fledged adult.

According to Levinson, middle adulthood commences in the early 40s with the midlife transition period. During this time, the life that was pursued so intensely during early adulthood is reappraised, possibly with a great deal of turmoil and agony. Levinson and his associates concluded that 80 percent of the men and 85 percent of the women in their samples experienced a moderate or severe crisis during the midlife transition. Why do some people begin such a painful reevaluation during the early or mid-40s? Levinson points to the significance of three related factors. First, even modest decline in bodily functioning around age 40 may be interpreted as a loss of youthful vigor and may stimulate an increasing awareness of one's mortality. The opportunity to make a lasting contribution to the world can be threatened by the realization that one's life is half over. Second, a generational shift normally occurs in the 40s. People in their 20s and 30s are apt to view someone in his or her forties as a member of the "older" generation. With the possibility of teenage children at this point and the likelihood of ailing or deceased parents, the person in his or her 40s feels pushed into senior status in the adult world and fears that youth (and all that it stands for) is largely completed.

Also, by the 40s, a person has experienced enough of life to assess progress toward the youthful Dream. A person who has failed to accomplish this Dream must deal with the failure and make some choices for the future. The person who has accomplished the Dream may begin to doubt whether the quest was worth it. The choices made in the 30s may have emphasized certain aspects of the self (for example, objective career success, achievement, power, competition) over others (for example, family, friendships, nurturance, spiritual development).

Levinson speculates that the midlife transition is followed by a stable period in which a person must try to fashion a satisfactory life for the middle years. This period, in turn, is followed in the early 50s by another transitional period during which time the person works further on the issues raised and the new goals developed during the midlife transition. The late adult transition (age 60–65) terminates middle adulthood and begins late adulthood.

A key aspect of Levinson's model is the proposed existence of four eras of the human life cycle in which a number of stable and transitional periods enable the individual to work on the major developmental tasks of each era. Despite the plausibility of the model, a number of questions over the years have become evident. How closely are the eras and the transitional periods linked to age? Is the sequence of periods fixed or can people "skip" periods? How universal are the periods? Are these periods applicable to both men and women in modern, industrialized societies?

First, Levinson believed that the periods are closely related to age. Although the participants in his samples showed some variation in the onset or termination of a period, the range was rather small, perhaps two years on either side of the average. Thus, Levinson believed that there is a close, but by no means perfect, correspondence between chronological age and period of life development for both men and women. Levinson also believed that each person goes through each period in a fixed sequence. This does not mean that a person actively or successfully deals with each developmental task in each period—only that the developmental tasks present themselves in a fixed order. The ability to generalize Levinson's model to all people in all societies has also been questioned. Although Levinson acknowledged that the answer to this question is unknown, he argued in favor of universal applicability. He cited literature from ancient Chinese, Greek, and Hebrew civilizations to support his view.

Perhaps the most intriguing issue in Levinson's model is the role of gender in adult life development. Daniel Levinson and his colleagues believed that women go through the same developmental periods as men, although some of the specific issues might differ between men and women. However, many women face a delicate "balancing act" between the pursuit of career progress and the demands of motherhood that makes the very nature of life development different for men and women. In this sense, it is possible that the sequence of developmental issues is reversed for women and men. For many women, the early adulthood stage can involve a preoccupation with balancing career, family, and dual-career issues. Even the pursuit of career success for women in their 30s is coupled with concerns about balancing multiple life roles and expectations. On the other hand, middle adulthood, when many men are reducing their involvement in work, can be a period of professional involvement and accomplishment for women as they become more independent and somewhat freer of family demands.

It is our opinion that Daniel Levinson's model of life development continues to be relevant, in a general sense, more than four decades after his initial work was published. While career progression in the 21st century is far more complex than in the 1970s, the notion of period-related developmental tasks still seems applicable to present day adulthood, and the alternating stable and transitional periods seem to permit continued growth and development throughout the lifespan. Finally, the three eras of adulthood—early, middle, and late—offer a useful structure for examining career-related issues during one's lifetime.

Generational Differences in Adult Life Development

Building upon the seminal works of Donald Super, Erik Erikson, and Daniel Levinson, a great deal of research attention has been devoted to variations in the career experiences and work attitudes of different age-based generations of employees.[69] The importance of the study of generations of individuals is based on the belief that each generation has certain characteristics, experiences, and shared life events that make it unique compared with other generations.[70] In addition, intergenerational interactions can influence individual and organizational outcomes such as turnover intentions, level of socialization and teamwork, acceptance of change, and degree of conflict.[71] Even though there is some disagreement over the terminology used to describe each generation of employees, the most commonly used terms are: the "baby boomers," or those born during the two decades after the end of World War II; "Generation X," or those born during the period from mid-1960s until the end of the 1970s; and the "Generation Y," or "Millennials" consisting of those born in the final 20 years of the 20th century. Overall, the linkage of a generational view of adult development with the stage-based view is fairly clear cut. Based on the age ranges, individuals in the baby boom demographic either are in, or are quickly approaching, a later stage of career and life. In contrast, members of the Generation X cohort are mostly in their 40s, indicating a midlife status in careers and life. Finally, the Millennial generation is under the age of 40, reflecting a group of people in the early phase of life and careers.

In general, and consistent with the research on career stages, the careers literature on generations of employees has focused on whether individuals born during certain eras display common background characteristics, values, attitudes, and cultural experiences, have similar expectations, and encounter related outcomes in terms of work and life experiences.[72] In addition to these within-generation analyses, studies have also looked at differences between the generations in terms of attitudes toward work and related career outcomes.[73]

While some conflicting results have been found,[74] these intergenerational studies show that the Generation X and Y individuals, in comparison with the older baby boom generation, rate work as less meaningful to their total lives, tend to value leisure time, self-enhancement, and extrinsic work values such as salary more highly, show a greater degree of openness to change, express a lower work ethic, and consistently score higher in individualistic traits.[75] Given the seemingly heavier emphasis on self-fulfillment and gratification in life and career outcomes, these findings have led some commentators to refer to the Millennial generation as "Gen Me" or the "Narcissistic Generation."[76] However, members of the Millennial generation also place a premium on such traditional work attributes as the prospects for advancement, solid training and developmental opportunities, working with and for upstanding and ethical people, and achieving work–life balance.[77]

It is not surprising that the baby boom generation has received the greatest degree of attention given its demographic size and its influence on the world of work, on society as a whole, and on governmental programs.[78] Although estimates vary, it is believed that in the U.S. the baby boom generation consists of roughly 78 million people, all of whom will be of the retirement age of 65 by the year 2030. Given their age, baby boom employees face a number of challenges in terms of career management, including maintaining competency in an era of rapid technological change, making important contributions to their work organizations even when faced with limited or nonexistent mobility opportunities, dealing with potential health issues, and preparing both emotionally and financially for retirement. These challenges are mostly unique to this older cohort of individuals.

For organizations, baby boom workers represent a critical resource given their years of experience, embedded work knowledge, leadership abilities, and consistency and reliability in the commitment to their jobs. Going forward, organizations will need to continue to engage and retain baby boom workers in view of the forecasted shortage of skilled and unskilled labor in the industrialized world over the next few decades. Simultaneously, baby boom workers can be seen as a burden for organizations because plateaued boomers can block the upward mobility of younger Generation X and Millennial workers who are presumably more technologically proficient.[79]

As with adult life and career stages, an understanding of the attitudes, needs, and motivations of different generations of employees certainly has implications for organizations in terms of the recruitment, development, and retention of individual workers as well as fostering positive group interactions and communication. These generational differences and the implications for organizations will be discussed in more detail in Chapters 7–9.

Stages of Career Development

In Chapter 1, we defined career development as an ongoing process by which an individual progresses through a series of stages, each of which is characterized by a relatively unique set of issues, themes, and tasks. While the concepts of life development and career development are compatible, there is a greater emphasis on work-related issues in career development models. This book views development of a career in terms of four stages. This view and the delineation are based on the more traditional perspectives on adult life development as well as the growing body of literature on generations of individuals. The four stages of this model are summarized in Table 2.3 and are discussed below.

Stage 1: Occupational and Organizational Choice

From a career perspective, the initial set of tasks in this stage are to form and refine an occupational self-image, explore the qualities of alternative occupations, develop at least a tentative occupational choice, and pursue the type of education or training required to implement the choice. The accomplishment of these initial career tasks requires considerable insight into one's own abilities, interests, values, and desired lifestyle, as well as the requirements, opportunities, and rewards associated with alternative occupational fields. Indeed, for younger adults, choosing an occupation involves the formation of an image of oneself and an increased understanding of the world of work. The model of career management that will be described in Chapter 4 is based on continual exploration and discovery, and many people develop second or third occupational choices during the course of their work lives. Because occupational choices can occur at other stages, the tasks associated

Table 2.3 Four Stages of Career Development

1. **Occupational and Organizational Choice**
   Typical Age Range: Initially 18–30; then variable
   Major Tasks: Develop occupational self-image, assess alternative occupations, develop initial occupational choice, pursue necessary education, obtain job offer(s) from desired organization(s).
2. **Early Career**
   Typical Age Range: 25–45
   Major Tasks: Learn job, learn organizational rules and norms, fit into chosen occupation and organization, increase competence, pursue career goals.
3. **Midcareer**
   Typical Age Range: 40–60
   Major Tasks: Reappraise early career and early adulthood, reaffirm or modify career goals, make choices appropriate to middle adult years, remain productive in work.
4. **Late Career**
   Typical Age Range: 55–Retirement
   Major Tasks: Remain productive in work, maintain self-esteem, prepare for effective retirement, both financially and mentally.

with occupational choice can reappear throughout one's lifetime. Chapter 7 focuses extensively on the occupational choice process.

Once an occupation has been selected, the second set of tasks in this stage focus on selecting and entering an organization, and landing a job that can satisfy one's career values and utilize one's talents. The organizational choice and entry process can take several months to complete and often depends on the number of years of education one has pursued, the accumulated set of skills, and the availability of employment opportunities. Although the entry process is experienced initially by persons who are moving directly from school to their first career-related work assignment, people can enter a new organization at any age; therefore, the age range can be quite variable. Chapter 7 elaborates on the tasks associated with the organizational choice and entry process. It also reviews how individuals can identify, evaluate, and choose organizations; highlights several obstacles to a match between the individual and the organization; and suggests ways to manage the organizational entry process effectively.

Stage 2: The Early Career—the Establishment and Achievement Phases

This career stage, which really encompasses two periods, reflects the dominant issues of early adulthood: finding a niche for oneself in the adult world and striving to "make it" along the chosen path. Having already focused on an occupation and an initial job, a critical first task of the early career is to become established in that career. The new employee must not only master the technical aspects of his or her job but must also learn the norms, values, and expectations of the organization. In this establishment period of the early career, the individual's major task is to learn about the job and the organization and to become accepted as a competent contributor; in other words, to make a place for himself or herself in the occupation and the organization.

It may seem odd that the early career can extend all the way up to age 45. But the entire stage, in our view, does reflect the early career in that the individual typically continues to pursue youthful aspirations as yet unencumbered by the sometimes-painful reappraisal of the midlife transition. In addition, career disruptions, high levels of job insecurity, and the rise of the gig economy with nonpermanent alternative work arrangements mean that individuals might take a greater amount of time to become established in a job and a career. Thus, it is suggested that the dominant theme of the early career, becoming established and making it (however defined), can maintain itself in one form or another for a significant period of time. Chapter 8 examines issues pertaining to the early career in considerable depth.

Stage 3: The Midcareer

A number of tasks and concerns characterize the midcareer years. First, as Levinson observed, the individual is likely to reappraise the lifestyle and demands that dominated his or her early career. Next, it is necessary to begin to form a lifestyle (with its career implications) to move fully into middle adulthood. Regardless of whether the new lifestyle is consistent with the prior one or constitutes a minor or radical departure, there are a number of specific work-related issues that confront the individual in midcareer.

Chapter 9 examines midcareer issues. Among the major concerns treated are the potential for a distinctive (and possibly trying) midlife transition, the dynamics associated with the pursuit of a midcareer change, the dangers of obsolescence, and the outcomes of, and responses to, midcareer plateauing. As with the other career stages,

Chapter 9 considers individual and organizational actions that can contribute to effective functioning during midcareer. Notice that the midcareer period can extend all the way to the age of 60. With people all over the industrialized world living longer and retiring later, it is possible that the "middle period" of a career can last longer than would traditionally be expected.

Stage 4: Late Career

There are two major tasks that dominate this stage. First, the individual must continue to be a productive contributor to the organization and maintain his or her sense of self-worth and dignity. However, the maintenance of productivity and self-esteem is often hindered by changes within the individual and by society's bias against older people. Second, the individual in late career must anticipate and plan for an effective retirement, so that either partial or full disengagement from work is not devastating to the individual and that the post retirement years are meaningful and satisfying. The issues that dominate the late career will also be examined more thoroughly in Chapter 9.

Difficulties in Applying a Career Stage Perspective

This chapter has outlined four career stages, which are organized around typical—although approximate—age ranges. We are not claiming that this is the only or the best way to view career development, but it does seem to structure our knowledge about careers in a meaningful manner. Nonetheless, there are several factors that complicate the use of stages as a predominant method of viewing career progression. One question concerning career stages is whether, in today's era of employment uncertainty, there is a clear linkage of the stages to chronological age. To answer this question, it is important to recognize that all age ranges are approximations. The onset, duration, and termination of stages can vary. Thus, a high school graduate might accept a first full-time job at age 18, whereas a Ph.D. graduate may take a first academic post at age 28 or later. Some approaches to career development define career stages on the basis of work activities, relationships, and psychological issues rather than on the basis of age. Despite the many valuable contributions of that approach, we take the position that age, or more generally life experience, strongly shapes career aspirations, experiences, and concerns, and therefore plays a critical role in the identification of career stages.

A second issue concerns the assumption that the stages of a career cycle depict development in a "normal" career; that is, a career in which a person chooses an occupation at an early age and remains continually in the same career field (or in the same organization) for the duration of one's work life. The idea of long and sequential career stages is based in large part on the assumed pursuit of traditional organizational careers that were prevalent when career stage theories were first proposed in the 1950s, 1960s, and 1970s. There is an emerging view, as we move through the early part of the 21st century, that career stages or cycles not only vary in duration but also reoccur periodically over the course of a person's career.[80] It is thought that career cycles are now compressed because of the frequent and dramatic changes or transitions associated with pursuing a boundaryless career.[81] Michael Arthur and his colleagues have identified three career cycles or "modes"—fresh energy, informed direction, and seasoned engagement—that are generally consistent with the early, middle, and late career stages, respectively.[82] Although fresh energy is typically displayed in the early career, informed direction in midcareer, and seasoned engagement in late career, Arthur and his colleagues demonstrated how individuals periodically "recycle" back to earlier modes as they change projects, jobs, employers, or industries.[83]

What are the complications in defining career stages that arise from deviations from a traditional organizational career? Consider the following illustrations:

- A 42-year-old woman accepts paid employment for the first time in nearly 20 years. Is she beginning her midcareer years or is she entering the establishment period of her early career?
- A 38-year-old banker pursues a promotion to senior vice-president with a different bank. Is he deeply entrenched in the achievement period of his early career or is he beginning another organizational entry stage?
- A 55-year-old computer executive leaves Silicon Valley to become a novelist. Is she approaching her late career or is she struggling to establish herself in the early career stage of her new literary pursuits?

These kinds of classification problems are inherent in all age-related theories of career development, but they may not be problems after all. Our aim is not merely to classify an individual into a particular stage but to understand how careers unfold and how people relate to work at different points in their lives. The newly employed woman primarily has to deal with the early career issues of socialization and establishment, but from the perspective of a 42-year-old. The 38-year-old banker does have to deal with the problems of organizational entry, but with the experience and work–life concerns of a person who is advanced in his early career and is "on the move." The 55-year-old former computer executive does, in most respects, have to establish herself in her new career field, but from the vantage point of a woman nearing later adulthood.

We should not bemoan these deviations from a neat classification system, because they reflect the rich diversity of careers and lives. In Table 2.4, we attempt to portray this diversity by linking the tasks of career development with the three eras of adulthood. Notice that the selection of an occupation, the entrance into an organization, the establishment of

Table 2.4 Relationship between Career Development Tasks and Stages of Adulthood

	Stages of Adulthood		
Career Development Tasks	*Early Adulthood*	*Middle Adulthood*	*Late Adulthood*
Occupational/Occupational Choice	XXX	XX	X
Early Career			
Establishment	XXX	XX	X
Achievement	XXX	XX	X
Midcareer			
Reappraisal	X	XXX	XX
Remain Productive	X	XXX	XXX
Late Career			
Remain Productive	X	XXX	XXX
Prepare for Retirement	X	XX	XXX

XXX Very Frequently

XX Frequently

X Occasionally

oneself in a new setting, and the striving for achievement in that setting occur most prominently in early adulthood. However, the selection of a different occupation or organization can occur during middle adulthood or late adulthood, necessitating renewed establishment and achievement concerns in the different career field or organization. Conversely, the tasks most closely aligned with midcareer and late career (reappraisal, remaining productive, preparation for retirement) may also occur to some extent during early adulthood. Perhaps our aim should be to understand the typical issues that people generally experience at each career stage, and then consider the possible variations that can occur at each stage. This approach will be followed in Chapters 7–9 when we delve more deeply into the different career stages.

Summary

This chapter presented a number of different perspectives from which a career and career management can be viewed. Traditional organizational careers, wherein one strives for and expects job stability, security, and upward advancement, have been supplanted by careers that are far less certain. The protean, boundaryless, and other more recent career concepts take into account the increased uncertainty in people's work lives. These newer ways of looking at careers recognize that individuals will likely work for multiple organizations (rather than just one or two organizations), that the nature of the psychological contract with their employer will likely be transactional (rather than relational), that the individual will be challenged to develop multiple skills that can be transported from one work setting to another, and that the individual (rather than the organization) has ultimate responsibility for his or her career management. This emphasis on flexibility and adaptability in the individual's career does not necessarily mean that the boundaryless career is the only or the dominant career model, but rather that an increasing segment of the population is likely to pursue a career with boundaryless characteristics. This pursuit either can occur through conscious design or be forced on the individual by the job insecurity and job loss that result from an uncertain and dispassionate world of work.

This chapter also recognized that careers and career choices do not occur in a vacuum. Social institutions, such as a person's family and community groups, have a significant influence on an individual's interests, values, and preferences that eventually translate into specific career choices. Research on careers also recognizes the role that social networks play in career decision-making and advancement. By engaging in these networks, individuals build social capital that facilitates connections with people of influence who can help the individual in various career-related tasks.

Contemporary career concepts expand the meaning of career success. Traditionally, career success was viewed primarily in objective terms, with such tangible outcomes as compensation level, job title, promotion record, and executive perks being seen as indicators of success. It is now recognized that career success also has a subjective component that takes into account an individual's feelings of success in his or her career. The subjective element can include feelings of satisfaction with the individual's career accomplishments or with his or her total life. This expansion in the meaning of career success recognizes that individuals have multiple demands both from the work and nonwork spheres of their lives and that they take into account accomplishments in both areas when gauging their success.

The research of Erik Erikson and Daniel Levinson suggests that the early, middle, and late stages of adulthood present somewhat different tasks and challenges that need to be addressed. Early adulthood is characterized by a preoccupation with establishing oneself as an adult and "making it" in the adult world. Middle adulthood often involves a reappraisal of one's life situation and a concern with building a lasting contribution to the world. In late adulthood, one needs to come to terms with the meaning and value of one's life. More recent research has focused on the varying career experiences and the challenges faced by people in different generations as based on the years when those individuals were born. As with career stages, a person's chronological age and generation can influence attitudes toward work, the desire for leisure and family time, the level of work ethic, and a host of other dispositions and outcomes.

Four stages of career development were identified: (1) occupational and organizational choice, during which time one develops an occupational self-image, explores alternative occupations, forms an occupational decision, and selects and enters an organization; (2) early career, in which one is concerned with establishing himself or herself in a career field and achieving competence and recognition; (3) midcareer, during which time one may need to reexamine the course of one's career and life and perhaps make adjustments for the future; and (4) late career, in which one needs to maintain a satisfactory level of productivity and self-esteem and plan for an effective retirement. These four career stages provide the structure for Chapters 7–9 of the book.

Career Management *for Life*: Work–Life Implications from Chapter 2

- Protean-oriented careerists often adopt a "whole-life perspective," by which they seek success and fulfillment in work *and* nonwork pursuits, and make career decisions with an awareness of how these decisions affect other parts of their life.
- One manifestation of pursuing a boundaryless career is permitting family or personal considerations to influence a career-related decision, as in rejecting a promotion for fear that it would interfere with family or personal commitments.
- A customized career is a nontraditional career path that employees pursue in response to their family or personal needs. A customized career may involve a reduced workload arrangement, the pursuit of noncontinuous employment with occasional interruptions, or a temporary or contract relationship with an employer.
- Subjective assessments of career success can depend on how successful an individual is in balancing work with other parts of life.
- Each career stage and life stage challenges individuals to make effective career decisions. Career management is not a one-shot activity but rather should be engaged in "for life."

Assignments

1. Interview a friend, acquaintance, co-worker, or relative who is in a different generation (or career stage) than you are. What career-related tasks and activities is this person currently undertaking? What are the issues and concerns that are uppermost in his or her mind? In what ways are these issues and concerns consistent or inconsistent with the approach to life development and career development proposed in this chapter?

2. Chart the career histories of a male and female friend, acquaintance, co-worker, or relative. Are the two career histories parallel and similar to each other? Do employment gaps exist in either career history? If so, ask whether these employment gaps have had any effect on the individual's career.

Discussion Questions

1. Given the high level of uncertainty in today's job market and the shift toward transactional psychological contracts between employers and employees, do you think a "traditional" career is still possible? Why or why not?
2. Do you think that making a great deal of money and advancing to high levels of an organization (achieving objective career success) necessarily produces feelings of subjective career success? Are there trade-offs that one would have to make in life in order to achieve such objective career success?
3. Many people experience a crisis during their middle career years. What factors are responsible for a midlife crisis? Do you think that the majority of people experience a midlife crisis, even though the intensity and outcomes might be different depending on the person? Why or why not?
4. Do you think the majority of people follow the same developmental path through adulthood? What environmental and individual factors could disrupt a normal progression through the career stages as described in this chapter?

Chapter 2 Case: Kevin at the Crossroads

By everyone's account, Kevin has the ideal life. At the age of 39 he has attained the title of vice-president of corporate planning for XO Engineering Services Inc. (fictitious name), a mid-sized engineering firm specializing in providing support for large-scale infrastructure projects around the world. Kevin has spent his entire professional career at XO.

At the age of 23 Kevin received his bachelor's degree in mechanical engineering from one of the top universities in the United States. While he looked at a number of engineering companies prior to graduation, he was most impressed with XO right from the start. By Kevin's estimation, XO was a progressive organization that had outstanding growth prospects and really seemed to care about its employees. During the interview process, he was surprised by how many times he heard that XO was like a family. Many of the employees whom Kevin met during his site visit had spent their entire careers at XO and some had been with the company for its entire 30-year existence. Another selling point in favor of XO was that its corporate headquarters was in a Virginia suburb right outside of Washington, D.C. Kevin had grown up in northern Virginia and really wanted to stay in the metro Washington, D.C. area. For all of these reasons, the choice of XO as an employer was a "no-brainer" for Kevin.

Kevin's Early Career

Kevin's work ethic, intelligence, and charisma were recognized by XO's senior management early in his tenure with the company. In every assignment and project, Kevin's superiors would give him glowing evaluations. Kevin's rise up the corporate hierarchy was meteoric, at least by XO's standards. He went from a junior to a senior engineering position in two years and to a project manager two years after that. With XO's encouragement, Kevin had gotten an executive MBA from a top-notch business school in Washington. By the time he was 30, Kevin was an assistant vice-president, and at the age of 34 he was promoted to vice-president of engineering services. At age 38 he was moved to his present position. His current salary and bonus now totals over $200,000 per year. He is financially well off and he knows that XO's senior management and board of directors see him as a future senior officer, maybe even the CEO someday. His decision to take a job with XO many years ago has paid off for Kevin. He is in a secure, stable career with a solid company and he has great prospects for further advancement.

Kevin's Nonwork Life

While an undergraduate, Kevin met and began dating Anne, a fellow student pursuing a degree in education. After three years of dating, they got married. While Kevin was starting his career at XO, Anne began teaching seventh grade English in a school district close to their home. The two-career relationship worked well, with both Kevin and Anne enjoying much success in their careers. And their dual incomes afforded them a comfortable lifestyle.

Kevin and Anne agreed that they wanted to have children as soon as they could. Two years after they got married they had their first son and two years later they had another son. Their dual-earner relationship resulted in a fair number of childcare challenges and stresses when the two boys were younger, but Anne's job meant that she could be counted on to get home in the afternoon and she had her summers off. Both Kevin's and Anne's parents lived relatively close by, and they took turns watching the boys when needed. Once the two boys started school, the childcare challenges became less difficult to manage. With his career on the fast track, Kevin did not get too involved in child-rearing activities—he just did not have the time. His job required him to travel about 30 percent of the time, so he was often away from home, and when he was at the corporate headquarters he usually put in some long hours.

As his sons got older, Kevin became involved in helping coach their sports teams. Both boys enjoyed athletics and they started playing baseball and football as soon as they were old enough. Kevin had played both sports in high school and he was quite pleased that his sons gravitated to these two sports. When he was not traveling, Kevin really enjoyed the time he spent coaching. He always looked forward to the practices and games, not only because he could spend time with his two sons, but he also believed that he had a positive influence on all the players he coached.

Just recently, several parents approached Kevin about becoming the manager of the travel baseball team for the next season. The travel team, of which Kevin's older son was a member, consisted of the top players in that age group. Because of the higher caliber of play, the travel team usually practiced twice a week and also played two games per week. While Kevin was flattered by the invitation to manage the team, he knew that his job demands would make it impossible for him to consider the offer seriously. Nevertheless, he really did want to manage the team and found himself bitter that his job was getting in the way of something that he really wanted to do.

Kevin's Dilemma

For at least the past three months Kevin has been having a difficult time being motivated about his work. After 17 years at XO the job is not as challenging as it once was and the same old routine has gotten to be a hassle. The regular travel overseas is the worst part because it takes him away from his family for several days at a time. When he is away he has a hard time focusing on his work—he just counts down the days to when he can get back home. His work has not really suffered yet, mainly because his technical and managerial skills are still sharp, but he worries that if he doesn't get his act together soon his performance might begin to slip.

Deep down, Kevin really envies his wife and her career. He sees Anne's teaching and counseling of children as fulfilling work, at least when compared with engineering. And unlike himself, it seems as if his wife is always motivated for her job. She also gets to spend a much greater amount of time with their children than he does. When he daydreams, Kevin secretly wonders what it would be like to be a teacher. One of the local colleges has been running ads for a program that would allow individuals who already have a bachelor's degree to get a teaching degree with only a year's worth of coursework. And he sees listings in the local newspapers for math and science teachers. Kevin is certain he would be a great teacher with his technical skills and all of his real-world experience.

His daydreams often fade quickly though, especially when he considers all that he would be giving up if he were to change careers. For one thing, his starting salary as a teacher wouldn't even be a third of what he is making as an executive with XO. Plus, if he were to leave XO now, he would be leaving a tremendous amount of potential future income "on-the-table" so to speak given his chances for further promotions and compensation increases with XO. Longer-term, if he were to leave XO before he hit the age of 50 he would also forgo a substantial amount of pension income in his retirement. He hasn't spoken with Anne about his daydreams and even if he did discuss the idea with her he isn't sure how she would react. She seems happy with the current situation and the successes they have achieved together. To willingly take a significant step backward in their household finances might not sit too well with her.

While in the midst of one of his daydreams, Kevin was brought back to reality by a knock at his office door. It was the CEO of the company and he wanted to know if Kevin was free for lunch that day. Kevin wasn't sure if the invitation to lunch was a good thing or not—after all, his boredom in his work might have finally caught up with him. To Kevin's surprise, the lunch with the CEO wasn't negative at all; in fact it should have been looked at as good news. The CEO explained to Kevin that XO's senior officers, with the blessing of the board of directors, had decided to make a major expansion of the company's operations into South America. Kevin knew that the expansion was possible, given that he had actually made the formal proposal to the Board. While XO already had an office in Brazil, this new strategy would significantly expand operations in that country and throughout the region.

The purpose of the lunch was to gauge Kevin's interest in taking over the expanded operations in South America. The CEO explained how much confidence he and the board of directors had in Kevin and that he was the clear-cut choice to head this mission. The CEO hinted that if he were successful in this venture he would be the heir apparent to the CEO position in two or three years. Of course, the move would mean a promotion to the senior vice-president level and a major increase in compensation. The CEO further explained that Kevin would need to move to Brazil, but the expatriate assignment would likely only be for two years. The CEO asked Kevin to think about the offer and also discuss it thoroughly with Anne. He asked Kevin to get back to him in a week or so. The company needed to move quickly, because if Kevin wasn't interested, they would likely go through an external search to fill the position.

After the lunch, Kevin sat at his desk in stunned silence. As he was about to leave and head home, he remembered that he had to go directly to the football field for his younger son's practice that evening—the team has a big game this weekend and they need Coach Kevin to help get them prepared.

Case Questions

1. Based on the definition and the description of the protean and boundaryless perspectives of careers as provided in this chapter, do you think Kevin has adopted these approaches to his career? Why or why?
2. Do you think Kevin sees himself as successful in his career? Why or why not?
3. What social and nonwork factors are influencing Kevin's career choices? How big a role should these factors play in the career decisions of an individual? Should they play a role?
4. Do you think Kevin's age and the fact that he is approaching midcareer are having an effect on his "daydreaming" and the questioning of his future career direction? Why or why not?
5. If Kevin sought your help, what advice would you give him in terms of the management of his career? If you had to make a prediction, what career choices do you think Kevin will make?

Notes

1 Greenhaus, J. H. & Callanan, G. A. (2012). Career dynamics. In Wiener, I., Schmitt, N. W. & Highhouse, S. (Eds.), *Comprehensive handbook of psychology, volume 12: Industrial and organizational psychology*, 2nd ed. (pp. 593–614). Hoboken, NJ: Wiley.

2 Sullivan, S. E. & Baruch, Y. (2009). Advances in career theory and research: A critical review and agenda for future exploration. *Journal of Management*, *35*, 1542–1571.

3 Cappelli, P. H. (2015). Skill gaps, skill shortages, and skill mismatches: Evidence and arguments for the United States. *ILR Review*, *68*, 251–290. Callanan, G. A. & Greenhaus, J. H. (1999). Personal and career development: The best and worst of times. In Kraut, A. I. & Korman, A. K. (Eds.), *Evolving practices in human resource management: Responses to a changing world of work* (pp. 146–171). San Francisco: Jossey-Bass.

4 Greenhaus, J. H., Callanan, G. A. & DiRenzo, M. S. (2008). A boundaryless perspective on careers. In Cooper, C. L. & Barling, J. (Eds.), *Handbook of organizational behavior* (pp. 277–299). Thousand Oaks, CA: Sage.
5 Sullivan & Baruch (2009).
6 Kulick, R. B. (2006). Occupational professionalization. In Greenhaus, J. H. & Callanan, G. A. (Eds.), *Encyclopedia of career development* (pp. 563–567). Thousand Oaks, CA: Sage.
7 Duffy, R. D. & Dik, B. J. (2013). Research on calling: What have we learned and where are we going? *Journal of Vocational Behavior, 83*, 428–436; Wrzesniewski, A. & Tosti, R. B. (2006). Career as a calling. In Greenhaus, J. H. & Callanan, G. A. (Eds.), *Encyclopedia of career development* (pp. 71–75). Thousand Oaks, CA: Sage.
8 Ibid.
9 Biemann, T., Zacher, H. & Feldman, D. C. (2012). Career patterns: A twenty-year panel study. *Journal of Vocational Behavior, 81*, 159–170.
10 Rodrigues, R., Guest, D., Oliveira, T. & Alfes, K. (2015). Who benefits from independent careers? Employees, organizations, or both? *Journal of Vocational Behavior, 91*, 23–34.
11 Hall, D. T. (1976). *Careers in organizations*. Glenview, IL: Scott Foresman.
12 Waters, L., Briscoe, J. & Hall, D. T. (2014). Using protean career attitude to facilitate a positive approach to unemployment. In Coetzee, M. (Ed.), Psycho-social career meta-capacities (pp. 19–33). London, UK: Springer; Waters, L., Briscoe, J. P., Hall, D. T. & Wang, L. (2014). Protean career attitudes during unemployment and reemployment: A longitudinal perspective. *Journal of Vocational Behavior, 84*, 405–419; Briscoe, J. P. & Hall, D. T. (2006). The interplay of boundaryless and protean careers: Combinations and implications. *Journal of Vocational Behavior, 69*, 4–18; Briscoe, J. P., Hall, D. T. & DeMuth, R. L. F. (2006). Protean and boundaryless careers: An empirical exploration. *Journal of Vocational Behavior, 69*, 30–47.
13 DiRenzo, M. S., Greenhaus, J. H. & Weer, C. H. (2015). Relationship between protean career orientation and work–life balance: A resource perspective. *Journal of Organizational Behavior, 36*, 538–560.
14 Ibid.
15 For a brief history of the development, explication, and application of the boundaryless career concept, see Arthur, M. B. (2014). The boundaryless career at 20: Where we stand, and where we can go? *Career Development International, 19*, 627–640. See also Greenhaus et al. (2008); Tams, S. & Arthur, M. B. (2006). Boundaryless career. In Greenhaus, J. H. & Callanan, G. A. (Eds.), *Encyclopedia of career development* (pp. 44–49). Thousand Oaks, CA: Sage.
16 Inkson, K. (2006). Protean and boundaryless careers as metaphors. *Journal of Vocational Behavior, 69*, 48–63.
17 Arthur, M. B. & Rousseau, D. M. (1996). Introduction: The boundaryless career as a new employment principle. In Arthur, M. B. & Rousseau, D. M. (Eds.), *The boundaryless career* (pp. 3–20). New York: Oxford University Press.
18 Ibid.
19 Greenhaus et al. (2008).
20 Arthur & Rousseau (1996); DeFillippi, R. J. & Arthur, M. B. (1994). The boundaryless career: A competency-based perspective. *Journal of Organizational Behavior, 15*, 307–324; Greenhaus et al. (2008).
21 Briscoe & Hall (2006); Inkson (2006).
22 Greenhaus et al. (2008).
23 Briscoe & Hall (2006).
24 Briscoe et al. (2006).
25 Inkson (2006).
26 Ibid.
27 Briscoe, J. P., Henagan, S. C., Burton, J. P. & Murphy, W. M. (2012). Coping with an insecure employment environment: The differing roles of protean and boundaryless career orientations. *Journal of Vocational Behavior, 80*, 308–316; Greenhaus et al. (2008); Tams & Arthur (2006); Waters et al. (2014); DiRenzo et al. (2015).
28 DiRenzo et al. (2015).
29 Sullivan & Baruch (2009); Mainiero, L. A. & Sullivan, S. E. (2005). Kaleidoscope careers: An alternative explanation for the "opt-out generation." *Academy of Management Executive, 19*, 106–123.
30 Valcour, M., Bailyn, L. & Quijada, M. A. (2007). Customized careers. In Gunz, H. & Peiperl, M. (Eds.), *Handbook of career studies* (pp. 188–210). Thousand Oaks, CA: Sage.
31 Valcour et al. (2007); Greenhaus, J. H. & Kossek, E. E. (2014). The contemporary career: A work–home perspective. *Annual Review of Organizational Psychology and Organizational*

Behavior, *1*, 361–388; Kossek, E. E., Ollier-Malaterre, A., Lee, M. D., Hall, D. T. & Pichler, S. (2011). Managerial gatekeeping rationales for customized work arrangements: Evidence of the changing employee–organization relationship. Paper presented at the Annual Meeting of the Organization for Industrial and Organizational Psychology. Chicago, IL.
32 Arthur, M. B., Khapova, S. N. & Richardson, J. (2017). *An intelligent career: Taking ownership of your work and life*. New York: Oxford University Press.
33 Inkson, K., Dries, N. & Arnold, J. (2014). *Understanding careers: Metaphors of working lives*, 2nd ed. Thousand Oaks, CA: Sage.
34 Krumboltz, J. D. & Jacobs, J. M. (2006). Social learning theory of career development. In Greenhaus, J. H. & Callanan, G. A. (Eds.), *Encyclopedia of career development* (pp. 756–759). Thousand Oaks, CA: Sage.
35 Jepsen, D. A. (2006). Family background and careers. In Greenhaus, J. H. & Callanan, G. A. (Eds.), *Encyclopedia of career development* (pp. 313–317). Thousand Oaks, CA: Sage.
36 Ibid.
37 Benson, V., Filippaios, F. & Morgan, S. (2010). Online social networks: Changing the face of business education and career. *International Journal of e-Business Management*, *4*, 20–33.
38 Murphy, W. M. & Kram, K. E. (2010). Understanding non-work relationships in developmental networks. *Career Development International*, *15*, 637–663.
39 For extensive reviews of research on networking, see: Porter, C. M. & Woo, S. E. (2015). Untangling the networking phenomenon: A dynamic psychological perspective on how and why people network. *Journal of Management*, *41*, 1477–1500; Tasselli, S., Kilduff, M. & Menges, J. I. (2015). The microfoundations of organizational social networks: A review and an agenda for future research. *Journal of Management*, *41*, 1361–1387; Carpenter, M. A., Li, M. & Jiang, H. (2015). Social networking research in organizational contexts: A systematic review of methodological issues and choices. *Journal of Management*, *38*, 1328–1361; Gibson, C., Hardy, J. H. & Buckley, M. R. (2014). Understanding the role of networking in organizations. *Career Development International*, *19*, 146–161. See also Colakoglu, S. N. (2006). Networking. In Greenhaus, J. H. & Callanan, G. A. (Eds.), *Encyclopedia of career development* (pp. 536–537). Thousand Oaks, CA: Sage.
40 Porter & Woo (2015).
41 Payne, G. T., Moore, C. B., Griffis, S. E. & Autry, C. W. (2011). Multilevel challenges and opportunities in social capital research. *Journal of Management*, *37*, 491–520; Adams, S. M. (2006). Social capital. In Greenhaus, J. H. & Callanan, G. A. (Eds.), *Encyclopedia of career development* (pp. 746–750). Thousand Oaks, CA: Sage.
42 Ng, T. W. H. & Feldman, D. C. (2010). The effects of organizational embeddedness on development of social capital and human capital. *Journal of Applied Psychology*, *95*, 696–712.
43 Ibid.
44 Ramarajan, L. & Reid, E. (2013). Shattering the myth of separate worlds: Negotiating nonwork identities at work. *Academy of Management Review*, *38*, 621–644.
45 Seibert, S. E. (2006). Career success. In Greenhaus, J. H. & Callanan, G. A. (Eds.), *Encyclopedia of career development* (pp. 148–154). Thousand Oaks, CA: Sage.
46 Dries, N. (2011). The meaning of career success. *Career Development International*, *16*, 364–384.
47 Shockley, K. M., Ureksoy, H., Rodopman, O. B., Poteat, L. F. & Dullaghan, T. R. (2016). Development of a new scale to measure subjective career success: A mixed-methods study. *Journal of Organizational Behavior*, *37*, 128–153.
48 Greenhaus & Kossek (2014); Hall, D. T., Lee, M. D., Kossek, E. E. & Heras, M. L. (2012). Pursuing career success while sustaining personal and family well-being: A study of reduced-load professionals over time. *Journal of Social Issues*, *68*, 741–766.
49 Greenhaus & Callanan (2012); Eby, L. T., Butts, M. & Lockwood, A. (2003). Predictors of success in the era of boundaryless careers. *Journal of Organizational Behavior*, *24*, 689–708.
50 Abele, A. E. & Spurk, D. (2009). How do objective and subjective career success interrelate over time? *Journal of Occupational and Organizational Psychology*, *82*, 803–824.
51 Greenhaus & Kossek (2014).
52 Callanan, G. A. (2003). What price career success? *Career Development International*, *8*, 126–133.
53 Ng, T. W. H. & Feldman, D. C. (2014). Subjective career success: A meta-analytic review. *Journal of Vocational Behavior*, *85*, 169–179; Maurer, T. J. & Chapman, E. F. (2013). Ten years of career success in relation to individual and situational variables from the employee development literature. *Journal of Vocational Behavior*, *83*, 450–465.
54 Erikson, E. H. (1963). *Childhood and society*. New York: W. W. Norton; Freud, S. (1959). *Collected papers*. New York: Basic Books; Kohlberg, L. (1964). Development of moral character

and moral ideology. In Hoffman, L. & Hoffman, L. W. (Eds.), *Review of child development research: Vol. 1* (pp. 383–431). New York: Russell Sage Foundation; Piaget, J. (1952). *The child's conception of number*. London, England: Routledge & Kegan Paul.
55 Agronin, M. E. (2014). From Cicero to Cohen: Developmental theories of aging, from antiquity to the present. *The Gerontologist*, *54*, 30–39.
56 Low, C. H., Bordia, P. & Bordia, S. (2016). What do employees want and why? An exploration of employees' preferred psychological contract elements across career stages. *Human Relations*, *69*, 1457–1481.
57 Finkelstein, L. M., King, E. B. & Voyles, E. C. (2015). Age metastereotyping and cross-age workplace interactions: A meta view of age stereotypes at work. *Work, Aging, and Retirement*, *1*, 26–40.
58 Ng, T. W. H. & Feldman, D. C. (2013). Employee age and health. *Journal of Vocational Behavior*, *83*, 336–345.
59 Finkelstein et al. (2015); Ng, T. W. H. & Feldman, D. C. (2013). How do within-person changes due to aging affect job performance? *Journal of Vocational Behavior*, *83*, 500–513; Ng, T. W. H. & Feldman, D. C. (2012). Evaluating six common stereotypes about older workers with meta-analytical data. *Personnel Psychology*, *65*, 821–858; Callanan, G. A. & Greenhaus, J. H. (2008). The baby boom generation and career management: A call to action. *Advances in Developing Human Resources*, *10*, 70–85; Keene, J. (2006). Age discrimination. In Greenhaus, J. H. & Callanan, G. A. (Eds.), *Encyclopedia of career development* (pp. 10–14). Thousand Oaks, CA: Sage.
60 Ng & Feldman (2013).
61 For a summary of the positive contributions of older workers in organizations see: James, J. B. & Pitt-Catsouphes, M. (2016). Change in the meaning and experience of work in later life: Introduction to the special issue. *Work, Aging, and Retirement*, *2*, 281–285; Zacher, H. (2015). Successful aging at work. *Work, Aging, and Retirement*, *1*, 4–25; Peterson, S. J. & Spiker, B. K. (2005). Establishing the positive contributory value of older workers: A positive psychology perspective. *Organizational Dynamics*, *34*, 153–167.
62 Sverko, B. (2006). Super's career development theory. In Greenhaus, J. H. & Callanan, G. A. (Eds.), *Encyclopedia of career development* (pp. 789–792). Thousand Oaks, CA: Sage; Super, D. (1980). A life-span, life-space approach to career development. *Journal of Vocational Behavior*, *16*, 282–298; Super, D. (1957). *The psychology of careers*. New York: Harper & Row.
63 For thorough reviews and discussions of Erikson's theory of adult psychosocial development see Kivnick, H. Q. & Wells, C. K. (2014). Untapped richness in Erik H. Erikson's rootstock. *The Gerontologist*, *54*, 40–50; Adams, G. R. (2006). Erikson's theory of development. In Greenhaus, J. H. & Callanan, G. A. (Eds.), *Encyclopedia of career development* (pp. 295–298). Thousand Oaks, CA: Sage.
64 Erikson, E. H. (1982). *The life cycle completed*. New York: W. W. Norton.
65 Bischof, L. J. (1976). *Adult psychology*. New York: Harper & Row; quote is on page 32.
66 Levinson, D. J., Darrow, C. N., Klein, E. B., Levinson, M. H. & McKee, B. (1978). *Seasons of a man's life*. New York: Knopf.
67 Levinson, D. J. (1986). A conception of adult development. *American Psychologist*, *41*, 3–13; Levinson et al. (1978).
68 Levinson, D. J. (1996). *Seasons of a woman's life*. New York: Knopf.
69 Greenhaus & Callanan (2012).
70 Joshi, A., Dencker, J. C., Franz, G. & Martocchio, J. J. (2010). Unpacking generational identities in organizations. *Academy of Management Review*, *35*, 392–414.
71 Joshi, A., Dencker, J. C. & Franz, G. (2011). Generations in organizations. *Research in Organizational Behavior*, *31*, 177–205.
72 Arnett, J. J. (2013). The evidence for generation we and against generation me. *Emerging Adulthood*, *1*, 5–10; Ng, E. S. W., Schweitzer, L. & Lyons, S. T. (2010). New generation, great expectations: A field study of the millennial generation. *Journal of Business and Psychology*, *25*, 281–292.
73 Becton, J. B., Walker, H. J. & Jones-Farmer, A. (2014). Generational differences in workplace behavior. *Journal of Applied Social Psychology*, *44*, 175–189; Lyons, S. & Kuron, L. (2013). Generational differences in the workplace: A review of the evidence and directions for future research. *Journal of Organizational Behavior*, *35*, 139–157; Twenge, J. M., Campbell, S. M., Hoffman, B. J. & Lance, C. E. (2010). Generational differences in work values: Leisure and extrinsic values increasing, social and intrinsic values decreasing. *Journal of Management*, *36*,

1117–1142; Hess, N. & Jepsen, D. M. (2009). Career stage and generational differences in psychological contracts. *Career Development International*, *14*, 261–283; Sullivan, S. E., Forret, M. L., Carraher, S. M. & Mainiero, L. A. (2009). Using the kaleidoscope career model to examine generational differences in work attitudes. *Career Development International*, *14*, 284–302; Cennamo, L. & Gardner, D. (2008). Generational differences in work values, outcomes and person–organisation values fit. *Journal of Managerial Psychology*, *23*, 891–906; Dries, N., Pepermans, R. & De Kerpel, E. (2008). Exploring four generations beliefs about career: Is "satisfied" the new "successful"? *Journal of Managerial Psychology*, *23*, 907–928; Wong, M., Gardiner, E., Lang, W. & Coulon, L. (2008). Generational differences in personality and motivation: Do they exist and what are the implications for the workplace? *Journal of Managerial Psychology*, *23*, 878–890.

74 Arnett (2013); Becton et al. (2014).

75 Twenge et al. (2010); Lyons, S. T., Higgins, C. & Duxbury, L. (2007). An empirical assessment of generational differences in basic human values. *Psychological Reports*, *101*, 339–352.

76 Arnett (2013).

77 Ng et al. (2010).

78 Callanan & Greenhaus (2008).

79 Ibid.

80 Greenhaus & Callanan (2012).

81 Arthur, M. B., Inkson, K. & Pringle, J. K. (1999). *The new careers: Individual action & economic change*. London: Sage.

82 Ibid.

83 Ibid.

3 Work–Life Challenges and Opportunities

Implications for Career Management

Employees' ultimate work–life challenge is how to combine different spheres of life in a way that enables them to feel engaged, effective, and satisfied in those parts of life that really matter to them.[1] Look at your situation, or if you are not employed, perhaps the situation of your parents. How would you (or they) respond to the following question about how you (or they) feel about how different parts of life come together?

- Frustrated, because there's just not enough of me to go around: my job, my family, my friends, my community, let alone myself. I feel like I am frequently ignoring something that is important to me.
- Good about the way different parts of my life fit together. It is not always easy, but I am there for my job, my family, my friends, my community, and myself. If it's important, I make it work.

Do you (or they) feel that different parts of life come together nicely in a satisfying way, or do you (or they) believe that important parts of life are being shortchanged because of lack of time, energy, or resources? Employees who are able to combine different parts of life reasonably well—not necessarily perfectly—experience a healthy level of work–life balance, which promotes a feeling of well-being.[2]

We noted in Chapter 1 that career management requires an understanding of the impact of our career on other parts of our life such as family, community, and personal interests as well as the effects of these other parts of life on our career. This chapter elaborates on that point. We discuss the concept of work–life balance, and then demonstrate the many ways in which our work and nonwork lives affect each other, negatively (as "enemies") and positively (as "allies"). We then show how the society in which we live and the organization in which we work can make it easier—or more difficult—to achieve a reasonable level of work–life balance. We also explain how employees and their families play a vital role in achieving more balance in life, and we offer suggestions to help them make better decisions. The aim of this chapter is to provide insights into work–life challenges and opportunities that you can apply to the career management process in the chapters that follow. In fact, an essential message that we reinforce throughout this book is that managing our career effectively requires us to pay attention to *all* parts of our lives, not only our work.

Work–Life Balance

Despite its popularity in the media and professional journals, the notion of work–life balance is often misunderstood. It does *not* mean spending exactly the same amount of time on different parts of life, such as work, family, friends, or community. Nor does it necessarily mean performing superbly or experiencing extraordinary satisfaction in each and every part of life.

Instead, we view *work–life balance* as the overall positive feeling that results from being engaged, effective, and satisfied in different arenas of life that we value highly.[3] Balance is a subjective feeling seen through our own eyes. For some, it means being highly engaged, effective, and satisfied in our work and family lives because nothing else matters nearly so much to us. For others, it means devoting ourselves primarily to our family, community, and religion. We all have our own priorities and values (which can change over the course of our life), and experiencing a strong sense of work–life balance means that we are sufficiently engaged in those parts of life that are of highest priority to us. When we combine work with other parts of life in a balanced way, we feel a sense of completeness or wholeness in our life.

Experiencing a strong sense of balance can be difficult to achieve, and if achieved, difficult to maintain. Just as a juggler knows that one ball tossed in the air may affect the trajectory of the other balls, so too must we realize that our work touches other parts of our lives in many ways, sometimes for the better and sometimes not.[4] Think of how a career can affect family and personal life; how a good (or bad!) day at work can affect a person's mood at home, or the times when a person misses a child's music recital or a workout at the gym because of job demands. Think also of how family or community responsibilities can affect how willing we are to spend countless evenings or weekends in the office rather than with family or friends, or how we might be reluctant to accept a job relocation if it jeopardizes a spouse's career, community ties, or children's friendships.

It is no wonder that work–life balance is a hot topic on the nation's social agenda. A number of the changes discussed in Chapter 1, such as flatter organizations with streamlined workforces, have left many people with more work to do and fewer resources with which to do it. Articles on flextime, parental leave legislation, "mommy and daddy tracks," and childcare arrangements filled the pages of the popular press and the professional journals in the 1980s and 1990s, and have continued with even greater frequency in the new millennium. Individuals and families are increasingly concerned with finding ways to "juggle" their work with other commitments in life.

The need to balance work with other parts of life has also become intense in recent years because more individuals are simultaneously pursuing a career and committed to their family. In 2015, about 24 percent of the households with children under 18 were single-parent households (85 percent headed by the mother), often placing extensive work and caregiving demands on the head of the household. In addition, the dual-earner family, in which both partners are employed has become a dominant lifestyle in the United States. Indeed, in 2015 both partners were employed in 61 percent of the married-couple families with children,[5] and many other countries throughout the world are witnessing similar trends.

Advances in communication technology have also increased the work pressures of employees in many organizations. The proliferation of smartphones, laptops, and other forms of electronic communication often makes employees feel "on call" 24 hours a day, seven days a week, at the whim of organizations that require their immediate action.[6] This electronic tethering of employees to their organizations represents a modern form of encroachment of work on home and personal life—"work creep"—even during vacations.[7] The need to be responsive to electronic communication after work hours blurs the boundaries between work and home domains and requires many employees to make choices about where to devote their time and attention even when at home. Moreover, an increasingly global economy requires many employees to communicate with colleagues, suppliers, and clients in different parts of the world and consequently in different time zones. Making or taking a 3:00am telephone call in the United States to speak with a colleague in Asia during the colleague's normal work hours can put additional strain on an already harried business person and disrupt sleep patterns. Further, as will be discussed in

Chapter 13, the proliferation of international careers can result in short- and long-term foreign assignments that require overseas travel or relocation.

Complicating matters further, many employees' lives extend far beyond their work and family commitments. For example, much of the U.S. population volunteers on a regular basis,[8] and participation in athletic activities—whether in formal competitions such as triathlons[9] or informal workouts at the local gym—is popular as well. Indeed, many people identify as strongly or more strongly with community, religious, leisure, or self-development activities than with work or family pursuits, what Ellen Kossek and her colleagues have referred to as "nonwork-eclectics."[10]

Work–Life Conflict: When Work and Life Are "Enemies"

There are many times when our work is in conflict with another part of our life. *Work–life conflict* exists when pressures from work and other life roles are mutually incompatible; that is, when participation in one role interferes with participation in another role.[11] Sometimes our work responsibilities interfere with our family or personal lives (known as work-to-life conflict), whereas at other times our family or personal lives interfere with our work (life-to-work conflict).[12] We will use the term work–life conflict when referring to the general notion of conflict between work and other life roles, and use the more specific terms of work-to-life conflict or life-to-work conflict when referring to the specific direction of the conflict or interference. Research has revealed three different forms of work–life conflict: time-based conflict, strain-based conflict, and behavior-based conflict.

Time-based conflict occurs because the activities we pursue in life compete for a precious commodity—time. The time spent in one role generally cannot be devoted to another role. Out-of-town business meetings or late evenings at the office can interfere with family dinners, parent–teacher conferences, or community volunteer activities. It is simply impossible to be in two places at once. Time-based work-to-life conflict is likely to be most prevalent for employees who work long hours, travel extensively, frequently work overtime, have inflexible work schedules, and receive little support from their boss or co-workers. All of these work situations can increase or fix the time at work that cannot be spent on family, community, or personal activities.

Time pressures that arise from domains other than work can also produce conflict. Employees who experience the most life-to-work conflict tend to have extensive family responsibilities (for example, they are married or have partners, have young children, have large families, have primary responsibility for childcare or eldercare, or have partners who hold demanding jobs), receive little support from family or friends, or have other extensive commitments outside of work. All of these pressures increase the amount of time devoted to family, community, or personal pursuits, which can interfere with work-related activities.

Strain-based conflict exists when psychological strain produced within one role affects our functioning in another role. Work stressors can produce strain symptoms such as tension, irritability, fatigue, depression, and apathy, and it is difficult to be an attentive partner, a loving parent, an understanding friend, or an enthusiastic volunteer when one is depressed, anxious, fatigued, or irritable. Strain-based work-to-life conflict is likely to be most intense for employees who experience conflict or ambiguity within the work role; who are exposed to extensive physical, emotional, or mental work demands; whose work environment is constantly changing; who work on repetitive, boring tasks; or who receive little support in the workplace. All these stressful conditions can produce a "negative emotional spillover" from work to other parts of life.[13] Of course, many sources of strain can arise from roles outside of work as well. Individuals who experience difficulties with partners, children, parents, friends, or members of community or religious organizations may find that these stresses intrude into their work life. It is difficult to devote oneself fully to work when preoccupied with a stressful family or personal situation.

Sometimes behavior that is effective in one role is simply inappropriate in another role. It has been suggested, for example, that managers at work are expected to be self-reliant, aggressive, detached, and objective. Family members and friends, on the other hand, may expect that same person to be warm, nurturing, and attentive in their interactions with them. If people cannot shift gears when they enter different roles, they are likely to experience *behavior-based conflict* between the roles. Behavioral styles that employees exhibit at work (logic, objectivity, power, and authority) may be incompatible with the behaviors desired by family and friends on the home front, who do not appreciate being treated like subordinates![14]

As this discussion shows, a variety of role pressures can produce work–life conflict. Some of these pressures demand excessive time commitments, others produce extensive stress, and many produce both. From where do these pressures emanate? Some come from role senders, persons with whom we interact in our work and nonwork lives. Bosses, colleagues, partners, children, and friends are all role senders who place demands on us to finish projects, attend weekend meetings, wash the dishes, and mow the lawn. People tend to experience more conflict when there are strong penalties for failing to comply with these demands from work and nonwork roles. If a boss insists that we attend a Saturday work meeting, and a partner refuses to change vacation plans by one day, we are caught between the proverbial rock and a hard place. If either the boss or the partner permits latitude to deviate from expectations, there is room to maneuver.

However, many pressures to participate or excel at work or in nonwork activities come not from other people, but from the expectations we place on ourselves. For example, employees who exhibit a Type A personality and who place tremendous pressure on themselves to work long hours and be highly successful, tend to experience more work–life conflict than those with a more relaxed Type B personality.[15] Outside of work the desire to be the "perfect" partner, parent, friend, or neighbor can place pressure on us that goes far beyond any pressure that others can muster. The pressures we put on ourselves can depend on the importance of the particular role to our self-concept. For example, if work is a central part of our life, we are more demanding on ourselves to participate fully and competently in that role, thereby exacerbating the degree of conflict. Those of us who are highly involved in both work *and* nonwork roles may experience the most conflict.[16] We want to be highly productive in all parts of our life and we feel guilty if we cannot achieve such high standards.

There is also evidence that our personality can affect the amount of work–life conflict we experience. People tend to experience less work–life conflict if they are agreeable, extraverted, open to new experiences, optimistic, proactive, self-confident, and hold generally positive attitudes toward life. It is possible that these qualities enable people to cope more resiliently with pressures from different spheres of life or make it more likely that they receive support from other people in their life.[17]

Table 3.1 presents a scale that measures work–life conflict. Strong agreement with an item reflects a relatively high level of work–life conflict. Therefore, the higher the score the more extensive is the conflict. Take a look to see whether you see a pattern in your responses to the different items.

Extensive work–life conflict can detract from our performance or satisfaction with our family, job, and life, and can produce physical or psychological health problems.[18] That is why chronic work–life conflict can serve as an enemy of work–life balance. When one part of life (work, for example) regularly interferes with our commitments to other parts

Table 3.1 Inventory of Work–Life Conflict

Below are 12 statements about the relationship between your work life and your family, home, or personal life. Indicate your agreement or disagreement by placing the appropriate number in front of each statement:

1=Strongly Disagree
2=Disagree
3=Uncertain
4=Agree
5=Strongly Agree

Work-to-Life Conflict

1. ____ My work schedule often conflicts with other parts of my life
2. ____ After work, I come home too tired to do some of the things I'd like to do
3. ____ On the job, I have so much work to do that it takes time away from my personal interests
4. ____ My family dislikes how often I am preoccupied with my work when I am at home
5. ____ Because my work is demanding, at times I am irritable at home
6. ____ The demands of my job make it difficult to be relaxed when I get home
7. ____ My work takes up time that I'd like to spend with my family, friends, or hobbies
8. ____ My job makes it difficult to be the kind of spouse or parent I'd like to be

Life-to-Work Conflict

9. ____ My family or personal life takes up time I would like to spend working
10. ____ My personal interests take too much time away from my work
11. ____ The demands of my family or personal life make it difficult to concentrate at work
12. ____ At times, my personal problems make me irritable at work

Modification of a scale initially developed by Kopelman, R. E., Greenhaus, J. H. & Connolly, T. F. (1983). A model of work, family, and interrole conflict: A construct validation study. *Organizational Behavior and Human Performance, 32,* 198–215.

Questions 1–8 refer to the extent to which work interferes with family, home, community, or personal life. Questions 9–12 refer to the extent to which family, home, community, or personal life interferes with work.

of our life, our involvement, performance, and satisfaction in these nonwork roles may decline, making it difficult to experience a feeling of balance or completeness in our life.[19] However, this does not mean that everyone who experiences work–life conflict necessarily experiences stress, diminished performance, dissatisfaction, and a feeling of imbalance. A certain level of conflict is inevitable in a society in which women and men are required to juggle work with other life responsibilities. Problems are probably most pronounced when the level of work–life conflict is so intense that it exceeds individuals' capacities to cope with the conflict.

Work–Life Enrichment: When Work and Life Are "Allies"

Although many of us experience work–life conflict—sometimes rather intensely—we should not conclude that work is always at odds with other parts of life.[20] When they are allies, work can strengthen our nonwork lives, and nonwork experiences can improve our work lives. We refer to these beneficial effects of work and nonwork on one another as *work–life enrichment*.[21]

There are two paths to work–life enrichment: the instrumental path and the affective path.[22] The *instrumental path* involves the acquisition of resources in one role that are used to improve our performance and satisfaction in the other role. A resource is an asset that can be used to solve a problem or master a challenging situation. Participating in a role—nonwork or work—provides opportunities to acquire resources from that role. These resources include the

- Development of *new skills*;
- Development of *new perspectives*, by forming novel ways of looking at situations and solving problems;
- Enhancement of our *self-confidence* as a result of performing well in our duties;
- Accumulation of *social capital*, the network of relationships we develop with other people who provide us with information or advice and who can use their influence to help us reach our goals;
- Acquisition of *material resource*s such as money and gifts.

We can acquire these resources in any role in which we participate. For example, as a family member, friend, neighbor, or community volunteer:

- We might improve our problem-solving *skills* as we learn to work effectively with our spouse or partner to solve daily problems, our listening skills in helping our toddler communicate his or her needs to us, or our multitasking skills in juggling our many commitments to our children, neighbors, friends, and spouses with our own personal needs.
- Our experiences with our child or with a brother or sister might produce a *new perspective* on working with others; for example, to let people try to solve problems on their own at first and not offer advice until it is requested.
- We may become more *self-confident* as we master the challenges of taking on a new volunteer role or a new hobby, caring for children, solving problems as a couple, or helping parents with a knotty housing problem.
- We may have access to the wisdom, advice, and social support of a family member or friend as we accumulate *social capital* in our lives.
- We may have access to *financial* resources such as a spouse's income, a parent's inheritance, or an in-law's generous gift.

It is not difficult to imagine how the resources acquired from our nonwork life can be beneficial to our work. For example:

- The problem-solving and listening *skills* honed as a spouse, parent, or friend may make us more effective members of work teams.
- The *new perspective* regarding the importance of letting people try to solve problems before offering advice may make us more effective supervisors or mentors at work.
- The *self-confidence* we have acquired as a result of solving a challenging problem outside of work may enable us to approach our tasks at work with more confidence and resilience.
- A *knowledgeable* neighbor or friend may provide us with excellent career advice or even use his or her influence to help us land a new job or acquire a business loan from a local bank.
- A substantial gift or family inheritance could be used to *bankroll* a new business.

All of these examples illustrate life-to-work enrichment whereby resources acquired outside of the work domain are successfully applied to our work lives. An important series of studies by Marian Ruderman and her colleagues has demonstrated how women managers' home and family experiences strengthen their professional lives.[23] When asked what aspects of their personal life enhanced their professional lives, many women replied that the resources gained from nonwork experiences improved their functioning at work. The most frequently mentioned resources were: improved interpersonal skills; psychological benefits such as self-esteem, emotional support and advice; and handling multiple tasks. In addition, the more psychologically committed the women managers were to their home roles, the greater the task and interpersonal skills they exhibited at work.

Just as our nonwork experiences can strengthen our work life, so too can the resources acquired at work enrich our lives outside of work. For example:

- An employee uses the *communication skills* she acquired in a management development workshop to develop a closer and more supportive relationship with her sister.
- An individual applies a newly appreciated *perspective* on work team dynamics to suggest that his volunteer organization begin to solve problems collectively as a group.
- A boost in self-esteem from succeeding on a challenging job assignment gives an individual the *self-confidence* to solve neighborhood problems more assertively.
- Discussions with a colleague at work provide an employee with *useful suggestions* on finding suitable care for elderly parents.
- Sizeable *salary increases* are used to purchase such essentials as quality childcare, education, and medical care for the entire family.

In addition to the instrumental path to enrichment, which involves the transfer of resources from one role to another, work–life enrichment also takes place when the positive emotions or feelings experienced in one part of life spill over to enhance performance and satisfaction in another part of life. This *affective path* occurs when people carry a positive emotion (e.g., joy, happiness, satisfaction) from one role to another and as a result become more highly engaged in the latter role. As Nancy Rothbard has explained, when we experience positive emotions in a role, we are more psychologically available to other people, we hold an outward focus that attends to other people's needs, and our energy expands, all of which can promote high performance and positive feelings in that role.[24] For example, an employee who experiences positive feelings at work is likely to bring those positive feelings home, interacting more effectively with family, friends, or neighbors.

For employees to experience work–life enrichment, they must acquire resources and/or experience positive emotions in one part of life and transfer the resources or positive emotions to another part of life. Not surprisingly, employees who are highly engaged in their work and family pursuits and who receive substantial support from others at work and outside of work tend to experience high levels of enrichment, presumably because engagement in an activity and support from others enable individuals to acquire resources.[25] Additionally, conscientious, extraverted, positive, and optimistic people—whose personalities enable them to acquire resources and experience positive emotions—also experience more extensive work–life enrichment.[26] In turn, experiencing a high level of work–life enrichment can: enhance job performance; promote greater job, family, and life satisfaction; and heighten employees' physical and mental health.[27] In sum, when work and nonwork are allies, we can experience more effectiveness and greater satisfaction in those parts of our life that matter, thereby producing a greater feeling of work–life balance.

Reducing work–life conflict and increasing work–life enrichment can both contribute to a stronger sense of balance because employees feel engaged, productive, and satisfied in those parts of life that are most important to them. In the following sections, we discuss what societies, work organizations, employees, and families can do to increase the chances that workers experience more balance and families experience enhanced well-being.

Societal Responses to Work–Life Challenges

Countries vary greatly in the extent to which they pass legislation and develop public policies to help their citizens to balance their work responsibilities with other parts of life. In countries that provide substantial work–life supports of the types discussed below, employers may follow suit by providing supportive policies to their employees,[28] and employees can experience a stronger sense of balance in their lives.[29]

Societal supports for work–life balance take a variety of forms, the most prominent of which are shown in Table 3.2. Some of these supports (for example, parental leaves and public expenditures for dependent care) are targeted to caregivers, whereas other supports, such as mandates regarding the availability of part-time work and the provision of vacations and holidays, are not necessarily limited to caregivers.

Each of the societal supports can provide specific benefits to a subset of the country's population. For example, providing paid maternity leaves can enable women to return to work when they and their child are ready for the reentry. Providing paid paternity leave, especially in countries such as Sweden that incentivize men to take leave, enables fathers to participate more extensively in caring for the infant, which leads them to feel a greater sense of responsibility for the child's well-being.[30] The availability of part-time jobs enables many caregivers (especially women who represent the majority of part-time employees in almost every country[31]) to remain in the workforce if they wish rather than stay home full-time with their children, the provision of affordable childcare similarly enables many parents to continue to be employed, and mandated paid vacations and holidays allow all employees to devote more time and attention to nonwork commitments, be they family, community, or leisure activities.

Table 3.2 Societal Work–Life Support

Types of Societal Support	*Examples of Societal Support*
Parental supports	
• Parental leaves	Paid or unpaid maternity and/or paternity leaves
• Health supports for pregnant or nursing women	Mandated nursing breaks; ban on hazardous or unsafe work for pregnant or nursing employees
Mandates regarding part-time work	Legal right to convert a full-time job to a part-time job; ban on discrimination against part-time employees
Public expenditures on dependent care	Provision of pre-school services such as kindergarten; tax credits for the cost of child care arrangements
Mandates regarding vacations and holidays	Require employers to provide paid vacation time; guarantee of a minimum number of paid holidays

The typology and examples of work–life support are based on a discussion in Greenhaus, J.H. & Powell, G. N. (2017). *Making work and family work: From hard choices to smart choices.* New York: Routledge.

All of the supports described in the table are relevant to work-family issues, although some of the laws or public policies (e.g., part-time work, vacations, and holidays) have direct implications for balancing work with commitments to friends, communities, religion, and personal self-development as well as family.

We do not contend that all countries must provide all of the supports identified in Table 3.2. For one thing, countries need to enact laws and public policies that are consistent with cultural norms to assure their citizens' approval of the supports.[32] Moreover, societal supports could have unintended negative consequences for some portion of the country's population.[33] For example, taking an extended parental leave may be seen in some countries or companies as a signal of low commitment to work, part-time jobs may have lower status and fewer benefits and may limit advancement opportunities, and public expenditures on dependent care will likely raise citizens' taxes. Instead, the point to be made is that employees' opportunities to experience greater balance between work and other parts of life are influenced, at least in part, by the norms, values, laws, and public policies of the culture in which they live.

Organizational Responses to Work–Life Challenges

Employees' opportunities to achieve greater balance in life are also affected by the practices of the organization for which they work. In this chapter, we discuss why organizations may choose to support their employees' efforts to balance their work with other parts of life, and briefly highlight the ways in which organizations can provide such support. In Chapter 14, we provide an examination of these practices in the context of an organization's human resource management system.

Why Provide Support?

Many, if not most, employers realize that it is in their best interest to help their employees to balance their work with other important parts of their life. What used to be considered a "woman's issue" is increasingly recognized as an employee issue and a business necessity. What accounts for this shift in attitudes among the nation's largest employers?

First, more employees are struggling to balance their work, family, and personal commitments than in prior years. As discussed earlier, the emergence of the dual-earner lifestyle and the large number of single-parent households require parents to coordinate their work demands with their family and personal responsibilities. In addition, employees are demanding opportunities to attain more balance in life, and a sizeable number are willing to make sacrifices in their careers to achieve a higher quality of life. More and more job-seekers are raising the issue of work–life balance in their employment interviews. And substantial numbers of men and women are refusing promotions, relocations, and jobs with extensive pressure or travel because of the strains these positions would put on their family or personal lives.[34]

These changes are playing havoc with the effectiveness of organizations' staffing practices. For one thing, organizations are losing the services of many talented young women managers and professionals who leave their jobs following the birth of a child. Many of these "career-and-family"-oriented women want to continue their career, but not with 50–60-hour work weeks and extensive travel requirements.[35] Because employers have not traditionally provided highly flexible work schedules, employees often leave. This represents a substantial blow to employers who have invested time and money, and now face extensive recruiting and training costs to replace these valued employees. This is especially problematic because the talent pool is increasingly female. The labor force participation rate of women in the U.S. is approximately 60 percent, up from around 30 percent at the beginning of the 1950s,[36] and about 46 percent of the total labor force are women.[37] In addition, with increasing numbers of women receiving bachelor's, master's, legal, and medical degrees, employers find that many of their best and brightest job candidates are women. Extensive turnover among this group results in high costs and low productivity.[38] Moreover, caregivers of both sexes who remain in the workforce are often preoccupied with the difficulties of balancing work with family and personal responsibilities, and the resultant work–life conflict can produce high levels of absenteeism and extensive stress,[39] both of which can detract from an organization's productivity.

Despite the demographic changes in the workforce discussed in this chapter, many employers have run their operations on the assumption that their managerial and professional employees conform to the organization's stereotype of an "ideal worker";[40] someone who devotes as many hours as necessary to complete a project (including evenings and weekends), travels at the drop of a hat, and relocates, either domestically or internationally, whenever it is to the advantage of the organization and the employee's career progress.

Nobody likes to change assumptions, attitudes, and behaviors, especially if they have been working well for a long time. Employers are no exception. However, this resistance to change is weakening as more companies experience difficulties attracting and retaining valued employees, and organizations see the benefits of implementing supportive practices. Not surprisingly, some of the leading reasons why employers initiate such practices include the desire to recruit and retain employees, to support employees and their families, and to enhance employee commitment and productivity.[41]

What Types of Support do Organizations Provide?

Organizational support around work–life issues can take three forms. Organizations can offer formal work–life policies to their employees, they can encourage supervisors to provide informal support to their employees, and they can establish a family-supportive or "life-supportive" organizational culture.

Table 3.3 summarizes a variety of formal work–life policies and practices that have been adopted by organizations in response to the issues discussed in this chapter. We classify

Table 3.3 Organizational Formal Work–Life Policies

Maternity and Paternity Supports	*Dependent Care Supports*	*Flexibility Supports*	*Informational and Social Supports*
Paid or unpaid maternity leaves	Child care resource and referral	Flextime	Employee assistance programs (EAPs)
Paid or unpaid paternity leaves	Child care centers	Compressed work week	Workshops and seminars
Work time off for prenatal health care	Financial assistance for child care or elder care	Telecommuting (telework)	Employee network groups (support groups)
Provision of hygienic nursing facility	Sick child care	Reduced work load (part-time work)	Support hotlines
Restraints on shift work, overtime hours, and hazardous or unhealthy work for pregnant or nursing employees	Elder care resource and referral	Personal & family leaves	
		Flexible career systems	
		Job sharing	

This table was reproduced from Greenhaus, J. H. & Powell, G. N. (2017). *Making work and family work: From hard choices to smart choices.* New York: Routledge.

these organizational actions into four broad categories of support: maternity and paternity, dependent care, flexibility, and informational and social.[42]

Maternity and paternity supports provide time for prenatal health care or for the care of the newborn child, as well as a hygienic, healthy work environment for pregnant or nursing employees. *Dependent care* supports range from providing information and referrals for childcare and eldercare resources to providing financial assistance in purchasing these services. *Flexibility* supports generally provide employees with some degree of control over when they work (flextime or flexible work schedules, personal and family leaves), where they work (telework or work-at-home), or how much they work (reduced load, job sharing) to help them meet their family or personal commitments while at the same time fulfilling their responsibilities at work. An additional form of flexibility support is the provision of flexible careers systems that allow employees to pursue an alternative career path that is more compatible with their family and personal lives than a traditional "promotion-oriented" vertical career path, and that enables employees to decrease (or increase) their commitment to work as their family and personal responsibilities expand (or subside). Finally, as the term suggests, *informational and social* supports consist of a variety of programs in which employees receive information, advice, counseling, and/or help on issues related to managing work, family, and other parts of life. Although quite different from each other, all four types of formal support aim to help employees meet their job's responsibilities as well as to other important parts of their life.

In addition to offering employees access to formal policies and programs, supportive organizations also encourage their supervisors to provide employees with *informal* support to supplement the support provided by the formal programs or to compensate for the absence of formal programs. Because of the critical role of the supervisor in fostering employee development, a great deal of attention has been paid to the "family-supportive supervisor" who is committed to helping the employee achieve greater balance between work and family or personal life.[43]

Leslie Hammer and her colleagues have identified four types of assistance provided by family-supportive supervisors.[44] A supervisor's *emotional support* includes showing care for employees and their feelings, and providing a comfortable and supportive environment in which employees can freely discuss personal and family issues that concern them. *Instrumental support* refers to tangible assistance such as permitting employees to adjust their work hours, take time off for family or personal matters, or work from home on an as-needed basis. Supportive supervisors also engage in *role modeling* behaviors (e.g., responding to a family or personal emergency during work time) that employees can emulate in managing their own work–life challenges. Supportive supervisors engage in *creative work–family management* when they develop department or team systems and procedures (e.g., working with a team to redesign its work process and meeting times) that enable the group to meet its work responsibilities as well as team members to meet their personal or family needs.

Employees who work for family-supportive supervisors not only participate more extensively in formal work–life programs,[45] but also experience less work–life conflict than employees who do not work for supportive supervisors.[46] Receiving support from their supervisor enables employees to experience more balance in their lives,[47] and promotes positive feelings toward their job and their organization.[48] Moreover, co-workers can provide some of the same types of assistance to employees as supervisors. For example, our co-workers can listen to us and show that they understand our difficulties (emotional support), offer to cover for us when we face a situation outside of work that requires our immediate attention (instrumental support), or role model behaviors or strategies (e.g., learning how to say no to unreasonable requests) that have worked for them.

However, work–life practices are not likely to be used unless understanding and flexible managers and supervisors implement them in a supportive environment.[49] In other words, the most supportive employers provide formal and informal work–life practices within a culture that respects employees' family and personal lives. Such organizations have revised their cultures to eliminate outdated assumptions that are not in tune with the needs of the contemporary workforce. Some cultural assumptions that need to be revised include the following:[50]

- "Keep your personal problems at home."
- "Put in long hours regardless of family responsibilities."
- "Travel when and where the organization dictates."
- "Relocate without concern for family needs."
- "Presence [at the workplace] equals performance."

The responsive organization replaces these assumptions with a more supportive culture. Central components of this culture are the recognition of the legitimacy of family and personal issues to all employees as well as the significance of work–life issues to the organization itself. The supportive organization understands that many employees value their career *and* their life outside of work. As a result, it develops policies like those shown in Table 3.3, it encourages employees to use these policies without jeopardizing their career, and it encourages managers and supervisors to provide their employees with informal support so they can be effective at work and at home.

Employee Responses to Work–Life Challenges: Work–Life Decision-Making

Governments' laws and policies and employers' formal and informal practices can help employees balance their work responsibilities with other parts of their life, but employees also play an important role in achieving a satisfying level of balance. In this section of the chapter, we discuss the actions that employees can take to reduce work–life conflict, increase work–life enrichment, and ultimately achieve a greater balance in life.

Actions that employees take to protect or increase their balance can be seen as a series of *work–life decisions*; that is, decisions in one part of life that are influenced or informed by circumstances in another part of life.[51] Because this book focuses on career management, we will highlight examples of decisions regarding work and career that are influenced by a consideration of family, community, or other nonwork domains. For example:

- Sam turns down a challenging assignment on his job because he is concerned that the assignment's extensive workload and travel requirements would restrict the amount of time he could spend with his young children.
- Kristen quits her job and accepts a position with another company that has a flexible work schedule policy so she can stay active on an important church committee that often meets during regular work hours.

Sam and Kristen each made a work–life decision because their work-related choices (to decline an assignment, to change employers) were influenced by a commitment to spending more time with the family (Sam) or the church (Kristen). These decisions were probably not based *solely* on nonwork factors—Sam may have concluded that turning down the assignment would not irreparably harm his career with the company, and Kristen may have determined that the more flexible job was about as good as her current job in most other respects—but the decisions were influenced by Sam and Kristen's values and interests outside of work. Moreover, both decisions were motivated by the desire to avoid or reduce work–life conflict. Sam wanted to prevent his job from overly interfering with quality family time, and Kristen wanted to ensure that her work schedule would not prevent her from contributing her time to her church.

Some work–life decisions are not motivated by the desire to reduce work–life conflict but rather to increase work–life enrichment, as in the following examples:

- Rocco decides to accept a two-year international assignment in Europe because he and his spouse believe that their children would benefit greatly from living abroad, learning about a different culture, and traveling to another part of the world.
- Saroj decides to relocate to a warmer climate so her 12-year-old son, a rising golf star, can hit the links year-round.

Again, these decisions were not based solely on family considerations. Rocco calculated that the international assignment would also increase his visibility in his company and expose him to his firm's global operations, and Saroj concluded that her new job would be interesting and represent a good fit with her skill set. Still, in making their decisions, Rocco and Saroj factored in the positive impact that their decision would have on their nonwork life, in this case their children.

Work–life decisions can involve leaving one work role for another as Kristen and Saroj did, changing a career path as Rocco did, or modifying or declining a work assignment, as Sam did. There are many other choices that might represent work–life decisions, such as choosing to telecommute several days a week, leaving or reentering the workforce, switching from full-time to part-time employment (or vice versa), making a career change, or pursuing (or declining) a promotion, to mention a few.

We believe that work–life decision-making is a critical element of effective career management because many of the career decisions that we encounter have implications—positive or negative—for other parts of our life. We do not suggest that employees should base career decisions *exclusively* on their effects on family, community, or personal commitments. Instead, we believe that they should factor nonwork considerations into their decision-making process to make a choice that is based on an informed judgment about the impact of the career decision on their entire life, not just their work and career. We apply this logic to the specific steps in the career management process that we discuss in Chapters 4, 5, and 6.

In effect, we advocate that employees adopt a *whole-life perspective* to the management of their careers. Originally discussed by Douglas Hall and colleagues,[52] we view a *whole-life perspective* as

> the extent to which an individual (i) seeks effectiveness and satisfaction in multiple life roles rather than solely in the work role, and (ii) makes career decisions with an awareness of their impact on other aspects of one's life. According to this view, an individual who adopts a whole-life perspective desires balance among different parts of life and understands the consequences of career decision making for achieving balance.[53]

How Employees Can Make Effective Work–Life Decisions

Factoring nonwork considerations into a career decision does not guarantee that the decision will be effective. That is, it does not assure that the decision will help us achieve more balance between work and other parts of our life. Here we present several suggestions for what employees can do to make effective work–life decisions:

- *Understand ourselves.* To understand whether a career decision will have a positive or negative impact on other parts of life, we have to understand not only our career values and aspirations, but also what we value and want to accomplish outside of work. What kind of spouse, parent, friend, community member, and person do we want to be, and what does work–life balance mean to us? Unless we understand our aspirations in all phases of our life, it would take blind luck to make a career decision that enables us to achieve our goals and experience balance. In Chapters 4 and 5, we elaborate on the importance of what we call "self-exploration."
- *Understand our environment.* In addition to understanding our values and motives, we need to understand our options. When deciding whether to telecommute, volunteer for a special assignment, accept a promotion, adjust our travel schedule, or quit our job, we need to have a pretty good handle on the consequences of these options. That requires understanding as best we can the pros and cons of telecommuting, the potential demands and rewards of the special assignment, the nature of the job into which we will be promoted, the advantages and disadvantages of different travel schedules, and the risks and rewards of quitting a job. We are not likely to have complete information on these options, but we need to engage in sufficient environmental exploration to gain as much insight as possible, again a topic to which we return in Chapters 4 and 5.
- *Counteract our decision-making biases.* Making any work–life decision is subject to human bias. Sometimes, we make a decision without seeing all of the pluses or minuses of a particular choice; sometimes we are so attentive to one aspect of a choice (e.g., a job's starting salary) that we don't pay attention to other factors (e.g., the organization's long work-hours culture). Sometimes, we substantially overestimate our chances of making a decision work ("I can definitely meet my massive work responsibilities and still have time for other parts of my life"). Of course, it is impossible to have a complete awareness of all of the implications of making a choice in advance of actually making the decision. However, we can be aware of the biases we tend to have and try to reduce them as much as possible.
- *Communicate and problem-solve with others.* Decisions should not be made in a vacuum because understanding our values and our options often requires us to communicate and negotiate with others. Understanding whether we can work one day a week from home, have more flexible work hours, hold occasional virtual meetings rather than travel, be relieved of some household tasks, or participate in a community activity in a less demanding way often requires that we share our concerns and negotiate with stakeholders at work and outside of work, often finding that these concerns can be resolved to the satisfaction of all parties.[54]
- *Craft experiments.* Sometimes, decisions are frightening because we don't have all the answers and the consequences of making a mistake are severe. Should we open our own business, change our career path from finance to marketing, return to school for an MBA degree, or accept a long-term international assignment? Crafting an experiment involves taking small and low-risk steps to try something on for size before committing to making a decision.[55] In these instances, crafting an experiment might mean shadowing an owner of a recent start-up (or working one evening a week in the business), conducting informational interviews or taking a temporary assignment in marketing, taking an online graduate course as a non-matriculated student, and looking for opportunities for short-term international travel. Experiments such as these can help individuals make more well-informed decisions down the road.

All of these suggestions require proactive strategies for managing work and life. One such approach to successful life management, called selection-optimization-compensation, emphasizes the importance of goals, strategies, and alternate plans to overcome obstacles to goal achievement.[56] We add that the usefulness of specific goals, strategies, and back-up plans rests on a foundation of understanding (ourselves, our environment, our biases), a willingness to communicate and problem-solve with others to meet mutual goals, and often a readiness to try out potential options on a small scale to gain insights while minimizing risks.

Family Responses to Work–Life Challenges

The "traditional" household, as embodied in television shows of the 1950s and 1960s, with an employed husband, a stay-at-home wife, and two or more children, currently represents only a small percentage of U.S. families in the contemporary world. Instead, there are a great variety of lifestyles, including single-parent households, childfree couples, "house-husbands" tending to the domestic front, and of course dual-earner families. We define a *dual-earner* couple as two people who share a lifestyle that includes an ongoing love relationship (heterosexual or same-sex), cohabitation, and a work role for each partner.[57] Each partner need not necessarily hold a professional or managerial job or a job that is emotionally absorbing. We focus this section of the chapter on dual-earner couples because this family structure has become so prominent in many parts of the world.

Certainly, one attractive feature of a dual-earner relationship is the financial security derived from two incomes. Many couples believe they need two incomes to acquire and maintain a desired standard of living. However, money does not tell the whole story. Each partner's quality of life can be enriched as well. When each partner works, his or her employment can satisfy a whole range of needs—achievement, challenge, variety, and power—that may not be as easily satisfied in a stay-at-home role. In fact, women's employment has been found to enhance their self-esteem and emotional well-being, especially if their job provides opportunities for challenging, interesting work.[58] Moreover, the pursuit of a career can promote independence and self-sufficiency that is healthy in its own right and critical if the relationship dissolves or a partner dies. By the same token, participation in a dual-earner relationship often involves considerable responsibility at home, especially for women, but increasingly for men. A more extensive involvement in child-rearing can provide a closer bond with the children and expand the enjoyment in life. Moreover, because one partner in a dual-earner relationship is not solely responsible for the financial well-being of the family, he or she may feel less pressure to "succeed" and so have more freedom to leave a dissatisfying job.

The dual-earner lifestyle can also benefit the quality of the relationship between the two partners. Dual-earner relationships provide opportunities for a more egalitarian sharing of participation in family roles.[59] Moreover, the employment of both partners can increase their mutual respect as equals, bring them closer together, and make for a more interesting, compatible couple.[60]

Sources of Stress in a Dual-Earner Relationship

The preceding section does not imply that dual-earner relationships are free of stress. Indeed, there are a number of significant issues that need to be faced in such relationships. This section examines these issues, recognizing that they are not equally relevant to all dual-earner couples.

Work–Life Conflict

Whether parents or childfree, straight or gay, married or cohabitating, dual-earner partners may find that their work demands conflict with commitments in other parts of their life because the couple is juggling two careers as well as home and family and perhaps other life commitments. Women in heterosexual relationships still bear the brunt of the responsibility for homemaking and childcare. Moreover, even when husbands do increase their participation in these domestic roles, they are often seen as "helping out" rather than assuming primary responsibility for the activities. Even relationships that start out with an equitable sharing of home responsibilities might revert back to a gender-based division of labor after the birth of a child[61] if the husband's career takes priority over his wife's.

The overload and stress experienced by dual-earner partners can threaten the relationship in several ways. First, parents may experience guilt over not spending enough time with their children.[62] Second, the couple may simply not have the time to nurture their own relationship. Work demands and children's needs leave partners with little time for each other. The absence of shared time can pose a threat to the romantic and emotional relationship and can estrange partners from one another. Third, family and work responsibilities frequently leave little time for individuals themselves. Time to relax, reflect, engage in community service, exercise, or pursue other leisure activities does not come easily, if at all.

In short, partners in dual-earner relationships often lead hectic, frenetic lives, especially if there are children in the family. There are work pressures, carpools, overnight business trips, children's dance lessons, demanding bosses, housework—the list seems endless. The dual-earner lifestyle can be extremely rewarding, but it is not easy.

Restricted Career Achievements

The dual-earner lifestyle may restrict or slow down one or both partners' career accomplishments. This has traditionally been the case for women, especially when there are children in the family. Many mothers reduce their involvement at work in an attempt to ward off unacceptable levels of work-to-life conflict, cutting back on the number of hours they work, turning down career development opportunities that would conflict with their family or other responsibilities, refusing promotions that require extensive travel or relocation, or putting their career "on hold" by leaving the workforce for a period of time. In this respect, dual-earner mothers may incur a "family penalty" because their extensive family responsibilities limit their career progress.[63] This penalty is partly self-imposed in the sense that dual-earner mothers often "voluntarily" cut back on their career involvement in order to meet their family responsibilities. However, we should not necessarily conclude that these actions are what women necessarily prefer. In many instances, cutting back on work is due more to a lack of support from the organization or the spouse than the women's personal wishes.[64] Of course, not all women experience a family penalty. In fact, a study of managers and executives found that women's psychological commitment to their spousal role did not restrict their job performance. Moreover, their commitment to their role as mother was associated with *higher* levels of performance on their job.[65]

Whereas some mothers may experience a family penalty that impedes their career success, men can experience a "family bonus" that actually helps their career. One study found that fathers earned more money, reached higher levels in their organization, and were more satisfied with their careers than men without children.[66] Why? Because fathers experienced more autonomy on their jobs than did their childfree colleagues. Although it is possible that the fathers in this study sought additional autonomy, employers may also have granted fathers more autonomy, because they perceive them to be more responsible and stable than men without children. However, not all men experience a family bonus. Men who are highly involved in their family lives—who believe that their family time is a critical part of their lives—may cut back on their involvement in work, just as many mothers in dual-earner families do.[67] Such men may switch careers, limit travel, and turn down promotions or relocations for family reasons.

The extent to which career achievements are restricted in dual-earner families may depend, in part, on the time commitment required in a particular job. A man or woman may not experience obstacles to career progress in a job that has reasonable, predictable, and flexible hours. On the other hand, performance and career progress may suffer in a job requiring extensive and inflexible work hours and heavy travel. In addition, career achievements may depend on the relative importance of each partner's career, each partner's commitment to the family, the availability of outside help for housework and childcare, the support received from the partner, and the employer's flexibility in addressing work–life concerns.

In sum, the pressures and constraints of a dual-earner relationship may impede the career progress of one or both partners, especially if career progress is defined as rapid mobility up the organizational ladder. However, researchers found that dual-earner professional women often experienced significant career accomplishments, although at a somewhat later stage in their lives than their single or childfree counterparts.[68] It would not be surprising if the same trend holds true for men. In the long term, then, career accomplishments may not be seriously hampered, at least not in occupations and organizations that permit flexibility in the pace of career growth.

Competition and Jealousy

The division of labor in the so-called traditional family makes for a neat, noncompetitive world. One partner (typically the man in heterosexual relationships) achieves competence in the work world, the other partner (typically the woman) masters the domestic demands, and comparisons of relative success in their respective ventures are unlikely. However, when both partners are employed, it is likely that one partner will eventually become more "successful" than the other partner. Jealousies on the part of the less successful partner, if left unattended, can threaten the stability of the relationship.

The effect of a partner's career success on feelings of competition and jealousy probably depends on the orientations of the two partners. Perhaps the most intense feelings of competition and jealousy are experienced by individuals who place substantial importance on their own career success, yet are insecure about their sense of worth. Under these conditions, a partner's career accomplishments can be particularly threatening. We must add, however, that in extensive discussions with undergraduate and graduate business students, we have found few men or women who believed that a partner's career success would provoke intense feelings of competition or jealousy.

The Impact of Dual-Earner Status on Children

According to a *Fortune* survey of working parents conducted about 30 years ago, a majority of men (55 percent) and women (58 percent) believed that "children of working parents suffer by not being given enough time and attention."[69] However, most of these same parents also believed that children benefit by having working parents as role models. Perhaps these findings reflected the ambivalence experienced by many dual-earner parents at that time. A more recent national survey, however, reveals less ambivalence: 67 percent of men and 80 percent of women believe that an employed mother can have just as good a relationship with her child as a mother who does not work outside the home.[70]

Research has shown that high-quality outsourced childcare (pre-school, after-school, or daycare) can be helpful for many children,[71] and the results of a Harvard Business School study suggest that working mothers have more successful daughters and more caring sons.[72] Ellen Galinsky, co-founder of the Families and Work Institute, persuasively argues that we should not view a mother's employment in "either/or" terms; that it is either bad or good for children. She concludes, "It depends on the people and the circumstances of their lives. And what's right for one person may not be right for another."[73] Ultimately, the impact of a dual-earner lifestyle on children's adjustment probably depends on such factors as the quality of the parent–child relationship, the quality of childcare, and the personal satisfaction of the parents.

How Families Can Make Effective Work–Life Decisions

Family *work–life decisions* are choices made by partners in a relationship that are intended to meet each partner's needs *and* to promote the well-being of the family as a whole.[74] These decisions generally relate to each partner's level of involvement in work and other life activities. Like employee work–life decisions, family decisions are often choices about work that take into account other parts of their life, such as their responsibilities as partners and parents.

Taylor and Leslie are in their early 30s with two pre-school-aged children. After their first child, they decided that they would both continue to work full-time in their respective jobs—for financial reasons, of course, but also because Taylor and Leslie both enjoy their work and are highly regarded by their employers. A combination of childcare three days a week and doting grandparents eager to watch the children on the other two days was a great help. Still, raising two young children while pursuing demanding careers was not easy, yet the couple tried to adapt. Time pressures were mounting, work-related travel was expanding, coordinating their schedules was getting increasingly more difficult, and they began wondering whether their hectic lifestyle enabled them to be the kind of employees, partners, and parents they wanted to be.

After extensive thought and discussion, Taylor and Leslie made several important decisions as a couple. They would both remain on their jobs but negotiate with their managers to have more flexible schedules. Taylor would go on a reduced load (20 hours a week) and work exclusively from home, and Leslie would have the discretion to start work two hours later, work through lunch, and most importantly limit travel. Because weekends were essential for family bonding and recharging their batteries, Taylor and Leslie cut back a little on socializing and community volunteering at least temporarily, and swore off doing any work (including answering work-related texts or emails) on Saturdays and Sundays. As a result, they were able to substantially limit outsourced childcare and rely on grandparents only for an occasional emergency. They found that they were just as effective at work, and not surprisingly, they were spending more quality time together as partners and parents.

Partners in dual-earner relationships make two types of work–life decisions: anchoring decisions and daily decisions.[75] *Anchoring* decisions are generally long-term decisions about one or both partners' involvement in work and other life roles that are consistent with the couple's overall strategy for managing their work–life interface. For example, Taylor and Leslie's initial determination that they would both continue to work full-time, use childcare for three days a week, and grandparents for the other two days is an example of an anchoring decision that is consistent with the type of family life they wanted to achieve. Decisions regarding whether a partner will quit a job, leave the workforce, switch career fields, or accept a promotion are other illustrations of anchoring decisions. Work-related anchoring decisions are influenced by considerations outside of work as, for example, when a couple decides that they will not relocate because of deep roots in their community or when they decide that both partners will cut back on their work hours to spend more time with their children.

A couple's anchoring decisions create a framework or strategy within which they can make more frequent daily decisions.[76] To illustrate:

> A couple's anchoring decision that one partner work in a demanding full-time job and the other work in a less demanding part-time job is likely to determine who will be available to pick up a child from school or take an elderly parent to the doctor on a particular day.[77]

Over time, partners may reevaluate anchoring decisions when circumstances change or when the daily decisions based on the anchoring decision are just not working.[78] For example, Taylor and Leslie's decision to change their work arrangements (Taylor working part-time at home and Leslie adopting a more flexible work schedule) arose from their belief that the initial decision to rely on childcare for the entire week was not working for the family.

As with employee work–life decisions, the decisions that families make may not necessarily be effective. We next present several suggestions regarding what partners can do to make work–life decisions that meet their goals and enhance the well-being of the family.[79]

Understand Identities

Making effective work–life decisions that meet the partners' needs requires both partners to understand how they identify with their family role. Each partner may hold a caregiving orientation, a career orientation, or a combination caregiving-and-career orientation to his or her family identity.[80] Partners who hold a caregiving orientation see their role in the family primarily in terms of providing nurturing and support to other family members. Partners who hold a career orientation view their role in the family primarily in terms of being an economic provider (breadwinner) or a role model of career success that their children can emulate. And, of course, some partners (caregiving-and-career) provide an equal emphasis on both components of their family identity.

It is important for partners to understand and accept their family identities so that they can make work–life decisions consistent with that identity.

> For example, caregiving-oriented partners who understand the specific activities that are most important to them (nurturing a child, providing emotional support to a partner, giving tangible assistance to a parent) will be in a better position to allocate their time and attention in identity-appropriate ways than those who have only a vague sense of what it means for them to be a good parent, partner, or child.[81]

Partners also need to be on the same page to make decisions that work for them and their family. For example, if one partner interprets the other partner's strong career focus as selfish rather than a way to help the family, the partners are likely to disagree on a division of home and caregiving responsibilities that work for both partners and they may begin to resent each other's contributions to the family.

Understand the Challenges in the Environment

Employers do not make it simple for caregiving-oriented employees to meet their responsibilities at home. Many organizations encourage their employees to make work their top priority and reward those who work long hours and place their family's needs on hold.[82] Partners need to understand the constraints they face at work and also the leverage they have to change the work environment; for example, by working out an "idiosyncratic deal"[83] or customized arrangement with their manager to have more flexible work hours while maintaining their high level of job performance. Partners also should understand whether they are receiving sufficient support at home to enable them to meet their work and nonwork needs. As we will see in Chapters 4 and 5, a critical element of career management is to assess the environment and be willing to seek changes that help us meet our needs.

Know what Constitutes Family Well-being

Families differ in the importance they place on material possessions, travel, community service, and quality time with family members, to mention just a few considerations of what constitutes a "good life" in their eyes. As a result, a decision—for example, for both partners to pursue a fast-track and fully absorbing career—that works for families that emphasize professional accomplishment and financial success will not necessarily work for families that stress extensive nurturing of children or frequent service to their community. Therefore, it is essential for partners to understand and agree on what family well-being means to them. Otherwise, work–life decisions may not help partners achieve what is most important to them and their family.

Seek Support

Social support can enable partners to address work–life challenges effectively and is strongly associated with partners' well-being.[84] Communication and mutual support are essential ingredients in a successful dual-earner relationship.[85] *Emotional* support, especially from family members, is particularly important because the partners are involved in a lifestyle that requires compromises and can produce identity problems, jealousies, and guilt. Nearly 50 years ago, Robert and Rhona Rapoport spoke of the understanding and caring "facilitating husband" as a major contributor to the success of a dual-earner relationship,[86] a point of view that rings true to this day. However, men also need the support of an understanding, "facilitating" partner. Indeed, support must be mutual, in that each partner must provide as well as receive support.

Because many dual-earner couples frequently experience unfamiliar situations, partners benefit from *information and advice* on problems so that relationship difficulties do not become too intense. Moreover, partners need to contribute tangibly by providing assistance in home and childcare responsibilities. Perhaps it is most important that dual-earner partners view their involvement and their partner's involvement in family-related activities as fair and equitable.[87] Finally, support can provide each partner with useful *feedback*. Partners may find it difficult to assess how well they are balancing work with other life roles, whether the children are handling the situation satisfactorily, and how the relationship between the two partners is faring. Accurate, constructive feedback can serve as a confirmation of each partner's efforts and as a way to improve the functioning of the family unit.

Beyond the support they receive from each other, partners also need support from other family members, friends, community services, and their employers. Moreover, partners often need to be assertive in seeking the support they require. Consider the following:

> Organizations without formal flexibility policies may be willing to provide flexibility to select, high-performing employees—but only if they assertively request the flexibility. Friends and parents may not think to offer support but will gladly provide support if requested. It also may take some digging to uncover community-based support that is not widely known, such as a municipal or federal program to aid families with emotionally-challenged children. And as much as two partners love each other, they are not mind readers who always recognize when support is required. Therefore, partners need to engage with each other and with other important people in their lives—at home and at work—to understand others' expectations of them, share their own concerns, and seek feedback, guidance, and support if required.[88]

Make Collaborative Work–Life Decisions

All work–life decisions do not necessarily need to be made collaboratively by partners. However, we believe that partners should collaborate in making those decisions that are most important and have the most substantial consequences to the family. The decision to stay late in the office one particular evening to finish a project need not be made by both partners, although consultation with the other partner is recommended. However, more consequential anchoring decisions such as switching career fields, quitting a job, or moving to a reduced-load work arrangement should be made collaboratively for several reasons.

First, collaborative decisions are likely to be of superior quality than unilateral (or coercive) decisions because each partner may have a unique and insightful perspective on the situation that can get incorporated into the decision. For example, a partner considering changing career fields can benefit from the other partner's experiences, knowledge, and perceptions about the impact of the decision on the partner's career as well as on the family as a whole. Second, collaborative decisions are more likely to be accepted—bought into—by both partners because they believe that their voices have been heard, they understand why the decision was made, and they believe that they had some input into the final decision. Third, collaborative work–life decision-making can strengthen the bond between the partners because of the trust that develops when partners listen to and support each other in making decisions together for the benefit of the entire family.[89]

Be Flexible

Making effective work–life decisions requires a great deal of flexibility on the part of all members of a family. Seeing problems from another person's perspective and changing behavior or attitudes that are outmoded are hallmarks of an effective coping style. Rigid patterns of behavior, by definition, are not conducive to the resolution of stressful situations. In Chapter 2, we discussed the notion of a protean career to illustrate the importance of flexibility. A protean career involves experiencing greater control over one's work life in which career success is judged by internal or subjective standards (satisfaction, achievement, or a balanced life), rather than the traditional external or objective standards of salary and promotions in an organizational structure. We can also speak of a *protean family*, which focuses on the growth and development of all family members, relatively unrestricted by society's norms and expectations. The protean family is willing to be flexible to meet the needs of family members, whether that involves one or both partners reducing work hours, sharing the care of dependents more equitably, or living apart a portion of the time.[90]

Understand and Resist Traditional Gender Roles

Flexible families also reverse traditional gender roles within the relationship when appropriate. Traditional gender norms emphasize women's primary involvement in the family role and men's primary involvement in the work role. Although these traditional norms have become increasingly blurred, many women feel principally responsible for home and family just as many men feel primarily responsible for playing the financial provider role within the family.

Although there is nothing inherently wrong with a woman investing most heavily in family and a man in work, it becomes problematic when partners' allocation of time and energy to work and family are driven by the gender role expectations of society and employers rather than by the partners' own preferences. Therefore, partners in heterosexual relationships should "resist the mandates of gender roles as best they can"[91] and instead encourage each other to make decisions based on their own personal values and needs. This requires that individuals understand their partner's underlying preferences and values and provide their partner with support (emotional, tangible assistance, information, advice, and feedback) so they can make work–life decisions that help their family while also meeting their own needs and values.

Moving from "Me" to "We"

In sum, couples should develop collaborative strategies to make decisions that address the needs of the family as a whole, moving from a "me" orientation (self-interest, coercion, and suppression of conflict) to a "we" orientation (mutual goals, encouragement, a healthy expression of differences, and a willingness to compromise).[92] Of course, what works for one couple may not work for another; there is no cookbook formula for success. However, what is applicable from one situation to another is the need to establish a climate of communication and problem-solving. Hall and Hall suggested the following strategy to establish such a climate: talk about problems regularly, listen to your partner and express your own feelings, discuss goals and explore expectations, practice problem-solving, and practice negotiating compromises. These actions take time, skill, and practice, but they are essential if problems are to be identified and managed. Problem-solving and compromise are necessary to prevent gender-role stereotypes or old behavior patterns from disrupting a couple's attempt to find fresh solutions to novel problems.

Summary

Work, family, and personal lives affect each other in a variety of ways. Each role can enrich another role because resources and/or positive emotions experienced in one role can be transferred to the other role, improving performance and heightening positive feelings in that role. In addition, there are times when the roles conflict with one another because the time spent in one role interferes with the requirements of another role, the stress aroused in one role diminishes experiences in another role, or the behavior that is appropriate in one role is dysfunctional when applied to another role. Whereas work–life enrichment can promote feelings of work–life balance, work–life conflict detracts from feelings of balance.

Societies can help employees achieve more balance in life through their supportive legislation and public policies. Additionally, organizations can provide their employees with various forms of formal work–life policies including maternity and paternity support, dependent care assistance, flexible work arrangements, and informational and social support. Employers' actions will be most effective when supervisors also provide informal work–life support in a culture that understands and respects employees' attempts to balance their work with other life commitments.

Employees and their family can also take actions to increase the balance in their lives as well as their family's well-being. Individuals should take family, community, or other personal circumstances into account when making work-related decisions, and there are a number of ways employees and their families can make these decisions effectively.

Career management requires employees to pay attention to *all* parts of their lives when making career decisions. They need to understand the effects of their career on family, friendships, community, and leisure activities, as well as the effects of these other commitments on their career. Employees should take a whole-life perspective to their career in which they make career decisions that take into account their other life commitments. We reinforce and illustrate these points throughout the remainder of this book.

Assignment

Complete the following questions and discuss them with someone significant in your life.

1. Are you as involved, effective, or satisfied in each of the following parts of life as you would like to be? Circle one response, yes or no, for each role in life.

Career	Yes	No
Family	Yes	No
School	Yes	No
Leisure	Yes	No
Community	Yes	No
Religion	Yes	No
Self-development	Yes	No
Other	Yes	No

2. If yes, what have you done to achieve this? If not, why are you not as involved, effective, or satisfied as you would like?
3. Develop a plan or devise an "experiment" to become more involved, effective, and satisfied with a part of your life.

- What do you need to do to become more involved, effective, and satisfied?
- How might it affect other parts of your life?
- Who can help you?
- How can you monitor your progress?

Discussion Questions

1. Develop a profile of the type of person most likely to experience extensive work–life conflict. Identify work pressures, family or other life pressures, and personal characteristics most likely to produce work–life conflict.

2. You are likely to become a partner in a dual-earner relationship at some point in your life. Perhaps you are already. What might be the major sources of stress in the relationship? Do the stresses outweigh the potential advantages of a dual-earner relationship? Why or why not?
3. It has been suggested that men and women may approach their careers in somewhat different ways: men might be more focused on personal goal achievement and make career decisions designed to enhance their career growth, whereas women might be more focused on relationships and make career decisions that take the needs of their family into account. From your personal observation or experience, are men and women similar or different in how they approach their work and nonwork lives? Why or why not?
4. Dual-earner couples cope most effectively when they adopt a collaborative orientation rather than a "me-first" orientation. Explain how partners in a dual-earner relationship can develop a more collaborative orientation toward work–life issues.
5. Defend or refute the following statement: "Being successful in your career inevitably harms your family or personal life." Provide the reasoning behind your position.

Chapter 3 Case: The Prized Promotion

Doug Sanders is a 38-year-old plant manager for Johnson Electronics, a medium-sized company that manufactures.computer components. He can't wait for dinner tonight to tell Lisa, his wife of 17 years, and Steve, his 15-year-old son, about his promotion.

It's been a long time coming, and Doug believes he richly deserves to be promoted to vice-president for manufacturing at Johnson. He's been with the company for nearly ten years, the first five as a mechanical engineer, and he has certainly paid his dues. For the past five years, since Doug was named plant manager, he has put in 12- and 13-hour days at the plant on a regular basis and is on emergency call 24 hours a day. Not to mention his willingness to fly to corporate headquarters in Denver whenever his boss thinks it is necessary. Besides, Doug's plant has reached new heights in productivity and profitability each year since he took over.

Doug is really looking forward to the new position. True, the hours are going to be just as long—if not longer—than his current job. But the 30 percent salary raise is nothing to sneeze at. Lisa can finally have her dream house! And Doug will have a lot more responsibility—he will finally be able to call the shots, at least as far as manufacturing is concerned. Doug suspects that the company is grooming him for even better things in the future. The relocation to headquarters in Denver is the icing on the cake. Doug and Lisa have always enjoyed their trips to Denver and Steve will be able to ski all the time.

Doug can't wait to break the news to the family tonight. He told Mr. Johnson that he would get back to him in a few days with a "definite yes" and a lot of plans have to be made in a hurry. Lisa will have to give notice on her job at the museum. She should be able to find something in Denver without much trouble. It's a bustling city that has culture on its mind.

The change will be good for Steve too. Always a pretty good student, his grades—and his attitude toward school—have been slipping this past year. Doug realizes that he has been rough on Steve lately, putting on the pressure about grades, but the boy hasn't pushed himself hard enough. He can't afford any more screw-ups if he is going to have a shot at a top-notch university. Anyway, Doug has found from his own business experience that you've got to tighten the screws if you want to get the most out of people.

Doug thinks that the promotion is coming at just the right time. He has been pretty tense and preoccupied at home lately because of the union problems and the pressure for cost-cutting. A change of scenery might be just what the doctor ordered. Doug can't wait to see Lisa's and Steve's faces when he gives them the good news at the dinner table.

Lisa Sanders knows she has a lot to be grateful for. Doug is a good husband and father, and her son Steve is a really nice kid. Her family is very important to her and it was not easy for her to go back to work a few years ago when Steve entered middle school. It wasn't that she particularly needed the money, but she wanted to accomplish something in addition to caring for Steve and Doug.

Lisa remembers that it was pretty difficult finding a job that matched her bachelor's degree in art history. She finally found a clerical position at the Art Museum and the rest is history. Although she doesn't consider herself to be ambitious, she welcomed the promotions that ultimately brought her to her current position, assistant director of the museum. She absolutely loves the job! She is doing what she enjoys the most—developing new cultural programs for the museum—the pay is pretty good, the hours are flexible, and most important, she is appreciated as a competent, creative, productive person. It feels very good. It's a "one in a million" job and she knows it.

Lisa can't wait to tell Doug about her newest project—her idea—that would make the museum more accessible to the elderly and the handicapped. Not that Doug would really appreciate the project. He knows little—and cares less—about art and hasn't shown much inclination to learn more about it in the past three years. Besides, he's been so preoccupied—no, obsessed—with his job recently that he doesn't seem to pay attention. He's always at the plant and when he's home his mind is somewhere else. If his tension and moodiness keep up much longer, maybe Doug should see a doctor or something. Lisa thinks she should suggest that to him one of these days.

Lisa thinks lovingly about her son. Steve is bright, caring, and sensitive. It wasn't easy at first for him to adjust to Lisa's working, but he's become more independent and resourceful by necessity. He's doing OK, although adolescence can be a tough time for anyone. Actually, his grades have slipped a little lately—nothing serious—but he seems to find time for everything but studying. Maybe a little talk is in order to build up his self-confidence. He's always done so well in school. Lisa wishes that Doug wouldn't push Steve so hard about the studying. Putting too much pressure on Steve could easily backfire. Doug and Steve are at each other's throats—when they talk!

Lisa hopes that tonight's meal will be pleasant. Maybe Doug will be relaxed and will be interested in hearing about the museum project.

Steve Sanders is a high school sophomore and things are going pretty well. He has made a lot of real good friends and, probably for the first time in his life, Steve feels that he fits in at school. The teachers are tolerable, the kids are great, and he's got a new girlfriend, Lori. Steve loves his parents, although sometimes he thinks it is easier to love his mother than his father.

Steve thinks a lot about his dad. He's always at the plant and when he does come home he's usually angry—mostly at Steve. Steve feels that his father has been on his case since his last report card. It wasn't terrible, but it wasn't as good as he's done before and it certainly wasn't up to his father's standards. Steve considers himself a pretty good student who had a bad term. Steve knows he should work harder, but he can't stand it when his father gets on his back about school. He doesn't listen to Steve or doesn't want to know why Steve's grades started slipping or what problems he has. He just yells, probably like he yells at the workers in his plant.

Steve thinks about his mom a lot too. He's really happy that she's doing so well at the art museum. She loves her job, but she always has time for his dad and him. Steve feels bad that his father never really seems interested in her job or spends much time with her. Steve realizes that his father doesn't have much time for him either. Steve wonders whether that's the way it is when you're a big shot in the business world.

Steve is optimistic that things will start looking up again soon. He realizes that he's got great friends and parents who love him. And he has promised himself that he'll start hitting the books again... college is right around the corner.

The Dinner

Dinner was anything but pleasant! Doug was astounded at Lisa and Steve's reaction to the news about his promotion. He thought they were downright hostile. Lisa was angry and shocked; this is the first she had heard that Doug was even up for a promotion. And Steve didn't know what to think, although he flatly told his parents that he's not moving no matter what. After about an hour, they all started repeating themselves and figured that dinner was over.

They all left the dinner table in bewilderment and anger. But Doug promised to hold off making a firm commitment to Mr. Johnson. And Lisa promised to sleep on it and continue the conversation tomorrow morning. Steve didn't promise anything.

Case Questions

1. If you were Lisa or Steve, how would you have reacted to Doug's announcement of his promotion? Why?
2. If you were Doug, how would you have reacted to Lisa and Steve's anger and resistance? Why?
3. What could Doug have done differently in his conversations with his company and his family?
4. What does the Sanders' situation illustrate about the special challenges faced by dual-earner families?
5. What should the family do next?

Notes

1 Greenhaus, J. H. & Foley, S. (2007). The intersection of work and family lives. In Gunz, H. & Peiperl, M. (Eds.), *Handbook of career studies* (pp. 131–152). Thousand Oaks, CA: Sage; Greenhaus, J. H. & Powell, G. N. (2017). *Making work and family work: From hard choices to smart choices*. New York: Routledge.

2 We use the term "work–life balance" to refer to the balance between work and other parts of life, such as family, friends, community, religious activities, leisure, and self-development. Work–life balance is broader than work–family balance, which refers only to the work and family roles. Work–life is an awkward term because it seems to contrast work and life whereas work is part of life. Nevertheless, we use the term work–life because of its breadth and its frequent use in everyday life. Evidence relating balance with such positive well-being indicators as job satisfaction, organizational commitment, family satisfaction, family performance, and family functioning can be found in Carlson, D. S., Grzywacz, J. G. & Zivnuska, S. (2009). Is work–family balance more than conflict and enrichment? *Human Relations*, *62*, 1459–1486.

3 Greenhaus, J. H. & Allen, T. D. (2011). Work–family balance: A review and extension of the literature. In Quick, J. C. & Tetrick, L. E. (Eds.), *Handbook of occupational health psychology*, 2nd ed. (pp. 165–183). Washington, DC: American Psychological Association; Greenhaus & Powell (2017); Casper, W. J., Vaziri, H., Wayne, J. H., DeHauw, S. & Greenhaus, J. H. (In Press). The jingle-jangle of work–nonwork balance: A comprehensive and meta-analytic review of its meaning and measurement. *Journal of Applied Psychology*.

4 For summaries of the connections between work and other parts of life, see Eby, L. T., Casper, W., Lockwood, A., Bordeaux, C. & Brinley, A. (2005). Work and family research in IO/OB: Content analysis and review of the literature (1980–2002). *Journal of Vocational Behavior*, Monograph, *66*, 124–197; Greenhaus, J. H., Allen, T. D. & Spector, P. E. (2006). Health consequences of work–family conflict: The dark side of the work–family interface. In Perrewe, P. L. & Ganster, D. C. (Eds.), *Research in occupational stress and well-being*, Volume 5 (pp. 61–98). Amsterdam: JAI Press/Elsevier; Greenhaus & Foley (2007). Greenhaus, J. H. & Parasuraman, S. (1999). Research on work, family, and gender: Current status and future directions. In Powell, G. N. (Ed.), *Handbook of gender and work* (pp. 391–412). Newbury Park, CA: Sage; Greenhaus, J. H. & Powell, G. N. (2006). When work and family are allies: A theory of work–family enrichment. *Academy of Management Review*, *31*, 72–92; Michel, J. S., Kotrba, L. M., Mitchelson, J. K., Clark, M. A. & Baltes, B. B. (2011). Antecedents of work–family conflict: A meta-analytic review. *Journal of Organizational Behavior*, *32*, 689–725.

5 Statistics available at the United States Department of Labor, Bureau of Labor Statistics at www.bls.gov (www.bls.gov/news.release/pdf/famee.pdf) under the menu item "Employment Characteristics of Families—2015," released on April 22, 2016.

6 Butts, M. M., Becker, W. J. & Boswell, W. R. (2015). Hot buttons and time sinks: The effects of electronic communication during nonwork time on emotions and work–nonwork conflict. *Academy of Management Journal*, *58*, 763–788; Johnson, D. (2006). It's all a blur: Techno-stress, "negative spillover" & you (reports on handheld electronics usage), *Industrial Safety & Hygiene News*, *5*, 6.

7 Greenhaus & Powell (2017); Perlow, L. A. (2012). *Sleeping with your smartphone: How to break the 24/7 habit and change the way you work*. Boston, MA: Harvard Business Review Press; Frase-Blunt, M. (2001). Busman's holiday. *HR Magazine*, *46*, 76–80; Rosato, D. (2003). Handy blackberry can be addictive. *USA Today*, June 6, E.13.

8 Bureau of Labor Statistics (2014). Civilian noninstitutional population age 15 and over [Table A-1]. American Time Use Survey. Retrieved from www.bls.gov/tus/home.htm#tables.

9 USA Triathalon (2009). The mind of the triathlete: Market research report. Retrieved from www.usatriathalon.org.

10 Kossek, E. E., Ruderman, M. N., Braddy, P. W. & Hannum, K. M. (2012). Work–nonwork boundary management profiles: A person-centered approach. *Journal of Vocational Behavior*, *81*, 112–128.

11 Greenhaus, J. H. & Beutell, N. J. (1985). Sources of conflict between work and family roles. *Academy of Management Review*, *10*, 76–88.

12 Frone, M. R. (2003). Work–family balance. In Quick, J. C. & Tetrick, L. E. (Eds.), *Handbook of occupational health psychology* (pp. 143–162). Washington, DC: American Psychological Association.

13 Evans, P. & Bartolome, F. (1980). *Must success cost so much?* New York: Basic Books; Greenhaus & Parasuraman (1999); Edwards, J. R. & Rothbard, N. P. (2000). Mechanisms linking

work and family: Clarifying the relationship between work and family constructs. *Academy of Management Review*, *25*, 178–199.
14 Greenhaus & Beutell (1985).
15 Allen, T. D., Johnson, R. C., Saboe, K. N., Cho, E., Dumani, S. & Evans, S. (2012). Dispositional variables and work–family conflict: A meta-analysis. *Journal of Vocational Behavior*, *80*, 17–26; Burke, R. J. (2006). Type A behavior pattern. In Greenhaus, J. H. & Callanan, G. A. (Eds.), *Encyclopedia of career development* (pp. 828–831). Thousand Oaks, CA: Sage.
16 Frone, M. R. & Rice, R. W. (1987). Work–family conflict: The effect of job and family involvement. *Journal of Occupational Behaviour*, *8*, 45–53.
17 Allen et al. (2012).
18 Greenhaus, J. H., Allen, T. D. & Spector, P. E. (2006). Health consequences of work–family conflict: The dark side of the work–family interface. In Perrewe, P. L. & Ganster, D. C. (Eds.), *Research in occupational stress and well-being*, Volume 5 (pp. 61–98). Amsterdam: JAI Press/Elsevier.
19 Greenhaus & Allen (2011).
20 Friedman, S. D. & Greenhaus, J. H. (2000). *Work and family—allies or enemies? What happens when business professionals confront life choices*. New York: Oxford University Press.
21 Friedman & Greenhaus (2000); see also Greenhaus & Powell (2006). Although we choose to use the concept work–family enrichment to refer to the positive effects that work and family roles have on each other, others have used similar concepts such as work–family facilitation and work–family positive spillover.
22 Greenhaus & Powell (2006).
23 Graves, L., Ohlott, P. & Ruderman, M. (2007). Commitment to family roles: Effects on managers' attitudes and performance. *Journal of Applied Psychology*, *92*, 44–56; Ruderman, M., Ohlott, P., Panzer, K. & King, S. (2002). Benefits of multiple roles for managerial women. *Academy of Management Journal*, *45*, 369–386.
24 Rothbard, N. P. (2001). Enriching or depleting? The dynamics of engagement in work and family roles. *Administrative Science Quarterly*, *46*, 655–684.
25 Lapierre, L. M., Li, Y., Kwan, H. K., Greenhaus, J. H., DiRenzo, M. S. & Shao, P. (In Press). A meta-analysis of the antecedents of work–family enrichment. *Journal of Organizational Behavior*.
26 Ibid.; Michel, J. S. & Clark, M. A. (2009). Has it been affect all along? A test of work-to-family and family-to-work models of conflict, enrichment, and satisfaction. *Personality and Individual Differences*, *47*, 163–168.
27 McNall, L. A., Nicklin, J. M. & Masuda, A. D. (2010). A meta-analytic review of the consequences associated with work–family enrichment. *Journal of Business and Psychology*, *25*, 381–396; Masuda, A. D., McNall, L. A., Allen, T. D. & Nicklin, J. M. (2012). Examining the constructs of work-to-family enrichment and positive spillover. *Journal of Vocational Behavior*, *80*, 197–210; Van Steenbergen, E. F. & Ellemers, N. (2009). Is managing the work–family interface worthwhile? Benefits for employee health and performance. *Journal of Organizational Behavior*, *30*, 617–642.
28 Den Dulk, L., Groeneveld, S., Ollier-Malaterre, A. & Valcour, M. (2013). National context in work–life research: A multi-level cross-national analysis of the adoption of workplace work–life arrangements in Europe. *European Management Journal*, *31*, 478–494.
29 Valcour, M. (2007). Work-based resources as moderators of the relationship between work hours and satisfaction with work–family balance. *Journal of Applied Psychology*, *92*, 1512–1523.
30 ILO; Rehel, E. M. (2014). When dad stays home too: Paternity leave, gender, and parenting. *Gender & Society*, *28*, 110–132; O'Brien, M. (2009). Fathers, parental leave policies, and infant quality of life: International perspectives and policy impact. *Annals of the American Academy of Political and Social Science*, *624*, 190–213; More hands to rock the cradle. (2015, May 16). *The Economist*. Retrieved November 23, 2015, from www.economist.com.
31 Greenhaus & Powell (2017).
32 Kim, J. S. & Faerman, S. R. (2013). Exploring the relationship between culture and family-friendly programs (FFPs) in the Republic of Korea. *European Management Journal*, *31*, 505–521.
33 Greenhaus & Powell (2017).
34 Malcolm, H. (2016, April 14). Millennials will take a happier workplace over better pay. *USA Today*, April 14. Retrieved November 6, 2016, from www.usatoday.com/story/money/personalfinance/2016/04/14/millennials-workplace-happy-salary-pay/82943186/.
35 Schwartz, F. N. (1989). Management women and the facts of life. *Harvard Business Review*, 65–76; Schwartz, F. N. (1992). *Breaking with tradition*. New York: Warner Books.

36 U.S. Department of Labor, Bureau of Labor Statistics (2015b). Labor force statistics from the Current Population Survey, table 2. Retrieved October 13, 2015, from www.bls.gov/cps; Powell, G. N. (2011). *Women and men in management*, 4th ed. Los Angeles: Sage.
37 Approximately 46 percent of the U.S. labor force were women in 2014. Retrieved November 8, 2016, from http://data.worldbank.org/indicator/SL.TLF.TOTL.FE.ZS.
38 Table 570. Civilian Labor Force and Participation Rates with Projections: 1980–2014, U.S. Census Bureau; also, see Schwartz (1992).
39 Frone, M. R. (2006). Work–family conflict. In Greenhaus, J. H. & Callanan, G. A. (Eds.), *Encyclopedia of career development* (pp. 867–869). Thousand Oaks, CA: Sage.
40 Williams, J. (2000). *Unbending gender: Why family and work conflict and what to do about it.* New York: Oxford University Press.
41 Bond, J. T., Galinsky, E., Kim, S. S. & Brownfield, E. (2005). *National study of employers.* New York: Families and Work Institute.
42 Greenhaus & Powell (2017).
43 Thomas, L. T. & Ganster, D. C. (1995). Impact of family-supportive work variables on work–family conflict and strain: A control perspective. *Journal of Applied Psychology, 80*, 6–15. Quotation is on p. 7.
44 Hammer, L. B., Kossek, E. E., Yragui, N. L., Bodner, T. E. & Hanson, G. C. (2009). Development and validation of a multidimensional measure of family supportive supervisor behaviors (FSSB). *Journal of Management, 35*, 837–856.
45 Thompson, C. A., Beauvais, L. L. & Lyness, K. S. (1999). When work–family benefits are not enough: The influence of work–family culture on benefit utilization, organizational attachment, and work–family conflict. *Journal of Vocational Behavior, 54*, 392–415.
46 Kossek, E. E., Pichler, S., Bodner, T. & Hammer, L. B. (2011). Workplace social support and work–family conflict: A meta-analysis clarifying the influence of general and work–family-specific supervisor and organizational support. *Personnel Psychology, 64*, 289–313.
47 Greenhaus, J. H., Ziegert, J. C. & Allen, T. D. (2012). When family-supportive supervision matters: Relations between multiple sources of support and work–family balance. *Journal of Vocational Behavior, 80*, 266–275.
48 Bagger, J. & Li, A. (2014). How does supervisory family support influence employees' attitudes and behaviors? A social exchange perspective. *Journal of Management, 40*, 1123–1150; Hammer et al. (2009).
49 Allen, T. D. (2001). Family-supportive work environments: The role of organizational perceptions. *Journal of Vocational Behavior, 58*, 414–435; Brewer, A. M. (2000). Work design for flexible work scheduling: Barriers and gender implications. *Gender, Work and Organization, 7*, 33–44; Powell, G. N. & Mainiero, L. A. (1999). Managerial decision making regarding alternative work arrangements. *Journal of Occupational and Organizational Psychology, 72*, 41–56; Roehling, P. V., Roehling, M. V. & Moen, P. (2001). The relationship between work–life policies and practices and employee loyalty: A life course perspective. *Journal of Family and Economic Issues, 21*, 141–171; Thompson et al. (1999).
50 Friedman, D. E. (1990). Work and family: The new strategic plan. *Human Resource Planning, 13*(2), 79–89; Magid, R. Y. (1986). When mothers and fathers work: How employers can help. *Personnel*, 50–56.
51 Greenhaus & Powell (2017) refer to work–family decisions. We extend the notion to work–life decisions to represent the process by which work-related decisions are informed not only by family considerations but also by a variety of other nonwork roles, such as community, friendship, or personal self-development.
52 Briscoe, J. P., Hall, D. T. & DeMuth, R. L. (2006). Protean and boundaryless careers: An empirical exploration. *Journal of Vocational Behavior, 69*, 30–47; Hall, D. T. (2004). The protean career: A quarter-century journey. *Journal of Vocational Behavior, 65*, 1–13; Hall, D. T. & Chandler, D. E. (2005). Psychological success: When the career is a calling. *Journal of Organizational Behavior, 26*, 155–176.
53 DiRenzo, M. S., Greenhaus, J. H. & Weer, C. H. (2015). Relationship between protean career orientation and work–life balance: A resource perspective. *Journal of Organizational Behavior, 36*, 538–560. Quotation is on p. 543.
54 Friedman, S. D. (2008). Be a better leader, have a richer life. *Harvard Business Review, 86*(4), 112–118.
55 Ibarra, H. (2002). How to stay stuck in the wrong career. *Harvard Business Review, 80*(12), 40–47.

56 Baltes, B. B. & Heydens-Gahir, H. A. (2003). Reduction of work–family conflict through the use of selection, optimization, and compensation behaviors. *Journal of Applied Psychology*, *88*, 1005–1018; Wiese, B. S., Freund, A. M. & Baltes, P. B. (2002). Subjective career success and emotional well-being: Longitudinal predictive power of selection, optimization, and compensation. *Journal of Vocational Behavior*, *60*, 321–335.
57 Hall, F. S. & Hall, D. T. (1979). *The two-career couple*. Reading, MA: Addison-Wesley.
58 Barnett, R. C. & Hyde, J. S. (2001). Women, men, work, and family: An expansionist view. *American Psychologist*, *56*, 781–796.
59 Gilbert, L. A. (2006). Two-career relationships. In Greenhaus, J. H. & Callanan, G. A. (Eds.), *Encyclopedia of career development* (pp. 822–828). Thousand Oaks, CA: Sage.
60 Parasuraman, S. & Greenhaus, J. H. (1993). Personal portrait: The life-style of the woman manager. In Fagenson, E. A. (Ed.), *Women in management: Trends, issues, and challenges in managerial diversity*, Vol. 4 (pp. 186–211). Newbury Park, CA: Sage.
61 Campbell, B. M. (1986). *Successful women, angry men*. New York: Random House.
62 Cho, E. & Allen, T. D. (2012). Relationship between work interference with family and parent–child interactive behavior: Can guilt help? *Journal of Vocational Behavior*, *80*, 276–287.
63 Friedman & Greenhaus (2000).
64 Greenhaus & Powell (2017).
65 Graves et al. (2007).
66 Friedman & Greenhaus (2000).
67 Ibid.
68 Poloma, M. M., Pendleton, B. F. & Garland, T. N. (1982). Reconsidering the dual-career marriage: A longitudinal approach. In Aldous, J. (Ed.), *Two paychecks: Life in dual-earner families* (pp. 173–192). Beverly Hills, CA: Sage.
69 Chapman, F. S. (1987). Executive guilt: Who's taking care of the children? *Fortune*, February 16, 30–37.
70 Galinsky, E., Aumann, K. & Bond, J. T. (2008). *Times are changing: Gender and generation at work and at home*. New York: Families and Work Institute.
71 Broberg, A. G., Wessels, H., Lamb, M. E. & Hwang, C. P. (1997). Effects of day care on the development of cognitive abilities in 8-year-olds: A longitudinal study. *Developmental Psychology*, *33*, 62–69; Durlak, J. A., Weissberg, R. P. & Pachan, M. (2010). A meta-analysis of after-school programs that seek to promote personal and social skills in children and adolescents. *American Journal of Community Psychology*, *45*, 294–309; Howes, C. (1988). Relations between early child care and schooling. *Developmental Psychology*, *24*, 53–57.
72 See http://qz.com/434056/working-moms-have-more-successful-daughters-and-more-caring-sons-harvard-business-school-study-says/, retrieved December 4, 2016.
73 Galinsky, E. (1999). *Ask the children: What America's children really think about working parents*. New York: William Morrow and Company.
74 Greenhaus & Powell (2017).
75 Radcliffe, L. S. & Cassell, C. (2014). Resolving couples' work–family conflicts: The complexity of decision making and the introduction of a new framework. *Human Relations*, *67*, 793–819.
76 Radcliffe & Cassell (2014).
77 Greenhaus & Powell (2017). Quotation is on p. 116.
78 Radcliffe & Cassell (2014).
79 These suggestions are largely based on material presented in Greenhaus & Powell (2017), pp. 124–131.
80 Masterson, C. R. & Hoobler, J. M. (2015). Care and career: A family identity-based typology of dual-earner couples. *Journal of Organizational Behavior*, *36*, 75–93.
81 Greenhaus & Powell (2017). Quotation is on p. 124.
82 Humberd, B., Ladge, J. J. & Harrington, B. (2015). The "new" dad: Navigating fathering identity within organizational contexts. *Journal of Business and Psychology*, *30*, 249–266; Kramer, K. Z., Kelly, E. L. & McCulloch, J. B. (2015). Stay-at-home fathers: Definition and characteristics based on 34 years of CPS data. *Journal of Family Issues*, *20*, 1–23.
83 Hornung, S., Rousseau, D. M. & Glaser, J. (2008). Creating flexible work arrangements through idiosyncratic deals. *Journal of Applied Psychology*, *93*, 655–664.
84 Friedman & Greenhaus (2000).
85 Gilbert (2006).
86 Rapoport, R. & Rapoport, R. N. (1971). Further considerations on the dual career family. *Human Relations*, *24*, 519–533.

87 Gilbert (2006).
88 Greenhaus & Powell (2017). Quotation is on p. 126. See also Friedman (2008).
89 The potential effectiveness of collaborative work–life decision-making is based largely on the literature on conflict management and negotiations. See Greenhaus & Powell (2017).
90 For information on how couples engage in problem-solving to achieve more sharing of home and family responsibilities, see the ThirdPath Institute website at www.thirdpath.org.
91 Greenhaus & Powell (2017).
92 Hall & Hall (1979).

4 A Model of Career Management

To manage a career is to make a decision or, more accurately, a series of decisions. Should you pursue a career in information technology, marketing, or accounting? Should you accept a position with a major corporation or obtain a graduate degree instead? Should you move into general management or stay in a staff position? Should you accept a transfer to manage a subsidiary in a foreign country? How can you obtain employment after an unexpected job loss? If you pursue early retirement, will you do volunteer work or start your own company?

Although these illustrations are all unique in some respect, they do possess a basic similarity; they all require active career management and decision-making. As was stated in Chapter 1, if we do not actively manage the direction of our careers and lives, then we leave our futures up to chance or whim. In today's less certain business environment, we all need to be proactive and responsible for our careers. Career management is the process by which individuals can make reasoned, appropriate decisions about their work in the context of their total life. It is also an approach to problem-solving that can be used to address a wide variety of career decisions.

In this chapter, we discuss a model of career management. First, an overview of the model and the research that forms the basis of the model are presented. Next, the value of using the career management process in a continual manner is articulated. Finally, four indicators of effective career management are outlined. In Chapters 5 and 6 we will delve more deeply into the career management process and emphasize the pragmatic application of the model to career decision-making. These chapters will include specific guidelines to apply the career management model, as well as learning exercises to practice the skills required by the model.

An Overview of the Career Management Model

In the social sciences, a model is a picture or representation of reality.[1] A model contains a set of variables that are related to each other in a specified manner to allow for a better understanding of some piece of the world. The model of career management considered in this book is *normative* in nature; that is, it describes how people *should* manage their careers. Not everybody manages a career in this fashion, but the activities represented in the model can lead to desirable outcomes for the individual. The reasons for this assumption will become clear as the model unfolds.

The career management model is portrayed in Exhibit 4.1. Before defining the key components in a formal sense, the career management cycle is introduced with a brief example.

A young chemical engineer is pondering her future in her company. Although she enjoys her position as a staff engineer, a career in management has intrigued her for a while. She could lay low and follow the company's "plan" for her. However, she decides to take a more active role in the management of her career. She has some decisions to make.

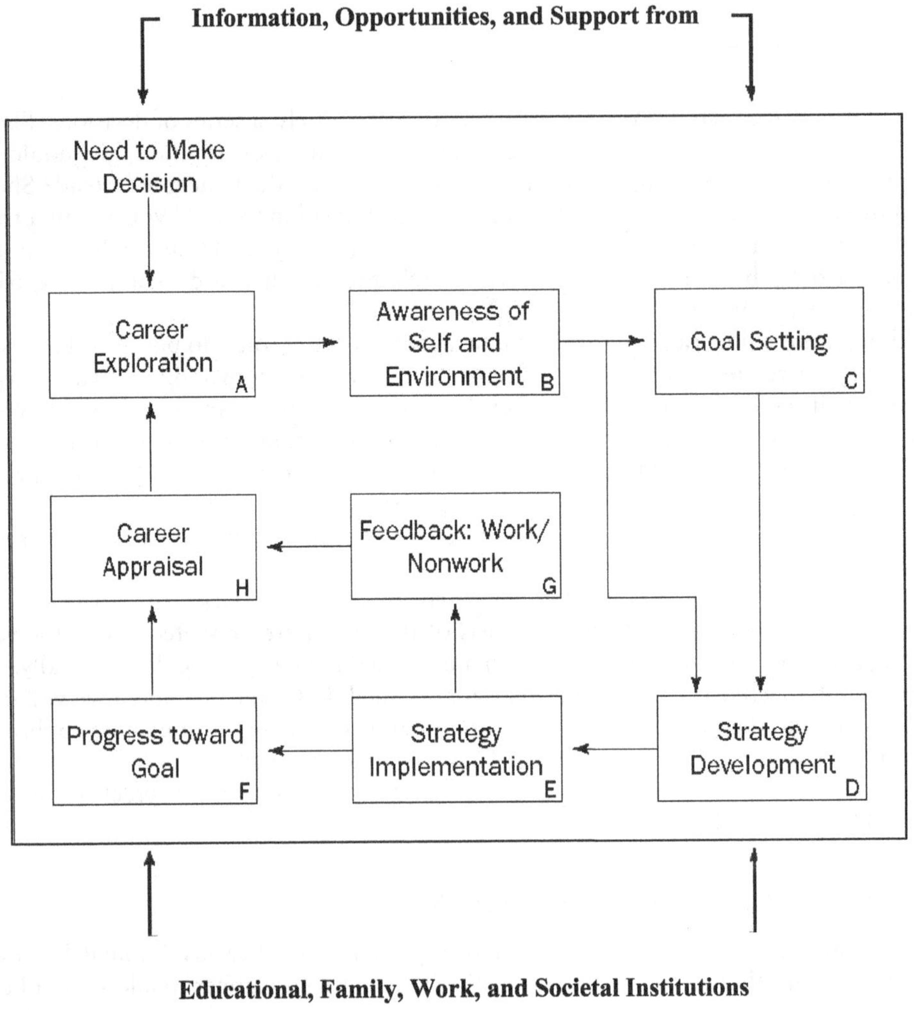

Exhibit 4.1 Model of Career Management

The first step in the career management model indicates that the engineer should engage in career exploration (Box A in Exhibit 4.1). That is, she should begin gathering information. She might collect information about herself (what she enjoys doing, where her talents lie, the importance of work in her total life), about alternative jobs inside or outside the organization (what does a plant manager really do, anyway? What are the salaries of veteran chemical engineers?), and about her organization (or other organizations) as a total system (is it possible to move from staff to line in this company? How do you get promoted around here?).

Career exploration, if conducted properly, should enable the engineer to become more fully aware of herself and her environment (Box B). She ought to gain insight, for example, into her values, interests, and abilities in both her work and nonwork lives. She should become more aware of job options and their requirements and of opportunities and obstacles that exist both with her current employer and with other companies.

A greater awareness of herself and her environment can help the engineer choose a career goal or goals to pursue (Box C). First, greater self-awareness should prompt the engineer to set reasonable conceptual goals. A conceptual goal represents a general summary of the nature of the work experiences or outcomes the individual intends to attain, without specifying a particular job or position. In this sense, the conceptual goal is a manifestation of the individual's significant values, interests, and preferences. For example, the engineer might have a conceptual goal to attain substantial managerial responsibility as a means to influence corporate direction.

In addition, greater awareness of the work environment should assist in the setting of operational goals. An operational goal translates the conceptual goal into a specific or targeted job and is based on the individual's understanding of the internal and external work environments. To extend the above example, the engineer might have a longer-term operational goal to be the assistant vice-president (AVP) of technical support, which would satisfy her conceptual goal to exert managerial responsibility that influences corporate direction. Of course, she could have interim operational goals that could take her to the AVP level. She might first set a more reasonable operational goal of being a team leader for a high-profile engineering project. Or she might have a short-term goal to remain in her current position for the foreseeable future as a means to gain more experience, establish a record of accomplishment, and build a set of transportable skills.

The establishment of realistic conceptual and operational goals can facilitate the development (Box D) and implementation (Box E) of career strategies; that is, courses of actions designed to attain the desired career goals. For example, if the engineer's primary operational goal is to become the AVP of technical support, she might enroll in one or more management development seminars sponsored by the company, encourage her boss to assign her more managerial tasks in her present position, learn more about the operation of the entire plant, or seek information through the Internet describing the responsibilities of an AVP of technical support.

The implementation of reasonable career strategies can produce progress toward the stated conceptual and operational career goals (Box F). If the engineer chooses wise plans of action, she is more likely to attain her goals than if she did not pursue any career strategies or if she developed inappropriate strategies.

The implementation of career strategies can provide useful feedback to the person. This feedback, in conjunction with feedback from other work and nonwork sources (Box G), can enable the engineer to appraise her career (Box H). The additional information derived from career appraisal becomes another vehicle for career exploration (see the arrow from Box H to Box A) that continues the career management cycle. For example, the engineer might discover that she has performed poorly on the newly acquired managerial portions of her job. This appraisal might lead the engineer to consider changing her goal; she may no longer wish to enter management. Or she may retain the goal but revise the strategies (see the arrow from B to D). For example, she might choose to pursue a graduate degree in management to hone her skills.

In sum, the career management cycle is a problem-solving, decision-making process. Information is gathered so individuals can become more aware of themselves and the world around them. Goals are established, plans or strategies are developed and implemented, and feedback is obtained to provide more information for ongoing career management.

Individuals who follow this approach to career management do not live in a vacuum. As indicated by the border around Exhibit 4.1, the usefulness of exploration, goal-setting, strategies, and feedback often depends on the support received from various people and organizations. For example, advice, love, and support from families can all contribute to effective career management.[2] Studies have shown that individuals who receive social support from family and friends feel more secure and are better able to progress in their career development.[3] Other forms of support and influence can come from internship and counseling programs provided by colleges, formal and informal performance appraisals, self-assessment workshops, mentoring and training programs offered by work organizations, assistance from supervisors or co-workers, and Internet-based information and advice on career management.

The successful application of this career management model depends both on the individual and the organization. It involves an exchange of information among employees, current and potential employers, co-workers, friends, and families. Individuals must be willing to take on the task of being proactive and responsible for their careers. It takes effort to gather the information needed to make appropriate career decisions. Organizations must also be willing and able to share information with employees, to make the necessary resources available, and to support employees in their attempts to manage their careers. Subsequent chapters will consider what individuals and organizations can do to stimulate career growth and effective career management.

Theory and Research on the Career Management Process

In this section, we examine the theory and research that form the conceptual base for the model of career management. We discuss, in turn, career exploration through career appraisal, defining key terms, offering a rationale for each component of the model, and summarizing relevant research.

This model is based on the assumption that people are more fulfilled and more productive when their work and life experiences are compatible with their own desires and aspirations. Extensive research has shown that people are more satisfied with their career choices and jobs when their work experiences are consistent with their values, interests, personality, abilities, and lifestyle preferences.[4] Moreover, performance in a career is enhanced when the job requires the application of skills and abilities that the individual possesses. For these reasons, the career management model attempts to optimize the compatibility or "fit" between individuals and their jobs, work environments, and organizations.

Career Exploration

Career exploration is the collection and analysis of information regarding oneself and the environment that foster the career management process.[5] Most people need to gather information so they can become more keenly aware of their own values, interests, and abilities, as well as the opportunities and obstacles in their environment. It is assumed that the more extensive and more appropriate the career exploration, the more likely people will become aware of different facets of themselves and the world of work.

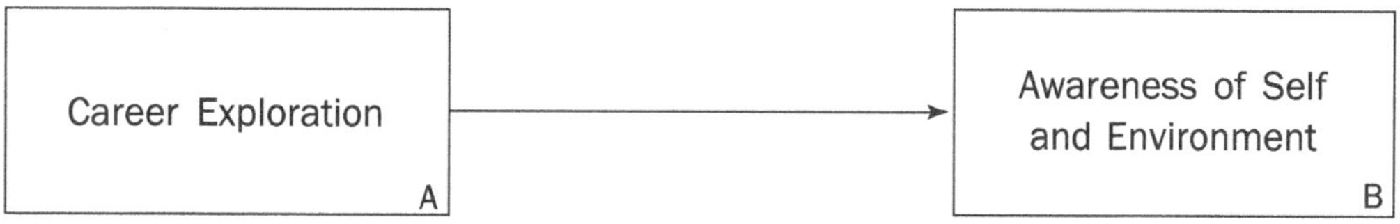

Why does career exploration promote awareness? First, people may not know themselves nearly as well as they think they do. For example, they may not have a clear understanding of what they really want from a job or from life. Perhaps they have not given it much thought, or possibly past decisions were guided more by what others wanted for them than what they wanted. People often need to collect the necessary data to increase awareness in these areas.

Second, people's insights into their personal qualities might be incomplete. They may never have thought, for example, that success as the advertising manager of the high school yearbook was a reflection of their persuasive and interpersonal skills, or that accomplishments on a special task force at work reveal substantial leadership qualities. Oftentimes, individuals hold rigid ideas about appropriate work roles based on their gender or upbringing; therefore, they may allow biases, rather than factual data, to determine what they think their abilities are.

Third, individuals may on occasion overestimate strengths in certain areas and judge themselves to be more talented than they really are. Conversely, some people may persistently underestimate their competence. For these reasons, career exploration can provide an individual with a more complete and accurate picture of himself or herself. The ability to be self-aware, that is, one's ability to reflect on and accurately assess one's demonstrated behaviors and skills in the workplace, has been linked to effective job performance.[6]

In a similar vein, knowledge of different occupations, organizations, and career opportunities can also benefit from an active exploration of the environment. It is known, for example, that people can develop expectations about jobs and organizations that are not realistic. Again, a thorough exploration of the world can help clarify alternatives and options, and aid adaptability.

Types of Career Exploration

It is helpful to think of career exploration in terms of the type of information that is sought. For example, self-exploration can provide a greater awareness of personal qualities (see Table 4.1). People may come to possess a deeper understanding of the activities they like and dislike (interests) and their unique individual persona (personality). They may examine how much challenge (or security, money, or travel) they want from a job (work values). As noted earlier, self-exploration can also provide substantial information about strengths, weaknesses, talents, and limitations. Finally, self-exploration can provide a better understanding of the balance of work, family, and other activities that best suit a preferred lifestyle.

Environmental exploration, as the name implies, helps one learn more about some aspect of the environment. For a student (or someone considering a career change), environmental exploration is likely to be occupationally and organizationally focused. What does a

Table 4.1 Types of Career Exploration

Self-Exploration	*Environmental Exploration*
• Interests • Talents Strengths Weaknesses • Work Values Job challenge Job autonomy Security Work/life balance Money Working conditions Helping others Power or influence	• Types of occupations • Types of industries • Necessary job skills • Job alternatives • Company alternatives • Impact of career decision on family or personal life • Impact of family or personal life on career

systems analyst really do? What skills are required for a career in electrical engineering? What is the difference between careers in private and public accounting?

For employees, environmental exploration might be oriented more toward alternative jobs within a particular organization or industry. In this context, exploration can provide information on one's current job or alternative future jobs. For what jobs would I qualify in two to three years? What experiences are needed to move from my current line position to a particular staff assignment? Is my current career path likely to come to a dead end within a few years?

Environmental exploration can provide employees with information about their current organization. Who in the organization is willing and able to be my sponsor? Who really gets rewarded in the organization? What training and development opportunities are available to me? For someone in the job market, whether by choice or by necessity, environmental exploration can provide information about the relative merits of working in one industry versus another or about the likelihood of career advancement in one company versus another. What organizations give the best chances for advancement? Which ones offer tuition reimbursement or have progressive family-friendly policies?

Another important aspect of the environment for many employees is their family. For example, knowing your spouse's willingness to relocate might help you to make a decision to pursue career opportunities 2,000 miles away or accept a temporary expatriate assignment. Therefore, environmental exploration can also provide useful information about a family's needs and aspirations, a spouse's career values, and about the relationship between one's work and other parts of life.

The Impact of Career Exploration on Career Management

Research suggests that career exploration has a beneficial effect on career management. The most immediate consequence of career exploration is an enhanced awareness of self and environment. A number of studies demonstrate that as individuals engage in more career exploration, they become more aware of themselves and their chosen career and they can increase the amount of information they acquire during the job-search process.[7] Research also indicates that career exploration can help people develop career goals, although it is likely that the focus and the quality of the exploration, rather than its mere quantity, facilitate goal-setting. Moreover, individuals' occupational decisions tend to be more appropriate or satisfying when their decisions are preceded by extensive career exploration.[8] Prior studies have also demonstrated the usefulness of career exploration for people engaged in job search behaviors and pursuing job prospects.[9] Students who engage in extensive exploration generate more job interviews and offers, obtain higher salary offers, and develop more realistic job expectations. Career exploration can also help people develop more extensive career strategies and perform more effectively in job-interview situations.

In short, career exploration can help people become more aware of themselves and the world of work. As a result, they are "ready" (or vocationally mature enough) to handle the formidable task of formulating career goals, and are able to develop strategies necessary to accomplish these goals. This does not mean that career exploration is either easy or guaranteed to provide profound and useful information. It does suggest, however, that career management can be more effectively conducted if it is based on a solid foundation of accurate information.

The purpose of this section was to examine the meaning and relevance of career exploration. Specific career exploration techniques will be presented in Chapter 5.

Awareness

In a career management sense, awareness portends a relatively complete and accurate perception of one's own qualities and the characteristics of one's relevant environment. In our model of career management, a deep awareness of self and environment enables a person to set appropriate career goals and to develop appropriate career strategies. As such, awareness is a central concept in career preparedness and development.[10]

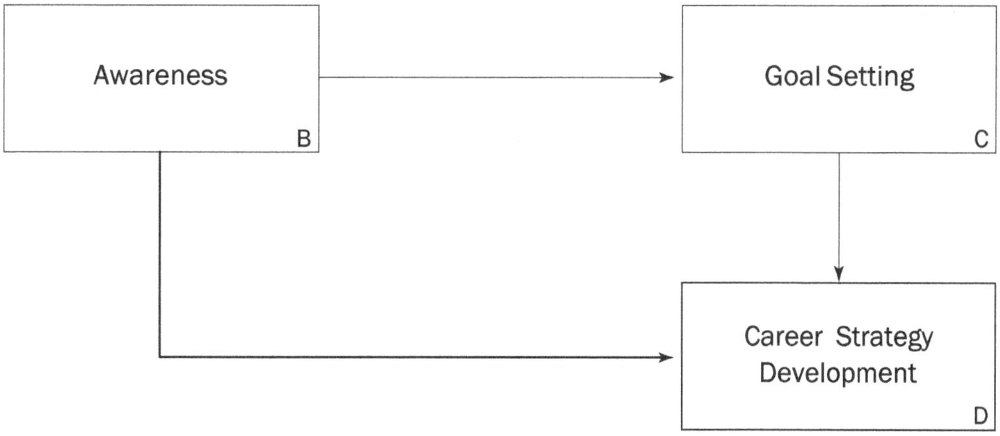

Indeed, it would be difficult to set realistic goals in the absence of an accurate view of oneself and the world of work. How can we set a realistic goal to become an actuary, for example, without a clear picture of the duties, requirements, and rewards of actuarial positions as well as a clear assessment of our talents and interests in those relevant areas? To extend this illustration further, how can we reasonably decide whether to remain an actuary or move into a general management track without understanding our motives and abilities that might help or hinder a career in management? This does not mean that people are always aware of themselves and their options when they set a goal or make a decision. In fact, we can all think of many career decisions that were based on stereotyped, biased, or distorted information. The point is that goals are likely to be more appropriate and more realistic when they are based on an accurate picture of self and environment.

Support for this notion comes from several sources. Researchers have found that students who reported extensive awareness of their values and their chosen field tended to establish more satisfying occupational goals than those who were relatively unaware of self and career field.[11] Information and awareness are likely to enhance the presence and clarity of career plans. Furthermore, information acquired about oneself or one's environment can help one develop realistic job expectations and attain higher levels of job satisfaction. Thus, research evidence suggests that awareness can have a positive effect on career management.[12]

Career Goal

A career goal is a desired career-related outcome that a person intends to attain. One of the most consistent research findings in the organizational behavior literature is that employees who are committed to specific, challenging task goals outperform those who do not have goals or have a weak commitment to established goals.[13] The advantage of establishing a career goal is that a person can direct his or her efforts in a relatively focused manner. Research has found that once goals are in place, complementary behaviors and attitudes that reinforce these goals occur.[14] For example, a sales representative who sets an operational goal to become the regional marketing manager can begin to plan a strategy around attainment of the goal. Without an explicit goal, a plan of action is difficult to develop.

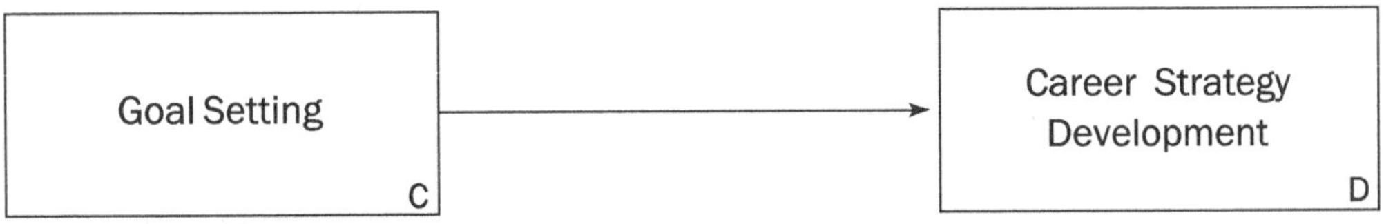

In our view, an operational career goal need not imply a promotion or an increase in salary. Certainly, an appropriate career goal may be a lateral move within the same or a different organization. In fact, a career goal does not have to involve a job change at all. A staff engineer's goal may be to remain in the same position while increasing technical skills and job responsibilities.

Up to a point, the more specific the operational career goal, the greater the likelihood of developing an effective strategy to achieve the goal. For instance, a financial analyst whose operational goal is to become a department manager within three years can ask what training or educational experiences, job assignments, and visibility will help to attain that position.

Although many writers on career management discuss the virtues of goal-setting, there is little research in the area of career goals. There is some evidence that a specific career goal can lead to greater optimism about one's career and that a higher degree of commitment toward one's goal can allow for the development of an extensive career strategy.[15] Indeed, clear career goals and plans have been associated with increasing levels of career effectiveness, career resilience, job involvement, and successful job search.[16] Edwin Locke and his associates have conducted extensive investigations as to why certain individuals perform better on the job than others. These researchers have found that individuals are motivated to perform better when they set challenging but achievable goals.[17] In addition, active monitoring of progress toward achieving established goals can motivate the ultimate attainment of those goals.[18] In Chapter 6 we will examine in more detail the characteristics of different types of career goals and specific techniques for developing realistic and effective goals.

Career Strategy

A career strategy is a sequence of activities designed to help an individual attain a career goal.[19] Organizations develop explicit strategic plans that enable them to pursue their goals successfully, and the same principle of strategic planning is applicable to individual career management. Much of the research on career strategies can be traced to Melville Dalton's seminal observation that managers' advancement within a manufacturing plant seemed less influenced by their formal education or years of service than by such "strategic" behaviors as joining a prestigious social or political organization.[20] Eugene Jennings's classic analysis revealed that highly mobile managers developed rather conscious strategies to move into the "executive suite," and successful managers took an active part in managing their careers and did not rely on the "loyalty ethic" of dutiful hard work, uncritical subordination to superiors, and undying respect for the corporate community.[21] While this loyalty-based approach may have worked in the past, today's companies require employees with the right experiences and competencies, not merely longevity with the company.

Research has sought to identify the kinds of strategies employees use (or think they should use) to improve their chances of career success and advancement.[22] An examination of these studies suggests that there are several general types of career strategies. These strategies include competence in one's present job, putting in extended hours, developing new skills, developing new opportunities, attaining a mentor, building one's image and reputation, and engaging in organizational politics.[23] A more detailed discussion of these specific strategies along with guidelines for development of career strategies is provided in Chapter 6.

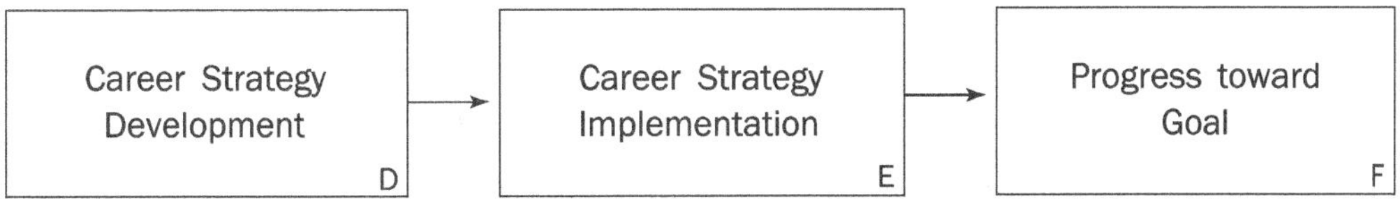

Career Appraisal

Career appraisal is the process by which people evaluate and reconsider career choices and then use this feedback to facilitate further planning.[24] The career appraisal process is portrayed in Exhibit 4.2. In work, as in all of life, people need to know how well or poorly they are doing.

Constructive feedback enables people to determine whether their goals and strategies still make sense. Career appraisal, which enables a person to monitor the course of a career, represents the adaptive, feedback function of career management.

Feedback can come from a number of different sources. The very act of implementing a career strategy can provide feedback regarding work and nonwork lives. For

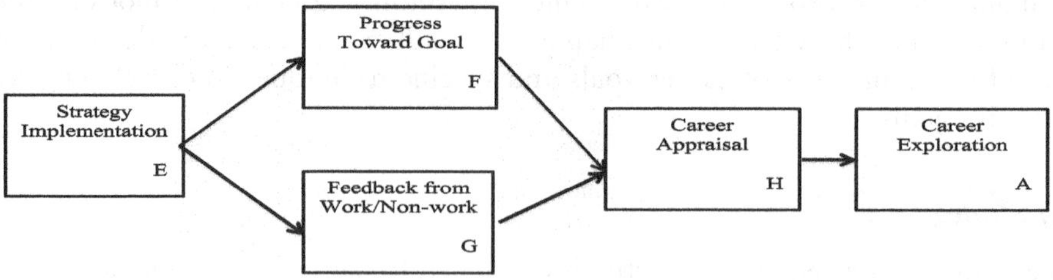

Exhibit 4.2 Career Appraisal Process

example, spending weekends in the office (extended work involvement) can provoke praise from a boss and hostility from a family. Participating in a training session or developing a close mentor relationship can teach people valuable lessons about themselves as well as about jobs and organizations. In addition, feedback about progress toward specific goals can be obtained from a superior in a coaching or performance-appraisal session, from peers, or from other significant persons. The information derived from career appraisal closes the career management cycle by becoming another piece of exploratory information that can enhance one's awareness of self and environment.

As noted earlier, the career appraisal process may lead to a reexamination of career goals. The feedback one obtains from work or nonwork sources can reinforce or lead to modification of a goal. An enthusiastic response to a training seminar or an outstanding performance review on a new project, for example, might convince an employee that his or her goal to reach the next management level remains desirable and feasible. Disappointments in the outcome of such activities, on the other hand, could prompt a person to shift goals.

Career appraisal can also affect strategic behavior. For example, in the course of a performance feedback session, an employee and his or her superior may conclude that additional formal training is unnecessary, but that greater exposure to key managers through a new work assignment is essential. In this case, the goal remains intact, but the strategy is revised. An ability to monitor and revise career strategies can lead to greater career mobility.

In short, career appraisal provides a feedback loop that perpetuates career exploration and the entire career management cycle. The usefulness of feedback for learning and performing tasks has been repeatedly demonstrated in the literature. Feedback's function as a self-corrective mechanism is equally applicable to the management of careers.

Career Management for Life: An Ongoing Process

There are a number of reasons why career management should be a regular, ongoing process. First, because work is such a central part of life, a satisfying career can promote feelings of fulfillment, whereas a string of poor career decisions can have a devastating effect on a person's sense of well-being. In addition, it is not easy to develop a deep understanding of our place in the world of work. Goals are often unrealistic, and strategies are frequently ill-conceived. Without continual, conscious, active career management, past errors might very well be prolonged and repeated.

Complicating the matter further, people often continue their commitment to a prior decision—even as they face repeated failure and frustration—to prove to themselves and others that their initial decisions were correct. Such people may fool themselves into believing their past failures will be reversed and their prior efforts will therefore be justified. These individuals may actually create alternative explanations or further self-justifications as to why their initial career decisions were correct.[25] Active career management on an ongoing basis, including feedback from many sources, is necessary as a way to avoid digging deeper holes from which one may never emerge.

Furthermore, in line with the boundaryless and protean career concepts, changing environments demand ongoing career management. As was discussed in Chapter 1, a variety of changes within one's organization and in the external environment can all affect a person's career. Employees who are not sensitive to the implications of such changes may find themselves unaware of their options.

People change as well. Goals that were so important during one time of life may require reexamination in later stages. Parts of jobs that were exhilarating at age 30 may be tedious or even aversive at 50. New talents and values can emerge with age, maturity, and experience, and changing family demands and situations can create constraints and opportunities to careers. Again, those who are insensitive to changes in themselves and their family will be missing a chance to make career decisions that are compatible with current values and lifestyle preferences.

For these reasons, career management should be a continual, problem-solving process. This is not to say that people must constantly be conducting self-assessment activities or revising their goals or strategies every week or every month. However, people should generally be attuned to changes in themselves and their environment. As will be seen in subsequent chapters, there are periods when active career management is particularly critical. The choice of a college major and an initial career field, the job-search process, the decision to remain specialized or to broaden one's experiences, the reaction to job loss, and the decision to reevaluate involvements in work and other life roles all require accurate information, realistic goals and plans, and an openness to feedback from the environment.

Indicators of Effective Career Management

How can people tell whether they are managing their careers effectively? Because career management is a problem-solving, decision-making process, it is tempting to examine the outcomes of career decisions at a particular point in time to assess the effectiveness of career management practices. We could, for example, look at our advancement in title or responsibility, or level of job performance to gauge the effectiveness of our career management. These temptations should be avoided because at least in the short run, career advancement and job performance are merely outcomes (although important ones) that do not necessarily reflect the process by which the outcomes were reached. They do not address the dynamics of our career decision-making.

Because career management is an ongoing, adaptive process, a snapshot view of a person's performance, status, or mobility does not necessarily reveal the manner in which the career has been managed. Following are four indicators of effective career management that can serve as a review of the career management model itself:

1. Effective career management requires a *deep knowledge of oneself and an accurate picture of the environment*. Some people have little insight into themselves and alternatives in the work environment. Without such knowledge, they may be fortunate enough to fall into a job that meets their needs and permits the use of valued abilities. Over the long run, however, we cannot count on luck alone. A career is composed of many decisions during the course of a person's life. Accurate knowledge about self and

environment enables the individual to take an active role in making appropriate career decisions.

2. Effective career management requires the development of *realistic conceptual and operational goals that are compatible with one's values, interests, abilities, and desired lifestyle.* While gaining accurate knowledge about self and the environment is a necessary process, it is not enough for effective career management. This knowledge has to be translated into a decision to pursue particular goals that, if accomplished, have a reasonable chance of meeting one's personal needs. There is a tendency for some people, especially college students making initial career plans, to choose career goals that others (parents, spouses, professors, supervisors) think are appropriate, regardless of whether the goals meet their own needs. It is the compatibility or fit of goals and accomplishments with personal needs and values that characterizes effective career management.
3. Effective career management requires the development and implementation of *appropriate career strategies.* It is one thing to develop valid career goals; it is another to attempt to accomplish the goal according to a plan. Again, some people may, on occasion, achieve a goal without any conscious strategic plan, but such good fortune is not likely to recur regularly. Since careers require many diverse types of decisions to be made over the long haul, skills in the development and implementation of career strategies are essential for effective career management.
4. Perhaps most important, effective career management requires a *continual feedback process* that permits adaptation in the face of changing circumstances. No one possesses totally accurate information about themselves or the environment, especially when people, families, and the world are in a state of flux and change. Moreover, goals and strategies may need fine-tuning or even a major overhaul. At different points, we might feel stuck in our careers, or feel as if we have hit a roadblock. A situation like this may help us to realize that our career goals or strategies are inappropriate in light of a dynamically changing work and nonwork environment. It is not incomplete awareness or even inappropriate goals or strategies per se that signal ineffective career management. The real problem is a person's inability to recognize these difficulties and do something constructive about them. Effective career management, therefore, is a striving process in which imperfect information and decisions are replaced by better (yet perhaps still imperfect) information and decisions.

For these reasons, it is not easy to assess the effectiveness of a person's career management practices. Certainly, the external trappings of "success" tell us little about the accuracy of a person's information or the appropriateness of his or her goals and strategies. Nor does a person's apparent satisfaction with work tell the whole story, since people can become "satisfied" by meeting other people's needs or be satisfied with work but completely unhappy with his or her family or personal life because of the overwhelming demands of work. Rather, effective career management represents a process of using information and insight to attain outcomes capable of satisfying personally meaningful values and aspirations.

At this juncture, the reader may wonder whether we are advocating a purely "rational" approach to career management. In a very real sense, our career management model is based on rational thinking and actions. We recommend that individuals explore themselves and their environment in a systematic manner, select career goals and strategies in a conscious way, and pay close attention to changes in themselves and the world around them. A rational approach to career decision-making can be useful, and a proactive, self-confident orientation to career management can reap lifelong benefits.

Nevertheless, to say that career management should be rational and systematic does not mean that it is mechanical, unemotional, or clear-cut. Career management is, by its very nature, a "messy" endeavor. Information is never complete, awareness is difficult and can come in fits and spurts, and goals and strategies may have to be revised many times before they make sense. Most significantly, events in the environment and in our personal and professional lives can cause major career disruptions and obviate even the best-laid plans. Accordingly, individuals should not become robots when managing their careers, and "gut" feelings should, at times, take precedence over analytical procedures.

Please keep these thoughts in mind when you examine the specific guidelines for applying the career management model in Chapters 5 and 6, and when you work on the learning exercises throughout the book. View the guidelines as just that—guidelines—rather than as unbending rules. Look for incremental advances in awareness, not instant insight. Accept the fact that you might make mistakes and might occasionally have to take two steps backward before progress is experienced. And most important, remember that career management is, at its core, a learning experience. Learning is occasionally rapid but is more often sporadic. It can be exciting but is frequently frustrating, and it is usually hard work. So relax, be patient with yourself, ask for support from those around you, and try to enjoy the process.

Summary

This chapter presented a model of career management and developed a rationale for each component in the model. Career exploration, the driving force of the model, involves the collection and analysis of career-related information. This information can increase awareness of personal qualities (interests, values, personality, talents, and lifestyle preferences) as well as the environment (the world of occupations, jobs, organizations, and family).

Awareness of self and the environment enables people to set realistic career goals. The development of conceptual and operational career goals can help individuals choose and implement appropriate career strategies designed to help them attain these goals. However, no particular strategy is likely to be effective in every situation. Hence the need for ongoing career appraisal in which career-related feedback is acquired and used. Such feedback can help people reexamine the effectiveness of their strategies and the appropriateness of their goals.

Because people and environments can change over time, career management should be an ongoing process. Four indicators of effective career management were identified: knowledge of self and the environment; the development of career goals that are consistent with values, interest, talents, and desired lifestyle; the development and implementation of appropriate career strategies; and a continual feedback loop that permits adaptation in the face of changing circumstances.

Career Management *for Life*: Work–Life Implications from Chapter 4

- One element of self-awareness is an understanding of the importance of work in our overall life.

- One component of environmental awareness is an appreciation of different facets of our nonwork life (family, friends, community, and leisure) and how they affect and are affected by our career.
- In establishing a career goal, we should consider whether the accomplishment of the goal would help or hinder our family and personal life.
- Similarly, in developing a career strategy, we should consider how implementing the strategy would affect our life outside work.
- Because circumstances and people change over time, career management should be a continual, problem-solving process. We should manage our career "for life."

Assignment

Interview a friend (perhaps a classmate or a co-worker) about his or her career management activities. Has your friend recently engaged in career exploration? What is his or her level of awareness of self and environment? Has your friend set a career goal? Developed a career strategy? Why or why not? What should he or she be doing next?

Discussion Questions

1. Why is career exploration such a critical component of career management? How, if at all, can people develop insights into themselves and their environment in the absence of deliberate attempts to seek information? What career exploration activities have you undertaken in the past year? In the past three years? How successful have they been?
2. Should career management be primarily a rational, systematic process? What are the advantages and disadvantages of adopting a highly rational approach to career management?
3. Why is it important to monitor and periodically appraise your career? How frequently should you conduct a career appraisal? How do individuals and environments change in ways that can influence a person's career? What role does family play in career appraisal?

Chapter 4 Case: Michele Terry, the Aspiring Banking Executive

Michele Terry is a 45-year-old assistant vice-president of marketing services at Federal Bank (fictitious name), a medium-sized financial institution. The fact that some of the staff she once hired have been promoted above her in recent years is a daily reminder that Michele's longtime ambition to become an executive vice-president at Federal Bank is not likely to be fulfilled. Her recent performance appraisal meetings with her 40-year-old superior, a senior vice president, left no doubt in Michele's mind about Federal's plans: she will most likely retire at her current level.

In fact, the handwriting had been on the wall for more than five years. During this time, Michele reexamined her original goal. How important was it for her to become an executive vice-president with Federal or some other commercial bank? Her conclusion was that it was still a personally important goal. As a result, Michele had at least 15 interviews during the past five years with other banks. In each case, she got a polite but negative response. All of the institutions were hiring MBAs, and Michele had only a bachelor's degree. More important, Michele was competent enough but did not have sufficiently varied experiences in the financial services industry and did not seem to project the image of a higher-level officer, let alone an executive vice president. In a state of dismay, she also spoke with officers of other institutions in the financial services industry. The reactions to these inquiries were all similarly negative.

Last year, several conversations with Federal's senior officers and her husband convinced Michele to give up her dream of becoming an executive vice-president at the bank. It was simply out of the question. Although there was a chance of further advancement, Michele concluded that it was slim. In the meantime, Michele reexamined why she always wanted to become a senior officer at the bank. In addition to money and status, she wanted the opportunity to affect broad policies as a way to make changes in the services that banks provide to the community. Therefore, she concentrated on broadening the scope of her current position by looking for ways to influence the bank's approach to community reinvestment. Michele enrolled in several training seminars on community reinvestment and convinced her boss that she should chair a task force on new market development. She also began to serve as a mentor to several of Federal's younger managers, helping them get their careers established and perhaps avoid some of the mistakes she may have made earlier in her career.

On the home front, Michele seems more relaxed than she has been in quite some time, and she is better able to enjoy her family. She has encouraged her husband to switch to a more personally satisfying career field, has freely given him advice and support, and seems to enjoy the success her husband is beginning to experience in his rejuvenated career. Michele is also spending more time with her children and her infant grandchild and has rekindled her interest in the local political scene.

Michele's most recent performance appraisal was outstanding. Although she doesn't put in nearly so many weekends and evenings as she had in the past, her job performance has not suffered. On the contrary, her marketing group is working on several innovative projects, the task force she heads is making real progress, and she is deriving great satisfaction from her mentoring relationships with several of the bank's younger managers. Although Michele is periodically frustrated over her lack of advancement, she is a respected contributor at the bank and, little by little, is coming to terms with her disappointment.

Case Questions

1. Identify the specific career exploration activities that Michele undertook to gather information about herself (her values, needs, abilities, interests, and desired lifestyle) and her environment (different jobs, employers, industries, her family). What could she have done to acquire more information?
2. Does Michele currently have conceptual and operational career goals? If so, what are they? If not, explain why you believe that Michele does not currently have career goals.

3. What specific career strategies did Michele implement? Were they effective? Why or why not?
4. To what extent has Michele received useful feedback regarding her career? Should Federal Bank have been more proactive in helping Michele manage her career? What could the Bank have done to help her?
5. If you were advising Michele, what recommendations would you give her to help her effectively manage her career going forward?

Notes

1 Dubin, R. (1983). Theory building in applied areas. In Dunnette, M. D. (Ed.), *Handbook of industrial and organizational psychology* (pp. 17–39). New York: Wiley.

2 Amundson, N. E., Borgen, W. A., Iaquinta, M., Butterfield, L. D. & Koert, E. (2010). Career decisions from the decider's perspective. *Career Development Quarterly*, *58*, 336–351.

3 Greenhaus, J. H. & Kossek, E. E. (2014). The contemporary career: A work–home perspective. *Annual Review of Organizational Psychology and Organizational Behavior*, *1*, 361–388; Ferguson, M., Carlson, D., Zivnuska, S. & Whitten, D. (2012). Support at work and home: The path to satisfaction through balance. *Journal of Vocational Behavior*, *80*, 299–307.

4 Chen, P., Sparrow, P. & Cooper, C. (2016). The relationship between person–organization fit and job satisfaction. *Journal of Managerial Psychology*, *31*, 946–959; Hardin, E. E. & Donaldson, J. R. (2014). Predicting job satisfaction: A new perspective on person–environment fit. *Journal of Counseling Psychology*, *61*, 634–640; Gabriel, A. S., Dienfendorff, J. M., Chandler, M. M., Moran, C. M. & Greguras, G. J. (2014). The dynamic relationships of work affect and job satisfaction with perceptions of fit. *Personnel Psychology*, *67*, 389–420.

5 Zikic, J. & Hall, D. T. (2009). Toward a more complex view of career exploration. *Career Development Quarterly*, *58*, 181–191; Zikic, J. (2006). Career exploration. In Greenhaus, J. H. & Callanan, G. A. (Eds.), *Encyclopedia of career development* (pp. 103–107). Thousand Oaks, CA: Sage.

6 Chang, C., Ferris, D. L., Johnson, R. E., Rosen, C. C. & Tan, J. A. (2012). Core self-evaluations: A review and evaluation of the literature. *Journal of Management*, *38*, 81–128; Fletcher, C. (2003). Assessing self-awareness: Some issues and methods. *Journal of Managerial Psychology*, *18*, 395–404; Luthans, F. & Peterson, S. J. (2003). 360-degree feedback with systematic coaching: Empirical analysis suggests a winning combination. *Human Resource Management*, *42*, 243–256.

7 Ibid.

8 Ibid.

9 Boswell, W. R., Zimmerman, R. D. & Swider, B. W. (2012). Employee job search: Toward an understanding of search context and search objectives. *Journal of Management*, *38*, 129–163.

10 Lent, R. W. (2013). Career-life preparedness: Revisiting career planning and adjustment in the new workplace. *Career Development Quarterly*, *61*, 2–14.

11 Singh, R. (2006). Self-awareness. In Greenhaus, J. H. & Callanan, G. A. (Eds.), *Encyclopedia of career development* (pp. 709–713). Thousand Oaks, CA: Sage.

12 Ibid.

13 Locke, E. A. & Latham, G. P. (2013). *New developments in goal setting and task performance.* New York: Routledge; Locke, E. A. & Latham, G. P. (2006). Building a practically useful theory of goal setting and task motivation: A 35 year odyssey. *American Psychologist*, *57*, 705–717; Locke, E. A. (2004). Goal-setting theory and its applications to the world of business. *Academy of Management Executive*, *18*, 124–125.

14 Ibid.

15 Greenhaus, J. H. (2006). Career goal. In Greenhaus, J. H. & Callanan, G. A. (Eds.), *Encyclopedia of career development* (pp. 107–109). Thousand Oaks, CA: Sage.

16 Ibid.

17 Locke & Latham (2006, 2013); Locke (2004).

18 Harkin, B., Webb, T. L., Chang, B. P. I., Prestwich, A., Conner, M., Kellar, I., Benn, Y. & Sheeran, P. (2016). Does monitoring goal progress promote goal attainment? A meta-analysis of the experimental evidence. *Psychological Bulletin*, *142*, 198–229.
19 Callanan, G. A. (2006). Career strategy. In Greenhaus, J. H. & Callanan, G. A. (Eds.), *Encyclopedia of career development* (pp. 146–148). Thousand Oaks, CA: Sage.
20 Dalton, M. (1951). Informal factors in career advancement. *American Journal of Sociology*, *56*, 407–415.
21 Jennings, E. E. (1971). *Routes to the executive suite*. New York: Macmillan.
22 Laud, R. L. & Johnson, M. (2012). Upward mobility: A typology of tactics and strategies for career advancement. *Career Development International*, *17*, 231–254.
23 Callanan (2006).
24 Larson, L. M. & Bailey, D. C. (2006). Career appraisal. In Greenhaus, J. H. & Callanan, G. A. (Eds.), *Encyclopedia of career development* (pp. 69–71). Thousand Oaks, CA: Sage.
25 Drummond, H. (2014). Escalation of commitment: When to stay the course? *Academy of Management Perspectives*, *28*, 430–436; Sleesman, D. J., Conlon, D. E., McNamara, G. & Miles, J. E. (2012). Cleaning up the big muddy: A meta-analytic review of the determinants of escalation of commitment. *Academy of Management Journal*, *55*, 541–562.

5 Applications of the Career Management Model

A Guide to Career Exploration

Chapter 4 presented a model of career management and provided a theoretical rationale for each component of the model. This chapter takes a pragmatic look at career exploration, the driving force of the model. In particular, we will identify the underlying principles of career exploration, discuss self- and environmental exploration activities, provide the reader with opportunities to participate in career exploration activities, and offer guidelines for successful career exploration. Chapter 6 will examine the remaining components of the career management model—goal-setting, strategy development, and career appraisal.

Career exploration refers to the collection and analysis of information on career-related issues.[1] As noted in Chapter 4, it can provide information about one's own qualities (self-exploration) as well as information about the environment: occupations, jobs, organizations, industries, and nonwork domains (such as family or community). The purpose of career exploration is to help the individual develop a greater awareness of self and the environment so that realistic goals can be established and appropriate strategies developed. Exploration activities have become more critical in recent years as increased uncertainty and reduced job security mandate that individuals be adaptable and flexible in their approaches to career management.[2] Knowing yourself and understanding the work environment can help you set reasonable and meaningful goals and can prepare you for career changes, regardless of whether these alterations are planned or not. Indeed, the ability to be prepared for career change and disruptions is the essence of managing the boundaryless career as we discussed in Chapter 2.

We next discuss the goals of self-exploration and highlight three steps that are central to effective self-exploration: collecting data, organizing the data into consistent themes,[3] and developing an understanding of our "preferred work environment." We then turn to the goals and techniques of environmental exploration, and conclude the chapter with a set of guidelines for conducting effective career exploration.

Goals of Self-Exploration

When one engages in self-exploration, information is sought about a variety of personal qualities that are relevant to career decision-making. These qualities include values, interests, personality factors, talents or abilities, weaknesses or areas for further development, and lifestyle preferences. To develop an accurate career identity and set meaningful career goals, it is essential to understand what one wants from work and nonwork roles and what skills and abilities can be brought to (or developed in) the work environment. The intended outcome of the self-exploration process is self-awareness, or the attainment of a relatively complete picture of one's individual qualities.[4] Given the importance of self-exploration and self-awareness to the career management process, we will examine values, interests, personality, abilities, and lifestyle preferences in more detail.

Values

Values represent the goals (or beliefs) about the qualities of human life that an individual wants to attain, and as such can serve as the guiding principles for behavior.[5] They highlight individual differences in preferences for what ought to be in terms of a job, a career, or life in general.[6] People, regardless of country or culture, tend to set values in priority order and use them as a way to explain, coordinate, and justify their attitudes and actions.[7] A substantial amount of research has been devoted to the study of life values as well as the more targeted values relevant to the work domain.[8] Shalom Schwartz and his colleagues identify four "higher-order" values that serve as overarching guideposts for behavior. As shown in Table 5.1, the four higher-order values include **self-transcendence**, where the person "transcends" his or her own individual concerns and looks to improve the well-being of others; **conservation**, where one seeks out certainty in various aspects of life; **self-enhancement**, indicating a desire for improving personal qualities or status; and **openness to change**, reflecting a willingness to undertake new or uncertain intellectual or behavioral directions.[9]

As shown in Table 5.1, the four higher-order values can then be delineated into ten discrete value types that are relevant to the work domain.[10] *Benevolence* reflects a desire for the preservation and enrichment of welfare of others with whom a person is in regular contact while the value *universalism* deals with enhancing the welfare of all peoples. *Conformity* gets at the exercise of restraint and a need to follow societal norms. *Tradition* reflects a respect for, and commitment to, historical customs and culture. The value *security* indicates a desire for safety, harmony, and well-being within oneself and society. Those who value *power* seek out status, prestige, and authority and control over others and resources. *Achievement* reflects the drive for success through demonstrated competence and tangible accomplishments, while *hedonism* gets at the need for self-indulgence and gratification. *Stimulation* indicates a desire for excitement, novelty, and challenge in life and work. Finally, *self-direction* reflects a need for autonomy and independence in thoughts and actions.

Each person probably has a unique combination of values that are personally significant. Understanding one's value structure can provide considerable insight into career aspirations. Indeed, people can differ substantially in the importance they place on different values such as power, tradition, and security. Moreover, occupations and specific jobs vary in the extent to which they satisfy these values. It is not surprising that people tend to be more satisfied with jobs in which they have an opportunity to attain their significant work values. While some people might place a high value on helping others (benevolence) or gaining power, others are more concerned with maintaining existing standards and customs (tradition) or discovering knowledge or creating something new (self-direction). To take an extreme example, a person who strongly values material accomplishments and the exercise of power is unlikely to be happy in an occupation with limited tangible rewards or with little opportunity to exercise leadership qualities.

Career planning programs encourage individuals to examine their values carefully. People can learn about their values by analyzing their life history, identifying the kinds of career decisions they have made, and examining the reasons behind these decisions. Often, such informal analyses are supplemented by more structured value inventories.[11] These structured assessments of values will be discussed later in this chapter.

Table 5.1 Illustrations of Work Values, Interests, and Abilities

*Work Values**	*Interests***	*Abilities****
Self-Enhancement	Realistic	Cognitive
Power	Nature & Agriculture	General Intelligence
Achievement	Computer Hardware & Electronics	Verbal Reasoning Skills
Hedonism	Athletics	Logical Reasoning Skills
Openness to Change	Protective Services	Memory
Stimulation	Mechanics & Construction	Writing Skills
Self-Direction	Military	Reading Skills
Self-Transcendence	Investigative	Psychomotor
Universalism	Science	Precision of Movement
Benevolence	Mathematics	Manual Dexterity
Conservation	Medical Science	Finger Dexterity
Conformity	Research	Reaction Time and Speed
Tradition	Artistic	Athleticism and Coordination
Security	Visual Arts & Design	Sensory
	Performing Arts	Visual
	Culinary Arts	Auditory
	Writing & Mass Communications	Perceptual
	Social	Stimuli Response
	Counseling & Helping	Physical
	Teaching & Education	Muscular Strength
	Social Sciences	Cardiovascular Endurance
	Healthcare Services	Movement Quality
	Religion & Spirituality	
	Human Resources & Training	
	Enterprising	
	Politics & Public Speaking	
	Entrepreneurship	
	Marketing & Advertising	
	Sales	
	Law	
	Management	
	Conventional	
	Office Management	
	Taxes & Accounting	
	Finance & Investing	
	Programming & Information Systems	

* The 10 values from Schwartz, S. E. (1999). A theory of cultural values and some implications for work. *Applied Psychology: An International Review*, 48, 23–47. Values are arranged according to the 4 higher-order values. See Cieciuch, J., Davidov, E., Vecchione, M. & Schwartz, S. H. (2014). A hierarchical structure of basic human values in a third-order confirmatory factor analysis. *Swiss Journal of Psychology*, 73, 177–182.

** The 30 Basic Interest Scales included in the Strong Interest Inventory arranged by the six Holland Interest Types. Taken from Herk, N. A. & Thompson, R. C. (2012). *Strong Interest Inventory Manual Supplement.* Mountain View, CA: Consulting Psychologists Press.

*** Adapted from: Rotundo, M. (2006). Abilities. In Greenhaus, J. H. & Callanan, G. A. (Eds.), *Encyclopedia of career development* (pp. 1–5). Thousand Oaks, CA: Sage.

Interests

Interests refer to likes and dislikes attached to specific activities or objects.[12] Interests, therefore, are expressions of what a person likes to do, and are derived from such factors as values, family life, social class, culture, and the physical environment.[13] While they are reflective of values, interests are attached to particular tasks or activities. For example, two people might each value the expression of creativity in their work. While one person might have strong scientific interests and the other might be interested in literary activities, both sets of interests can serve the broader creative value for each person. Understandably, people who choose career fields that are compatible with their interests tend to be more certain, satisfied, and motivated over their choice than those whose chosen career is incompatible with their interests.[14] Further, congruence between interests and career choice is broadly related to subsequent performance and tenure in the job.[15]

In his seminal work, John Holland identified six general interest orientations that reflect one's personality, values, and preferred lifestyle.[16] Holland's theory assumes that vocational interests are an important expression of personality and that the six orientations correspond with specific personality factors.[17] The six orientations include: realistic, investigative, artistic, social, enterprising, and conventional. The six interest orientations form a well-known acronym referred to as the RIASEC wheel or hexagon. Individuals who have a realistic orientation tend to be more practical and task-oriented, while investigative types are more scientific, scholarly, and research-oriented. Artistic people prefer unstructured situations, where creativity and self-expression are possible. Individuals in the social category are more humanistic, personal, and value-oriented, and show an attraction to interpersonal relations. An enterprising designation indicates a preference for entrepreneurial, managerial, and goal-centered activities. Finally, the conventional style reflects an orientation toward structure, tradition, and detail.

In the 1920s, Edward Strong of Stanford University developed an inventory of interests that reflected specific occupational preferences. Strong believed that interests supply something that is not disclosed by ability or achievement.[18] They point to what individuals want to do and what they consider satisfying. The current version of the Strong Interest Inventory (SII) includes descriptions of a person's interests in 30 basic areas that are grouped according to Holland's six occupational orientations described above.[19] Table 5.1 lists the interests according to occupational orientation. The SII provides information on the similarity of one's interests to those of members of different occupational types. Use of the SII and other interest assessment instruments as tools for individual self-exploration will be discussed later in this chapter.

Personality

One's basic personality is another area of self-exploration that can influence career choices. Personality refers to relatively stable psychological characteristics that embody such elements as thoughts, emotions, interests, habits, and behaviors.[20] Significant prior research has isolated five basic personality factors, often referred to as the "Big Five" or the Five-Factor Model.[21] The five factors are typically classified as extraversion, agreeableness, conscientiousness, emotional stability, and openness to experience.

- *Extraversion* indicates the degree to which a person seeks interpersonal stimulation. Individuals with a high degree of extraversion are drawn to seek social situations where they can interact with others. Individuals scoring low on this dimension are described as more introverted, quiet, and reserved.

- *Agreeableness* signifies individual characteristics such as likeability, kindness, courteousness, and nurturance. Individuals scoring high on this dimension are described as amicable, cooperative, sensitive, and caring and are interested in helping others. Individuals scoring low on this dimension can be described as more self-centered and inwardly focused.
- *Conscientiousness* refers to the cluster of individual traits relating to achievement, dependability, and persistence. Individuals scoring high on this personality trait tend to be organized, follow rules and norms, and are persistent in goal-directed behavior. Individuals scoring low on conscientiousness are comparatively less organized, irresponsible, and undependable.
- *Emotional stability* refers to an individual's tendency to remain calm and centered. Emotionally stable individuals are typically relaxed, self-assured, and calm. People who score lower on this factor tend to be more anxious, sensitive, and obsessive.
- *Openness to experience* describes individual differences in tolerance for and an attraction to the unfamiliar. Individuals who score high on this dimension are described as being imaginative, creative, and insightful. They prefer complexity and change over familiar and stable situations. In contrast, individuals who score lower on this factor are described as more conventional, down-to-earth, and less imaginative.

Other researchers have isolated a sixth personality factor that exists in addition to the Big Five dimensions, creating what has been referred to as the HEXACO model of personality.[22] This sixth factor is identified as *honesty-humility*. Individuals who score highly on this dimension demonstrate sincerity, modesty, fairness, and greed-avoidance. Individuals scoring low on this dimension would be more materialistic and less humble.[23] Regardless of whether five or six factors are observed, these models serve as the basis for personality questionnaires that are used by individuals for gathering self-information and by organizations for personnel selection, employee development, and individual assessment. We will discuss some of the well-known personality inventories later in the chapter.

Abilities

A person's abilities are another significant component to be taken into account in career management. Abilities (or talents) refer to the aptitudes, capacities, or proficiencies that allow an individual (sometimes with proper training and development) to perform a wide range of tasks.[24] Accordingly, they can set constraints on our potential accomplishments. And it is clearly necessary to consider our abilities and talents when making career decisions. Unfortunately, many people choose occupations or jobs that either require abilities they do not possess or do not take advantage of the talents they do have. Therefore, many career planning programs provide the opportunity for participants to assess their own strengths and weaknesses. Abilities and talents can be appreciated by reviewing accomplishments in school, work, and other parts of our lives.

The broad categories and types of abilities are shown in Table 5.1. Notice that four general categories of abilities are listed, **cognitive**, **psychomotor**, **sensory**, and **physical**, with each of the four having a number of sub-components. Depending on the nature of the occupation and the organization, particular abilities might be more critical in terms of success and performance on the job. In many careers, intelligence, and especially working memory, are important predictors of successful work performance.[25] In contrast, certain careers might require specific skills and abilities for success. For example, a career in construction might require a high level of logical reasoning skills along with physical strength or a career in performance art might demand a high level of precision of movement. Clearly, abilities play an important role in the career decision-making process given their linkage to successful work performance and satisfaction. Common assessment instruments for abilities will be discussed later in the chapter.

Values, interests, personality, and abilities are interrelated in several respects.[26] First, as indicated above, interests are rooted in deeper values. But it is also true that interests are related to abilities. People come to enjoy activities at which they excel. Through practice, they may also become more proficient at those activities they enjoy. Therefore, although it may be convenient to separate values, interests, abilities, and personality, at some point they must be appreciated as a coherent whole. Edgar Schein's concept of a **career anchor** probably comes closest to capturing this notion of a coherent whole.[27] Schein introduced the concept of the career anchor to recognize different forms of orientation toward work. A career anchor is a cluster of self-perceived talents, motives, and values that forms the nucleus of a person's occupational self-concept. An anchor also can provide the basis for career choices, because a person is likely to make job and organizational selections that are consistent with his or her own self-image and preferences.[28] It is only through a number of years of work experience and many reality tests that a person can fully clarify and understand his or her career anchor. Using his long-term research program with alumni from the Sloan School of Management at the Massachusetts Institute of Technology (MIT), Schein identified the following eight career anchors:

1. *Technical/Functional Competence* anchor, in which the primary concern is the actual content of the work. Employees who hold this anchor typically want to remain within their technical/functional area (e.g., finance, human resources, marketing).
2. *General Managerial Competence* anchor, in which the major goal is general line management rather than a particular functional area within the organization. For individuals who possess this anchor, the dominant concerns are the integration of the efforts of others, accountability for total results, and the tying together of different functions in the organization.
3. *Autonomy/Independence* anchor, in which the primary concern is with freeing oneself from organizational rules and restrictions in favor of a career in which one can decide when to work, on what to work, and how hard to work. People with this anchor would be willing to turn down a promotion in order to retain autonomy.
4. *Security/Stability* anchor, in which long-term career stability is the underlying drive. The need for security may be satisfied by remaining in the same organization, the same industry, or the same geographical location. People with this anchor generally prefer stable and predictable work.
5. *Entrepreneurial/Creativity* anchor, in which the major goal is to create something new, involving such demands as overcoming obstacles, running risks, and the achievement of personal prominence. People with this anchor want the freedom to build and operate their own organization in their own way.
6. *Service/Dedication* anchor, in which the primary concern is to achieve some valued outcome, such as improving the lives of others, perhaps by working in a "helping" occupation.

7. *Pure Challenge* anchor, in which the primary work demands involve solving seemingly unsolvable problems or surmounting difficult obstacles. Individuals with this anchor primarily seek novelty, variety, and stimulation in their work.
8. *Lifestyle Integration* anchor, in which the dominant theme is achieving balance in all the major sectors of one's life. Specifically, individuals with this anchor want harmonious integration of career activities with nonwork roles such as family, friendships, community, and self-development.

The eight career anchors identified by Schein are not mutually exclusive and it is clear that there are linkages between them. As one example, given their descriptions, an individual who indicates autonomy/independence as a primary anchor could also exhibit a high score on the entrepreneurial/creativity anchor. Indeed, research has shown that individuals can display more than one anchor as dominant at any one time.[29] Regardless of any correlation between them, the importance of career anchors is that they represent a combination of individual factors that develop and evolve over time and can guide an individual's career decision-making.

Lifestyle Preferences

As important as work is for many people, it is only one of many significant roles in life. What type of family life do you want? In what way can you express your spiritual needs? How can community or leisure activities satisfy your basic values? How important is climbing the corporate ladder and making a large sum of money in your total life? In short, what type of lifestyle is most desirable?

A thorough exploration of nonwork involvements is critical for a number of reasons. First, it is likely that some basic values may be difficult or impossible to satisfy through work. Second, some career fields or jobs can take so much time or emotion that little is left for private life. To make appropriate career decisions, the importance and variety of nonwork interests and values need to be examined. For example, as we saw with the Kevin case at the conclusion of Chapter 2, a parent strongly devoted to coaching his or her child's sports team would find a job requiring extensive travel frustrating. Third, the importance of community, leisure, or other nonwork activities can fluctuate over the course of a person's life. We must be sensitive to such changes to make career decisions that are consistent with as many parts of our life as possible.

The relationship between work and nonwork lives was treated in detail in Chapter 3. As it applies to self-exploration, an accurate picture of work and nonwork aspirations should produce an awareness of a **desired lifestyle** that the individual wishes to attain; that is, a pattern of involvement in work and nonwork pursuits that enables one to satisfy underlying values, participate in activities that one finds interesting, and find expression for personally meaningful talents. Therefore, an understanding of a desired lifestyle requires answers to the following questions:

1. What are my significant life values?
2. What kinds of activities do I like and dislike?
3. What are my talents, and which ones are significant and personally meaningful?
4. Which of my values, interests, and talents are best met in the world of work?
5. Which of my values, interests, and talents are best met outside of work?
6. How strongly do I identify with work?
7. How strongly do I identify with various nonwork roles, such as family, friendships, community, and spiritual activities?

8. How can I achieve a balance of work and nonwork involvements to find expression for my most significant values, interests, and talents?

In addition to consideration of family, friendships, spirituality, and community, individuals also should take into account their leisure interests as they seek to understand their lifestyle preferences. Leisure interests are an important component in developmental models of career decision-making and vocational choice, and occupational health psychologists have recognized the importance of leisure interests to mental and physical health and overall life satisfaction.[30] Research has identified four different leisure categories, including artistic and intellectual pursuits (e.g., gardening, cooking, crafts, writing, and dancing), competition and sports (e.g., card games, team sports, and individual sports), social (e.g., partying, shopping, and socializing with friends), and outdoors (e.g., hunting, fishing, camping, and adventure sports).[31] It is obvious that the passion for a particular leisure activity will play a substantial role in career choices. As a simplistic but clear example, someone who enjoys surfing and is devoted to it would likely be unhappy in a job far away from an ocean.

As noted earlier, self-exploration contains three steps. We now turn to the first step—the collection of relevant data or information—that serves as the foundation for the subsequent identification of themes and appreciation of one's preferred work environment.

Collection of Data for Self-Exploration: Step 1

The first step in self-assessment is to gather data on one's values, interests, personality, abilities, and lifestyle preferences. Techniques for gathering information and the sources of data are both quite varied. Overall, the techniques and sources can be broken down into four general categories: individual assessment instruments, integrated career planning approaches, organizational programs, and informal means of assessment.

Individual Assessment Instruments

There are literally hundreds of assessment instruments available to assist individuals in gaining a better understanding of themselves. A few of the more prominent and most widely used for self-exploration purposes are discussed below. For a fuller discussion of each of these instruments, please refer to the publisher's own documentation. Also note that nearly all assessment instruments must be administered and interpreted by professional counselors. In addition, all of the more modern assessment instruments are available both in paper-and-pencil form and computer-based through the Internet.

Assessment of Values

The *Rokeach Value Survey* consists of two lists of values (18 in each list).[32] Individuals rank the values on each list on the basis of how important each one is as a guiding principle in their life. The first list covers "terminal" values, or those values that relate to what one wants out of life, while the second list consists of "instrumental" values that relate to ways of behaving in the world. A significant aspect of this instrument is the relative ordering of the values, in that individuals must rely on their own internal value system to guide them in the choices they make.

The *Schwartz Value Survey* was developed by Shalom Schwartz and was utilized in the isolation of the ten value types as discussed earlier and as shown in Table 5.1.[33] The survey consists of 57 items with a total of 45 value items. For each item in the survey, the respondent reacts to a short description of the item by indicating the degree to which the value serves as a guiding principle in the person's life. The higher the number assigned to the value indicates the greater importance of that value in the respondent's life.

Super's Work Values Inventory-Revised (SWVI-r), as originally developed by Donald Super, attempts to measure the relative importance of a number of work values thought to be most important in career choice and development.[34] A total of 12 work values are assessed, and individuals are provided with a profile showing the 12 values listed in rank order of importance. The 12 work values are *Achievement*, *Co-workers*, *Creativity*, *Income*, *Independence*, *Lifestyle*, *Mental Challenge*, *Prestige*, *Security*, *Supervision*, *Work Environment*, and *Variety*. The SWVI-r is available exclusively online at www.kuder.com. The website also provides a linkage of results from the SWVI-r with the work values embodied within various occupations.[35]

Originally developed in 1931, the *Allport-Vernon-Lindzey Study of Values* (SOV) is a longstanding tool for the assessment of values.[36] The SOV identifies six value orientations: theoretical (discovery of truth), economic (that which is useful), aesthetic (form and harmony), social (love of people), political (power in all realms), and religious (unity of life). Respondents are asked to react to questions describing various familiar life situations. The SOV measures the relative strength of each of the six value orientations based on the answers to these questions. In reaction to difficulties and limitations with the earlier versions of the SOV, a newer fourth edition was created and published in 2003.[37] The properties of the most recent and the earlier editions of the SOV were found to be almost identical.

Assessment of Interests

The *Strong Interest Inventory* (SII) is perhaps the best known of the tools available to isolate interests and related occupations.[38] The SII consists of 291 questions that measure various dimensions related to one's vocational interest pattern. Output from the SII consists of three related sections—General Occupational Themes, Basic Interest Scales, and Occupational Scales.[39] The General Occupational Themes are based on the six basic vocational interest orientations of Holland as discussed earlier in this chapter. The 30 Basic Interest Scales from the SII (see Table 5.1) measure the strength and consistency of the individual's interests in specific areas, such as investigative or artistic activities. The Occupational Scales reflect the degree of similarity between the individual's interests and those of women and men employed in 260 different occupations. Thus, the SII attempts to link an individual's fairly broad interest orientation (one of the six Occupational Themes) with the somewhat more specific interests (one or more of the Basic Interest Scales) and with specific occupational titles. Detailed information on the SII is available at www.cpp.com.

The *Self-Directed Search* (SDS) and the *Vocational Preference Inventory* (VPI) are two other occupational assessment instruments, developed by John Holland, that are used in individual self-exploration.[40] Both of these instruments are conceptually similar to the SII in that they are based in part on the notion that well-adjusted and satisfied individuals within specific occupational fields possess common psychological characteristics, interests, and preferences. All three instruments—the SII, the VPI, and the SDS—attempt to measure one's pattern of interests and then link it to specific occupations that are satisfying to individuals with the same interest pattern. Also, like the SII, the VPI and the SDS utilize Holland's six major interest orientations as the link between individual characteristics and specific occupations. Detailed information on the SDS and the VPI is available at www4.parinc.com.

The *Fundamental Interpersonal Relations Orientation-Behavior* (FIRO-B) is an assessment tool that looks at how an individual's needs affect his or her behavior toward other people.[41] The FIRO-B offers insights into a person's compatibility with other people, as well as related individual characteristics. In essence, the FIRO-B assesses three interpersonal needs as follows:

1. *Inclusion*, or the extent of contact and prominence an individual seeks and wishes from others.
2. *Control*, or the extent of power or dominance that a person seeks or wishes from others.
3. *Affection*, or the amount of closeness that a person seeks and wishes from others.

The FIRO-B measures the degree to which an individual wishes to express each of these needs and the extent to which an individual is comfortable in receiving another person's expressed need. Detailed information on the FIRO-B is available at www.cpp.com.

The *Kuder Career Planning System*[42] is based on the interests measure originally developed by Frederic Kuder and first published in 1939. The current version of the instrument measures a respondent's interests in six different areas: Arts/Communication, Business Operations, Outdoor/Mechanical, Sales/Management, Science/Technology, and Social/Personal Services. The Kuder system also uses a "person match" that allows individuals to be electronically matched with persons who have similar interest profiles. The test-taker can then read mini-autobiographies of the person with whom they are matched to get an idea of the requirements of the job held by that person. The variety of job titles represented in the database for the matching process allows the test taker to investigate multiple career possibilities. Detailed information on the Kuder Career Planning System is available at www.kuder.com.

The *Campbell Interest and Skill Survey* (CISS) was developed by David Campbell and published in 1992. It is intended to measure self-reported interests and associated skills.[43] As with other standard interest inventories, the CISS interest scales are reflective of an individual's attraction for specific occupations and vocational areas. Similar to the Strong Interest Inventory, the CISS contains seven interest orientation scales (influencing, organizing, helping, creating, analyzing, producing, and adventuring) that are derived from 25 basic scales. The seven interest orientations are conceptually similar to the six RIASEC dimensions from John Holland. The instrument also includes 60 occupational scales that tie into the 25 basic scales. Detailed information on the CISS is available at www.pearsonassessments.com.

Assessment of Personality

The *Myers-Briggs Type Indicator* (MBTI) is the most well-known of the personality assessment instruments that are available commercially. The MBTI was developed by a mother-and-daughter team, Katherine Briggs and Isabel Myers. Based on the work of Carl Jung, a Swiss psychiatrist, the MBTI looks at eight separate personality preferences that all people use at different times.[44] The eight types are organized into four bipolar scales. The four preferences that are identified as most like you (one from each scale) are combined into what is called a type. Included among the four personality dimensions are: how a person energizes, how a person perceives information, how a person makes decisions, and the person's lifestyle preference. For the energizing scale, the two categories are extraversion and introversion. Extroverts have an affinity for drawing energy from the outside world of people, activities, or things. Introverts draw energy from their own internal world of ideas, emotions, or impressions. The two perception categories are designated as sensing and intuition. Sensing individuals prefer to gather information through the five senses by noticing what actually is. Intuitive individuals gather information through a "sixth" sense and notice what possibilities are available. The decision-making dimension includes thinking and feeling orientations. Thinking types prefer organizing and structuring information to make decisions in a logical fashion. Feeling types prefer to make decisions in a personal and value-oriented way. For the lifestyle preference, the two types are judgment and perception. The judgment type prefers living a planned and organized life, while the perception type prefers spontaneity and flexibility. The four bipolar scales result in 16 possible personality types. The MBTI is often used in conjunction with interest inventories and other elements of self-information. Detailed information on the MBTI is available at www.cpp.com.

The *Sixteen Personality Questionnaire* (16PF) was originally developed by Raymond Cattell in 1949.[45] Now in its fifth edition, the 16PF measures 16 personality dimensions as follows: level of warmth, reasoning ability, emotional stability, dominance, liveliness, rule-consciousness, social boldness, sensitivity, vigilance, abstractedness, privateness, apprehension, openness to change, self-reliance, perfectionism, and tension. The 16 factors can be further grouped into five global personality categories: extraversion, anxiety, tough-mindedness, independence, and self-control.

The full 16PF questionnaire consists of 185 items. In terms of career planning, the 16PF can be used to create a career development profile that allows individuals to gain greater insight into personality as it relates to their personal and career interests. The profile consists of six sections detailing one's patterns for: problem-solving, coping with stressful conditions, interpersonal interactions, organizational role and work patterns, and career activity interests and lifestyle considerations. As with the MBTI, the 16PF is used extensively in organizations as a tool to help employees assess preferences and ultimately manage their careers. Detailed information on the 16PF is available at www.pearsonclinical.com.

The *NEO PI-R* is another well-known questionnaire designed to measure the Five Factor elements of personality as well as the traits or facets that define each of the five dimensions.[46] In total, the NEO provides results for the five domain scales and 30 underlying facet scales. The NEO Job Profiler is an available tool that assists individuals by linking personality traits with personal qualities that are required for certain occupations. Information on the NEO PI-R is available at www4.parinc.com.

The *Minnesota Multiphasic Personality Inventory-2* (MMPI-2) is a 567-item personality measurement instrument set up in a true-or-false format.[47] The original version of the MMPI was published in 1943 and was initially used for clinical screening. It contained ten scales for measuring personality dimensions, primarily dealing with psychoneurotic concerns. In 1989, development of the revised (or second) version of the MMPI was completed and it has gone through later revisions and updates. While the new version contains the same scales, there were changes in interpretation of some scales and items were updated. The MMPI-2 is the most widely used and researched test of adult psychopathology. It is primarily used by clinicians to assist with the diagnosis of mental disorders and the selection of appropriate treatment. However, the MMPI-2 has also been used in career assessment in a number of ways, including measuring the degree of emotional adjustment and general personality functioning.[48] Detailed information on the MMPI-2 is available at www.pearsonassessments.com.

The *California Psychological Inventory* (CPI) is an assessment tool that measures personality and personal style.[49] Originally published in 1956, the CPI consists of 434 items and measures 20 dimensions of personality. A number of special-purpose scales are included with the CPI including managerial potential, work orientation, and leadership. The CPI has been used in a number of career development applications, including career decision-making and maturity.[50] Detailed information on the CPI is available at www.cpp.com.

Assessment of Abilities and Talents

The *General Aptitude Test Battery* (GATB) was developed by the U.S. Employment Service, a division of the Department of Labor, for employment service counseling and placement by various agencies of the U.S. government. The GATB, the original version of which dates back to 1947, is designed to measure cognitive, perceptual, and psychomotor skills.[51] It is one of the most frequently used tests and is unequaled in the size of its occupational database. The GATB consists of 11 timed tests that measure nine abilities: verbal ability, arithmetic reasoning, computational skill, spatial ability, form perception, clerical perception, motor coordination, manual dexterity, and finger dexterity. The basic aptitudes and capabilities measured by the GATB can be compared with occupational aptitude patterns that have been established for hundreds of different occupations.

The *O*Net Ability Profiler* is conceptually similar to the GATB in that it assesses the same nine ability categories. However, the O*Net Ability Profiler was designed and validated strictly for use in career exploration and planning. It is important to note that the O*Net Ability Profiler also ties into the O*NET-SOC occupation profiles, which allows individuals to compare assessment profiles obtained from the O*Net Ability Profiler to specific O*NET-listed occupations. Information on the O*Net Ability Profiler is available at www.onetonline.org.

The *Armed Services Vocational Aptitude Battery* (ASVAB) is the most widely used multiple-aptitude test used in the United States and is given to all applicants to the U.S. military.[52] Originally introduced in 1968, the ASVAB measures nine knowledge and skill sets: general science, arithmetic reasoning, word knowledge, paragraph comprehension, auto and shop information, mathematics knowledge, mechanical comprehension, electronics information, and assembling objects. Combinations of these skill sets can be used to measure other categories of abilities, such as general intelligence. It is administered annually to more than one million military applicants, high school and post-secondary students, and helps predict future academic and occupational success in the military. Information on the ASVAB is available at http://official-asvab.com.

The *Bennett Mechanical Comprehension Test* (BMCT) is designed to assess aptitude in comprehending mechanical applications in realistic situations.[53] Originally developed in 1940, the BMCT looks at practical problem-solving ability, the application of physical laws, and various mechanical operations. The current BMCT has standard results for such activities as engineering, installation, maintenance and repair, automotive, aircraft or general mechanical positions, transportation or machine operators, skilled trades, and others. Detailed information on the BMCT is available at www.pearsonclinical.com.

Assessment of Lifestyle Preferences

An important goal of self-exploration is to understand what would constitute a personally satisfying pattern of involvement in work and nonwork pursuits. Unlike the other areas of self-exploration (e.g., values, interests), there are no standardized measures that specifically assess an individual's preferences regarding how to combine work and nonwork activities in a satisfying manner. However, there are instruments that measure the level of work–life conflict, enrichment, and balance that one currently experiences.[54] As we will see shortly, Learning Exercise 1D will provide opportunities for you to explore the importance you place on different parts of your life and what you can do to achieve a satisfying balance between your career and other life commitments.

In summary, value surveys, interest inventories, personality measures, ability tests, and other assessment tools can be particularly helpful for career exploration, both with students making an initial career choice and with employees considering a career change. Nonetheless, psychological tests and assessment instruments have limitations. Accordingly, the results of these tests should be used as discussion guides and as a reference for theme identification and future decision-making. They are not intended to be, nor should they be used as, the conclusive answer to one's career decisions and direction.

Integrated Approaches to Self-Exploration

There are a number of sophisticated and integrated assessment methods that are designed to further individual growth with regard to career planning and decision-making. While most of these systems have as a central focus one or more of the primary assessment instruments discussed earlier in this chapter, the ultimate goal is to take the individual through the process of self-exploration to the point of having a higher degree of certainty over a college major or possible career paths. Integrated self-exploration programs can be offered through different venues, including a classroom, a counselor's office, a career resource center or placement office, the human resources department of an organization, or through the Internet.

Computer-based career support systems allow efficient and personalized access to self-exploration information.[55] These programs fulfill a number of career management needs, including information on various career topics, personality and skills assessment, listings of job vacancies, and career decision-making support. Most Internet-based career support systems are available for free or for the cost of a basic registration. The widespread availability of Internet-based career assistance programs offers convenient and practical tools for helping individuals in the career exploration and development process.

Curricular-based programs incorporate many aspects of career planning, including self-assessment, in a classroom setting. Most curricular programs are designed to span a number of weeks as the student or client builds a better understanding of self and the work environment over time. Indeed, many schools and universities offer a career course for academic credit where students use an entire semester of study to gain a better understanding of themselves and the career management process.

Individuals should be careful not to choose a career direction prematurely based solely on the results of an integrated career planning program. As with individual assessment instruments, these programs should be used as one of several aids for gaining a better understanding of one's personal preferences and needs. They certainly should not be used as the definitive guide to career selection.

Organization-Sponsored Self-Exploration Programs

One of the most effective methods for employees to gain a better understanding of their interests and abilities is through career management assistance programs offered at work. In an ideal sense, organization-sponsored programs should have benefits both for the individual employee and for the company.

Various researchers have noted a number of organizational career management tools that can enhance employees' self-knowledge.[56] These programs include individual self-assessment through such activities as career planning workshops, career workbooks, and organizational career assessment centers. These self-exploration programs offered by organizations will often use, as part of the total package, one or more of the commercial assessment instruments described earlier in this chapter. A brief profile of each technique is offered below:

- **Career-planning workshops** use a structured, interactive group format where participants formulate, share, and discuss with each other personal data concerning such factors as strengths, weaknesses, values, and other personal information.[57] The ultimate goal of the workshops is for individuals to take personal responsibility for their careers by setting realistic career goals and implementation plans to achieve their goals.
- **Career workbooks** are intended to fulfill the same basic objectives as a group career workshop, but do so in an individual, self-directed fashion rather than on a participative, interactive basis. The workbooks, which could be offered in a computer-based format or as a paper-and-pencil exercise, use a series of assignments and reference materials to guide employees through the individual assessment process. Also, the workbooks are designed to be completed by the individual alone and are self-paced.
- **Assessment centers** were traditionally used to assess employee career potential, wherein the focus was primarily on quantifying the hiring potential or the promotability of selected employees. In today's business world, these centers play multiple roles ranging from the assessment of personality traits and job-specific competencies to group exercises where individuals receive feedback on observed competencies and real or potential weaknesses.[58] In this sense, the results from assessment center ratings can be used for career decision-making and employee development purposes.[59] Nonetheless, while the results might prove insightful, individuals should ensure that conclusions from assessment center evaluations are valid and that the design of the center and the exercises are in accordance with international standards.[60]

In addition to the above programs, employees have other options for obtaining self-information through the organization. For example, periodic performance appraisals and supervisory feedback can offer insight into personal strengths and weaknesses that can add to the employee's exploration process. Many of the more prominent executive development programs use the 360-degree evaluation technique that provides feedback to the individual from a wider perspective. This fuller perspective, which includes assessments from superiors, subordinates, and peers, can give more extensive information on personal strengths and weaknesses, especially in the work role.[61]

Informal Self-Exploration

A variety of informal techniques are open to individuals in their self-exploration journey. These can include such activities as:

1. Ranking significant work values.
2. Analyzing "high-point" and "low-point" experiences in life.
3. Developing a present and future obituary notice.
4. Analyzing one's current job satisfactions and dissatisfactions.
5. Describing an ideal job.
6. Fantasizing about one's future life.

It is also important to informally share the results of one's exploration activities with other trusted individuals as another means of gaining additional personal insight. These other individuals might include parents, spouse or significant other, other family members, close friends, co-workers, and a manager.

> Learning Exercise 1 is included in the Appendix at the end of this chapter. It includes activities designed to help you collect self-related data. Although you may examine Learning Exercise 1 at this stage, it is recommended that you finish reading Chapter 5 before you begin the exercise.

Theme Identification for Self-Exploration: Step 2

Information is most useful when it is organized into coherent, understandable units. Therefore, it is necessary to make sense out of the data supplied by various inventories, exercises, and feedback. You will need to ask what you have learned about yourself and whether there are consistencies that cut across the results from different sources of information. You need to discover, in other words, what themes have emerged from the data.

A significant theme (such as "I want to get my own way," "I need to work cooperatively with other people," and "My family always comes before my work") can combine values, interests, personality, and abilities into meaningful wholes. The identification of themes is an inductive process. Much like a detective, the individual scrutinizes the specific data for clues about what it is saying, reaches preliminary conclusions about the presence of certain themes, and tests the data further to confirm or reject what has been learned.

The following steps could be helpful in identifying themes:[62]

1. Thoroughly examine each assessment activity for the presence of common elements. Highlighting key words or phrases is a helpful technique.
2. Look for data across different self-assessment activities that support or refute the presence of a theme. The more consistently the theme emerges from the data, the more likely the theme is important.
3. Label the themes in as descriptive a fashion as possible.
4. Assess the accuracy and importance of the themes. How much data support the theme? In how many different devices has the theme been identified? How much, if any, contradictory evidence has been found? (The fewer the contradictions, the more accurate the theme.)

Theme identification is clearly an active process, but it is rarely simple and straightforward. This is understandable, because the results of self-exploration activities may prove insufficient, inconclusive, or contradictory. Further, self-assessment, as a process of uncovering personality and psychological attributes, could produce feelings of anxiety and doubt. Nonetheless, the results of exploration activities are important and necessary in the setting of career goals and in the management of one's career. Thus, self-exploration must be conducted, even though the process may at times be uncomfortable.

> Learning Exercise 2 is included in the Appendix at the end of this chapter. It provides an opportunity for you to identify themes that emerged from the data collected in Learning Exercise 1. Although you may examine Learning Exercise 2 at this time, it is recommended that you finish reading Chapter 5 before you begin the exercise.

Understanding the Preferred Work Environment: Step 3

Once a set of themes is identified and confirmed, it is helpful to develop an understanding of your *preferred work environment*; that is, the kinds of work experiences that will be personally meaningful and interesting, will meet your significant values, will allow you to use those abilities and talents that are important to you, and will provide a satisfying balance between work and nonwork activities. Your statement about a preferred work environment is a summary of what you have learned from the self-exploration process. Based on the analyses of the themes that emerged from your self-assessment, you should try to identify the type of work environment (*not* a specific job in a particular company) that seems most compatible with your own qualities. The preferred work environment summary should touch on the following issues:

1. What types of *tasks or activities* are most interesting to you? For example, do you enjoy analytical activities, mechanical tasks, helping others, or scientific projects?
2. What *abilities and talents* do you wish to use in your work? Interpersonal? Quantitative? Creative? Writing skills?
3. How much freedom from supervision and *independence* do you want in your work?
4. What type of *working relationships* with other people do you prefer? Do you prefer working alone or with other people? How do you feel about exerting power or influence over other people?
5. What type of physical work setting is desirable (e.g., factory, office, outdoors)?
6. What is the role of money and security in your life?
7. How important is work in your total life, and what relationship do you desire between your work and other parts of your life?

> Learning Exercise 3 is included in the Appendix at the end of this chapter. It provides an opportunity to develop a statement about your preferred work environment. Although you may examine Learning Exercise 3 at this time, it is recommended that you finish reading Chapter 5 before you begin the exercise.

Goals of Environmental Exploration

Self-exploration is an essential ingredient in effective career management because it provides the information that is needed to answer a number of related questions: What do I find interesting? What are my strengths and weaknesses? What rewards are important to me? What do I want from my work and nonwork lives?

But self-assessment represents only half of the equation. Careers are embedded in occupations, jobs, and organizations. It is through interaction with the work environment that values are met, talents are utilized, and interests are stimulated.[63] Moreover, work environments differ in the extent to which they are compatible with a person' particular pattern of values, interests, and abilities. Research has shown that compatibility between the person (interests, abilities, preferences, etc.) and the work environment has a strong influence on such outcomes as job satisfaction, tenure, and career success.[64] In addition, research supports the "gravitational" view of employment, which states that individuals will, over the course of their labor market experiences, try to seek out jobs that are compatible with their values, interests, and abilities.[65] That is, individuals seek positions for which there is a good fit. Finally, given the overlap between work and nonwork domains brought on by advanced forms of communication technology and increased work demands, there is a need to consider how the individual self is defined by work and how that affects their identity and life.[66] Accordingly, self-awareness needs to be accompanied by an active exploration of one's environment.

Although there are many facets to the environment, four are particularly important in career management: **occupations, jobs, organizations**, and **nonwork roles**. The aim of environmental exploration is to learn enough about these facets to make decisions about occupational fields, jobs, career paths, and different organizations in the context of one's work *and* nonwork values and aspirations. Effective environmental exploration should enable a person to identify the setting in which he or she is most likely to meet significant values and to find expression for interests, abilities, and preferred lifestyle.

The most relevant facet of the environment in terms of the aims and activities of exploration will depend on the type of decision that is required in a particular situation. A student who is about to graduate and is looking for an entry-level job, a middle-aged employee who is seeking a new opportunity with a different employer, and a person trying to find reemployment after a job loss will need to focus their search and exploration activities in different ways.[67] Regardless of the particular decision to be made, individuals need to explore the potential of a match between a particular environment and desired work setting and lifestyle. To accomplish that task, environments need to be understood in light of the information derived from self-exploration. That is, a bridge should be built between self-exploration and alternative environments. This section of the chapter considers how such a bridge can be constructed. Specific applications of these principles to the choice of an occupation, organization, and career path will be discussed in subsequent chapters.

Table 5.2 summarizes the types of information relevant to each sub-environment. First of all, occupations differ in the particular tasks that need to be performed. Physicists and social workers, for example, engage in different activities. These activities have implications for a person's values, interests, and abilities. Someone who values intellectual stimulation, creativity, and independence, has interests in scientific activities, and has strong conceptual skills might be drawn to a research career in theoretical physics. Someone who strongly values social welfare, enjoys working closely with other people, desires variety in work, and has strong interpersonal skills may find a career in social work more attractive. Knowledge of occupationally related tasks is basic to linking self-assessment to career decisions.

In addition to task differences, occupations frequently differ in context or environment. Economic rewards, such as income and job security, are not equally distributed across all occupations. Similarly, the physical setting of the work, the degree and type of interaction with other people, and even the dress code can vary substantially from one occupational field to another.

Because occupational fields require different tasks, provide different rewards, and take place in different physical and social settings, they often have implications for different lifestyles. Two particular lifestyle considerations that should be examined are an occupation's time demands and its associated stresses and strains. Extensive time commitment to a job and/or exposure to extremely stressful work environments can produce conflicts between work and other parts of life. Therefore, occupations that require an extraordinary time involvement (e.g., extensive travel or a 60-hour work week) and are highly stressful may be incompatible with a lifestyle that attempts to achieve a balance between work and family or personal activities.

Table 5.2 also summarizes the type of information relevant to jobs and organizations. Notice first the similarity between occupational information and job information. Because

Table 5.2 Illustrative Information Relevant to Environmental Exploration

Occupations	Jobs
Task activities	Task variety
Ability/training requirements	Task significance
Amount of independence/autonomy	Ability/training requirements
Financial rewards	Amount of independence/autonomy
Occupational stability/security	Financial rewards
Social relationships	Job security
Physical setting	Social relationships
Lifestyle considerations	Physical setting
• Time commitment to work	Lifestyle considerations
• Degree of work stress	• Time commitment to work
	• Degree of work stress
	Relation to other jobs
Organizations	**Non-work Environment**
Industry outlook	Family
Financial health of the organization	• Spouse's career aspirations
Business strategies	• Spouse's emotional needs
Career path flexibility	• Children's needs
Supportive of family and personal life	• Family's financial needs
Career management practices/policies	• Family's desired lifestyle
Size and structure	• Self and spouse career stage
Reward system	• Family stage
Level of international operations	• Extended family members' needs
Mentoring programs	Friendships
	Community organizations
	Spiritual/religious organizations
	Leisure or self-development opportunities

a specific job (e.g., market research analyst in Company X) is essentially a vehicle for pursuing an occupation (e.g., market research), the similarity in information needs is understandable. However, a thorough occupational exploration does not preclude the need for additional job exploration. To illustrate, design engineers in one company do not necessarily perform the same activities with the same rewards as those in another company. Therefore, exploration focused on jobs and positions within particular organizations is essential.

In addition, notice that several additional pieces of information are relevant to job exploration. First, job autonomy can vary substantially between organizations or even between two units of the same organization. Sales representatives in two different companies may have essentially the same duties, but more autonomy in decision-making may be granted in one company than in the other. This knowledge is particularly important since autonomy can satisfy one's values for intellectually stimulating, independent, and creative work. Second, it is critical to examine the relationship between a particular job and other jobs in the same or different organizations. Some jobs, in effect, are "dead end" in that lateral or hierarchical movement to other jobs is extremely limited. Some jobs, in other words, provide more options than others.

It should be clear by now that nearly all jobs are inextricably connected to organizations. Therefore, whether one is entering a first full-time job or is currently employed, it is important to realize that:

1. The outlook of the industry or industries served by an organization can affect career possibilities.

2. The financial health of the organization can place limits on career opportunities.
3. The company's business strategy affects the type of human resources required and, therefore, the nature of career opportunities.
4. An organization's size and structure can affect mobility opportunities. Also, the degree to which a company has global operations or worldwide interests will dictate whether opportunities for an international career are possible.
5. Organizations differ in the extent to which they support career management through such practices as training and development programs, performance-appraisal systems, job postings, and career seminars.
6. Organizations vary in the degree to which they provide flexible career paths that enable employees to move in a number of different career directions. They also differ in terms of the flexibility and control they provide to help employees balance work with other parts of life.
7. Organizations differ in the importance they place on various financial, social, and intrinsic rewards. Some companies, for example, may pay high salaries but offer few chances for challenging work.

In short, the culture, outlook, and financial health of an organization affect the nature of specific career opportunities. Business plans and strategies, assumptions about people, and reward systems all have significant consequences for career management. In reality, the exploration of jobs and organizations is naturally intertwined in career decision-making. For example, a graduating MBA normally examines alternative jobs and organizations at the same time. A student interviewing for a sales position in Company A and one in Company B needs to examine the two jobs in detail as well as the characteristics of the two companies. Similarly, a manager considering his or her future in an organization needs to consider alternative jobs within that organization as well as in different organizations. Chapter 7 provides an in-depth discussion of the occupational choice and organizational entry processes.

Table 5.2 also specifies a range of information relevant to the nonwork environment. Information regarding one's family is prominently displayed because the family role is a central consideration for many if not most employees. Whether the primary focus is on gathering information about occupations, jobs, or organizations, it is essential to understand the needs and feelings of family members. Understanding the family's emotional and financial needs, career aspirations, and desired lifestyle is necessary if one wants to achieve satisfying work and nonwork lives. As was discussed in Chapter 3, the most significant source of information about the family's needs is the family itself—people need to talk and listen to the important people in their lives. However, because other aspects of life outside work are important to many employees, we need to understand the opportunities for satisfying experiences in the community, religious or spiritual activities, leisure or self-development pursuits, and friendships, and how these nonwork experiences can affect or be affected by our career.

Techniques for Effective Work Exploration

Essentially, the exploration of the work environment can be broken down into two categories, external and internal. Exploration of the **external work environment** involves gathering of information on specific occupations, jobs, organizations, and industries. Students just entering the workforce and employees interested in locating a job with another organization would engage in exploration of the external work environment. It is important to recognize that the Internet has helped external environmental exploration immensely in recent years. Substantial amounts of industry, organizational, and occupational information now reside on the World Wide Web.

Information on specific occupations and occupational classes is available from a number of sources, such as occupational classification systems that use various schema for grouping jobs and job data.[68] Experts use accumulated knowledge about the realm of jobs and sophisticated statistical techniques to create hierarchies of occupations and positions that take into account such factors as required skill and knowledge levels, work functions, job titles, and other related information. A few of the key occupational classification systems are listed here:

- The *Standard Occupational Classification* (SOC) was developed by the U.S. Department of Commerce.[69] It serves as the single classification system for all occupations in the U.S. economy, including public, private, and military jobs, regardless of whether the work is performed for pay. The SOC system is used by all federal agencies as the basis for the collection and reporting of jobs data. Occupational classifications are based on work performed as well as the skills, education, and training needed to perform the work at an acceptable level.[70] The SOC contains a hierarchy of occupations, moving from 23 general occupational groups to 97 more distinct groupings to 461 broad occupations to 840 detailed occupational titles.[71]
- The *Occupational Information Network* (O*NET) is seen as the most comprehensive resource for occupational information. It is an online resource that provides detailed, research-based descriptions of more than 1,100 occupations using hundreds of potential job characteristics and descriptors.[72] Occupation-specific information includes titles, alternate titles, specific tasks, and tools and technology used in the occupation. In addition, occupational descriptors include worker characteristics (interests, values, and abilities of the typical worker), worker requirements, occupational requirements, and training and education needs. The O*NET Interest Profiler allows individuals to link their interest assessment profiles to the O*NET-SOC occupational profiles and to identify careers for exploration.[73] The comprehensive O*NET Resource Center (available at www.onetcenter.org) provides online access to the O*NET database, career exploration tools, and related activities.
- The Department of Labor's *Occupational Outlook Handbook* (OOH) is another widely used source for occupational information.[74] The OOH describes job duties, work activities, qualifications, and projected openings for more than 500 occupations. The database also includes information on entry-level education, on-the-job training, projected number of new jobs becoming available, the growth rate in the occupation, and the median salary. The OOH, which is available at www.bls.gov/ooh, allows for a detailed and interactive sharing of occupational information.
- Many other reference materials are available in bookstores, libraries, and over the Internet that describe specific jobs and occupations. In addition, popular interest inventories, as described earlier in this chapter, include connections to specific occupations associated with various interest profiles.

Information on different organizations and industries is also available from multiple sources. For example, a company's website typically includes a description of the organization, corporate philosophies and goals, possible career paths, and the job application procedures. In addition, an organization's annual 10K filing with the U.S. Securities and Exchange Commission and its annual corporate report offer information on financial performance, key decision-makers within the company, and the products and services the company provides. Outplacement and career-counseling firms also provide information on different companies as part of the services they give to their clients. On the Internet, websites exist that provide unvarnished reviews (both positive and negative) of various companies from current and former employees that can help in the process of evaluating an organization. In addition, social media sites such as LinkedIn and Facebook can offer an avenue to directly and indirectly learn more about a company. More broadly, profiles and summaries of particular industries are available through the North American Industry Classification System (NAICS) and through other sources.

In a less formal sense, one's family, friends, and former coworkers employed in different companies and industries can provide substantial information on occupations and contacts that might not be available through formal sources. In addition to those sources listed above, public libraries in several states have centers that offer occupational information and advisement.

Internal work exploration involves the gathering of career-related information within one's own firm. There are a number of organizational career development tools that could be utilized to gather data on jobs and opportunities within one's organization, including: job posting programs, career ladders and career path planning, career resource centers, and in-house seminars and workshops. Other employees, including mentors and other supportive colleagues, can also provide information on jobs and opportunities within other departments and subsidiaries owned by the company.

> Learning Exercise 4 is included in the Appendix at the end of this chapter. It provides an opportunity to practice environmental exploration. Although you may examine Learning Exercise 4 at this time, it is recommended that you finish reading Chapter 5 before you begin the exercise.

Guidelines for Overcoming Obstacles to Career Exploration

Despite the logical role of self-exploration and environmental exploration in the career management process, it should not be assumed that exploration is always effective. That is, it does not always produce an enhanced awareness of self and/or the environment. Following is a list of potential obstacles to effective career exploration and guidelines for overcoming them.

1. Incomplete Exploration

Career exploration sometimes does not provide a sufficient amount of information to be useful. In other cases, a person may participate in little or no exploration, despite a recognized need for information. There are at least three reasons for inadequate exploration: complacency, hopelessness, and fear.

First, people may complacently accept the status quo. If they uncritically accept their course in life, there is no need to collect additional information. One explanation for this complacency is that people do not see the significance of career decisions. They often do not understand that a decision does have consequences in terms of future rewards and life's enjoyments.

Furthermore, some people attach little importance to the role that work plays in their overall lives, which leads to the belief that career exploration and career decisions are not going to make much difference in their present and future existence. An uncritical complacency with things as they are or as they might be is unfortunate because decisions have to be made regardless of participation in career exploration. Students still have to choose majors, graduates still have to choose jobs and employers, and even the most indifferent employees have to make decisions about their work lives.

Even if employees are not complacent, they may forgo career exploration if they perceive it to be useless. For example, a manager who perceives limited mobility opportunities in his or her organization is unlikely to participate in extensive career exploration within that organization.[75] In a sense, people who believe that they have little control over their opportunities may engage in inadequate exploration. Unfortunately, this aversion to career exploration creates a vicious cycle in which decisions made by others (by default) reinforce the view that control over one's fate is impossible.

Finally, fear may block an active approach to career exploration. People who fear that their exploration will fail to provide useful information may avoid risking such failure and simply not pursue exploration activities. Those with low self-esteem may fear confronting their own weaknesses and thereby reduce their participation in exploratory activities.

Even among those who initiate career exploration, it may be tempting to bring exploration to a premature halt to gain a sense of security. This may be a false sense of security, however, because exploration may raise issues that take time to understand or resolve. Therefore, one key ingredient to successful career exploration is the ability to tolerate a certain amount of ambiguity and frustration. Sometimes it is important to be persistent in career exploration.

Integrated and organizationally based career planning programs, as described earlier, can often provide information and support to overcome these forms of resistance to career exploration. Interactions with other more experienced career planners can help participants:

- Realize career-related choices have a significant effect on the course of their lives; decisions do matter;
- Recognize that they can exert sufficient control over their careers to make career exploration worthwhile;
- Understand that fear of the unknown is natural but should not stifle their attempts to understand themselves and their environment.

2. *Coerced Exploration*

Despite the need to acquire additional information, coercion is not a useful stimulant to successful exploration. While pressure from a manager, spouse, relative, or friend might be sufficient to initiate participation in career exploration, people tend to learn and change when the motivation comes from within and when there is a personal commitment to the learning process.

3. *Random and Diffuse Exploration*

This is exploration that is unfocused, jumps haphazardly from activity to activity, and does not build on the results of prior exploration activities. Effective exploration requires intentionality and focus, which are based on a combination of skill and practice. Therefore, some instruction in these skills through classes or workshops would help many people develop a more systematic approach to career exploration. This does not mean that career exploration, or career management in general, requires constant participation in formal programs, but rather that some initial, structured experience would be helpful in developing the appropriate skills.

4. *Ineffective Forms of Career Exploration*

As this chapter has shown, people committed to career exploration have choices to make about the manner in which they will seek information. Should they consult a mentor, see a counselor, speak to friends or family members, attend a career workshop, search the Internet, seek part-time employment, contact professional organizations, or pursue some of these activities in combination?

There is not sufficient evidence at this point to indicate which of these (or other) exploratory activities are most effective for a particular person in a specific situation. Indeed, the most potentially useful exploratory activities are not necessarily the ones that are engaged in the most frequently. It is likely that some people pursue the most easily accessible or the most comfortable exploratory activities and shy away from those that are more difficult to pursue or are more threatening. Although this is a natural and understandable tendency, it could result in a false sense of security.

Perhaps the most critical task is to estimate the likelihood that a particular activity will meet your informational needs. Although there is no easy solution to this problem, it is important not to equate ease with quality. Again, a structured experience can help provide guidance on the most useful, constructive forms of exploration.

5. *Defensive Self-Exploration*

In self-exploration, people need to obtain information from an activity and process it accurately and constructively. Clearly, some people are better able to accomplish this task than others. In particular, highly anxious people may not profit extensively from self-exploration.[76] It has been suggested that such people, when facing career decisions, focus on their own anxious feelings rather than on the information at hand. Therefore, people who are anxious about themselves or their careers may react defensively to threatening self-related information; may ignore, distort, or misinterpret the information; and may generally not utilize career exploration effectively. In terms of career decision-making, highly anxious people might feel compelled to reach a premature or hastily contrived decision, or may avoid the decision entirely.

The solution to this problem would seem to involve reducing feelings of anxiety to the point where they do not interfere with productive exploration. Fortunately, stress management programs have been found to stimulate exploratory behavior. It is also possible that group-oriented career planning workshops can help people become less anxious in career decision-making situations.

6. *Exclusion of Nonwork Considerations*

As we have repeatedly asserted, effective career exploration requires attention to all segments of life. Work experiences can affect the quality of one's family or personal life positively or negatively. Too many people fail to examine the implications of work-related decisions for other parts of their lives. Occupations are chosen, jobs are sought, and promotions are accepted without consideration of their consequences for *all* parts of life. Work, family, community, leisure, and other important nonwork roles all need to be examined in order to (1) identify one's lifestyle preferences and (2) test the compatibility of different occupations, jobs, and career paths with these preferences. The learning exercises included in this chapter periodically remind you to consider the impact of work experiences on your family and other significant parts of your life.

Self-Exploration and Environmental Exploration: A Reciprocal Relationship

Career exploration provides an awareness of self and environment that enables a person to set valid, realistic career goals. Although our discussion has separated self-exploration and environmental exploration, in practice they are connected.

First, a particular exploratory activity may provide useful information about both self and environment. For example, a student who accepts a part-time or summer position as an accounting intern not only will learn about the work life of an accountant but will also test the compatibility of his or her abilities and interests with the field of accounting.[77] A performance appraisal review with a boss not only can provide information about one's performance and progress in the organization, but can also suggest alternative opportunities for future mobility. Therefore, individuals need to be sensitive to the full range of information that can be acquired through a particular activity.

Second, there is a reciprocal relationship between self-exploration and environmental exploration; each can and should influence the direction of the other. For example, it is reasonable to engage in a certain amount of self-exploration before extensively exploring the environment. Self-awareness of interests, values, abilities, and lifestyle preferences can guide one's search for information regarding occupations, jobs, organizations, industries, or nonwork activities. Self-awareness also provides a framework for environmental exploration. Extensive environmental exploration without sufficient understanding of self is likely to be aimless and random.

However, because gaining self-awareness is often a fragmented process, it is impractical to complete the task of achieving substantial self-insight before beginning an assessment of the environment. Moreover, environmental exploration may highlight the need to engage in additional self-exploration. For example, exploring the viability of two jobs in different organizations might reveal that a position in one organization requires much more extensive travel than a similar position in the other organization. This piece of information might stimulate the person to consider the impact of travel (positive or negative) on his or her desired lifestyle.

In reality, people need to use self-exploration to direct environmental exploration and vice versa. Individual differences in terms of values, personality, and abilities are linked with success in academic pursuits, work, and in life in general.[78] Therefore, the more one learns about oneself, the more likely that certain questions about the environment become relevant to ensure that individual factors can be assessed and evaluated to help ensure success in different endeavors. In a similar fashion, the more information acquired about an occupation, a job, or an organization, the more one has to think about the relevance of that information for one's values, interests, abilities, and lifestyle preferences.

Summary

Career exploration is directed at learning more about yourself and gaining additional knowledge about the broader environment. Self-exploration requires (1) the collection of information about values, interests, personality, abilities, and desired lifestyle; (2) the organization of this information into meaningful themes; and (3) the identification of the implications of these themes for the formulation of one's preferred work environment that is most likely to satisfy important values, offer interesting tasks, utilize individual talents, and provide a desired lifestyle.

Environmental exploration can help us learn more about different occupations, organizations, and industries as well as the needs of our family and other parts of life (e.g., community) outside of work. The two forms of exploration, self- and environmental, can reinforce each other by suggesting different areas in which we need to collect additional information. Learning exercises are included at the end of this chapter to provide the opportunity to practice career exploration.

A number of obstacles to effective career exploration were discussed in this chapter, including incomplete exploration, coerced exploration, random and diffuse exploration, ineffective forms of exploration, excessive defensiveness, and exclusion of nonwork considerations. Suggestions were made for overcoming each obstacle.

Now that you have finished reading Chapter 5, it is time to complete Learning Exercises 1, 2, 3, and 4, which are included in the Appendix at the end of this chapter. Be thoughtful and patient in the completion of these exercises. You will refer to them as you complete later chapters in this book.

Career Management *for Life*: Work–Life Implications from Chapter 5

- An essential part of self-exploration is to become aware of the desired lifestyle that we wish to attain; that is, a satisfying pattern of involvement in work *and* nonwork pursuits that enables us to satisfy our values, participate in activities that we find interesting, and find expression for our talents.
- An essential part of environmental exploration is to determine the compatibility or fit of different occupations, jobs, career paths, and organizations with the type of lifestyle we want to achieve.
- People, occupations, jobs, and organizations are likely to change over time. Therefore, it is critical that we regularly engage in career exploration *for life*, not just when faced with a decision or a crisis

Assignments

1. Take a few moments to reflect on the things you like to do, the things you believe are important, your preferences, your competencies, and your weaknesses. On a separate worksheet, prepare a list of what you see as your interests, values, talents, and weaknesses. You can use the information provided in Table 5.1 to help guide you in the preparation of the list. Ask a friend, family member, or colleague to review your list and give you feedback on whether or not they see it as an accurate reflection of you. Ask them to explain any differences they see. How do you think the list you prepared and the feedback you received could help you in your career management process?
2. Take a few minutes to carefully review the descriptions of each of the eight career anchors developed by Edgar Schein presented earlier in this chapter. Once you have read each description, think about which one best fits you and your orientation toward work. Identify why you think this career anchor best describes you. Which career anchor describes you the least and why? How might you be able to use this information on career anchors in your self-exploration process and in theme development?

Discussion Questions

1. What are the differences among values, interests, personality, and abilities? How are they also related to one another? How does an understanding of these factors help us manage our career effectively?
2. How important is work in your total life? What makes you feel that way? Has the importance of work in your life changed in recent years? Do you think it will remain the same in the future? In what ways could your desire for a specific type of lifestyle affect your career decisions?
3. Do you believe that career exploration is worth the effort? Because the world can change so rapidly, will the information collected through career exploration be irrelevant and/or outdated within a short period of time?
4. Reexamine the six obstacles to effective career exploration. Which of them have you experienced in the past? How can you overcome these obstacles in the future?

Chapter 5 Case: Joe Francis the Sales Executive

At age 39, Joe Francis should have been pleased. In fact, he has been proud of his rapid rise to the position of vice-president of sales at Infotek (fictitious name), an established computer software development firm. Having started as a sales representative at Infotek upon graduation from college, Joe's sales performance at the district and regional levels was legendary. However, his promotion to the vice-presidency came as a surprise. He did not seek the position, always preferring sales to pencil-pushing and administration. But it was hard to turn down the promotion with its hefty salary increase and the other executive perks.

Although he has not complained to anyone, Joe has had gnawing doubts about his work. For one thing, he has had strong reservations about the quality of Infotek's products. He has found it increasingly difficult to get enthusiastic about software systems that fall short of personal and industry standards. Joe's comments to the Research and Marketing Departments have fallen on deaf ears. In fact, he has offered suggestions in a number of areas that the company seems unwilling to consider seriously. In addition, his fears about getting drowned in paperwork and administration have been realized. Joe has been bored for quite a while. Moreover, although the travel was enjoyable initially, the seemingly constant business trips of the past few years have left him tired, irritable, and with little time for his family.

Joe has had to suppress many of these feelings. After all, his salary and bonus reach well into six figures. His family has expensive consumption habits, two of his children are nearing college age, and his family wants a larger summer house at the lake. He doesn't dare even discuss his feelings with his family, who have become pretty accustomed to "the good life."

Although he dreads going to work, Joe believes that he must do it for the sake of his family. He is unhappy much of the time but has been pleased with his status in the company. Anyway, Joe has found that the traveling isn't so bad after four stiff drinks on the flight. For the sake of his wife and kids, Joe decided he would stay put for the next 15 or 20 years until early retirement.

Case Questions

1. What specific career exploration activities has Joe undertaken to gather information about himself (his values, needs, abilities, interests, and desired lifestyle) and his environment (different jobs, employers, industries, family and other nonwork domains)? What should he have done to acquire more information?
2. How much insight does Joe currently have about himself and his environment?
3. Is Joe successful in his career? Do you think if Joe conducted more extensive career exploration, it would lead to more positive career outcomes for him?
4. If Joe sought your help, what advice would you give to help him manage his career effectively?
5. If you had to make a prediction, where do you think Joe will be in his career five years into the future?

Appendix for Chapter 5: Learning Exercises 1–4

Each learning exercise involves a different aspect of career exploration. By investing time in these exercises, you can develop and practice critical career exploration skills. We recommend that you use electronic files in which to write your responses to these exercises. An electronic career management notebook provides the flexibility to add more information to an exercise at a later point. Although it may be possible to complete all exercises in one sitting, it is less tiring and more effective to allow some time for reflection in between them.

Learning Exercise 1

Self-Exploration: Data Collection

Learning Exercise 1 contains a number of activities designed to provide self-assessment data. Be as thorough as possible in answering all questions. Remember that the more you write, the more self-assessment information will be available for you to interpret.

Learning Exercise 1A: An Autobiography

Here you are today—a college undergraduate or graduate student, an employee with substantial work experience under your belt, or someone ready to reenter the job market after an absence of several years. Think of all the yesterdays that made you what you are today.

Given all that you know about yourself, write an autobiographical story that traces your history up to now. Divide the story into chapters, each chapter should cover a five-year period, starting with birth to five years old, five to ten years old, and so on. In each chapter, try to answer the following questions if they are relevant: Who were the important people in your life and why were they important? What was your family life like at the time? What were your school experiences like and how did you react to school? What were your work experiences like and how did you react to work? Did you develop hobbies and interests and what did you like about them? To what extent did your parents influence the activities you've pursued and the choices you've made? How have other family relationships shaped your experiences? What happened to you during this period that changed the course of your life?

Write as much as you can about each question. Don't worry about whether these chapters have anything to do with your career—you'll find that out later. If you are in doubt about whether or not to include something, include it. The more you write, the better.

Learning Exercise 1B: Focus on School

Now identify your favorite and least favorite courses and subjects, those subjects in which you did best and worst, and significant extracurricular activities (e.g., sports, music, clubs) in which you participated.

High School

Favorite Courses

Least Favorite Courses

Courses in Which You Did Best

Courses In Which You Did Worst

Extracurricular Activities:

College

Favorite Courses

Least Favorite Courses

Courses in Which You Did Best

Courses in Which You Did Worst

Extracurricular Activities:

What do your responses tell you about your interests and particular strengths and weaknesses?

Learning Exercise 1C: Focus on Work

Think about the best job you ever had. It could be your current job or a prior job, and either part-time, full-time, or temporary.

What do (did) you like most about the job? Be specific in terms of tasks, people, and other aspects.

What do (did) you dislike about the job? Again, be specific.

On what specific tasks or projects did you accomplish something significant? Why were you able to accomplish it?

On what specific tasks or projects did you not perform as well as you would have liked? What was the reason?

Now think about the worst job you ever had. It could be your current job or a prior job, and either part-time, full-time, or temporary.

What do (did) you dislike most about the job?

What do (did) you like about the job?

On what specific tasks or projects did you accomplish something significant? Why?

On what specific tasks or projects did you not perform as well as you would have liked? What was the reason?

Now describe your conception of an ideal job. What would it be like? Be specific in terms of the kinds of tasks, other people, rewards, and anything else that are important to you.

Next rank the following ten factors in terms of how important each is to you for a career-related job. Enter a 1 next to the factor that is most important to you, a 10 next to the least important factor, a 2 next to the second most important, a 9 next to the second least important, and so on until you have ranked all ten factors.

How important is it that your job...

☐ Permits you to work on a wide variety of tasks?
☐ Gives you the opportunity to help others?
☐ Provides you with a great deal of independence in deciding how the work gets done?
☐ Enables you to make a great deal of money?
☐ Offers you a secure future?
☐ Gives you the opportunity to develop friendships at work?
☐ Provides pleasant working conditions?
☐ Allows you sufficient time to spend on family or other nonwork activities?
☐ Provides you with power and influence over other people?
☐ Gives you a feeling of accomplishment?

Indicate any other job factors not listed above that are important to you.

Learning Exercise 1D: Life Roles

How important are different parts of your life? Rank the following five life roles from 1 (most important) to 5 (least important):

☐ Your career
☐ Your religious and spiritual life

☐ Your family life
☐ Your participation in community service activities
☐ Your leisure and recreational pursuits

Explain why each of these life roles is important (or unimportant) to you:

Your career:

___

Your religious and spiritual life:

___

Your family life:

___

Your community service:

___

Your leisure and recreational pursuits:

___

Will pursuing your career interfere with the opportunities you have to find satisfaction in other parts of your life? Why do you feel that way?

___

Will pursuing your career increase the opportunities you have to find satisfaction in other parts of your life? Why do you feel that way?

___

What will you do to make sure that you find satisfaction in your career and in other important parts of your life?

___

Learning Exercise 2

Self-Exploration: Theme Identification

Now that you have generated data about yourself in Learning Exercise 1, and perhaps have gathered other self-assessment information, the next step is to derive a set of themes based on your data. Review the steps for identifying themes presented in Chapter 5. You should be able to identify at least five themes from your data—if you have more than five themes that is fine, just write down all of the themes that you have along with the supporting evidence. Jot down your preliminary thoughts first, and then list your final set of themes along with supporting evidence.

Theme 1:

___

Evidence:

___

Theme 2:

Evidence:

Theme 3:

Evidence:

Theme 4:

Evidence:

Theme 5:

Evidence:

Other Themes:

Learning Exercise 3

A Summary of Your Preferred Work Environment

As indicated in this chapter, a preferred work environment (PWE) is a summary of the work experiences you find desirable, for example, the kinds of tasks you find interesting, the talents you wish to express, the importance of autonomy and freedom on the job, and so on. Reexamine your responses to Learning Exercises 1 and 2, and write down a comment for each component of the PWE listed below. For example, under tasks and activities, you might write, "I enjoy working on tasks that are technical in nature and that require a great deal of analysis."

Tasks and activities most interesting to you

Significant talents you want to express at work

Importance of independence and autonomy on the job

Work relationships (Work alone, with others, supervise?)

Physical work setting

Importance of money

Importance of job security

Relationship between work and other parts of your life

Other components of preferred work environment

Learning Exercise 4

Environmental Exploration

You can practice environmental exploration by completing either Learning Exercise 4A or 4B. If you are not currently employed, you should complete Learning Exercise 4A, which will give you an opportunity to explore occupations. If you are employed, you might find Learning Exercise 4B (job exploration) more useful. Examine the exercises before you decide which one to complete.

Learning Exercise 4A: Occupational Exploration

Choose an occupation about which you would like to learn more. Maybe it is one you are considering pursuing. Or perhaps you are pretty sure you want to pursue a certain occupation and would like to examine it in more detail. If you are completely undecided about an occupation at this time, read Chapter 7 (especially "The Development of Accurate Occupational Information") to help you decide which occupation to explore in this exercise. Write down the name of the occupation you have chosen to explore.

Review the preferred work environment (PWE) statement you constructed in Learning Exercise 3. Then look at the suggested sources of occupational information described in Chapter 5. Using as many sources as possible, collect information relevant to each component of your PWE in relation to the occupation you have chosen to explore. Summarize the information and the sources (so you can reexamine the raw data) in the format shown below. Remember to use as many different sources of information as you can.

Name of Occupation

Components of the PWE	*Relevant Information about Occupation*	*Information Source*
What tasks and activities are performed?		
What talents are required? Do you possess them or can you learn them?		

(Continued)

Name of Occupation (Continued)

Components of the PWE	*Relevant Information about Occupation*	*Information Source*
How much freedom and autonomy can be obtained?		
What type of working relationships with other people are likely?		
What is the physical work setting?		
How much money can be earned in the long term and short term?		
How much job security is likely?		
Effect of pursuit of occupation on family, leisure, religion, community		
Other significant issues (e.g., job prospects, opportunities for mobility)		

Learning Exercise 4B: Job Exploration

If you are employed, choose a job in your organization other than the one you currently hold. It could be a job you expect to enter next or a job you would like to learn more about. Write down the job title.

Review the preferred work environment (PWE) summary you constructed in Learning Exercise 3. Consider the following sources of information about a job: a written job description, the suggested sources of occupational information described in Chapter 5, your supervisor, employees who hold or previously held the job, members of the human resources department, and people who hold or held a similar job in a different organization. Using as many sources as possible, collect information relevant to each component of your PWE. Summarize the information and the sources (so you can reexamine the raw data) in the same format shown below. Remember to use many different sources of information.

Name of Occupation

Components of the PWE	*Relevant Information about Occupation*	*Information Source*
What tasks and activities are performed?		
What talents are required? Do you possess them or can you learn them?		
How much freedom and autonomy can be obtained?		
What type of working relationships with other people are likely?		
What is the physical work setting?		

Components of the PWE	*Relevant Information about Occupation*	*Information Source*
What is the physical work setting?		
How much money can be earned in the long term and short term?		
How much job security is likely?		
Effect of pursuit of occupation on family, leisure, religion, community		
Other significant issues (e.g., prospects of being offered job, usefulness of job for desired career path)		

Notes

1 Zikic, J. & Hall, D. T. (2009). Toward a more complex view of career exploration. *Career Development Quarterly*, *58*, 181–191; Zikic, J. (2006). Career exploration. In Greenhaus, J. H. & Callanan, G. A. (Eds.), *Encyclopedia of career development* (pp. 103–107). Thousand Oaks, CA: Sage.

2 Lee, B., Porfeli, E. J. & Hirschi, A. (2016). Between- and within-person level motivational precursors associated with career exploration. *Journal of Vocational Behavior*, *92*, 125–134.

3 Kotter, J. P., Faux, V. A. & McArthur, C. C. (1978). *Self-assessment and career development*. Englewood Cliffs, NJ: Prentice-Hall.

4 Singh, R. (2006). Self-awareness. In Greenhaus, J. H. & Callanan, G. A. (Eds.), *Encyclopedia of career development* (pp. 709–713). Thousand Oaks, CA: Sage.

5 Cieciuch, J., Davidov, E., Vecchione, M. & Schwartz, S. H. (2014). A hierarchical structure of basic human values in a third-order confirmatory factor analysis. *Swiss Journal of Psychology*, *73*, 177–182; Hartung, P. J. (2006). Values. In Greenhaus, J. H. & Callanan, G. A. (Eds.), *Encyclopedia of career development* (pp. 843–847). Thousand Oaks, CA: Sage.

6 Tamir, M., Schwartz, S. H., Cieciuch, J., Riediger, M., Torres, C., Scollon, C., Dzokoto, V., Zhou, X. & Vishkin, A. (2016). Desired emotions across cultures: A value-based account. *Journal of Personality and Social Psychology*, *111*, 67–82; Schwartz, S. H., Cieciuch, J., Vecchione, M., Davidov, E., Fischer, R., Beierlein, C., Ramos, A., Verkasalo, M., Lönnqvist, J., Demirutku, K., Dirilen-Gumus, O. & Konty, M. (2012). Refining the theory of basic individual values. *Journal of Personality and Social Psychology*, *103*, 663–688.

7 Boer, D. & Fischer, R. (2013). How and when do personal values guide our attitudes and sociality? Explaining cross-cultural variability in attitude–value linkages. *Psychological Bulletin*, *139*, 1113–1147; Hartung (2006).

8 Cieciuch, J., Davidov, E., Vecchione, M. & Schwartz, S. H. (2014). A hierarchical structure of basic human values in a third-order confirmatory factor analysis. *Swiss Journal of Psychology*, *73*, 177–182; Jin, J. & Rounds, J. (2012). Stability and change in work values: A meta-analysis of longitudinal studies. *Journal of Vocational Behavior*, *80*, 326–339; Leuty, M. E. & Hansen, J. C. (2011). Evidence of construct validity for work values. *Journal of Vocational Behavior*, *79*, 379–390.

9 Cieciuch et al. (2014).

10 Ibid.; Schwartz, S. E. (1999). A theory of cultural values and some implications for work. *Applied Psychology: An International Review*, *48*, 23–47.

11 Zytowski, D. G. (2006). Work values. In Greenhaus, J. H. & Callanan, G. A. (Eds.), *Encyclopedia of career development* (pp. 863–864). Thousand Oaks, CA: Sage.

12 Borgen, F. H. (2006). Interests. In Greenhaus, J. H. & Callanan, G. A. (Eds.), *Encyclopedia of career development* (pp. 393–396). Thousand Oaks, CA: Sage.

13 Ibid.

14 Johnson, V. A. & Beehr, T. A. (2014). Making use of professional development: Employee interests and motivational goal orientations. *Journal of Vocational Behavior*, *84*, 99–108; Tracey, T. J. G., Wille, B., Durr, M. R. & De Fruyt, F. (2014). An enhanced examination of Holland's

consistency and differentiation hypotheses. *Journal of Vocational Behavior*, *84*, 237–247; Wille, B., Tracey, T. J. G., Feys, M. & De Fruyt, F. (2014). A longitudinal and multi-method examination of interest–occupation congruence within and across time. *Journal of Vocational Behavior*, *84*, 59–73; Tracey, T. J. G. (2010). Relation of interest and self-efficacy occupational congruence and career choice certainty. *Journal of Vocational Behavior*, *76*, 441–447.

15 Van Iddekinge, C. H., Roth, P. L., Putka, D. J. & Lanivich, S. E. (2011). Are you interested? A meta-analysis of relations between vocational interests and employee performance and turnover. *Journal of Applied Psychology*, *96*, 1167–1194; Oleski, D. & Subich, L. M. (1996). Congruence and career change in employed adults. *Journal of Vocational Behavior*, *49*, 221–229.

16 Shahnasarian, M. (2006). Holland's theory of vocational choice. In Greenhaus, J. H. & Callanan, G. A. (Eds.), *Encyclopedia of career development* (pp. 352–356). Thousand Oaks, CA: Sage; Holland, J. L. (1997). *Making vocational choices*, 3rd ed. Odessa, FL: Psychological Assessment Resources.

17 Wille, B. & De Fruyt, F. (2014). Vocations as a source of identity: Reciprocal relations between big five personality traits and RIASEC characteristics over 15 years. *Journal of Applied Psychology*, *99*, 262–281; McKay, D. A. & Tokar, D. M. (2012). The HEXACO and five-factor models of personality in relation to RIASEC vocational interests. *Journal of Vocational Behavior*, *81*, 138–149; Strack, S. (1995). Relating Millon's basic personality styles and Holland's occupational types. *Journal of Vocational Behavior*, *45*, 41–54; Tokar, D. M. & Swanson, J. L. (1995). Evaluation of the correspondence between Holland's vocational personality typology and the five-factor model of personality. *Journal of Vocational Behavior*, *46*, 89–108.

18 Dik, B. J. (2006). Strong interest inventory. In Greenhaus, J. H. & Callanan, G. A. (Eds.), *Encyclopedia of career development* (pp. 778–785). Thousand Oaks, CA: Sage; Strong, E. K. (1943). *Vocational interests of men and women*. Stanford, CA: Stanford University Press.

19 Herk, N. A. & Thompson, R. C. (2012). *Strong interest inventory manual supplement*. Mountain View, CA: Consulting Psychologists Press.

20 Crant, J. M. (2006). Personality and careers. In Greenhaus, J. H. & Callanan, G. A. (Eds.), *Encyclopedia of career development* (pp. 627–634). Thousand Oaks, CA: Sage.

21 Hough, L. M. & Johnson, J. W. (2012). Use and importance of personality variables in work settings. Wiener, I. Schmitt, N. W. & Highhouse, S. (Eds.), *Comprehensive handbook of psychology, volume 12: Industrial and organizational psychology*, 2nd ed. (pp. 211–243). Hoboken, NJ: Wiley; Dilchert, S., Ones, D. S., Van Rooy, D. L. & Viswesvaran, C. (2006). Big five factors of personality. In Greenhaus, J. H. & Callanan, G. A. (Eds.), *Encyclopedia of career development* (pp. 36–42). Thousand Oaks, CA: Sage.

22 Ashton, C. & Lee, K. (2009). The HEXACO–60: A short measure of the major dimensions of personality. *Journal of Personality Assessment*, *91*, 340–345; Ashton, M. C. & Lee, K. (2005). Honesty–humility, the big five, and the five-factor model. *Journal of Personality*, *73*, 1321–1353.

23 Ashton, C. & Lee, K. (2008). The prediction of honesty-humility-related criteria by the HEXACO and five-factor models of personality. *Journal of Research in Personality*, *42*, 1216–1228.

24 Rotundo, M. (2006). Abilities. In Greenhaus, J. H. & Callanan, G. A. (Eds.), *Encyclopedia of career development* (pp. 1–5). Thousand Oaks, CA: Sage.

25 Drasgow, F. (2012). Intelligence and the workplace. In Wiener, I., Schmitt, N. W. & Highhouse, S. (Eds.), *Comprehensive handbook of psychology, volume 12: Industrial and organizational psychology*, 2nd ed. (pp. 184–210). Hoboken, NJ: Wiley.

26 Wille & De Fruyt (2014); McKay & Tokar (2012); Armstrong, P. I. & Anthoney, S. F. (2009). Personality facets and RIASEC interests: An integrated model. *Journal of Vocational Behavior*, *75*, 346–359; Ackerman, P. L. & Beier, M. E. (2003). Intelligence, personality, and interests in the career choice process. *Journal of Career Assessment*, *11*, 205–218; Larson, L. M., Rottinghaus, P. J. & Borgen, F. H. (2002). Meta-analyses of big six interests and big five personality factors. *Journal of Vocational Behavior*, *61*, 217–239.

27 Schein, E. H. (2006). Career anchors. In Greenhaus, J. H. & Callanan, G. A. (Eds.), *Encyclopedia of career development* (pp. 63–69). Thousand Oaks, CA: Sage.

28 Chapman. J. R. (2015). Fostering career management using career anchor theory. In Hartung, P. J., Savickas, M. L. & Walsh, W. B. (Eds.), *APA handbook of career intervention, volume 2: Applications* (pp. 507–520). Washington, DC: American Psychological Association; Rodrigues, R., Guest, D. & Budjanovcanin, A. (2013). From anchors to orientations: Toward a contemporary theory. *Journal of Vocational Behavior*, *83*, 142–152.

29 Chapman. J. R. & Brown, B. L. (2014). An empirical study of the career anchors that govern career decisions. *Personnel Psychology*, *43*, 717–740.

30 Hansen, J. C. (2006). Leisure interests. In Greenhaus, J. H. & Callanan, G. A. (Eds.), *Encyclopedia of career development* (pp. 468–469). Thousand Oaks, CA: Sage.
31 Ibid.
32 Rokeach, M. (1973). *Nature of human values*. New York: Free Press; Rokeach, M. (1979). *Understanding human values: Individual and societal*. New York: Free Press.
33 Schwartz, S. H. (1992). Universals in the content and structure of values: Theoretical advances and empirical tests in 20 countries. *Advances in Experimental Social Psychology*, *25*, 1–65; Schwartz, S. H. (1994). Are there universal aspects in the structure and content of human values? *Journal of Social Issues*, *50*, 19–45.
34 Leuty, M. E. (2013). Stability of scores on Super's Work Values Inventory-Revised. *Measurement and Evaluation in Counseling and Development*, *46*, 202–217; Robinson, C. H. & Betz, N. E. (2008). A psychometric evaluation of Super's Work Values Inventory-Revised. *Journal of Career Assessment*, *16*, 456–473; Zytowski, D. G. (2006). Work Values Inventory. In Greenhaus, J. H. & Callanan, G. A. (Eds.), *Encyclopedia of career development* (pp. 865–866). Thousand Oaks, CA: Sage.
35 Zytowski, D. G. (2006). *Technical manual for Super's Work Values Inventory-Revised*, Version 1.0. Available at www.kuder.com.
36 Kopelman, R. E. & Rovenpor, J. L. (2006). Allport-Vernon-Lindzey Study of Values. In Greenhaus, J. H. & Callanan, G. A. (Eds.), *Encyclopedia of career development* (pp. 15–18). Thousand Oaks, CA: Sage.
37 Kopelman, R. E., Rovenpor, J. L. & Guan, M. (2003). The study of values: Construction of the fourth edition. *Journal of Vocational Behavior*, *62*, 203–220.
38 Dik (2006).
39 Herk & Thompson (2012).
40 Holland, J. L. & Messer, M. A. (2013). *Self-directed search*, 5th ed. Lutz, FL: Psychological Assessment Resources; Reardon, R. C. & Lenz, J. G. (2006). Self-directed search (SDS). In Greenhaus, J. H. & Callanan, G. A. (Eds.), *Encyclopedia of career development* (pp. 717–719). Thousand Oaks, CA: Sage; VPI Manual (2016). *Vocational Preference Inventory*. Lutz, FL: Psychological Assessment Resources; Taber, B. J. (2006). Vocational preference inventory (VPI). In Greenhaus, J. H. & Callanan, G. A. (Eds.), *Encyclopedia of career development* (pp. 849–851). Thousand Oaks, CA: Sage.
41 *FIRO-B interpretive report for organizations* (2007). Mountain View, CA: Consulting Psychologists Press; Hammer, A. L. & Schnell, E. R. (2000). *FIRO-B Technical Guide*. Mountain View, CA: Consulting Psychologists Press; Schnell, E. R. (2006). FIRO-B. In Greenhaus, J. H. & Callanan, G. A. (Eds.), *Encyclopedia of career development* (pp. 321–322). Thousand Oaks, CA: Sage.
42 Toman, S. (2006). Kuder career assessments. In Greenhaus, J. H. & Callanan, G. A. (Eds.), *Encyclopedia of career development* (pp. 451–452). Thousand Oaks, CA: Sage.
43 Boggs, K. R. (2006). Campbell Interest and Skill Survey. In Greenhaus, J. H. & Callanan, G. A. (Eds.), *Encyclopedia of career development* (pp. 58–60). Thousand Oaks, CA: Sage.
44 Schaubhut, N. A., Herk, N. A. & Thompson, R. C. (2009). *MBTI Form M Manual Supplement*. Mountain View, CA: Consulting Psychologists Press. Hammer, A. L. (2006). Myers-Briggs Type Indicator. In Greenhaus, J. H. & Callanan, G. A. (Eds.), *Encyclopedia of career development* (pp. 524–527). Thousand Oaks, CA: Sage.
45 Cattell, H. E. P. & Mead, A. D. (2008). The Sixteen Personality Factor Questionnaire (16PF). In Boyle, G. J., Matthews, G. & Saklofske, D. H. (Eds.), *The Sage handbook of personality theory and assessment personality measurement and testing (volume 2)* (pp. 135–159). Thousand Oaks, CA: Sage; Chernyshenko, O. S. & Stark, S. (2006). Sixteen Personality Factor Questionnaire (16PF). In Greenhaus, J. H. & Callanan, G. A. (Eds.), *Encyclopedia of career development* (pp. 743–746). Thousand Oaks, CA: Sage.
46 McCrae, R. R., Costa, P. T. & Martin, T. A. (2005). The NEO–PI–3: A more readable revised NEO Personality Inventory. *Journal of Personality Assessment*, *84*, 261–270.
47 Butcher, J. N. & Perry, J. N. (2006). Minnesota Multiphasic Personality Inventory-2 (MMPI-2). In Greenhaus, J. H. & Callanan, G. A. (Eds.), *Encyclopedia of career development* (pp. 505–507). Thousand Oaks, CA: Sage.
48 Ibid.
49 Donnay, D., Gough, H. & Bradley, P. (2002). *Technical brief for the CPI 260 instrument*. Mountain View, CA: Consulting Psychologists Press; Fuqua, D. R. & Newman, J. L. (2006). California Psychological Inventory. In Greenhaus, J. H. & Callanan, G. A. (Eds.), *Encyclopedia of career development* (pp. 57–58). Thousand Oaks, CA: Sage.

50 Ibid.
51 Converse, P. D. & Oswald, F. L. (2006). General Aptitude Test Battery (GATB). In Greenhaus, J. H. & Callanan, G. A. (Eds.), *Encyclopedia of career development* (pp. 331–333). Thousand Oaks, CA: Sage.
52 Baker, H. (2006). Armed Services Vocational Aptitude Battery (ASVAB). In Greenhaus, J. H. & Callanan, G. A. (Eds.), *Encyclopedia of career development* (pp. 25–26). Thousand Oaks, CA: Sage.
53 Leuty, M. E. & Hansen, J. C. (2006). Bennett Mechanical Comprehension Test. In Greenhaus, J. H. & Callanan, G. A. (Eds.), *Encyclopedia of career development* (p. 33). Thousand Oaks, CA: Sage.
54 Examples of assessments of work–life conflict, enrichment, and balance can be found respectively in Carlson, D. S., Kacmar, K.M. & Williams, L. J. (2000). Construction and initial validation of a multidimensional measure of work–family conflict. *Journal of Vocational Behavior*, *56*, 249–276; Carlson, D. S., Kacmar, K. M., Wayne, J. H. & Grzywacz, J. G. (2006). Measuring the positive side of the work–family interface: Development and validation of a work–family enrichment scale. *Journal of Vocational Behavior*, *68*, 131–164; Valcour, M. (2007). Work-based resources as moderators of the relationship between work hours and satisfaction with work–family balance. *Journal of Applied Psychology*, *92*, 1512–1523.
55 Harris-Bowlsbey, J. (2013). Computer-assisted career guidance systems: A part of NCDA history. *Career Development Quarterly*, *61*, 181–185; Khapova, S. N. & Wilderom, C. P. M. (2006). Computer-based career support systems. In Greenhaus, J. H. & Callanan, G. A. (Eds.), *Encyclopedia of career development* (pp. 191–193). Thousand Oaks, CA: Sage.
56 Baruch, Y. (2006). Organizational career management. In Greenhaus, J. H. & Callanan, G. A. (Eds.), *Encyclopedia of career development* (pp. 572–580). Thousand Oaks, CA: Sage.
57 Shivy, V. A. (2006). Career-planning workshops. In Greenhaus, J. H. & Callanan, G. A. (Eds.), *Encyclopedia of career development* (pp. 132–133). Thousand Oaks, CA: Sage.
58 Hoffman, B. J., Melchers, K. G., Blair, C. A., Kleinmann, M. & Ladd, R. T. (2011). Exercises and dimensions are the currency of assessment centers. *Personnel Psychology*, *64*, 351–395.
59 Woehr, D. J. (2006). Assessment centers. In Greenhaus, J. H. & Callanan, G. A. (Eds.), *Encyclopedia of career development* (pp. 27–31). Thousand Oaks, CA: Sage.
60 Jackson, D. J. R., Michaelides, G., Dewberry, C. & Kim, Y. (2016). Everything that you have ever been told about assessment center ratings is confounded. *Journal of Applied Psychology*, *101*, 976–994; International Taskforce on Assessment Center Guidelines (2015). Guidelines and ethical considerations for assessment center operations. *Journal of Management*, *41*, 1244–1273.
61 Prochaska, S. (2006). Three-hundred-sixty-degree (360°) evaluation. In Greenhaus, J. H. & Callanan, G. A. (Eds.), *Encyclopedia of career development* (pp. 807–810). Thousand Oaks, CA: Sage.
62 Kotter et al. (1978).
63 Lent, R. W. (2013). Career-life preparedness: Revisiting career planning and adjustment in the new workplace. *Career Development Quarterly*, *61*, 2–14.
64 Gabriel, A. S., Diefendorff, J. M., Chandler, M. M., Moran, C. M. & Greguras, G. J. (2014). The dynamic relationships of work affect and job satisfaction with perceptions of fit. *Personnel Psychology*, *67*, 389–420; Hardin, E. E. & Donaldson, J. R. (2014). Predicting job satisfaction: A new perspective on person–environment fit. *Journal of Counseling Psychology*, *61*, 634–640; Walsh, W. B. (2006). Person-environment fit (P-E Fit). In Greenhaus, J. H. & Callanan, G. A. (Eds.), *Encyclopedia of career development* (pp. 622–625). Thousand Oaks, CA: Sage; Bretz, R. D. & Judge, T. A. (1994). Person–organization fit and the theory of work adjustment: Implications for satisfaction, tenure, and career success. *Journal of Vocational Behavior*, *44*, 32–54.
65 Judge, T. A., Klinger, R. L. & Simon, L. S. (2010). Time is on my side: Time, general mental ability, human capital, and extrinsic career success. *Journal of Applied Psychology*, *95*, 92–107; Wilk, S. L., Desmaris, L. B. & Sackett, P. R. (1995). Gravitation to jobs commensurate with ability: Longitudinal and cross-sectional tests. *Journal of Applied Psychology*, *80*, 79–85.
66 Ramarajan, L. & Reid, E. (2013). Shattering the myth of separate worlds: Negotiating nonwork identities at work. *Academy of Management Review*, *38*, 621–644.
67 Boswell, W. R., Zimmerman, R. D. & Swider, B. W. (2012). Employee job search: Toward an understanding of search context and search objectives. *Journal of Management*, *38*, 129–163; Blustein, D. L. (2011). A relational theory of working. *Journal of Vocational Behavior*, *79*, 1–17.
68 Bublitz, S. T. & Levine, J. D. (2006). Occupational classification systems. In Greenhaus, J. H. & Callanan, G. A. (Eds.), *Encyclopedia of career development* (pp. 554–558). Thousand Oaks, CA: Sage.

69 Cosca, T. & Emmel, A. (2010). Revising the Standard Occupational Classification system for 2010. *Monthly Labor Review*, *133*, 32–41.
70 Ibid.
71 Ibid.
72 Allen, M. T., Tsacoumis, S. & McCloy, R. A. (2011). *Updating occupational ability profiles with O*NET content model descriptors*. Alexandria, VA: Human Resources Research Organization; Smith, T. J. & Campbell, C. (2006). The structure of O*NET occupational values. *Journal of Career Assessment*, *14*, 437–448; Hartman, R. O. (2006). Occupational Information Network (O*NET). In Greenhaus, J. H. & Callanan, G. A. (Eds.), *Encyclopedia of career development* (pp. 559–560). Thousand Oaks, CA: Sage; Eggerth, D. E., Bowles, S. B., Tunick, R. H. & Andrew, M. E. (2005). Convergent validity of O*NET Holland code classifications. *Journal of Career Assessment*, *13*, 150–168.
73 Gregory, C. & Lewis, P. (2016). *Linking client assessment profiles to O*NET® Occupational Profiles within the O*NET Interest Profiler Short Form and Mini Interest Profiler (Mini-IP)*. Raleigh, NC: National Center for O*NET Development.
74 Hartman, R. O. (2006). Occupational outlook handbook. In Greenhaus, J. H. & Callanan, G. A. (Eds.), *Encyclopedia of career development* (pp. 560–561). Thousand Oaks, CA: Sage.
75 Sugalski, T. D. & Greenhaus, J. H. (1986). Career exploration and goal setting among managerial employees. *Journal of Vocational Behavior*, *29*, 102–114.
76 Greenhaus, J. H. & Sklarew, N. D. (1981). Some sources and consequences of career exploration. *Journal of Vocational Behavior*, *18*, 1–12.
77 Callanan, G. A. & Benzing, C. (2004). Assessing the role of internships in the career-oriented employment of graduating college students. *Education + Training*, *46*, 77–83.
78 Kuncel, N. R., Ones, D. S. & Sackett, P. R. (2015). Individual differences as predictors of work, educational and broad life outcomes. *Personality and Individual Differences*, *49*, 331–336.

6 Applications of the Career Management Model

Goals, Strategies, and Appraisal

In this chapter, we focus on career goal-setting, career strategy development, and career appraisal. As in the previous chapter, we will stress the pragmatic application of the career management model. Additional learning exercises are provided in the Appendix at the end of this chapter to help the reader develop and practice key career management skills. We also offer guidelines for effective goal-setting, strategy development, and career appraisal.

Career Goal-Setting

We all know or have heard stories of individuals who declared that they were going to be a millionaire by the time they were 30. Or perhaps we know someone who expressed a strong desire to become a senior executive of a corporation, or a top trial lawyer, or a surgeon, or a master carpenter. Most children begin projecting careers for themselves at young ages—"I'm going to be a police officer" or "I'm going to be a ballet star." Even employees on the verge of retirement often set plans to open their own business or perhaps get involved with some type of volunteer work.

The common theme in these examples is the setting, however tentative or ill-defined, of a career goal. A goal has been defined as the object or aim of one's actions. The usefulness of goal-setting is based on the belief that goals regulate human action.[1] Goals can affect behavior and performance in a number of ways.[2] First, they can spur high levels of effort that lead to attainment. Second, they can give focus or direction to effort because a specific goal provides a particular target toward which to strive.[3] Third, goals can produce high levels of persistence on a task. Fourth, a specific goal can help one develop a useful strategy for accomplishing the task. Finally, because of their concrete nature, goals provide opportunities for feedback on how well one is progressing. We define a career goal as *a desired career-related outcome that a person intends to attain.*

Even with its acknowledged positive attributes, one can question, especially in this era of non-permanent employment and economic uncertainty, whether career goal-setting is still a relevant exercise.[4] Some scholars have argued that with the current unsettled environment, goal-setting is futile at best, and harmful at worst. Under this view, the work world is seen as so uncertain that setting any kind of goal is useless, with the person setting the goal subject to possible bitterness and disappointment. Further, it could be argued that career goals promote rigidity in terms of actions and strategies, when what is really needed is flexibility and "boundarylessness" in being able to pursue other options or career directions.

In our view, career goal-setting is, in most cases, a useful and productive process. As we noted, goals provide direction and they serve as a benchmark against which progress can be measured. In addition, the presence of a career goal, in and of itself, should not cause inflexibility in the management of one's career. The career goal is simply a descriptive target toward which one aims; it does not specify how one gets to the desired end-state. Further, goals can, and should, change as conditions dictate.

Even though career goals have beneficial aspects, there are times when the setting of goals could be counterproductive. Later in this chapter we will discuss how *not* setting career goals is an appropriate response when a person does not have sufficient knowledge to make an informed decision.

With the preceding introduction as background, this section will examine several components of career goals, discuss the career goal-setting process, and provide a set of guidelines for effective goal-setting.

Components of Career Goals

A career goal can be viewed in two fundamental ways: by its conceptual and operational components and by its time dimension.

Conceptual Goal versus Operational Goal

A *conceptual* career goal summarizes the nature of the work experiences one intends to attain without specifying a particular job or position. It should reflect the person's significant values, interests, personality, abilities, and lifestyle preferences. For example, an individual's conceptual goal may be to hold a marketing job that involves extensive research and analysis, offers a great deal of responsibility, is broad and varied in pace, requires interaction with a variety of clients, does not chronically interfere with family and personal commitments, and is situated in a small, growth-oriented company in a warm weather climate. This conceptual goal addresses the nature of the task, interpersonal and physical settings, and total lifestyle concerns. The conceptual career goal should also take into account the intrinsic enjoyment one derives from goal-related experiences. In this sense, conceptual goals are appropriate to the extent to which their accomplishment permits a person to engage in enjoyable, fulfilling, and satisfying work activities; use his or her valued talents at work; and experience a satisfying lifestyle.

On the other hand, an *operational* career goal is the translation of a conceptual goal into a specific job or position. An operational career goal often embodies an *instrumental* element in the sense that the accomplishment of the operational goal can lead to (or is instrumental in) the attainment of a subsequent goal or goals. In the example described above, the operational goal may be to attain the position of marketing research manager at Company X, and the attainment of the goal of marketing manager may help the person to achieve his or her next goal of vice-president of marketing. For another individual, an operational goal might be to remain in his or her current position for the foreseeable future. It is important to realize that an operational goal is simply a vehicle for meeting an underlying conceptual goal. And it is helpful for career goals to be stated both in conceptual and in operational terms.

Short-Term versus Long-Term Career Goals

Career goals have a time dimension in that they can be distinguished between a short-term and long-term focus. Of course, what is considered short versus long is rather arbitrary. However, a short-term goal is usually thought to have a more immediate focus, perhaps

Table 6.1 Short-Term and Long-Term Goals for an Assistant Human Resource Manager

	Short-Term Goal	*Long-Term Goal*
Conceptual	More responsibility for administering human resources operation. Broad exposure to all facets of human resources. More interaction with line management.	Involvement in human resource planning activities. Involvement in corporate long-range planning. Involvement in policy development and implementation.
Operational	Manager of Human Resources within 1–3 years.	Director of Corporate Human Resources within 3–7 years.

one to three years, whereas a long-term goal is generally considered to have a time frame of *three to seven years.* Table 6.1 illustrates hypothetical short-term and long-term goals for an assistant manager in a human resources department. Notice that the conceptual goals focus on responsibilities and opportunities to acquire skills, whereas the operational goals identify specific jobs or positions.

Development of Long-Term and Short-Term Conceptual Goals

Ideally, the first step in setting a career goal is to identify a long-term conceptual goal. As an outgrowth of the self-exploration process, the long-term conceptual goal takes into account the person's values, interests, abilities, and expectations and should reflect the themes that were derived from self-exploration. It should, therefore, touch on job duties, degree of autonomy, type and frequency of interaction with other people, the physical environment, and lifestyle concerns. A long-term conceptual goal is, in effect, a projection of one's preferred work environment into a specific three- to seven-year timeframe. Ask yourself what type of job duties, activities, rewards, and responsibilities you would like to experience in the longer-term future.

Next, consider a short-term conceptual goal. Remember, the short-term conceptual goal should support the long-term one. To derive a short-term goal from a long-term goal, you should ask the following kinds of questions: What type of work experiences will prepare me to attain the long-term goal? What talents need to be developed or refined? What type of visibility is useful to reach a subsequent goal? These questions raise strategic issues. That is, the decision to pursue a particular short-term goal because of its value in attaining the long-term goal is an illustration of a career strategy.

A short-term conceptual goal should represent the qualities one hopes to express in work. Quite apart from its value as a stopping point, it must be viewed in terms of its capacity to provide important personal rewards, interesting and meaningful tasks, and the possibility of a desired lifestyle. As with the long-term goal, a short-term conceptual goal should be consistent with the significant elements of one's preferred work environment. For example, as shown in Table 6.1, the assistant human resource manager's short-term conceptual goal involves gaining more responsibility, exposure, and interaction as a means to fulfill the long-term conceptual goal of being involved in long-range planning and the implementation of human resource and corporate strategies.

Development of Long-Term and Short-Term Operational Goals

An operational goal is the translation of a conceptual goal into a specific job or position. Environmental exploration is required to convert conceptual goals into operational ones: What specific occupation (or job or organization) will provide an opportunity to meet your significant values, interests, abilities, and lifestyle requirements (i.e., your conceptual goal)?

There is no automatic formula that can (or should) dictate the selection of an operational goal. Your judgment (with input from trusted others) about the desirability and practicality of each operational goal should be your guide. You should, however, attempt to estimate the likelihood that an operational goal will enable you to satisfy the significant elements of your conceptual goal. For example, as shown in Table 6.1, the assistant human resource manager's short- and long-term operational goals involving upward movement in title in the human resources department are designed to allow for the attainment of greater responsibility and the exertion of greater influence in setting corporate policy (the conceptual goals). Thus, by examining these estimates for one or more operational goals, you can begin to assess the appropriateness of each operational goal.

The conversion of a goal from conceptual to operational terms clearly cannot be conducted in a vacuum. Instead, extensive information is required to assess the activities and rewards associated with each operational goal. This information cannot come simply from introspection. The individual needs data, much of which can be provided by the employer or potential employer. The role of the employer in providing such assistance is treated in subsequent chapters. Through the career appraisal process (discussed later in this chapter), the accomplishment or non-accomplishment of a goal can serve as an additional piece of career-related information.

Is a Long-Term Career Goal Necessary?

The goal-setting process assumes it is possible to develop long-term conceptual and operational goals. However, it is not always feasible to project three to seven years into the future with any sense of accuracy or confidence. In such cases, the person should attempt to formulate at least a partial conceptual goal, even if it is somewhat vague and even if it cannot be associated with a specific operational goal at the present time. Consider the following example:

> Jose, who is 28 years old, hopes to work in an environment where he can help others, work with clients as individuals and in group settings, and develop educational programs for the community, all in a setting where weekend and evening work could be kept to a minimum. This constitutes his long-term conceptual goal.
>
> Extensive environmental exploration indicates that a position in social work will likely enable Jose to achieve his conceptual goal. This long-term operational goal (to become a social worker) is admittedly vague, but the vagueness is appropriate at the present time. What type of social work position is most suitable for him? Should he work with children, adults, or a wide range of age groups? Should he work in a hospital, a school, a mental health clinic, or industry? At this time in the career planning process, these factors are unknowns.
>
> As vague as his long-term goal is, it can enable Jose to develop an appropriate short-term conceptual goal: to acquire the relevant education, experiences, and credentials to become a qualified social worker. His short-term operational goal is equally relevant: to obtain a master's degree in social work within two to three years.

Jose's experiences illustrate that one does not always have to develop a highly specific and elaborate long-term goal to develop a sensible short-term goal. It is important to think through the long-term future, develop a sense (however tentative) of the work and non-work experiences that would contribute to a desired lifestyle, and develop a short-term goal that is most consistent with this future, however hazy.

One can think of many situations in which a long-term goal is vague or uncertain. A mechanical engineer does not know whether she would like to remain in an engineering position or move into general management within five years. An accountant does not know whether he should remain at the firm in which he currently works or start his own small CPA practice. An upper-level manager is uncertain whether the rewards of being a company president outweigh the costs. The engineer, the accountant, and the manager may not have formulated clear, certain long-term goals at this point, but they will be better able to identify short-term goals and appropriate strategies if they examine the long-term future and alternative options than if they have not given any serious thought to such issues.

Learning Exercise 5 is included in the Appendix at the end of this chapter. It provides an opportunity to practice developing career goals. Although you may examine Learning Exercise 5 at this time, it is recommended that you finish reading Chapter 6 before beginning the exercise.

Overcoming Obstacles to Goal-Setting: A Set of Guidelines

Like career exploration, the goal-setting process is not without obstacles. Ultimately, the quality of a career goal depends on whether the achievement of the goal is compatible with the individual's preferred work environment and whether the goal can be realistically attained. Listed below are a number of obstacles to effective goal-setting and suggestions for overcoming them.

Goals that Belong to Someone Else

The achievement of a career goal is meaningless if the goal does not meet your needs and values, if the tasks are not interesting to you, and if the talents needed to be successful are not possessed and valued by you. It is your work, your career, and your life. Yet some people seem to develop career goals to please someone else—a parent, a professor, a spouse, or a boss. They place little value on meeting their own needs and rely on others to decide what is appropriate for them. In what is probably an unconscious process, such people, in effect, say, "I'm not important, I don't know what's best for me," or "I don't really deserve to get my own needs met." Ultimately, such people may choose occupations or jobs that do not take advantage of their own abilities and that are not personally interesting or rewarding. In the long run, such goals, even if accomplished, will likely produce frustration and alienation rather than fulfillment and growth.

The solution to this problem is twofold. First, people must be in touch with their own values, interests, abilities, and lifestyle preferences. Second, they must recognize the importance of meeting goals that are compatible with these qualities. Regarding the first point, virtually all self-assessment procedures provide opportunities for awareness of personal characteristics. Autobiographical statements, value clarification exercises, and analyses of life experiences hopefully enable the individual to separate personal abilities and desires from others' wishes and to separate personal values from society's expectations.

The more difficult task is acting constructively on this awareness. Career-planning programs can go only so far. Perhaps the ultimate answer is feeling good enough about yourself to pursue goals that are relevant to your own personal aspirations and values. Discussions with family, friends, and colleagues about the importance of meeting personal needs would be a significant first step.

Goals that Exclude Total Lifestyle Concerns

Many people pursue a career goal without regard for its impact on other parts of their lives. It is only after marital difficulties or a personal tragedy that some people recognize the relationship between work life and private life. Many people in midcareer become particularly aware of the trade-offs between work responsibilities and family or personal activities. Nevertheless, work and nonwork roles interact at all phases of a person's life.

The effective career manager anticipates the interrelationships between work and nonwork lives and sets career goals consistent with a desired total lifestyle. Although some career planning programs include considerations of lifestyle, it is still easy to focus so narrowly on job challenges, rewards, and prestige that one's family life and religious, leisure, and community roles are virtually ignored. It takes a conscious effort to retain a total lifestyle perspective in career goal-setting.

Goals that Fail to Take into Account One's Current Job

A career goal (either short-term or long-term) need not involve job mobility. Any particular job is merely a vehicle for the satisfaction of more basic values (i.e., the conceptual goal). If goals are first stated in conceptual terms, the current job's capacity to meet these values can be examined thoroughly. Often, successful career management is based on understanding the conceptual goal and the ability to use the current job to achieve that goal.

On too many occasions, however, individuals focus so narrowly on pursuing other jobs that they ignore their current job as a source of career growth and satisfaction. This myopic preoccupation with job mobility could be a serious problem in today's work environment where promotions or lateral moves are in short supply or where such moves, if attained, could have negative consequences for family or personal life (e.g., where another job requires relocation or extensive travel). A number of approaches to career planning include an examination of the ways in which one's current job can be improved, perhaps through increased responsibility or a greater variety of projects. This requires a constructive interaction between the career planner and his or her supervisor. This is a healthy focus that can be usefully incorporated into many career management activities.

Goals that are Overly Vague

It is well understood that specific goals are generally more useful than vague ones. Because they present a particular target toward which to strive, specific goals can direct one's efforts more efficiently than vague goals. In addition, a specific goal offers a greater opportunity for feedback because progress toward the goal is easier to detect.

Consider the vague conceptual goal "to do things that are interesting to me." It would probably be more useful to specify what kinds of activities are considered personally interesting; for example, working with detailed statistics, writing reports, or meeting frequently with colleagues and clients. A set of specific conceptual goal elements can be more easily translated into an operational goal than a vaguely stated conceptual goal. Moreover, stating a conceptual goal in specific terms forces a person away from generalizations and toward a deeper understanding of his or her aspirations.

There are also advantages to setting a specific operational goal. It is difficult to compare a vague operational goal to one's conceptual goal. To "move into marketing" is probably too vague to be helpful because different marketing jobs may match one's conceptual goal to varying degrees. An operational goal "to become a market research analyst in the consumer goods industry" is more specific and more useful because its connection to the underlying conceptual goal is more explicit and the path to goal attainment is more easily determined. As noted earlier, however, it might not be possible or desirable to develop a highly specific long-term goal in many circumstances. Perhaps the litmus test on whether a goal is specific enough is to determine whether the goal provides enough information to guide your behavior in a useful way.

Preoccupation with Instrumental Elements of an Operational Goal

Despite its many advantages, a specific operational goal can create tunnel vision. In the quest to accomplish a specific goal, people could forget why they wanted to reach the goal in the first place. They may also become so committed to the goal that they resist new information that runs counter to the value of the goal. Perhaps most important, striving for a sequence of goals, each of which is designed to accomplish a subsequent goal, can rob people of the enjoyment of the here-and-now. In effect, people can be driven and tyrannized by the desire to reach some end-state. Preoccupation with the destination, in other words, can make the voyage joyless.

This possibility presents a dilemma. On the one hand, an operational career goal can enhance future career growth and satisfaction. However, focusing exclusively on attaining a future operational goal can, in some circumstances, detract from the intrinsic satisfaction of the present. Perhaps the solution is to maintain an equal concern for the present and the future, enjoying current work experiences and at the same time targeting future experiences one wants to attain.

Consider the case of an engineering school graduate who, early in his career, set his sights on the presidency of a large manufacturing organization. Every job assignment, every promotion, every transfer was chosen for its instrumental value. His commitment to this operational goal was so strong that he could not allow himself the luxury of reexamining its importance. Nor could he stop and ask whether all of the intermediate goals and accomplishments were enjoyable, satisfying, and fulfilling, or whether they played havoc with his family or personal life. Mortgaging the present for the future is a risky business.

A healthy concern for the enjoyable, intrinsic quality of career goals is therefore an essential part of career management. This requires an ongoing focus on conceptual goals. There is nothing inherently satisfying about a company presidency or any other operational goal. The tasks, activities, opportunities, and rewards associated with an operational goal, however, can be intrinsically satisfying. A simultaneous concern for present satisfaction and future direction is critical. This can only come from an ongoing assessment of oneself and the environment.

Goals that are Too Easy or Too Difficult

Feelings of psychological success, which are essential for individual development and satisfaction, are experienced when accomplishing tasks that are challenging and meaningful.[5]

Therefore, career goals that are too easy are unlikely to provide a real sense of accomplishment and success. Whether a goal is directed toward one's current job (e.g., to improve in certain areas) or attaining a different job, it must be challenging enough so that the achievement of the goal produces feelings of real success.

However, goals that are too difficult are unlikely to be accomplished. As we saw with the Michele Terry case at the end of Chapter 4, the inability to reach a desired goal can bring a deep sense of frustration and failure. There is a fine line between a goal that is challenging and one that is virtually impossible. Detecting the fine line requires insight into one's own talents, the ability to develop new talents, and an understanding of the opportunities and obstacles in the work environment. Therefore, when selecting an extremely difficult goal, one should understand the risks involved and be willing to assume those risks.

Inflexible Career Goals

Although goal-setting is intended to be a flexible process, flexibility is often lost in practice. For one thing, as we noted earlier, people can become highly committed to a course of action to which they have devoted significant time, energy, and emotional involvement.[6] Second, the orientation toward the future built into goal-setting tends to emphasize the end result and make it an "objective reality" that an individual might find difficult to question. Moreover, because change can be hard for most people, a thorough reexamination of career goals and a possible change in career direction could be particularly threatening.

Yet as we've stressed previously, flexible goals are essential to effective career management and are at the heart of the boundaryless career perspective. Because the work milieu and people inevitably change over time, goals that have been appropriate in the past might no longer be valid at present or in the future. In today's world of economic uncertainty and rapid technological change, the setting of a concrete long-term career goal might not be advisable. Indeed, because of employment uncertainty in nearly all companies, individuals may find flexibility in the setting and changing of career goals to be a more appropriate action. For example, jobs and career paths may disappear or change as organizations restructure or develop new strategic plans, thereby leaving inflexible employees out in the cold. Similarly, technological and structural changes can give birth to new career routes that may require revisions in an individual's career goals.[7] In the broadest sense, people need to learn from their work and life experiences so that career goals can remain relevant and realistic. Career appraisal, discussed in a later section of this chapter, is the process by which learning and feedback provide flexibility and adaptability to career management.

Inability to Set Career Goals: Career Indecision

Although we have suggested that career goal-setting is a critical part of the career management process, for many people, both students and employees, the selection of a career goal is a difficult (or even impossible) task. Individuals are considered career undecided if they have either not established a career goal or if they have set a career goal over which they experience significant uncertainty or discomfort.[8] Because the selection of a career goal is viewed as a paramount task in the career management process, one would presume that the presence of career indecision would be both unsettling and detrimental to career success. As this section will show, however, career indecision should not be viewed as necessarily inappropriate, just as career decidedness (i.e., the selection of a career goal) should not be viewed as necessarily appropriate. It has been estimated that 10–30 percent of college students could be classified as undecided, but in many cases this state of career indecision is part of the normal developmental process.[9]

Given the importance of understanding career indecision, this section will discuss three related topics: the underlying causes and sources of career indecision, the existence of different types of career indecision, and the possible actions that could be taken to allow individuals to become career decided.

Causes and Sources of Career Indecision

Research on the career indecision of high school and college students found a variety of underlying reasons why individuals could not select a specific occupation or career goal.[10] In general, this research identified four sources of career indecision: lack of information about oneself, lack of information about the work environment, lack of self-confidence in decision-making, and the presence of psychological conflicts. Research conducted on managers and professionals identified seven sources of indecision that were somewhat more refined than those listed above.[11] Put differently, managers and professionals can be career undecided for one or more of the following reasons;

1. **Lack of self-information** reflects the individual's insufficient understanding of his or her interests, strengths, values, and lifestyle preferences.
2. **Lack of internal work information** reflects insufficient knowledge of career opportunities and job possibilities within one's current organization.
3. **Lack of external work information** reflects insufficient knowledge of opportunities outside of one's organization, including other occupations, companies, and industries.
4. **Lack of decision-making self-confidence** reflects insufficient self-assurance in making career-related decisions.
5. **Decision-making fear and anxiety** reflects decisional paralysis resulting from fear and anxiety over making a career decision.
6. **Nonwork demands** reflect individual conflicts between personal career desires and nonwork (e.g., family) pressures.
7. **Situational constraints** reflect individual career constraints produced by financial strain, age, and years invested in a given career direction.

In general, the first three sources—lack of self-information and the lack of information on the internal and external work environments—reinforce the discussion in Chapter 5, which stated that an awareness of self and the work environment is an essential requirement in career decision-making. In contrast to the information-related sources that could be resolved with increased exploration, the lack of self-confidence and decision-making fear and anxiety may reflect more deep-seated personality dispositions and psychological conditions. Finally, nonwork demands and situational constraints could place limitations on personal career choices and desires and may either impair the setting of a career goal or cause substantial uncertainty or discomfort over a selected goal. Exhibit 6.1 contains examples of items adapted from a more extensive instrument that can help you assess where you stand on the seven career indecision sources.[12]

Types of Career Indecision

Past research on the career decision-making of students indicated two forms of career indecision.[13] "Being undecided" was viewed as stemming from limited experience and knowledge, whereas "being indecisive" was seen as reflecting a more permanent

Lack of Self-Information	"I know exactly what I want most from a job (e.g., a lot of money, a great deal of responsibility, travel)."*
Lack of Internal Work Information	"I have a good understanding of where my organization is heading in the next 5 to 10 years."*
Lack of External Work Information	"I have a good grasp of what career opportunities might exist for me with a different employer."*
Lack of Self-Confidence	"I am confident that I can make career decisions that are right for me."*
Decision-Making Fear and Anxiety	"The idea of making a career-related decision frightens me."
Nonwork Demands	"Family pressures conflict with the direction that I would like my career to follow."
Situational Constraints	"The number of years I have invested in my current career prevents me from considering other careers that hold more appeal."

Notes

Sources identified in Callanan, G. A. & Greenhaus, J. H. (1990). The career indecision of managers and professionals: Development of a scale and test of a model. *Journal of Vocational Behavior, 37*, 79–103. Items are scored on a scale of 1 (Strongly Disagree) to 5 (Strongly Agree). The asterisk (*) indicates that the item is reverse scored.

Exhibit 6.1 Selected Items for the Seven Sources of Career Indecision

inability to make a career decision. The "being undecided" type was later termed *developmental indecision*, while the "being indecisive" type was termed *chronic indecision*. The study of managers and professionals previously mentioned also found support for the existence of developmental and chronic indecision.[14] Developmentally undecided employees were younger, had limited knowledge about the internal and external work environments, and experienced extensive nonwork demands. The chronically undecided group was comparatively older than their developmentally undecided counterparts. In addition, they lacked sufficient self-information, had lower self-confidence, displayed more extensive decision-making fear and anxiety, and experienced extensive situational constraints.

This research also isolated two types of career-decided managers; that is, managers who had selected a career goal.[15] Borrowing from the typology developed by Irving Janis and Leon Mann,[16] the researchers isolated a hypervigilant type and a vigilant type of career decidedness. The hypervigilant group had selected a career goal, but their profiles indicated that the decision might have been made with insufficient information and/or was hastily contrived due to pressure and anxiety. On the other hand, the vigilant group had likewise selected a career goal, but their profile showed that the decision was made in a well-informed manner with low levels of stress and anxiety.

Brief examples might help clarify the differences among the four types:

Annie is a 35-year-old internal audit manager for a consumer products company located in New York. After nearly 12 years with the firm she is dissatisfied with her present responsibilities and believes her chances for further advancement within the organization are limited. Moreover, the "rat race" of the big city has started to wear

(*Continued*)

on her and her family. Consequently, Annie is not really sure what she wants to do with her career. Annie has taken the Myers-Briggs Type Indicator and other assessment instruments that show she has an entrepreneurial personality. In fact, managing her own business has quite an appeal for Annie. She has also begun to look at a couple of interesting business ventures back in her home state of Mississippi.

Sanjay is a 27-year-old sales representative for a paper products company. He has held four different jobs in the six years since he graduated from college with a degree in business administration. Sanjay cannot seem to set goals for himself, and he still is not sure about what type of career he should pursue. Making decisions has always been difficult for Sanjay because he becomes anxious and "tenses up" whenever the need to make a commitment arises. Right now, Sanjay is unsure of how to go about selecting a longer-term career goal, but he is certain that his current sales position is not for him.

Jennifer is 26 and has just completed law school. Her whole family is excited about her future career as a lawyer. Her father, who is an attorney himself, is especially pleased that his daughter has decided to follow in his footsteps. Unfortunately, amid the euphoria and hoopla over her graduation, Jennifer is beginning to think that she may have been prematurely "pushed" into selecting the legal profession as a career. Jennifer's parents put undue pressure on her to enter law school. They were visibly upset when her two older brothers decided not to pursue legal careers, and Jennifer did not wish her parents to be disappointed again. Because of her quick selection of law as her vocation, Jennifer never really explored her own interests and values and didn't look at other possible occupations. At present, her life is full of stress because she is concerned about her future happiness as a lawyer.

At age 48, Dan is as happy as he has ever been. As a high school math teacher, Dan enjoys the chance to work with young people and he really does like teaching such subjects as algebra and geometry. Although Dan has been teaching for only four years, he is pleased that he made the difficult decision to get out of his former career as a systems analyst. Dan is certain that his satisfaction with teaching is due to the painstaking and thorough job he did of selecting it as his career goal. Dan took the time to reexamine his interests and values. He knew he loved to work with numbers and apply logical thinking, but he also liked working with young people. With some exploration, he learned that the local school district had a shortage of qualified math teachers. After discussing his thoughts with his fiancée and receiving her encouragement, Dan decided to try to become a teacher. Once he received his teaching certificate, Dan was set. He hasn't regretted the move.

These four scenarios represent the different types of career indecision/decidedness. In the first case, Annie could be described as developmentally undecided because she doesn't have a career goal but is actively exploring her interests and opportunities. On the other hand, Sanjay could be considered chronically undecided given his ongoing inability to set career goals and his associated high level of anxiety. In the third case, Jennifer is representative of the hypervigilant decided type. Her decision to pursue a law career was made prematurely, and she did not consider her own interests, abilities, and talents. She chose to pursue the career that would please her parents instead of herself. Dan represents the vigilant type. His decision to pursue the teaching of math as his career goal was the product of a thorough assessment of his interests and lifestyle preferences, as well as the work environment.

As these examples show, the usefulness and appropriateness of setting a career goal depend on the circumstances. There are times when the selection of a career goal is beneficial (as with Dan), and there are times when it can be harmful (as with Jennifer). For an individual such as Annie, who lacks sufficient decision-making information, being developmentally undecided is appropriate, whereas being chronically undecided (as with Sanjay) is problematic. Career goals should not be set until the individual is sufficiently aware of self and the environment and is confident that the goal is capable of providing compatibility with personal qualities.

Possible Steps to Becoming Career Decided

As stated in Chapter 5, the key activity that precedes the setting of a career goal is exploration. Individuals should engage in various forms of career exploration to enhance awareness of themselves and their environment. This heightened awareness of self and environment should enable individuals to set realistic career goals that are compatible with their preferred work environment. Certainly, being developmentally undecided is beneficial as long as you are in the process of learning more about yourself and your environment. For those who tend to be chronically undecided, the accumulation of additional information may be helpful, but it might not be enough to allow the selection of a career goal. In the chronic case, individuals must find ways to break the "paralysis" brought on by the high degrees of unproductive fear and anxiety and situational constraints. Career counseling programs and other activities that reduce debilitating stress and anxiety and improve self-confidence could prove useful in overcoming chronic indecision. Other career planning activities as described in Chapter 5, such as career workshops and the informal sharing of personal feelings and beliefs, could serve to reduce stress and promote exploration behavior and career goal-setting. It should be noted that the complete elimination of anxiety and stress is not necessarily advisable because some degree of anxiety or stress may in fact facilitate career exploration behavior.[17]

For those who are decided on a career goal, the key consideration is whether the selection was made in a well-informed fashion (the vigilant type), or was conducted in a tense and hasty manner (the hypervigilant type). The premature selection of, and commitment to, an inappropriate career goal could have unfavorable consequences, such as negative work attitudes and extensive life stress.[18] Hypervigilant individuals should be encouraged to slow down and consider whether their choices are truly consistent with their abilities, interests, and aspirations.

In summary, career indecision is a multifaceted state that can be a function of an individual's informational needs, personality, and environmental circumstances.[19] The important lesson to be learned from the discussion on career indecision is that the selection of a career goal is not positive or negative per se, but is dependent on the circumstances. Being undecided about one's career because of a lack of sufficient information (i.e., developmentally undecided) is appropriate. In contrast, being career decided but ignoring one's true interests and talents, could prove to be a source of dissatisfaction for the individual and ultimately harm the organization as well. In an ideal sense, all career decision-making should be performed in a "vigilant" fashion, wherein the career goal is selected with substantial knowledge and awareness. In this regard, universities and employers should strive to offer programs that encourage vigilant career decision-making.

Implications of Goal-Setting for Organizations and Their Employees

Employees who set career goals in a vigilant manner—based upon insights into themselves and their alternatives as well as a balanced concern for their present and future—should have the greatest likelihood of achieving productive and satisfying careers.[20] Organizations can promote a vigilant approach to career goal-setting in a number of ways.

Facilitate Self-Awareness

Reasonable and appropriate career goals are unlikely to be developed without a foundation of accurate information regarding one's talents, values, interests, and lifestyle preferences.[21] Organizations can promote self-awareness by providing mentoring, career counseling, and career planning activities. However, considerable self-insight can also be derived from everyday work experiences within organizations. Effective performance appraisal and feedback systems, education and training activities, temporary assignments, job changes, and an expansion of the current job can all serve as potential learning experiences. Employees can gain from these activities most effectively when they have an opportunity to discuss the insights they have acquired with other knowledgeable people, especially their own manager or a mentor.

Facilitate an Awareness of the Environment

Extensive information about the environment is necessary to set realistic and appropriate career goals. What rewards are associated with a market research position? How much travel is required for a product manager in this company? What skill areas are most critical for success as a sales manager? What is this company going to look like in one to two years or in three to five years?

An organization can promote an awareness of the environment by providing employees with access to key information about alternative jobs in the organization, such as duties, responsibilities, required skills, travel, and time commitment pressures. This requires that the organization itself understand the *behavioral* requirements of different jobs and career fields so that this information can be provided to employees. In addition, the organization should communicate its mission, structure, and culture to employees who are trying to determine the presence of a fit between the organization's needs and their needs.

In today's decentralized environment, it is likely that many employees will move outside their functional areas for their next jobs. Networking—either through formal or informal corporate sponsorship—encourages employees to broaden their horizons with regard to setting future career goals. An alternative is to provide exposure through ad hoc groups or taskforces as well as temporary positions or lateral moves. These opportunities provide a flexible approach for employees to learn about other areas and functions of the organization.

Encourage Experimentation

Much learning about oneself and the environment comes from active experimentation. People can learn a great deal from trying on new roles. A financial analyst or a salesperson contemplating a move into management should be encouraged to incorporate managerial responsibilities into his or her current job, perhaps through a special assignment or project. Experimentation can also take the form of seeking information from previously unfamiliar sources. Speaking with a counselor about a career dilemma, joining a support group for newly transferred employees, attending a seminar on marketing in the financial services industry, or enrolling in a graduate course or program can all stimulate an employee to think about his or her future from a different perspective.

Respond to Chronic Indecision

Our prior suggestions are based on a rather critical assumption that the undecided employee simply needs to learn more about himself or herself, the environment, or alternative courses of action; that is, the employee is "developmentally" undecided. Perhaps recent changes in an employee's work situation, family pressures, or career interests triggered a reevaluation of his or her future. Or changes in the individual's personal life (aging and feelings of mortality), work environment (merger or acquisition, change in corporate strategy), or family environment (empty nest, spouse retirement) have produced major uncertainties regarding career aims. Career indecision in the face of such changes suggests that an adaptive, developmental process is helpful in achieving career decidedness.

However, as noted earlier, some employees may be indecisive about making a career decision because of an extraordinarily high level of anxiety and stress surrounding the decision-making process. Managers should learn to recognize when indecision about a career direction represents a kind of chronic indecisiveness and paralysis. Observations about prior career moves might be helpful in this respect. In addition, discussions with the employee about his or her career attitudes might reveal a considerable degree of stress about making a career decision. The employee might be reluctant to make any career decision for fear of making a poor one. The employee might claim that more information is needed to make a decision (more testing, more counseling, more coursework), when in reality no amount of additional information is likely to move the employee closer to a decision.

This is not to suggest that managers become therapists, but rather that they probe the basis for employees' indecision and recommend appropriate courses of action. For example, because chronically undecided employees tend to be anxious and lack confidence in their decision-making, they might benefit from career counseling on a one-to-one basis as a supplement to company-sponsored workshops. Because chronically undecided individuals may also manifest high levels of life stress, a critical aspect of counseling is to determine whether part of the problem involves a need for a more comprehensive form of support, such as financial management skills or stress reduction, before undertaking any career goal-setting. In short, simply providing more information to chronically undecided employees might not be enough.

Discourage Career Hypervigilance

Hypervigilant employees tend to make career decisions in a reactive mode without adequate time for reflection, preparation, and thinking through their options and alternatives. Often this results in a decision that is not compatible with the employee's values, talents, and interests, thereby setting up a cycle of dissatisfaction or failure. For such individuals, getting away from everyday pressures and concerns to have proper time to reflect is critical. Effective career management programs should help these employees distinguish conceptual and operational career goals and understand the importance of choosing goals that can meet personal values. As the employees reflect on what may be truly fitting choices and goals, some combination of seminars, workshops, computer-based programs, and individual mentoring may be especially useful.

Benefits to the Organization

While it might be desirable for employees to set realistic career goals, there has to be some tangible benefit for the organization to promote such activities. One major incentive for an organization to encourage career goal-setting is that its employees learn to take responsibility for their careers. A second advantage is that when employees become involved in career goal-setting they are likely to become more highly skilled and more useful to the organization.

Moreover, many career goal-setting programs include analyses of employees' skills not only by the individuals themselves but by their superiors and peers as well. Understanding how others view their strengths and weaknesses further encourages employees to improve, particularly when these views do not threaten their self-concept. Taking stock of one's plans can aid in determining what types of training and development activities are needed. Such activities should be viewed in a positive light as they frequently result in more highly skilled employees. And in the event of a downsizing or other reorganization, the employee has a skills portfolio to take along to another job or organization.

For these reasons, career goal-setting is often in the best interest of the employee and the organization. Although there are certainly risks to the individual (e.g., disappointment) and the organization (the potential loss of talented individuals), we would argue that the advantages justify the risks. As with any development program, support from the organization's top management is necessary for success. Of particular importance is the creation of a work climate where individuals feel safe enough to engage in career goal-setting. All too often in today's business environment, employees are not willing to openly voice an interest in career goal-setting out of a belief that showing an interest in future career plans calls into question their loyalty to their present position and boss. In other cases, senior executives make positive statements about career issues while managers ignore them in practice.

In our view, it is important for companies and their managers to show a strong commitment to continued employee development through career planning. Even under turbulent conditions, employees should be expected to consider options and alternatives. Often, however, managers believe that while they are encouraged to develop their employees, they themselves are forgotten. Therefore, it is important for organizations to promote career management across the various hierarchical levels of the organization. The best way to ensure this outcome is to incorporate subordinate career growth into each manager's reward system. In light of our previous discussion, the most appropriate criterion to apply is *not* whether the subordinate has set a career goal or is ready for a promotion but whether the subordinate is being encouraged to explore himself or herself and the environment and is being provided with useful feedback, guidance, and support.

Finally, it is important for organizational managers to recognize the need for consistency between the strategic needs of the company on the one hand and the career management practices used by the firm on the other. More precisely, an organization's business strategies and other competitive factors normally will dictate the type and hierarchical level of individuals who are employed. The career management practices described in this chapter can help fulfill these human resource needs by linking individual aspirations with organizational staffing responsibilities.

Knowledge of individual career goals can also aid senior organizational managers in the critical task of succession planning. Individuals with career goals that fit the demands of top management positions can be targeted and groomed for these posts. Thus, a company can take advantage of the embedded knowledge of its existing personnel by deploying them in areas and in jobs that mesh with individual aspirations in the form of career goals. Without knowing individual differences, organizations are apt to make unwarranted or haphazard job assignments.

In summary, we believe that organizations and their employees can benefit from well-designed and maintained career management programs. We have articulated how career goals that are the product of a thorough assessment of one's own interests, abilities, and lifestyle preferences, as well as an examination of the work environment, can produce positive work attitudes. We also stated that career goals that are set without benefit of this thorough assessment can be counterproductive. Organizations that implement career management programs to help individuals explore themselves and their work environment can reap rewards in the form of potentially more productive employees and a more efficient matching of employee desires with corporate human resource requirements. Chapter 14 provides a more extensive discussion on why organizations should establish human resource management systems that have a focus on the career management of their employees and also describes specific programs that can be offered.

Developing Career Strategies

The model of career management advocated in this book is, in large part, based on the idea that individuals must be adaptable and flexible in the actions they pursue and the changes they make in the management of their careers. It also reflects the boundaryless career notion that the "single" organizational career, with job security taken for granted, is an unlikely proposition.[22] Indeed, as we discussed in Chapter 1, careers are increasingly less certain, tend to be less permanent with low job security, and are dominated by mobility between firms rather than within one particular firm. Employees in the United States and other parts of the industrialized world who are just entering the workforce or who are early in their careers are likely to be employed by a wide variety of organizations over their work lives. With this environment as a backdrop, it becomes even more critical for individuals to be assertive in their career management. Specifically, individuals must be proactive in their career management by setting career goals and pursuing career strategies that give them the greatest chances of personal and professional success and satisfaction.

One important objective for the deployment of career strategies is to attain and maintain employability over the course of the career.[23] The importance of employability cannot be overemphasized. In fact, when reviewing career-related research over the past several decades, "employability" is the term with the highest degree of academic emphasis.[24] Employability is defined as "the capacity to control one's employment options through the creation, identification, and realization of career opportunities."[25] As such, it reflects an action-oriented, proactive, and adaptive approach to career management.[26] Employability requires individuals to enact various career strategies to ensure that they have the ability not only to find employment or reemployment quickly, but also to achieve their career goals.

We define a career strategy as any behavior, activity, or experience designed to help a person meet career goals.[27] A career strategy represents a conscious choice by an individual as to the type of investment he or she is willing to make in attempting to reach career objectives. Ideally, people pursue a particular career strategy based on the expectation that it will give them the opportunity to enhance employability, accomplish career goals, and attain career success and satisfaction. Thus, career strategies involve conscious individual choices as to which human capital investments to make and which to avoid.

Types of Career Strategies

There are a number of broad types of career strategies that individuals can use to enhance their chances of career success, fulfillment, and employability. The strategies include attaining competence in the current job, putting in extended work hours, developing new skills, developing and pursuing new mobility opportunities, gaining a mentor, building one's image and reputation, and engaging in organizational politics. Table 6.2 presents a summary of the career strategies.

Attaining competence in the current job is a basic and somewhat obvious career strategy because organizations make appraisal and promotion decisions, at least in part, on employees' performance in their present job. In addition, the skills acquired

Table 6.2 Major Career Strategies

I. **Attaining Competence in the Current Job**
Meaning: Effectively developing and using skills in one's current job to improve present and future employability.

II. **Putting in Extended Hours**
Meaning: Devoting considerable amounts of time, energy, and emotion to one's work role. It is often considered a contributor to competence in the present job. It might also interfere with family and personal life.

III. **Developing New Skills**
Meaning: Acquiring or enhancing work-related skills and abilities through education, training, and/or job experience. It is intended to help one's performance on one's current job or could be used on a future job.

IV. **Developing and Pursuing New Mobility Opportunities**
Meaning: Actions designed to have one's interests and aspirations known to others and to become aware of opportunities that are consistent with those aspirations, including self-nomination, networking, and the building of social capital.

V. **Gaining a Mentor**
Meaning: Actions designed to seek, establish and use relationships with a significant other to receive or provide information, guidance, support, and opportunities. Although a major function of the mentoring process is to receive (or give) information, the mentoring relationship goes beyond the mere exchange of information and has a deeper emotional meaning.

VI. **Building One's Image and Reputation**
Meaning: The attempt to communicate the appearance of acceptability, success, and/or potential for success. It also can include the acceptance and completion of high-profile assignments that build one's reputation within the organization.

VII. **Engaging in Organizational Politics**
Meaning: The attempt to use flattery, conformity, coalition, and trading of favors and influence as a means for attaining desired outcomes. It can include overt and covert actions, such as sabotage and other self-serving behaviors, that raise one's standing in the organization possibly at the expense of others.

or honed in one job might be essential for performance in another job either with one's current employer or with another organization. The concepts underlying the protean and boundaryless career philosophies make it necessary for individuals to have relevant skills at the times when those skills are required by employers. Focusing on developing abilities in a current job can improve an individual's chances for employability in the future.

Putting in extended hours either at work or when away from the work site is a popular career strategy, especially in the early career when an employee is proving himself or herself to a company. Working beyond normal hours can enhance performance in the current job and can signify to the organization that one is committed to the job and capable of taking on large volumes of work. This is not to suggest that extended work involvement is always necessary or even productive or useful. We all know of organizations where many employees are present evenings and weekends because it is expected, not necessarily because any real work gets accomplished. Putting in extended work hours can also result in negative consequences. Not only might they interfere with other important parts of life, such as family or community, but they can also impinge on the time employees have to disengage mentally from work for a while, which would enable them to recharge their batteries and recover from the stresses of their job.[28]

Developing new skills is a career strategy that involves the acquisition or enhancement of work abilities that either improve performance in the present job or will be required in a subsequent position. Michael Arthur and his colleagues refer to this career strategy as "knowing how."[29] They note that skill development can involve formal occupational training as well as experiential learning. Skill development can include such activities as participation in training seminars, degree or non-degree university programs, or attendance at a leadership development workshop. Employees also develop skills by acquiring additional responsibilities on their current job, by working with an experienced colleague, or by joining occupational associations that sponsor continuing education. In essence, a commitment to skill development and lifelong learning helps ensure that a person's work abilities and knowledge are kept relevant with present work demands and are transferable to other organizations.

Developing and pursuing new mobility opportunities is comprised of a number of more specific strategies that are designed to increase one's career options. As an example, self-nomination is a frequently observed strategy that involves the willingness to inform superiors of accomplishments, aspirations, and desired assignments. Self-nomination is intended to enhance one's visibility and exposure to those in more senior positions within the organization, which can bring recognition, special assignments, and sponsorship.

Another relevant activity that can facilitate career goal accomplishment and offer information on alternative employment opportunities is networking.[30] In their typology, Michael Arthur and his colleagues refer to this career strategy as "knowing whom."[31] Networking represents focused behavior on the part of the individual that takes place within and outside of one's current organization and involves the development, reciprocal cultivation, and utilization of various interpersonal relationships.[32] In terms of career management, networking entails the identification of, and communication with, a group or groups of relevant acquaintances, friends, co-workers, and industry participants who can provide information, advice, friendship, and support regarding career opportunities and overall individual development.[33] Individuals typically have access both to formal and informal networks that exist inside and outside of work organizations,[34] and entry into these networks can occur both through face-to-face contact and through online, Internet-based connections. The company normally sanctions formal networks within an organization, and their formation is based on a certain theme or a cohort of employees. For example, an organization could have a formal network for working parents or newly hired employees. In contrast, informal networks usually develop within organizations organically and can have a significant influence on the attitudes, behaviors, and career opportunities of those with access to the network.[35]

While participating in face-to-face internal and external networks is still an important strategy to develop new career mobility opportunities, the primary mechanisms for initiating and maintaining network connections in the contemporary world is through online means. Although there are innumerable Internet-based sites that allow for networking on a worldwide basis, the most well-known of these online providers are LinkedIn and Facebook. LinkedIn, which began in 2003 with a mere 4,500 members, today has a membership approaching 500 million individuals who live and work in nearly every country in the world.[36] LinkedIn allows users to create an online account profile that can easily be updated and can be seen by others within a specified network of other users who can best help them professionally.[37] LinkedIn also has a job search application (app) and other tools that allow users to look for employment opportunities based on job title, location, and specified keywords and also make personal connections with other users who work for a targeted company. Facebook, which was founded in 2004, is easily the most well-known Internet site that connects people from around the world. With more than one billion users, Facebook's mission is to "give people the power to share and make the world more open and connected."[38] As a networking tool, Facebook allows individual users to become connected to groups that are focused on specific industries, occupational interests, and particular companies.

In summary, developing new mobility opportunities has traditionally been seen in terms of progress within a specific organization, i.e., in terms of intra-organizational mobility. However, in today's environment, with the virtual elimination of the relational psychological contract between employer and employee, this strategy should be viewed more broadly. More precisely, individuals should work on cultivating opportunities both in the internal and in the external labor markets. Depending on one's career stage, actively seeking out opportunities in the external labor market can prove beneficial, especially in terms of mobility and advancement in compensation.[39]

Gaining a mentor as a career strategy has received considerable attention in recent years given its recognized importance in attaining career success and satisfaction. Mentoring is defined as relationships between junior and senior colleagues, or between peers, that provide various career development and psychosocial functions.[40] The mentoring role can be filled by a variety of individuals, not by just one person, and can come from within one's internal work organization or from external social and professional networks. The mentor typically provides coaching, friendship, sponsorship, advice, and role modeling to the younger, less experienced protégé. In the process, the mentor can satisfy his or her need to have a lasting influence on another person's life and also improve his or her job satisfaction.[41]

Two types of mentor–protégé relationships exist—informal and formal. An informal relationship is one that develops organically over time, usually based on shared interests and identities or a common background between the two parties.[42] In contrast, as a way to ensure that all younger employees have access to a mentor, many organizations deploy formal programs where the newer employee is "assigned" a mentor whose job it is to provide career support.[43] Formal and informal mentoring relationships, including the pros and cons of each, will be discussed more extensively in Chapter 8.

Building one's image and reputation is a career strategy in which the individual attempts to convey an appearance of success and suitability. For example, being married, participating in community activities, and dressing properly have traditionally been viewed as providing a positive public image that could bring career rewards. While this type of strategy is not necessarily important in all or most situations, a significant number of employees make the investment in image-building because of the perceived high value to career advancement. Building one's work reputation is an important strategy because it is presumed that an individual's past experiences and accomplishments bode well for future performance. Thus, a focus on building a strong work reputation can improve a person's employability regardless of the employer.[44] One can build a positive reputation by accomplishing such tasks as engineering a turnaround of an unfavorable work situation or by showing leadership on a particular assignment.

Related to the strategy of building one's image and reputation is the concept of impression management, the process by which people attempt to influence the images that others have of them. Impression management involves many strategies that individuals use in trying to be seen in a certain way or to create a particular impression in others' minds.[45] It reflects the basic human motive to be viewed favorably (and to avoid being viewed unfavorably) by others. The need to manage impressions is especially high when the impression one makes is critical for attaining career outcomes, and the more people want certain outcomes the more likely they are to manage impressions in an effort to obtain them.[46] For example, job applicants and those seeking promotions would typically engage in impression management activities as a career strategy to achieve an operational career goal. More broadly, individuals seeking inter-organizational mobility opportunities through social networking sites would also utilize a variety of impression management techniques to improve their chances of external employment.[47] Although many impression management behaviors have been identified in the literature, William Turnley and Mark Bolino cite the following five strategies as those that are most often used as assertive actions,[48] although we emphasize that individuals may find some of these actions personally objectionable and unacceptable.

1. *Ingratiation*, where individuals seek to be viewed as likable by doing favors for others, agreeing with others, or flattering others.
2. *Exemplification*, where people seek to be viewed as dedicated by being a good role model and going beyond the call of duty.
3. *Intimidation*, where individuals seek to appear dangerous by making threats or signaling their power to punish or create pain and discomfort.
4. *Self-promotion*, where individuals hope to be seen as competent by playing up their abilities and accomplishments.
5. *Supplication*, where people seek to be viewed as needy or in need of assistance by "playing dumb" or advertising their shortcomings and weaknesses.

Another concept related to the strategy of building one's image and reputation is the development of social capital. Social capital is defined as the potential resources derived from an individual's interpersonal relationships as well as the valued resources available from the within the organization of that network of relationships.[49] The establishment of social capital is a way to gain valuable information about an organization or a job opening that otherwise might not be readily available, create trust between members in the social network, raise one's status relative to peers, and open opportunities for advancement or a job shift. Building and then tapping into social capital can provide a number of positive career outcomes and allow for the fulfillment of career goals.[50] Of course, relationships in the social network need to be nurtured in order to create trust and open communication between the members. In this sense, individuals need to pay attention to and invest in their social connections, both inside and outside of the work organization, that can lead to the creation of social capital.

Engaging in organizational politics includes activities that also fall under the tactic of impression management as described previously. Organizational politics involves the use of targeted influence to facilitate individual and organizational goals and covers such diverse activities as agreeing with or flattering one's supervisor, advocating company practices, not complaining about rules or regulations, and forming alliances or coalitions with others in the organization.[51] More extreme and often personally unacceptable political practices can include sabotaging another person's work or spreading rumors about a colleague. In many organizations, becoming involved in organizational politics and engaging in impression management activities are career strategies that are necessary for career advancement, although certain behaviors might be viewed as unethical or reprehensible. Nonetheless, depending on the organizational context, strategies involving organizational politics may have beneficial effects on individual promotability and career growth.[52]

Research suggests that developing a variety of skills and having a diverse number of work experiences can significantly improve one's chances of meeting career goals and attaining career accomplishments.[53] In addition, self-nomination and networking strategies can also contribute to an individual's career success. Nevertheless, the usefulness of a particular career strategy is dependent on a number of factors, including the nature of the job, the industry, and the culture and norms of the particular organization. Indeed, a career strategy that might be successful in one case may not work in another. In addition, changes in economic conditions and technological advancements can quickly affect the utility of any one strategy because career paths can be eliminated, necessitating strategic adjustments.[54] Finally, while advancements in communication technology facilitate several career strategies, they also open a range of concerns. For example, participation in social networking sites can help build social capital and expedite the job search process, but can simultaneously allow employers to violate employee privacy rights, and can also lead to such unethical practices as discrimination based on an applicant's digital footprint and profile.[55] Given the potential for negative consequences, individuals should be cautious when using social media as a career strategy.

Guidelines for the Development of Career Strategies

We offer the following observations and suggestions on the development of career strategies:

- There is no "one best" strategy that is equally effective in all situations.
- The effectiveness of a particular strategy depends on the nature of the career goal. A person striving to reach the presidency of an organization, for example, is likely to benefit from different strategies than one whose goal is to become an engineering project manager.
- The effectiveness of a strategy depends on the organization's norms and values. For example, some organizations may encourage secrecy and political machinations, whereas others may reward openness and collaboration.
- Individuals should not limit themselves to one single strategy but should engage in a variety of strategic behaviors.

- Strategies should be used not only to reach a career goal but also to test one's interest and commitment to a goal. For example, the strategy of developing new skills by taking a graduate course in cost accounting might reveal to the individual that a goal of attaining a management position in financial management is (or is not) appropriate depending on how the individual reacts to the course. In this way, planning can be viewed as a process of learning more about the environment and ourselves.
- Career strategies should reflect steps to be taken, as well as areas to be avoided. Individuals should pursue positive career strategies that lead to career success, and avoid negative or inappropriate strategies that could cause career failure, are unethical or personally unacceptable, or that harm our family or personal life.

It is impossible (and undesirable) to specify in advance each and every component of a career strategy. An essential part of the career management process is "learning by doing." As a person begins to develop and implement a strategy, additional strategic behaviors may become more obvious than they were before the process began.

Five-Step Process for Developing Career Strategies

1. **Reexamine your long-term goals.** Make sure you understand what the goals represent in terms of desired activities, rewards, and lifestyle (conceptual goal) and why a particular operational goal (e.g., an occupation or a specific job) is appropriate for meeting the conceptual goal.
2. **Identify behaviors, activities, and experiences that will help you reach long-term goals.** Two questions need to be raised regarding each element of a career strategy: Will it help you attain your goals? Regardless of its usefulness, do you want to engage in that behavior? One first needs to estimate the potential usefulness of a set of activities. The most useful sources of information are discussion and observation. Conversations with others in the organization, for example, may provide helpful information and dispel myths about certain strategies (for example, that everyone must follow the same career path to a particular job).

   A person can profit the most from conversations with others who have more experience in the organization such as a manager, a mentor, or a more established colleague. Since there can be an element of rivalry between superior and subordinate that prevents information-sharing in some circumstances, a mentor is sometimes the more appropriate source of information about the potential usefulness of certain career strategies. In fact, the establishment of a mentor relationship is itself a career strategy. Nonetheless, formal feedback from superiors through such activities as collaborative goal-setting and performance appraisal can serve to identify career strategies and developmental activities.

Consider as an example the case of Beth, a 28-year-old manager in the accounting department of a medium-sized insurance company. At the age of 22, Beth received a bachelor's degree in accounting from a large state university. After working two years in the billing department of a hospital, Beth accepted an accounting analyst position with the insurance company. In her four years there, she advanced quickly, assuming the position of manager at a comparatively young age. She enjoys working at the insurance company, and her longer-term goal is to be a vice-president by age 35. During her annual performance review, Beth asked her supervisor, the officer-in-charge of the department, what actions she could take to facilitate further advancement. Her supervisor willingly offered several ideas. First, he told her that the company normally filled officer positions with employees who had earned an MBA. In addition, the supervisor stated that officers generally would have to show competence in a variety of skills and should have a broad range of experience in other departments within the organization. Finally, he stated that working on assignments that would give her exposure to the firm's senior management would help her chances for promotion. With this information in hand, Beth set about to develop specific career strategies, including enrollment in an MBA program, monitoring the company's job postings to increase awareness of opportunities in other departments, and requesting high profile assignments that would give her a chance to work with senior management.

The second issue involves a person's decision to engage in a strategic behavior regardless of its apparent usefulness. Some behaviors may help attain one element of a career goal but interfere with the attainment of other elements. For example, frequent job changes and accompanying relocations may enable a person to acquire useful experiences and skills but may interfere substantially with family or personal life. Therefore, the effectiveness of a particular career strategy must be judged in a holistic sense. Moreover, certain strategies may be useful but personally distasteful. Forming political alliances, making oneself look good at the expense of a colleague, and loyally supporting an organization's questionable practices may violate ethical and/or religious values. A career strategy cannot simply be viewed in utilitarian terms.

One should emerge from this process with a relatively small list of critical and acceptable strategic plans, and with statements of purpose and approximate timeframes if possible. Table 6.3 presents a statement of hypothetical career strategies for a person seeking advancement in a human resources department.

3. **Examine short-term goals.** Examine the fit between short-term goals and long-term goals. Do your short-term goals still appear instrumental to the attainment of your long-term ones? If not, you may want to revise your short-term goals to improve the fit.
4. **Identify behaviors, activities, and experiences that will help you attain the short-term goals.** As with step 2, potential usefulness and personal acceptability should be twin criteria by which a strategy is evaluated. Develop a small list of critical and acceptable strategic plans for accomplishing short-term goals.
5. **Combine the lists of strategies for short-term and long-term goals.** It is likely that strategies designed to attain both types of goals are particularly critical and should remain at the top of the combined list. Keep the list manageable by ordering the strategic activities in a logical time sequence.

The planning and implementation of a career strategy is not nearly as mechanical as this five-step process might suggest. First, the five steps overlap somewhat in time. It is artificial to separate discussions about goals, long-term strategies, and short-term strategies. Second, strategies cannot always be specified in advance. You might have to implement one part of a strategy to determine the next step. The important outcome of this process is an appreciation of how different strategies relate back to your significant goals. The essential ingredient in this process is openness to information and a willingness to reexamine and possibly revise goals and/or strategies; in short, to monitor and appraise your career.

Table 6.3 Statement of Career Strategies for an Assistant Human Resources Manager

Strategies to Achieve Long-Term Goal of Director of Corporate Human Resources		
Activity	*Purpose*	*Time Frame*
Perform effectively on current job	To remain productive, grow on job	Ongoing
Receive promotion to manager of human resources	To gain competence, experience, and visibility in company	2–3 years
Receive MBA degree with specialization in human resources	To gain specialized knowledge and credibility	3–4 years
Strategies to Achieve Short-Term Goal of Manager of Human Resources		
Activity	*Purpose*	*Time Frame*
Perform effectively on current job	To remain promotable, grow on job	Ongoing
Take beginning courses in MBA program	To gain greater knowledge of labor relations	0–6 months
Discuss career goals with supervisor	To make supervisor aware of career aspirations, obtain feedback and suggestions	0–6 months
Obtain information on possible human resources manager opening in company	To assess likelihood of achieving short-term goal	0–6 months
Contact search firm	To assess likelihood of achieving short-term goal in another company	6–12 months
Attempt to initiate quality of work–life program in conjunction with current human resources manager and operations	To enhance productivity, develop relationships with line management, gain experience in quality of work life	1–2 years

Learning Exercise 6 is included in the Appendix at the end of this chapter. It provides an opportunity to practice developing a career strategy. Although you may examine Learning Exercise 6 at this time, it is recommended that you finish reading Chapter 6 before beginning the exercise.

Career Appraisal

If career management is to be a flexible, adaptive process, there must be some way for people to adjust to new information about themselves or the environment. Career appraisal serves this function. We define career appraisal as *the process by which career-related feedback is gathered and used.*

The feedback obtained through career appraisal has three specific functions. First, it can test the appropriateness of a career strategy. Is the strategy effectively moving a person closer to his or her goals? Second, feedback can test the appropriateness of a goal itself. The individual can assess whether the career goal is still relevant and attainable, and if it is not, reengage in one that is more appropriate.[56] Third, appraisal can lead to career adaptability on the part of the individual. Adaptability is a career competency that allows the individual to make alterations in career goals, strategies, and behaviors in light of new insight gained from appraisal.[57] In essence, adaptability is at the heart of successful career appraisal since it reflects a willingness to make necessary career changes in order to increase the chances of achieving career success and satisfaction.[58]

Consider the situation of a 36-year-old high school history teacher who has become increasingly bored with his job. After extensive self-assessment, he has concluded that he should seek work in an educational setting that is more varied than his current position, that offers the opportunity for greater financial rewards, and that takes advantage of his skills in working with people on an individual basis (the conceptual goal). After reading materials on careers in education and talking with several people in the field, his conceptual goal is translated into a specific operational goal: he intends to move into secondary school administration within the next three years.

The teacher's strategy was two-pronged. First, he applied for admission to a part-time master's program in educational administration at the local university. Completion of the graduate program would enable him to be certified in administration and eligible for future openings in administrative positions. Second, he obtained permission to represent his school at local and state conferences and parent–teacher organization activities. The latter strategy was designed to give him a broader perspective on his school's operations. His strategy was developed as much to test his interests and talents in administration as to prepare him for his future career shift.

The teacher's graduate school experiences were enlightening. After one semester, he realized he was less interested in administering a school (he hated the courses in budgeting, personnel, and curriculum development) than in helping kids on an intensive one-on-one basis. Two psychology electives in the second semester reinforced his recent discovery. Because of these revelations, he applied to a doctoral program in school psychology.

As the teacher's experiences indicate, career appraisal reflects the problem-solving and adaptable nature of career management. With an effective appraisal process, career management becomes a learning experience in which one looks for signs that either confirm or disconfirm prior decisions. These signs are pieces of information that close the career management cycle by re-instigating career exploration. The teacher's disillusionment with his initial master's program was the result of a strategic experience that heightened his awareness of his own interests as well as the day-to-day duties of a school administrator. It was this awareness, gained through strategy-based exploration, that enabled him to be adaptable in his decision-making and to redirect his goal in a more suitable direction.

Types and Sources of Information Derived from Career Appraisal

An individual open to his or her environment can acquire a great deal of information relevant to goals and strategies. Although information cannot be pigeonholed so neatly, career-related feedback can conveniently be classified in terms of the following:

1. **The conceptual goal:** What has the individual learned about values, interests, talents, and desired lifestyle? Is this information consistent or inconsistent with the person's conceptual goal? For example, the history teacher's strategic experiences essentially reinforced his conceptual goal of greater variety, opportunities for more money, and more individualized work with other people.
2. **The operational goal:** What has the individual learned about the appropriateness of the operational goal? Is a match still possible between the conceptual goal and the operational goal? Put another way, is it still believed that the targeted job is

compatible with the conceptual goal? Note that the history teacher's most significant conclusion was that a career in school administration would not necessarily meet his values and interests.

3. **Strategy:** What has the individual learned about the appropriateness of the strategy? Is it working? Does the individual experience a sense of progress toward the goal? If the goal involves gaining additional competencies in the current job, has it been reflected in favorable performance appraisals? If the career goal involves a different job, does the organization still view the person as a viable candidate for the job? In the teacher's case, he realized that although his strategy was appropriate for his initial goal, it would have to be revised if he were to pursue a career in psychology. His application to a doctoral program in psychology was the first step of this revised strategy.

Feedback regarding goals and strategies can come from a variety of sources. One source consists of social interactions with other people who have either observed the person's behavior or undergone similar experiences themselves. Supervisors, subordinates, mentors, clients, family members, friends, and acquaintances would fall into this category.

A second source of feedback resides in observing the work and nonwork environments. A salesperson losing out on three consecutive sales can gain insights into his or her job performance. Production rates, quotas reached, and patents established can all provide useful information, as can the observation that five of your colleagues (but not you) have received recent promotions. The observation of an improved or deteriorated family life can also be a significant environmental cue. In other words, people's observations can serve as a powerful source of feedback, especially in conjunction with discussions with others in the work and nonwork domains.

Guidelines for Effective Career Appraisal

Successful career appraisal requires the individual to be vigilant in detecting as early as possible when a strategy is or is not working as expected. This early warning orientation is likely to be more helpful than simply carrying a strategy to completion before examining its usefulness. The ongoing feedback effort suggested in the career management model requires a consistent monitoring of activities and their consequences.

Ongoing career appraisal can be aided by considering the following guidelines:

1. The most basic principle, and perhaps the most difficult to follow, is the willingness to see the world clearly and to make revisions in goals and strategies when appropriate. An "escalation effect" can occur when people persist in a course of action despite its lack of success.[59] People are sometimes willing to continue their commitment to a "losing cause" to justify to themselves and others that their prior decision was sound. This practice is inconsistent with effective career management, which requires people to incorporate new data and revise prior decisions when necessary. Therefore, be honest with yourself. If things are not working well, seriously consider the possibility that either your prior decisions were faulty or circumstances have changed.
2. Use your career strategies to provide benchmarks of accomplishments. Statements of strategies should include purposes and desired outcomes. Test the usefulness of the strategies against these specific benchmarks. Usually, strategies are neither completely appropriate nor totally useless. The establishment of benchmarks can help identify specific strengths and weaknesses of a strategy.

3. Strategies are as much learning opportunities as they are vehicles for accomplishment. Periodically review the appropriateness of career goals in light of what you have learned in the process of implementing strategies so that you can make the necessary adjustments to your goals or strategies.
4. If you are employed, structure your interactions with your supervisor to acquire desired information. Come into a performance appraisal meeting with your own agenda to supplement (not replace) your supervisor's. What can you learn from your manager about your current performance, your strengths and weaknesses, and the organization's needs that will help you appraise your goals and strategies? What should your manager know about your aspirations that will help him or her provide useful feedback?
5. Share experiences and feelings with trustworthy people. Frank discussions among peers can be beneficial to all parties. First, others may see parts of you that are hidden to yourself. Second, verbally articulating goals, desires, reservations, and strategies may help clarify your own feelings. Third, others may be willing to share their own successes, failures, and revelations that bear on your circumstances. In effect, try to form a network, either inside or external to the work organization, that provides mutual feedback, guidance, support, and stimulation. In doing this, choose colleagues with whom you can communicate freely. Because it is often difficult to reveal sensitive career matters, the members of the network need to build trust and openness, a climate that takes time and patience to develop. Whether such a network is offered and sanctioned by the organization or whether it takes place informally is less important than the members' willingness to share and help each other.
6. Seek feedback from nonwork sources. Work and nonwork lives, as we stressed in Chapter 3, affect one another. Therefore, career strategies should be examined for the impact they have on life outside of work. For example, one part of a person's career strategy might be to demonstrate competence and loyalty by working extraordinarily long hours. It might initially have been assumed that these work hours would not adversely affect family relationships. After some time, however, it is necessary to examine the accuracy of that assumption. Because a person can easily misperceive a family's feelings and attitudes, candid sharing of information is often necessary to balance work and nonwork activities.

Career Management: Formal *and* Informal Activities

It might appear that the career management process is highly structured and formal. There are group sessions to attend, autobiographies to write, goals to list, and exploratory interviews to conduct. Must it require an endless stream of seminars and forms? Career management does have its structured side. Formal programs include vocational counseling and testing, career planning seminars or workshops, and self-administered career planning exercises. Of course, many programs combine these activities in various ways.

Career management activities, however, need not always be formally organized, structured programs. Indeed, any activity that is pursued to develop or act upon career-related information is a form of career management. For example, one can learn about one's interests and strengths through coursework (how many pre-med students switch majors after the first course in organic chemistry?), part-time or full-time work experiences, leisure activities, conversations with colleagues, family members and friends, or conscious introspection and reflection. Because career management is an ongoing process, informal activities are probably more potent in the long run. What is most helpful is to translate daily experiences into learning opportunities.

James Clawson and his colleagues have suggested three types of periodic career management activities that vary in formality and intensity.[60] They recommend an annual *year-end assessment* of accomplishments and satisfactions in various aspects of work and life that can be linked with one's annual performance appraisal. Second, they suggest a more intense analysis every 3–4 years that can involve participation in a formal career planning seminar. Finally, they recommend an even more intense major career reassessment every 7–10 years that involves participation in a variety of structured programs (e.g., assessment centers, 3–4-month university development programs). At each level of intensity, informal conversations with colleagues, family members, friends, and other contacts should supplement the more formal activities.

Career Management: With the Head *and* the Heart

It might also appear that career management always involves a great deal of systematic analysis: collecting information on oneself and the environment, setting goals, developing strategies to attain the goals, and processing feedback to adjust goals and/or strategies if necessary. Indeed, our model of career management does emphasize a great deal of systematic, cognitive activity that is necessary to understand ourselves and our circumstances and to plan and pursue our future.

However, there is also a role for intuition and gut-level feelings in searching for awareness and deciding what steps to take in the future. In fact, research has shown that the most awareness is achieved and the most effective decisions are made when individuals use their head *and* their heart; that is, when they use a combination of systematic and intuitive decision-making.[61] In other words, we need to be attuned not only to the facts but also to our feelings. We will elaborate on this point in the next chapter when we discuss decisions regarding choosing an occupation or career field. But we would be remiss if we didn't make explicit what you might already realize: effective career management is not a mechanical application of analyses devoid of our emotions.

The real importance of career management lies in a way of thinking and feeling. The core of effective career management is a mental set, an awareness of ourselves and the world around us, an alertness to changes in self and the environment, and a willingness to make conscious decisions and to revise them accordingly. This philosophy of active and adaptable career management utilizes our head and our heart, and should serve as a foundation for lifelong learning.

Summary

Career exploration paves the way for the establishment of career goals. A career goal should not focus exclusively on a specific job or position but should be conceived more broadly in terms of desired work experiences. A career goal should also (a) focus on the intrinsic enjoyment derived from work experiences, (b) include total lifestyle concerns, (c) consider one's current job as a source of satisfaction and growth, (d) be sufficiently challenging and flexible, and (e) be capable of meeting one's own needs and values, not other people's expectations. A general procedure was outlined for establishing career goals, and learning exercises are provided to practice this procedure.

Career indecision was defined as the inability to select a career goal, or subsequently to experience significant uncertainty or discomfort over a selected goal. A variety of factors can cause career indecision, including insufficient self-awareness, a lack of information on the internal and external work environments, low self-confidence, decisional fear and anxiety, nonwork demands, and situational constraints. Different types of career indecision and decidedness have been observed, indicating that the appropriateness of being undecided or decided depends on the underlying circumstances. Individuals should strive to achieve vigilance in their career decision-making, such that their career goals are selected confidently and patiently, and are based on sufficient knowledge of self and the work environment.

Career strategies are actions designed to help individuals attain their career goals. The development of a career strategy is itself a learning experience that encourages individuals to reexamine their career goals and identify key behaviors, activities, and experiences that can help them reach their goals. It is helpful to specify the purpose of each part of a career strategy and an approximate timeframe for accomplishment. Observation as well as conversations with peers, managers, and other knowledgeable people can help people devise reasonable plans. A learning exercise is provided to practice career strategy development.

However reasonable a career strategy may appear, it is essential to monitor and appraise its effectiveness. As a strategy is implemented, the individual should ask whether the initial goal still makes sense and whether the strategy still appears capable of helping in the achievement of the established goal. Individuals should be willing to revise goals and strategies when necessary.

Career management is a blend of formal and informal activities that should be pursued throughout a person's working life. Periodic reappraisals of career accomplishments and aspirations are useful. The essence of active career management is a willingness to assume responsibility for one's career, take the necessary steps to influence the course of one's career, and make revisions in plans and strategies when appropriate. Moreover, these actions should be based on analysis (our head) and feelings (our heart).

Now that you have completed reading Chapter 6, it is time to begin Learning Exercises 5 and 6, which can be found in the Appendix at the end of this chapter.

Career Management *for Life*: Work–Life Implications from Chapter 6

Career Exploration

- Assess the importance of work, family, community, self-development, and leisure roles in your life.
- Share your life priorities with significant people in your life.
- Understand the effect of your work experiences on your physical and psychological health.
- Be aware of the implications of different jobs, career fields, and career paths on your family and personal life.
- Be aware of the impact of your family and personal aspirations on your career.

Career Goal-Setting

- Set a conceptual goal that incorporates your desired balance between work and other important parts of your life.

- Understand how the achievement of your career goal would affect your family and personal life, and how your family situation might affect the likelihood of achieving your career goal.

Career Strategies

- Recognize the implications of specific career strategies (for example, extended work involvement, rapid mobility, relocation) on your family and personal life.
- Discuss career strategies with significant people in your life before and during their implementation.
- Always consider the personal acceptability of a strategy as well as its instrumental value. Avoid strategies that violate ethical or moral beliefs.

Career Appraisal

- Seek feedback from different people regarding various parts of your life.
- Discuss changes in personal and career values with family members.
- Examine the effects of career strategies on your work and nonwork lives on an ongoing basis.
- Be willing to admit mistakes and make changes to your career or family or personal life if necessary.

Assignment[62]

Think about where you will be in your career and your life five years into the future. Create a list of the jobs that you think you will have, the additional skills you might develop, and the further education you will pursue. Using this list, prepare a résumé for yourself that reflects where you believe you will be in five years. Once you have prepared the résumé, share it with someone in your family or with a close friend. Ask them for their insight as to whether the résumé is an accurate portrayal of where they think you will be in five years. If their opinion is different from yours, can you determine why? How might this information factor into your present and future career decision-making?

Discussion Questions

1. Why is it *inadvisable* to focus on operational career goals to the exclusion of conceptual goals?
2. Career goal-setting involves the development of conceptual and operational goals. To what extent should emotions and "gut-level feelings" play a role in goal-setting? Why do you feel that way?
3. Have your career decisions and aspirations been based primarily on your own needs and values, or have you been heavily influenced by other people's hopes and expectations for you? What can you do to ensure that future career decisions are guided by goals that are personally meaningful to you?
4. Why can career goals easily become rigid and inflexible? Have you ever continued to pursue a goal that no longer makes sense? Why? Why are inflexible goals inconsistent with the model of career management presented in this book?

5. Do you think that you are presently experiencing career indecision? If you are, what do you see as the primary cause(s)? If you are career decided, do you consider yourself vigilant or hypervigilant? Why?
6. Although some strategies may help you achieve your career goals, they may be unacceptable to you on other grounds. What factors should be considered when judging the personal acceptability of a career strategy? Have you (or someone you know or have read about) pursued, avoided, or abandoned a career strategy that was personally unacceptable? What were the consequences of this decision?
7. Why is career appraisal such an important part of the career management process? Do you think that career appraisal inevitably leads to a change in career strategies or goals? Why or why not?

Chapter 6 Case: Kimberly the Graduating College Student

Kimberly was starting to get worried. In less than two months she would be graduating from college and she wasn't even close to finding a full-time job for after graduation. The problem was that Kimberly didn't really know what job or company would be right for her. She had developed a résumé and a standard cover letter, but what good were they when she had no idea where to send them? She was really questioning her decision to major in business management. As her advisor had told her, a degree in management didn't really qualify her for any specific position. She envied her friends who majored in accounting. They all seemed to know exactly what jobs they wanted and for what companies they wanted to work—in fact, many of them already had jobs lined up.

Kimberly had gone to a few of the on-campus interviews that were hosted by the university's Career Center, but most of the companies were looking for financial sales professionals and she didn't think that she had the aggressive personality that these companies wanted. It wasn't as if she didn't have "people" skills, but the high-pressure world of financial sales was just not right for her. With 18 credits in her final semester, Kimberly was finding it difficult to devote time to her job search and to start considering opportunities for interviews off campus.

Kimberly was a solid B student who did much better in her junior and senior years than she did early in her college studies. She really liked her management courses, especially the ones dealing with individual behavior and leadership. She had also taken a course in industrial and organizational psychology that she found interesting. In the back of her mind, Kimberly even thought about switching majors to psychology and perhaps pursuing a career in that field. One thing she knew was that she didn't want a job where she had to deal with numbers—she had really struggled with her math and statistics courses and she wouldn't be happy in that type of job. She also wanted to find a job close to where she grew up. She really valued the relationships she had with her family and friends and would never want to take a job that would force her to move to another geographic area. One reason she chose to go to a local state university was so she could continue to live at home and commute to school.

For the past three years Kimberly had worked as a waitress at a chain restaurant located near the campus. About a year ago she had been promoted to an assistant manager and given responsibility for running the restaurant during her scheduled shifts. The job was demanding, but it had given her first-hand management training. Kimberly had done so well in the assistant manager's position that the chain offered her a full-time position upon her graduation. Once she graduated, the company would send her for training and then would assign her to a full-time management position at a restaurant in the area. They also had a nice benefits package, including full tuition reimbursement for graduate courses. Kimberly thought that she might want to get an MBA sometime in the next few years and would want to work for a company that paid for graduate coursework.

Although she liked working at the restaurant and the management responsibilities that came with it, Kimberly had never seen it as a "career-oriented" or professional job—it was just something she did to earn money to pay for her college expenses. Besides, her parents were expecting her to get a job with a major corporation so that she could get on the fast-track to advancement. They probably wouldn't be too thrilled with their daughter taking a job as a restaurant manager, especially after the thousands of dollars they had invested in her education. But Kimberly wasn't convinced that a job with a big corporation would be right for her either. She dreaded the thought of ending up in "cube world" for several years as she tried to climb the corporate ladder. Kimberly had never been the type of person who could "sit still" for long periods of time; she needed to be on the move. That is why she thrived in the fast-paced environment of the restaurant.

Kimberly was in a quandary over where to turn for advice. She didn't think her family would be of much help, and most of her friends were in the same boat as she was. The university's Career Center was good at coordinating job interviews, but they didn't seem that interested in working with individual students. She tried to think of family friends who might be able to set her up with an interview at a company in the area, but she was coming up empty. Kimberly knew she needed some guidance, and soon. The queasy feeling she got in her stomach when she thought about her future was not going away until she was set on her career choice.

Case Questions

1. Do you think that Kimberly is experiencing career indecision? Why or why not? Based on the definitions and descriptions of the four subtypes of career indecision and career decidedness, what category do you think best describes her?
2. Do you think Kimberly has any career goals at this point? If you think she does, what are her goals?
3. Do you think Kimberly has begun formulating any career strategies? If you think she has, what are her strategies?

4. Do you think Kimberly has done enough self- or environmental exploration to make informed career decisions? What other information about herself or the work environment should she be seeking at this point in her college career? To whom (or where) could she go to get help and advice on her career options?
5. If Kimberly sought your help, what advice would give her in terms of the management of her career?

Appendix for Chapter 6 Learning Exercises 5 and 6

Learning Exercise 5

Goal-Setting

So far, you have developed a summary of your preferred work environment (PWE) (Learning Exercise 3) and have begun to explore the relevant work environment (Learning Exercise 4). In Learning Exercise 5, you will practice identifying and evaluating career goals. Before you begin, reread the discussion of career goal-setting in this chapter, and take another look at Table 6.1 for examples.

The first step is to develop a long-term (3–7-year) conceptual goal. In formulating it, try to address all of the significant elements of your PWE. List the elements of your long-term conceptual goal below and consult Learning Exercise 3 to verify that all of the important elements of your PWE are incorporated in the long-term conceptual goal. Remember that your long-term conceptual goal need not be very precise at this time. Simply be as specific as you can.

Elements of Your Long-Term Conceptual Goal

1. ______________________________
2. ______________________________
3. ______________________________
4. ______________________________
5. ______________________________
6. ______________________________

Next, determine how well different long-term operational goals may help you achieve your long-term conceptual goal. To do this, choose two long-term operational goals (occupations or specific job positions) in which you think you might be interested and identify them in the spaces below:

Long-term Operational Goal A: ______________________________

Long-term Operational Goal B: ______________________________

Then, for each of the two long-term operational goals, list all of the positives (advantages), that is, how the operational goal can help you achieve your conceptual goal and all of the negatives (disadvantages), that is, how the operational goal might hinder you from achieving your conceptual goal.

Long-Term Operational Goal A

Positives

1. ______
2. ______
3. ______
4. ______
5. ______
6. ______

Negatives

1. ______
2. ______
3. ______
4. ______
5. ______
6. ______

Long-Term Operational Goal B

Positives

1. ______
2. ______
3. ______
4. ______
5. ______
6. ______

Negatives

1. ______
2. ______
3. ______
4. ______
5. ______
6. ______

If you are still not sure which (or if either) operational goal is appropriate for you, do not be concerned. The important thing is that you are thinking about your long-term future and have identified goals for further thought and action.

The next step is to identify a short-term (1–3-year) conceptual goal. Reexamine the summary of your PWE as well as your analyses above about your long-term conceptual and operational goals. To formulate a short-term conceptual goal, think about the following question: What type of work, educational, and other experiences and responsibilities would help prepare you to attain your long-term conceptual and operational goals? List the elements of your short-term conceptual goal below:

Elements of Your Short-Term Conceptual Goal

1. ______________________________
2. ______________________________
3. ______________________________
4. ______________________________
5. ______________________________
6. ______________________________

Next, determine how well different short-term operational goals may help you achieve your short-term conceptual goal. This time, choose two short-term operational goals (occupations or specific job positions) in which you think you might be interested and identify them in the spaces below:

Short-term Operational Goal A: ______________________________

Short-term Operational Goal B: ______________________________

Then, for each of the two short-term operational goals, list all of the positives (advantages), that is, how the operational goal can help you achieve your conceptual goal and all of the negatives (disadvantages), that is, how the operational goal might hinder you from achieving your conceptual goal.

Short-Term Operational Goal A

Positives

1. ______________________________
2. ______________________________
3. ______________________________
4. ______________________________
5. ______________________________
6. ______________________________

Negatives

1. ______________________________
2. ______________________________
3. ______________________________
4. ______________________________
5. ______________________________
6. ______________________________

Short-Term Operational Goal B

Positives

1. ______________________________
2. ______________________________
3. ______________________________
4. ______________________________
5. ______________________________
6. ______________________________

Negatives

1. ______________________________
2. ______________________________
3. ______________________________
4. ______________________________
5. ______________________________
6. ______________________________

Hopefully, this exercise has helped you gain insight into personally meaningful short-term and long-term goals. If you are still not sure which short-term and/or long-term operational goal is more appropriate for you, it would be helpful to examine the goals in more detail. In fact, a significant part of your career strategy in Learning Exercise 6 should include plans for additional data gathering.

Learning Exercise 6

Career Strategy Development

In this exercise, you will develop strategies to help you attain long-term and short-term operational career goals. First, select a long-term operational career goal you identified in Learning Exercise 5. Then, reexamine Tables 6.2 and 6.3 for illustrations of career strategies, follow the five-step process for developing career strategies described in this chapter, and enter the relevant information below. Then, use the same procedure to develop a strategy to achieve a short-term operational career goal.

Strategy to Achieve Long-Term Operational Goal (Goal = ________________)

Activity	*Purpose*	*Time Frame*

Strategy to Achieve Short-Term Operational Goal (Goal = ________________)

Activity	*Purpose*	*Time Frame*

Activity	*Purpose*	*Time Frame*

Now, combine the lists of strategies for the short-term and long-term goals. Keep the final list manageable by ordering the strategic activities in a logical time sequence. What should evolve from this activity is an overall plan of action—what you will be doing, why, and when. Briefly describe the overall plan of action below.

Notes

1 Locke, E. A. & Latham, G. P. (2006). New directions in goal-setting theory. *Current Directions in Psychological Science*, *15*, 265–268.

2 For a broad-based discussion of goal-setting and its outcomes, see Locke, E. A. & Latham, G. P. (Eds.) (2013). *New developments in goal setting and task performance*. London, UK: Routledge; Latham, G. P. & Locke, E. A. (2006). Enhancing the benefits and overcoming the pitfalls of goal setting. *Organizational Dynamics*, *35*, 332–340.

3 Harkin, B., Webb, T. L., Chang, B. P. I., Prestwich, A., Conner, M., Kellar, I., Benn, Y. & Sheeran, P. (2016). Does monitoring goal progress promote goal attainment? A meta-analysis of the experimental evidence. *Psychological Bulletin*, *142*, 198–229.

4 Ordóñez, L. D., Schweitzer, M. E., Galinsky, A. D. & Bazerman M. H. (2009). Goals gone wild: The systematic side effects of overprescribing goal setting. *Academy of Management Perspectives*, *23*, 6–16.

5 Hall, D. T. & Foster, L. W. (1975). A psychological success cycle and goal setting: Goals, performance, and attitudes. *Academy of Management Journal*, *20*, 282–290.

6 Sleesman, D. J., Conlon, D. E., McNamara, G. & Miles, J. E. (2012). Cleaning up the big muddy: A meta-analytic review of the determinants of escalation of commitment. *Academy of Management Journal*, *55*, 541–562; Wong, K. F. E., Yik, M. & Kwong, J. Y. Y. (2006). Understanding the emotional aspects of escalation of commitment: The role of negative affect. *Journal of Applied Psychology*, *91*, 282–297.

7 Cappelli, P. (2006). Churning of jobs. In Greenhaus, J. H. & Callanan, G. A. (Eds.), *Encyclopedia of career development* (pp. 165–167). Thousand Oaks, CA: Sage.

8 Callanan, G. A. & Greenhaus, J. H. (1990). The career indecision of managers and professionals: Development of a scale and test of a model. *Journal of Vocational Behavior*, *37*, 79–103.

9 Foley, P. M., Kelly, M. E. & Hartman, B. W. (2006). Career indecision. In Greenhaus, J. H. & Callanan, G. A. (Eds.), *Encyclopedia of career development* (pp. 109–115). Thousand Oaks, CA: Sage.

10 Ibid.

11 Callanan & Greenhaus (1990).

12 Ibid.

13 Santos, P. J., Ferreira, J. A. & Gonçalves, C. M. (2014). Indecisiveness and career indecision: A test of a theoretical model. *Journal of Vocational Behavior*, *85*, 106–114.

14 Callanan, G. A. & Greenhaus, J. H. (1992). The career indecision of managers and professionals: An examination of multiple subtypes. *Journal of Vocational Behavior*, *41*, 212–231.

15 Ibid.

16 Janis, I. L. & Mann, L. (1976). Coping with decisional conflict. *American Scientist*, *64*, 657–667.

17 There is some evidence that anxiety or stress may lead to increased career exploration, especially exploration of the work environment: Greenhaus, J. H. & Sklarew, N. (1981). Some sources and consequences of career exploration. *Journal of Vocational Behavior*, *18*, 1–12; Blustein, D. L. & Phillips, S. D. (1988). Individual and contextual factors in career exploration. *Journal of Vocational Behavior*, *33*, 203–216.
18 Callanan & Greenhaus (1992).
19 Burns, G. N., Morris, M. B., Rousseau, N. & Taylor, J. (2013). Personality, interests, and career indecision: A multidimensional perspective. *Journal of Applied Social Psychology*, *43*, 2090–2099.
20 Greenhaus, J. H., Callanan, G. A. & Kaplan, E. (1995). The role of goal setting in career management. *The International Journal of Career Management*, *7*, 3–12.
21 White, N. J. & Tracey, T. J. G. (2011). An examination of career indecision and application to dispositional authenticity. *Journal of Vocational Behavior*, *78*, 219–224.
22 Callanan, G. A. & Greenhaus, J. H. (1999). Personal and career development: The best and worst of times. In Kraut, A. I. & Korman, A. K. (Eds.), *Evolving practices in human resource management: Responses to a changing world of work* (pp. 146–171). San Francisco, CA: Jossey-Bass.
23 Koen, J., Klehe, U. & van Vianen, A. E. M. (2013). Employability among the long-term unemployed: A futile quest or worth the effort? *Journal of Vocational Behavior*, *82*, 37–48; DiRenzo, M. S. & Greenhaus, J. H. (2011). Job search and voluntary turnover in a boundaryless world: A control theory perspective. *Academy of Management Review*, *36*, 567–589.
24 Baruch, Y., Szűcs, N. & Gunz, H. (2015). Career studies in search of theory: The rise and rise of concepts. *Career Development International*, *20*, 3–20.
25 DiRenzo & Greenhaus (2011). Quotation is on page 571.
26 Fugate, M. (2006). Employability. In Greenhaus, J. H. & Callanan, G. A. (Eds.), *Encyclopedia of career development* (pp. 267–271). Thousand Oaks, CA: Sage.
27 Callanan, G. A. (2006). Career strategy. In Greenhaus, J. H. & Callanan, G. A. (Eds.), *Encyclopedia of career development* (pp. 146–148). Thousand Oaks, CA: Sage.
28 Sonnentag, S. (2012). Psychological detachment from work during leisure time: The benefits of mentally disengaging from work. *Current Directions in Psychological Science*, *21*, 114–118.
29 Arthur, M. B., Claman, P. H. & DeFillippi, R. J. (1995). Intelligent enterprise, intelligent careers. *Academy of Management Executive*, *9*, 7–20.
30 Porter, C. M. & Woo, S. E. (2015). Untangling the networking phenomenon: A dynamic psychological perspective on how and why people network. *Journal of Management*, *41*, 1477–1500; Dobrow, S. R., Chandler, D. E., Murphy, W. M. & Kram, K. E. (2012). A review of developmental networks: Incorporating a mutuality perspective. *Journal of Management*, *38*, 210–242.
31 Arthur et al. (1995).
32 Tasselli, S., Kilduff, M. & Menges, J. I. (2015). The microfoundations of organizational social networks: A review and an agenda for future research. *Journal of Management*, *41*, 1361–1387; Gibson, C., Hardy, J. H. & Buckley, M. R. (2014). Understanding the role of networking in organizations. *Career Development International*, *19*, 146–161.
33 Colbert, A. E., Bonon, J. E. & Purvanova, R. K. (2016). Flourishing via workplace relationships: Moving beyond instrumental support. *Academy of Management Journal*, *59*, 1199–1223; Colakoglu, S. N. (2006). Networking. In Greenhaus, J. H. & Callanan, G. A. (Eds.), *Encyclopedia of career development* (pp. 536–537). Thousand Oaks, CA: Sage.
34 Murphy, W. M. & Kram, K. E. (2014). Understanding non-work relationships in developmental networks. *Career Development International*, *15*, 637–663.
35 Dabos, G. E. & Rousseau, D. M. (2013). Psychological contracts and informal networks in organizations: The effects of social status and local ties. *Human Resource Management*, *52*, 485–510.
36 For a full description of LinkedIn, see the company's website: www.linkedin.com.
37 Taub, E. A. (2013). The path to happy employment, contact by contact on LinkedIn. *The New York Times*, December 4.
38 For a full description of Facebook, see the company's website: www.facebook.com.
39 Stumpf, S. A. (2014). A longitudinal study of career success, embeddedness, and mobility of early career professionals. *Journal of Vocational Behavior*, *85*, 180–190; Lam, S. S. K., Ng, T. W. H. & Feldman, D. C. (2012). The relationship between external job mobility and salary attainment across career stages. *Journal of Vocational Behavior*, *80*, 129–136.
40 O'Brien, K. E., Biga, A., Kessler, S. R. & Allen, T. D. (2010). A meta-analytic investigation of gender differences in mentoring. *Journal of Management*, *36*, 537–554; Allen, T. D. (2006).

Mentoring. In Greenhaus, J. H. & Callanan, G. A. (Eds.), *Encyclopedia of career development* (pp. 486–493). Thousand Oaks, CA: Sage.
41 Ghosh, R. & Reio, T. G. (2013). Career benefits associated with mentoring for mentors: A meta-analysis. *Journal of Vocational Behavior*, *83*, 106–116.
42 Humbred, B. K. & Rouse, E. D. (2016). Seeing you in me and me in you: Personal identification in the phases of mentoring relationships. *Academy of Management Review*, *41*, 435–455.
43 Weinberg, F. J. & Lankau, M. J. (2011). Formal mentoring programs: A mentor-centric and longitudinal analysis. *Journal of Management*, *37*, 1527–1557.
44 Arthur, M. B. (1994). The boundaryless career: A new perspective for organizational inquiry. *Journal of Organizational Behavior*, *15*, 295–306.
45 Turnley, W. H. & Bolino, M. C. (2006). Impression management. In Greenhaus, J. H. & Callanan, G. A. (Eds.), *Encyclopedia of career development* (pp. 374–378). Thousand Oaks, CA: Sage.
46 Ibid.
47 Harrison, J. A. & Budworth, M. (2015). Unintended consequences of a digital presence: Employment-related implications for job seekers. *Career Development International*, *20*, 294–314.
48 Turnley & Bolino (2006).
49 Adams, S. M. (2006). Social capital. In Greenhaus, J. H. & Callanan, G. A. (Eds.), *Encyclopedia of career development* (pp. 746–750). Thousand Oaks, CA: Sage.
50 DiRenzo, M. S., Greenhaus, J. H. & Weer, C. H. (2015). Relationship between protean career orientation and work–life balance: A resource perspective. *Journal of Organizational Behavior*, *36*, 538–560.
51 Liu, Y., Liu, J. & Wu, L. (2010). Are you willing and able? Roles of motivation, power, and politics in career growth. *Journal of Management*, *36*, 1432–1460.
52 Sibunruang, H., Garcia, P. R. J. M. & Tolentino, L. R. (2016). Ingratiation as an adapting strategy: Its relationship with career adaptability, career sponsorship, and promotability. *Journal of Vocational Behavior*, *92*, 135–144; Liu et al. (2010).
53 Laud, R. L. & Johnson, M. (2012). Upward mobility: A typology of tactics and strategies for career advancement. *Career Development International*, *17*, 231–254.
54 Simosi, M., Rousseau, D. M. & Daskalaki, M. (2015). When career paths cease to exist: A qualitative study of career behavior in a crisis economy. *Journal of Vocational Behavior*, *91*, 134–146.
55 Roth, P. L., Bobko, P., Van Iddekinge, C. H. & Thatcher, J. B. (2016). Social media in employee-selection-related decisions: A research agenda for uncharted territory. *Journal of Management*, *42*, 269–298.
56 Creed, P. A. & Hood, M. (2014). Disengaging from unattainable career goals and reengaging in more achievable ones. *Journal of Career Development*, *41*, 24–42.
57 Savickas, M. L. & Porfeli, E. J. (2012). Career adapt-abilities scale: Construction, reliability, and measurement equivalence across 13 countries. *Journal of Vocational Behavior*, *80*, 661–673; Klehe, U. C., Zikic, J., van Vianen, A. E., Koen, J. & Buyken, M. (2012). Coping proactively with economic stress: Career adaptability in the face of job insecurity, job loss, unemployment, and underemployment. *Research in Occupational Stress and Well-Being*, *10*, 131–176.
58 Zacher, H. (2014). Individual difference predictors of change in career adaptability over time. *Journal of Vocational Behavior*, *84*, 188–198.
59 Sleesman et al. (2012); Wong et al. (2006).
60 Clawson, J. G., Kotter, J. P., Faux, V. A. & McArthur, C. C. (1992). *Self-assessment and career development*. Englewood Cliffs, NJ: Prentice-Hall.
61 Singh, R. & Greenhaus, J. H. (2004). The relation between career decision-making strategies and person-job fit: A study of job changers. *Journal of Vocational Behavior*, *64*, 198–221.
62 This assignment is adapted from an exercise originally developed by Laker, D. R. & Laker, R. (2007). The five-year resume: A career planning exercise. *Journal of Management Education*, *31*, 128–141.

Part II

Stages of Career Development

7 Choosing Occupations and Organizations

This chapter examines several critical steps in the career management process. First, the chapter discusses different views on the occupational choice process, or how people go about finding a suitable occupation, hopefully one that fits their personal characteristics. After reviewing theory and research on occupational choice, we examine several obstacles to occupational decision-making and offer recommendations for improving the process. The second part of the chapter discusses how individuals choose an organization in which to work and how they cross the boundary from outside to inside the organization. The organizational choice process consists of two simultaneous activities: individuals assess an organization to determine whether a job in that organization is likely to meet their work and nonwork needs and values, and concurrently organizations assess candidates' qualifications so they can select those with the highest likelihood of succeeding in the firm.[1] Just as candidates make decisions about organizations, organizations make decisions about job candidates.

Occupational Choice

Take a moment to consider the following four scenarios:

- Jessica is a 22-year-old woman who is excited about accepting her first full-time position upon graduation. As a newly hired junior accountant at an industrial products company, Jessica is finally about to embark on her career. She believes that her college degree in accounting and her summer internship jobs have prepared her to be successful in this new position. She is hopeful that there will be long-term growth opportunities at the firm.
- Tom is a 34-year-old commercial lending officer for a large bank who has just tendered his resignation after 11 years with the firm. Tom determined that his career in banking, while thus far financially rewarding, wasn't turning out the way he expected. In Tom's view, the bank's bureaucracy imposed needless constraints and restrictions that went against his entrepreneurial spirit. Moreover, with the many mergers in the industry, Tom wasn't sure about his prospects for keeping his job in the future. Consequently, Tom adjusted his career goals and has accepted a new job as a sales representative for a small medical products company. Tom believes that he can express his entrepreneurial spirit in this new position.
- Wilma is a 46-year-old woman whose youngest child just started high school, and she has decided to reenter the workforce full-time. While she wasn't sure what job she should pursue, Wilma was certain she wanted to work in an environment where she could demonstrate her impressive computer graphics skills. Computers have been a passion for Wilma and she has tinkered with them while being a stay-at-home parent. After taking web developer certification classes, she began her job

search. Two months later, Wilma landed a position as a web designer for the local school district.

- Antonio is a 58-year-old man who was told three months ago that his job as a production supervisor at a specialty chemical company was being eliminated in a cost-cutting move. Working with the outplacement firm that his company provided, Antonio assessed what he wanted to do with the rest of his career until he would retire in ten years or so. After evaluating all of his options, and considering his active involvement in strength training and weightlifting competitions, Antonio decided to apply for a personal trainer position at his local gym. He also began investigating what steps he could take to become a private trainer.

These four cases are distinct examples of people choosing occupations and specific jobs. While it is generally accepted that occupational choice is a key activity in the early phases of career development, these examples show that the dynamics of occupational selection can be relevant at each career stage. The experiences of Jessica, Tom, Wilma, and Antonio illustrate that the choice of an appropriate occupation (either initially or as a career change) is a pivotal task in the career management process, one that can take place really at any point in one's life.

Are you in the process of selecting an occupation? If you are, are you confident that you will make the right decision, or do frequent doubts enter your mind? Do you know where to turn for information and insight? Have you thought about how to select an occupation from among competing alternatives?

Theories of Occupational Choice

An *occupation* is a group of similar jobs found in several establishments.[2] This longstanding definition distinguishes a specific job in a particular organization (e.g., a marketing research analyst at Procter & Gamble) from the broader notion of an occupation (marketing research). Therefore, we can think of such diverse occupations as accounting, sales, computer web design, and personal training, each of which has a somewhat unique set of requirements and rewards.

A comprehensive review of the theories of occupational choice is beyond the scope of this book and is available elsewhere.[3] Instead, we present four significant themes that can help us understand the manner in which people make occupational choices and appreciate the variety of psychological, social, economic, and cultural factors that enter into occupational decisions:

1. Occupational choice as a matching process.
2. Occupational choice as a developmental process.
3. Occupational choice as a decision-making task.
4. Occupational choice as a function of social and cultural influences.

For each theme, we review the relevant research, highlight important findings, and illustrate its significance to our model of career management.

Occupational Choice as a Matching Process

Most theories of occupational choice contend that a person, consciously or unconsciously, chooses an occupation that "matches" his or her unique set of needs, motives, values, and talents. One of the earliest approaches to occupational choice, the trait and factor theory, is perhaps most explicit in this regard. According to this view, a person identifies his or her abilities, needs, interests, and values, and then chooses an occupation thought to be most compatible with his or her unique qualities.

The work of John Holland is the most well-known and influential theory that views occupational choice as a process of matching occupations and people.[4] Holland's theory proposes that people express their personalities in making an occupational choice, and individuals can be classified in terms of their similarity to the six personality types that were described in Chapter 5. Recall that these types were realistic, investigative, artistic, social, enterprising, and conventional. Each personality type is characterized by a common set of activity preferences, interests, and values. For example, as Table 7.1 indicates, enterprising personality types perceive themselves as adventurous, ambitious, and energetic, whereas conventional types see themselves as efficient, obedient, practical, and calm.

Holland proposes that occupational environments can also be classified into these six categories. Each environment is dominated by a particular personality type and reinforces those qualities possessed by that type as noted above. Moreover, Holland classified specific occupations into the same six environments as he had classified the personality types. For example, realistic occupations include engineering and construction work, investigative occupations include the physical and biological sciences, artistic occupations include music and art, social occupations include teaching and the ministry, enterprising occupations include public relations and advertising, and conventional occupations include administrative work.

Table 7.1 Illustrations of Holland's Typology of Personality and Occupations

Realistic
- **Personal Characteristics:** Shy, genuine, materialistic, persistent, stable
- **Sample Occupations:** Mechanical engineer, drill press operator, aircraft mechanic, dry cleaner, waitress

Investigative
- **Personal Characteristics:** Analytical, cautious, curious, independent, introverted
- **Sample Occupations:** Economist, physicist, actuary, surgeon, electrical engineer

Artistic
- **Personal Characteristics:** Disorderly, emotional, idealistic, imaginative, impulsive
- **Sample Occupations:** Journalist, drama teacher, advertising manager, interior decorator, architect

Social
- **Personal Characteristics:** Cooperative, generous, helpful, sociable, understanding
- **Sample Occupations:** Interviewer, history teacher, counselor, social worker, clergy

Enterprising
- **Personal Characteristics:** Adventurous, ambitious, energetic, domineering, self-confident
- **Sample Occupations:** Purchasing agent, real estate salesperson, market analyst, attorney, personnel manager

Conventional
- **Personal Characteristics:** Efficient, obedient, practical, calm, conscientious
- **Sample Occupations:** File clerk, CPA, typist, teller

Note: The entries are selected illustrations. For a complete classification, see Holland, J. L. (1985). *Making vocational choices: A theory of vocational personalities and work environments.* Englewood Cliffs, NJ: Prentice-Hall.

One of John Holland's major assumptions is that individuals seek out work settings that allow them to showcase their skills and abilities, express their interests and values, and take on relevant assignments.[5] A number of websites are available that can help a person determine in which of the Holland categories he or she falls.[6]

It is expected that people's stability in an occupational area depends on the fit or match between personality type and occupational environment. For instance, social personality types who find themselves in electrical engineering (an investigative occupation) could become dissatisfied with the occupation and might choose another occupation more consistent with their social orientation. Research has found that congruence between personality and occupational environment can lead to such favorable outcomes as higher job and career satisfaction, improved job stability, and increased job involvement and work engagement.[7] In addition, a mismatch between one's personality and occupational choice could be a reason to pursue a career change.

In general, traditional or classic views on the matching of individuals with occupations are based on the notion of "supplementary" congruence, or the matching of individuals with environments in which they are similar to people already in those environments.[8] However, some researchers have noted the possibility of a "complementary" congruence wherein personality characteristics and abilities of the individual can serve to complement personal characteristics and abilities already present in the work environment.[9] In this sense, the strengths of the individual might fill a void in a given work environment and thereby improve overall group performance.

Donald Super's extensive work is also based on the notion of a match between individuals and occupations. The key concept in his model is the self-concept; that is, how individuals see or perceive themselves and their many qualities.[10] Our self-concept, in other words, consists of the attributes we believe we possess: our abilities, personality traits, needs, interests, and values.

Super believes that an occupational choice enables a person to play a role appropriate to the self-concept. People implement their self-concept in developing an occupational choice; that is, they select an occupation that is compatible with significant parts of their self-concept. In effect, people develop a self-concept, form images or beliefs about a series of occupations, and take steps to enter the occupation that is most compatible with their self-concept. Indeed, a great deal of evidence supports the notion that people prefer and choose occupations that are compatible with their self-concept.[11] In our introductory vignettes, Antonio is starting a second career that is consistent with his avocation—weightlifting and strength training—and matches his interest in promoting good health.

Although an individual's self-concept includes elements that relate to the work domain—how I see myself as an accountant (or nurse or business owner) and what I value at work—it also includes self-perceptions of nonwork life, such as how I see myself as a spouse (or parent or sibling or child) and as a member of my community. As a result, when individuals contemplate the compatibility of different occupations with their self-concept, they consider (or should consider) work *and* nonwork elements of their self-concept. Some occupations may be consistent with work-related elements of their self-concept (e.g., as one who thrives on challenge and responsibility), but they may be inconsistent with nonwork elements of their self-concept (e.g., as an involved parent or community volunteer) because the occupations are so demanding that they leave little time or energy for life outside work.

In line with the linkage between self-concept and occupational choice, both sociologists and psychologists have noted that occupational choice is also driven by a person's work orientation, or the subjective meaning we place on work.[12] Specifically, a *work orientation* is considered a psychological construct that describes a person's general relationship with work.[13] Three distinct work orientations have been identified—as a *job*, a *career*, and a *calling*, each of which generally displays a different perspective on work.

Individuals with a *job orientation* view work as an instrumental activity to provide the necessary financial resources for other life activities. For these individuals, work represents a means for earning material benefits, so they can then enjoy their time away from the job and the workplace. In contrast, individuals with a *career orientation* are personally invested in their work, and consider it a source of self-esteem that can be gained through achievement and advancement in a chosen occupation. For them, work is a means toward obtaining long-term personal success and recognition. They typically have a deep personal investment in their work and mark their achievements through monetary gains and through future advancement. Finally, individuals with a *calling orientation* view work as a purposeful end unto itself, with less emphasis on extrinsic rewards. For these individuals work provides meaning and fulfills a mission in life. This *calling orientation* allows them to discover fulfillment in their work by providing social value and advancing the greater good.[14]

As with other personal characteristics, work orientation can serve as a key factor in attempting to match a person to an occupation. The three work orientations represent distinct ways of looking at a potential occupation, and each has implications as to whether work will be satisfying and enjoyable. For example, it is possible that someone with a strong *job orientation* could be dissatisfied in an occupation or a position with an upward striving component, with the associated time demands and pressures. It is also important to recognize that a person's work orientation can change over time. An individual who has a *career orientation* in his or her 20s and 30s could, through maturation and a change in life outlook, pursue a change in occupations that reflects a *calling orientation.*

Occupational Choice as a Developmental Process

Although people strive to match or implement their self-concept in choosing an occupation, one's selection of an occupation does not take place at a single point in time. The decision to become an accountant, as with Jessica in our opening vignettes, does not begin and end when a high school junior or senior decides to attend a college with a strong business program.

The choice of an occupation can be considered a developmental process that evolves over time. For one thing, the decision to pursue a particular occupation is really a series of decisions that span a significant portion of one's life. The accountant-to-be may have accompanied her mother on a "take your daughter to work day" while in fifth grade, decided to take an accelerated mathematics program in middle school, been chosen to join the business club in high school, and sought summer employment at a local company where she could assist with bookkeeping tasks. These educational and vocational decisions and activities build upon one another and ultimately culminate in an occupational choice.

Second, as Super and others have indicated, one's self-concept is formed, clarified, and modified over an extended period of time. It takes time and experience for talents to emerge and for interests and values to crystallize. Time is also required for people to learn about the world of work. Misinformation is hopefully replaced by more accurate perceptions as we learn about different occupations and jobs. Potential occupations are pursued or discarded as new information becomes available to the child, adolescent, young adult, and seasoned employee.

For these reasons, it is proper to view occupational choice as an unfolding, gradual, evolving process. As we indicated earlier in this chapter with the examples of Jessica, Tom, Wilma, and Antonio, the need to make occupational choices can occur throughout the life cycle. Likewise, the gathering of information and the gaining of personal insights relevant to one's occupational choice can occur through the various career stages.

People learn about themselves and the work world through exploratory behavior. High school and college years provide time for maturation. Our self-concept becomes more stable, clearer, and more realistic. For example, part-time and summer employment provide substantial opportunities for reality testing—a firsthand look at ourselves. By waiting tables, clerking, or selling, we not only can test our talents and interests, but we also can learn what it is like to work outside the home. In addition, the completion of temporary work assignments, including internships, cooperative education programs, and apprenticeships, is designed to help students develop an accurate self-concept, gain a realistic understanding of various career fields and organizational environments, and allow a check for fit between individual characteristics and the demands of different jobs.[15] In our earlier vignettes, Jessica's selection of accounting as an occupation was a product of her developing as a person, learning from earlier job-related experiences, and knowing her likes, dislikes, and special competencies.

Lifelong learning and personal development have become the mantras of the workplace. Adults continue to gain personal insights over the later stages of the life cycle. We continually reassess ourselves and our achievements in relation to our career goals. Incongruities between expectations and reality can lead to changes in career goals and alterations in occupational preferences. From our earlier vignettes, Tom's decision to make a midcareer change reflected his dissatisfaction with his work environment and his desire to achieve greater fit by choosing a job in which he could express his entrepreneurial orientation.

Transitions and changes in life roles can also necessitate the making of occupational choices. Our example of Wilma, who returned to work after the demands of caring for younger children had diminished, illustrates how changes in a nonwork role (in this case, her role as a parent) affected her decision to reenter the workforce as a full-time employee. Finally, organizational actions can force a change in one's occupational field. Downsizings, mergers and acquisitions, and business failures can serve to make new career goals and occupational choices a necessity. Loss of one's job, as given in the example of Antonio, is a powerful if not overwhelming inducement to seek a new occupation.

Occupational Choice as a Decision-Making Task

We have seen how occupational choice can be viewed essentially as a developmental process in which experiences and increasing maturity enable a person to develop, modify, and clarify the self-concept, gain further insights into the world of work, and attain a match between a chosen occupation and one's self-perceived interests, abilities, needs, and values.

Given a set of alternative occupations, how does one choose which occupation to pursue? According to the career management model presented in Chapter 4, a person should engage in career exploration, acquire a greater awareness of self and of alternative occupations, and develop a career goal. In the context of occupational choice, the operational career goal is to enter a particular occupation. But this does not explain *how* individuals select a particular occupational field. How, for example, does one determine whether finance or accounting will provide a better match? What psychological process guides one in the selection of a particular occupational field?

A number of models of vocational decision-making have been developed to address this very issue.[16] Although there are several differences among them, most are based on some form of psychological decision theory where it is generally assumed that individuals use compensatory or trade-off approaches in which unfavorable aspects of a given job are offset by the favorable elements.[17] Under one view, occupational choice could be based on a rational, deductive, and programmed decision-making process wherein people choose courses of action that are expected to produce desirable consequences.[18] With this decision-making approach, individuals become aware of a variety of potential outcomes or rewards that may be associated with an occupation (e.g., advancement opportunities, salary, flexible work hours, or interesting work) and then assess the personal value that they place on each of these outcomes. The individual then searches to identify occupations that would provide the outcomes they value, and then systematically chooses the occupation with the highest likelihood of providing these valued outcomes.

However, finding an occupation that has a high probability of meeting valued outcomes is not the same as choosing to enter that occupation. There may be many attractive occupations (e.g., professional athlete, politician, brain surgeon) that we ultimately reject for one reason or another. Perhaps we believe we do not have the right mix of talents for a particular occupation or that our financial resources (or our patience) are not adequate for the extensive training required. Thus, we also assess the likelihood of actually gaining entrance into the identified occupations, and are most likely to select an occupation that we not only find attractive but also have a decent chance of entering.

Do people really choose occupations in such a rational, calculative manner? Do people compare possible occupations and choose occupations that maximize the likelihood that they will obtain desirable outcomes and avoid undesirable outcomes? Our occupational preferences and decisions do seem to be guided by our desire to seek maximum rewards from work. However, a competing view of occupational decision-making suggests that occupational choice is neither as rational nor as systematic as we have described above. Individuals, when confronted with real-life choices, often use decision-making strategies wherein the first option that fulfills minimally acceptable standards on specific occupational attributes is chosen. This "unprogrammed" approach means that people do *not* initially assess a job regarding a long list of potential outcomes but rather focus on one or two particularly significant outcomes. Jobs that fail to reach an acceptable level on these significant outcomes are rejected from further consideration, even if they would provide many other desirable outcomes. The jobs that survive this cut would not be compared to one another, but rather are placed on an "active roster" of acceptable alternatives. From this active roster, the person often makes an "implicit" decision (unknown even to oneself) to favor one alternative over the others, based on just one or two outcomes.

There has not been sufficient research from which to draw sound conclusions about the relative usefulness of the rational, programmed and the unprogrammed decision-making approaches to occupational choices, although research seems to indicate the efficacy of structured, rational decision-making strategies as a way to improve the quality of a decision.[19] While the jury is still out, these approaches share one important principle, namely, that choices are based on perceptions of different occupations or jobs. Whether the choice is based on one or two critical outcomes or on a longer list of outcomes weighted by their respective value, beliefs about an occupation's ability to provide these outcomes determine occupational preferences. If beliefs and perceptions are unrealistic, occupational decisions are likely to be faulty, which will lead to disappointment and disillusionment in the job. The implications of these unmet expectations will be discussed in detail later in this chapter.

Social and Cultural Factors that Influence Occupational Choice

As we discussed in Chapter 2, our careers and career decision-making are shaped considerably by social influences. Consistent with the adage that behavior is a function of the person *and* the environment, the choices we make are reflections of our personal characteristics as well as the environment in which we live. The occupational choice process is no exception to this general rule. Most of the research on occupational choice seems to focus on the person as an active agent in the formulation of occupational plans and decisions. Certainly, our model of career management emphasizes what one can or should do to plan, manage, and appraise a career. Much of the psychologically oriented theory and research discussed so far consider personal goals and intentions, awareness, information seeking, and strategy development as key influences on occupational decision-making.

However, there are other approaches to the study of occupational choice and decision-making. In particular, the sociological approach to careers reflects the idea that circumstances beyond the individual's control can exert considerable influence on the course of his or her life and occupational choices.[20] Undoubtedly, social influences from the environment—both past and present—play a major role in occupational decision-making. A person's prior environment includes family of origin, social class, income, and place of residence. The present environment includes the economic, political, and cultural climates, and the family situation in which a person lives.

First, consider the ways in which a child's social background can influence his or her orientation to the work world. Although some countries like the United States may be less class-conscious than other cultures, there can be distinct lifestyles associated with membership in different socioeconomic classes. Social class and economic status not only affect the availability of resources for one's career choice, but also affect the attitudes, customs, and expectations to which we are exposed, and the network of support we receive.[21]

Studies have shown that differences in values and attitudes, especially occupational and educational aspirations, can be explained, in part, by one's socioeconomic status.[22] Accordingly, a parent's occupation can determine the kind of people met and admired during childhood. Growing up as a child of a physician is likely to expose one to different role models than growing up as a child of a firefighter—not better or worse, but different. Selective exposure to different adults can stimulate widely different occupational aspirations. In addition, social status and access to economic resources can influence the career decision-making self-confidence of individuals, such that someone who grows up in a more affluent environment might have a comparatively higher degree of confidence in his or her occupational choices.[23]

Moreover, social class can affect the values we hope to attain at work. A father or mother who has lived through some unstable time (a strike or extended layoff, lapses in continued employment caused by downsizings, or the Great Recession) may encourage a child to value security above all else in a job. A college professor or scientist may encourage a life of study and research, a social worker or physician a life of service, and an entrepreneur a life of competition. This is not to say that a child automatically adopts a parent's work values, but that the opportunity to identify with parents and internalize their values is certainly present.

One's family background has a significant effect on occupational choice and aspirations.[24] Parents' occupations can influence the development of their children's interests and skills in certain areas, particularly regarding the choice of white- or blue-collar jobs. An automobile mechanic's son or daughter is likely to get an early introduction to the world of "things" and mechanical operations. A doctor's daughter may accompany her mother to the office or hospital and develop an interest and ability in working with people in emergency situations. In addition, parents' occupations affect family income. A wealthy family can provide the resources to pursue special hobbies and perhaps develop some latent interests and skills. Financial resources also make it easier for the child to attend college and perhaps graduate or professional school.

Parents' occupations and income can also influence the type of neighborhood in which a family lives. A place of residence is influential because it determines whom we meet and with whom we interact in our daily lives. Because of their residents' backgrounds and values, neighborhoods differ in their emphasis on athletic achievements, academic attainments, and occupational success. Peer pressure among children can work to encourage or discourage educational accomplishments and aspirations.

In addition to the cultural norms of a particular social class or neighborhood, the geographical location of one's residence can affect occupational decisions. Young people growing up in a city may have little knowledge of the life of a forest ranger, and someone from a tropical climate might not seriously consider a career in ski resort management. These geographical considerations do not pose insurmountable barriers (a Miami-bred college student at a New England university could develop an interest in and proficiency at skiing), but they do restrict a view of what constitutes a feasible career.

Beyond the influences of family, social class, and geography, career decisions are also made in the context of the larger society and culture within which one lives. For example, the ethnic culture in which one grows up can influence an individual's values, interests, and job choices.[25] Moreover, members of some underrepresented ethnic minority groups may perceive barriers to entering certain educational institutions and occupations that are not experienced by others, and women may avoid male-dominated occupations because of the absence of female role models or the lack of encouragement by others who adhere to sex-role stereotypes.[26]

In addition, economic conditions and consumer preferences promote certain industries and occupations over others. The growth in many service industries is a result of increased consumer buying power and preference for a more leisurely lifestyle. Technological changes create positions that were unheard of just a few years before. Moreover, the role of "accidents" in career decision-making must not be forgotten. If you hadn't attended that political rally, you never would have met your fiancé, who couldn't have introduced you to his cousin, who wouldn't have asked you to go to the conference in social planning, which ultimately stimulated your interest in public administration. These kinds of "random" accidental events occur all the time and can easily influence the course of our lives.

In summary, one's social background can stimulate or suppress certain skills, values, and abilities. Social class has been found to be related to beliefs about one's ability and control over a situation, as well as the importance of work to one's identity.[27] One's social background provides or withholds financial resources and, to a large extent, determines the people who will play a major role in one's early life. Moreover, the cultural environment reinforces certain values, legitimizes certain career aspirations, and places occupational decisions in a larger economic, political, and technological milieu. In short, the environment can influence how people view themselves, their future, and the world of work.

Guidelines for Effective Occupational Decision-Making

Despite our position that occupational choice is primarily a matching process, observation and common experience tell us that many people do not necessarily choose occupations that are compatible with their talents, values, and interests. Some choose occupations that fail to utilize their talents, that provide for little satisfaction of their needs and values, and that involve job duties in which they have little or no interest. In this section, we apply the career management model by examining several factors that can contribute to the choice of an appropriate occupation.

Development of Self-Awareness

Self-awareness is the cornerstone of effective career management. In the absence of a deep understanding of one's values, interests, personality, abilities, work orientation, and preferred lifestyle, one would require considerable luck to fall into a compatible occupation. The major obstacles to the development of self-awareness were discussed in Chapter 5. At this time, it is appropriate to consider your degree of self-awareness. Review your responses to Learning Exercises 1 (data collection), 2 (theme identification), and 3 (preferred work environment) provided at the end of Chapter 5. Do the themes still make sense to you? Is your preferred work environment summary consistent with these themes? Does your summary touch on all eight of the elements listed in Exercise 3? If not, ask yourself why certain elements are missing. Consider, once again, the importance you place on family, spiritual life, community, and leisure, and how you want work to fit in with other parts of your life that are important to you.

Learning Exercise 7 appears in the Appendix at the end of this chapter. It provides an opportunity for you to revise or complete your preferred work environment statement. If you believe you need more information in certain areas, indicate how you can go about obtaining the information. Consider the possibility of seeing a vocational counselor, taking tests, reading materials on self-assessment, and speaking to friends, relatives, spouse, colleagues, coworkers, or professors. Remember that self-exploration is a process; it is never really completed. Therefore, a periodic appraisal of your preferred work environment can be helpful.

Development of Accurate Occupational Information

Self-awareness needs to be combined with a satisfactory understanding of alternative occupations. However, lack of relevant work experience, stereotypes of occupations, and unfamiliarity with certain occupational fields all detract from development of a solid base of occupational information.

Actually, there are two related steps in occupational exploration. The first is to identify a number of occupations that may be potentially compatible and satisfying. Then, collect more in-depth information on each occupation. Obviously, one can go back and forth between the two steps, but some form of screening is necessary. As was discussed in Chapter 5, effective screening of various occupations can be accomplished by consulting sources that provide information on a wide range of occupations. Once some initial screening has been conducted, it is possible to collect more extensive information on a smaller number of occupational alternatives. Again, an understanding of one's preferred work environment can help focus one's information search.

Other people in one's social network, such as counselors, professors, friends, relatives, and work associates, can provide information on specific occupations. In addition, personal or family contacts can frequently identify individuals who are currently employed in a particular occupation and are willing to share their experiences and opinions. Seminars, which can also provide useful information on specific occupations (e.g., "Careers in Advertising"), are often sponsored by student groups (e.g., the Society for the Advancement of Management), counseling offices, and professional associations. Finally, work experience, which has frequently been mentioned as a source of information about oneself and the world of work, is also helpful. For students, cooperative work assignments, internships, and part-time or summer jobs can provide insights into different occupational fields. For employees, volunteering in the community, shadowing someone who works in a field of interest to you, working on a part-time job in another field, or taking on a project at work unrelated to your current job can increase knowledge about other occupations. Whether student or employee, individuals can conduct "informational interviews" with someone in a career field or a company in which they are interested. An informational interview is an informal way to gain information about a prospective job or company without the pressure of trying to sell oneself, as in a formal interview process.[28] The informational interview can be used as a way to gain knowledge about a career field or a company and its business lines and, in a preliminary way, test for a fit with a particular job or the organization as a whole.

Effective Goal-Setting

One of the most significant components of the career management process is the development of realistic and appropriate career goals. In the context of occupational choice, the goal is to enter a specific occupational field. Assuming that a person has conducted sufficient self- and occupational exploration, how should he or she decide from among alternative occupations?

Learning Exercise 5, included at the end of Chapter 6, provided an opportunity for you to develop long-term and short-term operational goals. If you identified specific occupations in Learning Exercise 5, this would be a good time to reexamine the advantages and disadvantages you listed for each occupation. If you did not identify specific occupations in Exercise 5, you should do so at the present time. List the elements of your conceptual goal (long-term or short-term), identify two occupations in which you have some interest, and then list the advantages and disadvantages of each occupation.

The choice of an occupation is, in the end, a subjective, emotional experience, and no absolute criteria are available to determine what represents a "good" career choice. No easy, automatic formulas exist (or should exist) to eliminate the subjective element. However, a systematic collection and analysis of relevant information can provide a realistic database in making such decisions.

Development of Career Strategies

Once a goal to enter a particular occupational field is selected, we need to identify strategic behaviors, activities, and experiences that help to achieve the goal, such as completing a degree program, changing majors, obtaining an advanced degree, or achieving certification. As noted in Chapter 4, enacting a career strategy can also help test the viability of a career goal. For example, pursuing a master's degree or taking elective courses in a particular area may confirm or disconfirm the wisdom of our occupational choice. Regardless of which strategies are used, it is important to understand the purpose of each activity, sequence the activities, and establish timetables for completion. It is also necessary to be flexible in developing and implementing a career strategy. No list of strategies should ever be considered final. Even if goals remain the same, specific strategic behaviors should be added or deleted as necessary. Most important, people should take advantage of the feedback and appraisal functions of strategies. Periodically ask yourself whether your chosen occupation still makes sense to you. If the evidence is consistently and convincingly negative, be prepared to change your course of action—or pay the price somewhere along the line.

Learning Exercise 8 appears in the Appendix at the end of this chapter. If a strategy to enter an occupation (or change occupations) is relevant to you at the present time, use Learning Exercise 8 to formulate the strategy.

Choosing and Entering an Organization

Once a person has settled upon a particular occupation, the next step is to find a job and successfully gain entry into an organization. As with occupational choice, organizational choice involves trying to find a match between an individual's values, interests, abilities, work orientation, and lifestyle preferences and the requirements, rewards, and other characteristics of a job in a particular organization that has its unique mission, products, and culture. Organizational choice is a multistage process involving activities undertaken by the individual job-seeker (such as researching a company, preparing a résumé and cover letter, and lining up professional references) and simultaneous efforts by the organization (such as posting or advertising available job openings, participating in job fairs, and establishing appropriate screening tools).[29]

Past research has identified four phases in the organizational choice and entry process, with each phase having different but related tasks for the job candidate and the hiring organization; recruitment, selection, orientation, and socialization.[30] *Recruitment* is defined as the process of mutual attraction between the individual and the organization. At this stage, the individual locates information on job sources and firms, while the organization is concerned with finding and attracting job candidates. *Selection* involves the process of mutual choice. Individuals in this phase must deal with job interviews, assessments, and making choices among job offers. For the hiring organization, the key task is a person–job fit assessment of candidates for future job performance and retention. *Orientation* is defined as the period of initial adjustment once the person has actually entered the organization. For the individual, this means coping with the stress of entry, while the organization must attend to the emotional and informational needs of newcomers. The last stage, or *socialization*, is termed the process of mutual adjustment. During this phase, the individual moves through typical work stages and experiences various successes. The organization employs socialization techniques and tactics to influence newcomers' behavior and ensure their assimilation into the organization. This chapter will cover the recruitment and selection processes, and Chapter 8 will discuss orientation and socialization.

The ultimate objective of organizational choice/entry is to attain a match between the individual and the organization. The candidate's capabilities and the job's requirements must match, as should the individual's needs and the organization's rewards or reinforcements. The capability–job requirement match can affect an employee's level of job performance, whereas the need–reinforcement match can influence an employee's level of job satisfaction.[31] Both matches can affect the contribution a new employee makes to the organization.

Consequences of a mismatch can be severe. From the employee's perspective, a mismatch can produce dissatisfaction and disappointment, can be a threat to self-esteem, and might result in a decision to pursue another job in a different organization. From the organization's point of view, poor performance can detract from the organization's effectiveness, and extensive turnover can be costly because replacements need to be recruited, selected, trained, and developed into productive employees.[32] For these reasons, it is important to understand how individuals choose jobs in organizations, the role of expectations in the organizational entry process, and the steps individuals and organizations can take to increase the likelihood of successful organizational entry.

Theories of Organizational Choice

The basic approaches an individual can take when deciding on an employer are similar to those used in occupational choice. Specifically, job candidates are attracted to an organization that is most likely to provide desirable outcomes and they avoid those organizations that would likely result in undesirable outcomes. In one sense, the job-seeker could take a programmed approach to organizational choice by systematically gathering all relevant information during the recruiting process and then using this information to estimate the likelihood that alternative employers will provide the desired set of outcomes. The individual then systematically assesses the desirability or value of each potential outcome from alternative employers, and accepts a job offer from the firm that is most compatible with one's values, interests, and preferred lifestyle; that is, the job most likely to provide valued outcomes such as interesting work, pleasant working conditions, advancement opportunities, and flexible work schedules.

In contrast with this programmed approach to organizational choice, a job candidate could be considerably less thorough or systematic in the selection process. According to this alternative (or unprogrammed) view, candidates initially become attracted to organizations that are acceptable according to just one or two particularly critical outcomes (not a long set of outcomes), develop an implicit (often unconscious) choice of an organization, and then engage in perceptual distortion in favor of the organization they have already implicitly chosen.[33] Organizational choice, in this view, is based on the subjective perception that an organization can provide a satisfactory opportunity to attain just one or two highly significant outcomes.

Which approach, programmed or unprogrammed, more accurately describes the organizational choice process? Although research has supported the efficacy of both types of decision-making, one can argue that the more thorough the search and the greater the number of outcomes and organizations considered, the greater the likelihood of a favorable match and success in the job search process.[34] Perhaps the most relevant question is not which type of job search is more typical, but which type is more beneficial for the individual and the organization. It should not be surprising that a programmed approach with a thorough search for extensive information enables a candidate to be more confident and satisfied with the organizational entry process.

The Role of Expectations in Organizational Choice and Entry

Both approaches to organizational choice—programmed and unprogrammed—reflect a matching process in that people choose jobs that will satisfy significant values. In effect, candidates develop expectations about an organization's capacity to provide valued outcomes. These expectations guide people toward or away from various job opportunities. Thus, a person's attraction to a certain job is based on the expectations that the job will provide desirable outcomes such as interesting work and autonomy on the job. Whether accurate or not, these expectations strongly influence a person's choice of jobs in organizations. Indeed, an organization's "corporate image" has a strong influence on an individual's choice to pursue employment with that organization.[35]

Yet job expectations—for interesting work, advancement opportunities, financial security, and the like—may not be realized when a candidate actually enters the organization as a new employee. In fact, job-related expectations can be unrealistically inflated upon organizational entry, and the more abstract the topic (e.g., opportunity for personal growth), the more unrealistic the applicants' expectations. New employees often experience "reality shock," a sense of disillusionment, disappointment, and dissatisfaction upon recognizing that the reality of the job and the organization do not quite match their preconceived expectations.

Several typical expectations held by job-seekers as they embark on their job search are identified in Table 7.2, alongside the realities of being a new employee. It is not suggested that all candidates hold these expectations or that all new employees experience the same realities. However, there is certainly an opportunity for a gap between naïve expectations and day-to-day job experiences.

Development of Unrealistic Expectations

What happens when expectations prove to be unrealistic? It has been argued that candidates who hold such expectations become dissatisfied when faced with the realities of a job and, ultimately, may choose to leave the organization.[36] For example, if a job candidate is told during the interview process that working extended hours or on weekends is rarely required, but then finds out after accepting a job that long hours are the norm, that person will likely be dissatisfied, disillusioned, and tempted to leave the organization. The reasons for the devastating effect of unrealistic expectations will be examined in a later section. For now, assume that recruits who hold unrealistic expectations about a job and organization will, at the very least, be surprised when they confront a reality on the job that does not confirm their expectations, and this surprise may be accompanied by dissatisfaction and disillusionment if the job experiences are generally undesirable.[37] Indeed, as one would expect, if a recruit's image of a company (as defined as expectations around issues such as pay, development, flexibility, and security) is not based on reality,

Table 7.2 Comparisons of Expectations and Experiences

A Recruit May Expect That...	*A New Employee May Experience That...*
• "I will have a great deal of freedom in deciding how my job gets done."	• "My boss pretty much determines what I do and how I do it."
• "Most of my projects will be interesting and meaningful."	• "It seems like I have an endless stream of trivial, mundane tasks."
• "I will receive helpful, constructive feedback from my boss."	• "I really don't know how I am doing on the job."
• "Promotions and salary increases will be based on how well I do my job."	• "Promotions and money are tight, and they appear to be based on factors other than my performance."
• "I will be able to apply the latest techniques and technologies to help the organization."	• "People resist adopting my suggestions, even though the old ways are antiquated and inefficient."
• "I will be able to balance my work and nonwork responsibilities without much difficulty."	• "My job and my nonwork responsibilities often interfere with one another."

then the result could be a heightened level of job dissatisfaction as well as intention to terminate employment.[38]

If we assume for the moment that unrealistic expectations can have a negative effect on new employees, we need to pose certain questions: *Why do people develop unrealistic expectations? Where do these expectations come from? Why do they end up being unrealistic?* We answer these questions by identifying a number of factors that can lead to unrealistic expectations.

Career Transitions

Perhaps the most fundamental explanation for unrealistic expectations is that the path from the job-seeker role to the employee role represents a career transition. A *career transition* is a period in which a person either changes career roles (inter-role transition) or changes orientation to a current role (intra-role transition). For example, when a person leaves school and enters a work organization (an inter-role transition), there are many differences between the old and the new settings: differences in tasks, required behaviors, norms, and expectations. Indeed, the lives of students and employees are vastly different. Even a job change, within the same organization or from one organization to another, represents a career transition, although the differences in settings may not be as severe as those between student and employee roles.

In short, many new employees, whether coming directly from school or from another organization, have to face a set of demands with which they may be unfamiliar. New employees must confront such experiences as reliance on other people (bosses, peers, customers), low levels of freedom and autonomy, extensive resistance to changes they might suggest, too much or too little job structure, and the politics of organizational life.[39] The organization is not typically going to change to accommodate a new employee. Oftentimes, close supervision, mundane tasks, little responsibility, and tight controls are an organization's way of ensuring the satisfactory performance of new, untested employees.

Organizations' policies and practices might explain the nature of the job experiences a new employee confronts, but they don't explain how the employee developed unrealistic expectations. Why do so many people expect to have considerable freedom in a job, to get promoted in a short time, to be appraised and counseled by a supportive, caring boss, and to obtain challenging, meaningful, and rewarding assignments? Where do people get such ideas in the first place? To answer this question, several other critical influences on unrealistic expectations must be explored.

The Recruitment Process

Even though organizations commit substantial resources to recruiting, the recruitment process has often been viewed as the most significant source of unrealistic expectations. In essence, it is claimed that organizations often portray jobs in overly optimistic terms, thus inducing unrealistic expectations on the part of the job candidate. To understand why this occurs, one must appreciate that the organization's goal is to attract qualified candidates. To keep qualified candidates interested in the organization, recruitment often focuses on "selling" the organization and the job opportunity.[40] This is accomplished by presenting incomplete or overly flattering accounts of what it is like to work in the organization.

For instance, even a cursory examination of recruiting brochures or corporate websites illustrates how companies emphasize the positive: challenging and exciting work, rewards based on job performance, good opportunities for promotion, and timely, constructive feedback from your boss. Of course, there is the question of whether organizations can deliver on these promises. Even if they could, these descriptions omit some of the less flattering qualities that characterize almost any job in any organization. The delivery of overly positive messages during recruitment is a key source of unrealistic expectations.

This is not to say that organizations deliberately lie, but in their effort to put their best foot forward, they can easily slant their presentations in favor of positive information. Moreover, the employees responsible for recruitment often have little direct line experience in the organization. Accordingly, they might also believe these glowing accounts of the organization and, in the process, pass on these unrealistic expectations to job candidates.

Of course, individual candidates have their own goal during recruiting: to keep the organizations interested in them so they may select the most appropriate organization for which to work. To keep an organization interested, candidates are likely to emphasize their strengths and omit potential weaknesses or reservations. This all amounts to a "mutual sell" in which each party (the candidate and the recruiting organization) may be reluctant to reveal less desirable qualities. These goal conflicts are hardly conducive to an open, complete sharing of information during recruitment and selection. As a later section of this chapter will show, organizations can choose to modify their recruitment practices to offer candidates a realistic job preview that is intended to convey a more complete, accurate picture of the organization than traditional recruitment normally permits.

Organizational Stereotypes

Many candidates hold images and stereotypes of certain companies or industries even before they have had extensive contact with the organization. For example, research has found that job candidates hold specific stereotypes of small companies that differ substantially from those of big firms.[41] In addition, candidates can hold highly specific images of particular companies. Job candidates perceive a company's image in terms of its job opportunities, products, labor relations posture, administrative practices, geographical location, pay practices, and financial performance. Moreover, as noted earlier, a positive image of a company is an important factor in a candidate's decision to pursue a job with that company.[42]

In a sense, then, stereotyped images breed expectations, and because stereotypes are, by definition, partially incomplete or inaccurate, the resulting expectations may not be particularly realistic. A candidate who holds a stereotype about Company X ("Company X has a great reputation—people are promoted quickly with good money, lots of challenge, and flexible time off") may not bother to test out these assumptions during recruiting or may not pay close attention to any discrepant information a company provides.

Educational Process

Specific coursework at the undergraduate or graduate level often does not sufficiently prepare students for the reality of the work world. For example, technically oriented courses in engineering or business rarely dwell on the problems inherent in working within an organizational structure as a new employee. Moreover, many colleges try to instill in their students a sense of pride in themselves and an ardent enthusiasm for their chosen career field. Under these conditions, it is not surprising that many graduates emerge with an inflated, unrealistic picture of what they will face in their first job. The resulting disillusionment may be particularly severe when employers deliberately hire overqualified job candidates, who are likely to see themselves as underutilized on the job.

Lack of Prior Work Experience

Job candidates without extensive prior work experiences may be particularly susceptible to the development of unrealistic expectations. Job candidates with a variety of prior work experiences are more likely to engage in a more thorough information search during recruiting than candidates without such experience. Presumably, varied work experiences teach people that all organizations are not the same; hence the need for obtaining more information about each potential employer.

Self-Delusion

We also must consider the possibility that some people fool themselves into believing what they want to believe. Why the tendency to fool ourselves during a job search? First, candidates who are initially attracted to a job may distort or ignore negative information because they do not want to be confronted with anything unfavorable about a job they have already decided they prefer. Also, candidates with few alternative opportunities may hear only the positives of a job that they believe they might ultimately be forced to take.

Distortions also may be due to the feelings of dissonance or tension people experience after having reached an important decision. When individuals make a choice, they normally reject one alternative in favor of another. They may then engage in distortion or selective attention to convince themselves of the wisdom of their decision. In the process, however, they set themselves up for disillusionment since the overly glowing picture of the chosen organization could not be matched by the realities of the first year of employment. Thus, one source of unrealistic expectations is our own natural tendency to see the world through rose-colored glasses; that is, to see it as we would like it to be.

Organizational Choice and Entry in Later Adulthood

In Chapter 2, we discussed the view that specific age ranges can demarcate career stages. Organizational choice and entry normally would be experienced in the earliest period of adulthood. Of course, with the rise of nontraditional and impermanent work arrangements, the need to make career changes or job switches, either by choice or by circumstance, makes the issues surrounding organizational choice and entry relevant at any age. Thus, while an individual may be in the middle or late adulthood stages in a chronological sense, he or she could be looking for a new job or accepting a new position, thereby facing the demands of recruitment, selection, orientation, and socialization that come with organizational choice and entry. The important distinction is that older adults confront these demands from a different, more experienced perspective. In other words, recruitment, establishment, and socialization are still important tasks for older adults, but they are addressed in hopefully a wiser and more mature fashion. Consider the following example:

Sharon never thought she would have to prove herself again. After all, in the first 22 years of her career, she had built a record of significant accomplishment—several promotions, ultimately to the level of vice-president for planning and development; an annual salary of $200,000; an executive MBA degree from a top school; a recognized leadership position in the organization, with admiration from her peers and subordinates alike; and the opportunity to help map her company's future. In the 23rd year, Sharon's fast track rise came to an abrupt end. Her company was purchased in a hostile takeover and the new company saw Sharon's position as expendable. At the age of 46, Sharon found herself out of a job. Working with an executive search firm, Sharon put together a new résumé and pursued several promising leads. With few managerial- and executive-level jobs available, Sharon found the competition to be intense for the open positions that fit her background and experience. Sharon made sure she was well prepared for each interview by researching each prospective company extensively on the Internet. After several months of job search, Sharon accepted the position of business planning and forecasting manager for a small automotive products retailer. The salary and status were comparatively much lower than her previous job, but Sharon was convinced that her new employer was a good match for her.

Even though Sharon is in middle adulthood, she was forced to "cycle back" by confronting the variety of tasks associated with finding a new employer and gaining entry. In this sense, she was like a graduating college student looking for a first professional position. She had a résumé to prepare, companies to research, questions to ask, and offers to assess. But Sharon approached these tasks from a more mature perspective. Her 23 years of corporate experience had provided extensive knowledge of her own talents and interests, as well as an understanding of the inner workings of business organizations. Accordingly, she was clear on the type of work situation she wanted, and she also knew which conditions to avoid. Because of her experience, Sharon was less prone to developing unrealistic expectations about her new job. Thus, while Sharon was forced to endure the rigors of organizational choice and entry, she was able to negotiate the process from the vantage point of an experienced employee.

Organizational Actions During the Entry Process

Organizations have three major tasks to accomplish during the organizational entry process. First, they need to attract talented and qualified candidates into the applicant pool and keep them interested in the organization. Second, they need to attract candidates in such a way as to minimize the development of unrealistic job expectations on the part of the candidates. Third, they must assess candidates accurately and extend offers to those who are likely to succeed in the organization. Organizations use a multitude of techniques, to varying degrees, in the attraction, recruitment, assessment, and selection processes.[43] This section discusses several approaches that organizations can use to attract and select candidates in an effective, realistic manner.

Attraction of Job Candidates

Certainly, organizations will not be able to staff themselves properly unless they can induce talented candidates to enter and remain in the recruitment process. Research on recruitment has identified a number of issues that have significant implications for organizations.[44]

Impact of the Recruiter

For many candidates for managerial, professional, and technical positions, the first formal contact with the organization is with the recruiter, and the initial activities are submitting a résumé, filling out an application, and sitting for the screening interview. Below are a few of the desirable qualities of this initial interaction between the candidate and the organization.[45]

First, candidates' reactions to interviews are most positive when the recruiter is perceived as knowledgeable. Recruiters who are familiar with the candidate's background and understand the organization and job qualifications in detail are viewed favorably. Given the straightforward nature of this fact, it would seem surprising that recruiters are often perceived as unprepared and/or unknowledgeable. However, the lack of interview preparation and knowledge may be a function of the way organizations train and prepare their recruiters, and some companies fail to offer recruiter training programs or ensure that their recruiters are properly prepared prior to beginning their recruitment assignments.

In addition to adequate knowledge and preparation, recruiters' behavior during the interview affects candidates' attitudes.[46] Recruiters who ask relevant questions, answer candidates' questions accurately, and discuss career paths and job qualifications produce positive responses from candidates. Finally, the perceived qualities of the recruiter play a prominent role in the interview setting. A warm, enthusiastic, perceptive, and thoughtful recruiter understandably affects the recruit's reactions affirmatively.

Although there is no direct evidence on the frequency of poorly conducted interviews, it is clear that interviews can cause negative reactions among job candidates. One possible explanation for this phenomenon is recruiters' apparent lack of awareness of job candidates' values, needs, and aspirations. Recruiters can overestimate or underestimate the significance that individuals attach to specific aspects of the job (e.g., salary) and the organization (e.g., its reputation for ethical behavior). It seems unlikely that recruiters can present favorable information on topics of special significance to candidates if they misjudge the importance of these topics. Therefore, organizations need to pay sufficient attention to the initial interview process to ensure that proper information about the organization is presented to candidates. To present this information satisfactorily, recruiters need to understand candidates' concerns better, develop a deeper knowledge of the organization, and project a positive, concerned image. Careful selection and training of recruiters is certainly one place for an organization to begin.

Follow-up Activities

Upon completion of the initial screening interview with a candidate, organizations decide whether to carry the process to the next step (normally a site visit) or to terminate the relationship with the candidate. Often, job candidates hold unrealistic expectations regarding the selection process,[47] including the time it takes for an organization to make a go/no-go decision on whether to continue the recruitment process. Organizations can take three weeks or more to make a decision on a potential employee, depending on the number of interviews to be conducted as well as the number of layers of management approval that are required to further the recruitment process. Clearly, many companies could profit by shortening the lag time between the interview and the go/no-go decision and, at the very least, indicate during the initial interview what the time lag is likely to be.

The organization should also pay close attention to the site visits for candidates who survive the initial screening. Positive attitudes regarding the visit have been associated with the opportunity to meet with supervisors and peers, to ask questions and to have them answered frankly, and to receive sufficient information about the job, the company, and the specifics of the on-site activities in advance of the visit. Organizations have an opportunity at each phase of recruitment to create a *workplace brand*, defined as the "*process of building an identifiable and unique employer identity that... differentiates it from its competitors.*"[48] The workplace brand allows the firm to distinguish itself through recruitment (and other HR) practices that are perceived as desirable, effectively creating a positive brand image.[49] Organizations must also be mindful of how they handle the job offer. Candidates hold more positive attitudes toward offers when the organization contacts them after the offer to provide additional information, is open to candidates' questions, and is willing to discuss specific terms of employment.[50]

In summary, organizations can take more effective steps to attract candidates during the recruitment process. The importance of the recruiter and the initial interview cannot be overemphasized. Also, the manner in which the site visit is planned and the way in which the job offer is extended can influence the candidates' attitudes toward the organization. All of these activities contribute to the brand image an organization projects to the public. The fact that an organization's brand image and reputation can attract or repel potential candidates is a reminder of the importance of the recruitment process.

Realistic Recruitment

The preceding section examined ways for organizations to project an attractive image to job candidates. However, as previously discussed, an organization's brand image can be "too positive" if it is not based on reality. Because the recruitment process is an important source of candidates' unrealistic job expectations, it is a prime target for reexamination and possible revision.

Realistic recruitment means presenting candidates with relevant and undistorted information about the job and the organization, even when this information might be seen as negative or unflattering to the hiring organization.[51] The vehicle through which realistic information is conveyed to candidates has been called the *realistic job preview* or RJP. As the term indicates, an RJP presents job candidates with a balanced, realistic preview of the job and the organization. An RJP may be presented through a company's website, films, booklets, lectures, or one-on-one discussions. An RJP is often contrasted with a *traditional job preview* (TJP), wherein the organization paints an overly optimistic (and hence unrealistic) picture of the job and its requirements. Not surprisingly, given their lack of realism, TJPs tend to produce higher levels of organizational attractiveness to job candidates,[52] an attraction that is likely to diminish when reality on the job sets in.

The presentation of realistic information to job candidates should reduce the level of voluntary turnover among candidates who ultimately join the organization. Several arguments have been advanced to support such a position. *First*, realistic previews lower candidates' expectations to more appropriate levels—expectations that are more likely to be met on the job.[53] Employees whose expectations have been met tend to be satisfied with their jobs, and satisfied employees are less likely to quit than are dissatisfied employees. According to this "met expectations" view, RJPs function by deflating initial expectations so that new employees experience little disappointment, disillusionment, and dissatisfaction when they confront reality.

A *second* explanation views a realistic preview as presenting a dose of reality about the job that allows for the development of coping strategies to help the new employee deal with the potentially disappointing and dissatisfying aspects of the job. For example, candidates who learn during recruitment that a job requires a great deal of close supervision may prepare themselves by rehearsing how they would deal with close supervision or perhaps by convincing themselves that the close supervision of a newcomer to the organization may not be so terrible after all.

A *third* explanation is that RJPs convey an air of honesty to job candidates. This can have two effects. First, candidates may admire and respect an organization that is candid enough to "tell it like it is." This attitude can bond a new employee to the organization and reduce the likelihood of turnover. For example, one study found that turnover may be minimized by offering oral or written RJP discussions delivered post-hire and designed to signal organizational honesty.[54] In addition, candidates who accept a job after receiving an honest disclosure of its negative qualities can become committed to the job and organization because they believe they made their decision with full knowledge of the facts and without coercion or distortion on the part of the organization.

Fourth, it has been suggested that realistic previews offer candidates a basis to self-select out of the recruitment process. In other words, they should enable candidates to determine whether a job will meet their significant values. Faced with an accurate, balanced portrayal of a prospective job, some candidates might choose to reject a job offer because they don't perceive a match between their needs and values and the organization's rewards and opportunities.

Do Realistic Job Previews Work?

The major objective of realistic recruitment is to reduce voluntary turnover among new employees. Therefore, a fair test of an RJP's effectiveness is to compare the turnover rates of new employees who received an RJP during recruitment with a comparable group who did not. Several reviews have evaluated the overall effectiveness of RJPs.[55] Studies suggest that RJPs can reduce turnover significantly, which can provide considerable savings to organizations that have to recruit, select, and train fewer new employees to replace those who terminate employment.

However, there are two caveats. First, RJPs do not significantly reduce turnover in every case. If the turnover rate of a job is high because of its undesirable qualities (e.g., poor pay, boring work), then even an RJP is not likely to reduce turnover.[56] Thus, the impact of RJPs on turnover can vary from setting to setting. Second, there is little evidence to support any of the four mechanisms (met expectations, coping, air of honesty, self-selection) that presumably explain the effectiveness of RJPs. Taken together, these two problems indicate that it is not fully understood when and why RJPs are effective.

However, there are a number of circumstances in which RJPs are likely to be most effective. First, when job candidates have alternative employment opportunities, they can be selective about accepting a job offer and feel less compelled to accept an unappealing job, thereby permitting an RJP's self-selection mechanism to operate. In contrast, people who see few alternative opportunities may distort or discount negative information during recruitment, thus rendering an RJP less effective. Second, when job candidates would have held unrealistic expectations in the absence of an RJP, a realistic preview can be an eye-opener. Third, an RJP may be of particular value when job candidates would have had difficulty coping with the job demands in the absence of a realistic preview. In this regard, the negative information included in an RJP can lower employee expectations about the job and also allow the establishment of behaviors to cope effectively with undesirable features of the job.[57] Finally, the effectiveness of an RJP can increase when the information presented to the prospective employee touches on topics that are particularly significant or relevant to the candidate.

In conclusion, realistic job previews are potentially valuable ingredients in an organization's recruitment program that present an image of the organization as an honest, caring employer that may also reduce turnover among new employees. Moreover, the concept of the RJP is not limited to new hires. It can be extended to situations in which employees are faced with a promotion, job transfer, and/or geographical relocation. In each of these situations, a realistic forewarning of future circumstances may be helpful to the individual and the organization.

Regardless of an organization's recruitment practices, some reality shock is inevitable. There are many sources of unrealistic expectations besides organizational recruitment. Organizational entry is a career transition, and there are going to be some unpleasant surprises and required adjustments. The first 6–12 months on a new job challenge the new employee and the organization. These challenges will be examined in more detail in Chapter 8.

Assessment and Selection

Once prospective job candidates have been attracted and realistically recruited, the next step for the organization is final assessment and selection. This section will discuss briefly the process by which organizations assess and select their employees. More extensive treatments of this topic are available in other published works.[58]

In the selection of individuals for employment, organizations first attempt to achieve a match or fit between the knowledge, skills, and abilities of the individual and the specific requirements of the job. In addition, some recruiters also try to assess the fit between the job candidate and such broader organizational factors as strategy, culture, and corporate values.[59] Ideally, organizations should use selection techniques (and make actual selections) that are based on the accomplishment of both match-ups. In this sense, the "total" person is selected, one who is hired not only to meet the challenges of a particular job, but also to "fit" with the work and cultural environment of the organization. In this regard, many organizations are taking advantage of social media in assessing candidates and in making selection decisions.[60] By searching social media sites, such as Facebook and LinkedIn, employers can gather additional information on a prospective employee that goes beyond what is available through a résumé, employment application, or personal interview. Although the search of social media sites is controversial and could be viewed as an invasion of privacy, it is a tool that can offer insights, both positive and negative, on an applicant.[61]

In contrast to the "total" person view of hiring, some organizations make hiring decisions using a single criterion (or a limited number of criteria) such as the degree of conscientiousness or level of intelligence.[62] While there can be arguments for using a limited number of criteria in making hiring decisions (such as the simplification of the assessment process), we believe that the total person strategy of matching individual to organization is the more appropriate approach to ensure longer-term satisfaction for the individual and the hiring organization. Nonetheless, it is obvious that individual intelligence and character do play a critical role in most, if not all, hiring decisions and have been found to be consistent predictors of individual job performance.[63]

Overall, the selection of individuals whose abilities and personal characteristics match the job and the work environment can have positive consequences for the organization in terms of lower turnover, a more involved and committed workforce, and enhanced task performance.[64] Thus, it is in the best interests of the organization (and the individual) to utilize selection methods that serve to ensure a proper person–environment fit.

Individual Actions During the Choice and Entry Process

From an individual's perspective, the primary aim of organizational entry is to obtain a job that is reasonably consistent with his or her preferred work environment. In this regard, an individual can take certain steps to improve the likelihood of a positive outcome and an appropriate adjustment to a new work role.[65] This section considers several major tasks people need to confront during organizational choice and entry, including the identification of prospective employers, the use of effective job interview behavior, the assessment of organizations, and the choice of an organization for which to work. In each task area, we provide guidelines for effectively managing the organizational entry process.

Identification of Prospective Employers

There are a number of sources for job leads, including college placement offices, unsolicited direct contacts, personal associates, advertisements in newspapers, social media, personnel agencies and search firms, Internet employment websites, and corporate websites. Much has been written about each source and its relative advantages and disadvantages.

Although college placement offices are a widely used source of job leads for college students, the importance of personal associates and contacts for everyone looking for employment cannot be overestimated. For professional, managerial, and technical employees, personal contacts often provide the most useful information about potential employers. There exist two broad types of personal contacts: (1) family members, friends, and social acquaintances and (2) work contacts such as present or past bosses, colleagues, and teachers. As we discussed in Chapter 2, the accumulation of social capital allows individuals to use personal contacts within a "social network" to learn of job openings or to put them in touch with others who might know of openings.[66] That is, they know many people who are either aware of job openings or know others who are. Certainly, social media networking using LinkedIn, Facebook, Twitter, and other sources can provide useful entrées.[67]

It is generally more difficult for younger people to use personal contacts because their social networks are not as extensive as older, more experienced people. Nevertheless, it is never too early to begin to establish networks and build social capital. Part of the challenge is identifying potential sources of information. Faculty members, fellow students, relatives, and friends of the family may all possess useful information. Connecting with them on a social networking site such as LinkedIn may be the first step to building a professional relationship. Participation in campus clubs and student professional organizations also may provide job leads and future contacts. However, meeting people is not enough. We also have to communicate our needs, values, and aspirations so others are aware of them. This requires an assertive posture that is essential to all aspects of career management.

In recent years corporate websites, social media, and Internet recruitment have become key mechanisms for the attraction, application-filing, testing, and assessment of prospective job candidates.[68] Websites provide an efficient way to deliver a company's recruitment, diversity, and work–life messages, as well as basic information about corporate strategy and mission. They also allow interested job candidates instant access to learn about open positions. When combined with electronic employment screening and screening via social media networking sites,[69] these websites let companies quickly identify individuals for further assessment and simultaneously eliminate those who do not meet the basic requirements for a position. For the job candidate, corporate websites and social media networking sites provide a wealth of information about a prospective employer.

Effective Job Interview Behavior

Just like an organization, a job candidate has multiple goals during recruitment. Candidates need to make a favorable impression to receive a job offer, and they must gather useful information about companies so they can assess alternatives. Sometimes these goals can conflict with one another. This section will examine impression management, and the next section will turn to the accurate assessment of jobs and organizations.

Although companies scrutinize candidates' educational and work experiences and often administer psychological and integrity tests, the most widely used assessment procedure is the personal interview. Therefore, job candidates should be aware of the factors that contribute to a successful interview. In general, interviews are judged most effective when the interviewee knows about the company, has specific career goals, asks good questions, is socially adept, and is articulate. These five factors seem to reflect two underlying dimensions of interviewee behavior: preparation/knowledge and effective interpersonal communication skills.

The first dimension underscores the need for candidates to conduct thorough research on the organization. There are many possible information sources. In addition to commonly available documentation (such as newspaper articles, annual reports, and corporate websites), these sources include potentially knowledgeable people, such as friends, family members, members of professional and social organizations, and people with contacts or who know people with contacts.

People who work in the company of interest can be particularly helpful, and may be found via social media networking sites. It is recommended that job candidates conduct informational interviews with such people; that is, interviews that are designed to obtain useful information, not necessarily to obtain a job.[70] Moreover, candidates should enter these interviews with questions that are relevant to their preferred work environment. A relatively clear understanding of desired tasks, rewards, and opportunities should enable a candidate to identify many of the relevant features of an organization and its jobs.

The second dimension, effective interpersonal communication skills, reflects social skills and articulation. Although there is no guaranteed way to become articulate and socially adept, candidates can work toward reducing their anxiety so that their positive qualities can emerge during the interview. Employment interviews are anxiety-provoking situations for most people. They are somewhat unpredictable and can play a major role in one's career. However, there are a number of ways to reduce anxiety to appropriate and manageable levels:

- Know yourself. People who know what they want can be more relaxed during an interview and can respond more naturally and effectively to questions about career goals and expected contributions to the organization.
- Research the company thoroughly and prepare salient questions to ask.
- Participate in programs designed to enhance interview and speaking skills, job search focus, and assertiveness. Many such programs are available through college placement offices or organizationally sponsored training activities.

In short, adequate planning and preparation for interviews can make a candidate more relaxed and effective in recruitment situations.

Assessing Organizations

To make a realistic job choice, a candidate needs to assess organizations carefully and systematically. A useful organizational assessment requires the collection and analysis of data from varied sources. Table 7.3 lists several different types and sources of information that would be helpful in organizational assessment and interview preparation.

It may be difficult to obtain some of the information shown in Table 7.3 for two reasons. First, candidates may be so preoccupied with making a positive impression and obtaining a job offer that they don't seek information or pay attention to information that is provided. Second, organizations may be unable or unwilling to provide some important pieces of information. Job candidates can overcome these potential obstacles in several ways. *First*, they should be conscious of their own motives and goals during recruitment. They must recognize that their desire to impress a company may possibly distract them from their task of collecting critical information. Candidates must understand that it is possible to impress and assess simultaneously. Indeed, companies may not even be impressed with candidates who fail to ask significant and perceptive questions.

Second, candidates must see the connection between their preferred work environment and the assessment of an organization. Otherwise, the questions they ask may turn out to be irrelevant or trivial. Candidates should review their preferred work environment summary before each interview and identify the specific information they will need to assess the compatibility of the organization with their values, interests, talents, and desired work–life balance.

Third, candidates should understand the most appropriate data collection techniques. Observing prospective supervisors and colleagues in their work environment can give some clues about their competence, cooperativeness, and attitudes toward the organization and each other. Even if one's observations cannot provide conclusive evidence, they can suggest areas to be pursued with direct questioning. In other words, take advantage of the site visit to understand the people, their communication patterns, the organization, and its facilities. In addition, as noted in Table 7.3, there are websites that students and job-seekers can use to learn about organizations in an independent way.[71] Specifically, these websites provide commentaries on, and "unvarnished" reviews of, a given company penned by current and former employees. Further, popular social media sites, such as LinkedIn and Facebook, can also serve as a source of information on a particular organization. Of course, information

Table 7.3 Types and Sources of Information for Organizational Assessment and Interview Preparation

Types of Information
• Line(s) of business conducted by the organization • Size of the organization • Structure of the organization • Outlook of the industry(ies) in which the organization does business • Financial health of the organization • Organization's business plans for the future • Location of the organization's headquarters and major facilities • Availability of training and development opportunities • Opportunities for flexibility in work schedules and locations (telework) • Promotion and advancement policies (e.g., promotion from within) • Descriptions of jobs and plans for individuals within jobs (if available)
Sources of Information
• Documents such as corporate annual reports, 10K and 10Q filings with the Securities and Exchange Commission, and newspaper articles • Corporate social media accounts, including Facebook and Twitter • Reviews of a company posted on reputable Internet sites • Friends, family members, coworkers, and former or current employees of the company

Table 7.4 Sample Questions Asked by Interviewee

Sample Target Job: Financial Analyst

Sample Interview Questions

1. What is the role of a financial analyst in this company?
2. What training opportunities are available?
3. Do financial analysts work on a variety of projects at one time?
4. How much responsibility and independence do financial analysts have in their work?
5. What technical support is available?
6. What long-term career opportunities are available for financial analysts?
7. How are salary increases and promotions determined?
8. How much travel is involved?

and reviews gained through Internet sites should be viewed as just another source of data that can help in the assessment of a prospective employer.

In addition, it is important to understand that the way in which a question is asked can affect the impression you make and the likelihood that you will obtain useful information. Members of the organization are human beings who can become defensive if they believe the questions are personally threatening or embarrassing. Therefore, questions should be asked in a sensitive, nonthreatening manner. Table 7.4 provides a set of sample questions that might be used during the interview process by a job candidate for a financial analyst position.

A *fourth* obstacle for a job candidate to overcome is an overload of information at the completion of an interview or a visit to an organization. To prevent information loss, candidates should complete a brief set of notes immediately after a recruitment interview to record their reactions to the interview as well as objective data, such as the time and place of the interview and the interviewer's name. Also, during breaks on the day of the interview, it might be possible to make notations on a personal computer or tablet. Items on a notes log should be tied to the important elements of one's preferred work environment (e.g., "Will the job take advantage of my talents?" "Is there enough flexibility on the job to meet my family and personal responsibilities?" "Are there training opportunities?"). Not only would this practice help one assess alternative organizations, it also would permit one to identify issues for which further information is needed. In addition, job candidates should request business cards or another form of contact information from the individuals they meet during the interview process or the site visit, which can help prevent information loss, provide key data such as phone numbers and email addresses, and be a guide to the position titles of the people who conducted the interviews.

Choosing Organizations

Like the choice of an occupation, the selection of a job with a particular organization should not be a mechanical "by-the-numbers" decision. Nor should it be speculative or unsystematic. On the basis of one's preferred work environment, one should identify a set of desirable and undesirable outcomes, and then estimate the compatibility of each alternative job with each outcome. Some job offers (or potential job offers) may be discarded quickly, whereas others may require more information and a more thorough analysis of the data.

Of course, if the individual has only one job offer, it might be difficult to "discard" that job because there is no alternative that is readily available. In this case, the job offer and the organization have to be evaluated based on other possibilities and whether the job-seeker can afford to wait longer to see whether another, perhaps more attractive, offer is forthcoming. Accepting a job offer simply because it is the only one available might set the person up for longer-term disappointment if that job and organization do not fit with individual interests, values, and abilities.

Evaluating alternative jobs on the basis of expected outcomes should stimulate individuals to think about their values and aspirations, and the likelihood that competing jobs will meet their preferred outcomes. Lists of advantages and disadvantages of each job can also help to visualize the relative attractiveness of each alternative. Nevertheless, there is a subjective, emotional element in job choice that should not be suppressed. Although this book emphasizes the systematic collection and analysis of information, the decision to accept one job over another also has to "feel" right. In this regard, we should not rely too heavily on other people's views of our needs and values. Although it is important to obtain input from a wide variety of people, it is our needs and values that must be met, not other people's visions of what we should want from work.

Summary

Four themes capture much of the thinking and research on the occupational choice process: (1) occupational choice is a matching process in which individuals seek an occupation that is consistent with their talents, values, interests, and desired work–life balance; (2) occupational decisions evolve over time as people develop and refine their knowledge of themselves and the work world; (3) occupational choice is a decision-making task in which people evaluate the likelihood that alternative occupations will provide desirable outcomes; and (4) individuals' occupational decisions are influenced by their social background and the current economic, political, and technological environment.

Self-awareness, the cornerstone of career management, is a necessary ingredient in effective occupational decision-making. In addition, people need to develop a solid base of information to screen alternative occupations for potential appropriateness. The choice of an occupation from a set of alternatives should maximize the compatibility of the chosen occupation with one's conceptual goal. Career strategies particularly relevant to occupational choice include competence in current activities, self-nomination, networking, and seeking guidance.

Organizational entry is the process by which a job candidate moves from outside to inside an organization. Its objective is to attain a match between individual talents and needs and a job's demands and rewards. Candidates develop expectations that guide their selection of jobs and organizations. Often, however, these expectations prove to be unrealistically inflated. The development of unrealistic job expectations can be due to a radical career transition (e.g., moving from school to work), the recruitment process itself, stereotypes that candidates hold about particular organizations, the nature of candidates' prior educational and work experiences, and candidates' natural tendency to see things as they would like them to be, not necessarily as they are. New employees can become disillusioned and dissatisfied if they see that the reality of the job doesn't live up to their lofty expectations.

Organizations should develop recruitment techniques that attract candidates effectively. At the same time, organizations should consider developing realistic recruitment procedures in which candidates are given a balanced picture of the job—both the positive and the negative features. Under certain conditions, realistic recruitment can reduce dissatisfaction and turnover among new employees.

Individuals also need to manage the organizational entry process. In particular, candidates should understand their own preferred work environment, develop networks to identify prospective employers, develop or refine job interview skills, conduct accurate assessments of organizations, and make job choices based on sound information and self-knowledge.

Career Management *for Life*: Work–Life Implications from Chapter 7

- Occupations can differ in terms of their compatibility with a person's lifestyle preferences and desired form of work–life balance.
  - Some occupations require longer work hours or more travel than others.
  - Some occupations can be more stressful than others.
- Therefore, individuals in the process of selecting an occupational field should understand what they want to accomplish in different parts of life (work, family, community, leisure) and try to determine whether a particular occupation is compatible with *all* of these aspirations.
- Similarly, jobs in some organizations require longer work hours, have more inflexible hours, demand more travel, or are more stressful than similar jobs in other organizations.
- Therefore, individuals engaged in the job search process should learn as much as possible about job requirements and the supportiveness of the organization (e.g., availability of flexible work arrangements) to determine whether a particular job will help or hinder their achieving work–life balance.

Assignments

1. Think about an organization in which you worked. List the characteristics of the organization that you evaluated before you made the choice to work there. In making the choice, did you consider just one or two important characteristics of the company (as with unprogrammed decision-making), or did you evaluate more thoroughly a longer list of salient characteristics (as with programmed decision-making)? In retrospect, were you satisfied with the organizational choice you made? Do you think your approach to decision-making influenced your subsequent satisfaction with the organizational choice you made? Explain why or why not.
2. Interview your parents, spouse/partner, and/or other relatives to understand how your family background can influence (or has already influenced) your career choices. Think back to when you were younger. Specifically consider how the ideals and aspirations of your parents or others in your social network (such as other relatives and/or friends) influenced your personal development. How has your family income, neighborhood, sports programs, and religious training affected your views and attitudes toward work? Try to trace the significance of all of these factors to your current career plans and choices.

Discussion Questions

1. Do most people choose occupations that match their talents, values, interests, and desired work–life balance? What are some obstacles to establishing such a match?
2. What is the role of emotion or "instinct" in deciding on an occupation? What weight should be given to a formal, rational analysis of a job versus a more subjective, emotional appraisal?

3. What can you do to develop realistic expectations about a job in which you are interested? Identify as many sources of information as possible.
4. To what extent have your educational and/or prior work experiences given you a realistic picture of what it would be like to enter a new organization? How could colleges and universities help individuals develop more realistic job expectations?
5. What are the advantages that accrue to organizations that practice realistic recruitment? Are there any risks involved? In your prior attempts to seek employment, did organizations provide you with a balanced, realistic picture of the job and the organization? What were your reactions to the recruitment procedure?
6. Why is an understanding of one's preferred work environment so critical to effective job search and organizational entry? What does a job candidate risk if he or she lacks self-insight in this area?
7. What can you learn about a job or an organization by visiting its facilities? How can you prepare for a visit to maximize the amount of useful information you receive? How can you assess whether a prospective employer will fit with your preferred work environment?

Chapter 7 Case: Natalie the Retail Manager (Part A)

Natalie graduated from a large state university with two important possessions—a combined marketing and management degree and high aspirations. She believed that her education, abilities, and ambition would lead to a rewarding career in management. As she interviewed with several companies for her first postgraduate job, it seemed that retail organizations offered the best opportunity for a quick rise to the management ranks. Also, retail firms seemed to give her a good chance to apply her dual majors. The "fast-track" program offered by Enigma (fictitious name), a chain of upscale department stores, was especially intriguing to Natalie. The program included an intensive training course for aspiring managers combined with challenging on-the-job assignments. The recruiter told Natalie that those selected for this program could expect an unencumbered rise to upper management. Natalie was also impressed by what she had seen in the literature the recruiter had used to describe Enigma's proactive development programs and corporate culture.

Natalie was so pleased with her choice of Enigma as her first employer that in all the excitement she didn't get much of a chance to talk to her parents or friends about it. Also, the preparations for graduation and the end-of-year parties didn't leave much time for her to check into Enigma as an employer. In Natalie's view, the recruiter gave her a fairly balanced overview of the company. One month after graduation, Natalie began the three-month course that blended textbook learning with real-life, store-based training at the company's Dallas headquarters.

Natalie found the training course to be quite demanding. Substantial emphasis was placed on individual initiative and accomplishments, often pitting trainees against one another in business simulations. Natalie thought the emphasis on individual action to be somewhat strange since the recruiter had stressed that Enigma's success was based on teamwork and esprit de corps. Although she was in a class with 40 other trainees, Natalie found it difficult to make friends with her cohorts. The rigors of the training and the emphasis on individual competitiveness left little time or inclination for personal bonds to be established. Near the end of the training period Natalie received her first performance evaluation. The instructors saw her intelligence and technical skills as strong points, but also noted that she needed to be more decisive, become more sensitive to customer needs, and develop a "killer instinct" when dealing with difficult employee behavior. Even though the training wasn't exactly what she had expected, Natalie still believed that she was well prepared for a regular store assignment.

After completion of the training course, Natalie was filled with confidence as she began her career as an assistant manager at one of Enigma's busiest and most profitable stores in an East Coast suburban location. While the competitiveness of the training course was a surprise, she looked forward to the assignment because it was close to her parents' home and it was within easy driving distance to major metropolitan areas. As an assistant manager, Natalie was given significant responsibility for the housewares department. She was told that her duties covered all aspects of the department, including inventory control, customer service, staff scheduling and hiring, and merchandise presentation. It was explained to Natalie that her "normal" work week would be Tuesday through Saturday, from 9:30am to 6:30pm, but that Enigma's culture dictated that the managers see their responsibility to their stores as being 24 hours a day, seven days a week.

One Year Later

Natalie has really begun to dread these visits to the doctor's office. The regular migraine headaches she developed from the very beginning of her time at Enigma were bad enough, but now the heartburn and stomach distress are almost unbearable. While she sat in the doctor's office, Natalie began to reflect on the past year at Enigma. The first six months had been really overwhelming. It took her a while to comprehend Enigma's use of a Darwinian "survival of the fittest" approach to employee development and retention. She had been thrown into the housewares department with virtually no advance preview of the workings of the operation or the personnel. When she did meet with her boss in the afternoon of her second day, Natalie was told, for the first of many times, that this is a "sink or swim assignment, so you better dive in and start swimming."

The staff in housewares included a mixture of full- and part-time employees. Generally, the full-time staff members were assigned to housewares on a permanent basis, while part-timers could be assigned to any department in the store depending on such factors as absenteeism or promotional campaigns. From the start of her assignment, Natalie felt a sense of hostility toward her from three full-time staff members, each of whom had been with Enigma for more than five years. Natalie believes that the hostility, which had subsided somewhat just in the last few weeks, resulted from two factors. First, the longer-tenured staff resented her being given the job of assistant manager without having paid any "dues" on the front lines of the department. Second, nearly all of the staff at the Enigma store had a negative view of management, primarily because of what were seen as Enigma's abusive demands and "factory-like" approaches to the supervision of its employees.

Natalie could accept the first factor since it was true that she was only out of college for less than six months and she was supervising people who had been with the store for many years. Natalie was dismayed over the second factor, but saw its validity. During her recruitment, Enigma portrayed itself as a progressive and caring organization that was concerned about the quality of life of its employees. Yet the three-month training program and her work experiences clearly pointed to a different organization, one that saw its employees as nothing more than human capital that could be used up and then replaced. Horror stories (and turnover) were commonplace. Employees were regularly called upon to work ridiculous hours or abandon personal plans at the last minute because they were needed at the store. Also, the managerial culture dictated that employee difficulties were dealt with in an aggressive and dispassionate way. The abusive attitude toward the staff and the culture were troubling to Natalie because they went against the grain of her personality. She had always viewed herself as a friendly and caring person, but the store demanded that she think and act differently or risk being seen as not a team player.

Natalie's relationships with her boss and her fellow assistant managers were strained, to say the least. The competitiveness that was fostered in the training program carried over into operations of the stores. Natalie's boss, a woman in her mid-30s, was overly ambitious, and she had no qualms about telling everyone who would listen that her goal was to be a vice-president and regional manager by the time she was 40. The boss appreciated the contributions of the people who worked for her, but only to the extent that they could be instrumental in taking her to the next level. Natalie believed that if she showed too much ambition or in any way tried to question the established procedures or culture, she would be seen as a threat and labeled a maverick and not supportive of the management team or Enigma's mission. So, Natalie learned to implement changes and improvements in her department in a quiet fashion. Also, she tried to create a new culture within housewares that encouraged teamwork as a way to improve performance. Through her efforts, housewares had shown steady performance gains, and by the end of Natalie's first year, it was one of the top two departments in the store.

When it came to her relationships with her contemporaries, Natalie continued to find it difficult to create any sort of personal or emotional ties with the 11 other assistant managers. The encouragement of individualistic behavior, brought on by the store's penchant for inter-departmental performance comparisons, created a working environment where everyone was most concerned with his or her own performance, not the performance of the store in total. This environment also led to a variety of political behaviors being used, from backstabbing to outright sabotage. Although it took a little while, Natalie caught on to the self-serving games and had learned how to act when confronted with political behaviors.

In her personal life, it was tough for Natalie to engage in any social activities, let alone find an intimate relationship. She had been putting in 70-hour work-weeks throughout her first year with Enigma, and the grueling schedule left little time for leisure or exercise. She realized that her health problems were partly attributable to a lack of outside interests that could have served to reduce stress. Just within the last two months,

Natalie has vowed to spend more time in activities outside of work. She joined a health club and started socializing more with family and friends.

Despite all the tribulations of the past year, Natalie believed that she had grown in the managerial position at Enigma. The work culture wasn't real positive, and she still felt some residual hostility from her subordinates, but she had learned to cope and had actually been successful in putting her own imprint on the workings of her department and the store. After six months on the job she had wanted to quit, but now, even with the migraines, the heartburn, and the advice of her doctor to find a less stressful job, she thought she would stick it out for a while longer. (Part B of the Natalie case is at the end of Chapter 8.)

Case Analysis Questions

1. Critique the process Natalie went through in her selection of Enigma as an employer. Do you think the selection of Enigma was right for her? What could she have done differently in her job search? What aspects of her work–life balance did she consider?
2. Do you think Enigma was right in the approaches it used to recruit Natalie? Should an employer have a moral obligation to always use realistic recruitment?
3. Do you believe that the "survival of the fittest" approach that Enigma used in developing its managers was an appropriate strategy? Do you think Natalie should have been more forceful in trying to correct managerial and cultural wrongs that she observed?
4. Do you agree with Natalie's decision to "stick it out for a while longer" with Enigma after she had been on the job for a year? Should Natalie have been more proactive in considering other employment options at this point in her career?

Appendix for Chapter 7: Learning Exercises 7 and 8

Learning Exercise 7: Reexamination of Preferred Work Environment (PWE)

Reread your responses to Learning Exercises 1, 2, and 3 before completing Exercise 7.

Component of PWE	*Is PWE accurate?*	*Is PWE complete?*	*Where can you get more information?*
What tasks do you find interesting?	Yes/No	Yes/No	
What talents do you want to use?	Yes/No	Yes/No	
How much freedom and independence do you want?	Yes/No	Yes/No	

Component of PWE	*Is PWE accurate?*	*Is PWE complete?*	*Where can you get more information?*
What type of relationships with others do you want?	Yes/No	Yes/No	
What physical work setting do you prefer?	Yes/No	Yes/No	
How important is money?	Yes/No	Yes/No	
How important is security?	Yes/No	Yes/No	
How important is balance of work, family, and leisure?	Yes/No	Yes/No	

Learning Exercise 8: Formulation of Career Strategy to Enter a Specific Occupation

List each activity that you deem necessary to prepare yourself to enter a specific occupation you wish to pursue. To guide task accomplishment, also identify the purpose of each activity and the general timeframe needed for completion. Realize that the formulation of a strategy is an important step in preparing to enter an occupation that you are considering. Be thorough in identifying your needed activities. For a listing of the different types of career strategies, please consult Table 6.2. And for examples of specific strategies, you might want to review Table 6.3.

If there are two different occupations you are considering, feel free to complete Learning Exercise 8 twice, first for one occupation and then for the other occupation.

Activity	*Purpose*	*Time Frame*

Notes

1 Callanan, G. A. (2006). Organizational entry. In Greenhaus, J. H. & Callanan, G. A. (Eds.), *Encyclopedia of career development* (pp. 586–588). Thousand Oaks, CA: Sage; Wanous, J. P. (1992). *Organizational entry: Recruitment, selection, orientation and socialization of newcomers*. Reading, MA: Addison-Wesley.
2 Crites, J. O. (1969). *Vocational psychology*. New York: McGraw-Hill.
3 Pryor, R. G. & Bright, J. E. (2006). Occupational choice. In Greenhaus, J. H. & Callanan, G. A. (Eds.), *Encyclopedia of career development* (pp. 547–554). Thousand Oaks, CA: Sage.
4 Holland, J. L. (1966). *The psychology of vocational choice*. Waltham, MA: Blaisdell; Holland, J. L. (1985). *Making vocational choices: A theory of vocational personalities and work environments*. Englewood Cliffs, NJ: Prentice-Hall; Holland, J. L. (1997). *Making vocational choices: A theory of vocational personalities and work environments*, 3rd ed. Odessa, FL: Psychological Assessment Resources; Ohler, D. L. & Levinson, E. M. (2012). Using Holland's theory in employment counseling: Focus on service occupations. *Journal of Employment Counseling*, *49*, 148–159; Shahnasarian, M. (2006). Holland's theory of vocational choice. In Greenhaus, J. H. & Callanan, G. A. (Eds.), *Encyclopedia of career development* (pp. 352–356). Thousand Oaks, CA: Sage.
5 Ohler & Levinson (2012); Shahnasarian (2006).
6 Some of the more commonly available resources for the assessment of the Holland types include www.careerkey.org, www.self-directed-search.com, www.careeronestop.org, www.hollandcodes.com.
7 de Beer, L. T., Rothmann, S., Jr. & Mostert, K. (2016). The bidirectional relationship between person-job fit and work engagement: A three-wave study. *Journal of Personnel Psychology*, *15*, 4–14; Rehfuss, M. C., Gambrell, C. E. & Meyer, D. (2012). Counselors' perceived person–environment fit and career satisfaction. *Career Development Quarterly*, *60*, 145–151; Walsh, W. B. (2006). Person–environment fit (P–E fit). In Greenhaus, J. H. & Callanan, G. A. (Eds.), *Encyclopedia of career development* (pp. 622–625). Thousand Oaks, CA: Sage.
8 Super, D. E. (1963). Toward making self-concept theory operational. In Super, D. E., Starishevsky, R., Matlin, N. & Jordaan, J. P. (Eds.), *Career development: Self-concept theory* (pp. 17–32). New York: College Entrance Examination Board.
9 Muchinsky, P. M. & Monahan, C. J. (1987). What is person–environment congruence? Supplementary versus complementary models of fit. *Journal of Vocational Behavior*, *31*, 268–277.
10 Blustein, D. L., Kenna, A. C., Murphy, K. A. & Devoy Whitcavitch, J. E. (2006). Self-concept. In Greenhaus, J. H. & Callanan, G. A. (Eds.), *Encyclopedia of career development* (pp. 713–717). Thousand Oaks, CA: Sage; Sverko, B. (2006). Super's career development theory. In Greenhaus, J. H. & Callanan, G. A. (Eds.), *Encyclopedia of career development* (pp. 789–792). Thousand Oaks, CA: Sage.
11 Blustein et al. (2006); Chen, C. T., Chen, C. F., Hu, J. L. & Wang, C. C. (2015). A study on the influence of self-concept, social support and academic achievement on occupational choice intention. *The Asia-Pacific Education Researcher*, *24*, 1–11.
12 Bellah, R. N., Madsen, R., Sullivan, W. M., Swidler, A. & Tipton, S. M. (1985). *Habits of the heart: Individualism and commitment in American life*. Los Angeles: University of California Press; Wrzesniewski, A., McCauley, C., Rozin, P. & Schwartz, B. (1997). Jobs, careers, and callings: People's relations to their work. *Journal of Research in Personality*, *31*, 21–33.
13 Duffy, R. D. & Dik, B. J. (2013). Research on calling: What have we learned and where are we going? *Journal of Vocational Behavior*, *83*, 428–436; Wrzesniewski, A. E. (1999). *Jobs, careers, and callings: Work orientation and job transitions*. Unpublished doctoral dissertation, University of Michigan; Wrzesniewski et al. (1997).
14 Duffy & Dik, (2013); Elangovan, A. R., Pinder, C. C. & McLean, M. (2010). Callings and organizational behavior. *Journal of Vocational Behavior*, *76*, 428–440; Lan, G., Okechuku, C., Zhang, H. & Cao, J. (2013). Impact of job satisfaction and personal values on the work orientation of Chinese accounting practitioners. *Journal of Business Ethics*, *112*, 627–640; Steger, M. F., Frazier, P., Oishi, S. & Kaler, M. (2006). The meaning of life questionnaire: Assessing the presence of and search for meaning in life. *Journal of Counseling Psychology*, *55*, 80–93; Wrzesniewski et al. (1997).
15 Callanan, G. A. (2006). Anticipatory socialization. In Greenhaus, J. H. & Callanan, G. A. (Eds.), *Encyclopedia of career development* (pp. 20–21). Thousand Oaks, CA: Sage; Callanan, G. A. & Benzing, C. (2004). Assessing the role of internships in the career-oriented employment of graduating college students. *Education + Training*, *46*, 77–83.

16 Phillips, S. D. & Jome, L. M. (2006). Career decision-making styles. In Greenhaus, J. H. & Callanan, G. A. (Eds.), *Encyclopedia of career development* (pp. 94–96). Thousand Oaks, CA: Sage.
17 Osborn, D. P. (1990). A reexamination of the organizational choice process. *Journal of Vocational Behavior, 36*, 45–60.
18 Sauermann, H. (2005). Vocational choice: A decision making perspective. *Journal of Vocational Behavior, 66*, 273–303; Singh, R. & Greenhaus, J. H. (2004). The relationship between career decision-making strategies and person–job fit: A study of job changers. *Journal of Vocational Behavior, 64*, 198–221.
19 Kulkarni, M. & Nithyanand, S. (2013). Social influence and job choice decisions. *Employee Relations, 35*, 139–156; Singh & Greenhaus (2004); Van Hoye, G. & Lievens, F. (2007). Social influences on organizational attractiveness: Investigating if and when word of mouth matters. *Journal of Applied Social Psychology, 37*, 2024–2047; Van Hoye, G. & Lievens, F. (2009). Tapping the grapevine: A closer look at word-of-mouth as a recruitment source. *Journal of Applied Psychology, 94*, 341–352.
20 Kulkarni & Nithyanand (2013); Osipow, S. H. (1983). *Theories of career development*. Englewood Cliffs, NJ: Prentice-Hall; Van Hoye & Lievens (2007, 2009).
21 Canedo, J. C., Stone, D. L., Black, S. L. & Lukaszewski, K. M. (2014). Individual factors affecting entrepreneurship in Hispanics. *Journal of Managerial Psychology, 29*, 772–755; Giscombe, K. (2006). Socioeconomic status. In Greenhaus, J. H. & Callanan, G. A. (Eds.), *Encyclopedia of career development* (pp. 759–761). Thousand Oaks, CA: Sage; Stone, D. L., Johnson, R. D., Stone-Romero, E. F. & Hartman, M. (2006). A comparative study of Hispanic-American and Anglo-American cultural values and job choice preferences. *Management Research, 4*, 8–21.
22 Ibid.
23 Thompson, M. N. & Subich, L. M. (2006). The relation of social status to the career decision-making process. *Journal of Vocational Behavior, 69*, 289–301.
24 Jepsen, D. A. (2006). Family background and careers. In Greenhaus, J. H. & Callanan, G. A. (Eds.), *Encyclopedia of career development* (pp. 313–317). Thousand Oaks, CA: Sage.
25 Stone et al. (2006).
26 Fouad, N. A. (2006). Culture and careers. In Greenhaus, J. H. & Callanan, G. A. (Eds.), *Encyclopedia of career development* (pp. 214–220). Thousand Oaks, CA: Sage; Eby, L. T. (2006). Gender and careers. In Greenhaus, J. H. & Callanan, G. A. (Eds.), *Encyclopedia of career development* (pp. 325–331). Thousand Oaks, CA: Sage.
27 Brown, M. T., Fukunaga, C., Umemoto, D. & Wicker, L. (1996). Annual review, 1990–1996: Social class, work, and retirement behavior. *Journal of Vocational Behavior, 49*, 159–189; Stone et al. (2006).
28 Gonzalez, P. (2006). Informational interview. In Greenhaus, J. H. & Callanan, G. A. (Eds.), *Encyclopedia of career development* (pp. 387–389). Thousand Oaks, CA: Sage.
29 Callanan (2006); Wanous (1992).
30 Wanous (1992).
31 Ibid.
32 Griffeth, R. W. & Hom, P. W. (2001). *Retaining valued employees*. Thousand Oaks, CA: Sage.
33 Soelberg, P. O. (1967). Unprogrammed decision making. *Industrial Management Review, 8*, 19–29.
34 Lent, R. W., Ezeofor, I., Morrison, M. A., Penn, L. T. & Ireland, G. W. (2016). Applying the social cognitive model of career self-management to career exploration and decision-making. *Journal of Vocational Behavior, 93*, 47–57; Saks, A. M. (2006). Multiple predictors and criteria of job search success. *Journal of Vocational Behavior, 68*, 400–415.
35 Gatewood, R. D., Gowan, M. A. & Lautenschlager, G. J. (1993). Corporate image, recruitment image, and initial job choice decisions. *Academy of Management Journal, 36*, 414–427; Kolenko, T. A. (2006). Organizational image. In Greenhaus, J. H. & Callanan, G. A. (Eds.), *Encyclopedia of career development* (pp. 588–589). Thousand Oaks, CA: Sage.
36 Schreurs, B. H. J. & Syed, F. (2011). Battling the war for talent: An application in a military context. *Career Development International, 16*, 36–59; Wanous (1992).
37 Greenhaus, J. H., Seidel, C. & Marinis, M. (1983). The impact of expectations and values on job attitudes. *Organizational Behavior and Human Performance, 31*, 394–417; Schleicher, D. J. & Fox, K. E. (2006). Job satisfaction. In Greenhaus, J. H. & Callanan, G. A. (Eds.), *Encyclopedia of career development* (pp. 436–440). Thousand Oaks, CA: Sage.
38 Ito, J. K., Brotheridge, C. M. & McFarland, K. (2013). Examining how preferences for employer branding attributes differ from entry to exit and how they relate to commitment, satisfaction, and retention. *Career Development International, 18*, 732–752.

39 Lent, R. W. (2013). Career-life preparedness: Revisiting career planning and adjustment in the new workplace. *Career Development Quarterly, 61,* 2–14; Schein, E. H. (1978). *Career dynamics: Matching individual and organizational needs.* Reading, MA: Addison-Wesley.
40 Wilhelmy, A., Kleinmann, M., König, C. J., Melchers, K. G. & Truxillo, D. M. (2016). How and why do interviewers try to make impressions on applicants? A qualitative study. *Journal of Applied Psychology, 101,* 313–332.
41 Greenhaus, J. H., Sugalski, T. & Crispin, G. (1978). Relationships between perceptions of organizational size and the organizational choice process. *Journal of Vocational Behavior, 13,* 113–125; Ito et al. (2013).
42 Aiman-Smith, L., Bauer, T. N. & Cable, D. M. (2001). Are you attracted? Do you intend to pursue? A recruiting policy-capturing study. *Journal of Business and Psychology, 16,* 219–237; Gatewood et al. (1993); Cable, D. M. & Turban, D. B. (2003). The value of organizational reputation in the recruitment context: A brand-equity perspective. *Journal of Applied Social Psychology, 33,* 2244–2266.
43 Piotrowski, C. & Armstrong, T. (2006). Current recruitment and selection practices: A national survey of Fortune 1000 firms. *North American Journal of Psychology, 8,* 489–496.
44 Turban, D. B. (2006). Recruitment. In Greenhaus, J. H. & Callanan, G. A. (Eds.), *Encyclopedia of career development* (pp. 675–679). Thousand Oaks, CA: Sage.
45 Ito et al. (2013); Turban, D. B., Campion, J. E. & Eyring, A. R. (1995). Factors related to job acceptance decisions of college recruits. *Journal of Vocational Behavior, 47,* 193–213.
46 Celani, A. & Singh, P. (2011). Signaling theory and applicant attraction outcomes. *Personnel Review, 40,* 222–238; Chapman, D. S., Uggerslev, K. L., Carroll, S. A., Piasentin, K. A. & Jones, D. A. (2005). Applicant attraction to organizations and job choice: A meta-analytic review of correlates of recruiting outcomes. *Journal of Applied Psychology, 90,* 928–944.
47 Derous, E. (2007). Investigating personnel selection from a counseling perspective: Do applicants and recruiters' perceptions correspond? *Journal of Employment Counseling, 44,* 60–72.
48 Backhaus, K. & Tikoo, S. (2004). Conceptualizing and researching employer branding. *Career Development International, 9,* 501–517. Quotation is on p. 502.
49 Ibid; Celani & Singh (2011); Lievens, F., Van Hoye, G. & Anseel, F. (2007). Organizational identity and employer image: Towards a unifying framework. *British Journal of Management, 18,* S45–S59.
50 Turban et al. (1995).
51 Pane, S. S. (2012). Realistic job previews and performance: The mediating influence of personal goals. *Journal of Management Research, 12,* 163–178; Wanous, J. P. (2006). Realistic recruitment. In Greenhaus, J. H. & Callanan, G. A. (Eds.), *Encyclopedia of career development* (pp. 672–675). Thousand Oaks, CA: Sage.
52 Gardner, W. L., Reithel, B. J., Foley, R. T., Cogliser, C. C. & Walumbwa, F. O. (2009). Attraction to organizational culture profiles: Effects of realistic recruitment and vertical and horizontal individualism–collectivism. *Management Communication Quarterly, 22,* 437–472.
53 Buda, R. & Charnov, B. C. (2003). Message processing in realistic recruitment practices. *Journal of Managerial Issues, 15,* 302–316.
54 Earnest, D. R., Allen, D. G. & Landis, R. S. (2011). Mechanisms linking realistic job previews with turnover: A meta-analytic path analysis. *Personnel Psychology, 64,* 865–897.
55 Wanous (2006).
56 Ibid.
57 Pane (2012).
58 Gatewood, R. D., Feild, H. S. & Barrick, M. (2016), *Human resource selection,* 8th ed. Mason, OH: Cengage; Gowan, M. A. & Gatewood, R. D. (2006). Personnel selection. In Greenhaus, J. H. & Callanan, G. A. (Eds.), *Encyclopedia of career development* (pp. 634–638). Thousand Oaks, CA: Sage.
59 Bretz, R. D., Rynes, S. L. & Gerhart, B. (1993). Recruiter perceptions of applicant fit: Implications for individual career preparation and job search behavior. *Journal of Vocational Behavior, 43,* 310–327.
60 Roth, P. L., Bobko, P., Van Iddekinge, C. H. & Thatcher, J. B. (2016). Social media in employee-selection-related decisions: A research agenda for uncharted territory. *Journal of Management, 42,* 269–298.
61 Ibid.
62 Behling, O. (1998). Employee selection: Will intelligence and conscientiousness do the job? *Academy of Management Executive, 12,* 77–86.

63 Le, H., Oh, I., Shaffer, J. & Schmidt, F. (2007). Implications of methodological advances for the practice of personnel selection: How practitioners benefit from meta-analysis. *Academy of Management Perspectives*, *21*, 6–15.

64 Arthur, W., Jr., Bell, S. T., Villado, A. J. & Doverspike, D. (2006). The use of person-organization fit in employment decision making: An assessment of its criterion-related validity. *Journal of Applied Psychology*, *91*, 786–801; Chi, N. W. & Pan, S. Y. (2012). A multilevel investigation of missing links between transformational leadership and task performance: The mediating roles of perceived person–job fit and person–organization fit. *Journal of Business and Psychology*, *27*, 43–56; Hoffman, B. J. & Woehr, D. J. (2006). A quantitative review of the relationship between person–organization fit and behavioral outcomes. *Journal of Vocational Behavior*, *68*, 389–399; Iplik, F. N., Kemal, C. K. & Yalcin, A. (2011). The simultaneous effects of person–organization and person–job fit on Turkish hotel managers. *International Journal of Contemporary Hospitality Management*, *23*, 644–661; Saks, A. M. & Ashforth, B. E. (2002). Is job search related to employment quality? It all depends on fit. *Journal of Applied Psychology*, *87*, 646–654.

65 Kammeyer-Mueller & Wanberg (2003); Zikic, J. & Klehe, U. (2006). Job loss as a blessing in disguise: The role of career exploration and career planning in predicting reemployment quality. *Journal of Vocational Behavior*, *69*, 391–409.

66 Adams, S. M. (2006). Social capital. In Greenhaus, J. H. & Callanan, G. A. (Eds.), *Encyclopedia of career development* (pp. 746–750). Thousand Oaks, CA: Sage.

67 Zide, J., Elman, B. & Shahani-Denning, C. (2014). LinkedIn and recruitment: How profiles differ across occupations. *Employee Relations*, *36*, 583–604; Leonardi, P. M. & Vaast, E. (2016). Social media and their affordances for organizing: A review and agenda for research. *Academy of Management Annals*, *11*, 150–188.

68 Cober, R. T. (2006). Internet recruitment. In Greenhaus, J. H. & Callanan, G. A. (Eds.), *Encyclopedia of career development* (pp. 406–409). Thousand Oaks, CA: Sage; Williamson, I. O., Lepak, D. P. & King, J. (2003). The effect of company recruitment web site orientation on individuals' perceptions of organizational attractiveness. *Journal of Vocational Behavior*, *63*, 242–263; Zide et al. (2014).

69 Albrecht, W. D. (2011). LinkedIn for accounting and business students. *American Journal of Business Education*, *4*, 39–41; Philbrick, J. H., Sparks, M. R. & Arsenault, S. (2006). Electronic employment screening. In Greenhaus, J. H. & Callanan, G. A. (Eds.), *Encyclopedia of career development* (pp. 257–259). Thousand Oaks, CA: Sage.

70 Gonzalez (2006).

71 As just two examples, www.glassdoor.com and www.indeed.com provide anonymous reviews of companies by current and prior employees. These reviews include both positive and negative comments. While giving potentially valuable insight, these reviews, since they are anonymous, should be viewed with some degree of skepticism since the source or writer of the review could be offering biased commentary.

8 The Early Career Stage

Establishment and Achievement

In previous chapters, we discussed the process of forming career goals and choosing (or targeting) a job and an organization. This chapter examines the two dominant themes of the early career—establishing oneself in a career and then striving for additional achievement—and offers guidelines to advance career management at this stage.

In any new job, the first charge is literally to become established. There is much to learn in this phase. One must become accustomed to the day-to-day routine and demonstrate mastery of new assignments. Acceptance by one's colleagues and bosses is another important consideration. In short, the hope is that one can become competent, productive, satisfied, and recognized within the new occupation and organization. Of course, it may take several years to determine whether competence, productivity, satisfaction, and recognition are attained.

Once the establishment phase has passed, and the employee has gained a measure of self-confidence and acceptance, the next major task of the early career is to increase one's level of achievement and contribution to the employer (or employers). Several questions arise at this point. Should an employee move from his or her current functional area to another department? Should one make preparations to assume a managerial role? Are there sufficient opportunities at one's company to pursue a number of different options? If not, what opportunities with increased responsibilities are available at other companies? This second phase of the early career typically reflects a concern for, if not a preoccupation with, achievement and accomplishment. Of course, the pursuit of career achievement and accomplishment has become more complicated over the past several years as companies have taken a more "transactional" approach to hiring and upward mobility, and as individual careers have become more "boundaryless." Career disruptions, brought on by the ongoing shift to less permanent work arrangements as well industry consolidations and corporate mergers, make it difficult for individuals to follow a standard path toward achievement of career goals.

Table 8.1 identifies changes that typically occur during the course of the early career. Employees early in their tenure with an organization are somewhat dependent on the organization for guidance and also tend to exhibit a need for security. However, as these individuals gain years of experience, they become more confident, assertive, dominant, independent, and achievement-oriented, and less concerned with gaining approval from others. In addition, their achievement and self-fulfillment needs become more prominent. As individuals mature in the early career, they do so not in a vacuum, but develop a sense of self through competency in developing relationships with others.[1] In time, both the establishment and achievement themes enable men and women in the workplace to become competent contributors.

Although it is impossible to pinpoint the timing of the transition from establishment to achievement, such a shift is likely to occur. This fact does not suggest that neophyte

Table 8.1 Changes During the Early Career

Establishment Themes	*Achievement Themes*
Fitting In	Moving Up
Dependence	Independence
Learning	Contributing
Testing Competence	Increasing Competence
Insecurity	Self-Confidence
Seeking Approval	Seeking Authority

employees care little about achievement, nor are veteran employees unconcerned about learning and gaining acceptance and security; it's a matter of relative emphasis. Moreover, because more senior individuals who are starting out in a new job might be concerned with establishing themselves in the new company, while their peers of the same age might be more concerned with achievement, the relative emphasis on establishment and achievement can fluctuate during the course of the early career.

The Establishment Phase

A person beginning—or redirecting—his or her career is traveling in unknown territory. An unproven commodity, the new employee needs to answer at least some of the following questions.[2] Will the job give me an opportunity to test myself? Will I be considered a worthwhile employee? Will I be able to maintain my individuality and integrity? Will I be able to balance my work life and home life? Will I learn and grow? Will I find the work environment stimulating and enjoyable? Will I "fit in" after being out of the workforce for several years raising my children? The employee at this point is a newcomer to the organization and has not yet acclimated to the organization psychologically. Therefore, there is a strong need to become accepted as a competent, contributing member of the firm, while exhibiting positive work habits and attitudes and establishing effective relationships with co-workers.[3]

At the same time, the organization must ensure that the new employee learns how to perform the job and how to fit into the company. Fitting in requires more than a mastery of task skills. It also requires learning how the organization operates, what actions are rewarded or punished, and the organization's values, culture, and social network. New hires and others in the establishment phase generally are the most receptive to information about the company and the ways they can make a contribution to it.

Just as a child growing up learns about society's values and norms (e.g., thrift, honesty, cooperation), so too must the newcomer learn how to function in the organization. Organizational *socialization* can be defined as "the process by which an individual learns appropriate attitudes, behaviors, and knowledge associated with a particular role in an organization."[4] It is generally believed that those who are well socialized into a firm are more likely to stay and develop their careers within the organization. They are more committed to the organization, more involved in their job, and, because they are able to adapt to their new environments, they are better performers.[5] The socialization process allows the employee to learn the functions, absorb the values, understand the hierarchy, and internalize the organization's culture.[6]

An organization's *culture* can be defined as "a pattern of basic assumptions invented, discovered or developed by a given group as it learns to cope with its problems of external adaptation and internal integration that has worked well enough to be considered valid and, therefore is to be taught to new members as the correct way to perceive, think, and feel in relation to those problems."[7] Socialization of new organizational members is the primary mechanism by which an organization can ensure the stability and perpetuation of its culture. Thus, proper socialization has an influential role in the longer-term survival of the firm because it serves to ensure continued adherence to the norms, ethics, values, and essential mission of the enterprise. By creating an environment in which the employee and the employer accept each other, the organization has properly socialized recruits and allowed them to be integrated into their new work environment.[8]

In essence, socialization is a learning process wherein the individual moves or changes from a former role (perhaps that of a college student, stay-at-home parent, or employee in a prior organization) into the new role of employee in the current organization. Evidence suggests that well-designed socialization processes can positively influence motivation, job and career satisfaction, compensation, job involvement, and organizational commitment.[9] Consequences of these positive influences include enhanced individual and organizational performance and lower levels of employee turnover.[10]

From the new employee's perspective, effective socialization is critical because it is difficult, if not impossible, to be competent and accepted without learning about and adjusting to the organization. Socialization is also essential to organizations. After all, organizations have histories and procedures that have been tested by time and tradition, and have ongoing work groups with established norms and priorities. Somehow, the newcomer must learn how to operate within an organization's established cultural system to become successful.

Content Areas of Socialization

Based on a review of the socialization literature and research, Georgia T. Chao and her colleagues identified six content areas of socialization.[11] The six areas represent the possible outcomes an organization would expect to result from the socialization process:

- **Proficient Performance**—the extent to which the individual has successfully learned the tasks involved on the job.
- **People**—the extent to which the individual has established flourishing work relationships with organizational members.
- **Politics**—the extent to which the individual has been successful in gaining information regarding formal and informal work relationships and power structures within the organization.
- **Language**—the extent to which the individual has learned the profession's technical language as well as the acronyms, slang, and jargon that are unique to the organization.
- **Organizational Goals and Values**—the extent to which the individual has learned the organization's culture, including informal goals and the values espoused by organizational members, especially those in powerful or controlling positions.
- **History**—the extent to which the individual understands and appreciates the organization's traditions, customs, myths, and rituals, as well as the personal backgrounds and work histories of important or influential organizational members.

Well-designed socialization programs attempt to address most if not all of the content areas listed above. Organizations can facilitate socialization through building a strong culture that then disseminates (either formally or informally) consistent lessons for newcomers. Organizations interested in attracting and retaining the best talent should purposefully manage the socialization process.[12] Nonetheless, a substantial amount of socialization takes place informally as individuals observe and monitor the behavior of others in the organization and as they are exposed to the inner workings of their employer.

Stages of Organizational Socialization

A number of researchers have proposed that socialization follows a sequence of three stages: Anticipatory Socialization, Entry/Encounter, and Change and Adjustment. These stages, described below, primarily reflect the need to become psychosocially and organizationally invested in the firm.[13]

Stage 1: Anticipatory Socialization

The socialization process can begin informally, even before the employee joins the organization on a full-time basis. Career choices are based initially on rough ideas of what a career will be like. Individuals gather these ideas from books, television shows, or Internet searches. Or they may be learned vicariously through interactions with others (family, teachers, and friends). Job candidates enter the recruitment process with specific expectations about organizational life and their future career. As discussed in Chapter 7, the major concern at this early career stage is that these expectations are realistic, so that individuals have a reasonable chance of meeting them and of utilizing their talents.

Because anticipatory socialization involves the learning that takes place prior to newcomers entering the organization, formal programs and activities can include internships, apprenticeships, cooperative educational assignments, and informational interviews. These programs provide positive developmental experiences for individuals entering the work world, and can improve career decision-making self-efficacy, strengthen one's self-concept, allow one to acquire job-related skills, and allow students a significant advantage in gaining options for well-paid full-time employment upon graduating.[14]

Stage 2: Entry/Encounter

The recruit begins employment and encounters a new environment. In fact, the environment is not only new, but may depart radically from the newcomer's expectations in many ways. This early learning environment includes a sense-making process, as the newcomer reconciles unmet expectations with the new reality of the job.[15] This may be true regardless of whether the newcomer also interned at the firm, because experiences of interns may be different from experiences of new employees.

There are also enormous learning requirements for the recruit. There are new tasks to learn, new relationships to cultivate, new work groups to enter, and new policies and procedures to grasp. In short, one needs to "learn the ropes." Organizational newcomers should recognize the need to take an active role in learning the work processes and culture of their new company. These learning activities can be both formal and informal in nature. Often, informal lessons may reinforce formal procedures, or they may influence individuals in directions that are not sanctioned by the firm.[16]

Organizations realize that newcomers have a great deal to learn. Often, this recognition is couched in terms of "breaking in" the new recruit. Although it is debatable whether the treatment of people deserves the same term as applied to a new pair of shoes, it cannot be denied that substantial changes and learning must take place during this early period of employment. But how do newcomers learn the ropes? Either consciously or unwittingly, organizations attempt to socialize newcomers in a variety of ways. Socialization tactics used by organizations can be broken down into two types: institutionalized and individualized. *Institutionalized socialization* consists of common programs and training experiences that are formally presented to all (or nearly all) new organizational members. On the other hand, *individualized socialization* consists of unique activities and learning experiences that are specifically targeted to a particular person.[17] It may be preferable for an organization to employ *institutionalized socialization* tactics to promote strong attachment to the job/organization, and also *individualized socialization* tactics to promote the clarification of job and role expectations. Thus, organizations might use a combination of institutionalized and individualized tactics in order to tailor their socialization to achieve positive outcomes. Listed below are some of the common organizationally sponsored socialization techniques:

1. **Recruitment** can be defined as activities engaged in by the firm with the purpose of attracting potential employees. Recruitment is considered a socialization technique because it enables organizations to select candidates whose talents and values are most compatible with the organization's requirements. In addition, realistic recruitment can be used to set candidates' expectations to more appropriate levels. Realistic recruitment usually offers information to the recruit that is important in order to complete job assignments upon full-time employment.[18]
2. **Training** activities are designed to provide instruction on job-related tasks and to orient the newcomer to the organization's goals and practices. Through planned learning programs, newcomers develop their competencies in order to perform to the best of their abilities. Training and development activities have evolved from one-on-one apprenticeship programs, to programs that blend classroom instruction, systematic job instruction, team-building, simulation, web-based or computer-based individualized instruction, and satellite videoconferencing. Research suggests that when companies offer a variety of newcomer training options, employees are able to choose the method that best fits their development needs.[19]
3. **Debasement experiences** are also used to socialize the newcomer.[20] In one version, "sink or swim," the employee is given a difficult assignment with little guidance or support. Organizations may also provide an "upending experience" by assigning tasks that are trivial or insoluble, thereby making it clear to the new employee that the organization is in control. Milder forms of debasement might include hazing and scut work designed to put newcomers in their place right from the start. Most people have played (or will play) the gofer role (go for coffee, etc.) that often befalls the lowest and newest person in the hierarchy. Regardless of the specific form, debasement strategies are intended to shake the newcomer's confidence so that the organization can influence or reshape his or her behavior. Successful completion of debasement strategies may be followed with initiation ceremonies and rites of passage that indicate the newcomer is no longer a rookie, but is now a full-fledged and welcome member of the organization.[21]
4. **Reward and control systems** also provide socialization experiences to the newcomer. New employees learn what an organization values by observing what activities or outcomes are rewarded. Objective market and financial indicators are used to monitor employees' accomplishments in such areas as increasing sales, improving profits, and serving as agents for change. Performance appraisals and promotions are normally related to progress along pre-established dimensions.

Organizations can offer multisource feedback by involving multiple raters (otherwise known as 360-degree feedback) when giving performance appraisals. This type of appraisal provides data from a variety of both internal and external constituents (customers, co-workers, supervisors, and subordinates). One goal of 360-degree evaluations is to eliminate the subjectivity associated with one person (the supervisor) assessing the employee. Rather, a variety of views are gained, thereby giving the employee a holistic appraisal that ideally offers specific opportunities for growth. Multisource feedback has been found to increase employees' job performance and knowledge-sharing, as well as organizations' financial performance.[22]

Stage 3: Change and Adjustment

We have discussed how newcomers encounter the reality of a new work environment and are subject to pressures to adapt to these realities. In what ways do they change as a result of encountering this new environment? Put another way, how do they know if the socialization process has been successful? Change and successful adjustment can take a number of forms:[23]

1. Has the employee learned the job? It is essential that task demands be sufficiently mastered so that the newcomer performs successfully and dependably and feels successful in the job role.
2. Has the employee been integrated into the work group? Successful integration requires an appropriate level of mutual trust and acceptance so the group can operate effectively. The recruit must typically adjust to the group's established practices, norms, and values. For example, a group that emphasizes cooperation and good-natured kidding is likely to put pressure on a new member to adopt these behaviors.
3. Has the employee achieved an acceptable level of role clarity? Can he or she handle the ambiguities and conflicts inherent in the organization? Conflicts may arise between work and other parts of life as well as between the expectations of the work group and other individuals or groups in the organization. The successful resolution of these conflicts is an important learning task for newcomers. An employer's use of institutionalized socialization tactics, such as job-related training, can lower role ambiguity, role conflict, and intentions to quit, and increase job satisfaction, organizational commitment, job performance, and perceptions of fit.[24]
4. Has the employee learned how to work within the system? Working within the system means dealing with one's manager and peers, overcoming resistance to new ideas, accepting initially low levels of responsibility, and understanding the reward system. Interestingly, experienced employees can learn much about their own roles and the organization when they socialize newcomers.
5. Does the employee understand and accept the organization's values? Is the recruit, for example, beginning to act, think, and feel like an integral part of the company? In other words, is the newcomer's self-concept changing to be more in line with the organization's values? Have the culture and norms of the organization been successfully transmitted? This is, in fact, the heart of the socialization process.

Edgar Schein distinguished pivotal or essential values (e.g., belief in free enterprise, acceptance of organizational hierarchy) from relevant values that are desirable but not absolutely essential for employee acceptance (e.g., dress codes).[25] One sign of *unsuccessful* socialization is a new employee's rejection of both pivotal and relevant organization's values and norms. Newcomers who react with such "rebellion" are unlikely to survive in the organization, unless their talent level is so high as to make their "rebellious" behavior tolerable. Schein also suggests that the blind acceptance of all values produces a level of conformity and sterility that can be disastrous for the individual and the organization. For example, newcomers who accept all values of an organization may become so tied to the system that they are incapable of making needed changes in the organization when they develop more influence later in their career.

Another response, what Schein calls creative individualism, is the most desirable outcome of the socialization process. In this case, pivotal values and norms are accepted, but the less essential ones may be rejected. By retaining portions of their own identity, such creative individualists should be able to make the most innovative contributions to the organization over time. While accepting the core goals and values of the organization, creative individualists are able to question some of the organization's less useful qualities and can effect changes in these qualities as they acquire more influence in the system.

Mutual Acceptance and the Psychological Contract

Successful socialization is signified by a sense of mutual acceptance. The individual accepts the organization by sustaining high levels of involvement, motivation, and commitment and by deciding to remain with the organization. Simultaneously, the organization accepts the newcomer as a trusted and valued member. Having survived the initial trials and obstacles, the individual has, to a certain extent, proven himself or herself in the eyes of the organization. Veteran employees signify their acceptance of the newcomer in a number of ways: by providing a positive performance appraisal, a more challenging assignment, a promotion, or a substantial salary increase; by introducing the newcomer to crucial social knowledge about the organization and its people; and by involving him or her more extensively in group interactions. Without being accepted into the work group, the newcomer is unlikely to be fully involved with the organization. The process of assimilation and acceptance enables all parties to be full organization members focused on achieving the organization's goals.[26]

Mutual acceptance also shows an initial approval of the psychological contract between the individual and the organization. *Psychological contracts* are the implied agreements between employer and employee that serve to specify the contributions an employer believes are owed to the organization, as well as the inducements the employee believes are owed in return from the organization.[27] The degree of consistency between perceived employer promises with pre-entry expectations can have an effect on how the psychological contract is experienced upon the newcomer's entry.[28] As we noted in Chapters 1 and 2, there exist two forms of psychological contracts: relational and transactional. The "traditional" view of careers assumed a *relational contract* between employer and employee involving a high degree of commitment to the relationship by both parties. In contrast, a *transactional contract* is more short-term in nature and is predicated on performance-based pay, involves lower levels of commitment by both parties, and allows for easy exit from the agreement. A transactional contract is economic and extrinsic, and usually remains stable and observable over the length of the relationship.[29]

But even with the shift from relational to transactional psychological contracts, the employee and organization still go through the process of testing one another. This testing puts each party in a better position to evaluate the viability of its expectations. The individual has a better sense of the organization's responses to his or her efforts, and the organization has a better idea of what it can expect from the employee. However short-lived, mutual acceptance represents a tentative approval of continued employment, or a ratification of the psychological contract, as illustrated below.

This case provides an example in which mutual acceptance is an outcome of the socialization process. But there are many situations in which a bad match is recognized by the individual and/or the organization—a violation, in a sense, of the initial psychological

Sarah started work in the budget department of a large department store chain a little more than a year ago. She was impressed with the company right from the start—everyone inside and outside of her department made her feel welcome. After two months with the company Sarah's career got a boost, although she didn't see it that way at the time. Specifically, the senior budget analyst who was in charge of tracking the company's capital expenditures and assessing future spending plans resigned suddenly. With no one else available to fill the void, Sarah stepped in and assumed the role. As a junior analyst with limited work experience, Sarah found the job of simultaneously learning the capital budgeting system and dealing with day-to-day expenditures to be extremely stressful. Her prior work experiences helped, and Sarah was determined to succeed. Sarah performed so well that the company promoted her to budget analyst after only six months and she received a 10 percent raise. Time and again her company's management has commented on her outstanding work. She has been identified as someone who can advance rapidly and she has been given added responsibilities. Sarah enjoys her work and socializes frequently with the other people in her department. After one year she is really committed to the company and, from all indications, the company is committed to her.

bond. Perhaps the individual did not live up to the organization's expectations, or the organization did not provide the kind of work setting the individual expected. In such situations, employees may become less productive and less satisfied, and may ultimately choose to leave the organization. In those cases, mutual acceptance does not occur, and a mutually satisfying psychological contract is never established.

Continuing Tasks of Establishment

Mutual acceptance does not really terminate the establishment period. Rather, it provides some concrete feedback to the individual and the organization. Schein identified four other general issues that must be addressed during this phase:[30]

First, the employee must continue to improve on the job. If a new assignment or promotion is granted, the employee needs to demonstrate continued capability at higher levels of complexity and responsibility.

Second, the employee normally develops competence in a specialization area (e.g., marketing, engineering, information systems) that will serve as a foundation for the future career. Businesses generally expect their managers to be specialists in their early career, regardless of whether they ultimately want to move into a more general management position.

Third, the employee must continue to learn how to work effectively as a less experienced member of the organization. The employee is still relatively new and may not receive all of the autonomy he or she would like. In essence, employees must appreciate their status and continue to learn how to work effectively within the constraints of the organization.

Fourth, employees should reassess their talents, values, and interests in light of their recent work experiences. There should be sufficient insight at this point to reevaluate the appropriateness of the chosen occupation and the opportunities within the organization. Decisions need to be made regarding whether to remain in, or leave, the career field and/or the organization.

Floundering: Learning Through Experience

The establishment period can evolve within one occupational field and one organization. However, there may also be considerable struggle and trial before a person finds a suitable line of work and a compatible organization in which to pursue the chosen work. People in their 20s may experience a "quarterlife crisis" when they graduate from college and confront the process of choosing a career, determining where they will live, carving out social relationships, and attempting to manage money. This period can indeed be rocky, especially when a young person has trouble finding a satisfying job. Young adults need to understand that part of the adjustment to adulthood is getting comfortable with one's self-identity—which in actuality is a process that continues throughout one's entire adult life.[31] Therefore, many people may try to establish themselves a number of times before they find a satisfying connection to the work world.

Consider the situation of Reginald, an MBA student, whose route to graduate school at age 30 demonstrates the tortuous path many people follow to establish a suitable career direction.

Reginald was an undergraduate management major who had given little thought to the kind of career he ultimately wanted. Because of limited job prospects, he accepted a position as a claims adjuster in a large insurance company, as an opportunity to learn about himself and the world of work. In time, he acquired the technical and interpersonal skills that made him a successful adjuster—so successful that after three years, he was offered a promotion to claims supervisor. This promotion opportunity forced Reginald to consider whether he really wanted a career in claims. Realizing that he wanted more autonomy and financial rewards than his current career path could offer, he declined the promotion and left the company shortly thereafter.

Reginald next accepted a sales position with a national manufacturer of office copiers. He quickly knew he had made the correct decision. He enjoyed sales immensely and became one of the top producers. However, a number of disturbing policy and personnel changes (including the promotion of a less-qualified peer) convinced him that this was not the kind of company where he could grow and develop.

Reginald changed employers so he could pursue what was crystallizing as a natural career goal—to become a sales manager at a progressive company. He accepted a district sales manager position for a distributor of copiers. Although he performed well in this position, he thought the company's management style was too authoritarian.

At age 26, Reginald wondered whether he could ever find the kind of company that would suit his values and career goals. He quit his position and went to work for a former boss, who was now regional manager at an office products firm. Although he started out as a sales representative, Reginald was promised the position of branch manager at the end of six months, when the current branch manager was to leave. Unfortunately, the job went to someone else, another old friend of Reginald's boss. Disillusioned and bitter, Reginald quit the office products firm and, along with four other aspiring entrepreneurs, founded an Internet-based marketing organization. He looked forward to testing his skills in marketing and selling an innovative service. After six months, though, clients were few and expenses drained the company's cash flow. Hope was vanishing rapidly.

In the midst of his risky business venture, Reginald began to establish a serious romantic relationship and was now considering marriage. He became more concerned with stability in his career and his life. After one year of slow growth and an uncertain future, Reginald cut his ties from the company he had helped to form.

Seeking a more stable career direction, Reginald accepted a sales position with an audiovisual production company. He performed well in this position and, for the first time in his career, worked closely with marketing people. After six consecutive months of reaching his sales quota, however, Reginald was fired in a cost-cutting move.

Reginald was plagued with self-doubt. Was he unlucky or was he a failure? Was he unrealistic in his career goals or did he just have a series of bad breaks? Two months short of his 30th birthday and nine months before his wedding, Reginald was desperate. His fiancée, Simone, was supportive and suggested he call up friends to get a better handle on different career opportunities. He scanned Internet employment boards for job openings. Disillusioned with his experiences in sales, he listened with interest and excitement when his fiancée suggested he consider a career in marketing. Having spoken to a number of people, he was optimistic that marketing would satisfy his career interests. But he also learned that an entry-level position in marketing often required either prior marketing experience or an MBA degree.

With some trepidation, Reginald returned to graduate school to pursue an MBA on a full-time basis. He joined the MBA Society, a student-run group, and attended a mentoring session in which alumni spoke to students about career opportunities in different fields. Conversations with an alumnus eventually led to a summer internship in the marketing department of a large, prestigious consumer products company. Having just successfully completed the internship, Reginald finally feels that he has direction in his career. At the age of 30, his establishment as a marketing professional is just beginning.

Reginald's situation illustrates the difficulties some people have in establishing their career. Finding a fit is not always easy. Career indecision, unrealistic expectations, personal shortcomings, lack of self-insight, organizational turmoil, and economic fluctuations can introduce considerable uncertainty and frustration into careers and lives.

On the positive side, however, people can learn from their experiences. Researchers at the Center for Creative Leadership (CCL) in Greensboro, North Carolina, examined the lives and work experiences of executives as they developed through their careers. Their studies have documented the important role that career difficulties, hardships, and traumas can have in promoting individual development. These hardships can include business failures and mistakes, career setbacks (e.g., demotions, missed promotions, dissatisfying jobs), subordinate personal or performance problems, and personal difficulties (e.g., divorce, work–family conflict, illness or death of a loved one or co-worker). Successful responses to these career challenges can be shown in a number of ways, including a greater degree of sensitivity to others, recognition of one's personal limits, awareness of the need for balance between work and nonwork lives, acceptance of the need to take charge of one's career, and the development of coping strategies. Known as experience-driven development, CCL suggests organizations apply life learning to work experiences by mapping competencies to stretch assignments, creating new experiences (cross-functional or cross-country), and promoting an experience-driven culture.[32]

No experience is really wasted, although it may appear so at the time. What Reginald had going for him was a considerable degree of self-insight, a determination to make his career work, a willingness to leave situations that no longer seemed tenable, a support system, and a strong belief that he could influence the course of his career. These qualities will serve Reginald well throughout his career, even though they were discovered through difficult experiences early in his career.

Organizational Actions During Establishment

Effective Recruitment

Discrepancies between job expectations and the realities of the organization can inhibit a new employee's adjustment to the organization. As we discussed in Chapter 7, realistic recruitment can play a significant role in helping newcomers establish themselves in their career and forge a healthy, candid relationship with the firm.

In addition, there is a tendency for organizations to select overqualified candidates for some positions because it is easier to choose the most qualified individuals than the best qualified. It is also easier to examine credentials than real job qualifications. Thus, college graduates might be sought to fill positions demanding a high school diploma, and MBAs are recruited for positions that require a bachelor's degree. In some instances, these high qualifications are justified because they are required for future jobs to which the employee might ultimately be promoted. In the meantime, however, many of these highly qualified newcomers may believe that their talents and training are underutilized in their first job and may leave (or become alienated) before they have had a chance to establish themselves. To avoid underutilization in these situations, organizations should provide the newcomer with sufficiently challenging, responsible tasks to maintain high levels of motivation and involvement. At the same time, organizations must be aware of *job creep*, where the extra time and energy required by continual increases in job responsibility intrude into the employee's nonwork life, in part because the employee feels pressured to take on additional work responsibilities and pressures in order to be seen by the organization as going above and beyond the call of duty.[33]

Organizations can improve attraction and retention of newcomers by offering work conditions that meet employee preferences and expectations and strengthen the employer–employee relationship. Although employers may not always be in a position to fulfill employee preferences, an explanation of the reasons why certain promises are not being kept will help both employee and employer gain a better understanding of mutual constraints and needs, as well assist in forming a stronger bond between both parties.[34]

Effective Orientation Programs

The first few days or weeks in an organization can be particularly critical in orienting the newcomer to the work environment. Effective orientation or "onboarding" programs can help new employees become part of the organization and inform them about the organization's policies, benefits, and services. Research has identified the following functions of onboarding programs:[35]

- Introduction to the company.
- Review of important policies and practices, benefits, and services.
- Completion of employment forms, including benefit plan enrollment.

- Review of employer expectations and development of accurate employee expectations.
- Introduction to peers and facilities.
- Introduction to the new job.
- Introduction to mentors.
- Follow-up feedback session after initial orientation.

Onboarding programs are designed to provide the newcomer with vital information (regarding people, processes, and technology) so that the person becomes integrated quickly into the organization.[36] Onboarding for millennials should be cognizant of the needs and learning styles of this generation by providing, for example, brief, job-relevant training that is visual and interactive, possibly through online activities, and that allows them to become part of a community.[37]

Onboarding programs also help the newcomer understand the organization's culture and the role the individual plays in making the company effective. The information provided should be responsive to newcomers' specific questions and needs, such as information on job-related questions or on potential career paths. Therefore, some portion of an onboarding/orientation program should involve small-group discussions and one-on-one sessions, where more attention can be devoted to individual concerns. For example, programs can work to combat high levels of anxiety that new employees may experience. This support should be offered anywhere from the first few weeks to the first year. The program should also offer follow-up by going through a checklist provided by human resources that identifies all the information that is essential to be shared with the newcomer. Honest feedback on the onboarding/orientation program should be solicited at this time.

Early Job Challenge

Most employees desire and expect high levels of challenge and responsibility on a new job, but many organizations are hesitant to provide early challenge and instead exercise tight supervision and control until newcomers are more experienced, skilled, and trusted.

However, when early job challenge is provided to new employees, the results can be quite beneficial and long-lasting. When new employees are given jobs that have high levels of challenge and autonomy, require a variety of skills, and are seen as significant, they experience higher job and career satisfaction, enhanced motivation to learn their new job, work harder and more creatively, and are more promotable.[38] Even pre-entry opportunities lead to positive experiences. Interns who are given challenging job assignments report higher organizational commitment and loyalty when they join the organization full-time.

Providing early challenge also enables a new employee to internalize high work standards. A recruit who is exposed to substantial challenge learns that the organization is demanding, that it expects people to assume responsibility for decisions, and that it holds people accountable for results. As newcomers come to appreciate this emphasis on challenge, responsibility, and accountability, they tend to accept these standards as their own and act in ways consistent with these standards.

It is also well documented that other people's expectations affect our behavior.[39] When supervisors expect their subordinates to be able to handle additional challenge, they build more challenge into the job; offer help, encouragement, and support; and find that their optimistic predictions are confirmed by their subordinates' accomplishments, a self-fulfilling prophecy in action. Douglas T. Hall proposed that employees who accomplish sufficiently challenging tasks experience a sense of psychological success (an internal feeling of being successful) that raises their self-esteem and sense of competence, increases their career involvement, and spurs them on to want even more challenge.[40] Hall's psychological success model explains how "success breeds success"—by giving employees a real opportunity to develop a positive self-image and to define success in their own subjective terms. Providing new employees with meaningful, challenging work right from the start may require the organization to reexamine its assumptions about recruits as well as its established traditions. Organizations also may have to reevaluate the most effective way to train recruits, perhaps moving in the direction of pre-entry programs such as internships, which have grown substantially in recent years.

Also, organizations should not permit their stereotypes to interfere with employees' early career growth. There is some evidence, for example, that women may be assigned to less challenging tasks than men, especially when the organization has had little experience working with women (or other underrepresented groups) in certain job classifications, or when the person making the assignment is male. These differences in early career experience may account for the wage and intra-firm mobility differences experienced by women.[41] The message should be clear: if women or other groups of employees are initially given less challenging assignments, their career growth may be unfairly stunted.

Frequent and Constructive Feedback

Although performance appraisal and feedback are important at all stages of career development, they are particularly crucial during the establishment years because of the newcomer's need to become competent and accepted. It is not enough to assign challenging tasks. Newcomers have to know how well (or poorly) they are performing on these tasks. Feedback must be sufficiently frequent so that employees can make changes in their behavior on an ongoing basis to maximize learning. Moreover, if the feedback is positive, it can serve as a powerful source of praise and reinforcement. Also, performance feedback sessions provide an opportunity for supervisors and subordinates to discuss their assumptions and expectations about each other—to clarify the psychological contract.

But feedback must be administered in a constructive, supportive manner if it is to be effective. Although employees seek feedback to improve their perceived career development, they may hold two simultaneous yet conflicting needs.[42] On one hand, they want honest feedback; they want to hear the truth. On the other hand, they also want to hear only good news to protect their sense of self-esteem and to receive extrinsic rewards. Sometimes, feedback is so negative and devastating that an adversarial and defensive relationship is created between supervisor and subordinate. In other cases, supervisors are so concerned about being "kind" that they provide no useful feedback to the subordinate. Perhaps most frequently, supervisors are so uncomfortable with performance appraisal that they simply avoid the process altogether.

As we noted earlier in the chapter, organizations can improve the appraisal and feedback process by using the 360-degree feedback technique, which allows the new employee to understand that the appraisal process is in fact for career development, rather than for punitive reasons. Such efforts involve developing more useful performance appraisal forms, encouraging newcomers to engage in self-appraisal, extending numbers of appraisers to include peers and others in and outside the organization, training supervisors in providing feedback, and separating discussions of performance feedback from discussions of salary and promotion decisions.[43]

The First Supervisor: A Critical Resource

A newcomer striving for competence and acceptance requires what has been called "supportive autonomy"; that is, sufficient challenge and autonomy to develop a sense of psychological success and a supportive environment in which to make mistakes, learn, and grow.[44] The newcomer's supervisor can play a major role in providing supportive autonomy.

Subordinates have a number of task and personal needs that the manager can fulfill at different career stages. It takes a certain type of manager to play the roles of coach, feedback provider, trainer, role model, and protector in an accepting, esteem-building manner. Managers must be personally secure and unthreatened by subordinates' training, ambition, and values. In effect, managers should be viewed as the career developers and coaches for their subordinates and should be trained and rewarded for fulfilling this role.[45] Consider the following example:

> Drew is an experienced retail manager in a large home goods store. He manages a group of 15 retail salespeople. He recently had two new salespersons join his group and it is obvious that the two newcomers have different needs as they try to become acclimated to their new retail environment. One newcomer, Doris, a mother of three, is in her early 40s. She had worked in another retail store for 11 years before she stopped working to raise her children. The other newcomer, Craig, is in his early 20s and recently graduated from a local university with a degree in design and merchandising. He has had relatively few work experiences, except for the summers when he worked part-time in a retail setting. Drew immediately saw Doris as a peer, but quickly recognized that he needed to coach Doris through the process of adjusting to the work setting and learning the intricacies of the company's computer systems. He has advised her to be patient as she becomes re-acclimated to full-time work and as she learns specific tasks. In contrast, Drew has tried to temper Craig's excitement about his new job, keep him focused on the tasks at hand, and help him to manage his time more wisely. As an enlightened manager, Drew consciously adapts his leadership style to meet the needs of his subordinates. Even though both Doris and Craig are newcomers, they have different requirements given their varying levels of work experience.

Encouragement of Mentor Relationships and Other Supportive Alliances

Mentoring can be defined as relationships between junior and senior colleagues, or between peers, that provide a variety of developmental functions.[46] The establishment of a relationship with a mentor is thought to be one of the critical events of early adulthood, and finding a mentor or sponsor is seen as a major developmental task of the early career.[47]

The term mentor can be traced to Greek mythology in which Odysseus, absent from home because of the Trojan Wars, charged his servant Mentor with the task of educating and guiding his son Telemachus. In fulfilling this obligation, Mentor—through the wisdom provided by Athena—acted variously as teacher, coach, taskmaster, confidant, counselor, and friend.[48] In this historical sense, the mentor-protégé relationship was comprehensive (it involved educational, occupational, physical, social, and spiritual development) and was based on a high degree of mutual affection and trust. In a similar vein, as illustrated in Table 8.2, mentors fulfill both career and psychosocial functions.

Most mentoring relationships are established when the protégé is in his or her early career, and some relationships may involve the protégé's immediate supervisor. A survey of executives revealed that more than 75 percent of the respondents reported having had at least one mentoring relationship during their career, and 71 percent of organizations offer formal mentoring programs.[49] Other studies have shown that individuals who had experienced a mentor relationship were earning more money at an earlier age, were better

Table 8.2 Mentoring Functions*

Career Functions (*primarily enhance career advancement*)	*Psychosocial Functions* (*primarily enhance sense of competence and effectiveness*)
Sponsorship	Role Modeling
Exposure and Visibility	Acceptance and Confirmation Counseling
Coaching	Friendship
Protection	
Challenging Assignments	

* Adapted from T. D. Allen. (2006). Mentoring. In Greenhaus, J. H. & Callanan, G. A. (Eds.), *Encyclopedia of career development* (pp. 486–493). Thousand Oaks, CA: Sage.

educated, and were more likely to follow a career plan than those who had not established a relationship with a mentor. In fact, research has consistently indicated that mentoring is related to a variety of positive work outcomes, including higher degrees of career and organizational commitment, career resilience and success, recognition, satisfaction, career mobility, and compensation.[50] And mentoring lowers work and nonwork stress. Thus, mentoring can have a positive effect on an individual's career and life.[51]

Most people would readily agree that employees striving to establish their career would benefit from coaching, support, exposure to senior executives, sponsorship, emotional support, and identification with a successful role model. The question is whether they need one mentor, or a constellation of mentors, to fulfill all of these roles. It is not clear that a single individual must fulfill, or is capable of fulfilling, all of these mentoring functions in the traditional sense. Research suggests that protégés establish a developmental network of mentors, so that mentoring functions can be provided from a variety of sources. Under the assumption that not every mentor can provide advice and support with the same intensity, the developmental network provides protégés with a range of sources from which they can receive career support, emotional closeness, sponsorship, and important information. It has already been indicated that the first supervisor is a critical career developer of the new employee, as a coach, trainer, and feedback provider. Others in the constellation could include subordinates, peers, and customers, who may also provide job-related feedback, professional advice, career strategy guidance, and emotional support.[52]

Organizations can stimulate such diverse relationships by making it easier for newcomers to interact with these multiple benefactors. Discussion groups, seminars, and social gatherings are among the vehicles that can be used. Further, organizations can promote access to other types of career management and assessment mechanisms to achieve understanding and growth among newer staff members who may not have access to a mentor.[53] These activities, which could serve either as a supplement to or as a substitute for a formal mentoring program, should include career counseling and coaching, 360-degree feedback, and other forms of assessment.

Companies with formal mentoring programs have observed several benefits, including: socialization of the protégé; better understanding of the organization's mission, values, structure, and informal systems; increased organizational communication; increased competence, motivation, and performance; greater organizational commitment and improved retention of new hires; identification of management talent; and enhanced diversity and well-being at work.[54] However, the "engineering" of relationships goes against the spontaneous and mutual attraction that normally characterizes mentoring alliances, and formal programs can cause anxiety and discomfort among participants, create pessimism about career prospects for those not chosen to participate, and overemphasize a single supportive relationship when in reality a constellation of developmental alliances is more enriching. Evidence suggests that the individual benefits received from formal mentoring relationships do not compare to the benefits received from informal relationships. However, the most important ingredient in formal relationships is the quality of the relationship, so organizations need to develop mechanisms to allow mentors and protégés to develop mutually supportive bonds.[55]

Whether formal or informal, mentors can play an important role by providing career and psychosocial support to protégés through a "work–family lens" that recognizes the challenges that protégés can face in balancing their work and nonwork lives.[56] Mentors who adopt a work–family lens discuss with their protégés the work–nonwork implications of achieving a particular career goal or enacting a specific career strategy, encourage protégés to examine the time pressures and stresses associated with different assignments or career paths, and protect their protégés from being stigmatized for using a flexible work arrangement or pursuing a nontraditional career path. We expect that protégés of mentors who adopt a work–family lens can successfully balance work with other important parts of their life.

Because the upper echelons of corporate America are still dominated by a white male majority, much has been written about the perceived and actual difficulties of women and minorities in finding and maintaining a mentor during the early career years.[57] We discuss these challenges for individuals and organizations in Chapter 11, when we focus on managing diversity.

Individual Actions During Establishment

We have seen that organizations can take actions to facilitate the employee's career establishment. Nevertheless, as stressed throughout this book, the individual has the ultimate responsibility to manage his or her career effectively. Following are some steps individuals can take.

Career Exploration and Goal-Setting

During the establishment years, it is essential that new employees understand their developmental needs and realize that this period is a time of mutual testing. Both the individual and the organization are assessing the presence or absence of a match. Without a conscious awareness of these issues, it is unlikely that useful information will be acquired and appropriate decisions made. It is, therefore, crucial for new employees to use their assignments, performance reviews, day-to-day observations, and informal relationships to learn more about themselves and the organization. With this knowledge and information, individuals should be willing and able to adjust career goals as necessary. Career management is a dynamic process, and one's goals can change as new insights are gained and organizational realities become clear.

Career Strategies—Influencing the Environment

Although the establishment period often requires the individual to adjust to the demands of the new environment, the newcomer is not a passive victim at the complete mercy of the organization. In fact, newcomers can play an active role in the ultimate success of the socialization process. Newcomers with a strong sense of self-competence can adopt active strategies and coping responses to understand the organization's culture and influence the environment.[58] Because information and help are not always offered when they are most needed, an assertive strategy is often required. Such an approach might include the following activities:

- Initiate discussions with your supervisor on ways to increase the level of challenge, responsibility, and variety in your job.
- Initiate discussions with your supervisor regarding your recent performance. If the feedback is not sufficiently specific or critical, politely but firmly seek greater detail.

- Analyze your supervisor's needs and discuss ways in which you can help your supervisor become more effective in his or her job.
- Seek information from peers who are in a position to observe your performance.
- Participate in formal programs to learn as much about the organization as possible.
- Read literature about the organization and seek answers to your questions.
- Develop informal contacts in the organization who can provide you with information, insights, and accumulated wisdom about the organization.
- Be prepared to share your perceptions and opinions with others. Mutual information-sharing is more likely to sustain relationships than one-sided communications.
- Try to learn where the organization is heading and what skills it will require in the future.
- Reexamine the compatibility between your values, interests, and talents and the values, requirements, and opportunities in the organization.

One of the ways these strategies can be implemented is through employee networks or affinity groups. These are groups of employees organized (either formally or informally) to provide individual members with information about the company, allow employees to feed information back to the company, and encourage career management activities. One company that has sponsored formal networks, known as Associate Resource Groups, is Avon Products, Inc. Avon believes that part of its corporate social responsibility is to provide avenues by which the employee can develop. Avon advocates workplace diversity and strives to create an environment that values and encourages the uniqueness of each employee. Avon is committed to creating a culture that supports employees as they balance their many, and sometimes competing, work and personal responsibilities. It has several groups around the globe, including a Women's Empowerment group, a Latino network, a Black Professional Association, an Asian network, and a Gay and Lesbian network. The networks act as liaisons between employees and management to bring voice to critical issues that influence the workplace and the marketplace. Goldman Sachs similarly hosts upward of 80 affinity networks, many similar to Avon's, but also a Veteran's network, a Disability Interest Forum, and a Religious Support group.[59] Early-career employees are likely to benefit both personally and professionally from participation in such networks.

The Achievement Phase

At some point during the early career, the concern with acceptance and "fitting in" subsides and striving for achievement and authority takes precedence. The shift from establishment to achievement is neither fixed in time nor abrupt, although it seems that a certain degree of security and acceptance may trigger achievement striving. It is also significant to recall that a large portion of the achievement period coincides with the period in adult development where the need to accomplish achievement-oriented goals becomes particularly strong.[60]

The achievement phase has been referred to as an "advancement" stage by several researchers, presumably because the desire for vertical mobility (i.e., promotions) is so strong. The term *achievement*, rather than advancement, is used here because it is a broader concept that can encompass many different forms of accomplishment. Achievement can mean different things to different people, and given the lack of quick vertical mobility for many employees, achievement is a more relevant concept today.

Indeed, with wide variations in career aspirations and orientations, the meaning of achievement, accomplishment, and career success rests on the individual's personal beliefs and attitudes. In addition, compatibility between a person's career orientation and job setting produces higher levels of job satisfaction, career satisfaction, and organizational commitment, and a lower intention to leave an organization.[61] Conversely, incompatibility can result in dissatisfaction and a corresponding desire to leave the particular work setting. Consider the following example:

> As Arun has discovered, there is a fine line between being in a satisfying work environment and a dissatisfying one. For the past four years, Arun has worked in a department where the manager encouraged his people to be independent-minded. The manager wanted his staff to be able to complete their assignments from start to finish based on their own knowledge and judgment, with the freedom to suggest and implement changes when they thought them necessary. Arun thrived in this kind of setting. He loved the independence and autonomy, which made him feel like a real contributor to the department's success. Unfortunately for Arun, a new manager took over the department five weeks ago. Since that time, Arun has seen a 180-degree turn in the way his work group is managed. New rules and procedures have been put in place requiring the daily monitoring of activities and accomplishments. On several occasions, Arun has had to justify his routine decisions, and has even been criticized for not seeking approval before taking action from the different layers of management. Arun has found the meddling from above and the strict approval process to be disconcerting. If a turnaround doesn't happen soon, Arun is certain he'll have to look for another job.

There are a number of general issues that are the focus of concern to many employees during the achievement period:

1. To demonstrate continued, increasing competence in work assignments.
2. To acquire additional levels of responsibility and authority in work assignments.
3. To determine the most appropriate type of contribution they can make to themselves, the occupation, and the organization, such as whether to remain in a specialized function or to move into general management.
4. To assess opportunities inside and outside the organization.
5. To develop long- and short-range career goals consistent with their career aspirations.
6. To develop and implement strategies to attain their career goals.
7. To use values to drive career decisions and to be proactive in making these decisions.
8. To remain flexible and adaptive to changing circumstances.
9. To understand that viable careers exist in and outside of "traditional" boundaries.
10. To understand the relative priorities they place on work, family, community, and other parts of life and to take these priorities into account in defining what they mean by a successful career.
11. To seek a mentor for psychosocial and career development support along the way.

Organizational Actions During Achievement

Provide Sufficient Challenge and Responsibility

During the establishment period, early job challenge enables newcomers to test their abilities and begin to make a real contribution to the organization. In the achievement period, employees have a greater urgency to enlarge their area of responsibility, to become more autonomous and independent, to "call the shots." Having spent a number of years learning and launching their career, employees are ready to acquire more responsibility.

Although additional responsibility can come through promotions and other forms of job mobility, the current job also can be used to this end. Jobs can be "enriched" to provide high levels of responsibility, complexity, and autonomy and to permit the employee to keep learning, growing, and stretching. Employees want to succeed on meaningful tasks and to feel that the work they do is significant. Enriched job characteristics, such as autonomy, variety, and significance, can all serve to enhance employees' level of work engagement. The organization, especially the immediate supervisor, must consider ways to provide these enriched job challenges and must know employees well enough to judge how much challenge they can handle. Participative goal-setting, schedule and budget control, additional discretion on how jobs get accomplished, and participation in special assignments are all ways to enhance the level of responsibility. Providing feedback on tasks allows employees to have knowledge of their results, and enables them to adapt as needed to achieve their goals. In addition, job rotation, especially among early-career employees, has a positive influence on such career outcomes as promotability, salary progression, and overall job performance. Firms also gain from job rotation when there is uncertainty about employees and their skills because it allows both the firm and the employee to better understand what strengths the employee has and what learning needs to take place.[62]

Employees who aspire to higher-level management positions require additional challenge and responsibility in their current job in order for them to test their capabilities and be groomed for future positions. Moreover, added challenge and responsibility enable employees who wish to stay in their functional area or even on their current job to remain competent, motivated, and involved. An international study of leadership development practices found that carefully managed on-the-job assignments and skill assessments, not necessarily formal training, were key factors in allowing optimum individual development and growth.[63] The most respected leadership behaviors include the ability to "bring in the numbers," to take "a stand and make tough decisions," and to "mobilize a team." Other skills and experiences needed for achievement-oriented individuals include:

- Strong interpersonal skills.
- Passion for results.
- Ability to bring out the best in people.
- Having a network of mentors or personal coaches.

Using the results from a number of studies on the developmental experiences of managers and executives, researchers from the Center for Creative Leadership identified 14 different components of managerial jobs that have important developmental consequences.[64] The 14 components of managerial jobs are shown in Table 8.3. The components are grouped according to whether they represent a job transition (a change in work role, job content, status, or location), the need to create change (such as starting an operation from scratch or engineering a turnaround), assuming higher levels of responsibility (moving to a job characterized by increased visibility and scope), exercising influence in non-authority relationships (participating in projects or serving on a team where negotiation skills and coordination are required), and overcoming obstacles (dealing with difficult situations or adverse business conditions).[65] All of these developmental

Table 8.3 Developmental Components of Managerial Jobs from Studies of On-the-Job Learning*

Development Task	*Component*
Job transitions	Line to staff Increases in job scope Radical job moves Changes in employers, status, or function
Creating change	Start-up operation Fix-it assignment
Assuming higher levels of responsibility	Organizational level Large-scale operations
Non-authority relationship	Serving on task forces Making deals and coordinating among departments
Overcoming obstacles	Difficult boss Negative experiences Experience with crises and diversity

*Adapted from McCauley, C. D., Ruderman, M. N., Ohlott, D. J. & Morrow, J. E. (1994). Assessing the developmental components of managerial jobs. *Journal of Applied Psychology*, *79*, 544–560.

experiences serve to increase the level of job challenge and autonomy afforded the individual employee.

Performance Appraisal and Feedback

The need to appraise performance never really ceases. Organizations must make a number of decisions about individual employees during their early career, including conclusions about promotability, training and development needs, and salary increases. These decisions are important not only for so-called "fast track" managers, but for other managers and non-managers as well. In addition, employees continue to need ongoing performance feedback, especially as it relates to their career goals.

Construction of Realistic and Flexible Career Paths

In a traditional sense, a career path is a sequence of job positions, usually related in work content, through which employees move during the course of their careers. A standard career path for someone in marketing might involve the following positions: marketing representative, product manager, a staff position at corporate headquarters, district marketing manager, regional marketing manager, and vice-president of marketing. The identification of career paths can be helpful to organizations in planning their staffing needs and it can provide a structure for employees in planning their personal careers. Nonetheless, it is important to recognize that this traditional view of career paths has been altered radically over the past several decades. The combined effects of mergers, downsizings, new technology, job restructurings, and new organizational designs either have eliminated (or mangled) career paths in many organizations or have made it difficult to formulate individual career plans that are based on a consistent path of jobs. As we have noted previously, these changes in the work environment and individuals' work orientations dictate that individuals be more proactive, boundaryless, and protean in the ways they attempt to manage movement along a career path. Consider the example of Roberto, who is in the achievement stage of his career, and is pursuing a more contemporary career path:

> Roberto has experienced a varied career in the information systems field since he finished up his undergraduate degree in computer science 17 years ago. While he was in the establishment phase of his career, his path was altered substantially by the economic fallout of the Great Recession. At the beginning of his professional work life, Roberto's career was more traditional. He worked for a small software company, but then after five years moved to an organization that was larger in size where he was part of the information services department. Unfortunately, his traditional career trajectory ended rather quickly. The larger company declared bankruptcy not long after the start of the Great Recession, and Roberto, like many of his contemporaries in the establishment phase, found himself unemployed. With no immediate job prospects, Roberto became a "gig" worker for an outsourcing firm, moving from client to client on a contractual basis.
>
> Now that he is in his later 30s, he has become more agile in his career management and displays the characteristics of a boundaryless perspective. Within the past three years he has made a number of self-initiated career moves. First, he went back to school and got an MBA in logistics and supply chain management. He simultaneously pursued career opportunities with consulting companies that specialized in helping clients manage global production and materials sourcing. Fortunately, he landed a position with a mid-sized consulting firm where his entrepreneurial spirit and prior work experience have allowed his career to take off. He is now firmly affixed in the achievement phase of his early career.
>
> Going forward, Roberto sees himself remaining with the consulting firm for at least the next few years, yet he realizes that many factors beyond his control could cause him to alter his plans. He continues to focus on enhancing his functional knowledge and skills, while networking with others in the industry. He keeps his eyes and ears open to other career opportunities, just in case he needs to quickly adjust to new circumstances.

Stimulate Career Exploration

Many organizations sponsor workshops, seminars, discussion groups, and counseling to aid the self-assessment process. Moreover, since much self-insight can be gained through ongoing job experiences, timely, constructive performance feedback and coaching sessions with a supervisor or other significant person is a useful ingredient in any self-assessment effort.

Organizations also can help employees gather information on alternative job opportunities. Effective job exploration requires up-to-date job descriptions that provide accurate information on job duties and behaviors, knowledge and skill requirements, demands, and rewards. However, information on jobs or career paths will not be useful unless it gets to the people who need it. Ideally, line managers should be provided with sufficiently detailed information on jobs and career paths to aid their subordinates' career planning efforts. Job posting programs and career days are other vehicles for disseminating job-related information. Today, many job postings are available on company intranets (available only to employees) or on the company website. These sites allow both employees and potential candidates to explore career options. An example of a company-sponsored job posting website is provided below:

> The Johnson & Johnson organization (J&J), headquartered in New Brunswick, New Jersey, uses a company-wide Global Job Posting program as a way to allow its employees to be aware of and apply for open positions that exist throughout its many varied divisions that are located all over the world. J&J sees the Global Job Posting program as a mechanism to promote its "commitment to the advancement and development of [its] employees by providing them transparency in job opportunities within Johnson & Johnson, and helps to create a strong foundation for ongoing development discussions between employees and managers."[66] On the company's website, all career opportunities are listed and are broken down by functional role, business segment, country location, and required experience level. Employees within the company are empowered to leverage J&J's global jobs network as a means to manage their careers and professional development.

Exploration designed to understand the organization—its goals and strategies, future human resource needs, mobility opportunities, reward systems, and the like—can be encouraged and aided in a number of ways. Although much of this type of learning takes place informally through mentoring relationships, organizations can provide information on their business and human resource plans. Organizations should provide realistic information on mobility patterns, a sort of realistic career preview, so that employees' expectations are in line with the reality of the organization's environment. Lateral movement within firms may be a sound mobility strategy for development of new competencies. While once considered a "kiss of death" to one's career, downshifting, or movement down the hierarchy, is now being used by individuals who want to redirect their careers and need to learn necessary skills to prepare for another position. Indeed, recent research suggests that both younger millennial workers and older baby boom workers are more willing, at least compared with earlier time periods, to accept lateral career moves to achieve an improved career direction.[67]

Individual Actions During Achievement

A great deal of advice has been offered to employees who aspire to higher-level positions in organizations. Common to all of these guidelines is the need for individual initiative and self-determination, an active approach to career management. A number of potentially useful actions recommended in the literature are discussed below.

Set Realistic Goals

Goal-setting procedures were examined extensively in Chapter 6. At this time, it is important to remember that if the employee does not establish goals, the goals will likely be established (or assumed) by the organization to fit its own needs. Therefore, it is in the employee's best interest to periodically reconsider established career goals (conceptual and operational), set new goals where necessary, and communicate these aspirations to the organization.

One important decision for many individuals is whether to remain in a specialized function within the organization or prepare to seek a general management position. The decision to contribute as a specialist versus a generalist should not only be based on the availability of positions in the current organization and other organizations, but also on the fit of the position with one's career orientation. Individuals who hold certain career orientations, such as a technical/functional career anchor, may wish to make their contribution as a specialist. Individuals who hold other orientations—the managerial competence anchor, for example—may see more challenge and rewards in a general management position. The achievement period of the early career can be a critical time to examine these kinds of alternatives. An analysis of one's cumulative work experiences and discussions with one's supervisor, mentor, colleagues, and/or significant other can help the employee assess his or her dominant career orientation.

Another issue to consider is that traditional advancement prospects, at least in a hierarchical sense, are far more limited in the current business environment. Intense competition, mergers and acquisitions, and the need to stay "lean and mean" are combining with the sheer number of people born in the baby boom generation to effectively restrict upward mobility opportunities. Due to these conflicting factors, achieving hierarchical success (through promotions) is becoming more uncommon, but ways to achieve subjective career success are infinite.[68] Recognizing this fact is a key to setting realistic, achievable career goals. Indeed, individuals should be less concerned with upward advancement and instead appreciate both the diversity in career paths that may satisfy their needs and the skill sets required to pursue these paths. This may involve planning and setting goals that include lateral moves, downward moves, higher degrees of specialization in a given function, and leaving the organization to join another organization, or to start one's own business. Moreover, these goals should take into account aspirations in work *and* nonwork parts of life. The point is that one's sense of accomplishment, satisfaction, and achievement can be gained in diverse ways, not only through hierarchical promotions. We will discuss this concept further in Chapter 9 when we cover possible reactions to career plateauing and obsolescence.

Performance and Responsibility on the Current Job

It is often observed that agile managers have learned to become a crucial subordinate to a busy boss. Being crucial means demonstrating technical competence, of course, but it also means developing skills that complement the boss's skills and make the boss look good.

This strategy requires that subordinates understand their superiors' skills, needs, and aspirations. It has been observed that a boss's needs depend on his or her own career stage.[69] For example, a boss in the establishment period needs technical and psychological support from the subordinate, whereas one in the achievement period requires loyal followership that enhances the performance and reputation of the boss. Subordinates should understand their needs, their boss's needs, and the constraints under which the boss operates, and establish a feedback and evaluation system for assessing the relationship between themselves and their bosses.

Individuals also must recognize that the types of job experiences and the length of tenure in high-responsibility jobs can play a critical role in determining career performance and progress. As discussed in Chapter 6, career strategies should take into account not only those assignments that are important for future advancement, but also recognize that there are certain jobs that can cause untoward disruptions in career progress and thus should be avoided if possible. Awareness of dead-end jobs and "derailment" type assignments is a critical factor in successfully managing one's career.[70] Derailment, or the movement off an established track of upward mobility, normally represents a mismatch between the demands of the work situation and one's personal skills. While derailment is caused by a multitude of issues, individual and contextual factors that can lead to derailment include the following: problems with interpersonal relationships and emotional intelligence, a failure to meet business objectives, an inability to build and lead a team, narcissistic tendencies and overplayed strengths, and an inability to develop or adapt to new work demands. Further, derailed managers have been found to be less self-motivating and less focused on continuous learning.[71] It is essential for employees to recognize that a derailment experience can serve as an opportunity to acquire new skills, knowledge, and abilities, and also be an opening to understand those behaviors that can lead to negative career outcomes.

Continued Development of Skills

It is essential to maintain and enhance the skills that are essential to perform effectively on your current job as well to develop additional skills that can help you now or in future positions you may hold in your organization or in a different organization. Seeking feedback from your boss, mentor, or colleagues can provide insights into your current performance level, the skills you need to refine or develop, and the most effective ways to enhance your skills (e.g., training programs, stretch assignments). Given the boundaryless nature of most contemporary careers, it is also important to consider the development or enhancement of portable skills that can be transferred from one job, career path, or organization to another.

Mobility Paths

Employees with upward mobility aspirations should be willing to nominate themselves for future positions. But not all job changes are equally useful. Highly mobile managers must understand the most promising paths (and the related career strategies) that will allow them to achieve their goals. In addition, they should apply the boundaryless and protean concepts of career management in that the career strategies they pursue for upward mobility are flexible enough to accommodate the inevitable twists and turns that are faced throughout their work lives.

While pursuing appropriate career strategies is critical to attaining career success, it is also important to recognize the role of individual personality in career management. A wide range of personality traits—for example, emotional stability, extraversion, proactivity, positive mood, and self-monitoring (awareness of social expectations and ability to modify behavior accordingly)—have been associated with various aspects of career success.[72] As Michael Crant has concluded from his review of personality and careers:

> Our personality fundamentally shapes who we are, how other people view us, and the situations that we choose to enter. By better understanding who we are and identifying the various elements of our own personality, we can make better decisions about careers.[73]

From our earlier vignette, Roberto was proactive in managing his career. And even though he had disruptions in the establishment phase of his career, he focused on developing career goals and strategies that allowed him to flourish as he moved into his achievement phase.

Attaining Sponsorship

Support and sponsorship from bosses, mentors, and other influential people are often crucial to goal attainment. Although high visibility and exposure are necessary to attain sponsorship, they are not sufficient. The sponsored individual should also be a high performer and be loyal and trustworthy to superiors. That is, the individual helps the supervisor attain organizational goals, minimizes risks for the supervisor, and prevents potentially embarrassing outcomes. In short, such an employee is a crucial subordinate. Developmental relationships and support are especially critical during the achievement phase of one's career. As discussed earlier, employee development can be supported by a constellation of individuals, including mentors, superiors, peers, subordinates, and friends both inside and outside one's current organization.[74]

A Word of Caution

Many of the strategies discussed above have a "chess like" quality in that they involve constant adjustments and frequent movement. Each move is made as a stepping stone to the next position. There is nothing wrong with this strategy as long as the jobs comprising this route to success are themselves satisfying and compatible with the person's needs and values. One must also determine whether career goals and strategies are consistent with the desired balance of work, family, community, self-development, and leisure activities. Extensive work involvement and frequent relocations may provide career success, but at the expense of personal failure on the home front.[75] Excessive levels of organizational and career commitment can have adverse consequences for employees and for those individuals around him or her. Stress and tension in social and family relationships and limited time for nonwork and leisure activities have negative consequences. The impact of work experiences on stress and quality of life will be examined in Chapter 10.

The Early Career: A Question of Timing

We have seen how the early career is initiated by a period of establishment followed by a dominant concern with achievement and accomplishment. We also positioned the early career within early adulthood. It is in the era of early adulthood that socialization into the work world, launching a career, and settling down to pursue one's dream generally take place.

However, one must recognize that the establishment–achievement cycle can be triggered by a career transition any number of times during adulthood. All job changes require resocialization to a somewhat unfamiliar task and interpersonal environment. Such resocialization is probably prerequisite to subsequent achievement and innovation. Changing employers or career fields would undoubtedly require some form of resocialization and reestablishment, because the new environments would be as unfamiliar as the previous environment originally was.[76]

Moreover, establishment and achievement concerns can be reactivated during middle or late adulthood. Individuals in their 40s, 50s, and 60s who change jobs, employers, or occupations are faced with similar pressures to establish themselves in a new environment. Recall our example of Sharon from Chapter 7. She had spent 23 years with one company, rising to the level of vice-president for planning and development. At the age of 46, she was fired by her employer, and eventually found a new job (albeit with lower prestige and responsibility) as business planning manager for a small automotive products retailer. In beginning this new position, Sharon had new people to meet, new rules and procedures to follow, and a new culture to comprehend so she could "hit the ground running" and prove her worth. Hopefully, Sharon and other seasoned veterans can successfully renavigate the tasks of establishment and achievement given their more extensive work and life experiences.

Thus, the dominant themes of the early career, establishment and achievement, are not strictly limited to people in their 20s and 30s. It follows that the organizational and individual actions recommended in this chapter can also be applied to a wider group of people beyond those in early career. Ultimately, it behooves individuals to understand their own developmental needs (whatever their age) and organizations to recognize the implications of these needs for the individual's career growth and the organization's effectiveness.

Summary

The early career poses two major tasks for an employee: establishment and achievement. The initial task of the early career is to establish oneself in a career field; that is, to gain competence in the job, to learn the ropes in an organization, and, ultimately, to gain acceptance as a valued contributor. An organization attempts to socialize new employees by providing job-related training, rewarding desirable behavior, and communicating and reinforcing its dominant values and norms through socialization tactics. The new employee who has undergone successful socialization is competent on the job, integrated into the work group, achieves a satisfactory level of role clarity, learns to work within the system, and internalizes the key values and norms of the organization.

Organizations can help new employees establish their careers by developing effective recruitment and orientation practices, offering important early job challenge, providing constructive performance feedback, and helping employees develop supportive relationships with their supervisor, mentors, and others who can guide their career development. At the same time, individual employees can engage in career exploration to understand themselves and their new environment, and can develop strategies to positively influence their career trajectory.

When a new employee becomes relatively secure and established in his or her career, the concern with fitting into the organization subsides, and the desire for increasing levels of achievement, authority, and responsibility takes over. During this period, the individual needs to maintain effective performance on the job, develop more insight into career and work orientations, set realistic career goals, understand the influence of different career paths and patterns on goal accomplishment, and obtain support from others both inside and outside their organization. To help individuals with these tasks, organizations can encourage career exploration, provide challenge and responsibility on the job, construct realistic and flexible career paths, provide constructive performance appraisals, and help employees formulate career management plans.

Career Management *for Life*: Work–Life Implications from Chapter 8

- The early career is demanding because newcomers feel the need to prove themselves to the organization and those in the achievement phase strive for even greater accomplishments. One result is the possibility of *job creep*, where the time and energy required by demanding jobs intrude into the employee's non-work life.
- Therefore, individuals need to understand the priorities they place on different parts of life so they can define what a successful career means to them and decide

the best way to achieve a desired balance between work and nonwork roles during their early career.

- Organizations also should be sensitive to the work demands they place on early-career employees to avoid high levels of dissatisfaction and turnover.
- The establishment of career goals should take into account aspirations in work *and* nonwork parts of life.
- Mentors who adopt a "work–family lens" that recognizes the challenges of balancing work and nonwork roles can help their protégés achieve more balance.

Assignment

If you are employed presently, take a few minutes and consider the programs your organization offers to help employees become established during the early part of their careers. What programs, if any, are being used? How would you rate the effectiveness of these efforts in assisting employees with the tasks of establishment?

If you are not employed currently, you may want to interview a close associate or relative about the programs at his or her organization.

Or, regardless of your employment status, if no programs are available for you to explore, do some exploration on the Internet to see what different companies offer. Then answer the assignment questions given above.

Discussion Questions

1. Why do organizations attempt to "break in" employees when they first join? Describe the major socialization practices used by organizations and relate them to experiences you have had as an organizational newcomer. Identify the signs of a successful and an unsuccessful socialization experience.
2. Reexamine the example of Reginald, the 30-year-old MBA student, as provided in this chapter. How effectively has he managed his early career? What, if anything, could he have done differently to shorten his period of floundering?
3. What are the advantages (and disadvantages) of providing a new employee with a challenging initial job assignment that provides considerable responsibility and autonomy? Why do many organizations have reservations about providing this type of assignment? What can organizations do to provide challenging, meaningful work to newcomers and, at the same time, address the reservations they hold?
4. Describe the significance of the mentor–protégé relationship. What functions does the mentor provide and how can they contribute to the development and growth of the protégé's early career? Do you agree with the proposition that mentoring functions can be provided by a constellation of individuals? Why or why not? What can individuals do who may not have access to a mentor?
5. Look at the eight career anchors proposed by Professor Edgar Schein that are shown in Chapter 5. How would you characterize yourself in terms of these career orientations? How can employees gain greater insight into their career orientation? How would such insight contribute to more effective career management?

Chapter 8 Case #1: Natalie the Retail Manager (Part B)

At the conclusion of Chapter 7, we provided Part A of the Natalie case. You may want to reread Part A of this case before reading Part B.

At the end of Part A, Natalie had just completed one year of employment with Enigma. After some uncertainty and soul searching, Natalie decided to stay with Enigma for a while longer. Part B describes Natalie's situation after five years with Enigma. (Remember, Enigma is a fictitious name and should not be confused with any real company.)

Five Years into Her Career at Enigma

Natalie's career at Enigma is now at a crossroads. She is confronted with some tough decisions concerning both her professional and her personal lives. Enigma has recently offered her the chance to become the manager of its Seattle store. She would be given complete responsibility for the store operations, would receive a 40 percent salary increase, and could garner a sizable performance bonus after one year. While flattered by the opportunity, Natalie has other factors to consider. She is engaged to be married and the wedding date is just eight months away. Her husband-to-be has made it clear that he is not in favor of a move to the West Coast. Besides, they had talked about starting a family in the next two years and a move to Seattle would take them far away from their parents and other relatives who would willingly satisfy any childcare needs that might arise if they did have children.

Natalie needed some time to ponder her choices. The past four years at Enigma had been an emotional roller coaster. She had thought about leaving Enigma on several occasions, but had never "tested the waters." She always believed that the pros of staying with the company outweighed the cons. The extensive demands of the job had kept her busy, and the corporate culture still served to create unnecessary animosity and obstacles. But Enigma showed that they believed in her ability by promoting her a year ago to deputy store manager and by paying for her to attend a number of executive development programs. Most of her friends from college were still trying to move into an initial management position. They were amazed at the experiences Natalie had already encountered. Natalie had likened her situation to being in quicksand, the deeper she had gotten into Enigma, the harder it was to get out. In the back of her mind, she often wondered whether other employers or another type of career would be a better fit for her and her aspirations. In fact, she often dreamed of becoming an entrepreneur by opening up a high-end housewares store. Five years of her life had been devoted to Enigma, five years of headaches, stress, and various political battles. But the five years of rewards had been there too: nice salary increases, bonuses, and a major promotion.

The West Coast regional manager wanted an answer in two days. If Natalie didn't take the promotion, it would please her fiancé and her family, but she knew it would be difficult to get another opportunity to be a store manager anytime soon. If she did take the promotion, she was looking at escalating demands, with even more stress and headaches. Natalie believed that if she really pressured her fiancé he would, reluctantly, agree to move to Seattle. And she rationalized that they could always find some sort of childcare arrangement out there when they did have kids. But she still hadn't ruled out the possibility of starting her own business. One way or another, this was the toughest decision she had ever faced in her life.

Case Analysis Questions

1. Is Natalie in the establishment or the achievement phase of her early career? What factors did you take into account in answering this question?
2. Identify all of the issues that Natalie needs to take into account in deciding whether to accept the offer to manage the Seattle store. How is Natalie's nonwork life influencing the decision that needs to be made? As an upwardly mobile manager in her early career, should Natalie even be concerned with these nonwork issues? Why or why not?
3. If you were in Natalie's shoes after five years with Enigma, what career and life choices would you be prepared to make? What are the most important factors that you considered in making your choices?
4. If you were to write a continuation to this case, what would you predict for Natalie for the future, say 10 or 15 years after her college graduation? Would it be a happy or an unhappy future?

Chapter 8 Case #2: Claudia the Star Performer

Throughout Claudia's senior year in college, she was actively recruited by a number of firms. As one of the top business students in her graduating class, Claudia believed that she could be choosy in selecting an employer. One of her strongest selection criteria was whether the hiring firm would pay for her MBA. Claudia eventually settled on a research assistant position with a medium-sized commercial bank. The salary was competitive and the bank would reimburse her for her graduate work.

Holding true to her goal, Claudia immediately began pursuing her MBA, attending one of the premier business schools in the country on a part-time basis. After two years, and an investment of well over $75,000 by her company, Claudia received an MBA in finance with a minor in international business.

Unbeknownst to her employer, Claudia had signed up for several of the on-campus interviews that were being held for graduating MBA students. She was especially interested in the large investment banking companies that were actively recruiting on campus. She was also interested in relocating to New York City. It wasn't that Claudia was displeased with her commercial bank; in fact, the opposite was true—the bank had treated her quite well, giving her challenging assignments and two promotions. Claudia just wanted to determine her market value and gain some leverage with the bank. Also, a job with one of the top investment banking firms would allow Claudia to continue advancing in her profession, and pursue her lifelong dream of living in New York City and attending the theater frequently.

Claudia was pleasantly surprised when she received offers from two prestigious New York investment banks. Both job proposals represented a 50 percent increase over her present salary and her relocation expenses would be covered. Claudia believed she had no choice but to ask the commercial bank if it would match the offers. Of course, she knew that the bank, with its rigid pay structure, would be loath to give her that kind of an increase. And her manager was not leaving his post anytime soon. True to her expectation, the bank refused to match the offer but stated that she would receive a generous increase at her next performance review. Claudia, believing that the bank offered her little choice, resigned the next day.

Claudia felt only a little remorse upon leaving the bank, rationalizing that the open labor market was the efficient, capitalistic way. Claudia also believed that this might be a one-time opportunity to pursue both personal and professional interests while living in New York City. The bank's management was bitter that it had lost one of its star performers and saw a significant investment go down the drain. And this was not the first time the bank lost a star performer to a competitor after the employee had received a graduate degree paid for by the bank. Indeed, at the most recent meeting of its executive management committee, the bank was considering dropping all support for graduate school tuition reimbursement, reviewing instead whether hiring MBAs from the outside was a more prudent course of action.

Case Analysis Questions

1. As a star performer and one who wanted to continue achieving in her profession, was Claudia wrong in seeking an opportunity from another employer? Given her track record and her MBA degree, if you were in Claudia's situation, what would you have done?
2. Do you think that Claudia acted ethically in quickly accepting the job from the investment bank? As an employee in the establishment phase of her early career, what alternatives should Claudia have considered in her pursuit of upward advancement? Should Claudia have given the bank a better opportunity to advance her in her career? Why or why not?
3. What are the economic implications for the bank with Claudia's departure? If you were a member of the executive management committee, what path would you have recommended at the meeting? How could the bank have better managed this important human resource?

Notes

1 Bray, D. W., Campbell, R. J. & Grant, D. L. (1974). *Formative years in business: A long-term AT&T study of managerial lives*. New York: Wiley; Coy, D. R. & Kovacs-Long, J. (2005). Maslow and Miller: An exploration of gender and affiliation in the journey to competence. *Journal of Counseling & Development*, *83*, 138–145; Hall, D. T. & Nougaim, K. (1968). An examination of Maslow's need hierarchy in an organizational setting. *Organizational Behavior and Human Performance*, *3*, 12–35; Surrey, J. L. (1991). The self-in-relation: A theory of women's development. In Jordan, J. V., Kaplan, A. G., Miller, J. B., Silver, I. P. & Surrey, J. L. (Eds.), *Women's growth in connection* (pp. 51–60). New York: Guilford Press.

2 Schein, E. H. (1993). *Career anchors*, 2nd ed. San Francisco, CA: Jossey-Bass Pfeiffer; Schein, E. H. (2006). Career anchors. In Greenhaus, J. H. & Callanan, G. A. (Eds.), *Encyclopedia of career development* (pp. 63–69). Thousand Oaks, CA: Sage.
3 Dix, J. E. & Savickas, M. L. (1995). Establishing a career: Developmental tasks and coping responses. *Journal of Vocational Behavior*, *47*, 93–107; Houghton, T. (2016). Establishing effective working relationships. *Nursing Standard*, *30*, 41–48; Jones, K. & Ewens, A. (2010). Achieving excellence in postgraduate community nurse practice placements. *British Journal of Community Nursing*, *15*, 604–610.
4 Chao, G. T. (2006). Organizational socialization. In Greenhaus, J. H. & Callanan, G. A. (Eds.), *Encyclopedia of career development* (pp. 596–602). Thousand Oaks, CA: Sage. Quotation is on p. 596.
5 Cohen, A. & Veled-Hecht, A. (2010). The relationship between organizational socialization and commitment in the workplace among employees in long-term nursing care facilities. *Personnel Review*, *39*, 537–556; Zhang, Y., Liao, J., Yan, Y. & Guo, Y. (2014). Newcomers' future work selves, perceived supervisor support, and proactive socialization in Chinese organizations. *Social Behavior and Personality*, *42*, 1457–1472.
6 De Cooman, R., De Gieter, S., Pepermans, R., Hermans, S., Du Bois, C., Caers, R. & Jegers, M. (2009). Person–organization fit: Testing socialization and attraction–selection–attrition hypotheses. *Journal of Vocational Behavior*, *74*, 102–107; Saks, A. M. & Gruman, J. A. (2011). Getting newcomers engaged: The role of socialization tactics. *Journal of Managerial Psychology*, *26*, 383–402.
7 Schein, E. H. (1990). Organizational culture. *American Psychologist*, *2*, 109–119. Quotation is on p. 111.
8 Myers, K. & Oetzel, J. G. (2003). Exploring the dimensions of organizational assimilation: Creating and validating a measure. *Communications Quarterly*, *51*, 438–457; Pucetaite, R., Novelskaite, A. & Markunaite, L. (2015). The mediating role of leadership relationship in building organisational trust on ethical culture of an organisation. *Economics & Sociology*, *8*, 11–31.
9 Bauer, T. M., Morrison, E. W. & Callister, R. R. (1998). Organizational socialization: A review and directions for future research. *Research in Personnel and Human Resource Management*, *16*, 149–214; Chao (2006); Chao, G. T., O'Leary-Kelly, A. M., Wolf, S., Klein, H. J. & Gardner, P. D. (1994). Organizational socialization: Its content and consequences. *Journal of Applied Psychology*, *79*, 730–743; Cohen & Veled-Hecht, (2010).
10 Saks, A. M., Uggerslev, K. L. & Fassina, N. E. (2007). Socialization tactics and newcomer adjustment: A meta-analytic review and test of a model. *Journal of Vocational Behavior*, *70*, 413–446; Zhang et al. (2014).
11 Chao et al. (1994).
12 Chao (2006); Saks & Gruman (2011); Zhang et al. (2014).
13 Chao (2006); Colakoglu, S. N. & Gokus, O. (2015). Mentoring functions' relationship with socialization facets and stages: A conceptual framework. *Journal of Organizational Culture, Communications and Conflict*, *19*, 1–13; Wanous, J. P. (1992). *Recruitment, selection, orientation and socialization of newcomers*. Reading, MA: Addison-Wesley; Zottoli, M. A. & Wanous, J. P. (2000). Recruitment source research: Current status and future directions. *Human Resource Management Review*, *10*, 353–382.
14 Callanan, G. A. (2006). Anticipatory socialization. In Greenhaus, J. H. & Callanan, G. A. (Eds.), *Encyclopedia of career development* (pp. 20–21). Thousand Oaks, CA: Sage; Chao (2006); Callanan, G. A. & Benzing, C. (2004). Assessing the role of internships in the career-oriented employment of graduating college students. *Education and Training*, *46*, 82–89; García-Aracil, A. (2015). Effects of college programme characteristics on graduates' performance. *Higher Education*, *69*, 735–757; Rigsby, J. T., Addy, N., Herring, C. & Polledo, D. (2013). An examination of internships and job opportunities. *Journal of Applied Business Research*, *29*, 1131–1143; Scholaris, D., Lockyer, C. & Johnson, H. (2003). Anticipatory socialization: The effects of recruitment and selection experiences on career expectations. *Career Development International*, *8*, 182–197.
15 Chao (2006).
16 Chao (2006); Cooper-Thomas, H., Anderson, N. & Cash, M. (2012). Investigating organizational socialization: A fresh look at newcomer adjustment strategies. *Personnel Review*, *41*, 41–55; Morrison, E. W. (1993). Newcomer information seeking: Exploring types, modes, sources, and outcomes. *Academy of Management Journal*, *36*, 557–589; Morrison, E. W. (2002).

Newcomers' relationships: The role of social network ties during socialization. *Academy of Management Journal, 45*, 1149–1160.
17 Saks et al. (2007).
18 Turban, D. B. (2006). Recruitment. In Greenhaus, J. H. & Callanan, G. A. (Eds.), *Encyclopedia of career development* (pp. 675–679). Thousand Oaks, CA: Sage; Wanous, J. P. (2006). Realistic recruitment. In Greenhaus, J. H. & Callanan, G. A. (Eds.), *Encyclopedia of career development* (pp. 672–675). Thousand Oaks, CA: Sage.
19 Arthur, W., Jr., Bennett, W., Jr., Edens, P. S. & Bell, S. T. (2003). Effectiveness of training organizations: A meta-analysis of design and evaluation features. *Journal of Applied Psychology, 88*, 234–245; Heames, J. T. (2006). Training and development. In Greenhaus, J. H. & Callanan, G. A. (Eds.), *Encyclopedia of career development* (pp. 817–818). Thousand Oaks, CA: Sage.
20 Schein, E. H. (1978). *Career dynamics: Matching individual and organizational needs*. Reading, MA: Addison-Wesley.
21 Wanous (1992); Wanous, J. P. & Reichers, A. E. (2000). New employee orientation programs. *Human Resource Management Review, 10*, 435–451.
22 Campion, M. C., Campion, E. D. & Campion, M. A. (2015). Improvements in performance management through the use of 360 feedback. *Industrial and Organizational Psychology, 8*, 85–93; Eichinger, R. W. & Lombardo, M. M. (2003). Knowledge summary series: 360-degree assessment. *Human Resource Planning, 26*, 34–44; Kim, K. Y., Atwater, L., Patel, P. C. & Smither, J. W. (2016). Multisource feedback, human capital, and the financial performance of organizations. *Journal of Applied Psychology, 101*, 1569–1584.
23 Ashforth, B. E. & Saks, A. M. (1996). Socialization tactics: Longitudinal effects on newcomer adjustment. *Academy of Management Journal, 39*, 149–178; Feldman, D. C. (1981). The multiple socialization of organization members. *Academy of Management Review, 6*, 309–319; Schein, E. H. (1964). How to break in the college graduate. *Harvard Business Review, 42*, 68–76; Schein (1978); Wanous (1992).
24 Saks et al. (2007).
25 Schein (1978).
26 Myers, K. K. (2006). Assimilation and mutual acceptance. In Greenhaus, J. H. & Callanan, G. A. (Eds.), *Encyclopedia of career development* (pp. 31–32). Thousand Oaks, CA: Sage; Schein (1978).
27 Low, C. H., Bordia, P. & Bordia, S. (2016). What do employees want and why? An exploration of employees' preferred psychological contract elements across career stages. *Human Relations, 69*, 1457–1481; Robinson, S. L., Kraatz, M. S. & Rousseau, D. M. (1994). Changing obligations and the psychological contract: A longitudinal study. *Academy of Management Journal, 37*, 137–152.
28 Tomprou, M. & Nikolaou, I. (2011). A model of psychological contract creation upon organizational entry. *Career Development International, 16*, 342–363.
29 Coyle-Shapiro, J. A. M. (2006). Psychological contract. In Greenhaus, J. H. & Callanan, G. A. (Eds.), *Encyclopedia of career development* (pp. 652–659). Thousand Oaks, CA: Sage; Robinson et al. (1994); Low et al. (2016); Rousseau, D. M. & Wade-Benzoni, K. A. (1996). Changing individual–organization attachments: A two-way street. In Howard, A. (Ed.), *The changing nature of work*. San Francisco: Jossey-Bass, 1995.
30 Schein (1978).
31 Klemm, C. (2007). Quarter-life crisis hits those in transition to adulthood. *Knight Ridder Tribune Business News*, June 24, 1; Griggs, J. (2013). Midlife, quarterlife—what are our life crises about? *New Scientist, 219*, 29; Robbins, A. & Wilner, A. (2001). *Quarterlife crisis: The unique challenges of life in your twenties*. New York: Putnam/Tarcher.
32 Gurvis, J., McCauley, C. & Swofford, M. (2016). *Putting experience at the center of talent management*. White Paper. Greensboro, NC: Center for Creative Leadership. www.ccl.org/articles/white-papers/putting-experience-at-the-center-of-talent-management/; Lindsey, E. H., Homes, V. & McCall, M. W. (1987). *Key events in executives' lives*. Greensboro, NC: Center for Creative Leadership; McCall, M. W. (1988). Developing executives through work experiences. *Human Resource Planning, 11*, 1–11; McCauley, C.D. & Van Velsor, E. (2004). *The Center for Creative Leadership handbook for leadership development*, 2nd ed. San Francisco: Jossey-Bass.
33 Kossek, E. & Ruderman, M. (2012). Work–family flexibility and the employment relationship. In Shore, L. M., Coyle-Shapiro, J. A. M. & Tetrick, L. E., (Eds.), *Understanding the employee–organization relationship: Advances in theory and practice* (pp. 223–253). London: Routledge/Taylor & Francis Group; Lam, C. F., Wan, W. H. & Roussin, C. J. (2016). Going the extra mile

and feeling energized: An enrichment perspective of organizational citizenship behaviors. *Journal of Applied Psychology, 101*, 379–391; Van Dyne, L. & Ellis, J. B. (2004). Job creep: A reactance theory perspective on organizational citizenship behavior as over-fulfillment of obligations. In Coyle-Shapiro, J., Shore, L., Taylor, M. S. & Tetrick, L. (Eds.), *The employment relationship: Examining the psychological and contextual perspectives* (pp. 135–160), Oxford, UK: Oxford University Press.
34 Low et al. (2016).
35 D'Aurizio, P. (2007). Onboarding: Delivering on the promise. *Nursing Economics, 25*, 228–229; Morel, S. (2007). Onboarding secures talent for the long run. *Workforce Management, 86*, 9; Smith, R. E. (1984). Employee orientation: 10 steps to success. *Personnel Journal, 63*, 46–48.
36 D'Aurizio (2007).
37 Ferri-Reed, J. (2013). Onboarding strategies to supercharge millennial employees. *The Journal for Quality and Participation, 36*, 32–33; Johnson, M. & Senges, M. (2010). Learning to be a programmer in a complex organization: A case study on practice-based learning during the onboarding process at Google. *Journal of Workplace Learning, 22*, 180–194.
38 De Pater, I. E., van Vianen, A. E. M., Bechtoldt, M. N. & Klehe, U. C. (2009). Employees' challenging job experiences and supervisors' evaluations of promotability. *Personnel Psychology, 62*, 297–325; Dixon, M. A., Cunningham, G. B., Sagas, M., Turner, B. A. & Kent, A. (2005). Challenge is the key: An investigation of affective commitment in undergraduate interns. *Journal of Education for Business, 80*, 172–180; Morrison, R. F. & Brantner, T. M. (1992).What enhances or inhibits learning a new job? A basic career issue. *Journal of Applied Psychology, 77*, 926–941; O'Shea, D., Monaghan, S. & Ritchie, T. D. (2014). Early career attitudes and satisfaction during recession. *Journal of Managerial Psychology, 29*, 226–245; Shalley, C. A., Gilson, L. L. & Blum, T. C. (2000). Matching creativity requirements and the work environment: Effects on satisfaction and intention to leave. *Academy of Management Journal, 43*, 215–223.
39 Carette, B., Anseel, F. & Lievens, F. (2013). Does career timing of challenging job assignments influence the relationship with in-role job performance? *Journal of Vocational Behavior, 83*, 61–67; Driskell, J. E. & Mullen, B. (1990). Status, expectations and behavior: A meta-analytic review and test of the theory. *Personality and Social Psychology Bulletin, 16*, 541–553.
40 Hall, D. T. (2004). The protean career: A quarter-century journey. *Journal of Vocational Behavior, 65*, 1–13.
41 Hideg, I. & Ferris, D. L. (2016). The compassionate sexist? How benevolent sexism promotes and undermines gender equality in the workplace. *Journal of Personality and Social Psychology: Interpersonal Relations and Group Processes, 111*, 706–727; Jones, K., Stewart, K., King, E., Whitney, B. M., Gilrane, V. & Hylton, K. (2014). Negative consequence of benevolent sexism on efficacy and performance. *Gender in Management, 29*, 171–189; Mai-Dalton, R. R. & Sullivan, J. J. (1981). The effects of manager's sex on the assignment to a challenging or dull task and reasons for the choice. *Academy of Management Journal, 24*, 603–612; Ransom, M. & Oaxaca, R. L. (2005). Intrafirm mobility and sex differences in pay. *Industrial & Labor Relations Review, 58*, 219–237.
42 Porter, L. W., Lawler, E. E. & Hackman, J. R. (1975). *Behavior in organizations*. New York: McGraw-Hill; Van der Rijt, J., Van den Bossche, P., Van de Wiel, M. W. J., Segers, M. S. R. & Gijselaers, W. H. (2012). The role of individual and organizational characteristics in feedback-seeking behaviour in the initial career stage. *Human Resource Development International, 15*, 283–301.
43 DeRue, D. S. & Wellman, N. (2009). Developing leaders via experience: The role of developmental challenge, learning orientation, and feedback availability. *Journal of Applied Psychology, 94*, 859–875.
44 Hall (2004).
45 Joo, B. K., Sushko, J. S. & McLean, G. N. (2012). Multiple faces of coaching: Manager-as-coach, executive coaching, and formal mentoring. *Organization Development Journal, 30*, 19–38.
46 Ragins, B. R. & Kram, K. E. (Eds.) (2007). *The handbook of mentoring: Theory, research and practice*. Thousand Oaks, CA: Sage.
47 Schein (1978).
48 Ragins & Kram (2007).
49 Bridgeford, L. C. (2007). Mentoring programs still have a place in the 21st century. *Employee Benefit News, 21*, 16; Catalyst (2004). *Women and men in U.S. corporate leadership: Same workplace, different realities?* New York: Catalyst.
50 Arora, R. & Rangnekar, S. (2014). Workplace mentoring and career resilience: An empirical test. *The Psychologist-Manager Journal, 17*, 205–220; Baugh, S. G., Lankau, M. J. & Scandura, T. A.

(1996). An investigation of the effects of protégé gender on responses to mentoring. *Journal of Vocational Behavior*, *49*, 309–323; Bozionelos, N., Bozionelos, G., Kostopoulos, K. & Polychroniou, P. (2011). How providing mentoring relates to career success and organizational commitment. *Career Development International*, *16*, 446–468; Colarelli, S. M. & Bishop, R. C. (1990). Career commitment: Functions, correlates, and management. *Group & Organization Studies*, *15*, 158–176; Dreher, G. F. & Chargois, J. A. (1998). Gender, mentoring experiences, and salary attainment among graduates of a historically black university. *Journal of Vocational Behavior*, *53*, 401–416; Dreher, G. F. & Cox, Jr., T. H. (1996). Race, gender and opportunity: A study of compensation attainment and the establishment of mentoring relationships. *Journal of Applied Psychology*, *81*, 297–308; Eby, L. T., Allen, T. D., Hoffman, B. J., Baranik, L. E., Sauer, J. B., Baldwin, S., Morrison, M. A., Kinkade, K. M., Maher, C. P., Curtis, S. & Evans, S. C. (2013). An interdisciplinary meta-analysis of the potential antecedents, correlates, and consequences of protégé perceptions of mentoring. *Psychological Bulletin*, *139*, 441–476; Fagenson, E. A. (1989). The mentor advantage: Perceived career/job experiences of protégés versus non-protégés. *Journal of Organizational Behavior*, *10*, 309–320; Godshalk, V. M. & Sosik, J. J. (2000). Does mentor–protégé agreement on mentor leadership behavior influence the quality of a mentoring relationship? *Group & Organization Management*, *25*, 291–317; Jyoti, J. & Sharma, P. (2015). Exploring the role of mentoring structure and culture between mentoring functions and job satisfaction: A study of Indian call centre employees. *Vision*, *19*, 336–348; Scandura, T. A. (1992). Mentorship and career mobility: An empirical investigation. *Journal of Organizational Behavior*, *13*, 169–174; Kirchmeyer, C. (2005). The effects of mentoring on academic careers over time: Testing performance and political perspectives. *Human Relations*, *58*, 637–660; Turban, D. B. & Dougherty, T. W. (1994). Role of protégé personality in receipt of mentoring and career success. *Academy of Management Journal*, *37*, 688–702.

51 O'Neill, R. M. (2002). Gender and race in mentoring relationships: A review of the literature. In Clutterbuck, D. & Ragins, B. R. (Eds.), *Mentoring and diversity: An international perspective* (pp. 1–22). Oxford, UK: Butterworth-Heinemann; Qian, J., Lin, X., Han, Z. R., Chen, Z. X. & Hays, J. M. (2014). What matters in the relationship between mentoring and job-related stress? The moderating effects of protégés' traditionality and trust in mentor. *Journal of Management and Organization*, *20*, 608–623; Sosik, J. J. & Godshalk, V. M. (2000). Leadership style, mentoring functions received, and job-related stress: A conceptual model and preliminary study. *Journal of Organizational Behavior*, *21*, 365–390; Tharenou, P. (2005). Does mentor support increase women's career advancement more than men's? The differential effects of career and psychosocial support. *Australian Journal of Management*, *30*, 77–110; Wallace, J. E. (2001). The benefits of mentoring for female lawyers. *Journal of Vocational Behavior*, *58*, 366–391.

52 Ghosh, R., Haynes, R. K. & Kram, K. E. (2013). Developmental networks at work: Holding environments for leader development. *Career Development International*, *18*, 232–256; Gregoric, C. & Wilson, A. (2015). Informal peer mentoring in early career researchers. *International Journal for Researcher Development*, *6*, 40–56; Haggard, D. L., Dougherty, T. W., Turban, D. B. & Wilbanks, J. E. (2011). Who is a mentor? A review of evolving definitions and implications for research. *Journal of Management*, *37*, 280–304; Murphy, W. M. & Kram, K. E. (2010). Understanding non-work relationships in developmental networks. *Career Development International*, *15*, 637–663.

53 Dreher, G. F. & Dougherty, T. W. (1997). Substitutes for career mentoring: Promoting equal opportunity through career management and assessment systems. *Journal of Vocational Behavior*, *51*, 110–124.

54 Benabou, C. & Benabou, R. (2000). Establishing a formal mentoring program for organizational success. *National Productivity Review*, *19*, 1–8; Butyn, S. (2003). Mentoring your way to improved retention. *Canadian HR Reporter*, *16*, 13–15; Farnese, M. L., Bellò, B., Livi, S., Barbieri, B. & Gubbiotti, P. (2016). Learning the ropes: The protective role of mentoring in correctional police officers' socialization process. *Military Psychology*, *28*, 429–447; Gibbs, S. (1999). The usefulness of theory: A case study in evaluating formal mentoring schemes. *Human Relations*, *52*, 1055–1075; Holt, D. T., Markova, G., Dhaenens, A. J., Marler, L. E. & Heilmann, S. G. (2016). Formal or informal mentoring: What drives employees to seek informal mentors? *Journal of Managerial Issues*, *28*, 67–82; Laiho, M. & Brandt, T. (2012). Views of HR specialists on formal mentoring: Current situation and prospects for the future. *Career Development International*, *17*, 435–457; Payne, S. C. & Huffman, A. H. (2005). A longitudinal examination of the influence of mentoring on organizational commitment and turnover. *Academy of Management Journal*, *48*, 158–168; Perrone, J. (2003). Creating a mentoring culture. *Healthcare*

Executive, *18*, 84–85; Singh, V., Bains, D. & Vinnicombe, S. (2002). Informal mentoring as an organizational resource. *Long Range Planning*, *35*, 389–405.
55 Baugh, S. G. & Fagenson-Eland, E. A. (2007). Formal mentoring programs. In Ragins, B. R. & Kram, K. E. (Eds.), *The handbook of mentoring at work: Theory, research and practice* (pp. 249–272). Thousand Oaks, CA: Sage; Ensher, E. A. & Murphy, S. E. (2011). The Mentoring Relationship Challenges Scale: The impact of mentoring stage, type, and gender. *Journal of Vocational Behavior*, *79*, 253–266; Holt et al. (2016).
56 Greenhaus, J. H. & Singh, R. (2007). Mentoring and the work–family interface. In Ragins, B. R. & Kram, K. E. (Eds.), *Handbook of mentoring at work* (pp. 519–544). Thousand Oaks, CA: Sage.
57 Blake-Beard, S. D., Murrell, A. & Thomas, D. (2007). Unfinished business: The impact of race on understanding mentoring relationships. In Ragins, B. R. & Kram, K. E. (Eds.), *The handbook of mentoring at work: Theory, research and practice* (pp. 223–248). Thousand Oaks, CA: Sage; McKeen, C. & Bujaki, M. (2007). Gender and mentoring: Issues, effects and opportunities. In Ragins, B. R. & Kram, K. E. (Eds.), *The handbook of mentoring at work: Theory, research and practice* (pp. 197–222). Thousand Oaks, CA: Sage.
58 Dix & Savickas (1995); Saks et al. (2007).
59 Retrieved from www.avoncompany.com/corporate-responsibility/people/diversity-inclusion/; www.goldmansachs.com/who-we-are/diversity-and-inclusion/employee-affinity-networks.html on January 19, 2017.
60 Levinson, D. J., Darrow, C. N., Klein, E. B., Levinson, M. H. & McKee, B. (1978). *Seasons of a man's life*. New York: Knopf; Levinson, D. J. & Levinson, J. D. (1996). *Seasons of a woman's life*. New York: Knopf.
61 Igbaria, M., Greenhaus, J. H. & Parasuraman, S. (1991). Career orientations of MIS employees: An empirical analysis. *MIS Quarterly*, *15*, 151–169; Maurer, T. J. & Chapman, E. F. (2013). Ten years of career success in relation to individual and situational variables from the employee development literature. *Journal of Vocational Behavior*, *83*, 450–465; Ng, T. W. H. & Feldman, D. C. (2014). Subjective career success: A meta-analytic review. *Journal of Vocational Behavior*, *85*, 169–179; Singh, R., Ragins, B. R. & Tharenou, P. (2009).What matters most? The relative role of mentoring and career capital in career success. *Journal of Vocational Behavior*, *75*, 56–67; Stumpf, S. A. (2014). A longitudinal study of career success, embeddedness, and mobility of early career professionals. *Journal of Vocational Behavior*, *85*, 180–190.
62 Campion, M. A., Cheraskin, L. & Stevens, M. J. (1994). Career-related antecedents and outcomes of job rotation. *Academy of Management Journal*, *37*, 1518–1542; Fox, M. L. (2006). Job design. In Greenhaus, J. H. & Callanan, G. A. (Eds.), *Encyclopedia of career development* (pp. 414–420). Thousand Oaks, CA: Sage; Kaymaz, K. (2010). The effects of job rotation practices on motivation: A research on managers in the automotive organizations. *Business and Economics Research Journal*, *1*, 69–86; Marinova, S. V., Peng, C., Lorinkova, N., Van Dyne, L. & Chiaburu, D. (2015). Change-oriented behavior: A meta-analysis of individual and job design predictors. *Journal of Vocational Behavior*, *88*, 104–120; Ortega, J. (2001). Job rotation as a learning mechanism. *Management Science*, *47*, 1361–1371; Zin, M. L. M., Shamsudin, F. M. & Subramaniam, C. (2013). Investigating the influence of job rotation on career development among production workers in Japanese companies. *International Journal of Business and Society*, *14*, 135–148.
63 Bernthal, P. & Wellins, R. (2006). Trends in leader development and succession. *Human Resource Planning*, *29*, 31–41.
64 For an overview of the work of the Center for Creative Leadership, see McCauley, C. D. (2006). Center for Creative Leadership. In Greenhaus, J. H. & Callanan, G. A. (Eds.), *Encyclopedia of career development* (pp. 162–164). Thousand Oaks, CA: Sage; For research on the components of managerial jobs, see McCauley, C. D., Ruderman, M. N., Ohlott, P. J. & Morrow, J. E. (1994). Assessing the developmental components of managerial jobs. *Journal of Applied Psychology*, *79*, 544–560.
65 McCauley et al. (1994).
66 Retrieved from www.careers.jnj.com.
67 Bown-Wilson, D. & Parry, E. (2013). Career progression in older managers. *Employee Relations*, *35*, 309–321; Kaye, B. & Farren, C. (1996). Up is not the only way. *Training & Development*, *50*, 48–54; Lyons, S. T., Schweitzer, L. & Ng, E. S. W. (2015). How have careers changed? An investigation of changing career patterns across four generations. *Journal of Managerial Psychology*, *30*, 8–21.
68 Enache et al. (2011); Ng & Feldman (2014); Seibert, S. E. (2006). Career success. In Greenhaus, J. H. & Callanan, G. A. (Eds.), *Encyclopedia of career development* (pp. 148–154). Thousand Oaks, CA: Sage.

69 Baird, L. & Kram, K. E. (1983). Career dynamics: Managing the superior/subordinate relationship. *Organizational Dynamics*, *11*, 46–64.
70 Kovach, B. E. (1989). Successful derailment: What fast-trackers can learn while they're off the track. *Organizational Dynamics*, *18*, 33–48; Ross, S. (2013). Talent derailment: A multidimensional perspective for understanding talent. *Industrial and Commercial Training*, *45*, 12–17; Van Velsor, E. (2006). Derailment. In Greenhaus, J. H. & Callanan, G. A. (Eds.), *Encyclopedia of career development* (pp. 225–226). Thousand Oaks, CA: Sage.
71 Ross (2013); Van Velsor, E. & Leslie, J. B. (1995). Why executives derail: Perspectives across time and cultures. *Academy of Management Executive*, *9*, 62–72; Yeh, Q. J. (2008). Exploring career stages of midcareer and older engineers—when managerial transition matters. *IEEE Transactions on Engineering Management*, *55*, 82–94.
72 Crant, J. M. (2006). Personality and careers. In Greenhaus, J. H. & Callanan, G. A. (Eds.), *Encyclopedia of career development* (pp. 627–634). Thousand Oaks, CA: Sage; Seibert (2006); Levine, S. P. (2006). Self-monitoring. In Greenhaus, J. H. & Callanan, G. A. (Eds.), *Encyclopedia of career development* (pp. 729–730). Thousand Oaks, CA: Sage.
73 Crant (2006). Quotation is on p. 633.
74 Greenhaus, J. H., Callanan, G. A. & DiRenzo, M. (2008). A boundaryless perspective on careers. In Barling, J. & Cooper, C. L. (Eds.), *The Sage handbook of organizational behavior*, Volume 1 (pp. 277–299). Thousand Oaks, CA: Sage; Ragins & Kram (2007).
75 Gaultier, A. (2002). Paying the price: The high cost of executive success. *New Zealand Management*, *49*, 34–38; Korman, A. K. (1988). Career success and personal failure: Mid- to late-career feelings and events. In London, M. & Mones, E. M. (Eds.), *Career growth and human resource strategies* (pp. 81–94). New York,: Quorum; Weerahannadige Dulini, A. F. & Cohen, L. (2011). Exploring the interplay between gender, organizational context and career. *Career Development International*, *16*, 553–571.
76 Colakoglu & Gokus (2015); Scholaris, D., Lockyer, C. & Johnson, H. (2003). Anticipatory socialization: The effect of recruitment and selection experiences on career expectations. *Career Development International*, *8*, 182–197.

9 The Middle and Late Career Stages

Career Challenges for Seasoned Employees

As we discussed in Chapter 2, from a chronological age sense, the midcareer years roughly span the period from the early 40s to the later 50s. The late career stage would normally include those who are in their later 50s and older. Of course, as we also discussed in Chapter 2, these age ranges are somewhat arbitrary as job losses and impermanent work arrangements, individual uncertainty with regard to future income streams, and longer life expectancies have all blurred the distinctions between what represents the middle and late career stages as well as the standard age at which the move toward full retirement from work occurs. Surveys show that across the United States the average age of retirement is 63 years old, but 6 percent of all Americans are still working at the age of 80 and beyond.[1]

It is fortunate that a good deal has been learned about midcareer and late career issues in recent years. The graying of America and other parts of the industrialized world is no myth. Clearly, the aging of the baby boom generation, the roughly 78 million people born in the United States during the nearly 20-year period after World War II, is having and will have a dramatic effect on work organizations, government institutions, and individual career management over the upcoming decades.[2] Demographic data present a vivid picture of the future labor force.[3] Over the next 30 years the percentage of the civilian labor force represented by the baby boom generation will drop steadily. It is likely that in the year 2020, baby boomers will represent roughly 25 percent of the U.S. labor force, but that rate will decline markedly over the ensuing decades as retirements take hold.[4] By the year 2050, when all of the baby boom generation will be 85 years of age and older, the entire cohort will essentially be out of the labor force.[5]

The implications of these forecasts are clear. With the aging of the baby boom generation, older workers will make up a large share of both the population and the labor force in the short run. Accordingly, organizations must become more attuned to the needs and experiences of midcareer and late career employees. As fewer younger employees enter the labor force, as demands for skilled labor prevent organizations from offering early retirement options, and as financial pressures coupled with longer life expectancies force people to delay retirement, more and more senior employees are expected to continue as active members of the workforce, at least over the next decade or more. These seasoned employees will have to make a number of significant decisions about the timing of retirement and the ways in which they would like to live their pre-retirement and retirement years.

In this chapter, we examine the middle and late stages of career development. We consider the tasks and challenges posed by each of these two career stages, examine some typical concerns experienced by individuals in these phases of their lives, and offer career management guidelines for organizations and individuals.

The Middle Career Years

The midcareer years pose two major career and life tasks. *Confronting the midlife transition* involves reappraising one's accomplishments relative to ambitions and dreams and reexamining the importance of work in one's life.[6] Indeed, many midcareer employees may have to learn to cope with the personal and professional stressors produced by the midlife transition. *Remaining productive* during midcareer requires employees to update and integrate their skills; exercise sufficient autonomy to express these skills; and develop new skills such as the mentoring of younger colleagues.

Confronting the Midlife Transition

According to Daniel Levinson and his colleagues, the midlife transition typically takes place between the ages of 40 and 45.[7] It can be triggered by a number of experiences: fear of lost youth and missed opportunities, awareness of aging and mortality, failure to accomplish significant career and personal life goals, the inability to achieve an acceptable balance between work and nonwork commitments, and the need to shed youthful illusions that propelled the earlier portion of one's career and life. The midcareer employee may also experience rivalries with more energetic, ambitious, and highly educated younger colleagues and may feel defensive and guilty about these hostile feelings. Technical or managerial obsolescence, common among midcareer employees, can add to these frustrations. The recognition that one may not advance further in the organization—that one has reached a career plateau—can undoubtedly intensify feelings of failure and cast a gloom over one's future career. Further exacerbating the situation, many individuals in midcareer often have a difficult time seeking reemployment when confronted with job loss. In addition, highly successful and work-focused employees may experience feelings of personal failure at midlife, reflecting the guilt and regret over having sacrificed family relationships and other personal interests, in the ambitious pursuit of career success.[8]

It is no surprise, then, that many midcareer employees become restless. Although some people may make drastic occupational changes or pursue alternate lifestyles, many more are psychologically conflicted. Some may exhibit renewed energy toward new career pursuits. Others may continue their direction toward fulfillment of longstanding goals, while still others may reduce their involvement in work, decrease work engagement, resist learning new things, and turn their attention and energies toward their families and/or themselves.[9]

We have painted a somewhat negative picture of the midlife transition. Indeed, Levinson and his colleagues concluded that 80 percent of the men and 85 percent of the women in their research experienced a crisis during this period.[10] However, other researchers have questioned whether the midlife crisis is universally experienced, arguing that feelings of frustration, mortality, and stress can occur at different times for different people, depending on their particular pattern of life experiences and the culture and point in history in which they live. In fact, major crises, such as financial burdens, job loss, or illness or divorce, can occur anytime throughout adulthood.[11] In contrast to Levinson's findings, other research involving middle-aged adults found that only 25 to 33 percent stated that they experienced a midlife crisis.[12]

Further, neuroscientists who have studied mental functioning have found that the human brain is more flexible and adaptable after the age of 40 than once thought. Studies suggest the right and left hemispheres of the brain become more integrated at midlife, and hence allow for greater creativity. The "use it or lose it" adage has been confirmed scientifically, suggesting that those who challenge themselves mentally throughout midlife continue to strengthen cognitive ability, report fewer physical health problems, and remain engaged in the workplace. In addition, better emotional regulation, mental health, increased wisdom and practical intelligence, and a strong sense of mastery are positive outcomes associated with midlife.[13] Thus, midlife is not universally seen as a period of trauma and change, and can be a positive time filled with personal growth and discovery.

What can be concluded about the midlife transition? First, the notion that people need to reappraise their lives as they enter middle adulthood is compelling. Coming to grips with this fact and making adjustments for the next era of life seem essential. Early adulthood and all that it entails—youth, feelings of immortality, dreams, and hopes—can never be relived. Whether these midlife issues arise between the ages of 40 and 45, as Levinson and his colleagues found, or possibly later as others suggest,[14] is still uncertain. However, it seems reasonable that these issues should surface in the "early" part of middle adulthood.

Second, it is unclear whether the feelings that accompany midlife appraisal are so intense as to constitute a crisis. Perhaps it is sufficient to state that the entrance into middle adulthood raises certain issues that may produce a variety of emotional reactions regarding social, psychological, and physical domains. It is important that the entry into middle adulthood is begun with a reappraisal of accomplishments and life goals. This reappraisal enables individuals to find constructive ways to remain professionally and personally productive and fulfilled throughout their midcareer years. It also facilitates an assessment of the many emotions associated with midlife. Perhaps this period of transition and self-assessment allows for adaptation to a middle-age adult life role. Ways in which individuals and organizations can address the midlife transition will be examined later in the chapter.

Remaining Productive: Growth, Maintenance, or Stagnation?

The second major task of midcareer is to remain productive. For many, the middle career years are characterized by maintenance of the status quo, where individuals experience little motivation to start in new directions, possibly from a lack of opportunity within their employing organization. This period has been dubbed *middlescence* because it can be as frustrating and confusing as adolescence.[15] Millions of midcareer employees are dealing with middlescence as they try to find new meaning in work, while balancing the responsibilities of job, family, community, and leisure. While many people desire growth and development during midcareer, others enter a period of maintenance or begin to stagnate and decline, essentially "checking out" of the organization. It is clear that the midcareer years can be fraught with challenges regarding work commitment and performance, changing health, and possibly motivation.[16] Two midcareer experiences, plateauing and obsolescence, can affect midcareer productivity and trigger feelings of stress.

The Career Plateau

Realistically, everyone plateaus at one time or another. Although plateauing can occur at any career stage, it is particularly relevant to the seasoned employee. For that reason, we consider the career plateau as a central issue in midcareer.

A career *plateau* has traditionally been defined as the "point in a career where the likelihood of additional hierarchical promotion is very low."[17] Researchers have identified various types and reasons for career plateaus. When an individual is unable to rise further within an organization—that is, when the likelihood of additional hierarchical promotions is low—the person is viewed as "structurally" plateaued. When growth opportunities associated with increasing responsibility on one's current job become unavailable, the person is "content" plateaued.[18] It is reasonable to believe that a person might be plateaued in both ways, with no opportunities to move up the corporate ladder and with few opportunities for growth in the current job.

When an individual becomes plateaued, it is normal to look for reasons as to why the plateau has occurred. In a basic sense, firms may plateau the employee, or the employee may choose to be plateaued. Firms often have two main reasons for why they plateau an employee.[19] First, the organization may have *constraints* it is facing and therefore cannot allow the employee to advance further up the hierarchy or cannot provide additional responsibilities associated with the current job. The employee might not be able to advance (structural plateau) due to the narrowing organizational pyramid, a reduction in upper-level positions due to downsizings that may be occurring, or increased competition for positions in the hierarchy. The employee may also not receive increased job responsibilities (content plateau) because of inflexible job descriptions or unavailable training in new technology. In these cases, it is the actions or situations within the organization that result in the employee being plateaued. Second, the organization may negatively *assess* the value and abilities of the employee, and hence plateau him or her. An employee may not receive promotions (structural plateau) because management believes the individual lacks the necessary experience, interpersonal skills, work ethic, commitment, or political savvy needed for higher-level jobs. Or the employee might not receive greater job responsibility (content plateau) because he or she is "not ready," "can't handle it," or lacks the desire or necessary skills. These negative assessments of the employee, valid or not, cause the employee to be plateaued. So, organizations may plateau employees for organizational *constraint* or *assessment* reasons.

Seasoned employees may choose to be plateaued for *personal-choice* reasons. This motive for plateauing may become more common as baby boom employees, many in dual-earner relationships, choose to stay in their current job instead of pursuing (or accepting) a higher-level job that requires additional responsibilities. The stress, travel, and potential relocation implications to, and interruptions of, one's nonwork life (e.g., family, health, leisure) may outweigh the additional compensation or prestige that the new job might bring. Depending on the firm's culture, some employees may explicitly make known their personal choice to be plateaued, while others may send ambiguous signals to management. Although the choice to become plateaued can go against the grain of organizational expectations, employees can make a conscious decision to be plateaued for *personal-choice* reasons.

In summary, why is plateauing such a universal experience?

1. At the most basic level, the pyramidal structure of most organizations provides fewer and fewer positions at higher levels of the hierarchy. The higher one rises in the organizational structure, the fewer the number of positions that are available for further advancement. As the pyramidal structure becomes flatter, fewer management levels are available through which one might advance.
2. There is increasing competition for these few positions because of the glut of baby boomers reaching middle or senior levels of management at the same time and the downsizing of the corporate structures that has taken place over the past several decades.
3. The degree of employee plateauing is exacerbated in organizations that are growing slowly, not growing at all, or contracting their operations and workforce. The outsourcing of jobs, either across state or country lines, has created more plateauing. Furthermore, a company's business strategy can affect the number

and type of growth opportunities and hence the incidence of plateauing in certain career paths.

4. The virtual elimination of mandatory retirement can clog career paths and prevent younger employees from progressing in the hierarchy.
5. Changes in technology may close certain career paths or open new paths for which employees are not prepared.
6. Some employees may be more likely to plateau structurally because they are thought to be too valuable in their present position and hence must stay. This restriction could cause individuals to experience a deterioration in their technical or managerial skills, and may limit their future career mobility.
7. A variety of factors can cause executives and others to become "derailed" off the fast track and end up plateaued. These factors include problems with interpersonal relationships, a failure to meet business objectives, a failure to build and lead a team, and an inability to change or adapt during transitions.[20]
8. As we noted above, the desire for a more balanced lifestyle has led an increasing number of employees to make the organization aware that they do not wish to be considered for further advancement or increased job responsibilities because of the potential conflicts with family, community, or leisure commitments.[21]

What are the consequences of plateauing? Many plateaued men feel like failures because they equate career success with masculinity. For some men, the sense of failure is tinged with guilt over the little time they have spent with their families during their pursuit of career success. Some women may feel betrayed if they have foregone marriage and/or family to concentrate on a career that now seems to be going nowhere. Plateaued employees might be stereotyped as "deadwood" and may be alienated within the firm. Other harmful psychological reactions include lower self-worth, lower skill assessment, and lack of acceptance by peers and supervisors due to perceptions of lower work contributions.[22]

It is not surprising that most individuals associate plateauing with negative outcomes. Plateaued employees can become less involved in their jobs and display decreased motivation in their work, especially if they believe that the organization has devalued their contributions. Ultimately, these employees may exhibit deteriorated performance and cause a decline in the performance of their department and organization. After all, the most powerful incentives that have motivated performance to this point, the promise of further advancement or increased job responsibilities, are no longer a feasible reward for effective performance. Individuals who perceive themselves as career plateaued tend to exhibit lower levels of satisfaction with their job, their career, and their personal development; experience higher levels of stress and emotional exhaustion; perceive less organizational support; and are more apt to leave their organization or consider early retirement.[23] However, some content-plateaued employees who have not experienced a hierarchical plateau could retain positive work attitudes due to the prospect of upward mobility, even if the chances are remote.[24]

Are negative outcomes inevitably linked to career plateauing? Given the relatively common occurrence of becoming plateaued, experiencing a career plateau may not be as embarrassing or stressful as it once was considered. Indeed, a leveling-off period (as represented by a career plateau) can have a positive influence on individual development and personal growth. Because a career plateau can represent a time of stability, plateaued individuals can master new work skills, pursue a more predictable family and personal life, become more psychologically involved in their nonwork commitments, and replenish psychic energy.[25] They may also use this time to take stock of their position and recount their accomplishments.

Consistent with these observations on the potentially positive aspects of career plateaus, researchers have concluded that many employees adapt to their career plateau without too much trouble by redefining career success.[26] Whether due to a real change of values or simply a rationalization of their current situation, the job performance and work attitudes of these adaptable employees may not suffer greatly. Consider the following example:

Jan emerged from her annual performance review feeling numb. For the third year in a row, she had received only a "good" rating—another indication that her promotion prospects were close to nil. It wasn't always like this for Jan. Earlier in her career she received "excellent" or "outstanding" evaluations and she was promoted every two or three years. She wasn't necessarily on the fast track, but she continued to advance at a steady pace.

In the course of her 25-year career, Jan could point to many accomplishments, both in her work and in her personal life. She had overseen the installation of a new automated system, had taken over an operation with poor performance and turned it around, and had made cost-saving recommendations to senior management that resulted in significantly reduced expenses. Moreover, Jan had obtained her MBA going part-time, had gotten married, raised two children, and gone through a divorce. Jan recently purchased her own townhome and is dating an executive at another company in town.

All in all, she was pleased with her professional and personal development. But with her latest evaluation, Jan is uncertain what to do next. She realizes she won't be receiving more promotions, and she is feeling the heat from younger staff members and colleagues who are eager to move up the ladder. Being on a career plateau has been a stressful experience for her. She could look for another job, but she has no idea of her prospects. Besides, she has asked herself why she would want to trade her current job, with good pay and benefits, for another job where she would be an unknown commodity and would have to prove herself all over again.

After a period of time, Jan began to accept her plateaued state. She realized that not having to compete for higher-level positions had benefits. She now had more time for her children and was able to pursue other outside interests. She had time to work on decorating her new townhome, and even began using the company's exercise facilities. At work, Jan refused to let her situation have a negative effect on her performance. She decided to do the best job she possibly could. Also, Jan looked for ways to expand her knowledge of new computer applications, thinking this would increase her value to the firm. Eventually, Jan spoke with her boss about the prospects for a lateral move to another department in the company. She stressed that she wanted to go into an area where she could gain new experiences. Jan's boss welcomed the idea and said she would see what she could do, but she also encouraged Jan to keep her eye on the posting board for opportunities.

Four months after the performance evaluation meeting, Jan posted out of the department. She is looking forward to putting her newly acquired computer skills to good use. She believes she can continue to contribute to the firm and is excited that she will have the opportunity to learn more in this new position.

Table 9.1 Model of Managerial Careers

Structurally Plateaued			
Yes		No	
Current Performance		Current Performance	
Low	High	Low	High
Deadwood	Solid Citizen	Learner	Star

Note: This typology of the career plateau is based on the work of Ference, T. P., Stoner, J. A. F. & Warren, E. K. (1977). Managing the career plateau. *Academy of Management Review, 2*, 602–612. Deadwoods and solid citizens are plateaued, whereas learners and stars are not plateaued.

Unlike Jan, some plateaued employees are more prone to deteriorated attitudes and performance. A model that addresses this issue, shown in Table 9.1, classifies employees along two dimensions: whether or not they are structurally plateaued, and how well they perform on their current job. Note that there are two kinds of structurally plateaued employees: the "solid citizens" like Jan, who are still performing effectively in their current job, and the "deadwood," whose job performance is substandard. Although the solid citizens perform the bulk of the organization's work, managerial attention and concern are frequently directed toward encouraging and rewarding the fast-track stars and punishing, shelving, or firing the deadwood. One major challenge for management, therefore, is to prevent solid citizens from becoming deadwood. Management actions relevant to this challenge will be considered later in this chapter.

Obsolescence

Like plateauing, obsolescence is not a uniquely midcareer issue, but it may be more pronounced and more devastating in midcareer than in earlier years.[27] Seasoned employees who cannot incorporate new developments into their work processes are susceptible to obsolescence, and could be considered by the organization as "past their prime." *Obsolescence* has been defined as the degree to which "workers lack the up-to-date knowledge or skills necessary to maintain effective performance in either their current or future work roles."[28] Personal changes that result from the midlife transition and other experiences could cause a reduced level of achievement orientation and a lower level of interest in work, which in turn may adversely influence the desire to stay current in one's job.

Obsolescence has its root in change. Research has identified several factors that can lead to obsolescence, including environmental disruptions, individual characteristics, the nature of work, and organizational climate.[29] Environmental disruptions encompass shifts in competitive balance between organizations that are typically associated with changes in technology. In this case, the adoption of new technology by one company causes competing companies to adopt the same technology to stay competitive. Workers in those companies must learn the new technology or the worker (and the company) can face obsolescence. Several individual characteristics can also cause obsolescence. For example, an employee's advancing age might reduce the desire to learn new skills or understand new technology. The nature of one's work, which encompasses the knowledge, skills, and abilities (KSAs) embodied in the job, can influence worker obsolescence. In this case, the KSAs change in such a way or so quickly that the employee cannot keep up. Finally, the organization's climate can also play a role in contributing to obsolescence. Organizations that allow a high degree of interaction and communication among colleagues and encourage participatory management styles tend to do a better job of keeping their workforces informed of new developments in their fields and related fields. In addition, organizational climates that encourage and reward professional growth and development, allow risk-taking behavior, and prize innovation usually discourage worker obsolescence. When workers see that the firm is rewarding advancement of knowledge, they typically direct their efforts toward keeping up-to-date in their field.

As the prior discussion shows, the individual and the work environment both play a critical role in averting obsolescence. Obsolescence is less likely to manifest itself when jobs are challenging, when job reassignments are made periodically to maintain stimulation and avoid overspecialization, when people are given sufficient responsibility and authority on their job, when colleagues interact freely, and when organizations reward employees for keeping up to date by providing challenging work, promotions, and salary increases. In fact, opportunities for continued learning and development, training, and on-the-job practice are probably the greatest deterrents to obsolescence and also can enhance performance at the same time.[30] Suggestions for combating obsolescence will be examined in more detail in a later section of this chapter.

Career Change

The popular press, TV shows, and movies would have people believe that middle-age restlessness almost inevitably leads to major career changes. Vivid examples of urban business executives who open bed and breakfast inns within a rural community, engineers who become artists, or accountants who leave their firms to pursue a career in organic farming merely reinforce this view. Although many people in midcareer do shift career direction, career change is neither an inevitable product of the midlife transition nor is it limited to the midcareer years.

Career change has been viewed as voluntary movement into a different occupation that is not part of a typical career path or is not part of a path that necessarily represents increasing financial gains.[31] More and more people are willing to consider different career fields during their lives. Moreover, although some career changes involve minimal movement in job demands and lifestyle, others represent major transitions. Scholars suggest that a "trigger event" may not necessarily cause a career change, but trigger events may precipitate personal exploration and experimentation with ideas that may lead to career change.[32] Indeed, research has found that getting laid off is not necessarily a sufficient cause for one to change a career path, but rather leads individuals to consider another type of career path.[33]

What are the compelling reasons for people to make career changes? Although the number of reasons may seem endless, they can be grouped into general categories. First, there are several individual factors that can influence a career change. While individual elements such as age, gender, health, interests, values, and skill transferability play a large role, researchers suggest that one's self-concept and professional identity may motivate one to deviate from an established career path. When individuals perceive that their job and their current sense of identity are no longer in balance, they may change careers to deal with the dissonance they feel. One's self-concept is not only a current state of being, but also a future state. Therefore, an individual's belief that their future possible self (or where they want to be) is disconnected from their current job, may precipitate a change in career.[34]

A personal dissatisfaction with one's current occupation or lifestyle can be a powerful stimulant to change. One source of this dissatisfaction is a lack of fit between current occupation and significant needs, desires, or goals. The skills that individuals brought to a job may no longer be required. Or as individuals develop, they may find that their interests and preferences have changed such that they now conflict with their chosen career.[35] In addition, career change could be aroused by the recognition that one has an underlying need for greater achievement and contribution beyond what the individual has accomplished in the current career field. Also, dissatisfaction with one's life in general can have a significant influence on job satisfaction and the desire for career change.[36] For example, discovering that other career fields would enable an individual to have more time and energy to devote to family, community, or leisure endeavors could prompt the individual to consider other career fields.

There are also a number of environmental factors that can induce career changes. Certainly, the loss of one's job, or even the threat of loss, can be a direct reason to change one's path, but there are many others. These additional environmental factors might include a technological change, economic forces, a corporate restructuring or downsizing, changes in a company's reward system, increased job demands, workplace bullying, and alterations to family relationships.[37]

In addition to these individual and environmental factors, there usually needs to be an *attractive alternative* to one's current situation in order for a career change to take place. The alternative would typically provide a better fit with one's needs, values, or abilities than the current occupation. For example, career changers frequently mention the opportunity for more personally meaningful work and a greater fit with personal values as important reasons for their changes.[38] Other factors associated with successful career change include: *confidence* that the change can actually be made, the *belief* that one is in control of one's fate during the change, and the *presence of support* from one's social network.[39] In fact, career change can be positively influenced by social networks that offer referral opportunities for attractive career alternatives.[40]

In all, the individual and environmental factors described above help explain why midcareer people decide to change careers. Given the dynamic and complex life situation that midcareer employees face, there are a number of "healthy" reasons for changing careers:

- Reaching a career plateau.
- Becoming obsolete.
- Feeling misutilized or underutilized.
- Recognizing that the original occupational choice was inappropriate.
- Realizing that one's skill set might be best used in another occupation.
- Appreciating that being satisfied is not determined only by financial wealth.

All of these reasons relate, in one way or another, to a lack of fit between one's current career status and one's self-concept, which is then likely to increase one's dissatisfaction with the current role if action is not taken. Such feelings of dissatisfaction may intensify during midcareer, when more general issues of aging, mortality, and missed opportunities are also surfacing. Before embarking on a midcareer change, people must understand their motives, their ideal self-concept, and the nature of the changes they will have to undergo if they decide to shift career direction. Career changers need to stay open to the range of job possibilities for which their experiences have qualified them, while remaining realistic about what they can achieve.[41] A career coach may serve the midcareer changer well. The career coach, or executive coach, can help to identify skills (or needed skills), develop career alternatives, and aid in career decision-making.[42] Often, the career coach can help an individual to determine whether the benefits of jumping to a new career field outweigh the loss of stature and credits one has built with one's current company. Coaches can reinvigorate midcareer and late career employees by helping them refresh and reprioritize their goals and then identify subsequent actions to achieve the goals.

There may be many challenges in changing careers, such as financial (a salary cut, loss of income in a new business venture, foregoing pension or health care benefits), time-related (the time required to train for a different occupation), and psychological (the uncertainty and insecurity about becoming competent in a different field). All the more important that individuals carefully consider the pros and cons of changing career fields. The next sections will consider more specific actions that organizations and individuals can take to resolve some of the midcareer issues discussed to this point.

Organizational Actions During Midcareer

We have reviewed the major developmental tasks of midcareer as well as the potential for plateauing, obsolescence, and career change. Next, we examine the actions that organizations can take to help employees manage their careers during this stage.

Help Employees Understand Midcareer Experiences

Before any organization can help employees understand their midcareer experiences, organizational managers must first appreciate the issues facing midcareer employees. In this way, organizations can avoid overreacting to employees who are having trouble adjusting to middle age and can offer useful programs to this cohort of employees. Moreover, educating managers on these issues can help improve the supervisor–subordinate relationship, when one or the other party is in midcareer. The organization must also recognize that there are likely to be considerable differences in how employees react to midcareer and the issues that are most critical to them. For example, those employees who are midcareer based on their age but are recycling through an early career phase because they have recently returned to work or because they have undergone a major career shift, might require the organization to help them become established in the new environment. Seminars and workshops can be used to educate upper-level managers on the importance of understanding midcareer dynamics, especially with so much of the workforce in midcareer.

Moreover, employees can cope more effectively with midlife transitions, plateauing, obsolescence, and restlessness when they understand that they are experiencing natural, normal reactions to a different career status. People need to work through these feelings to enter middle adulthood stronger and healthier. The failure to confront these feelings, doubts, or frustrations could produce even greater problems somewhere down the line. Seminars, workshops, and support groups can provide an opportunity for people to talk about their feelings and realize that they are not alone. Professional counseling or executive coaching might also be appropriate for some employees.

Provide Expanded and Flexible Mobility Opportunities

Because promotional opportunities may be limited during midcareer, alternative forms of career mobility can be used to keep midcareer employees stimulated, challenged, and motivated. *Career mobility* is a broad term that denotes all possible directional movements within one's career.[43] Lateral mobility may be particularly appealing to plateaued midcareer employees, especially when the moves do not involve geographical relocation. The judicious use of periodic mobility may prevent solid citizens from becoming deadwood and may deter obsolescence. Career mobility opportunities not only stretch and stimulate employees, but also might provide a different perspective on solving an organization's problems.

Lateral, and even downward transfers, are useful to the extent to which they bring additional challenge, skill utilization, and stimulation. Because extended time in one job can produce negative attitudes or stagnation, perhaps mobility in any direction, if handled properly, can promote positive attitudes and motivation. Of course, not all midcareer employees will experience a plateau. Many will hold realistic upward mobility aspirations and will need the organization's help in achieving these goals. Therefore, several of the organizational actions relevant to the achievement period of the early career—stimulation of career exploration, career pathing, and development planning to mention a few—are also appropriate for the mobile midcareer employee.

Utilization of the Current Job

Although many midcareer employees may no longer expect advancement, their needs for achievement and autonomy can remain strong. An alternative or supplement to lateral mobility during midcareer is the improvement of the current job by building in more variety, challenge, and responsibility.[44] Participation in taskforces, project teams, and temporary assignments can provide stimulation and recognition and should be welcomed by many in midcareer if the responsibilities do not cut too deeply into their personal and family lives. Providing sufficient challenge and responsibility throughout the midcareer years can be a primary deterrent to development of deadwood attitudes and behaviors.

One factor that characterizes the work experience of solid citizens is the presence of clear job duties and agreed-upon performance objectives. Moreover, clear and accurate performance feedback is essential to maintain the high performance of plateaued employees, even though the absence of promotional opportunities may make these performance discussions unpleasant for the supervisor. Accurate performance appraisals, particularly 360-degree feedback, are also important as a means to detect the presence or potential for obsolescence.[45]

Encourage and Teach Mentoring Skills

In Chapter 2, we noted that the generativity need (to guide the next generation) is particularly strong during middle adulthood. The long-term service and broad experiences of many midcareer employees may make them particularly suitable to mentor younger colleagues. However, before midcareer employees can help others, they must understand their own feelings about their careers and lives. Special lectures, group discussions, or coaching on midcareer issues can be developed to accomplish this. It is also likely that many midcareer employees will require some training on how to coach, counsel, and provide feedback as mentors.[46]

Training and Continuing Education

The use of training or retraining for plateaued or obsolescent employees has been suggested frequently in the literature,[47] although some management scholars have offered a rather critical evaluation of continuing education as a deterrent to obsolescence for several reasons.[48] First, although organizations may formally support and endorse continuing education, participation in such activities is often discouraged and unrewarded by individual supervisors as it may be considered a distraction from formally assigned tasks.

Second, it is not clear that participation in continuing education, in and of itself, can really help avert obsolescence. Instead, continual job challenge and periodic job rotation are normally viewed as the most effective deterrents to obsolescence. Well-planned, demanding, and innovative continuing education programs can help if employees are counseled to enter the right program at the right time to meet their own needs and goals, and if continuing education supplements rather than replaces stimulating, challenging job assignments. Continuing education that is relatively short in duration and focused on more specific topics has a comparatively better chance of helping to lower the degree of employee obsolescence.[49]

One significant function of continuing education is preparing midcareer employees who wish to engage in a career change. Continuing education can serve as a catalyst that encourages employees to consider the possibility of a different career field at some point in their future. In this sense, educational benefits provided by the organization are used to help interested employees prepare themselves for a career shift. Organizations can then creatively encourage their "surplus" employees to take early retirement to pursue the alternative career field or perhaps become an entrepreneur.[50]

Broaden the Reward System

Many of the following suggestions involve reexamination and expansion of the organization's reward system. Instead of focusing exclusively or primarily on promotions and increased compensation as the incentive for effective performance, alternative rewards should be considered by organizations.[51] Interesting and challenging jobs, stimulating reassignments (including international assignments), flexible work arrangements, recognition, praise, and financial rewards can all be used to maintain the effectiveness of employees experiencing midcareer plateaus. These steps can help prevent solid citizens from becoming deadwood.

Rewarding employees for lifelong learning and development, success in challenging jobs, and participation in appropriate continuing education programs are the most effective means for forestalling functional obsolescence. Offering mobility opportunities, providing the framework for becoming a mentor, and broadening the reward system to recognize a variety of contributions to the organization are other avenues by which midcareer employees can be engaged. Such approaches explicitly recognize the importance of long-term career performance, not simply vertical mobility through the hierarchy.

Individual Actions During Midcareer

Career Exploration

Self-assessment is critical in midcareer. In addition to exploring one's values, interests, and talents, it is essential to understand one's real feelings about middle age and any shifts in the relative priorities given to work, family, community, and self-development. Specifically, individuals should conduct periodic self-assessments and reappraisals to determine whether their interests, values, and skills are still in line with their established goals and plans. This awareness should empower individuals to better recognize and utilize opportunities as they arise, and can allow a more proactive response to changes in the work environment. If the organization does not provide a formal mechanism to stimulate this reappraisal, then the employee must take the initiative through discussions with colleagues, friends, family members, or counselors.

An examination of alternatives involves exploration of work and nonwork environments. In the work domain, reappraising career-related aspirations, reassessing one's current job for possible improvement, investigating lateral mobility opportunities, and adopting flexible work arrangements might be considered. Exploration of different occupations and organizations, as discussed in Chapter 7, also may be appropriate. Moreover, relationships with one's spouse and/or children might need to be examined, new priorities might need to be set, and more personal time might need to be allotted.[52] In fact, midcareer is an opportune time to reexamine opportunities to develop a range of new interests outside of work, including hobbies, volunteerism, and self-development.

Midcareer employees considering a career change not only need to understand their own motives and interests, but also must anticipate and examine the upside and the potential risks of a career change, as discussed earlier in the chapter, perhaps especially if the change is from an organizational career to an entrepreneurial venture, where the risk of failure may be high. Herminia Ibarra recommends that employees explore the potential fit of a different career field by "crafting an experiment," that is, trying out "new activities and professional roles on a small scale before making a major commitment to a different path."[53] These low-risk experiments—for example, shadowing someone already in the field, taking a part-time job or a temporary assignment in the new field, doing volunteer work in a different line of work—can provide insights into your potential fit with a different career field as well as help you develop contacts should you choose to make the change on a full-time basis. Although it is certainly wise to discuss a prospective change with people who know us well (e.g., family members, friends, and colleagues), Ibarra recommends that we also develop new connections with individuals who, because they are less familiar with our past, may be able to see us in a new light and provide feedback on what we can become in the future.[54]

Goal-Setting and Strategy Development

The goal-setting process during midcareer is not fundamentally different from other stages, although the goal itself may be less likely to involve hierarchical advancement. Of particular importance is the establishment of a conceptual goal that is not tied to a particular position; for example, to provide IT support to nonprofit organizations devoted to improving urban environments. Success in managing one's career throughout the midlife period is based on the ability to understand one's conceptual goal and to see the possibilities of satisfying that goal either in one's current position, or in other jobs or career fields.

Career strategies or action plans, as always, must be tied to goals and tested for feasibility. The development of active, realistic strategies of any type requires an awareness of goals, a willingness to communicate those goals to others, and a talent for observation, listening, and analysis. Participation in special skill-building sessions for those in midcareer might help promote a more active, realistic strategy for dealing with the issues raised in this chapter. Most important, perhaps, is the conviction that one can influence, to a considerable extent, the course of one's career at any period of development.

Job Crafting

Adding more variety, challenge, and responsibility into an employee's current job can be a strong source of motivation and satisfaction, especially for individuals who do not want (or will not receive) further hierarchical advancement. Although we have recommended that organizations take the initiative to enrich employees' jobs, it may not occur (or appeal) to them to do so. In these situations, we believe that it is the individual's responsibility to initiate the process proactively.

With job crafting, employees take the initiative to change or redesign their jobs,[55] the aim of which is to provide a better fit with their needs, values, talents, and aspirations. Job crafting could involve such actions as expanding the challenges on the job, increasing the amount of autonomy on the job, obtaining additional resources to enhance performance on the job, changing or improving relationships with other stakeholders at work, expanding one's skill set, and decreasing the more disagreeable parts of the job.[56] Job crafting has been found to relate positively to job satisfaction, work engagement, and job performance.[57] Not surprisingly, proactive employees are most likely to craft their job.[58] Because it is unlikely that individuals can craft their job in a vacuum, job crafters could benefit from the support of others in the organization who can assist them in their effort to improve their current job.

Idiosyncratic Deals

Idiosyncratic deals (or I-deals) are informal, customized arrangements negotiated between employees and employers for the benefit of both parties. From employees' perspective, the aim is to improve their work and/or nonwork lives in some way, and from employers' perspective, the aim is to improve employees' job performance or retention in the organization.[59] Typically initiated by employees, I-deals can take many forms. Two of the more frequently negotiated types of I-deals involve increased opportunities for flexibility in the hours or location of work (flexibility I-deals) and expansion of the opportunities for skill and career development on the job (developmental I-deals).[60] Each type of I-deal can be relevant to midcareer employees, flexibility I-deals for those who want to achieve greater balance in life and developmental I-deals for those who want more opportunities for growth in their jobs. The fact that employees' level of personal initiative increases the likelihood of negotiating an I-ideal[61] is consistent with the importance of proactivity and self-direction in career management advocated throughout this book.

Dealing with Job Loss

Loss of one's job can be a traumatic experience at any point in the life cycle, but it may be especially difficult and damaging for persons in the midcareer phase.[62] First, individuals in midcareer may be vulnerable to periods of self-doubt and questioning their competency and worth; job loss can only add to the magnitude (and trauma) of the questioning process. Second, individuals in midlife are most susceptible to financial strains, with a peak in such demands as household expenses, acquisition of material goods, planning for (or making) the payment of children's college tuition, possibly supporting family elders, and attempting to save for one's retirement. Again, the loss of one's job can only exacerbate the financial stress. Further, job loss can put strain on a marriage or a committed relationship that may already be on shaky ground due to the pressures of the midlife transition.

There are a number of well-documented reasons (or combination of reasons) why individuals are terminated by their employers. The most common causes include poor performance of the individual, a corporate-wide downsizing or a divestiture, unfavorable financial or economic conditions faced by the company, a violation of company policy, or some unethical behavior. It is important to understand that perceived performance may not necessarily indicate midcareer employee incompetence. Rather, it may reflect such factors as differences of opinion on priorities and corporate strategies, personality clashes, and organizational politics.[63]

Individual reactions to job loss can be varied, depending on such factors as financial resources, social contacts and status, the meaningfulness of work in the individual's life, and the person's level of confidence and self-esteem.[64] In essence, job loss can disrupt the established equilibrium in various facets of one's life, including economic, psychological, physiological, and social.[65] Reflecting the disrupted life equilibrium, some outcomes of job loss may include reduced happiness, increased depression, mental and physical illness, increased anxiety, disengagement, and loss of societal status and privileges. The thought that getting rehired by another firm at middle age will be difficult, will take much time, and may result in offers (if any) at a reduced income level, is a sobering situation to face.

Conversely, for some people, job loss can be a growth experience. Even though it may not be viewed as a worthwhile occurrence at the time, job loss can be a "blessing in disguise" because it can force people to reassess their interests and desires and look for new avenues for personal fulfillment.[66] When unemployed midcareerists pursue coping behaviors that focus on the specific demands of searching for a job, and have sound personal and financial support, they report greater life satisfaction and less unemployment stigma.[67] Regardless of one's financial and emotional state, the subsequent process of coping with job loss and landing a new job will likely follow a predictable series of stages.

In the first stage, individuals experience an initial response to the loss of a job. Researchers have identified four different types of initial response.[68] First, the individual may feel a sense of shock and disbelief, even when warning signs were in place to signal the impending termination. People often assume that job loss "won't happen to them." A second type of initial reaction is anger at the company, and its management, for the lack of loyalty and for allowing the termination to occur. A third response is a sense of relief, as the uncertainty and stress of potential termination is finally lifted. Lastly, individuals may show signs of escapism by displaying little or no emotion and attempting to divorce themselves totally from the difficult situation.

After the initial reaction subsides, individuals move into the second stage, where they confront the tasks of becoming reemployed. The campaign to secure a new position involves a multitude of activities including preparing and mailing (or emailing) up-to-date résumés, drafting cover memos and letters of introduction, working with an outplacement firm and joining job search clubs, identifying former work associates who can serve as job contacts and leads, and practicing proper interview performance. Updating the résumé may even include condensing the number of companies worked for over one's career, eliminating dates when diplomas or certifications were received; in essence "de-professionalizing" the résumé in order to compete in the younger labor market.[69] Some midcareerists are using a "free agent" mentality where they consider "renting" their skills for semi-permanent employment. While achieving the goal of reemployment, this option is often considered a temporary work role and might not reflect or lead to a permanent employment solution.[70]

For the majority of people, coping with job loss ends after the second stage, when a new work position is found. However, if the job search continues for an extended period, individuals may enter a third stage in which the frustration of not finding work results in vacillation about one's career, lingering self-doubt about one's abilities, and anger that can involve displaced aggression toward others.[71] Anger also exists when the midcareerist perceives discriminatory hiring practices, where companies prefer less expensive younger workers with different skill sets.[72] If individuals do not become reemployed, a fourth stage can occur in which they experience such dismay over not finding a new job that they resign themselves to being unemployed and begin withdrawing from activities, including those aimed at finding work.[73]

From the above discussion, it is clear that the second stage following job loss is the critical period in finding a new position. It is during this phase that one is likely to undertake a concerted job search effort. For this reason, it is important that the job-seeker apply the career management concepts discussed throughout this book. More precisely, individuals should first conduct a thorough appraisal of interests, talents, and lifestyle preferences. Second, the individual should assess the work environment, gathering information on alternative jobs, occupations, companies, and industries. Individuals should then develop conceptual goals and set tentative operational goals regarding the type of position (or positions) toward which they would like to target their reemployment efforts. Strategies would then be set on how to go about landing a preferred job.

Of course, no set of actions, regardless of how practical they are, guarantees that one will find a job in a timely fashion. Nevertheless, it is important that the career management model be followed to at least ensure that the individual is doing everything possible to locate a new job that is consistent with his or her interests and preferences. The career management model provides the individual with the ability to focus on the "problem" of finding a new job, while also establishing a mechanism for dealing with the emotional needs associated with reemployment as the individual seeks counsel and social support from friends and relatives. Both problem-focused and emotion-focused support are necessary for the individual to come up with options and navigate the job loss situation successfully.[74]

There are a variety of actions that organizations can take to assist their employees in coping with job terminations. Basic programs include advance notification, severance pay and extended benefits, retraining, outplacement assistance, and counseling. Because of the social responsibility and legal consequences of job layoffs, organizational leaders should also ensure that the process is procedurally fair.[75] Further, in the case of an across-the-board downsizing, it is recommended that the organization attempt to dispel the inevitable self-blame that individuals might place upon themselves as a means to minimize the loss of self-esteem and confidence that is likely to occur.[76] Also, it is important that organization-sponsored interventions to assist laid-off workers attempt to enhance confidence about finding another job. Without this confidence, seasoned employees often do not engage in extensive job search, which impedes chances for rehire.[77] Research also suggests that when job search assistance and social support are provided by employers, job-seekers report higher earnings with their new job, and usually acquire jobs more quickly than when that assistance is not provided.[78]

The Late Career

With the aging of the baby boom generation throughout the industrialized world, businesses cannot afford to cast off or take for granted their older workers. For one thing, older workers represent a substantial labor pool that will continue to grow as the baby boom generation ages. Second, legislation in the United States, including the Age Discrimination in Employment Act (ADEA),[79] protects workers age 40 and older from discriminatory employment practices. Third, as worldwide economic growth and the attendant need for more labor continues, the future projected shortage of younger workers will place a greater value on the older worker who can provide stability and continuity to an organization's workforce. Finally, it makes good and socially responsible business sense for companies to fully utilize all of their human resources. Ironically, even in the face of a growing labor shortage, corporate takeovers, restructurings, and other actions have led many large organizations to "ease out" senior employees through early retirement programs. Many of these programs are designed to reduce fixed operating costs by inducing the retirement of older, more expensive workers and replacing them with lower-cost younger workers.

Other ways seasoned employees might be eased out include job elimination and layoffs, and through a threatened change in pension benefits.[80]

It is clear that the treatment of the older worker will be a major management issue facing employers for at least the next three decades as the entirety of the baby boom generation reaches retirement age. A handful of late career employees must prepare themselves for senior leadership roles in their respective organizations. For the vast majority of employees in late career, however, the primary tasks are focused on two developmental needs: to remain productive and to prepare for effective retirement.[81]

Remaining Productive

Remaining competent and productive is important to the late career employee. Few people wish to be "carried" as excess baggage, but there are several obstacles to remaining productive during the late career. For one thing, rapid changes in technology and organizational demands pose a threat of obsolescence, especially to older workers with limited education and skills.[82] Unless midcareer obsolescence is prevented or reduced, the situation can only get worse during the late career. This becomes even more devastating when changes in an organization's mission, structure, or technology eliminate jobs, career paths, or even whole functions.

Second, the plateauing process discussed earlier can have negative effects on the performance of late-career employees. Although a plateau may initially be reached during midcareer, a solid citizen who is bored, unrewarded, and/or unmotivated may well become late-career deadwood. In other words, obsolescence and plateauing may have their roots in midcareer, but could eventually produce increasing deterioration during the late career.

Maintaining effective performance during the late career also can be jeopardized by society's stereotypes and biases against older people in general, and older workers in particular. Older workers have typically (and erroneously) been viewed as deficient in several areas: productivity, efficiency, ability to work under pressure, ambition, interest in promotion, receptivity to new ideas, adaptability, versatility, and the ability to develop new technological skills.[83] However, research demonstrates that stereotypes that inspire age discrimination are without merit; indeed, the majority of older workers are able to perform their work roles far beyond the typical age of retirement and well into later years in life.[84] There is no support for the presumption that increased age leads inevitably to declines in work engagement and performance, and to increases in workplace accidents and absenteeism.[85] As noted in Chapter 2, older workers tend to show higher levels of reliability and work commitment, display more adept social skills, and are equally as open to new experiences as compared with younger colleagues.[86]

Despite the inaccuracy of age stereotypes, such biases can have a significant effect on how organizations treat and manage the older worker.[87] A number of management actions, as listed below, can be traced to the negative stereotypes and myths concerning older workers:[88]

- If older workers are seen as rigid and resistant to change, then organizations will be less likely to help them improve their performance.
- If older employees are perceived as less motivated to keep up-to-date with changes, then organizations will be less willing to invest time and money in skill-development programs for them.
- If older employees are seen as less creative or innovative, then organizations are less willing to move them into a position requiring these qualities.

- If older employees are believed to be less productive, and organizations use only subjective appraisals of performance, then these older employees will have lower performance ratings.

These management assumptions can produce a self-fulfilling prophecy in which older workers, deprived of developmental experiences and mobility opportunities, never have the chance to disconfirm the original stereotypes. The inaccurate stereotypes can produce a negative attitude toward older workers that, in turn, produces bias in such areas as personnel selection, performance appraisal, and assignment to training. Additionally, in line with social identity theory, if a seasoned worker perceives himself or herself to be stereotyped as an "older worker," the worker will tend to identify with that group, display reduced organizational commitment, and disengage from the job, perhaps by pursuing early retirement.[89]

Daniel Feldman suggests two reasons for these negative stereotypes: (1) lower performance ratings of seasoned employees allow supervisors to give higher ratings to younger employees, thereby justifying the distribution of scarce financial resources to those younger employees; and (2) supervisors who try to block the upward mobility of senior employees thereby create fewer rivals for themselves.[90] In either case, if older employees perceive that their supervisors devalue their contributions, they may experience reduced satisfaction, feelings of depression and helplessness, and lower self-worth and self-esteem.

Organizations need to overcome these biases and recognize the value of their older workers for a number of reasons. First, senior employees are less likely to take time off except when absolutely necessary, and appear to be as engaged as younger counterparts. Second, seasoned employees are less likely to leave the organization voluntarily because of their well-paying jobs and pensions, the congruence between what they hope to get from their jobs and what they actually get, their satisfaction with their work and its tangible and intangible benefits, and their commitment to the organization. Thus, older workers can be dedicated, productive, and enthusiastic employees, but must be treated with dignity and respect and recognized for their value to the organization.

Preparation for Retirement

Retirement is a major career transition for most people because it can signify an end to 40, 50, or even 60 years of continual employment. *Retirement* is defined as the departure from a job or career path, taken by individuals after middle age, where the individual physically and psychologically withdraws from the workforce.[91] While this definition seems straightforward enough, the recent proliferation of available part-time positions and changes in attitudes toward working later in life can sometimes make it difficult to determine when someone is actually retired. In general, retirees can be differentiated from non-retirees based on the following: retirees tend to be older, usually over the age of 50; spend less of their time working for pay; are more likely to receive some income from sources that are specially designated for retirees; and are inclined to think of themselves as officially separated from the workaday world.[92]

Preparing for retirement involves deciding when to retire and planning for a satisfying, fulfilling life upon retirement. However, the decision to retire has been complicated in recent years by government and corporate actions. On the one hand, the ADEA has virtually eliminated any mandatory retirement age in the U.S. Essentially, the decision of when to retire is now a voluntary one for nearly all American workers. In addition, changes in the Social Security system in the U.S. can encourage (or force) employees to delay retirement. Older workers can begin taking Social Security benefits as early as age 62, although the longer one waits to take money from the system, the larger the amount one receives per month. Further, the age at which full Social Security benefits can be attained is gradually increasing. Traditionally, employees could collect full benefits (receiving 100 percent) at age 65, but for workers born between 1943 and 1960, the full-benefit retirement age is 66, and for workers born after 1960, the full-benefit retirement age is 67.[93] These actions provide older workers with new issues to consider in the timing and type of retirement they prefer.

Attitudes toward retirement are likely to be rooted in one's attitude toward work. Work fulfills so many human functions and can be such an important part of one's identity that to leave the work role may be akin to leaving one's self-concept behind.[94] Work provides a niche in society and a feeling of usefulness and purpose, and it allows people the opportunity to fulfill their basic needs for affiliation, achievement, power, and prestige. Work also provides financial rewards and a structure that helps people organize their daily lives. For many people, these tangible and intangible benefits are not easy to give up, and many seasoned workers speak of retirement as an ongoing process, not necessarily a one-time decision. In fact, many workers look forward to a phased retirement in which they will shift gradually from full-time employment to part-time employment to full retirement.[95]

On the other hand, many employees relish the thought of retirement and look forward to days without the pressures of deadlines, supervisors, and long hours. It is important to understand why some people seem to adjust more favorably to retirement than others. Satisfaction and well-being in retirement have been linked with a variety of factors, including: the extent to which the person had engaged in financial planning while still employed, the presence of a financially satisfying pension, experiencing good health, anticipated pursuit of hobbies or travel, the absence of emotional involvement with one's job, the ability to structure one's day, involvement in volunteer work, and high levels of self-esteem.[96]

Retirement intentions can take different forms given the variety of situations in which older workers might find themselves. The following are descriptions of various retirement options available to seasoned employees.

Early Retirement

Over the past three decades, the option for workers to retire "early" has become commonplace. While there is no consensus on a definition of early retirement, it is generally viewed as the decision to retire prior to the age at which one is eligible for full corporate or government sponsored pensions.[97] Across the globe, early retirement has been noted, generally, as a function of both "push" and "pull" factors. "Push" factors include reduced job opportunities created by poor economies, while "pull" factors include individual affluence and the financial incentives received in early retirement programs and offers.[98] Organizations offer early retirement packages as a way to reduce the size of the workforce and to effect cost savings in a less stressful manner than simple across-the-board reductions in staff. It is almost impossible to find one major corporation that has not offered some form of early retirement to its workers.

For individuals, the decision to retire early could be prompted by having a skill set that is obsolete, being dissatisfied with one's job, or facing periodic or chronic health problems. Or early retirement might be induced if the worker wishes to spend more time with family, to travel, to do volunteer work, or to pursue other vocational or business interests. Or it could be that the individual has acquired enough financial resources that he or she is able to retire, or has received such a generous financial incentive from his or her employer that it makes sense to retire early.[99]

Phased Retirement

Phased retirement normally means that an older worker remains with his or her employer while gradually working fewer hours per day, week, month, or year.[100] Long-tenured employees may be given the option to work fewer hours, have less responsibility, or both, as a stepping stone to full retirement. From the organization's perspective, phased retirement allows valued employees to stay engaged within the company for a longer period of time than would be possible if only a standard retirement, with full disengagement from work, were available. In addition, phased retirement represents a form of social responsibility on the part of the participating organization because it signifies that the organization is willing to make accommodations for its employees in the form of progressive employment practices.[101]

Although phased retirement appears to be a win-win option for employers and employees, there are several potential drawbacks. First, organizations might be reluctant to offer phased retirement on an unconditional basis because it is likely that only certain employees approaching retirement would have the right mix of abilities and attitude to be meaningful contributors to an organization in a phased retirement arrangement. In addition, employers might be reluctant to offer phased retirement because of policies that require a minimum number of hours to be worked in a year and restrictions that are imposed by defined benefit pension programs that calculate benefits based on earnings attained in the final years of a career with the organization.[102] To get around these restrictions, some employers offer a form of phased retirement called "retire-rehire." In this case, full-time workers officially retire from their firm and then return as part-time or temporary workers, where the time interval between retirement and rehiring can be a matter of days.[103]

Bridge Employment

An increasingly popular option for employers to attract older workers is to offer bridge employment. Bridge employment allows workers who have retired from a career-oriented job in one organization to move to a transitional work position typically in a different organization, which thus allows a "bridge" between one's long-term career and the entry into total retirement from all work.[104] Bridge jobs normally involve a combination of fewer hours, less stress or responsibility, greater flexibility, and fewer physical demands. From the workers' perspective, bridge employment contributes to their economic security by providing additional income and can enhance emotional and physical well-being. In this sense, the bridge job is viewed as an opportunity to do something meaningful in one's life and to have control over one's work role. In addition, bridge jobs allow employees to focus on the significant aspects of their work without concern over hierarchical advancement, job security, or organizational politics. Of course, bridge employment is not for everyone and is most often pursued by late-career individuals who are in good health and with a strong desire to continue some level of work involvement.[105]

Organizational Actions During Late Career

Reasonable attempts to manage older workers require sensitivity to late-career issues on the part of the organization's top management and human resource staff. This necessitates a clear understanding of the differences between the myths and realities of aging and recognition of the value differences among generations of workers.

Performance Standards and Feedback

Clear standards of effective performance should be developed and communicated to the seasoned worker. When confronting low productivity among older workers, performance problems should be stated in clear behavioral terms, the consequences of continued ineffective performance should be identified, and options to improve performance should be explored. Accurate, unbiased performance appraisals are essential to maintain effective performance, and real reasons for terminating an older worker, if necessary, must be documented.

Education and Job Restructuring

Many of the suggestions made to prevent or ameliorate midcareer obsolescence and to manage the midcareer-plateaued employee are also relevant to the employee in late career. Ongoing learning opportunities, through the integration of stimulating, responsible job assignments and continuing education, can play a major role in maintaining the vitality of the late career workforce.

In order to combat the obsolescence of older workers, two key factors must be addressed. First, the employee must believe that he or she can assert control over the career and its development. Second, the employee must believe that the work he or she is doing is meaningful and making a positive contribution to the organization. Yet, the requirements of the job must be seen as manageable by the older worker. Intention to retire was found to be related to the physical demands of the job, demonstrating that extending the careers of seasoned workers requires adaptations of their jobs in terms of how exhausting they may be.[106]

Education, training, and job restructuring activities should include some of the following components: (a) an assessment of employees' training and developmental needs, (b) a program of developmental experiences such as training for upgrading technical, managerial, and/or administrative skills, (c) a plan for redeploying workers to needed areas, (d) a review and evaluation of the training's effectiveness, and (e) long-range planning with employees to identify future retraining needs.[107] Although some employers with discriminatory attitudes can be reluctant to send older people to training, it is important for firms to offer formal learning activities to late career employees. Indeed, both formal and informal learning play an important role in allowing older employees to maintain their employability and achieve continued career development.[108]

Development and Enforcement of Nondiscrimination Policies

In the U.S., the ADEA forbids age discrimination in such areas as hiring and placement, compensation, advancement, and termination. Nondiscrimination makes good business sense and protects organizations from costly litigation. Likewise, training managers on the requirements of non-discrimination employment laws and regulations also makes good business sense and ensures that the organization is being socially responsible toward its older workers. This is especially true when younger managers reviewing seasoned employees may need counseling on working within ADEA employment guidelines.[109]

Development of Retirement Planning Programs

Well-planned and executed retirement planning programs can smooth the transition between work and retirement for older employees. Typically, retirement planning programs cover such topics as the challenge of retirement, health and safety, housing, time management, legal issues, and financial planning. Some recommendations for successful retirement planning programs are given below:[110]

1. Retirement planning programs should focus on both the extrinsic and intrinsic aspects of retirement. Extrinsic elements include financial security, retirement income, housing alternatives, and legal issues. Intrinsic factors associated with retirement include the various psychological, healthcare, and wellness issues related to disengagement from work. Organizations might want to offer "realistic retirement previews" that provide a balanced, accurate picture of retirement.
2. Programs should be run in small groups that encourage two-way communication and provide opportunities for counseling. In this way, the social and psychological consequences of retirement can be discussed in a more candid fashion.
3. Ideally, participation in retirement planning programs should begin at least five years prior to the anticipated retirement of the employee to allow adequate time to address all issues. Counseling activities should also be available for a specified period of time after retirement.
4. Previously retired persons can be used as information resources and role models during retirement planning sessions.
5. Spouse participation in retirement planning programs can be beneficial and should be encouraged.
6. Organizations should consider offering special retirement planning programs for those employees who have an especially strong commitment to work. These employees may have a particularly difficult time dealing with the prospect of retirement.
7. Retirement planning programs should be designed to help maintain positive attitudes and performance among pre-retirees, allow the organization to retain high-performing older employees, and educate older employees on the retirement options available to them (early retirement, phased retirement, regular retirement, and bridge employment). Such programs must be carefully evaluated to determine whether they are meeting the needs of the employees and the organization.

Establishment of Flexible Work Patterns

Undoubtedly, many organizations prefer that the more competent, adaptable late career employees continue working beyond "normal" retirement age and that others take early retirement. A system of flexible work patterns may enable both of these aims to be met.

High-performing employees nearing retirement age could be induced to continue employment if they had more options than simply remaining a full-time member of the organization in their current position. These options can include part-time employment, special consulting assignments, job sharing, flexible or compressed working hours, and job restructuring. Programs such as phased retirement could also help organizations retain the services of highly valued older employees while unclogging career paths for younger workers. Interestingly, studies have found that men are less likely to take phased retirement when compared to women, who are more open to flexible work options and volunteer work.[111]

The flip side of the retirement issue is the encouragement of low-performing or less adaptable workers to take early retirement. Here, too, innovative programs may serve the needs of the employee and the organization. These innovations can include supplementing the reduced Social Security benefits for employees who retire before full benefits are given, offering cash bonuses, maintaining fringe benefits for the employee until age 65, providing cost-of-living adjustments to pension benefits, and allowing for full pension benefits for early retirement.[112]

Hiring Seasoned Employees

The aging of the baby boom generation is creating a growing pool of retirement-aged individuals looking for alternative work arrangements. Accordingly, employers have an opportunity to hire from this external labor market as a means to fill current and future human resource requirements. Organizations will need to develop creative approaches to attract and recruit these workers. At a minimum, these approaches should involve taking the company's recruitment message to the potential workers, using marketing techniques to highlight company programs, and establishing an internal work climate that is attractive to older workers. Many organizations have developed creative approaches to reach out to workers over the age of 50.

Individual Actions During Late Career

Active career management is no less significant during the late career than during earlier periods of development. The suggestions made to midcareer employees earlier in this chapter are equally applicable to those in late career. Moreover, given the presence of age stereotypes, there may be a number of obstacles that older workers face in acquiring more challenging and responsible assignments or lateral mobility opportunities. Therefore, an awareness of one's current career needs and an assertive career strategy are necessary to ensure an individual–organizational fit during the late career.

Like many other career issues, retirement planning should be conducted by the individual employee, whether or not the employer offers a formal program. In addition, we recommend that the approaches individuals use to plan their retirement resemble the active approaches to career management as outlined throughout this book. Pre-retirees are encouraged to gather relevant information about their financial assets and expenses, preferred lifestyle, and social and psychological needs. The development of financial, social, and personal objectives and the identification of action steps are all part of this planning process. Financial advice from experts should be sought. Various types of software applications and websites can also help individuals set plans for retirement. In an overall sense, the planning for retirement should involve as much concern and attention to detail as the planning for earlier actions and events in the career.

Individuals making preparations for retirement should ask themselves a number of fundamental questions, such as: How might I live in retirement? What do I really care about? What is of value and worth? Do I want (or need) to participate in phased retirement or bridge employment for a period of time before full retirement? By probing in this fashion, pre-retirement employees can gain a clearer picture of what they wish to accomplish and the life they would like to lead in the years ahead.

Summary

The middle career years present employees with two major tasks—to confront the midlife transition and to remain productive in their work. The midlife transition serves as a bridge between early and middle adulthood. Triggered by an awareness of aging and a fear of lost youth, employees may need to reconcile their accomplishments in life with their youthful aspirations. Although not all midcareer employees necessarily experience a crisis during this period, some form of reappraisal of accomplishments and goals may be necessary to move into middle adulthood in a constructive, productive manner.

Productivity during midcareer can be hampered if employees realize that they have reached a career plateau in which future advancement opportunities or increases in job responsibility are unlikely. Although some midcareer employees react to the plateauing experience with frustration, guilt, and stagnation, others adapt by substituting other personal goals for vertical mobility. Midcareer employees may also fall prey to technological or managerial obsolescence and ultimately job loss if they lack sufficient and current knowledge and skills to maintain effective performance on their job.

Organizations can promote effective career management during midcareer by: (a) helping employees understand their midcareer experiences; (b) providing a variety of mobility opportunities, including lateral and downward transfers; (c) providing sufficient challenge and responsibility on the current job to maintain involvement and productivity; (d) providing training or retraining as a supplement to challenging job assignments; and (e) encouraging some midcareer employees to serve as mentors to their junior colleagues. Individuals need to develop insight into their values and motives, reassess their current career prospects, establish a conceptual career goal that can be achieved in a variety of jobs, and perhaps craft their current job to enhance its meaning in their life.

The late career also poses some potential threats to employee motivation and performance. Not only might seasoned employees have to deal with the aftermath of midcareer obsolescence or plateauing, but they may also have to contend with negative age biases that obstruct continued growth and development on the job. Moreover, the late career employee must begin to consider a number of issues regarding retirement. A variety of post-retirement job alternatives (volunteerism, phased retirement, or bridge employment) are available to the late career employee.

Organizations can help late career employees by (a) understanding their unique problems, (b) developing clear performance standards and offering concrete feedback, (c) providing job challenge and continual training to maintain motivation, (d) developing and implementing nondiscriminatory policies regarding older workers, (e) developing effective pre-retirement programs, and (f) establishing flexible work patterns for employees nearing retirement age. Individuals should maintain an active vigilance during the late career years and should plan their retirement with care and attention.

Career Management *for Life*: Work–Life Implications from Chapter 9

- Some work-focused employees may experience feelings of personal failure at midlife, realizing that they have sacrificed family relationships and other personal interests in the ambitious pursuit of their career.
- Midlife employees may choose *not* to pursue a promotion or seek additional responsibility in their current job to allow more time and energy for other parts of life, such as their family, community, or leisure activities.
- One reason why some midcareer employees change their career field is to achieve greater work–life balance.
- Employees can negotiate idiosyncratic deals (I-deals) to obtain more flexibility in the hours or location of their work to meet their responsibilities at work *and* at home.

- Late career employees may choose phased retirement or bridge employment to continue working at a lower level of involvement and also attend to other important parts of their life.
- Organizations should provide late-career employees with retirement planning programs that focus not only on financial issues but also on psychological, healthcare, and wellness issues related to disengagement from work.

Assignment

If you are 40 years of age or older, take a few introspective minutes and consider your career and life history. Do you believe that you have gone through (or are going through) a midlife transition? If the answer is yes, what kinds of issues did you deal with (or are you dealing with) during this transition period? Describe the changes that you have undergone (in work, family, or personal life) as a result of the midlife transition. Did you (or do you) view this period of time as a "crisis"? Why or why not? If you do not believe that you have experienced a midlife transition, why not? How would you reconcile that with Levinson's theory as discussed in Chapter 2 and this chapter?

If you are younger than 40 years old, interview a friend, relative, or colleague who is in his or her mid- to late 40s or early 50s. Determine whether the person has gone through a midlife transition. If the answer is yes, what kinds of issues did the person deal with during this transition period? Describe the changes that the person has undergone (in work, family, or personal life) as a result of the midlife transition. Did the person view this period of time as a "crisis"? Why or why not? If the person does not seem to have experienced the midlife transition, ask why not? How would you reconcile that with Levinson's theory as discussed in Chapter 2 and this chapter?

Discussion Questions

1. Defend or refute the following statement: "Reaching a plateau in the organization drastically reduces the productivity and satisfaction of employees." Describe the reasoning behind your position.
2. What characteristics distinguish a solid citizen from a deadwood plateaued employee in an organization? What can organizations do to prevent solid citizens from becoming deadwood? What forces may prevent organizations from taking these actions?
3. What triggers a desire to make a midcareer change, and what factors inhibit people from actually making such a change? When is a midcareer change an adaptive behavior and when do workers use it as a shield against their real problems?
4. What are some common stereotypes of the older employee? Do you think these stereotypes are generally accurate or inaccurate? How do stereotypes of aging affect the ways in which organizations manage their older employees?
5. Why do some older workers relish the thought of retirement while others dread the prospect of leaving their work life behind? What kind of planning should be conducted to prepare oneself for retirement? Why should retirement planning begin considerably before the anticipated retirement date?

Chapter 9 Case: George the Banker

George did not know what to think. The walk to the train, the train ride, and the drive home involved no effort at consciousness. His world was in turmoil and he did not know whether to feel anger or relief, exhaustion or despair.

George had what most would consider a "good job": vice-president in the accounting department of Obelisk Bank (fictitious name). Obelisk was a medium-sized regional bank with just over $4 billion in deposits. At 54 years of age, George had believed he would retire comfortably from Obelisk on his own terms and when he decided it was time. George had begun working at Obelisk nearly 23 years ago. After high school, he had spent four years in the Marines, and then used the GI bill to get his bachelor's degree in accounting. After spending six years in public accounting, during which time he gained his CPA, George joined Obelisk as an assistant controller. His early career at the bank had progressed nicely, but he had held his current position for the past eight years. George was generally pleased with his work and his record of achievements, although since his mid-40s a vague sense of unfulfillment and even disenchantment had taken hold. He knew that the lack of an MBA prevented him from advancing, and he recognized that he had been passed over for promotion, in deference to much younger colleagues, twice within the past four years. He even half-heartedly entertained the notion of returning to school for his MBA, but age and a lack of real desire, he believed, precluded this.

George's older daughter was graduating from college this year and she was planning to attend graduate school in the fall. His younger daughter was entering college as well. George was proud to tell his co-workers how he was putting his two daughters through college. George's wife returned to work five years ago, managing a gift shop. Her salary was a nice addition to the family income, but it really didn't go very far in paying the bills. College tuitions were a real financial strain, and there were still nine more years to go on the mortgage. As was the case with his father before him, George saw his primary life role as breadwinner of the family. For financial, emotional, and psychological reasons, George was nowhere near ready for retirement.

George had gone to work that morning as always. For the past three months, Obelisk had been abuzz with rumors that it was the object of a takeover by a large bank from another state. The bank's senior management had even written an open letter to the employees telling them, in no uncertain terms, that the bank wasn't for sale and that the management would resist any and all takeover bids. George felt encouraged by the letter to the employees. He personally believed that the bank's senior management would take whatever steps were necessary to keep the bank from being acquired.

George began to reflect back on one of the many maxims his high school football coach had told his players—"the worst hit in football is when you're blindsided, because you never see it coming and you really can't prepare for it." George now had a better appreciation than ever for his old coach's words of wisdom. In the late afternoon that day, he had gotten a call that the head of human resources needed to see him immediately. The message from the senior vice-president of human resources was delivered bluntly. Obelisk was cutting costs as a means to stave off the takeover, and several officers were being targeted for dismissal. George was given two options. The bank either would "credit" him with an additional three years of service so he could take early retirement and earn the full defined contribution pension when he turned 59.5 years of age, or it would give him a severance package of one year's salary, six months of medical coverage, and three months of outplacement services. George was given until the next day to make a decision, but with either option, his last day at Obelisk would be on Friday, just three days away.

When George got home, the house was empty. His two daughters were out and his wife was working until 10 o'clock that night. George rarely had a drink after work, but tonight was different. He eased back in his chair, sipped his drink, and thought. About 29 years ago his college roommate had prodded him to join his firm. The salary was about the same, but they would pay for his MBA degree. Also, the chances to move beyond accounting and into more general management were strong. Twelve years ago, George's cousin had encouraged him to join her at her fledgling CPA firm. He could have come in as her partner, but the income was less certain and the benefits were nowhere near as good as they were at Obelisk. George networked extensively when he was younger, which had led to other solid job opportunities over the past several years. But each time he had a chance to move, he would remember what he would be giving up by leaving Obelisk. The bank was like a rock. And he knew two things; the bank offered security and they would never let him go because he was too valuable. George became depressed as he grasped the reality that he had opted for security over opportunity every time.

George started feeling bitter. He had given his life to Obelisk, willingly working nights and weekends when necessary. He recalled the times he missed his daughters' school functions because he was so dedicated to the bank. He had never even taken more than one week of vacation at a time because he believed he was needed too much at the office to spare more than a week. George tried to figure out all the questions he needed to answer in the next few hours. They came to him quickly and in no logical order. How much is college tuition going to cost me over the next four years? How many more years am I going to live? Will my wife and I be able to travel the world like we had planned? What company would be willing to hire a 54-year-old accountant with a limited range of work experiences? Which severance package makes the most sense? Should I think about opening my own business? Should I hire a lawyer and hit Obelisk with an age discrimination lawsuit? Will my family think I'm a failure? Should we sell the house and move to something smaller?

George poured himself another drink. He heard the garage door closing and the familiar words, "Hi honey, how was your day?"

Case Analysis Questions

1. How would you rate Obelisk's approach to the dismissal of George? What could or should they have done differently?
2. Why do you think George was blindsided by his dismissal? Do you think there was any way he could have seen the dismissal coming?

3. Why do you think George "opted for security over opportunity every time"?
4. Do you think George has a right to be bitter at Obelisk?
5. Should George take the early retirement option or the severance package? What do you see as the key issues for George as he decides what to do with his career in the short run and over the longer term?
6. If you were to make a prediction, what do you think George's career and life will look like five years into the future?

Notes

1 Retrieved from https://smartasset.com/retirement/average-retirement-age-in-every-state-2016.

2 Callanan, G. A. & Greenhaus, J. H. (2008). The baby boom generation and career management: A call to action. *Advances in Developing Human Resources*, *10*, 70–85.

3 Colby, S. L. & Ortman, J. M. (2014). The baby boom cohort in the United States: 2012 to 2060. Retrieved from www.census.gov/prod/2014pubs/p25-1141.pdf; Toossi, M. (2012). Employment outlook: 2010–2020. Labor force projections to 2020: A more slowly growing workforce. *Monthly Labor Review*, January, 43–64.

4 Toossi, M. (2013). Labor force projections to 2022: The labor force participation rate continues to fall. *Monthly Labor Review*, December, 1–28.

5 Toossi, M. (2012). Projections of the labor force to 2050: A visual essay. *Monthly Labor Review*, October, 1–16.

6 Levinson, D. J., Darrow, C. N., Klein, E. B., Levinson, M. H. & McKee, B. (1978). *Seasons of a man's life*. New York: Knopf; Levinson, D. J. & Levinson, J. D. (1996). *Seasons of a woman's life*. New York: Knopf; Schein, E. H. (1978). *Career dynamics: Matching individual and organizational needs*. Reading, MA: Addison-Wesley.

7 Levinson et al. (1978, 1996).

8 Burke, R. J. (1999). Career success and personal failure feelings among managers. *Psychological Reports*, *84*, 651–654; Klehe, U. C., Koen, J. & De Pater, I. E. (2012). Ending on the scrap heap? The experience of job loss and job search among older workers. In Hedge, J. W. & Borman, W. C. (Eds.), *The Oxford handbook of work and aging* (pp. 313–340). New York: Oxford University Press; Nicholson, N. & de Waal-Andrews, W. (2005). Playing to win: Biological imperatives, self-regulation, and trade-offs in the game of career success. *Journal of Organizational Behavior*, *26*, 137–154; Vansteenkiste, S., Deschacht, N. & Sels, L. (2015). Why are unemployed aged fifty and over less likely to find a job? A decomposition analysis. *Journal of Vocational Behavior*, *90*, 55–65; Wanberg, C., Kanfer, R., Hamann, D. & Zhang, Z. (2016). Age and reemployment success after job loss: An integrative model and meta-analysis. *Psychological Bulletin*, *142*, 400–426.

9 Bal, A. C., Reiss, A. E., Rudolph, C. W. & Baltes, B. B. (2011). Examining positive and negative perceptions of older workers: A meta-analysis. *The Journals of Gerontology Series B: Psychological Sciences and Social Sciences*, *66*, 687–698; Billett, S., Dymock, D., Johnson, G. & Martin, G. (2011). Overcoming the paradox of employers' views about older workers. *International Journal of Human Resource Management*, *22*, 1248–1261; Goštautaitė, B. & Bučiūnienė, I. (2015). Work engagement during life-span: The role of interaction outside the organization and task significance. *Journal of Vocational Behavior*, *89*, 109–119; Heidemeier, H. & Staudinger, U. M. (2015). Age differences in achievement goals and motivational characteristics of work in an ageing workforce. *Ageing & Society*, *35*, 809–836.

10 Levinson et al. (1978); Levinson & Levinson (1996).

11 Cohen, G. (2006). The myth of the midlife crisis; It's time we stop dismissing middle age as the beginning of the end. Research suggests that at 40, the brain's best years are ahead. *Newsweek*, January 16, p. 82; Lachman, M. E. (2004). Development in midlife. *Annual Review of Psychology*, *55*, 305–331; Stark, E. (2009). Fractures, fissures, and fault lines: Challenges accompanying baby boomers retaining employment in a recovering U.S. economy. *Journal of Applied Management and Entrepreneurship*, *14*, 3–26; Strenger, C. & Ruttenberg, A. (2008). The existential necessity of midlife change. *Harvard Business Review*, *86*, 82–90.

12 Lang, S. S. (2001). *Crisis or just stress? Cornell researcher finds the midlife crisis is less common than many believe.* Retrieved from *Cornell Chronicle*, www.news.cornell.edu/stories/2001/03/midlife-crisis-less-common-many-believe.
13 Baltes, P. B., Staudinger, U. M. & Lindenberger, U. (1999). Lifespan psychology: Theory and application to intellectual functioning. *Annual Review of Psychology*, *50*, 471–507; Cohen (2006); Lachman (2004); Lachman, M. E. & Bertrand, R. M. (2001). Personality and the self in midlife. In Lachman, M. E. (Ed.), *Handbook of midlife development* (pp. 279–309). New York: Wiley; Ng, T. W. H. & Feldman, D. C. (2013). Employee age and health. *Journal of Vocational Behavior*, *83*, 336–345; Magai, C. & Halpern, B. (2001). Emotional development during the middle years. In Lachman, M. E. (Ed.), *Handbook of midlife development* (pp. 310–344). New York: Wiley; Matz-Costa, C. (2016). Productive aging in the workplace: Understanding factors that promote or impede subjective well-being at work. *Best Practices in Mental Health*, *12*, 43–62; Stark (2009); Stewart, A. J. & Osgrove, J. M. (1998). Women's personality in middle age: Gender, history and midcourse corrections. *American Psychologist*, *53*, 1185–1194.
14 Cohen (2006); Levinson et al. (1978).
15 Morison, R., Erickson, T. & Dychtwald, K. (2006). Managing middlescence. *Harvard Business Review*, March, 78–86.
16 Vasconcelos, A. F. (2015). Older workers: Some critical societal and organizational challenges. *Journal of Management Development*, *34*, 352–372.
17 Ference, T. P., Stoner, J. A. F. & Warren, E. K. (1977). Managing the career plateau. *Academy of Management Review*, 2, 602–612. Quotation is on p. 602.
18 Godshalk, V. M. (2006). Career plateau. In Greenhaus, J. H. & Callanan, G. A. (Eds.), *Encyclopedia of career development* (pp. 133–138). Thousand Oaks, CA: Sage; Godshalk, V. M. & Fender, C. M. (2015). External and internal reasons for career plateauing: Relationships with work outcomes. *Group & Organization Management*, *40*, *529–559*.
19 Ibid.
20 Ross, S. (2013). Talent derailment: A multi-dimensional perspective for understanding talent. *Industrial and Commercial Training*, *45*, 12–17; Van Velsor, E. (2006). Derailment. In Greenhaus, J. H. & Callanan, G. A. (Eds.), *Encyclopedia of career development* (pp. 225–226). Thousand Oaks, CA: Sage.
21 Godshalk & Fender (2015).
22 Bardwick, J. M. (1986). *The plateauing trap*. Toronto, Canada: Bantam Books; Godshalk (2006); Morison et al. (2006).
23 Allen, T. D., Russell, J. E. A., Poteet, M. L. & Dobbins, G. H. (1999). Learning and development factors related to perceptions of job content and hierarchical plateauing. *Journal of Organizational Behavior*, *20*, 1113–1137; Armstrong-Stassen, M. (2008). Factors associated with job content plateauing among older workers. *Career Development International*, *13*, 594–613; Chay, Y. W., Aryee, S. & Chew, I. (1995). Career plateauing: Reactions and moderators among managerial and professional employees. *International Journal of Human Resource Management*, *6*, 61–78; Godshalk & Fender (2015); Hofstetter, H. & Cohen, A. (2014). The mediating role of job content plateau on the relationship between work experience characteristics and early retirement and turnover intentions. *Personnel Review*, *43*, 350–376; Hurst, C. S., Kungu, K. & Flott, P. (2012). Stress, organizational citizenship behaviors, and coping: Comparisons among plateaued and non-plateaued employees. *Business and Management Research*, *1*, 17–27; Lee, P. C. B. (2003). Going beyond career plateau: Using professional plateau to account for work outcomes. *Journal of Management Development*, *22*, 538–551; Lentz, E. & Allen, T. D. (2009). The role of mentoring others in the career plateauing phenomenon. *Group & Organization Management*, *34*, 358–384; Nachbagauer, A. G. M. & Riedl, G. (2002). Effects of concepts of career plateaus on performance, work satisfaction, and commitment. *International Journal of Manpower*, *23*, 716–733; Wang, Y. H., Hu, C., Hurst, C. S. & Yang, C. C. (2014). Antecedents and outcomes of career plateaus: The roles of mentoring others and proactive personality. *Journal of Vocational Behavior*, *85*, 319–328.
24 McCleese, C. S. & Eby, L. T. (2006). Reactions to job content plateaus: Examining role ambiguity and hierarchical plateaus as moderators. *Career Development Quarterly*, *55*, 64–76.
25 Bown-Wilson, D. & Parry, E. (2013). Career progression in older managers. *Employee Relations*, *35*, 309–321; Godshalk (2006); Allen et al. (1999); Chay et al. (1995); Godshalk & Fender (2015).
26 Armstrong-Stassen (2008); Bown-Wilson & Parry (2013); Duffy, J. A. (2000). The application of chaos theory to the career-plateaued worker. *Journal of Employment Counseling*, *37*,

229–236; Hurst et al. (2012); Ng, T. W. H. & Feldman, D. C. (2014). Subjective career success: A meta-analytic review. *Journal of Vocational Behavior*, *85*, 169–179; Verbruggen, M. (2012). Psychological mobility and career success in the "new" career climate. *Journal of Vocational Behavior*, *81*, 289–297; Wang et al. (2014).

27 Fossum, J. A., Arvey, R. D., Paradise, C. A. & Robbins, N. E. (1986). Modeling the skills obsolescence process: A psychological/economic integration. *Academy of Management Review*, *11*, 362–374; Znidarsic, J. (2012). Continuous education of older employees: Cost or benefit? *The International Business & Economics Research Journal*, *11*, 911–922.

28 Kaufman, H. G. (2006). Obsolescence of knowledge and skills. In Greenhaus, J. H. & Callanan, G. A. (Eds.), *Encyclopedia of career development* (pp. 539–546). Thousand Oaks, CA: Sage. Quotation is on p. 539.

29 Ibid.

30 Ibid.

31 Sun, J. Y. & Wang, G. G. (2009). Exploring career transition in the transitioning Chinese context: A case study. *Human Resource Development International*, *12*, 511–528; Sun, J. Y. & Wang, G. G. (2011). Integrating disparate literatures on voluntary career transition and voluntary turnover. *Journal of Chinese Human Resources Management*, *2*, 23–42; Zimmerman, E. (2003). To veer in midcareer, away from the money. *The New York Times*, May 18, p. BU13.

32 Ibarra, H. (2006). Career change. In Greenhaus, J. H. & Callanan, G. A. (Eds.), *Encyclopedia of career development* (pp. 77–82). Thousand Oaks, CA: Sage.

33 Khapova, S. N., Arthur, M. B., Wilderom, C. P. & Svensson, J. S. (2007). Professional identity as the key to career change intention. *Career Development International*, *12*, 584–595; Kunda, G., Barley, S. & Evans, J. (2002). Why do contractors contract? The experience of highly skilled technical professionals in a contingent labor market. *Industrial and Labor Relations Review*, *55*, 234–261.

34 Barclay, S. R., Stoltz, K. B. & Chung, Y. B. (2011). Voluntary midlife career change: Integrating the transtheoretical model and the life-span, life-space approach. *Career Development Quarterly*, *59*, 386–399; Dacey, J. S. & Travers, F. F. (2004). *Human development across the lifespan*. New York: McGraw Hill; Donohue, R. (2007). Examining career persistence and career change intent using the Career Attitudes and Strategies Inventory. *Journal of Vocational Behavior*, *70*, 259–276; Ibarra, (2006); Khapova et al. (2007).

35 Ibid.

36 Judge, T. A., Boudreau, J. W. & Bretz, Jr., R. D. (1993). Job and life attitudes of male executives. *Journal of Applied Psychology*, *79*, 767–782; Judge, T. A. & Watanabe, S. (1993). Another look at the job satisfaction–life satisfaction relationship. *Journal of Applied Psychology*, *78*, 939–948; Kasprzak, E. & Brzuszkiewicz, K. (2012). Temperamental traits and life and job satisfaction. *Polish Psychological Bulletin*, *43*, 27–39; Khan, E. A., Aqeel, M. & Riaz, M. A. (2014). Impact of job stress on job attitudes and life satisfaction in college lecturers. *International Journal of Information and Education Technology*, *4*, 270–273.

37 Barclay et al. (2011); Donohue (2007); Khapova et al. (2007).

38 Duffy, R. D., Allen, B. A., Autin, K. L. & Bott, E. M. (2013). Calling and life satisfaction: It's not about having it, it's about living it. *Journal of Counseling Psychology*, *60*, 42–52; Duffy, R. D., Bott, E. M., Allen, B. A., Torrey, C. L. & Dik, B. J. (2012). Perceiving a calling, living a calling, and job satisfaction: Testing a moderated, multiple mediator model. *Journal of Counseling Psychology*, *59*, 50–59; Zimmerman (2003).

39 Heppner, M. J., Multon, K. D. & Johnston, J. A. (1994). Assessing psychological resources during career change: Development of the Career Transitions Inventory. *Journal of Vocational Behavior*, *44*, 55–74.

40 Ibarra (2006).

41 Strenger & Ruttenberg (2008).

42 Chung, Y. B. (2006). Career coaching. In Greenhaus, J. H. & Callanan, G. A. (Eds.), *Encyclopedia of career development* (pp. 83–84). Thousand Oaks, CA: Sage; Hewlett, S. A. (2013). *Forget a mentor, find a sponsor: The new way to fast-track your career*. Boston, MA: Harvard Business School Publishing.

43 Ng, T. (2006). Career mobility. In Greenhaus, J. H. & Callanan, G. A. (Eds.), *Encyclopedia of career development* (pp. 127–130). Thousand Oaks, CA: Sage.

44 Barclay et al. (2011); Donohue (2007); Hall, D. T. & Richter, J. (1990). Career gridlock: Baby boomers hit the wall. *Academy of Management Executive*, *4*, 7–22; Strenger & Ruttenberg (2008); Znidarsic (2012).

45 Campion, M. C., Campion, E. D. & Campion, M. A. (2015). Improvements in performance management through the use of 360 feedback. *Industrial and Organizational Psychology*, *8*, 85–93; Eichinger, R. W. & Lombardo, M. M. (2003). Knowledge summary series: 360-degree assessment. *Human Resource Planning*, *26*, 34–44; Kim, K. Y., Atwater, L., Patel, P. C. & Smither, J. W. (2016). Multisource feedback, human capital, and the financial performance of organizations. *Journal of Applied Psychology*, *101*, 1569–1584.
46 Morison et al. (2006).
47 Ibid.
48 Kaufman, H. G. (1995). Salvaging displaced employees: Job obsolescence, retraining, and redeployment. In London, M. (Ed.), *Employees, careers, and job creation: Developing growth oriented strategies and programs* (pp. 105–120). San Francisco: Jossey-Bass.
49 Larwood, L., Rodkin, S. & Judson, D. (2001). Retraining and the technological productivity paradox. *International Journal of Organizational Theory and Behavior*, *4*, 201–224.
50 Hodges, J. (2012). The transition of midlife women from organisational into self-employment. *Gender in Management: An International Journal*, *27*, 186–201; Morison et al. (2006); Templer, A., Armstrong-Stassen, M. & Cattaneo, J. (2010). Antecedents of older workers' motives for continuing to work. *Career Development International*, *15*, 479–500; Znidarsic (2012).
51 Gordon, J. R. & Whelan, K. S. (1998). Successful professional women in midlife: How organizations can more effectively understand and respond to the challenges. *Academy of Management Executive*, *12*, 8–24.
52 Ibid.
53 Ibarra, H. (2002). How to stay stuck in the wrong career. *Harvard Business Review*, *80*(12), 40–48. Quotation is on p. 44.
54 Ibid.
55 Rudolph, C. W., Katz, I. M., Lavigne, K. N. & Zacher, H. (2017). Job crafting: A meta-analysis of relationships with individual differences, job characteristics, and work outcomes. *Journal of Vocational Behavior*. *102*, 112-138.
56 Rudolph et al. (2017); Tims, M., Bakker, A. B. & Derks, D. (2012). Development and validation of the job crafting scale. *Journal of Vocational Behavior*, *80*, 173–186.
57 Rudolph et al. (2017).
58 Bakker, A. B., Tims, M. & Derks, D. (2012). Proactive personality and job performance: The role of job crafting and work engagement. *Human Relations*, *65*, 1359–1378.
59 Las Heras, M., Rofcanin, Y., Bal, P. M. & Stollberger, J. (2017). How do flexibility i-deals relate to work performance? Exploring the roles of family performance and organizational context. *Journal of Organizational Behavior*, *38*, 1280–1294; Rousseau, D. M. (2005). *I-deals: Idiosyncratic deals employees bargain for themselves*. New York: M. E. Sharpe; Rousseau, D. M., Ho, V. T. & Greenberg, J. (2006). I-deals: Idiosyncratic terms in employment relationships. *Academy of Management Review*, *31*, 977–994.
60 Ng., T. W. H. & Lucianetti, L. (2016). Goal striving, idiosyncratic deals and job behavior. *Journal of Organizational Behavior*, *37*, 41–60; Rousseau, D. M., Hornung, S. & Kim, T. G. (2009). Idiosyncratic deals: Testing propositions on timing, content, and the employment relationship. *Journal of Vocational Behavior*, *74*, 338–348; Hornung, S., Rousseau, D. M. & Glaser, J. (2008). Creating flexible work arrangements through idiosyncratic deals. *Journal of Applied Psychology*, *93*, 655–664.
61 Hornung et al. (2008).
62 Klehe et al. (2012); McKee-Ryan, F. M. (2006). Job loss. In Greenhaus, J. H. & Callanan, G. A. (Eds.), *Encyclopedia of career development* (pp. 427–432). Thousand Oaks, CA: Sage; Wolf, G., London, M., Casey, J. & Pufahl, J. (1995). Career experience and motivation as predictors of training behaviors and outcomes for displaced engineers. *Journal of Vocational Behavior*, *47*, 316–331; Wanberg et al. (2016).
63 Cascio, W. F. & Wynn, P. (2004). Managing a downsizing process. *Human Resource Management*, *43*, 425–436; Latack, J. C., Kinicki, A. J. & Prussia, G. E. (1995). An integrative model of coping with job loss. *Academy of Management Review*, *20*, 311–342; Marks, M. L. & deMeuse, K. P. (2005). Resizing the organization: Maximizing the gain while minimizing the pain of layoffs, divestitures, and closings. *Organizational Dynamics*, *34*, 19–35; Mendenhall, R., Kalil, A., Spindel, L. J. & Hart, C. M. D. (2008). Job loss at mid-life: Managers and executives face the "new risk economy." *Social Forces*, *87*, 185–209; Talbot, A. G., Tobe, E. & Ames, B. D. (2015). The experience of un- or underemployment and home foreclosure for mature adults: A phenomenological approach. *Journal of Family and Economic Issues*, *36*, 503–513.

64 Schneer, J. A. (1993). Involuntary turnover and its psychological consequences: A theoretical model. *Human Resource Management Review*, *3*, 29–47; Snell, D., Schmitt, D., Glavas, A. & Bamberry, L. (2015). Worker stress and the prospect of job loss in a fragmented organisation. *Qualitative Research in Organizations and Management*, *10*, 61–81; Wanberg et al. (2016).

65 Latack et al. (1995); Mendenhall et al. (2008); Power, S. J. (2010). Career management tactical innovations and successful interorganizational transitions. *Career Development International*, *15*, 664–686; Talbot et al. (2015); Wanberg et al. (2016).

66 Blumenstein, R. (2004). Older executives find job losses often mean having to retire early. *Wall Street Journal*, July 20, p. B1; Mendenhall et al. (2008).

67 Blau, G., Petrucci, T. & McClendon, J. (2013). Correlates of life satisfaction and unemployment stigma and the impact of length of unemployment on a unique unemployed sample. *Career Development International*, *18*, 257–280; Fasbender, U., Deller, J., Wang, M. & Wiernik, B. M. (2014). Deciding whether to work after retirement: The role of the psychological experience of aging. *Journal of Vocational Behavior*, *84*, 215–224; McKee-Ryan (2006); Wanberg et al. (2016).

68 Latack et al. (1995); Mendenhall et al. (2008).

69 McKee-Ryan (2006); Mendenhall et al. (2008).

70 Mendenhall et al. (2008).

71 Latack et al. (1995).

72 Mendenhall et al. (2008).

73 Latack et al. (1995).

74 McKee-Ryan, (2006).

75 Ibid.

76 Schneer (1993).

77 Eden, D. & Aviram, A. (1993). Self-efficacy training to speed reemployment: Helping people to help themselves. *Journal of Applied Psychology*, *78*, 352–360; Marks & deMeuse (2005); Vansteenkiste et al. (2015).

78 Westaby, J. D. & NicDomhnaill, O. M. (2006). Outplacement. In Greenhaus, J. H. & Callanan, G. A. (Eds.), *Encyclopedia of career development* (pp. 608–609). Thousand Oaks, CA: Sage.

79 Scidurlo, L. (2006). Age Discrimination in Employment Act of 1967 (ADEA). In Greenhaus, J. H. & Callanan, G. A. (Eds.), *Encyclopedia of career development* (pp. 14–15). Thousand Oaks, CA: Sage.

80 Jacobs, D. L. (2013). 11 sneaky ways employers get rid of older workers. *Forbes*, November 3. Retrieved from ww.forbes.com/sites/deborahljacobs/2013/11/03/11-sneaky-ways-companies-get-rid-of-older-workers/#57dab665206a; OECD Economic Outlook (2002). Increasing employment: The role of late retirement: Incentives for early retirement still exist, even after recent reforms. *OECD Economic Outlook*, *72*, 146–151; Stoll, J. D. (2007). GM starts first phase of buyouts. *Wall Street Journal*, December 19, p. A13.

81 Williams, C. P. & Savickas, M. L. (1990). Developmental tasks of career maintenance. *Journal of Vocational Behavior*, *36*, 166–175.

82 Kaufman (1995, 2006); Mahon et al. (2014).

83 Beehr, T. A. & Bowling, N. (2002). Career issues facing older workers. In Feldman, D. C. (Ed.), *Work careers: A developmental perspective* (pp. 214–241). San Francisco: Jossey-Bass; Boone, J., McKechnie, S., Swanberg, J. & Besen, E. (2013). Exploring the workplace impact of intentional/unintentional age discrimination. *Journal of Managerial Psychology*, *28*, 907–927; Bowen, C. E. & Staudinger, U. M. (2012). Relationship between age and promotion orientation depends on perceived older worker stereotypes. *Journals of Gerontology Series B: Psychological Sciences and Social Sciences*, *68*, 59–63; Dordoni, P. & Argentero, P. (2015). When age stereotypes are employment barriers: A conceptual analysis and a literature review on older workers stereotypes. *Ageing International*, *40*, 393–412; Greller, M. M. & Simpson, P. (1999). In search of late career: A review of contemporary social science research applicable to the understanding of late career. *Human Resource Management Review*, *9*, 309–347; Sterns, H. L. & Miklos, S. M. (1995). The aging worker in a changing environment: Organizational and individual issues. *Journal of Vocational Behavior*, *47*, 248–268.

84 Keene, J. (2006). Age discrimination. In Greenhaus, J. H. & Callanan, G. A. (Eds.), *Encyclopedia of career development* (pp. 10–14). Thousand Oaks, CA: Sage.

85 Ibid.

86 Bertolino, M., Truxillo, D. M. & Fraccaroli, F. (2013). Age effects on perceived personality and job performance. *Journal of Managerial Psychology*, *28*, 867–885; Van Dalen, H. P., Henkens, K. & Schippers, J. (2009). Dealing with older workers in Europe: A comparative survey of employers' attitudes and actions. *Journal of European Social Policy*, *19*, 47–60.
87 Dordoni & Argentero (2015); Roscigno, V. J., Mong, S., Byron, R. & Tester, G. (2007). Age discrimination, social closure, and employment. *Social Forces*, *86*, 313–334.
88 Feldman, D. C. (2006). Late career stage. In Greenhaus, J. H. & Callanan, G. A. (Eds.), *Encyclopedia of career development* (pp. 453–457). Thousand Oaks, CA: Sage; Greller & Simpson (1999).
89 Desmette, D. & Gaillard, M. (2008). When a "worker" becomes an "older worker": The effects of age-related social identity on attitudes towards retirement and work. *Career Development International*, *13*, 168–185.
90 Feldman (2006); Sterns & Miklos (1995).
91 Boveda, I. & Metz, A. J. (2016). Predicting end-of-career transitions for baby boomers nearing retirement age. *The Career Development Quarterly*, *64*, 153–168; Collins, G. (2006). Retirement. In Greenhaus, J. H. & Callanan, G. A. (Eds.), *Encyclopedia of career development* (pp. 693–696). Thousand Oaks, CA: Sage.
92 Boveda & Metz (2016); Riffkin, R. (2014). *Average U.S. retirement age rises to 62*. Retrieved from www.gallup.com/poll/168707/average-retirement-age-rises.aspx.
93 Social Security Administration (n.d.). *Full Retirement Age: If You Were Born Between 1943 and 1954*. Retrieved from www.ssa.gov/planners/retire/1943.html.
94 Mollica, K. (2006). Early retirement. In Greenhaus, J. H. & Callanan, G. A. (Eds.), *Encyclopedia of career development* (pp. 254–255). Thousand Oaks, CA: Sage.
95 Powell, R. (2014). How to phase into retirement. *USA Today*, September 6.
96 Hanisch, K. A. (1994). Reasons people retire and their relations to attitudinal and behavioral correlates in retirement. *Journal of Vocational Behavior*, *45*, 1–16; Kim, S. & Feldman, D. C. (2000). Working in retirement: The antecedents of bridge employment and its consequences for quality of life in retirement. *Academy of Management Journal*, *43*, 1195–1210; Kubicek, B., Korunka, C., Raymo, J. M. & Hoonakker, P. (2011). Psychological well-being in retirement: The effects of personal and gendered contextual resources. *Journal of Occupational Health Psychology*, *16*, 230–246; Lim, V. K. G. & Feldman, D. C. (2003). The impact of time structure and time usage on willingness to retire and bridge employment. *International Journal of Human Resource Management*, *14*, 1178–1191; Schmitt, N., White, J. K., Coyle, B. W. & Rauschenberger, J. (1979). Retirement and life satisfaction. *Academy of Management Journal*, *22*, 282–291; Topa, G. & Alcover, C. (2015). Psychosocial factors in retirement intentions and adjustment: A multi-sample study. *Career Development International*, *20*, 384–408.
97 Ibid.
98 Schlosser, F., Zinni, D. & Armstrong-Stassen, M. (2012). Intention to unretire: HR and the boomerang effect. *Career Development International*, *17*, 149–167.
99 Mollica (2006).
100 Hutchens, R. (2006). Phased retirement. In Greenhaus, J. H. & Callanan, G. A. (Eds.), *Encyclopedia of career development* (pp. 638–640). Thousand Oaks, CA: Sage; Quinn, J. F. & Cahill, K. E. (2016). The new world of retirement income security in America. *American Psychologist*, *71*, 321–333.
101 Callanan & Greenhaus (2008).
102 Quinn & Cahill (2016).
103 Callanan & Greenhaus (2008).
104 Boveda & Metz (2016); Ulrich, L. B. (2006). Bridge employment. In Greenhaus, J. H. & Callanan, G. A. (Eds.), *Encyclopedia of career development* (pp. 49–51). Thousand Oaks, CA: Sage.
105 Müller, A., De Lange, A., Weigl, M., Oxfart, C. & Van der Heijden, B. (2013). Compensating losses in bridge employment? Examining relations between compensation strategies, health problems, and intention to remain at work. *Journal of Vocational Behavior*, *83*, 68–77.
106 Munderlein, M., Ybema, J. F., Koster, F. (2013). Happily ever after? Explaining turnover and retirement intentions of older workers in the Netherlands. *Career Development International*, *18*, 548–568.
107 Kaufman (1995); Mahon & Millar (2014).
108 Billett, S. & Van Woerkom, M. (2008). Personal epistemologies and older workers. *International Journal of Lifelong Learning*, *27*, 333–348; Froehlich, D. E., Beausaert, S., Segers,

M. & Gerken, M. (2014). Learning to stay employable. *Career Development International*, *19*, 508–525; Grima, F. (2011). The influence of age management policies on older employee work relationships with their company. *International Journal of Human Resource Management*, *22*, 1312–1332; van Vianen, A. E. M., Dalhoeven, B. A. G. W. & De Pater, I. E. (2011). Aging and training and development willingness: Employee and supervisor mindsets. *Journal of Organizational Behavior*, *32*, 226–247.

109 Mahon & Millar (2014).

110 2016 Workplace Benefits Report: Empowering and encouraging employees to plan for their financial future. Bank of America Merrill Lynch, Workplace Insights, www.benefitplans.baml.com/IR/Pages/workplace-benefits-report.aspx; LaRock, S. (2000). Retirement planning programs should go beyond investment advice, especially for older workers. *Employee Benefit Plan Review*, *55*, 16–18; Wotherspoon, C. J. (1995). Plan now, enjoy later? A study of the use and effectiveness of formal retirement planning programs. *Benefits Quarterly*, *11*, 53–57.

111 Boveda & Metz (2016).

112 Collins (2006); Hutchens (2006).

Part III

Contemporary Issues in Career Management

10 Job Stress and Careers

The presence of job stress in the workplace is a major concern for both employees and organizational managers. Stress takes an immense toll on the physical and emotional health of individuals, as well as the bottom line profits of organizations. Indeed, stress can lead to such negative consequences as employee burnout, physiological and psychosomatic illnesses, and low job satisfaction.[1] Each year, job stress results in substantial costs to both American and international businesses due to increased absenteeism and turnover, lower productivity and organizational commitment, and higher medical costs.[2] Some estimates suggest that the stress-related expenditures that U.S.-based companies experience are upwards of $300 billion per year, representing nearly 10 percent of total U.S. spending on health care.[3]

The incidence and magnitude of stress experienced in today's business environment continues to escalate. Research indicates that a large percentage of employees believe that their work-related stress is increasing and that this stress results in related physical symptoms such as fatigue, headaches, upset stomach, and muscle tension. Pressures emanate from several sources—long hours and poor communication at work, greater job demands with little control over one's tasks and work scheduling, conflicts with co-workers, personal financial worries, and balancing work and nonwork lives.[4] From a career management standpoint, individuals need to be aware of the role that stress plays in their lives. Excessive levels of stress can seriously impair an employee's work performance and career success. Moreover, job stress will not go away by itself, and there is a need to understand the nature of job stress before attempts can be made to control or manage it. Finally, individuals should understand the support mechanisms that are available for coping with job stress.

In this chapter, we examine the implications of job stress. First, we define stress and identify its sources and consequences. We then examine three particular sources of job stress that have been subject to much scrutiny—Type A behavior, career transitions, and bias in the workplace. In addition, we discuss job burnout, technology-induced stress, and workaholism, three stress-related factors that have been described extensively in the popular press. We conclude the chapter by offering ways in which individuals can deal with stress as they manage their careers and their lives, as well as ways that organizations can help their employees in this process.

Job Stress: An Overview

Stress involves an interaction between a person and the environment that is perceived to be so trying or burdensome that it exceeds the person's coping resources. Stress can produce physiological, cognitive, emotional, and/or behavioral reactions to work, which may then threaten one's overall well-being.[5] Stress is aroused when a person is confronted with an opportunity, a constraint, or a demand.[6] An *opportunity* is a situation in which a person stands to gain additional gratification of his or her significant values or desires, as in a new work assignment or promotion. A *constraint*, on the other hand, threatens to block additional gratification, for example, when a job promotion is denied. A *demand* threatens to remove a person from a currently gratifying situation, as when one is fired from a job.

A particular situation can simultaneously represent an opportunity, a constraint, and a demand. A new, challenging work assignment, for instance, may represent an opportunity to develop skills and acquire needed exposure, but also constrain one from spending more time with family. It can also become a demand if it overloads one to the point that work effectiveness and satisfaction suffer. A situation—be it an opportunity, constraint, or demand—is stressful when it exceeds or threatens to exceed the individual's capacity to handle it.

For stress to be aroused, the individual must care about the particular outcomes of a given situation, but lack control over the circumstances or have a weak system of support.[7] If a person is indifferent toward future advancement within the work organization, then a new work assignment probably would not produce a significant amount of stress because the outcome (future advancement) does not hold a high degree of importance to the individual. Uncertainty, unpredictability, and fear of the unknown breed stress. If one knows for certain that a new job will be satisfying and stable, it will be far less stressful than if there is a degree of uncertainty about how satisfying the new job will be. In this sense, a person has to be emotionally involved in an uncertain situation for it to be stressful. Consider the case of Christie, a recent MBA graduate:

> Christie had spent several sleepless nights contemplating her first new product proposal before the executive management team of her employer. She had spent day and night for the past three weeks preparing the report and her presentation. She viewed the proposal as the first real test of her contribution to the organization, and if she succeeded, she would be considered as having managerial potential. Christie's presentation lasted five minutes and was followed by about ten minutes of questions from the management team. Christie was thanked for making a fine presentation and was then dismissed from the meeting by the company's president. As she left the room, she felt cold and realized she was sweating profusely. She quickly went to the nearest women's restroom and in a release of tension, shook uncontrollably. "All that work for 15 minutes," she thought as she felt a tear fall, "why do I let this get to me so much?"

Christie's presentation represented an opportunity to test herself and impress the management team, but it also posed a threat to her self-esteem and her reputation within the company. Although she did not know how well the presentation would go, she cared deeply about the outcome because it was important to her future career with the company. Under these circumstances, it is understandable why Christie experienced a high level of stress that was manifested in such a physical way.

Sources and Consequences of Stress

Exhibit 10.1 presents an overview of job stress. This model distinguishes environmental stressors from the perception of stress, from strain symptoms, and from the outcomes of stress.[8] Additionally, it notes that individuals may have internal or external resources that assist in dealing with stress.

Table 10.1 identifies a number of potential environmental stressors, which can emanate from work or nonwork situations, and can be understood as "stimuli that evoke the stress process."[9] Stress can be produced by work roles that are ambiguous, overload (or underload)

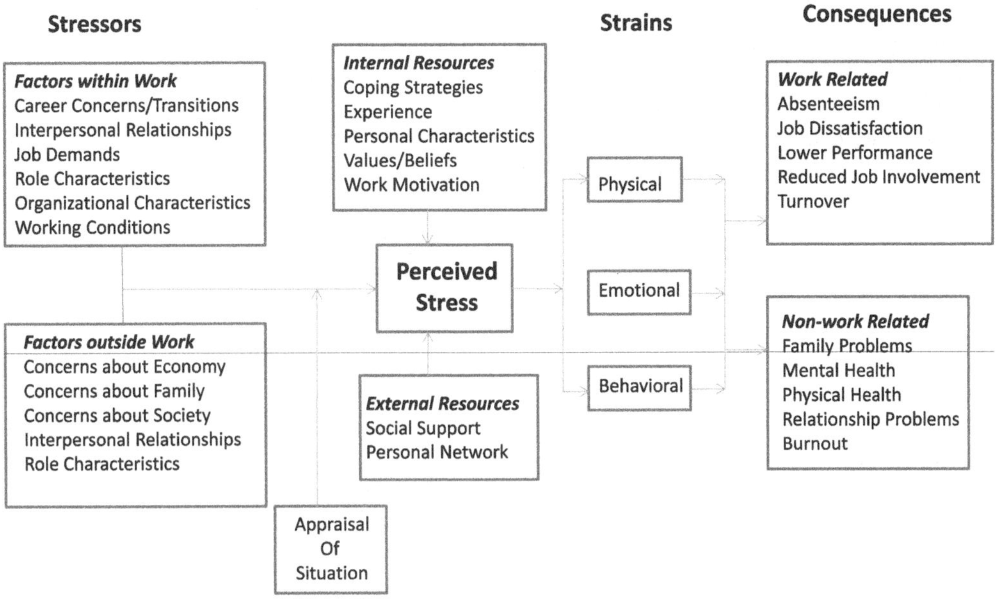

Adapted from Lu, Cooper, Kao, and Zhou (2003) and other sources; see end note 8.

Exhibit 10.1 Job Stress Model

Table 10.1 Illustrations of Environmental Stressors

Organizational Characteristics
Centralization, low participation in decision making
Poor communication
Pay inequities

Job Demands
Time pressure and deadlines
Responsibility for people
Repetitive work

Role Characteristics
Role conflict: caught between conflicting expectations
Role ambiguity: lack of clarity about expectations or performance
Role overload/underload: too much or too little work

Interpersonal Relationships
Conflict within and between groups
Competition
Inconsiderate or inequitable supervision

Working Conditions
Crowding
Noise
Excessive heat or cold

Career Concerns/Transitions
Change of job, employer, location
Obsolescence
Career plateau
Bias in the workplace
Loss of employment
Retirement

Nonwork Pressures
Family conflicts
Life changes, for example, divorce, illness or death of loved one, birth of child

Adapted from several sources, including: Brief, A. P., Schuler, R. S. & Van Sell, M. (1981). *Managing job stress.* Boston, MA: Little, Brown and Company; Spector, P. E. (2006). Stress at work. In Greenhaus, J. H. & Callanan, G. A. (Eds.), *Encyclopedia of career development* (pp. 771–778). Thousand Oaks, CA: Sage.

one's capacities, require extraordinary time commitments, or put one in the middle of two conflicting people or groups. Stress can have its roots in organizational policies or practices, in the demands of the job itself, and in the nature of the physical and social context of work. Individuals may become distressed due to the lack of career development opportunities, the lack of prestige associated with their job, the necessary time and travel associated with the occupation, or minimal advancement prospects for the future. As discussed in Chapter 3, there are stressors that emanate from outside of work, including the demands of the multiple roles we hold and concerns over the quantity and quality of the time spent with family and in other interpersonal relationships outside of work. Thus, stress can also occur in the nonwork environment, where personal factors such as family finances, health concerns, and social relationships can create substantial burdens and pressures.[10] As just one example, incivility within one's family has been linked to increased psychological distress, which carries over into the work role to have a negative impact on performance at work.[11]

Stressors may be perceived by individuals as hindrances or challenges. Hindrance-oriented stressors, which are thought to block the opportunity to achieve goals and personal growth (e.g., organizational politics, administrative red tape, role ambiguity, concerns about job security) are negatively related to job performance, whereas challenge-oriented stressors, which are thought to create opportunities to learn and achieve goals (e.g., high workload, time pressures, job scope or demands) can motivate workers, decrease turnover intentions, and relate positively to job performance even as they might evoke other strains such as fatigue and exhaustion.[12]

The presence of an environmental stressor does not inevitably produce stress. It depends on how the situation is interpreted or appraised. Some people may not see a situation as particularly important, thereby reducing the level of perceived stress. For example, if Christie's career were not so important to her, the presentation would not have produced much stress. Or one may be so confident about one's ability to handle a situation that it is not viewed as threatening or uncertain. Therefore, what is perceived as stressful by one person may not be seen as stressful by another. An individual's internal resources and characteristics, such as personality, motivation, or coping ability, can determine how one perceives and responds to stressors. For example, those high in neuroticism (emotional instability) are likely to be less able to handle stressful situations because they tend to show a strong emotional reaction when distressed and use avoidance or denial as ways to cope with a stressful situation.[13]

Certain personal characteristics can produce stress over and above the effects of particular environmental pressures. For example, highly anxious employees tend to experience high levels of stress, regardless of the environmental conditions.[14] Other personal qualities, such as a Type A personality (which we will discuss in more depth shortly), inflexibility, and intolerance of ambiguity can also heighten feelings of stress.[15] In addition, some individuals may simply have a personal disposition toward stress, whereby they experience stress regardless of the characteristics of the work situation.[16] The important point is that stress can be produced by a variety of situations that may be interpreted as threatening, as well as by a general personal tendency to perceive various life circumstances as stressful.

In addition, the amount of control an employee has over a work situation can determine whether that situation produces extensive stress. Individuals who have control over the particular tasks they perform (the way they complete the tasks or the time or place at which the tasks are undertaken) may be able to avoid a stressful incident, or perceive the incident as a challenge rather than a hindrance. Control may be particularly important on jobs that that are highly demanding.[17]

Perceived stress can produce a number of different strain symptoms. These strains may become manifest in a variety of physical, behavioral, and emotional outcomes (see Table 10.2). The impact of work stress on physical and psychological health is well documented. In fact, stress has been linked with pursuing an unhealthy lifestyle, elevated blood pressure, cardiovascular disease, gastrointestinal disorders, increased cortisol, susceptibility to viruses, and other related health problems. Stress can also result in behavioral symptoms such as under/overeating, drug and alcohol abuse, smoking, becoming less physically active, or becoming more violent in the workplace. Those who experience excessive stress may also be affected with greater emotional exhaustion, negativity, and irritability.[18]

Of course, not everyone who experiences stress will develop these strain symptoms. Some people have a naturally high capacity to handle stress. In addition, effective coping skills can help protect people from the ravaging effects of extreme stress. Further, the availability of support from others can help keep stress within manageable bounds so that people do not experience such negative reactions to trying situations. Coping strategies for stress will be discussed in a later section.

Extensive strain can reduce job involvement and productivity, and increase dissatisfaction, absenteeism, and turnover. In short, extensive work stress results in strains that may not only prove dangerous to one's physical and emotional well-being, but also produce dysfunctional consequences for the organization. Exposure to stress over a long period of time can be so debilitating that it has a significant impact on both health and productivity, and may result in burnout[19] as well as workplace harassment and violence and other deviant behaviors at work.[20]

It is important to recognize that stress per se is not necessarily harmful. In fact, a moderate level of stress enhances performance and health, but extreme levels of stress (low or high) can be distressful because they serve either to under-stimulate or over-stimulate the person. Optimal levels of stress can be challenging and produce *eustress* (positive feelings and high involvement) rather than *distress*. Therefore, it is helpful for employees to consider stressors as challenges (eustress), thereby creating a more positive interpretation of the stressors and minimizing the perception of distress.[21]

Type A Behavior as a Source of Stress

As noted earlier, personal needs, motives, and behavior patterns can produce stress. One such personality-related behavior pattern, known as Type A, is characterized by a hard-driving competitiveness, a sense of extreme impatience and time-urgency, the desire to live a fast-paced lifestyle, a preference for performing many activities simultaneously,

Table 10.2 Illustrations of Strain Symptoms

Physical	**Behavioral**
Short-term: heart rate, galvanic skin response, respiration,	Sudden change in use of alcohol/drug abuse
gastrointestinal disorders, susceptibility to virus, insomnia	Sudden change in smoking habits
Long-term: ulcer, blood pressure, cardiovascular disease	Sudden, noticeable weight loss or gain
Nonspecific: adrenaline, gastric acid production, difficulty breathing, increased cortisol	Less physically active during leisure time
Emotional/Psychological	Burnout
Apathy, boredom	Workplace harassment and violence
Inattentiveness, loss of ability to concentrate	
Irritability	
Negativism	
Exhaustion	

Adapted from a longer list developed by Schuler (1980), and added to by various recent studies in endnote 18. Schuler, R. S. (1980). Definition and conceptualization of stress in organizations. *Organizational Behavior and Human Performance*, *24*, 115–130.

and a constant striving for achievement and perfection.[22] In contrast, the Type B pattern has been characterized as having low or moderate levels of competitiveness, a higher degree of patience, and a less intense need for accomplishment and perfection. It is believed that the Type A pattern is produced by certain beliefs and fears that people hold about themselves and the world. For example, Type A individuals have higher perceptions of their intellectual ability, morality, and self-worth than Type Bs. In addition, Type A individuals tend to base their sense of self-worth on their attainment of material success.[23]

On the positive side, Type A students exhibit strong study habits and academic achievement, and Type A employees tend to be highly involved in their jobs and hold high levels of occupational success and self-esteem.[24] Moreover, Type As can be more productive than their Type B colleagues, largely because of their internal belief of self-competence, their willingness and ability to juggle multiple projects, and their tendency to develop high performance goals. On the other hand, Type A employees tend to experience comparatively higher levels of job stress and health-related problems such as coronary heart disease, and report higher levels of hostility and turnover motivations, and lower levels of optimism, job satisfaction, and organizational commitment.[25]

Programs have been developed to help Type As alter their more harmful behaviors. Many of these intervention programs involve self-appraisal, a reorientation of one's philosophy of life, behavior therapy, well-being therapy, and psychotherapy.[26] Additionally, Type A individuals who are at risk of cardiovascular ailments may benefit from educational programs on behavior control, stress management workshops, biofeedback, individual coaching and counseling, and relaxation techniques.[27] Might the reduction of Type A behavior, however, render the employee less productive on the job? Some researchers think not. Studies suggest that intervention techniques can allow for alteration of just the negative consequences associated with Type A behavior, where targeted interventions can achieve increases in the time Type As devote to relaxation, with an attendant reduction in stress-related psychosomatic symptoms.[28] The implications are that employees who successfully reduce their aggressiveness and impatience, and who increase their control over pressing demands, can reduce the likelihood of negative stress-induced outcomes without impairing their level of job performance.

Career Transitions as a Source of Stress

A *career transition* involves either a change in roles—as when a person takes a first job, is promoted, or changes employers—or a change in one's orientation to a role currently held, as illustrated by alterations in attitudes toward a job due to changes in duties, colleagues, or one's own behavior. All career transitions involve changes and contrasts between old and new settings. For example, a recently transferred and relocated employee has many adjustments to make: a new job, a new boss, a new group of colleagues, a new office, maybe even new work norms and expectations. There also is a different home in a different community, new neighbors, and, if there are children, new schools to enter and new friendships to form.

While career transitions usually require adjustments to new tasks, relationships, and expectations, do they really produce extensive stress? As was discussed in Chapter 9, one form of transition, job loss, has been linked to strain symptoms such as poor health, depression, insomnia, irritability, low self-esteem, and a feeling of helplessness. Beyond job loss, other forms of career transitions can produce high levels of stress as outlined below:

1. Undesirable career transitions are more likely to be stressful than desirable ones. Most employees desire promotions and the salary increases that generally accompany them.

As was indicated above, job loss and unemployment, on the other hand, can be devastating to one's financial security and sense of self-worth. Life transitions that have negative connotations produce more psychological distress. In fact, several researchers have discussed how individuals who see career plateauing as a "career failure" will experience job-related stress over time. Also, the reasons why employees perceive they are plateaued can affect the amount of stress they experience. For example, individuals who choose not to pursue a promotion experience less stress than those who believe that they have plateaued due to the organization not seeing them as worthy of a promotion.[29]

2. Career transitions that involve extensive changes, such as changing organizations or occupations, or relocating to another geographic region, can produce more stress and a greater need to cope than transitions that involve fewer or smaller changes.
3. Sudden, unexpected transitions may produce more shock and stress than gradual transitions. Also, uncertainty and fear over the effect of the transition can produce stress. Expected changes with more certain consequences allow the individual to prepare for the transition and develop more constructive coping responses.
4. Career transitions accompanied by other life transitions (e.g., marriage, divorce, birth of a child, serious illness in the family, financial hardship) are likely to be more stressful than career transitions unencumbered by other major life alterations or events.
5. Transitions that are forced on an individual may be more stressful than those under the individual's control. A forced transition is probably less desirable than a self-initiated one, mainly because the timing of such a change may be beyond the control of the individual. Indeed, transitions can be more stressful when the individual cannot control the onset or duration of the stress-producing situation. Many individuals experienced involuntary career transitions during and after the Great Recession of 2008–2009, and the loss of one's job or home, or an unanticipated transfer to a different geographic area for a new work opportunity, can all be stress-causing events.

In sum, transition-induced stress is likely to vary with the specific characteristics of the career transition, simultaneous life stresses, and the support and psychological resources available to the individual. Individual coping strategies can also help people deal with the changes and adjustments associated with transitions. A later section of this chapter will review the characteristics of effective coping behavior. Consider the following example that highlights the multifaceted nature of career transition-induced stress:

Isabel was feeling overwhelmed and desperate for help. Three months ago, she was unexpectedly promoted to quality assurance manager of her company. While the promotion was flattering, the time demands have been extraordinary. She has been putting in 70-hour work weeks, and there is no relief in sight. Compounding matters, Isabel's home and family life are in a state of flux. As the divorced mother of a three-year-old son, Isabel had relied on her mother to provide care for her child while she was at work. This childcare arrangement was ideal for Isabel because it gave her flexibility to work as many hours as she needed without worry or guilt over the adequacy of supervision for her child. Unfortunately, two weeks ago Isabel received a call at work from her sister at the local hospital—their mother had fallen and broken her hip. All at once, the stress in Isabel's life tripled—she had the demanding job, she lost the ideal childcare arrangement for her son, and she had to find a way to care for her ailing mother. She feels like her head is about to explode and she just doesn't know where to turn. With only her sister in the area, who is also busy with work and family, they will need to find a way to manage their mother's health and rehabilitation. She fears her new boss will be unsympathetic, and she is unaware of any programs at her company to help her deal with this crisis situation.

In this example, Isabel's promotion to a new job with excessive time demands represents, in and of itself, a stress-provoking career transition. On top of that, other events in Isabel's life are producing added stress and strain. At the moment, Isabel does not see a way out of her plight; that is, coping resources and support are not readily available to her. As we will discuss later in this chapter, innovative and socially responsible organizations are attuned to the needs of their employees who, like Isabel, are undergoing significant career and life transitions with related stress.

Employment Bias as a Source of Stress

While a wide range of organizational and personal characteristics can produce job stress, it is also possible that employees can experience stress if they face bias and discrimination within their organization. Although it is not clear whether women and people of color experience more stress than other employees, there is evidence to suggest that certain organizational and societal conditions can be particularly stressful for these groups.

Historically, research has found that women in male-dominated fields, especially professional women, are exposed to four unique stressors over and above others: employment discrimination, sex-role stereotyping, social isolation, and work–family conflicts.[30] In addition, many minority employees may be subject to race stereotyping, restricted advancement opportunities, and alienation. The potential link between discrimination and stress can lead to lower organizational commitment, reduced job satisfaction, and higher work tension among minority employees.

An employee exposed to bias, discrimination, and stereotyping becomes vulnerable to stress because of the lack of fit between talents/aspirations and organizational opportunities. A woman or person of color who occupies a token position is likely to feel social isolation or may be marginalized from the mainstream organization. And any "first"—for example, the first female or African American senior vice-president in an organization—is likely to experience intense pressure and stress. These stressors include not just being the "first" to achieve a particular position, but also having to deal with the potential biases of one's peers. Maintaining high levels of performance can create additional stress as women and minority group members are usually watched closely to see whether they are deserving of their new position.[31]

It is important to recognize that not all minorities face bias and isolation, and not all organizations stereotype and discriminate against minority group members. Rather, the research suggests the potential for these stressors exists, and indicates the need for individuals and organizations to understand and modify these stressors when they are present. Indeed, organizations must realize the high price paid for work-related stresses experienced by women and minority employees, which can negatively impact their well-being, and by implication, their productivity. Undoubtedly, there is a need for additional research that focuses on the individual and organizational consequences of the stress experienced by minorities and women. Employment bias will be discussed more thoroughly in Chapter 11.

Burnout

The legendary football coach Dick Vermeil began his career in the National Football League (NFL) in 1976 as the head coach of the Philadelphia Eagles. Coach Vermeil enjoyed much success in Philadelphia. He was named the NFL's Coach of the Year in 1980, and in 1981 he led the Eagles into Super Bowl XV. Many people were surprised when Coach Vermeil, at 46 years of age, suddenly retired after the 1982 season citing *burnout* as the reason for leaving the coaching ranks.[32] Coach Vermeil eventually returned to the NFL in 1997 to coach the St. Louis Rams, where he guided that team to a Super Bowl victory in 2000. Over the past several decades, expressions of burnout have been voiced by many other corporate, government, and sports figures, who felt that the pressures of their work lives were creating such a high level of stress that they could not continue in their jobs. Burnout is a complex phenomenon that may occur for a multitude of reasons, and may become manifest in a variety of ways.

Burnout is extreme psychological strain in response to chronic work stress.[33] Although initially it was thought that burnout was primarily associated with jobs with a high degree of human contact, such as those in the social services and health care sectors, it is now recognized that burnout is more widespread and can appear in many occupations and industries.[34] Burnout has been likened to job depression since emotional exhaustion is a symptom, and it also has been linked to Type A behavior as the irritability and impatience attributed to this personality type appear to heighten the effect of stressors that lead to burnout.[35]

Burnout has also been considered a problem related to motivation because it is associated with low engagement at work. In this sense, burned out individuals often become unable to perform their jobs, mostly because of the powerlessness they experience as a result of their burnout.[36] Interestingly, burnout also seems to cross over to one's spouse or to other employees at work. In this sense, burnout has a "contagion" effect whereby others at home and at work are negatively affected by the person suffering from burnout.[37]

In general, burnout consists of three interrelated components or psychological reactions.[38] First, continual contact with (and responsibility for) the problems of other people eventually produce a feeling of *emotional exhaustion*. Emotional exhaustion refers to feelings of being overextended and depleted of one's emotional and physical resources. To deal with the enervating features of their work, burned-out workers become cynical and callous toward others and begin to *depersonalize* relationships with the people they serve, treating them more like objects and less like people. Increasingly, the burned-out worker experiences a feeling of *low personal accomplishment* due to self-evaluations of incompetence resulting in a lack of achievement and productivity in work.[39]

Many of the causes of burnout can be traced to extensive job demands, that is, "those physical, psychological, social, or organizational aspects of the job that require sustained physical and/or psychological effort and are therefore associated with certain physiological and/or psychological costs"[40] such as high work pressure and emotionally demanding interactions with others at work. The availability of job resources, such as autonomy and performance feedback, can prevent extensive job demands from producing burnout,[41] whereas several personal characteristics (idealistic expectations, feelings of personal responsibility for failure, and a predisposition to stress) are likely to produce high levels of burnout.[42] For example, an idealistic technology consultant who wants to complete a project within the prescribed deadline, and who enthusiastically expects to help his or her clients receive adequate resources from their organization to implement a new information system, may feel frustrated when the resources are not forthcoming. The consultant may also begin to believe that his or her personal shortcomings are somehow responsible for the organization's unwillingness to provide these resources. Burnout would occur when this situation pushes the individual beyond his or her ability to cope with the stress being experienced.

The individual's predisposition to see the world in a positive or negative way is another personal characteristic that may induce burnout. The tendencies to perceive events with either positive or negative affectivity may influence one's perception of stress.[43] Individuals with negative predispositions have been found to experience high role stress, high emotional exhaustion and depersonalization, and to report low social support. They are also anxiety-prone, tend to feel insecure in their job, and perform poorly on tasks.[44] Furthermore, those who experience high levels of negative affect and burnout appear to perceive organizational support more as a demand, rather than as a resource, thereby diminishing any positive outcomes associated with the support that is offered.[45] Those with positive predispositions report a lower incidence of burnout, higher levels of personal achievement, greater levels of organizational commitment and job satisfaction, and lower absenteeism.[46] Thus, the manner in which one views life events may increase (or decrease) the chances for burnout.

Following are some commonly identified signs of burnout:[47]

- **Negative emotions.** While we all experience negative emotions, burned-out individuals are more anxiety-prone, experience negative emotions more often, ultimately resulting in emotional fatigue.
- **Interpersonal friction and withdrawal.** When emotionally drained, burned-out individuals have less empathy for those with whom they work and live. Communication with these individuals becomes strained, and burnout victims are apt to withdraw in order to cope. Burnout has a negative "spillover" effect in the work–family arena. Not only are workers who experience burnout viewed by their spouses more negatively than those who do not experience burnout, but, as we noted earlier, employees' burnout has a contagious effect that produces burnout in their spouse as well.[48]
- **Health suffers.** Burned-out individuals typically suffer severe fatigue resulting in energy erosion. As emotional reserves become depleted, so does physical resilience. Burnout victims often experience disturbed sleep patterns, metabolic/endocrine changes, gastrointestinal disturbances, muscle tension, colds, headaches, and backaches.
- **Declining performance.** As burnout progresses, individuals become bored and find it difficult to be enthusiastic and productive in their work. Job dissatisfaction is common. Burned-out individuals report low organizational commitment, high absenteeism and turnover, and a greater intention to leave the job. Studies have found that nurses experiencing higher levels of burnout were judged by their patients to provide a lower level of patient care.
- **Substance abuse.** To cope with stress, burnout victims may find themselves drinking more alcohol or coffee, using more drugs (prescription or otherwise), eating more (or less), and smoking more often.
- **Feelings of meaninglessness.** Burnout victims tend to become apathetic—thinking "so what" or "why bother?" Enthusiasm is replaced by cynicism. Burnout has been associated with the feeling of alienation, as well as powerlessness, isolation, and self-estrangement.
- **Increased violence in the workplace.** Workers who describe themselves as highly stressed or burned out experience a higher incidence of physical or emotional conflict than those who are less stressed.

Organizations concerned about the problem of burnout can attempt to change the environment that breeds this type of reaction to stress. Organizational managers need to realize that burnout is produced when employees experience high job demands, low control over the job, a lack of social support, and disagreements about values in the workplace.[49]

Employees in jobs with a high proclivity for burnout who are reassured of their worth and value and who receive supportive and considerate supervision show a lower incidence of burnout and increased organizational commitment. Indeed, while job demands are likely to increase the incidence of burnout, available resources can lower the negative effects. In light of these findings, organizations, especially those with jobs that have high susceptibility for burnout, should ensure that supervisors and others in leadership positions are able to recognize the signs of burnout among their employees; provide social support to their employees; offer organizational resources that help employees cope with burnout; and regularly acknowledge the value and worth of all employees. Organizational actions such as these can help prevent burnout from occurring and can help employees be more confident in their ability to accomplish their work objectives.[50]

One specific way organizations can help employees cope with burnout is through Employee Assistance Programs (EAPs), which can include counseling services focusing on the prevention and/or remediation of occupational stress experienced by employees or members of their families. These programs can have a positive effect on employee well-being and are perceived by employees as a desirable workplace resource.[51] Employers are also taking proactive steps towards creating less stress for their employees. Upwards of 70 percent of employers offer some type of wellness program, including on-site physicians and nurses, nutritious food options and free meals, nap rooms or chill zones, complimentary fitness centers, yoga and meditation classes, stress reduction programs, and a number of other related initiatives. Some companies even provide space for employees to bring pets to work, as well as space for table tennis or other activities that encourage employees to "burn off steam."[52] Obviously, these approaches are not mutually exclusive. Organizations should change their environment to reduce the likelihood of burnout while at the same time provide counseling and support to employees who experience burnout symptoms.

Technology-Induced Stress and the Potential for Workaholism

As was discussed in Chapter 3, the widespread use of smartphones, personal computers and tablets, and other communication technologies as common business tools has increased pressure on employees to be accessible to their employers 24 hours per day, seven days a week.[53] For many workers, the line between work hours and nonwork hours is blurred. Not only has technology allowed employees to be connected to their offices and work at all times, employers have become accustomed to having their employees available on a moment's notice. Both parties note that email and texting allow each one to "check in" on the other, regardless of physical location, or whether it is during "normal" office hours. This tethering to the workplace during traditional nonwork hours has the potential to produce significant amounts of stress.

Although electronic tethering is generally a response to organizations' expectations that employees be available on a regular basis, it may also be linked, in some cases, to employees' workaholism. People who show signs of workaholism have a compulsive need to work at the expense of everything else in their life. A *workaholic* is a person who is highly work-involved and is compelled to work because of inner pressures to do so.[54] It has been estimated that between 10 percent and nearly 25 percent of U.S. employees, particularly in professional roles, meet this definition.[55] Signs of workaholism are failure to use vacation time, refusal to stay home when ill, an inability to delegate work, a high level of perfectionism, and the tendency to seek control of group projects.[56] As might be expected, workaholism is linked both to high levels of work stress and to work–life imbalance, and it occurs equally among men and women.[57]

Although workaholism and burnout are two distinct concepts, just like with burnout, employees who experience workaholism need to learn coping techniques in order to create a balanced life and an equilibrium between work and other parts of life.[58] Organizations, too, need to be wary of creating a workplace climate that encourages or fosters individuals to overwork and become workaholics.[59]

Coping, Social Support, and Stress

No one can, or should, go through life free of stress. All people experience career transitions, some of them traumatic. Jobs may be pressure-packed or routine and repetitive. Family circumstances, midlife reappraisal, job loss, and threats to health and finances can all be stressful events. People who have survived life's trials are resourceful and have learned how to cope.

Coping behaviors enable individuals to reduce the harmful effects of stressful situations. Effective coping does not eliminate stress from our lives, but it hopefully helps to prevent the stress from producing severe emotional or physical strain. Three broad categories of coping responses have been identified.[60] First, one can use a *problem-focused* coping strategy by proactively attempting to change the situation that produces the stress, in other words, reduce or modify the actual stressors. Seeking clarification of job standards, reducing workload, requesting advice from others, taking on more varied assignments, or changing jobs are all examples of problem-focused coping responses designed to alter the environment or the person's role in it.

A second type of coping response attempts to change the meaning of the stressful environment without necessarily changing the stressors themselves. This approach is known as *cognitive restructuring* or "self-talk." People can make a situation less threatening by cognitively reappraising it, making a comparison (favorable, of course) with others' conditions, focusing on the positive features of the situation (i.e., seeing it as a challenge rather than as a hindrance), or changing work or life priorities to be more consistent with the situation in which they find themselves. With cognitive restructuring, the individual might need to accept burdensome parts of the job, but can mentally reorder the priority that the job holds in that person's total life. A plateaued manager who places a greater emphasis on community service rather than on further vertical mobility illustrates a cognitive restructuring technique in response to stress.

A third form of coping attempts to *manage the strain symptoms* themselves. Relaxation techniques such as meditation or biofeedback, deep breathing exercises, yoga, physical exercise, and recreation can effectively reduce the physical and emotional consequences of stress. Proper time management, keeping a journal, and using scheduling software applications can help the individual to stay ahead of daily pressures. Proper nutrition and repetitive prayer have been found to calm both mind and body.[61]

Employees can also manage their stress by psychologically detaching from work during nonwork hours. Psychological detachment from work involves refraining not only from job-related activities when not at work but also from thinking about job-related matters.[62] This mental disengagement or "switching off"[63] from work during nonwork hours enables individuals to replenish the resources that had been depleted during the work day, in effect, recharging their batteries. Psychological detachment from work during the evening or weekend enables individuals to recover from a stressful work situation, promotes heightened psychological well-being, and allows individuals to return to work in a more positive emotional state and more productive on the job.[64]

Table 10.3 Illustrations of Three Types of Coping Behaviors Used in Reaction to a Stressful Work Environment

Problem-Focused	*Cognitive Restructuring*
Seek clarification of job duties	Accept burdensome parts of job
Seek clarification of career prospects	Accept over-bearing boss
Seek feedback on job performance	Reappraise the work situation as a challenge
Seek more flexible work schedule	Mentally place more emphasis on nonwork pursuits and activities
Seek different organization or career field	Understand and accept stressful interactions with coworkers
Attempt to resolve conflicts with supervisor, peers, and/or subordinates	Rationalize unfair workplace situations (others getting promotions, variations in rewards)
Attempt to upgrade job skills through education and/or experience	
Managing the Strain Symptoms	
Undertake regular physical activity and exercise	
Pursue relaxation techniques, prayer, healthier lifestyle	
Do yoga and meditation techniques	
Practice time management and maintain a schedule	
Pursue a counselling program	
Attend stress management workshop	
Psychologically detach from work during after-work hours	

Table 10.3 presents illustrations of all three types of coping strategies.

It is unlikely that a specific type of coping response is universally effective in all situations. Rather, the usefulness of a coping strategy is contingent on many factors: the severity of the stress; the psychological and social resources of the individual; and the circumstances of the stressful situation. Therefore, a person should take a contingency approach to coping wherein the coping strategy selected meets the needs of the situation. This requires individuals to possess not only a repertoire of coping skills for different situations, but also positive attitudes toward themselves to help them manage stress. Indeed, the field of positive psychology suggests that there are human strengths that can act as buffers against occupational stress. These buffers include such attributes as courage, optimism, interpersonal skills, faith, hope, honesty, perseverance, resilience, and perspective. Employees who use positive thinking approaches report better psychological well-being and job performance. It appears that positive thinking and emotions assist individuals by enhancing their optimism and resiliency and allowing a more positive reaction to daily stress.[65] An appropriate combination of problem-solving, cognitive reappraisal, positive emotions, and physical exercise/relaxation may be particularly useful in reducing the negative effects of stress.

Edgar Schein developed a four-step method that is consistent with this contingency approach to coping.[66] Step 1 involves diagnosing the situation and correctly identifying the real source of the problem. In this step, one needs to understand whether the stress comes from work, family, personal concerns, or some combination of these sources. Step 2 involves self-assessment. It is essential to take (and make) the time to reflect on feelings and motives and to become familiar with "blind spots" or other defenses that shield people from an insightful understanding of themselves.

In Step 3, a coping response is selected. By talking with colleagues, family members, friends, neighbors, and community resources about problems and stresses and by establishing supportive relationships with others, one can choose an appropriate coping response. It is important to identify either an external coping resource (e.g., a confidant) or internal resource (e.g., personal characteristic such as hardiness) so that the appropriate coping response is selected. Coping resources aid the person in choosing a healthy response.[67] The chosen response may involve changing an aspect of the stressful environment, shifting one's priorities and the meaning of the environment, or managing the strain symptoms themselves. Finally, Step 4 involves understanding the effect (if any) of the coping response and making adjustments when necessary. Consider the following example:

Gene was scared. Over the past three months his health and physical well-being had gotten progressively worse. It started with recurring headaches and a nagging tightness in his back and shoulders. Over time, he experienced stomach distress, a shortness of breath, and chest pains. On top of it all, Gene had trouble sleeping, spending many nights just staring at the ceiling. The culmination of Gene's physical problems occurred one night while he was driving home from work, when he suddenly experienced an episode of tachycardia (a rapid heartbeat). He pulled off to the side of the road thinking his life was about to end. Eventually his heartbeat returned to normal, but the incident left him deeply concerned.

Gene called in sick the next day and saw his physician. He also began contemplating why these health problems were occurring. He concluded that his problems were the outcome of the stress he was experiencing in his life. He was recently transferred to another division of his company that, while not causing him to move his family, did double his commuting time. His commute now took one and a half hours each way. In addition to the demands of the new job, Gene has had to deal with turmoil at home. His 16-year-old son was having problems in school—skipping classes and being disruptive when he did attend. The principal of the school had threatened suspension unless his son's behavior changed. Gene was afraid his son's current difficulties might eventually lead to something far more serious.

Gene began thinking about what was causing him distress and what was really important in his life. His job allowed him and his family to live comfortably and gave them financial security, but the commuting and work demands left little time for leisure and family activities. Gene had considered speaking with his boss about the possibility of telecommuting on a regular basis, but he knew that his company had a fairly strict policy against that practice. In short, Gene concluded that the excessive time he gave to his job and its associated travel had a negative effect on his and his family's well-being. In talking to his wife about his thoughts, she confirmed what he already knew—his job was causing physical and emotional harm. His introspection and the conclusions he reached left Gene feeling a bit more at ease.

Gene began discussing his options with his wife. They agreed that Gene's work was important to him, but his family's well-being was essential. They considered that a new job, especially one closer to home, might give Gene the opportunity to spend more time with his family. He also knew that he needed to pay more attention to his diet and to begin an exercise program. With the support of his family, Gene started looking for a new job and he began playing tennis on a regular basis. Gene resolved that until he found a new position he would devote as much time as he could to his son. By being there to listen to what his son had to say, Gene hoped to help his son through the emotional turmoil of being a teenager.

Overall, Gene recognized that he likely would be sacrificing financial rewards by taking a new job, but the anticipated reduction in stress and increased time for family and leisure activities would be well worth it.

This example highlights the effective use of the contingency approach to coping with stress. The physical manifestations of Gene's stress forced him to take time to evaluate his situation. This set the stage for Gene to go through a period of self-assessment, examining his values and goals. His self-assessment allowed him to change the meaning of various aspects of his life; work was important, but his well-being and that of his family were more important. He then selected coping responses, such as finding a new work position, improving his diet and getting more exercise, and vowing to allow more time for his family. Finally, Gene sought to understand the effect of his intended actions, the potential trade-off between financial rewards and a lower level of stress.

Gene's story also emphasizes the importance of other people as sources of information and support. Social support has long been recognized as an invaluable aid to individuals undergoing conflict and stress, and the utilization of support is considered a form of problem-focused coping. Support from others can help reduce the stressfulness of the environment as well as protect individuals from the harmful effects of the stress that they do experience.[68]

Support to help deal with stress can come from many sources, both informal (family, friends, co-workers) and formal (self-help groups, mental health or other professionals, and childcare or other service providers). Researchers often distinguish four classes of supportive behaviors: emotional, instrumental, informational, and appraisal.[69] Definitions and illustrations of these four types of support are provided in Table 10.4.

Table 10.4 Definitions and Illustrations of Four Types of Social Support

Type of Support	*Meaning*	*Illustrations*
Emotional	Empathy, caring, trust, love	Boss praises your effective performance.
Instrumental	Provision of tangible aid and services that assist a person in need	Subordinate's improving performance relieves you of pressure. Boss provides you with a flexible work schedule
Informational	Advice or suggestions to be used by person to cope with problems	Co-worker gives you advice on how to discipline a subordinate.
Appraisal	Information that provides feedback for self-evaluation	Boss gives you constructive feedback on your most recent assignment. Close friend gives you her opinion of your interpersonal style.

Types and meanings of social support adapted from House, J. S. (1981). *Work stress and social support.* Reading, MA: Addison-Wesley; Heaney, C. A. & Israel, B. A. (2008). Social networks and social support. In Glanz, K., Rimer, B. K. & Viswanath, K. (Eds.), *Health behavior & health education, 4th Edition*, pp. 189–210. San Francisco: Jossey-Bass.

No magic formula exists to identify the sources and types of social support that are most useful in a specific situation. Therefore, it is important for individuals seeking support to understand their needs, determine the source of the stress, and identify the available resources. Not surprisingly, the responsiveness of the support to the recipient's needs is critical; the more responsive the support the more likely it leads to positive outcomes.[70] In addition, individuals should recognize that receiving support from multiple sources (e.g., supervisor and spouse) can be especially powerful in promoting well-being.[71] It is also essential to understand that supportive relationships are not a one-way street. We must be willing to give social support to receive it. Indeed, the amount of social support received is strongly related to the amount of social support given, especially from spouses, family, or friends.[72]

Organizational Actions

Organizations have developed a variety of programs to help employees reduce their level of stress. Using the distinction among the types of coping responses, organizations can either alter the stressful environment, work with employees to change their interpretation of the environment, or help them manage their strain symptoms.

Illustrations of these approaches are shown in Table 10.5. Any particular program is likely to incorporate some combination of the coping strategies. For example, a program designed to build supportive work groups may simultaneously try to change the stressful environment (by fostering constructive communication between individuals) as well as the meaning of the environment (such as understanding when competition is healthy and when cooperation is more appropriate).

Before any program is initiated, organizations must properly diagnose the extent and root causes of employee stress. Such diagnoses may be organization-wide or may be applied to select groups of employees based on level (e.g., senior executives), job category (e.g., air traffic controllers), location (e.g., employees at a nuclear power plant), or other relevant criteria. Organizational diagnoses can focus on the assessment of organizational stressors (e.g., workload), the degree of employee strain (e.g., physical health, burnout), and the employee characteristics that might modify or lessen the strain symptoms (e.g.,

Table 10.5 Illustrations of Organizational Actions to Reduce Employee Stress

Reducing Stressors	*Changing the Meaning of Stressful Situations*
Eliminate racial/gender stereotypes, biases, and discrimination	Offer counseling services to employees
Redesign jobs to be more in line with employees' capabilities and interests	Run programs to ameliorate Type A behavior, burnout
Clarify employee expectations through goalsetting program	Run programs on time management
Provide constructive performance feedback	Run social support groups for employees
Build supportive work groups	*Managing Strain Symptoms*
Train supervisors in interpersonal skills	Provide relaxation programs (e.g., meditation)
Eliminate noxious elements of physical working conditions	Provide facilities for physical exercise
Help employees with problem-solving/coping skills	Provide counseling and medical treatment
Develop flexible work schedules	Provide comprehensive "wellness" programs
Develop programs for transitioned (e.g., relocated) employees	

coping strategies). Organizations also need to be aware that techniques that work for one employee may not work for all employees.[73]

In the fast-paced, global economy of the 21st century, it is highly likely that the level of stress experienced by today's workers will continue to rise. The constant pressures of modern work life and technological engagement with work in combination with increasing responsibilities at home or in the community portend escalating levels of stress. Therefore, as shown in the following example, organizationally sponsored programs that help employees cope with stress and burnout can be especially beneficial:

IBM believes that part of its corporate social responsibility is the promotion of employee well-being; in fact, it first developed a formal policy on employee well-being more than a half-century ago, back in 1967. The current version of its Well-Being Management System (WBMS) is a global program that links the company's occupational medicine, industrial hygiene, safety, wellness, and health initiatives to its strategic mission of caring about the well-being of IBM employees around the world. Examples of country-specific IBM wellness programs include: Seven Habits of Highly Healthy People in Latin America; Quit Smoking for Life campaign in Japan; Physical Activity Flex Credit program rewards Canadian employees through a financial incentive for undertaking regular physical activity; and in the United States, the Children's Health Rebate is an action-oriented program designed to help parents support children in maintaining a healthy weight. IBM has also made a significant investment in helping their employees maintain work–life balance. In 2001, the company created the Global Work/Life Fund with a five-year, $50 million commitment. This fund addressed employee work–life issues on a global basis. The fund, which is now active in 42 countries, has an ongoing focus on increasing the supply and improving the quality of dependent care in communities where IBM employees work and live. IBM is committed to creating a supportive, flexible work environment that gives employees more control over their work as a means to achieve greater work–life balance.[74]

Summary

Stress is aroused when an individual faces an opportunity, a constraint, or a demand. A situation is likely to be most stressful when the outcome is uncertain but is important to the individual. Stress can be produced by a number of conditions in the work environment—organizational characteristics, job demands, low job control, the quality of interpersonal relationships, working conditions, and career concerns—as well as pressures arising outside of work. Because individuals have different needs, competencies, and perspectives, a situation that is stressful to one person may not be stressful to another. A high level of stress can manifest itself in physiological, emotional, and behavioral changes. It can ultimately lead to decreases in job satisfaction, involvement, and performance, and increases in absenteeism and turnover.

This chapter examined three particular sources of stress. The Type A behavior pattern, characterized by a hard-driving competitiveness and sense of time urgency, can be physically and emotionally destructive. In addition, career transitions (such as promotions, relocations, or terminations) can be stressful under certain conditions: when they require extensive, unwanted adjustments, when they are accompanied by changes in other parts of a person's life, when they are unexpected and forced on an individual, and when the individual's coping and social support mechanisms are absent or ineffective. It was also suggested that stress is likely to be experienced by women and minority group members who are exposed to bias and discrimination in their work environment.

Also examined was the concept of burnout, a stress reaction in which an individual in a highly charged work setting experiences emotional exhaustion, depersonalizes relationships with others, and begins to hold lower feelings of personal accomplishment. Burnout is most likely to be experienced by employees who initially held idealistic expectations about their job, who ultimately come to believe they are personally responsible for organizational failures, and who have a predisposition for stress. Workaholics were described as individuals who are highly work-involved, experience low work enjoyment, and are compelled to work because of inner pressures, and we noted that workaholism may detract from feelings of work–life balance.

People who survive stressful conditions have likely learned effective coping skills and/or have utilized supportive relationships with others. Because no single coping behavior is likely to be effective in all situations, individuals must learn to assess the situation and select appropriate responses. These coping responses may be directed toward changing the stressful environment, reappraising the environment, or reducing the resultant strain symptoms through such activities as relaxation and physical exercise. In a similar manner, organizations can help alleviate employee stress through a series of programs designed to change the stressful conditions, help employees adjust to the conditions, and/or reduce the negative strain symptoms.

Career Management *for Life*: Work–Life Implications from Chapter 10

- Stressors can arise from outside of work, including the demands of the multiple roles we hold and concerns over the quantity and quality of the time spent with family and in other interpersonal relationships outside of work.
- Career transitions that are accompanied by a substantial change in another part of life (e.g., marriage, divorce, birth of a child, serious illness in the family) are likely to be especially stressful.
- Employee burnout can cross over into the home, producing burnout and other negative reactions in spouses.
- Frequent electronic connection to work during traditional nonwork hours through smartphones, computers, and tablets can reduce the time and energy an employee has for other parts of life.
- Support provided by family members can help employees reduce or manage job-induced stress.

Assignment

Think about the work stress and nonwork stress you may be experiencing. What symptoms have you encountered? How successfully have you coped with the stressors in the work and nonwork domains?

Discussion Questions

1. Take a look at the descriptions of the four types of social support shown in Table 10.4. Provide examples of emotional, instrumental, informational, and appraisal support that you have received from others and that you have offered to others.
2. What levels of stress can you tolerate? What levels of stress are harmful to you (distress) and what levels of stress are beneficial (eustress)?
3. Investigate your company (or a company in which you are interested in working) to determine what types of wellness management programs it offers. Are companies obliged to offer such programs? Would you work for one that did not; why or why not?

Chapter 10 Case: Saachi the Stressed Saleswoman

Saachi, 29 years of age, has been selling telecommunications equipment to manufacturers since she graduated from college nearly eight years ago. She is obviously good at her job. Not only has she consistently met or exceeded her sales quota, but her customers report that she is knowledgeable about her products and continually puts in long hours keeping tabs on their needs and providing valuable consulting to them. Saachi's employer, GA Industries (fictitious name), recognizes her value to the organization and has rewarded her handsomely over the years.

The last few months have been rough on Saachi. She seems to be tired all the time. She has had trouble shaking a month-long cold, and, for the first time she can remember, she canceled an appointment with a customer because she just could not get herself out of her apartment that morning.

Saachi has also been short-tempered of late. Although it has not affected her sales volume yet, she has had to catch herself a few times from snapping at some thick-headed customers. How many times does she have to explain the same things to these people? But that cannot be the entire problem.

She has found herself getting into a lot of petty arguments with Anik, her fiancé. She just seems to be preoccupied with her job wherever she is. The plans for Saachi and Anik's wedding have taken a backseat to her work, and their wedding date has been put off a couple of times, much to Anik's dismay. On top of this dilemma, Saachi and Anik have had many discussions about where they will live, and if and when they will have children. They have not been able to come to agreement on these issues.

"Why am I so irritable?" Saachi keeps asking herself. She is doing well and still finds her job interesting and challenging. It is true that her boss, Maria, GA's industrial sales manager, keeps poking her nose into Saachi's business and giving her unneeded advice about how to handle customers. Maria wants her to put more pressure on several customers to purchase certain pieces of equipment they really do not need. Her customers would not tolerate a hard sell like that, but Saachi will avoid that issue as long as she can. She hardly sees Maria nowadays, maybe once every other week, and she is usually too busy to talk to her. Sometimes, Saachi wonders what Maria really thinks of her. Fortunately, her customers tell her how good she is at her job.

Saachi admits that she has been a little peeved at the company for expanding her territory six months ago. Not that she is uninterested in new business, but she cannot do a thorough job with such a large territory. And she's been finding herself out of town four, sometimes five, days a week. The larger territory has left Saachi drowning in paperwork, and she is beginning to wonder how she can ever maintain a relationship with her fiancé when they hardly ever see each other anymore. And then there are the wedding plans and pressures...

But the job is so challenging. And GA is coming out with a new product line next week. The whole sales force has been attending weekend meetings for about four weeks to learn more about these new products. It is exciting to introduce a new product on the cutting edge. Saachi just wishes she understood the new product line better. She has not been able to focus at the training classes, has not really understood the lectures at the meetings, and has been unable to make much sense out of the manuals. She probably should have taken a few more technical courses back in college. But that's water under the bridge.

Saachi would like to talk to someone about her feelings. But who? Talking to her boss Maria is out of the question. She would think Saachi was being ungrateful, and Maria is so self-focused she would not be able to relate to her. Saachi is convinced that her family and her fiancé just wouldn't understand the situation. The other salespeople, she guesses, would be pretty uncaring. But she does need to talk to someone. And soon!

Case Analysis Questions

1. What evidence is there that Saachi is experiencing job stress? What are the symptoms?
2. What conditions are producing Saachi's stress?
3. How is Saachi's job stress affecting her family and personal life? And are her family and personal life affecting her work?
4. If you were Saachi, what would you do? Identify as many alternative plans of action as possible and indicate the advantages and disadvantages of each. Which plan(s) of action would you choose? Why?
5. What types of social support (as shown in Table 10.4) would Saachi find most helpful: appraisal, instrumental, emotional, or informational? From whom should she seek such support? Why?
6. If you were the president of GA Industries and just heard Saachi's story, what, if anything, would you do? Why?

Notes

1 Ahmad, A. & Afgan, S. (2016). The relationship of job stress and turnover intention in commercial banks of Pakistan by assessing the mediating role of burnout. *Journal of Business Strategies*, *10*, 1–23; Azagba, S. & Sharaf, M. F. (2011). The effect of job stress on smoking and alcohol consumption. *Health Economics Review*, *1*, 1–14; Ganster, D. C., Fox, M. L. & Dwyer, D. J. (2001). Explaining employees' health care costs: A prospective examination of stressful

job demands, personal control, and physiological reactivity. *Journal of Applied Psychology*, *86*, 954–964; Hsieh, Y. & Wang, M. (2012). The moderating role of personality in HRM—from the influence of job stress on job burnout perspective. *International Management Review*, *8*, 5–18, 85; Leung, M., Chan, Y. S. I. & Dongyu, C. (2011). Structural linear relationships between job stress, burnout, physiological stress, and performance of construction project managers. *Engineering, Construction and Architectural Management*, *18*, 312–328; Perrewe, P. L. & Ganster, D. C. (Eds.) (2001). *Research in occupational stress and well being, exploring theoretical mechanisms and perspectives*, Volume 1. New York: JAI Press; Spector, P. E. (2006). Stress at work. In Greenhaus, J. H. & Callanan, G. A. (Eds.), *Encyclopedia of career development* (pp. 771–778). Thousand Oaks, CA: Sage; Reilly, E., Dhingra, K. & Boduszek, D. (2014). Teachers' self-efficacy beliefs, self-esteem, and job stress as determinants of job satisfaction. *The International Journal of Educational Management*, *28*, 365–378; ur Rehman, M., Irum, R., Tahir, N., Ijaz, Z., Noor, U. & Salma, U. (2012). The impact of job stress on employee job satisfaction: A study on private colleges of Pakistan. *Journal of Business Studies Quarterly*, *3*, 50–56; Wang, Y., Zheng, L., Hu, T. & Zheng, Q. (2014). Stress, burnout, and job satisfaction: Case of police force in China. *Public Personnel Management*, *43*, 325–339.

2 Anonymous. (2017, March 14). Workplace stress. Retrieved from www.stress.org/workplace-stress; Ahmad & Afgan, (2016); Enshassi, A., El-Rayyes, Y. & Alkilani, S. (2015). Job stress, job burnout and safety performance in the Palestinian construction industry. *Journal of Financial Management of Property and Construction*, *20*, 170–187; Goswami, T. G. (2015). Job stress and its effect on employee performance in banking sector. *Indian Journal of Commerce and Management Studies*, *6*, 51–56; Hsieh & Wang (2012); Ruzungunde, V. S., Murugan, C. & Hlatywayo, C. K. (2016). The influence of job stress on the components of organisational commitment of health care personnel in the Eastern Cape Province South Africa. *The International Business & Economics Research Journal (Online)*, *15*, 219–225; Pazzanese, C. (2016, July 12). The high price of workplace stress. Retrieved from http://news.harvard.edu/gazette/story/2016/07/the-high-price-of-workplace-stress; Sanjeev, M. A. & Rathore, S. (2014). Exploring the relationship between job stress and organizational commitment: A study of the Indian IT sector. *Management Research and Practice*, *6*, 40–56.

3 Smith, J. (2016, June 6). Here's why workplace stress is costing employers $300 billion a year. Retrieved from www.businessinsider.com/how-stress-at-work-is-costing-employers-300-billion-a-year-2016-6; and www.cms.gov/research-statistics-data-and-systems/statistics-trends-and-reports/nationalhealthexpenddata/nationalhealthaccountshistorical.html.

4 Greenhaus, J. H., Allen, T. D. & Spector, P. E. (2006). Health consequences of work–family conflict: The dark side of the work–family interface. In Perrewe, P. L. & Ganster, D. C. (Eds.), *Research in occupational stress and well-being*, Volume 5 (pp. 61–98). Amsterdam: JAI Press/Elsevier; Greenhaus, J. H. & Powell, G. N. (2017). *Making work and family work: From hard choices to smart choices*. New York: Routledge; Lambert, E. G., Pasupuleti, S., Cluse-Tolar, T., Jennings, M. & Baker, D. (2006). The impact of work–family conflict on social work and human service worker job satisfaction and organizational commitment: An exploratory study. *Administration in Social Work*, *30*, 55–74; Spector (2006); Warr, P. (2007). *Work, happiness and unhappiness*. Mahwah, NJ: Lawrence Erlbaum Associates.

5 Ahmad & Afgan (2016); Lu, L., Cooper, C. L., Kao, S. & Zhou, Y. (2003). Work stress, control beliefs and well-being in Greater China: An exploration of sub-cultural differences between the PRC and Taiwan. *Journal of Managerial Psychology*, *18*, 479–510; Spector (2006); Warr (2007).

6 Kahn, R. L. & Byosiere, P. (1992). Stress in organizations. In Dunnette, M. D. & Hough, L. M. (Eds.) *Handbook of industrial and organizational psychology*, Volume 3 (pp. 571–650). Palo Alto, CA: Consulting Psychologists Press.

7 Christie, A. & Barling, J. (2006). Careers and health. In Greenhaus, J. H. & Callanan, G. A. (Eds.), *Encyclopedia of career development* (pp. 158–162). Thousand Oaks, CA: Sage.

8 Eulberg, J. R., Weekley, J. A. & Bhagat, R. S. (1988). Models of stress in organizational research: A metatheoretical perspective. *Human Relations*, *41*, 331–350; Le Fevre, M., Matheny, J. & Kolt, G. S. (2003). Eustress, distress, and interpretation in occupational stress. *Journal of Managerial Psychology*, *18*, 726–744; Lu et al. (2003); van Vegchel, N., de Jonge, J. & Landsbergis, P. A. (2005). Occupational stress in (inter)action: The interplay between job demands and job resources. *Journal of Organizational Behavior*, *26*, 535–560.

9 LePine, J. A., Podsakoff, N. P. & LePine, M. A. (2005). A meta-analytic test of the challenge stressor-hindrance stressor framework: An explanation for inconsistent relationships among stressors and performance. *Academy of Management Journal*, *48*, 764–775. Quotation is on p. 764.

10 Greenhaus, J. H., Bedeian, A. G. & Mossholder, K. W. (1987). Work experiences, job performance, and feelings of personal and family wellbeing. *Journal of Vocational Behavior*, *31*, 200–215; Lu et al. (2003); Schaubroeck, J. & Ganster, D. C. (1993). Chronic demands and responsivity to challenge. *Journal of Applied Psychology*, *78*, 73–85; Xie, J. L. & Johns, G. (1995). Job scope and stress: Can job scope be too high? *Academy of Management Journal*, *38*, 1288–1309.

11 Lim, S. & Tai, K. (2014). Family incivility and job performance: A moderated mediation model of psychological distress and core self-evaluation. *Journal of Applied Psychology*, *99*, 351–359.

12 LePine et al. (2005); Podsakoff, N. P., LePine, J. A. & LePine, M. A. (2007). Differential challenge stressor–hindrance stressor relationships with job attitudes, turnover intentions, turnover, and withdrawal behavior: A meta-analysis. *Journal of Applied Psychology*, *92*, 438–454.

13 Bakker, A. B., van der Zee, K. I., Lewig, K. A. & Dollard, M. F. (2006). The relationship between the Big Five personality factors and burnout: A study among volunteer counselors. *Journal of Social Psychology*, *146*, 31–50; Heppner, P. P., Cook, S. W., Wright, D. M. & Johnson, W. C., Jr. (1995). Progress in resolving problems: A problem-focused style of coping. *Journal of Counseling Psychology*, *42*, 279–293; Van Heck, G. L. (1997). Personality and physical health: Toward an ecological approach to health-related personality research. *European Journal of Personality Research*, *11*, 415–443.

14 Cheung, T. & Yip, P. S. F. (2015). Depression, anxiety and symptoms of stress among Hong Kong nurses: A cross-sectional study. *International Journal of Environmental Research and Public Health*, *12*, 11072–11100; Liu, C., Spector, P. E. & Shi, L. (2007). Cross-national job stress: A quantitative and qualitative study. *Journal of Organizational Behavior*, *28*, 209–221; Lu, L. (1999). Work motivation, job stress and employees' well-being. *Journal of Applied Management Studies*, *8*, 61–72.

15 Bakker et al. (2006); Burke, M. J., Brief, A. P. & George, J. M. (1993). The role of negative affectivity in understanding relationships between self-reports of stressors and strains: A comment on the applied psychological literature. *Journal of Applied Psychology*, *78*, 402–412; Fortj-Cozens, K. (1992). Why me? A case study of the process of perceived occupational stress. *Human Relations*, *45*, 131–141; Jamal, M. (1990). Relationship of job stress and Type-A behavior to employees' job satisfaction, organizational commitment, psychosomatic health problems, and turnover motivation. *Human Relations*, *43*, 727–738.

16 Grant, S. & Langan-Fox, J. (2007). Personality and the occupational stressor–strain relationship: The role of the Big Five. *Journal of Occupational Health Psychology*, *12*, 20–33; Nelson, D. L. & Sutton, C. (1990). Chronic work stress and coping: A longitudinal study and suggested new directions. *Academy of Management Journal*, *33*, 859–869; Scott, C. (2005). Helping employees become wellness CEOs. *Workspan*, *48*, 76–83.

17 Spector (2006).

18 Bishop, G. D., Enkelmann, H. C. & Tong, E. M. W. (2003). Job demands, decisional control, and cardiovascular responses. *Journal of Occupational Health Psychology*, *8*, 146–156; Cohen, S., Frank, E., Doyle, W. J., Skoner, D. P., Rabin, B. S. & Gwaltney, J. M. (1998). Types of stressors increase susceptibility to the common cold in healthy adults. *Health Psychology*, *17*, 214–223; Ganster et al. (2001); Grunberg, L., Moore, S. & Anderson-Connolly, R. (1999). Work stress and self-reported alcohol use: The moderating role of escapist reasons for drinking. *Journal of Occupational Health Psychology*, *4*, 29–36; Habibi, E., Poorabdian, S. & Shakerian, M. (2015). Job strain (demands and control model) as a predictor of cardiovascular risk factors among petrochemical personnel. *Journal of Education and Health Promotion*, *4*, 1–7; Heikkilä, K., Fransson, E. I., Nyberg, S. T., Zins, M., Westerlund, H., Westerholm, P. & Kivimäki, M. (2013). Job strain and health-related lifestyle: Findings from an individual-participant meta-analysis of 118,000 working adults. *American Journal of Public Health*, *103*, 2090–2097; Kamarck, T. W., Muldoon, M. F. & Shiffman, S. S. (2007). Experiences of demand and control during daily life are predictors of carotid atherosclerotic progression among healthy men. *Health Psychology*, *26*, 324–332; Landsbergis, P. A., Dobson, M., Koutsouras, G. & Schnall, P. (2013). Job strain and ambulatory blood pressure: A meta-analysis and systematic review. *American Journal of Public Health*, *103*, E61–E71; Luciana, F. P., Luna, C. K., Rotenberg, L., Silva-Costa, A., Toivanen, S., Araújo, T. & Rosane, H. G. (2015). Job strain and self-reported insomnia symptoms among nurses: What about the influence of emotional demands and social support? *BioMed Research International*, 1–9; O'Connor, D. B., Jones, F. & Conner, M. (2008). Effects of daily hassles and eating style on eating behavior. *Health Psychology*, *27*, S20–S31; Raynor, D. A., Pogue-Geile, M. F., Kamarck, T. W., McCaffery, J. M. & Manuck, S. B. (2002). Covariation of psychosocial

characteristics associated with cardiovascular disease: Genetic and environmental influences. *Psychosomatic Medicine*, *64*, 191–203; Rystedt, L. W., Cropley, M., Devereux, J. J. & Michalianou, G. (2008). The relationship between long-term job strain and morning and evening saliva cortisol secretion among white-collar workers. *Journal of Occupational Health Psychology*, *13*, 105–113; Schaubroeck, J., Ganster, D. C. & Kemmerer, B. E. (1994). Job complexity, "Type A" behavior, and cardiovascular disorder: A prospective study. *Academy of Management Journal*, *37*, 426–439.

19 Ahmad & Afgan (2016); Enshassi et al. (2015); Bakker et al. (2006); Baruch-Feldman, C., Brondolo, E. & Ben-Dayan, D. (2002). Sources of social support and burnout, job satisfaction, and productivity. *Journal of Occupational Health Psychology*, *7*, 84–93; Halbesleben, J. R. B. (2006). Sources of social support and burnout: A meta-analytic test of the conservation of resources model. *Journal of Applied Psychology*, *91*, 1134–1145; Hsieh & Wang (2012); Lu (1999).

20 Driscoll, R. J., Worthington, K. A. & Hurrell, J. J., Jr. (1995). Workplace assault: An emerging job stressor. *Consulting Psychology Journal: Practice and Research*, *47*, 205–211; Nasurdin, A. M., Ahmad, N. H. & Razalli, A. A. (2014). Politics, justice, stress, and deviant behaviour in organizations: An empirical analysis. *International Journal of Business and Society*, *15*, 235–254; Schat, A. C. H. & Kelloway, E. K. (2003). Reducing the adverse consequences of workplace aggression and violence: The buffering effects of organizational support. *Journal of Occupational Health Psychology*, *8*, 110–122.

21 Le Fevre, M. L., Kolt, G. S. & Matheny, J. (2006). Eustress, distress and their interpretation in primary and secondary occupational stress management interventions: Which way first? *Journal of Managerial Psychology*, *21*, 547–565; Le Fevre, M., Matheny, J. & Kolt, G. S. (2003). Eustress, distress, and interpretation in occupational stress. *Journal of Managerial Psychology*, *18*, 726–744; Warr (2007).

22 Birks, Y. & Roger, D. (2000). Identifying components of Type-A behavior: "Toxic" and "non-toxic" achieving. *Personality and Individual Differences*, *28*, 1093–1105; Jamal, M. & Baba, V. V. (2001). Type-A behavior, job performance and well-being in college teachers. *International Journal of Stress Management*, *8*, 231–240.

23 McGregor, L., Eveleigh, M. & Syler, J. C. (1991). Self-perception of personality characteristics and the Type A behavior pattern. *Bulletin of the Psychonomic Society*, *29*, 320–322; Ryan, R. M. & Brown, K. W. (2006). What is optimal self-esteem? The cultivation and consequences of contingent vs. true self-esteem as viewed from the self-determination theory perspective. In Kernis, M. H. (Ed.), *Self-esteem issues and answers: A sourcebook of current perspectives* (pp. 125–131). New York: Psychology Press.

24 De la Fuente, J. & Cardelle-Elawar, M. (2009). Research on action–emotion style and study habits: Effects of individual differences on learning and academic performance of undergraduate students. *Learning and Individual Differences*, *19*, 567–576; Jamal, M. & Baba, V. V. (2003). Type A behavior, components, and outcomes: A study of Canadian employees. *International Journal of Stress Management*, *10*, 39–50; Ryan & Brown (2006).

25 Chida, Y. & Hamer, M. (2009). Chronic psychosocial factors and acute physiological responses to laboratory-induced stress in healthy populations: A quantitative review of 30 years of investigations: Correction to Chida and Hamer (2008). *Psychological Bulletin*, *135*, 793; Ganster, D. C., Schaubroeck, J., Sime, W. E. & Mayes, B. T. (1991). The nomological validity of the Type A personality among employed adults. *Journal of Applied Psychology*, *76*, 143–168; Jamal & Baba (2003); Kent, L. K. & Shapiro, P. A. (2009). Depression and related psychological factors in heart disease. *Harvard Review of Psychiatry*, *17*, 377–388; Mohan, J. & Singh, S. (2016). A study of Type A behavior in relation to hostility, stress and optimism among rural and urban male coronary heart disease patients. *Journal of Psychosocial Research*, *11*, 447–458.

26 Cooper, C. L. (2006). The challenges of managing the changing nature of workplace stress. *Journal of Public Mental Health*, *5*(4), 6–9; Fava, G. A., Cosci, F. & Sonino, N. (2016). Current psychosomatic practice. *Psychotherapy and Psychosomatics*, *86*(1), 13–30; Quick, J. C. & Quick, J. D. (1997). *Preventive stress management in organizations*. Washington, D.C.: American Psychological Association.

27 Ginsberg, J. P., Pietrabissa, G., Manzoni, G. M. & Castelnuovo, G. (2015). Treating the mind to improve the heart: The summon to cardiac psychology. *Frontiers in Psychology*, *6*, 1101–1104.

28 Cooper (2006); Mohan & Singh (2016); Warr (2007).

29 Frank, M. L. (2000). What's so stressful about job relocation? British researchers give some answers. *Academy of Management Executive*, *14*, 122–123; Godshalk, V. M. (2006). Career

plateau. In Greenhaus, J. H. & Callanan, G. A. (Eds.), *Encyclopedia of career development* (pp. 133–138). Thousand Oaks, CA: Sage; Godshalk, V. M. & Fender, C. M. (2015). External and internal reasons for career plateauing: Relationships with work outcomes. *Group & Organization Management*, *40*, 529–559; Joseph, J. (1992). *Plateauism and its effect on strain as moderated by career motivation and personal resources.* Unpublished doctoral dissertation, University of Iowa.

30 Nelson, D. L. & Quick, J. C. (1985). Professional women: Are distress and disease inevitable? *Academy of Management Review*, *10*, 206–218.

31 Bell, E. L. J. & Nkomo, S. M. (2001). *Our separate ways: Black and white women and the struggle for professional identity.* Boston, MA: Harvard Business School Press; Brewster, M. E., Velez, B., DeBlaere, C. & Moradi, B. (2012). Transgender individuals' workplace experiences: The applicability of sexual minority measures and models. *Journal of Counseling Psychology*, *59*, 60–70; Hackett, G. & Byers, A. M. (1996). Social cognitive theory and the career development of African American women. *The Career Development Quarterly*, *44*, 322–340; Lau, H. & Stotzer, R. L. (2011). Employment discrimination based on sexual orientation: A Hong Kong study. *Employee Responsibilities and Rights Journal*, *23*, 17–35; Lyness, K. (2006). Glass ceiling. In Greenhaus, J. H. & Callanan, G. A. (Eds.), *Encyclopedia of career development* (pp. 333–336). Thousand Oaks, CA: Sage; Mong, S. N. & Roscigno, V. J. (2010). African American men and the experience of employment discrimination. *Qualitative Sociology*, *33*(1), 1–21; Rabelo, V. C. & Cortina, L. M. (2014). Two sides of the same coin: Gender harassment and heterosexist harassment in LGBQ work lives. *Law and Human Behavior*, *38*, 378–391.

32 Anonymous (1983). Vermeil quits, saying he is "burned out." *The New York Times*, January 11.

33 Halbesleben (2006); Maslach, C., Schaufeli, W. B. & Leiter, M. P. (2001). Job burnout. *Annual Review of Psychology*, *52*, 397–422.

34 Maslach, C. & Leiter, M. P. (2008). Early predictors of job burnout and engagement. *Journal of Applied Psychology*, *93*, 498–512.

35 Hallberg, U. E., Johansson, G. & Schaufeli, W. B. (2007). Type A behavior and work situation: Associations with burnout and work engagement. *Scandinavian Journal of Psychology*, *48*, 135–142; Otero-Lôpez, J. M., Santiago, M. J., Castro, C. & Villardefrancos, E. (2010). Stressors rendering school coexistence difficult, personal variables and burnout: Towards an explanatory model. *European Journal of Education and Psychology*, *3*, 299–316.

36 Potter, B. A. (1998). *Overcoming job burnout: How to renew enthusiasm for work.* Berkeley, CA: Ronin Publishing.

37 Bakker, A. B., Demerouti, E. & Schaufeli, W. B. (2005). The crossover of burnout and work engagement among working couples. *Human Relations*, *58*, 661–689; Bakker, A. B., Schaufeli, W. B., Sixma, H. & Bosveld, W. (2001). Burnout contagion among general practitioners. *Journal of Social and Clinical Psychology*, *20*, 82–98; Bakker, A. B., Van Emmerik, I. J. H. & Euwema, M. C. (2006). Crossover of burnout and engagement in work teams. *Work and Occupations*, *33*, 464–489; Bakker, A. B., Westman, M. & Schaufeli, W. B. (2007). Crossover of burnout: An experimental design. *European Journal of Work and Organizational Psychology*, *16*, 220–239.

38 Greenhaus, J. H. (2006). Burnout. In Greenhaus, J. H. & Callanan, G. A. (Eds.), *Encyclopedia of career development* (pp. 51–52). Thousand Oaks, CA: Sage.

39 Cordes, C. L. & Dougherty, T. W. (1993). A review and integration of research on job burnout. *Academy of Management Review*, *4*, 621–656; Halbesleben (2006); Halbesleben, J. R. B. & Buckley, M. R. (2004). Burnout in organizational life. *Journal of Management*, *30*, 859–879; Maslach & Leiter (2008).

40 Bakker, B. B. & Demerouti, E. (2017). Job demands-resources theory: Taking stock and looking forward. *Journal of Occupational Health Psychology*, *22*, 273–285. Quotation is on p. 274.

41 Ibid.

42 Jackson, S. E., Schwab, R. L. & Schuler, R. S. (1986). Toward an understanding of the burnout phenomenon. *Journal of Applied Psychology*, *7*, 630–640.

43 Bouckenooghe, D., Raja, U., Butt, A. N., Abbas, M. & Bilgrami, S. (2017). Unpacking the curvilinear relationship between negative affectivity, performance, and turnover intentions: The moderating effect of time-related work stress. *Journal of Management and Organization*, *23*, 373–391; Burke et al. (1993); Judge, T. A. (1993). Does affective disposition moderate the relationship between job satisfaction and voluntary turnover? *Journal of Applied Psychology*, *78*, 395–401; Marchand, C. & Vandenberghe, C. (2016). Perceived organizational support, emotional exhaustion, and turnover: The moderating role of negative affectivity. *International Journal of Stress Management*, *23*, 350–375; O'Brien, A., Terry, D. J. & Jimmieson, N. L. (2008).

Negative affectivity and responses to work stressors: An experimental study. *Anxiety, Stress & Coping: An International Journal*, *21*, 55–83.

44 Bouckenooghe et al. (2017); Kaplan, S., Bradley, J. C., Luchman, J. N. & Haynes, D. (2009). On the role of positive and negative affectivity in job performance: A meta-analytic investigation. *Journal of Applied Psychology*, *94*, 162–176.

45 Marchand, C. & Vandenberghe, C. (2016). Perceived organizational support, emotional exhaustion, and turnover: The moderating role of negative affectivity. *International Journal of Stress Management*, *23*, 350–375.

46 Cropanzano, R., James, K. & Konovsky, M. A. (1993). Dispositional affectivity as a predictor of work attitudes and job performance. *Journal of Organizational Behavior*, *14*, 595–606; Haslam, S. A., O'Brien, A., Jetten, J., Vormedal, K. & Penna, S. (2005). Taking the strain: Social identity, social support, and the experience of stress. *The British Journal of Social Psychology*, *44*, 355–370; Iverson, R. D. & Erwin, P. J. (1997). Predictors of occupational injury: The role of affectivity. *Journal of Occupational and Organizational Psychology*, *70*, 113–128; Iverson, R. D., Olekalns, M. & Erwin, P. J. (1998). Affectivity, organizational stressors, and absenteeism: A causal model of burnout and its consequences. *Journal of Vocational Behavior*, *52*, 1–23; Latack, J. C., Kinicki, A. & Prussia, G. E. (1996). Response to "Negative affectivity and coping with job loss." *Academy of Management Review*, *21*, 331–332; Mak, A. S. & Mueller, J. (2001). Negative affectivity, perceived occupational stress, and health during organisational restructuring: A follow-up study. *Psychology & Health*, *16*, 125–137.

47 Åkerstedt, T., Kecklund, G. & Gillberg, M. (2007). Sleep and sleepiness in relation to stress and displaced work hours. *Physiology & Behavior*, *92*, 250–255; Burke, R. J. & Greenglass, E. R. (2001). Hospital restructuring, work–family conflict and psychological burnout among nursing staff. *Psychology and Health*, *16*, 83–94; Driscoll et al. (1995); Enginyurt, O., Cankaya, S., Aksay, K., Koc, B., Bas, O. & Ozer, E., (2016). Relationship between organizational commitment and burnout syndrome: A canonical correlation approach. *Australian Health Review*, *40*, 181–187; Froiland, P. (1993). What cures job stress? *Training*, *30*, 32–35; Frone, M. R. & Tidwell, M. O. (2015). The meaning and measurement of work fatigue: Development and evaluation of the three-dimensional work fatigue inventory (3D-WFI). *Journal of Occupational Health Psychology*, *20*, 273–288; Gloria et al. (2013); Jackson, S. E. & Maslach, C. (1982). After-effects of job-related stress: Families as victims. *Journal of Occupational Behavior*, *3*, 63–77; Leiter, M. P., Harvie, P. & Frizzell, C. (1998). The correspondence of patient satisfaction and nurse burnout. *Social Science & Medicine*, *47*, 1611–1617; Leiter, M. P. & Maslach, C. (2000). Burnout and health. In Baum, A., Revenson, T. & Singer, J. (Eds.), *Handbook of health psychology* (pp. 415–426). Hillsdale, NJ: Erlbaum; O'Brien et al. (2008); Nasurdin et al. (2014); Peterson, U., Demerouti, E. & Bergström, G. (2008). Work characteristics and sickness absence in burnout and nonburnout groups: A study of Swedish health care workers. *International Journal of Stress Management*, *15*, 153–172; Potter (1998); Powell, W. E. (1994). The relationship between feelings of alienation and burnout in social work. *Families in Society*, *75*, 229–235; Rumschlag, K. E. (2017). Teacher burnout: A quantitative analysis of emotional exhaustion, personal accomplishment, and depersonalization. *International Management Review*, *13*, 22–36, 101; Schat & Kelloway (2003); Sonnenschein, M., Sorbi, M. J. & van Doornen, L. J. P. (2007). Electronic diary evidence on energy erosion in clinical burnout. *Journal of Occupational Health Psychology*, *12*, 402–413; Vahey, D. C., Aiken, L. H., Sloane, D. M., Clarke, S. P. & Vargas, D. (2004). Nurse burnout and patient satisfaction. *Medical Care*, *42*, 57–66; Zedeck, S., Maslach, C., Mosier, K. & Skitka, L. (1988). Affective response to work and quality of family life: Employee and spouse perspectives. *Journal of Social Behavior and Personality*, *3*, 135–157.

48 Bakker, A. B., Demerouti, E. & Schaufeli, W. B. (2005). The crossover of burnout and work engagement among working couples. *Human Relations*, *58*, 661–689.

49 Lindblom, K. M., Linton, S. J., Fedeli, C. & Bryngelsson, I. L. (2006). Burnout in the working population: Relations to psychosocial work factors. *International Journal of Behavioral Medicine*, *13*, 51–59; Maslach, C. & Leiter, M. P. (1997). *The truth about burnout*. Chichester, USA: Wiley.

50 Charoensukmongkol, P., Moqbel, M. & Gutierrez-Wirsching, S. (2016). The role of co-worker and supervisor support on job burnout and job satisfaction. *Journal of Advances in Management Research*, *13*, 4–22; Halbesleben & Buckley (2004).

51 Levine, M. (2006). Employee assistance programs. In Greenhaus, J. H. & Callanan, G. A. (Eds.), *Encyclopedia of career development* (pp. 271–272). Thousand Oaks, CA: Sage; Kirk, A. K. & Brown, D. F. (2003). Employee assistance programs: A review of the management of stress and wellbeing through workplace counseling and consulting. *Australian Psychologist*, *38*, 138–143;

Reynolds, S. (1997). Psychological well-being at work: Is prevention better than the cure? *Journal of Psychosomatic Research*, *43*, 93–102.

52 Anonymous (2014, March 24). Seven ways employers can reduce stress in the workplace. Retrieved from www.businessreviewusa.com/leadership/3621/7-ways-employers-can-reduce-stress-in-the-workplace; Porter, J. (2015, Nov. 16). How Google and others help employees burn off stress in unique ways. Retrieved from www.fastcompany.com/3053048/how-google-and-other-companies-help-employees-burn-off-stress-in-unique-ways; Valet, V. (2015, July 8). More than two-thirds of U.S. employers currently offer wellness programs, study says. Retrieved from www.forbes.com/sites/vickyvalet/2015/07/08/more-than-two-thirds-of-u-s-employers-currently-offer-wellness-programs-study-says/#78db863c231d.

53 Anonymous (2007). Addicted to technology? There could be legal repercussions. *HR Focus*, *84*, 1–3; Anonymous (2008). Beware the dangers of workaholism. *HR Focus*, *85*, 9; Barley, S. R., Meyerson, D. E. & Grodal, S. (2011). E-mail as a source and symbol of stress. *Organization Science*, *22*, 887–906; Fender, C. M. (2010). *Electronic tethering: Perpetual wireless connectivity to the organization*. Unpublished doctoral dissertation, Drexel University; Paczkowski, W. F. & Kuruzovich, J. (2016). Checking email in the bathroom: Monitoring email responsiveness behavior in the workplace. *American Journal of Management*, *16*, 23–39; Perlow, L. A. (2012). *Sleeping with your smartphone: How to break the 24/7 habit and change the way you work*. Boston, MA: Harvard Business Review Press.

54 Spence, J. T. & Robbins, A. S. (1992). Workaholism: Definition, measurement, and preliminary results. *Journal of Personality Assessment*, *58*, 162–174.

55 Weissman, J. (2013, September). Is there such a thing as a workaholic? Retrieved from www.theatlantic.com/magazine/archive/2013/09/the-work-addiction/309437/#7.

56 Aziz, S. & Cunningham, J. (2008). Workaholism, work stress, work–life imbalance: Exploring gender's role. *Gender in Management*, *23*, 553–566; Porter, G. (2001). Workaholic tendencies and the high potential for stress among co-workers. *International Journal of Stress Management*, *8*, 147–164.

57 Andreassen, C. S., Hetland, J., Molde, H. & Pallesen, S. (2011). Workaholism and potential outcomes in well-being and health in a cross-occupational sample. *Stress and Health*, *27*, 209–214; Brady, B. R., Vodanovish, S. J. & Rotunda, R. (2008). The impact of workaholism on work–family conflict, job satisfaction, and perception of leisure activities. *The Psychologist-Manager Journal*, *11*, 241–263; Burke R. J. (2004). Workaholism, self-esteem, and motives for money. *Psychological Reports*, *94*, 457–463; Burke, R. J. & Matthiesen, S. (2004). Workaholism among Norwegian journalists: Antecedents and consequences. *Stress and Health*, *20*, 301–308; Douglas, E. J. & Morris, R. J. (2006). Workaholic, or just hard worker? *Career Development International*, *11*, 394–417; Holland, D. W. (2008). Work addiction: Costs and solutions for individuals, relationships and organizations. *Journal of Workplace Behavioral Health*, *22*, 1–15; Kubota K., Shimazu, A., Kawakami, N., Takahashi, M., Nakata, A. & Schaufeli, W. B. (2010). Association between workaholism and sleep problems among hospital nurses. *Industrial Health*, *48*, 864–871; Russo, J. A. & Waters, L. E. (2006). Workaholic worker type differences in work–family conflict. *Career Development International*, *11*, 418–439; McMillan, L. H. W. & O'Driscoll, M. P. (2004). Workaholism and health: Implications for organizations. *Journal of Organizational Change Management*, *17*, 509–519; Shimazu, A., Schaufeli, W. B. & Taris, W. T. (2010). How does workaholism affect worker health and performance? The mediating role of coping. *International Journal of Behavioral Mediation*, *17*, 154–160; Sussman, S. (2012). Workaholism: A review. *Journal of Addiction Research & Therapy*, *Suppl 6*, 4120–4138.

58 Greenhaus et al. (2006).

59 Mazzetti, G., Schaufeli, W. B. & Guglielmi, D. (2014). Are workaholics born or made? Relations of workaholism with person characteristics and overwork climate. *International Journal of Stress Management*, *21*, 227–254.

60 Latack, J. C. (1989). Work, stress, and careers: A preventive approach to maintaining organizational health. In Arthur, M. B., Hall, D. T. & Lawrence, B. S. (Eds.), *Handbook of career theory* (pp. 252–274). Cambridge, UK: Cambridge University Press; Latack, J. C. & Havlovic, S. J. (1992). Coping with job stress: A conceptual evaluation framework for coping measures. *Journal of Organizational Behavior*, *13*, 479–508; Shin, H., Park, Y. M., Ying, J. Y., Kim, B., Noh, H. & Lee, S. M. (2014). Relationships between coping strategies and burnout symptoms: A meta-analytic approach. *Professional Psychology: Research and Practice*, *45*, 44–56; Wallace, E. V. (2007). Managing stress: What consumers want to know from health educators. *American Journal of Health Studies*, *22*, 56–58.

61 Anonymous (2007). Taking control of stress. *Harvard Health Letter*, *32*, 3–4; Wallace (2007).

62 Sonnentag, S. (2012). Psychological detachment from work during leisure time: The benefits of mentally disengaging from work. *Current Directions in Psychological Science*, *21*, 114–118.
63 Ibid.
64 Ibid.
65 Avey, J. B., Luthans, F. & Jensen, S. M. (2009). Psychological capital: A positive resource for combating employee stress and turnover. *Human Resource Management*, *48*, 677–693; Gianakos, I. (2000). Gender roles and coping with work stress. *Sex Roles*, *42*, 1059–1079; Gianakos, I. (2002). Predictors of coping with work stress: The influences of sex, gender role, social desirability, and locus of control. *Sex Roles*, *46*, 149–158; Havlovic, S. J. & Keenan, J. P. (1991). Coping with work stress: The influence of individual differences. *Journal of Social Behavior & Personality*, *6*, 199–212; Ong, A. D., Bergeman, C. S., Bisconti, T. L. & Wallace, K. A. (2006). Psychological resilience, positive emotions, and successful adaptation to stress in later life. *Journal of Personality and Social Psychology*, *91*, 730–748; Siu, O., Chow, S. L. & Phillips, D. R. (2006). An exploratory study of resilience among Hong Kong employees: Ways to happiness. In Ng, Y. K. & Ho, L. S. (Eds.), *Happiness and public policy: Theory, case studies and implications*. New York: Palgrave Macmillan.
66 Schein, E. H. (1978). *Career dynamics: Matching individual and organizational needs*. Reading, MA: Addison-Wesley.
67 Latack, J. C., Kinicki, A. J. & Prussia, G. E. (1995). An integrative process model of coping with job loss. *Academy of Management Review*, *20*, 311–342.
68 Latack et al. (1995); Manning, M. R., Jackson, C. N. & Fusilier, M. R. (1996). Occupational stress, social support, and the costs of health care. *Academy of Management Journal*, *39*, 738–750; Shin et al. (2014).
69 See the pioneering work of James House in House, J. S. (1981). *Work stress and social support*. Reading, MA: Addison-Wesley.
70 Maisel, N. C. & Gable, S. L. (2009). The paradox of received social support: The importance of responsiveness. *Psychological Science*, *20*, 928–932.
71 Greenhaus, J. H., Ziegert, J. C. & Allen, T. D. (2012). When family-supportive supervision matters: Relations between multiple sources of support and work–family balance. *Journal of Vocational Behavior*, *80*, 266–275.
72 Acitelli, L. K. & Antonucci, T. C. (1994). Gender differences in the link between marital support and satisfaction in older couples. *Journal of Personality and Social Psychology*, *67*, 688–698; Jou, Y. H. & Fukada, H. (2002). Stress, health, and reciprocity and sufficiency of social support: The case of university students in Japan. *Journal of Social Psychology*, *142*, 353–370; Novin, S., Tso, I. F. & Konrath, S. H. (2014). Self-related and other-related pathways to subjective well-being in Japan and the United States. *Journal of Happiness Studies*, *15*, 995–1014.
73 Iverson et al. (1998); Quick & Quick (1997).
74 Adapted from the IBM website. Retrieved from www.ibm.com/ibm/responsibility/employee_well_being.shtml.

11 Workforce Diversity and Career Management

Societies throughout the industrialized world are becoming increasingly diverse; consequently, the workforces of organizations are becoming progressively diverse. Companies that can manage their diverse workforce effectively are likely to be more successful and competitive.[1] Within any one country or region of the world, the level of diversity can vary substantially. Indeed, fertility and immigration rates as well as life expectancies can play significant roles in determining the demographic composition of a population and, by extension, the overall workforce. Further, population and workforce diversity has been, and will be, influenced by a variety of demographic, economic, sociological, and governmental factors. Consider the following statistics and forecasts:[2]

- Although it is often difficult to neatly categorize individuals into ethnic groups, data and projections available from governmental agencies, such as the U.S. Bureau of Labor Statistics, offer insight into how the make-up of a given population and labor force can change over time.[3] With regard to specific ethnic groups in the U.S., in 1994 African Americans represented just over 11 percent of the labor force, moving to 12 percent in 2014, and are projected to be nearly 13 percent in 2024. The Hispanic population in the U.S. has grown substantially during the early part of the 21st century. In terms of the labor force, people of Hispanic origin were 9 percent of the U.S. labor force in 1994, moving to over 16 percent in 2014, and are expected to be nearly 20 percent in 2024. The percentage of the labor force of Asian descent was roughly 4 percent in 1994, climbed to nearly 6 percent in 2014, and is projected to be close to 7 percent in 2024. In contrast, the white non-Hispanics' share of the U.S. labor force has declined over time, moving from nearly 77 percent in 1994 to 65 percent in 2014 to a projection of roughly 60 percent in 2024. While the total white non-Hispanic population in the U.S. continues to grow in size, its percentage share of the total labor force is decreasing markedly due to increasing numbers of ethnic minorities in the population.
- Immigration into economically developed sectors of the world can substantially alter the diversity of the population of a given country or geographic region. Governmental policies, geopolitical unrest and persecution, disparities in wealth distribution, and a host of other factors can serve to encourage (or discourage) immigration. In the U.S., absent major changes in policy, net immigration is expected to continue to add more than one million people annually to the resident population.[4]
- The labor force participation rate of women in the U.S. grew substantially over the second half of the 20th century and into the 21st, moving from 33 percent in 1950, to a peak of over 60 percent in the early 2000s, to roughly 57 percent in 2017.[5] In contrast, the labor force participation rate for men has declined markedly over the

past seven decades, moving from 86 percent in 1950 to roughly 70 percent in 2017.[6] Women are also expected to work for a longer period over their lifetimes, into their 60s and 70s, due to a number of factors such as economic need, increased desire for greater career fulfillment, higher educational attainment, greater work experience, freedom from more intensive family responsibilities, and changes in marital status.[7]
- The labor force participation rate for persons with a disability was nearly 20 percent in 2017.[8] Roughly one-third of workers with a disability worked part-time, and disabled workers are comparatively more likely to be self-employed.[9]
- As we discussed in Chapter 9, the populations and workforces of the highly developed sectors of the world are getting increasingly older. In the U.S., the median age of the workforce has moved from 37.7 years in 1994 to an expected 42.4 in 2024 as the majority of the baby boom workforce continues to work its way to retirement age.[10] According to the Pew Research Center, in the year 2000, less than 13 percent of individuals in the U.S. aged 65 and older were still working full or part time, but a decade and a half later, the percentage was up to roughly 19 percent, or around nine million workers.[11] As the baby boom generation ages, and as economic necessity dictates, the total number and percentage of older workers in the labor force will undoubtedly rise.

The increasing diversity of the workforce in terms of race, ethnicity, gender, and age, as well as disability status, religion, veteran status, and sexual orientation requires organizations to recognize their dependency on a more varied employee base. There is justifiable concern about organizations' ability to manage employees who are not only different from the historically dominant white male managerial base, but are also different from one another in many respects. In part, this concern is due to the career difficulties experienced by many minority group members, especially women and people of color. Without question, the election in 2008 of Barack Obama as the first African-American President of the United States (as well as his reelection in 2012) and the presidential campaigns of Hillary Clinton in 2008 and *2016* underscore the progress in advancement and mobility achieved by African Americans and women over the last quarter-century in the U.S. Indeed, the numbers of women and people of color in management and executive positions have risen significantly over the past several decades.

Nonetheless, the progress in upward career mobility to the most senior titles has been slow. In terms of representation in leadership positions, including managerial and professional jobs, senior executive ranks, and board of directors' seats, women and minorities clearly lag behind white male counterparts and are underrepresented in comparison to overall population profiles. A report issued by the consulting company McKinsey entitled, *Women in the Workplace 2016*, indicates that within U.S. companies, women are underrepresented at every level; firms promote men 30 percent more frequently than women; women negotiate for promotions and raises as frequently as men, but receive more pushback when they do; and women of color report less access to opportunities than their white female counterparts.[12] Among Fortune 500 companies, women and minorities hold roughly one-third of all board of directors seats, which represents a gradual increase over time, but is still well below the commonly stated goal of 40 percent by the year 2026.[13]

Taylor Cox and Stacy Blake-Beard provided six arguments for why an organization can improve its competitive advantage through the effective management of its cultural diversity.[14] A brief summary of these six arguments is presented below:

1. **Cost argument.** Organizations have not been as successful in managing women and minorities as in managing white males. Therefore, organizations that are unable to

manage an increasingly dominant part of the workforce will incur considerable additional costs that will detract from their productivity.

2. **Resource-acquisition argument.** Organizations that have the most favorable reputation for managing a culturally diverse workforce will attract the most talented women and minorities into their ranks.
3. **Marketing argument.** Organizations that serve multinational or domestically multicultural consumers will benefit from a diverse workforce that brings a blend of insights and cultural sensitivities to the organizations' marketing efforts.
4. **Creativity argument.** The representation of varying perspectives in a culturally diverse workforce should enhance the level of creativity in the organization.
5. **Problem-solving argument.** The availability of various perspectives in a culturally diverse workforce should enable problem-solving groups to produce high-quality solutions and decisions.
6. **System flexibility argument.** Organizations that manage diversity effectively become more fluid and flexible, which enables them to respond to environmental changes more quickly and efficiently.

We return to these arguments later in this chapter. But first, we examine barriers to fairness in organizations, identify programs and policies that organizations can provide to manage diversity effectively, and propose actions that individuals can take to manage their careers in culturally diverse organizations.

Fairness in Organizations

As noted earlier, one reason for the concern about organizations' ability to manage diversity is the suspicion that women and people of color are not growing in their careers to a degree commensurate with their talents. If women and minorities have faced substantial obstacles in reaching the upper echelons of their organizations in the past, how can organizations manage an increasingly diverse group of employees in the future?

An organization is acting fairly when its employment decisions (regarding such issues as hiring, pay, and advancement) are based on job-related criteria rather than an individual's membership in a population subgroup (e.g., gender, race, religion, age).[15] Conversely, discrimination occurs when organizational practices have a negative effect on the employment of subgroup members that is not based on job-related factors. Two types of discrimination have been distinguished: access discrimination and treatment discrimination.

In cases of *access discrimination*, minority group members[16] are less likely to be hired for a particular job due to their demographic background than members of the dominant group despite the fact that they could have performed the job as effectively as members of the dominant group.[17] For example, if bias in employment interviews disproportionately rejects talented women (due to their gender) for a construction management position in favor of equally (or less) talented men, women (as a group) will have limited access to that particular job. Discrimination in hiring was the target of the early fair employment movement during the 1960s and 1970s.

Treatment discrimination occurs when the treatment of employees is based on their minority group status rather than on their merits or achievements; that is, when such employees receive fewer opportunities for development and career advancement than they legitimately deserve on the basis of job-related criteria.[18] For example, people of color, older employees, or women who are systematically excluded from key committee assignments or sponsorship opportunities experience treatment discrimination within their organization due to their status as minority group members.

Although access discrimination has certainly not been eliminated, women and people of color have been entering managerial and professional positions in increasing numbers. Thus, a key issue is how they are treated once they are in an organization. For this reason, we focus on understanding *treatment discrimination* in organizational settings. Moreover, because much of the concern regarding fairness is based on the more restricted career advancement historically experienced by people of color and women as compared to white men, we begin our discussion with career advancement and then move to an examination of those factors that may explain differences in career advancement between women and men as well as between minority and nonminority employees.

Career Advancement

Difficulties experienced by minority groups members in rising to the highest levels of management has often been attributed to the presence of a *glass ceiling* or "an invisible but impenetrable barrier that prevents qualified women and people of color from advancing to senior management jobs."[19] The presence of the glass ceiling serves to place limits on the opportunities for many women and people of color to develop in their careers and to attain top management positions.[20] Indeed, it is thought that black women experience a "concrete ceiling," which is even more challenging to overcome than a glass ceiling.[21]

What factors might produce a glass ceiling? One could argue that the limited representation of women and people of color in senior management is due to the fact that they entered the managerial pipeline later than their white counterparts. Although this may explain a portion of restricted career advancement, it is unlikely that it is the sole explanation. For example, research suggests that white employees' promotions outstrip minorities' promotions even when the two groups have accumulated comparable levels of human and social capital, suggesting that factors other than years of experience or education could explain the apparent glass ceiling.[22] The career advancement of women presents a similar picture. The underrepresentation of women at senior management levels suggests that many women do not move beyond jobs in lower and middle levels of management,[23] and there is evidence that the restricted promotion of women is not due to their age, tenure in the organization, or education, all proxies for their level of skill development.[24]

Another possible explanation for why people of color and women have experienced more restricted career advancement is that they perform less effectively in their current job assignments than white men. However, sex differences in job performance have been found to be either small[25] or nonexistent,[26] and gender-balanced firms tend to perform better than gender-homogeneous firms.[27] Therefore, it is unlikely that women's restricted advancement is due solely to the belief that they are ineffective in their current jobs.

Research on race or ethnic differences in job performance has observed a tendency for black employees to receive lower job performance assessments than white employees,[28] although these differences are generally quite small,[29] and can vary according to such factors as the particular racial groups compared, the aspect of job performance that is assessed, and the measures used to assess performance.[30]

Are assessments of job performance biased against racial minority employees? There is no simple answer to this question. The tendency to give higher performance ratings to subordinates of the same race[31] can harm minorities because the majority of supervisors in most organizations are white. Moreover, race differences in job performance ratings have been found to be more substantial in organizations where blacks make up a very small proportion of the workforce, suggesting that blacks in small numbers are "put under the microscope" in the assessment of their job performance.[32] Additionally, it is possible that African-American managers are not given as much "credit" for their job performance as white managers. One study revealed that when white managers perform well on the job, their boss tends to attribute the managers' performance to their ability, whereas when black managers perform well on the job, their boss tends to attribute it to the help and assistance the managers receive from other people.[33] These differential performance attributions might explain why the career advancement rate of racial minorities lags behind that of white employees even when controlling for level of job performance.[34]

In sum, there is evidence that the job performance of black employees is assessed somewhat lower than the job performance of white employees, and it is difficult to determine how much of this difference reflects true differences in job performance and how much represents bias in the evaluation process. As we discuss later in the chapter, organizations should carefully scrutinize their performance evaluation systems to ensure that they are not biased against any group. However, we cannot overemphasize that *there are talented and high-performing members of all groups* within an organization, and employment decisions should be based on talent and job performance, not membership in a particular group or category.

A Model of Organizational Fairness

We have seen that the career advancement of women and people of color has often lagged behind that of white men. It is important to emphasize that the restricted career opportunities discussed in this chapter are not experienced by all minority group members, and they are not experienced to the same degree in all organizations. Exhibit 11.1 presents a model of organizational fairness that proposes reasons why women and people of color may experience restricted career advancement opportunities. The model suggests that cultural dissimilarities between groups in organizations can produce stereotypes, feelings of psychological distance, and cultural misunderstandings, which, in turn, may result in differential treatment for women and people of color compared to white men. Differential treatment represents "lost opportunities"[35] for minority group members to develop human and social capital, which can detract from their job performance and dampen their career advancement prospects.

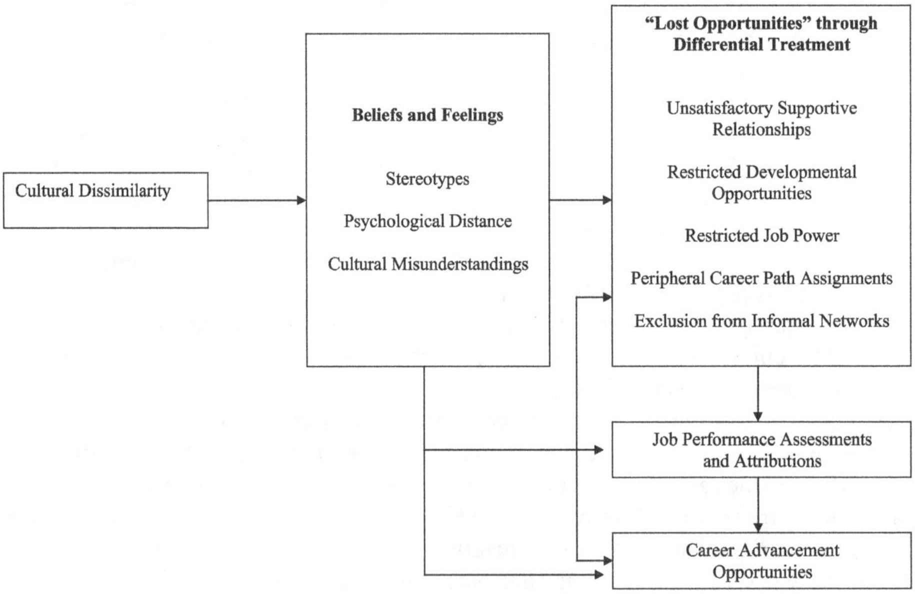

Exhibit 11.1 Model of Organizational Fairness in Career Advancement Opportunities

Beliefs and Feelings

Stereotypes

A *stereotype* is a preconceived perception or image one has of another person based on that person's membership in a particular social group or category. We may believe that Mary, an accountant, is logical and organized because we believe that accountants in general are logical and organized. We may perceive John, a social worker, to be compassionate and fair-minded because we perceive social workers to possess these characteristics. Of course, not all stereotypes are so flattering. For example, we may believe that investment broker Susan is unethical, and engineer Brad is narrow-minded because we perceive brokers and engineers to be unethical and narrow-minded, respectively.

Moreover, the actions we take in response to our stereotype can ultimately confirm the stereotype. For example, because of our belief that members of a particular group are lazy, we may not provide an individual from that group with attention or encouragement or with a great deal of challenge and responsibility on the job. The individual might respond to this lack of support by not appearing to care about the organization and by not expending much effort on the job. This reaction might well reinforce our original perception of the individual as lazy. Although neither party's actions necessarily operate at a conscious level, their consequences are quite real. Negative stereotypes can produce biased assessments of members of targeted groups and can play a role in decisions regarding job assignments, salary increases, and promotions.[36] Unfortunately, negative attitudes, stereotypes, and prejudice based on an individual's race or gender have not disappeared completely in contemporary society.[37] Historically, stereotypes have been a significant obstacle to the careers of black managers and the most difficult stereotypes to combat are those that malign a minority employee's ability and qualifications.[38]

Gender-based stereotypes, or our shared social beliefs about the normative attributes of women and men, also persist in contemporary society. Women are thought to possess a number of qualities that are seen as incompatible with success in many managerial and professional positions. For example, whereas men are often perceived as aggressive, dominant, and independent, women are likely to be perceived as compassionate, understanding, and warm. Research suggests that gender-based stereotypes continue to inhibit women's advancement in organizations. These stereotypes can be descriptive (what women are like) or prescriptive (what women should be like).[39] As a result of these stereotypes, women may be passed over for a job that is perceived to require "masculine" characteristics.[40] Women are also subject to gender-role stereotypes regarding the priorities they attach to their career and family responsibilities. Many men (and some women) believe that women should be primarily responsible for home and childcare activities. As a result of these beliefs, women with extensive family responsibilities may be stereotyped as less committed than men to their work and the organization. In fact, this bias against women may affect performance evaluations and career progress when prescriptive gender stereotypes are violated (i.e., women did not behave as they ought to).[41]

The Catalyst organization suggests that subtle gender bias still exists where viable female candidates are taken out of the running for executive jobs, based on the assumption that women cannot handle certain jobs and also handle family obligations. Catalyst found that many women, too, hold limiting beliefs that stand in their own way of career progress. Catalyst suggests gender-based bias can be demonstrated in different ways:[42]

- Women do not receive credit for their work performance, when credit is due them. Instead, male colleagues get the credit.

- Men are more often promoted on potential, whereas women need to demonstrate performance before promotion is available, which slows women's career progression.
- Competent women are often marked as unlikeable. In fact, the more accomplished women are, the more likely their reputations suffer. Many suggest Hillary Clinton experienced this bias during her quests to become president of the United States.

Psychological Distance

Cultural dissimilarity may produce feelings of psychological distance, which can cause misunderstandings between leaders and followers, and result in reduced communication, and a greater social distance, thereby lowering the quality of leadership exchanges.[43] It is possible that some white men feel more psychologically distant from women and people of color than they do from other white men.

Psychological distance can provoke mistrust and even fear because of the belief that people who are different from us are more difficult to understand and therefore more difficult to predict.[44] For example, if we feel different and distant from a person, we may not understand what motivates the person or how to influence the person. In organizational settings, supervisors can form an in-group of trusted and favored subordinates and relegate other subordinates who are less trusted to out-group status. It is possible that the placement of an individual into an out-group is attributable in part to the psychological distance a supervisor feels toward that individual. The resultant manifestation of an in-group/out-group mindset can "cause positive and negative discrimination, such as better jobs offered to members of the in-group, refusal of employment to a member of the out group, or lower wages paid to out-group members."[45]

Note that stereotypes can create psychological distance, and psychological distance can reinforce existing stereotypes. If we stereotype a subordinate as unmotivated or ineffective, we may accentuate the differences between that individual and ourselves, ascribe the individual out-group status, and provide few opportunities for the individual to demonstrate his or her strengths. The individual may assume (quite accurately) that he or she is not valued, and therefore show a reduced level of initiative or interest in improving job performance. This understandable reaction is likely to be interpreted as a lack of involvement in work, which will reinforce the initial stereotype, increase the feeling of psychological distance, result in a self-fulfilling prophecy, and likely create difficulty for the individual's career.

Cultural Misunderstandings

As a result of cultural differences, stereotypes, and psychological distance, there are many opportunities for people to misunderstand each other. For example, a man may perceive a woman's willingness to cooperate with a stubborn colleague as a sign of weakness and accommodation, rather than the strength and resolve it may actually represent. A supervisor unfamiliar with Asian culture might misinterpret the modesty and deference of an Asian as a lack of confidence or even as a lack of talent, rather than as a sign of respect for another person based on cultural norms. Cultural misunderstandings can be exacerbated by language differences that produce tension and conflict.

Lost Opportunities through Differential Treatment

Perhaps the most serious consequence of negative stereotypes, psychological distance, and cultural misunderstandings is the tendency to discount the present or future contributions of persons who come from different backgrounds. If we believe that members of a particular group are unqualified, not sufficiently assertive, exhibit language or cultural differences that pose insurmountable social obstacles, or are not committed to their careers, we will be unwilling to invest the time and the organization's resources to develop these individuals and groom them for additional responsibility.

An organization's unwillingness to invest time and resources in particular groups of employees can take several forms as shown in Exhibit 11.1—reluctance to encourage the exercise of power and authority on the job, exclusion from informal networks within the organization, provision of less extensive sponsorship or mentorship opportunities, assignment to fewer tasks or projects designed to build skills or visibility, and assignment to more peripheral (less central) career paths. We suggest that exclusion from these resources represents lost opportunities for minority group members to develop job-related skills and establish important career contacts,[46] which can reduce their work effectiveness over time, and diminish their opportunities for further growth, development, and advancement. Next, we briefly discuss several of these lost opportunities.

Restricted Job Power

There is some indication that minority group members have historically reported less authority and power in their jobs than white men, may be assigned to jobs that permit less authority and discretion, and are underrepresented in career paths involving line operations.[47] If women and people of color do possess (or perceive) limited authority in their job, their opportunity to develop new skills and exercise political clout is likely to be diminished.

Exclusion from Informal Networks

Traditionally, some of the most critical decisions affecting employees' career accomplishments are made over lunch, during the cocktail hour, or on the golf course. Historically, women and people of color were often excluded from these informal activities.[48] Although overt exclusion is less likely to occur in modern organizations, isolation from informal networks of information and power, when it occurs, can restrict the career opportunities of minority group members.

Mentoring and Other Developmental Relationships

In earlier chapters, we emphasized the importance of developmental relationships to an individual's career. At this point, we add that it is important to understand the complex role of gender and race in high-quality developmental relationships.[49] With the proliferation of formal mentoring programs adopted by modern organizations, it is not surprising that a number of studies indicate that minority group members are as likely to have had a mentor as white men.[50] Nonetheless, some women and racial minority executives and professionals may struggle to find mentors and establish career-enhancing relationships and support.[51] Perhaps it is not so much a question of the establishment of a mentor relationship, but rather the nature and quality of the relationship.

Because of the sheer numbers of white men in most organizational hierarchies, many people of color develop cross-race mentoring relationships (i.e., they have a white mentor), and many women have cross-gender mentoring relationships (a male mentor). Moreover, although cross-race relationships tend to provide career support to the protégés, they may provide less psychosocial support than same-race relationships. In fact, findings indicated that protégés of color with mentors of color reported more relationship satisfaction, interpersonal comfort, and psychosocial and instrumental support than protégés of color whose mentors were of a different race.[52] Cross-race relationships may add certain complications that inhibit the development of minority employees. Racial dynamics in developmental relationships indicate the many factors that determine success in such relationships, including the culture of the organization, the way the mentor and protégé deal with racial issues, and the level of trust in the relationship.[53]

Cross-gender developmental relationships also seem to provide the protégé with less psychosocial support than same-sex relationships, although the results are not entirely consistent in this regard, and in some cases, male and female protégés in same-gender relationships did not report being more satisfied than those in cross-gender mentorships.[54] It appears that cross-gender developmental relationships are more challenging than same-gender relationships because of the possibility of gender stereotypes and the potential misinterpretation of a relationship as having a sexual or romantic component.[55] However, it may be that career role salience is a stronger factor in cross-gender mentoring relationships than gender identity. A study revealed that protégés with a strong masculine identity placed greater salience on their career role and thus reported being satisfied with mentors who provided substantial career development support. On the other hand, protégés with a strong feminine identity valued socio-emotional career success and reported being satisfied with mentors who provided higher amounts of psychosocial support.[56] Additionally, an under-researched area that needs further study is the relationship between mentors and protégés in gay/lesbian/bisexual mentoring relationships.[57]

Despite these concerns, evidence suggests that those managers of color who advance the furthest in an organization share one characteristic—a strong network of mentors and powerful corporate sponsors who offer long-term, close, developmental support.[58] Mentoring can prove especially valuable for women and racial minorities in certain career fields and industries. As one example, women and members of certain minority groups tend to be underrepresented in the science and technology fields. In response, a variety of mentoring programs have been established so that women and racial minorities may be mentored throughout their education and pursue careers in science, technology, engineering, and mathematics (STEM) and computing.[59]

Tokenism

Although tokenism is not strictly a lost opportunity in the same sense that the other factors we have discussed, it is an experience that can produce lost opportunities. A *token* is a member of a particular subgroup that constitutes a very small percentage (perhaps 15 percent or less) of a population in an organization.[60] Tokens are highly visible because they are perceived to be different from members of the dominant group. This heightened visibility and attention can produce performance pressures because the token's performance is scrutinized more carefully than the performance of non-tokens.[61] Under these conditions, every performance problem experienced by a token may be magnified in the eyes of the organization's management. In addition, women and people of color may feel substantial stress because their accomplishments not only affect their own careers but may also influence management's attitude toward other women and racial minorities in the organization.

Token status can isolate minority group members from the mainstream organization as differences between tokens and non-tokens become exaggerated. Among people of color, this isolation can create racial micro-aggressions in the workplace, excluding tokens from informal social networks, and making it difficult for them to attract a mentor or sponsor.[62] Moreover, isolation from informal groups can reinforce existing stereotypes held by the dominant group, because there are not enough direct experiences with tokens to counteract the stereotypes, and negative stereotypes can cause decrements in tokens' job performance. This cycle can continue for minorities and has been noted to become detrimental to their career advancement.[63]

In sum, cultural differences within an organization can produce stereotyping, feelings of psychological distance, and misunderstandings. These beliefs and feelings may result in lost opportunities for women and people of color to cultivate developmental relationships and acquire needed skills and experiences. Not only can lost opportunities erode job performance over time, but stereotyping, distancing, and misunderstandings may bias the assessment of job performance for minority group members. Perceptions of ineffective performance and low potential, real or imagined, can curtail the career advancement of women and people of color.

In this section, we have emphasized the stereotyping, psychological distancing, and misunderstanding by white men because they have traditionally possessed the most power in organizations. However, it is also possible for women and people of color to stereotype white men, misunderstand their intentions, and experience psychological distance from them. Moreover, although diversity is most closely associated with race and gender, other forms of diversity are significant in contemporary organizations. For example, organizational diversity may be viewed in terms of differences in age, religion, national culture, language, sexual orientation, veteran status, and disability status, and significant diversity issues can also revolve around line-staff interactions and functional differentiation, such as engineering versus marketing, or production versus sales.[64] Although the specific concerns will vary depending on the dimension of diversity being considered, there are common elements as well to consider—different backgrounds and perspectives, stereotyping, distancing, and misunderstandings.

Is Diversity Inherently Valuable?

Broadly speaking, there are two schools of thought regarding why organizations should be concerned about managing diversity. According to one approach, the world and the workplace are becoming increasingly diverse and globalized. Because this trend is inevitable, it behooves the organization to cope with new demographic realities. Therefore, organizations must hire and develop the most talented individuals from all backgrounds in an effective and fair manner. It is not a question of whether diversity is inherently desirable or undesirable, but rather it is a fact of life. This approach is most consistent with the cost and the resource acquisition arguments presented earlier in the chapter.

The second approach, which goes beyond the demographic necessity of becoming more diverse, asserts that organizational diversity is healthy and beneficial in its own right. This approach, which is most consistent with the marketing, creativity, and problem-solving arguments, assumes that employees from different cultural groups bring different strengths and perspectives to an organization that can enhance its effectiveness. For example, it has been suggested that because of their unique socialization experiences, women view situations differently than men. Assuming women are more attuned to social relationships, they may be more likely than men to involve colleagues and subordinates in a collaborative manner, share power and information, and include others in decision-making.[65] The implication is that women possess certain qualities and skills (e.g., communication, cooperation, emotional expressiveness) that provide different perspectives on the management of organizations.[66] In a similar vein, it has been suggested that many racial and ethnic minorities have experienced the world differently than the dominant cultural group. As a result, they can bring different views, approaches, perspectives, and understandings to the solution of organizational problems.[67]

Are women and people of color substantially different from white men in how they view work-related tasks, approach problems, and relate to other people? In our view, the research does not provide a definitive answer to this question. Studies comparing men and women in managerial and professional careers have often revealed considerable similarity in personality, work-related values, and behaviors. Although this does not mean that men and women react identically in all situations, it does call into question the assumption that women in managerial roles *necessarily* bring different strengths and perspectives to the organization than men bring. In fact, it is likely that there is considerable variation in talents and perspective within each gender. What is apparent, however, is that there are many women who bring special strengths and perspectives to an organization not necessarily—or only—because of their gender, but rather because of their intelligence, education, training, and unique work and life experiences.

Similarly, it is not clear that people of color *necessarily* have unique perspectives on work-related issues by virtue of their race. However, even if there are not consistent and substantial race differences in managers' perspectives or behaviors, it is clear that there are many racial minority employees who bring special strengths and perspectives to an organization not necessarily—or only—because of their race but rather because of their intelligence, education, training, and unique work and life experiences.

The "different perspective" approach has been viewed critically by Stephen Carter, who states:

> Viewpoint, outlook, perspective—whatever word is used, the significance is the same. We have come to a point in the evolution of our ways of talking about race when it is not only respectable but actually encouraged for public and private institutions alike to make policy based on stereotypes about the different ways in which people who are white and people who are black supposedly think.[68]

Carter suggests that this view can put pressure on minorities (and we would add women) to represent the "minority perspective" (female perspective) and see things the way minorities (women) see things. This approach, in our view, runs the risk of replacing old race and gender stereotypes with new and different "perspective" stereotypes.

In sum, we do not claim that women and racial minorities are the same as white men in how they define issues and problems, see the world, or interact with other persons. However, we are not convinced at this time that there are substantial and consistent differences in "perspective" between women and men, or between different racial or cultural groups. Moreover, although several studies illustrate the potential advantages of sexually or racially diverse work groups, several reviews of the literature have found that groups with a substantial amount of demographic diversity (e.g., gender, race, age) do not necessarily perform more effectively than groups with more homogeneity along these dimensions.[69] We agree with an observation made by Roosevelt Thomas more than 25 years ago:

> Many individuals believe that there is richness in diversity that you can't get from a homogeneous workforce. This may be true, but it's not necessary to support managing diversity. Whether there is a richness or not, managers will have employees with significant differences and similarities. The compelling case for managing diversity lies in the fact that diversity is a reality—or soon will be. By focusing on the richness, you risk suggesting that the manager has a choice.[70]

It is clear that organizations desperately require talent, and talent is distributed amply across different groups. All organizations, regardless of size, need to recognize and develop the talents and contributions of all employees, regardless of their gender, race, religion, age, disability status, veteran status, or sexual orientation. Therefore, it is in the best interest of the employee, the organization, and society for all talent to be identified, developed, and rewarded.

Moreover, it is also apparent that there are sufficient differences in language, customs, and cultural experiences that can lead us into the trap of stereotyping and misunderstanding other people. Biases, conscious or not, run deep, and what is unfamiliar is often denigrated. With the inexorable shift to a globalized business world, organizations need to understand different groups and cultures to acknowledge similarities and to appreciate differences. As individual employees, we also need to understand our stereotypes and their effects on our behavior as well as on the behavior of others with whom we interact.

Whether or not there is inherent value in diversity, there is value in mutual understanding and respect, and there is certainly value in ensuring that *all employees* have the opportunity to demonstrate their talents and be rewarded for their accomplishments. With these thoughts in mind, we consider ways in which organizations can manage diversity.

The Multicultural Organization

A multicultural organization "seeks and values all differences and develops systems and work practices that support the success and inclusion of members of every group."[71] Key elements of a multicultural organization[72] are discussed below.

Elimination of Access Discrimination

As noted earlier in this chapter, access discrimination occurs when members of a particular subgroup are disproportionately excluded from joining an organization by virtue of their subgroup membership rather than job-related factors. Applicant qualifications, not race, gender, religion, national origin, sexual orientation, age, physical disability or veteran status, or any other nonperformance-related factors, must determine hiring decisions. An organization cannot even begin to utilize fully its human resources if it hires (or fails to hire) people on the basis of irrelevant personal factors.

Mutual Accommodation

We observed in Chapter 8 that the socialization process encourages new employees to learn and accept the organization's central assumptions, norms, values, and expectations—in short, to assimilate into the organization's dominant culture. We stressed that organizations possess established ways of accomplishing tasks—what should be done, how it should be done, and by whom it should be done—and that employees must adapt to the most crucial of these expectations to become accepted and successful.

Socialization has generally been viewed as a one-way street in which employees adapt and assimilate into the organization's culture. However, a multicultural organization realizes that members of cultural groups in today's society may not be willing to assimilate fully into the organization's culture. Moreover, it may not be in the best interest of the organization to demand full assimilation. If members of different groups do possess different views and perspectives (an assertion we consider an important proposition rather than an established fact), then organizations should encourage members of different groups to retain their uniqueness. Total accommodation to an organization's culture could reduce the contributions that members of different groups can make to the organization and could lead to dysfunctional decision-making outcomes such as groupthink. Of course, employees from diverse cultural backgrounds must assimilate and accommodate to some degree. For example, they must accept the mission of the organization and many of its most cherished norms and values.

Elimination of Treatment Discrimination

As we discussed earlier, an organization can intentionally or unwittingly discriminate against members of subgroups. Employees who are excluded from informal networks or experience restricted developmental opportunities, limited power, and peripheral career path assignments may prematurely plateau in their careers. These experiences diminish the opportunities for learning, skill development, and career contacts, and can dampen job performance and career advancement prospects.

The multicultural organization understands the potential for treatment discrimination.[73] It recognizes that discrimination not only impedes the progress of individual employees, but also prevents them from maximizing their contributions to the organization. Therefore, multicultural organizations develop mechanisms that aim to eliminate bias and discriminatory treatment, including "reverse discrimination."

Structural Integration

Structural integration refers to the representation of cultural groups at all levels and functions within the organization.[74] In some instances, members of certain cultural groups and women could be clustered at the lower levels of the organization or disproportionately represented in certain functional departments. Of course, there is nothing wrong with pursuing careers in certain departments or career fields. However, when there is a systematic overrepresentation (or underrepresentation) of subgroup members at specific levels or functions, it is essential to determine the factors that are responsible for these patterns of career achievement. The multicultural organization strives to ensure that members of all groups are at levels and in jobs that are commensurate with their talents and consistent with their aspirations. Artificial obstacles to full representation in different parts of the organization—stereotypes, bias, or treatment discrimination—must be removed.

Minimize Intergroup Conflicts

As Taylor Cox has noted, "Conflict becomes destructive when it is excessive, not well managed, or rooted in struggles for power rather than the differentiation of ideas."[75] Culturally diverse organizations are susceptible to potential conflicts between different cultural groups. Language difficulties, stereotyping, mutual misunderstanding, and resentments of perceived preferential treatment can also exacerbate intergroup conflict.

The multicultural organization recognizes the difference between healthy conflict (clash over ideas) and unhealthy conflict (clash over lifestyles or cultures). Because relationship and task conflict tend to be lower in gender-diverse groups that possess inclusive climates,[76] it is reasonable to expect that diverse groups with inclusive climates may reap the benefits of lower levels of conflict in the form of improved performance.[77] Therefore, the multicultural organization should take steps to ensure that unhealthy intergroup conflicts are minimized, and that those conflicts that occur are dealt with quickly and effectively so they do not fester into more extensive and damaging ones.

Respond to Work–Life Issues

As we discussed in Chapter 3, a significant source of diversity in contemporary organizations is the substantial representation in the workforce of women (and increasingly men) who are concerned with balancing their career involvement with other parts of life such as family, community, friendships, and leisure activities. If this concern is not reconciled properly, it could result in an employee's decision to leave an organization or to refuse assignments or promotions that involve excessive time commitments, travel, or relocation. It could also result in feelings of extensive conflict and stress. The multicultural organization acknowledges the connections and conflicts between work and other parts of life, and seeks to create a culture that legitimizes work–life issues and helps employees balance their involvements in different life roles.

Organizational Approaches to the Challenges of Diversity

We have presented a portrait of the multicultural organization in its idealized form. While much progress has been made in this regard, employers still need to look for ways to achieve the goal of multiculturalism and to learn from the experiences and best practices of other organizations. Before we discuss specific programs and policies, it would be helpful to describe three general approaches to the challenge of diversity: affirmative action, valuing differences, and managing diversity.[78]

Affirmative Action

Affirmative action is a public policy with the goal to eliminate systematic bias against members of underrepresented groups by requiring an organization "to take proactive steps toward ensuring that the demographic characteristics of its workforce are consistent with the demographic characteristics of the labor markets in which it recruits."[79] Organizations with 50 or more employees that conduct business with the United States federal government are required to submit written affirmative action plans, although other organizations can develop voluntary plans.

Affirmative action organizations whose workforce contains proportionately fewer women and/or minority group members in certain jobs than are available in the labor market are required to take "affirmative" steps to reduce the disparity. Affirmative action does not require organizations to develop quotas in hiring or promotions, but rather action plans, goals, and timetables to ensure progress toward achieving a better representation of the workforce to the labor market. Seven core components of many affirmative action plans include ensuring management accountability; examining organizational structures, cultures and systems; understanding representation; providing training; offering mentoring programs; promoting advocacy groups; and emphasizing shared values among all stakeholders.[80]

Roosevelt Thomas has argued that affirmative action, born during the civil rights movement of the 1960s, was based on five assumptions:[81]

1. Adult, white males make up the U.S. business mainstream.
2. The U.S. economy is solid and unchanging.
3. Women, minorities, and immigrants should be allowed to join organizations for reasons of common decency.
4. Extensive prejudice keeps women, minorities, and immigrants out of organizations.
5. Legal and social pressure is required to bring women, minorities, and immigrants into organizations.

According to Thomas, these five assumptions may no longer be valid. First, because of the demographic shifts we have discussed, the "mainstream" is already diverse. Second, the economy is anything but stable, and it has forced organizations to become more competitive and to seek talent from all segments of society. Third, the major problem is no longer getting women and minorities into organizations but rather fully utilizing their capabilities throughout the organization. Fourth, blatant prejudice on the basis of race and gender has generally been replaced by perceived concerns about education and skill qualifications. Finally, coercion is less likely to play a dominant role today.

Although affirmative action has been successful in many respects, it is unlikely to solve the long-term needs of organizations and employees in and of itself.[82] It is the object of strongly held (and varying) views by different groups in society and is increasingly under legal attack.[83] As organizations change their focus toward ensuring the full contributions of all members of a diverse organization, additional approaches are required.[84]

Valuing Differences

This approach goes beyond "meeting the numbers" of affirmative action by attempting "to encourage awareness and respect for diversity within the workplace."[85] Through various types of educational and training activities, the valuing differences approach attempts to improve interpersonal relationships in a diverse organization by achieving one or more of the following objectives:[86]

- An understanding of differences among people.
- An understanding of one's own feelings toward people who are different in some respect.
- An understanding of how differences among people can be an advantage to an organization.
- Improved working relationships between people who are different from one another.

Thomas points out that "valuing differences" activities can help improve the quality of relationships between employees and can reduce blatant forms of prejudice and discrimination. However, because an understanding and acceptance of diversity are not necessarily sufficient in and of themselves to maximize the contributions of all employees, a third approach—managing diversity—should also be considered.

Managing Diversity

In Thomas's view, "Managing diversity is a holistic approach to creating a corporate environment that allows all kinds of people to reach their full potential in pursuit of corporate objectives."[87] He believes that the need to manage diversity is derived from the following questions:

> Given the competitive environment we face and the diverse workforce we have, are we getting the highest productivity possible? Does our system work as smoothly as it could? Is morale as high as we would wish? And are those things as strong as they would be if all the people who worked here were the same sex and race and nationality and had the same lifestyle and value system and way of working?[88]

Organizational Programs and Policies

We now turn to a discussion of programs and policies that organizations can use to manage diversity. Some of these programs are derived from affirmative action, because the need to ensure equitable access to organizations has not yet disappeared. Other programs involve valuing differences because special efforts are often required for employees to understand their feelings about people who are different. But taken together, the programs represent a set of actions designed to manage diversity as Roosevelt Thomas has used the term: a comprehensive attempt to change the culture of an organization so that all employees can contribute to the productivity and profitability of the organization. Table 11.1 identifies key components of a comprehensive process to manage diversity.

In order to manage diversity effectively, an organization must understand what constitutes diversity in its world, and must signify the importance of managing diversity to the internal and external environment. Central to Thomas's views is the recognition that diversity goes beyond race and gender. Diversity includes all significant differences in the experiences, perspectives, and backgrounds of different groups within an organization's workforce. Many organizations experience difficulties establishing cooperative relationships between line and support functions, between manufacturing and sales, between exempt and non-exempt staff, or between older and younger employees. These difficulties may limit the contributions that certain segments of the workforce can and should make. Organizations should determine the relevant dimensions of diversity that need to

Table 11.1 Components of a Comprehensive Diversity Management Program

I.	Communication Regarding the Meaning and Importance of Diversity
	Expanded Meaning of Diversity
	Mission Statement
	Orientation
II.	Unbiased Hiring Systems
III.	Identification of Critical Diversity Issues
	Assessment of Organizational Culture
	Ongoing Research
	Diversity Task Forces
IV.	Diversity Training: Valuing Differences
V.	Language Policy and Programs
VI.	Sexual Harassment Policy
VII.	Full Utilization of Career Systems
	Career Planning
	Mentoring and Other Supportive Relationships
	Developmental Experiences
	Proactive Promotion Planning
	Ongoing Monitoring of all Systems
VIII.	Work–life Programs and Policies
	Maternity and Paternity Support
	Dependent Care
	Flexible Work Arrangements & Career Systems
	Legitimize Work–Life Issues
IX.	Leadership and Accountability

be managed successfully and communicate the processes pertaining to diversity-oriented procedures that may influence decision-making processes and the execution of the organization's diversity-related policies and practices.[89]

Having established the meaning of diversity, an organization must signify to all its stakeholders—for example, employees, the board of directors, stockholders, suppliers, and customers—that it is committed to managing diversity. The incorporation of a statement regarding diversity in its mission statement would communicate an organization's serious commitment in this area. Also, orientation programs represent an important vehicle for an organization to communicate significant elements of its culture to newcomers in the workplace. Such programs can be used to inform new employees about the meaning and significance of diversity in the organization, and can begin to lay the foundation for positive attitudes toward diversity.

Unbiased Hiring Systems

Organizations must constantly guard against discriminatory hiring practices. Not only is it illegal to discriminate against members of protected groups, but it is also unwise from a business perspective. As we have noted many times, an organization cannot afford to exclude effective employees from its workforce, and talent, motivation, and commitment are found in all groups within society, irrespective of race, gender, religion, national origin, age, sexual orientation, physical disability, or veteran status.

For these reasons, organizations must engage in aggressive recruiting practices to locate the most talented applicants from all groups within society. Then they must scrutinize each part of the hiring process—application blanks, interviews, psychological tests—to ensure that they are valid and nondiscriminatory.

Identification of Critical Diversity Issues

It is recommended that organizations seeking to manage diversity conduct an assessment of their diversity climate or culture.[90] An organization's culture includes its assumptions about people, its norms and values, and its expectations regarding what people should do and how they should do it. Certain assumptions and beliefs that emanate from organizational culture may not be conducive to the effective management of diversity. Companies can assess their culture by administering surveys, conducting interviews, and observing what goes on in the organization. A culture assessment can help to identify sources of bias and can determine what elements of the culture might have to be changed to create opportunities for all employees to develop in their careers and contribute effectively to the organization.[91]

In addition to a culture assessment, ongoing research into management practices and employee attitudes can help organizations identify problems associated with managing a diverse workforce. Employee surveys can cover a wide range of topics relevant to diversity: perceptions of advancement opportunities, usefulness of human resource practices (e.g., performance appraisal, mentoring), supervisor–subordinate relationships, and organizational reward systems. Focus groups can be conducted in which small groups of targeted employees (e.g., women, older employees) share their perceptions regarding the organization and the practices that have helped and hindered their career growth. Useful information can also be obtained from diversity task forces or committees.

Diversity Training and Learning

Diversity training programs are designed to enhance "the awareness, knowledge, and interpersonal skills required to work successfully with others who are different from oneself."[92] These programs frequently include presentations, role-playing activities, team-building experiences, and videos. Diversity training should not be a standalone activity that replaces other diversity initiatives. Nevertheless, it can be one valuable process that enables employees to hold more positive attitudes toward diversity in general, increase their knowledge about diversity issues, understand the basis for stereotyping, and perhaps develop the skills necessary to work more effectively with others from different backgrounds.[93] Consider the description of the following program:

> A deep commitment to diversity learning is demonstrated by Sodexo, Inc., a leading provider of food- and facilities-management services that has more than 136,000 employees in the United States and touches more than 75 million customers in 80 countries worldwide every day.[94] Because diversity and inclusion are central elements of Sodexo's business strategy, they are incorporated in all business and human resources initiatives and policies. One important aim of Sodexo's program is to enhance diversity competencies at all levels throughout the organization. These competencies include understanding the business case for diversity and inclusion, establishing and sustaining a diverse and inclusive work environment, utilizing diversity as a competitive advantage though the effective management of an increasingly diverse workforce, and securing and retaining diverse clients, customers, suppliers, and partnered relationships with women- and minority-run businesses.
>
> To achieve these competencies, Sodexo delivers numerous learning programs from the top management level (where diversity programs are conducted at senior management team meetings) to individual managers (who take an eight-hour introductory course on commitment to diversity and inclusion) and work teams (who can receive a customized learning program based on their unique needs; for example, selling to a diverse client base). Sodexo believes that its diversity learning initiatives have contributed to its effectiveness and growth. Sodexo has consistently earned "best place to work" awards, due to its diversity and inclusion strategies, and is proud of the quality of life experiences of women and minorities.

Language Policies and Programs

Companies, especially ones with significant global operations, can experience difficulties that arise from multiple languages spoken in the workplace. In the U.S., employees who do not speak English may misunderstand a supervisor's directive and may resent the fact that others in the organization have not taken the trouble to learn their native language. English-speaking employees, on the other hand, may resent the difficulties and inconveniences imposed by employees who do not communicate well (if at all) in English.

Organizations need to understand the difficulties stemming from language differences, and must be willing to provide flexible solutions. As one example, Roosevelt Thomas recommends that an organization that employs predominantly Hispanics asks, "Is there a compelling business reason for these workers to speak English? Does the nature of their work require it? Is it too much to ask me to speak English and Spanish?"[95] In fact, McDonald's is offering an English as a second language program called English under the Arches, and also offers multiple language courses at Hamburger University for employees who need to travel abroad. Language classes in Japanese, Spanish, German, French, and Mandarin Chinese are offered at Hamburger University. The intent of these programs is for employees to be better able to communicate with other employees across the globe.[96]

Sexual Harassment Policy

Sexual harassment is a form of gender discrimination in violation of Title VII of the Civil Rights Act of 1964. Title VII applies to companies with 15 or more employees. The Equal Employment Opportunity Commission has adopted the following definition of *sexual harassment*:

> Unwelcome sexual advances, requests for sexual favors (often considered "quid pro quo" or an exchange of "this for that"), or other verbal or physical conduct of a sexual nature constitute sexual harassment when this conduct explicitly or implicitly affects an individual's employment, unreasonably interferes with one's work performance, or creates an intimidating or hostile environment.

- The victim or harasser may be a woman or a man. The victim does not have to be of the other sex.
- The harasser can be the victim's supervisor, an agent of the employer, a supervisor in another area, a co-worker, a customer, supplier, or other non-employee.
- The victim does not have to be the person harassed but could be anyone else affected by the offensive conduct in the work environment.
- Unlawful sexual harassment may occur without economic injury to or discharge of the victim.
- The harasser's conduct must be unwelcome.[97]

Clearly, sexual harassment is a serious situation for all parties involved in the action. Not only does the target suffer a personal indignity, but the target's job satisfaction, career development, psychological well-being, and health may deteriorate as well.[98] Moreover, the harasser may be subject to severe disciplinary action, including termination, and the employer may be liable for the actions of its employees. Often, fear of backlash keeps victims from seeking organizational relief. Widespread mishandling of sexual harassment complaints erodes trust in the organization during the grievance process, which may in turn impede future victim responses to sexual harassment. It is important for organizations to be proactive and follow due process in properly handling sexual harassment claims; hand down punishments to harassers that match the severity of the infraction; and remain cognizant of the potential differences in the ways women and men respond to sexual harassment.[99]

It is likely that the most effective deterrent to sexual harassment is the knowledge that it will not be tolerated in the workplace. A strong sexual harassment policy statement that defines sexual harassment, indicates its seriousness, and specifies the consequences for the harasser is necessary. However, the credibility of the policy will be sustained only if the employer investigates complaints swiftly and fairly, and enforces the disciplinary action that is warranted.

Although perhaps not as well-known as sexual harassment, age harassment is a violation of the Age Discrimination in Employment Act of 1967 and the Civil Rights Act of 1964. Harassment on the basis of race, religion, or national origin is also a violation of the

Civil Rights Act of 1964. Clearly, any form of harassment is inconsistent with an appreciation of diversity and can perpetuate a culture of disrespect and mistrust.

Full Utilization of Career Systems

We have noted throughout this book that career growth is enhanced when employees actively manage their careers and when organizations provide support in the form of performance appraisal and feedback systems, mentoring, training, challenging jobs, developmental assignments, and promotion planning. According to Roosevelt Thomas, "Managing diversity is a comprehensive managerial process for developing an environment that works for all employees."[100] That is, by managing diversity, organizations attempt to create a culture in which all employees can benefit from the organizations' career systems, and in which individuals are not disadvantaged because of their cultural background.

Why do special attempts have to be made to ensure that some individuals are not disadvantaged in their pursuit of career growth? We have discussed the potential challenges that women and people of color may experience in receiving satisfactory opportunities for developing skills and career contacts. Whether or not the organization has intentionally favored one group over another, these lost opportunities can hamper the careers of affected individuals. Therefore, organizations should take steps to ensure that support and career opportunities are available to all employees through some or all of the following activities:

- Monitor the progress of all employees to determine whether the careers of women, people of color, and members of other underrepresented groups are disadvantaged in some respect.
- If it is discovered that the careers of some groups of employees are not flourishing relative to other groups, determine answers to the following questions:
    - Do employees perceive the organization's culture to be unsupportive and an obstacle to their career development?
    - Is the performance appraisal system biased?
    - Are some groups of employees provided with fewer opportunities to develop their skills through formal training or on-the-job assignments?
    - Are some groups of employees less likely to be mentored or less likely to be in an effective mentoring relationship?
    - Are some groups of employees less likely to be considered for promotions or special projects despite performing effectively on their jobs?
- Address problematic responses to the questions raised above by revising career development systems (e.g., performance appraisal, training and development, mentoring) to ensure inclusion and fairness.
- Hold ongoing discussions among senior managers to ensure that career systems are working for everyone and that the accomplishments of all employees are recognized and rewarded.

Effective diversity initiatives have several qualities in common. First, top management is committed to diversity and is actively involved in the process. Second, the companies are systematically tracking women and minorities to ensure that they are provided with useful developmental opportunities and to assess their progress in the organization. Indeed, one primary aim of such efforts is to make sure that talented candidates for promotion are not overlooked in the decision-making process.

Work–Life Programs and Policies

In Chapter 3, we discussed the need for organizations to help their employees to balance their work and nonwork lives, and we proposed several programs that organizations can provide:

- Maternal and paternal support.
- Dependent care (e.g., on-site childcare, eldercare).
- Flexible work arrangements (e.g., flexible work schedules, telework, and job sharing).
- Flexible career systems.
- Culture change to legitimize work–life issues.

You may wish to review the material on work–life balance discussed in Chapter 3 in the broader context of managing diversity.

Leadership and Accountability

A lack of commitment and responsibility on the part of an organization can be a major impediment to the successful management of organizational diversity.[101] Taylor Cox and Stacy Blake-Beard provide the following assessment of the role of organizational leadership in managing diversity:

> Top management support and genuine commitment to cultural diversity is crucial. Champions for diversity are needed—people who will take strong personal stands on the need for change, role model the behaviors required for change, and assist with the work of moving the organization forward. Commitment must go beyond sloganism. For example, are human, financial, and technical resources being provided? Is this item prominently featured in the corporate strategy and consistently made a part of senior level staff meetings? Is there a willingness to change human resource management systems such as performance appraisal and executive bonuses? Is there a willingness to keep mental energy and financial support focused on this for a period of years, not months or weeks? If the answer to all of these questions is yes, the organization has genuine commitment. If not, then a potential problem with leadership is indicated.[102]

Effective leadership is needed to establish and maintain an organizational environment that supports diversity management. This need is particularly important in highly homogenous environments where managing workforce diversity becomes a greater challenge. To confront this challenge, one option would be to have a person (or a group) within the organization with clear authority and accountability for ensuring that diversity management issues are given proper strategic attention.[103]

Managing Diversity: Opportunities and Competence

This section examines two additional questions regarding the diversity management process: (1) Should there be "special programs" for targeted groups within the organization? (2) Should organizations practice "preferential treatment"? Each question is complex, controversial, and politically sensitive, and neither question has an easy answer.

We have indicated throughout this chapter that the aim of diversity management is to enable all employees to contribute to the organization and reap the benefits of their accomplishments. Recall Roosevelt Thomas's observation that managing diversity helps an organization's management systems work for everyone. In an attempt to accomplish this aim, many organizations have developed programs for targeted groups, for example, a mentoring program for black managers or a career planning program for women professionals. Are programs targeted for select groups consistent or inconsistent with a philosophy of managing diversity?

On the one hand, it can be argued that if mentoring is so important, all employees (not just minority managers, for example) should be provided with an opportunity to participate in a mentoring program. Similarly, if career planning activities are vital to success, all employees (not just women professionals, for example) should be provided with career planning opportunities. To do otherwise, it is suggested, would be unfair to one group—white men—and would put this group at a disadvantage.

On the other hand, it can be asserted that special programs are needed because the existing systems that have worked for white men—developmental assignments, promotion planning, sponsorship—are not as available or are not as effective for other groups in the organization. It is suggested that bias, stereotyping, and neglect have historically excluded many women and minorities from the formal and informal systems that have served white men so well for so many years. According to this view, targeted programs are designed to level the playing field, not to give any group an unfair advantage.

It is our belief that organizations must determine whether their current practices and systems are effective for diverse groups. A combination of survey research, focus group interviews, observation, and deep soul searching should provide insight into this issue. If it is concluded that current systems are effective for all groups, perhaps no special programs are needed. On the other hand, if it is concluded that certain groups are disadvantaged by the current practices, then the organization has two options. One option is to provide programs or practices to all employees within a given job category (for example, all middle managers) and to ensure that no one is excluded from the program or practice by virtue of his or her membership in a subgroup. The second option is to provide programs especially targeted for selected groups. It is our opinion that the first option is the preferable long-term goal. However, targeted programs may be useful initially, especially if the group has special needs, or if the organization is concerned that the needs and the contributions of the group will simply not be recognized in a general program. One example is a successful mentoring program offered by the National Forum for Black Public Administrators that assists in the development of young, black managers into the next generation of senior public-sector administrators.[104]

A second and related issue concerns the perceived preferential treatment in career development and advancement accorded to women and minorities. We emphasize "perceived" because it is difficult to determine objectively the extent to which preferential treatment (often referred to as "reverse discrimination") is practiced.[105]

Companies committed to affirmative action typically set goals for the hiring and promotion of women and minorities. Given the powerful effect of goal-setting on task performance, the establishment of affirmative action goals is not unreasonable in and of itself—goals motivate action and often produce success. However, some observers believe that goals quickly become "quotas" and ultimately lower standards of job qualifications and job performance. We do not want to enter this fray, in part because "standards" are not always easily measured and because biases and stereotypes themselves can interfere with the objective assessment of standards. Moreover, other observers believe that affirmative action can be burdensome to employers with disabled applicants because the applicants do not need to disclose whether they have received prior accommodations when taking scholastic or selection tests. As a result, the employer may not be able to make well-informed selection decisions, which, at the same time, can create a high potential for failure on the job.[106]

It is important to reemphasize that most diversity advocates (and, we believe, a large segment of the public) firmly believe that decisions about hiring, training, development, and promotions must be made on the basis of competence rather than race, gender, or other social groupings. Managing diversity is entirely consistent with the ideology of meritocracy. Roosevelt Thomas has persuasively suggested that merit has three components:

task merit (capability to perform a task); cultural merit (capability to conform to the organization's culture); and political merit (capability to receive the endorsement of a powerful sponsor). Thomas believes that people who are "different" from the organization's power base often possess task merit but are not necessarily perceived to possess cultural merit or political merit. Moreover, all individuals, including (or especially) white men, have benefited from political assistance in their careers. As Thomas notes: "Managing diversity simply calls for the manager to ensure that cultural and political realities do not advantage or disadvantage anyone because of irrelevant considerations."[107]

Therefore, competence is and should be the major criterion for decisions affecting the careers of all employees. A key challenge in managing diversity is to provide sufficient attention and support to all individuals so that competence can be developed, recognized, and rewarded.

Individual Actions

In this section, we suggest actions for *all* employees pursuing careers in culturally diverse organizations based on the career management approach emphasized throughout this book.

Awareness of Self and Environment

- Understand the stereotypes you hold about members of other groups. Be willing to admit that you (like all people) may hold preconceived biases against people who are different from you.
- Understand other people, including those from backgrounds different from yours. Understand similarities and differences among people.
- Recognize that there is considerable variation in ability, interests, values, and personality within each group.
- Understand situations from other people's (and other groups') perspective.
- Understand your current organization's culture and its view of diversity. When seeking a new job in a different organization, assess its culture and view of diversity.
- Understand what it takes to be successful in your current work environment.
- Attempt to move your organization forward by identifying gaps and needs and by offering solutions. If you have the opportunity, establish accountability, commit resources, and measure progress towards an ideal environment.

Career Goal-Setting

- Set career goals that are personally meaningful to you.
- Pursue your vision of success and do not be constrained by what others think that you (as a woman, man, white, or person of color) are supposed to want.
- Communicate your goals to others inside and outside your organization.

Career Strategies

- Establish a broad network of social relationships inside and outside your organization. Look for opportunities for multicultural engagement that allow you to gain a better and broader appreciation of other peoples and cultures as a way to advance your personal development, skill set, and career prospects.[108]
- Do not compromise personal values in pursuing career goals.
- Be assertive in managing your career and in seeking new experiences and opportunities to develop new skills.
- Do not give up your uniqueness or cultural identity in trying to achieve success.

Career Appraisal

- Be willing to modify your attitude toward other people or groups as a result of your ongoing experiences with them.
- Be willing to change your own behavior toward people who are "different" from you.

Summary

Workforces within the developed sectors of the world have become increasingly diverse, and it is exceedingly important for organizations to manage diversity effectively. Organizations need to understand the reasons why members of different subgroups may experience restricted career opportunities. Stereotypes, feelings of psychological distance from people who are "different," and cultural misunderstandings can have subtle but important consequences for career achievement. Employees subjected to stereotyped attitudes may have difficulties establishing or maintaining supportive relationships, may not be provided with sufficient opportunities to develop or demonstrate their competence, may experience limited power on their jobs, and may be excluded from important informal (or formal) networks of mentors and support. These "lost opportunities" can have negative effects on employees' job performance and on their prospects for career advancement.

An organization seeking to manage diversity effectively should: develop a vision of multiculturalism that is central to the organization's mission and communicate that vision to all of the organization's constituencies; eliminate discrimination in hiring; identify the most salient issues that interfere with effectiveness in the diverse work environment; provide opportunities for employees to understand and appreciate differences among people; address significant language conflicts if they arise; develop and implement an effective sexual harassment policy; ensure that career policies and systems do not give unfair advantage or disadvantage to either gender, or to members of different racial or ethnic groups; develop work–life responsive programs and policies; and exercise consistent leadership and accountability for diversity throughout the organization.

Career Management *for Life*: Work–Life Implications from Chapter 11

- Many employees in contemporary organizations place a strong emphasis on achieving a greater balance between their work responsibilities and other parts of their life.
- Whereas balance for some employees is a matter of meeting work and family needs, other employees are concerned with balancing work with a variety of other life domains, including community and volunteer activities, friendships, spiritual involvement, and leisure and self-development pursuits.
- Organizations should recognize the diverse work–life needs of their employees, and—through formal and informal practices and a supportive culture—assist their employees in being productive and satisfied at work while meeting their needs in other parts of their life.
- Employees should manage their career with an understanding of the role that work, family, community, friendships, spiritual involvement, and leisure and self-development activities play in their life.

- Employees should understand that others may place different priorities on work, family, community, friendships, spiritual involvement, and leisure and self-development activities than they do.

Assignment

Interview an individual (e.g., a friend, classmate, or co-worker) who is not of the same gender or race/ethnicity as you are. Ask this individual about his or her values, career goals, and strengths and weaknesses. Then have the individual interview you on the same topics. Discuss the extent to which this individual's career experiences/career plans and your career experiences/career plans have been influenced by your respective backgrounds.

Discussion Questions

1. Examine Cox and Blake-Beard's six arguments regarding why the effective management of diversity can improve an organization's competitive advantage. Which arguments do you find most convincing and least convincing? Why?
2. To what extent do you believe that underrepresented employees experience the "lost opportunities" indicated in Exhibit 11.1: unsatisfactory supportive relationships, restricted developmental opportunities, restricted job power, peripheral career path assignments, and exclusion from informal networks? Do you think that lost opportunities are more likely to be experienced by members of some groups (such as those based on gender, race/ethnicity, age, sexual orientation, physical disability, religion, national culture, language, or veteran status) than other groups? Why or why not?
3. What stereotypes, if any, do you hold regarding members of the other gender? What stereotypes, if any, do you hold regarding individuals from different racial or ethnic groups? How accurate are these stereotypes and how do you think they were formed? What stereotypes do you think others hold of members of your gender and race/ethnic group? How accurate are these stereotypes?
4. Do you believe that a work group or organization that is culturally diverse (in terms of the gender and racial/ethnic composition as well as other aspects of diversity) is more effective than a culturally homogeneous group or organization? Why or why not?
5. Can discrimination be eliminated from the workplace? Why or why not? What should employers do to eliminate or reduce workplace discrimination? How much progress has been made in eliminating workplace discrimination in recent years? What do you predict for the next 5–10 years?

Chapter 11 Case: Dave the Aspiring Executive (Part A)

Dave began reflecting on the progress of his career over the past 12 years at the Xtel Corporation (fictitious name). He remembered how, early on, he received a great deal of support and assistance from Xtel, but those days seem to be long ago.

About 20 years ago, Xtel had instituted a program with two basic goals in mind: to help inner city minority youths gain access to a college education and to create a ready pool of minority college graduates to help Xtel satisfy affirmative action hiring goals. Under the program, Xtel would pay the college tuition of the minority students in exchange for a commitment to work summers for the corporation and to accept employment with the firm after graduation for a minimum of two years. Xtel would accept four new participants into the program each year, so that a maximum of 16 college students would be active at any one time.

Dave had always shown outstanding ability in math, winning awards in grade school and high school for his proficiency. During his junior year in high school Dave began looking at colleges in the area. He set his sights on the Ivy League school in the city. At the same time, Dave's high school guidance counselor told him about Xtel's assistance program. Dave applied immediately to the Xtel program, sending in a brief background statement, a sketch of his career interests, two letters of recommendation, and the newly arrived acceptance letter from the Ivy League school. After two months, Dave received a letter from Xtel stating he had been accepted into their program.

At college, Dave majored in computer science and did exceptionally well. He joined the Black Student Organization at the school and also worked for the college radio station. During his summer internships, Dave worked in a number of different departments at Xtel, mainly assisting in the development of computer applications in each function. Dave was impressed with the fact that even though Xtel was a Fortune 500 company, it was still caring for its employees—Dave had expected Xtel to be more impersonal in its treatment of employees.

In the middle of his senior year, Dave began discussing with Xtel's staffing manager where he would be working when he graduated. Dave was pleased that his first job would be in the audit department, working as a computer systems auditor. After two months of full-time work at Xtel, Dave had gotten a call from one of his former professors who inquired about his progress. During their conversation, she encouraged Dave to begin thinking about graduate school. With his grades, the professor was certain that Dave would have no trouble being accepted into the Ivy League school's Master of Science program in computer science. Dave sent an email to Xtel's head of Training and Development seeking company support for his pursuit of the master's degree—he was pleased that Xtel encouraged his attendance and also offered tuition reimbursement. Dave finished the degree in two years, again doing exceptionally well in his studies.

In his first five years at Xtel, Dave progressed rapidly, rising to the level of audit manager at the age of 28. Over this period, he had received challenging assignments and had even made a presentation to the audit committee of the company's board of directors. Now in his early 30s and with a wife and a young son, Dave was interested in continuing his advancement at Xtel, mainly to provide a nice income and financial security for his family. He hoped to be an officer within a year. But Dave was getting a subtle message from Xtel's upper management that maybe he had advanced as far as he could at Xtel—he was not receiving the challenging assignments or support anymore, and his latest performance review cryptically indicated the need for broader-based experience. One particular example of the lack of support stood out. Dave had thought that attendance at one of the premier executive management programs would be beneficial as a career advancement strategy. But Xtel refused to support Dave in this endeavor, indicating that they had already identified those individuals who would be attending executive programs. Of course, Dave knew that Xtel had never sent a minority employee to any executive management program.

Dave had never believed that his race had any influence on his treatment or career progress at Xtel, but he was beginning to wonder. Dave had seen Xtel's newly published five-year goals for affirmative action placement. He noted that the five-year objective for minority representation at the junior officer level had already been achieved. All at once Dave began to feel a little used. He questioned whether his progress at Xtel was truly a reflection of his ability and contributions, or was it more a function of helping to fulfill Xtel's affirmative action targets at successive levels in the hierarchy? He did find it interesting that the affirmative action targets were managed closely, with minority representation in a given grade usually hitting right on or near the target.

Dave thought about his situation for some time, contemplating his next step. His skills and educational background made him highly marketable. After a while, Dave decided to meet with Xtel's vice-president of human resources to discuss career prospects. At the meeting, Dave stated his strong desire to move up to the officer-level within a year; after all, some of his less qualified contemporaries had already reached that level. The lukewarm response Dave received from the vice-president gave him a clear message—his career at Xtel was in a holding pattern. Dave concluded it was time for a change. (Part B of Dave the Aspiring Executive is located at the end of Chapter 12.)

Case Analysis Questions

1. If Dave had the opportunity, what questions—if any—should he have asked the president of the Xtel Corporation regarding his recent treatment?
2. Do you believe that the Xtel Corporation has discriminated against Dave on the basis of his race? Why or why not?
3. To whom inside or outside Xtel could Dave have gone for social support? What types of support would have been most helpful: appraisal, instrumental, emotional, or informational? Why?

Notes

1 Cox, T. H. & Blake-Beard, S. (1991). Managing cultural diversity: Implications for organizational competitiveness. *Academy of Management Executive*, *5*, 45–56; Heet, J. A. (2006). Workforce 2020. In Greenhaus, J. H. & Callanan, G. A. (Eds.), *Encyclopedia of career development* (pp. 877–880). Thousand Oaks, CA: Sage; King, E. B., Dawson, J. F., West, M. A., Gilrane, V. L., Peddie, C. I. & Bastin, L. (2011). Why organizational and community diversity matter: Representativeness and the emergence of incivility and organizational performance. *Academy of Management Journal*, *54*, 1103–1118; Post, C. & Byron, K. (2015). Women on boards and firm financial performance: A meta-analysis. *Academy of Management Journal*, *58*, 1546–1571;

Robinson, G. & Dechant, K. (1997). Building a business case for diversity. *Academy of Management Executive, 11*, 21–31; Thomas, K. M. (2006). Diversity in organizations. In Greenhaus, J. H. & Callanan, G. A. (Eds.), *Encyclopedia of career development* (pp. 236–243). Thousand Oaks, CA: Sage; Thomas, R. R., Jr. (1991). *Beyond race and gender*. New York: AMACOM; Walsh, K., Fleming, S. S. & Enz, C. A. (2016). Give and you shall receive: Investing in the careers of women professionals. *Career Development International, 21*, 193–211.

2 Toossi, M. (2012). Employment outlook: 2010–2020. Labor force projections to 2020: A more slowly growing workforce. *Monthly Labor Review*, January, 43–64. Retrieved from www.bls.gov/opub/mlr/2012/01/art3full.pdf.

3 Toossi, M. (2015). Labor force projections to 2024: The labor force is growing, but slowly. *Monthly Labor Review*, U. S. Bureau of Labor Statistics, December, 1–33.

4 Bureau of Labor Statistics. (2017). Retrieved from www.bls.gov/news.release/empsit.t01.htm.

5 FRED Economic Data. (2017). Civilian labor force participation rate: Women. *Federal Reserve Bank of St. Louis*. Retrieved from https://fred.stlouisfed.org/series/LNS11300002.

6 FRED Economic Data. (2017). Civilian labor force participation rate: Men. *Federal Reserve Bank of St. Louis*. Retrieved from https://fred.stlouisfed.org/series/LNS11300001.

7 Goldin, C. & Katz, L. F. (2016). Women working longer: Facts and some explanations. *National Bureau of Economic Research, NBER Working Paper No. 22607*, September; Lusardi, A. & Mitchell, O. S. (2016). Older women's labor market attachment, retirement planning, and household debt. *National Bureau of Economic Research, NBER Working Paper No. 22606*, September.

8 Bureau of Labor Statistics. (2016b). The employment situation—January 2017. Retrieved from www.bls.gov/news.release/pdf/empsit.pdf.

9 Bureau of Labor Statistics. (2017). Retrieved from www.bls.gov/news.release/disabl.nr0.htm.

10 Toossi (2015).

11 DeSilver, D. (2016). More older Americans are working, and working more, than they used to. *Pew Research Center*. Retrieved from www.pewresearch.org/fact-tank/2016/06/20/more-older-americans-are-working-and-working-more-than-they-used-to.

12 McKinsey & Company. (2016). Women in the workplace. Retrieved from www.mckinsey.com/business-functions/organization/our-insights/women-in-the-workplace-2016.

13 Deloitte. (2017). Missing pieces report: The 2016 board diversity census of women and minorities on Fortune 500 boards. *Alliance for Board Diversity*, 1–25.

14 Cox & Blake-Beard (1991).

15 Avery, D. R. (2006). Racial discrimination. In Greenhaus, J. H. & Callanan, G. A. (Eds.), *Encyclopedia of career development* (pp. 667–671). Thousand Oaks, CA: Sage; Derous, E. & Ryan, A. M. (2006). Religious discrimination. In Greenhaus, J. H. & Callanan, G. A. (Eds.), *Encyclopedia of career development* (pp. 686–690). Thousand Oaks, CA: Sage; Gutek, B. A. (2006). Sex discrimination. In Greenhaus, J. H. & Callanan, G. A. (Eds.), *Encyclopedia of career development* (pp. 730–734). Thousand Oaks, CA: Sage; Keene, J. (2006). Age discrimination. In Greenhaus, J. H. & Callanan, G. A. (Eds.), *Encyclopedia of career development* (pp. 10–14). Thousand Oaks, CA: Sage.

16 In our discussion of discrimination, we often use the term minority group members broadly to include underrepresented minorities based on sex, race, ethnicity, age, or other demographic characteristics.

17 Bell, M. P., Berry, D. P., Marquardt, D. J. & Tiffany, G. G. (2013). Introducing discriminatory job loss: Antecedents, consequences, and complexities. *Journal of Managerial Psychology, 28*, 584–605.

18 Ibid.

19 Morrison, A. M. & Von Glinow, M. A. (1990). Women and minorities in management. *American Psychologist, 45*, 200–222. Quotation is on p. 200.

20 Thomas (2006). Quotation is on p. 240.

21 Catalyst. (1999). *Women of color in corporate management: Opportunities and barriers*. Retrieved from www.catalyst.org/knowledge/women-color-corporate-management-opportunities-and-barriers.

22 Avery (2006); Baxter, G. W. (2012). Reconsidering the black–white disparity in federal performance ratings. *Public Personnel Management, 41*, 199–218; Lyness (2006).

23 Lyness (2006); for a study that found no sex difference in promotions to senior management, see Powell, G. N. & Butterfield, D. A. (1994). Investigating the "glass ceiling" phenomenon: An empirical study of actual promotions to top management. *Academy of Management Journal, 37*, 68–86; McKinsey & Company (2016).

24 Yap, M. & Konrad, A. M. (2009). Gender and racial differentials in promotions: Is there a sticky floor, a mid-level bottleneck, or a glass ceiling? *Relations Industrielle*, *64*, 593–619.
25 Pulakos, E. D., White, L. A., Oppler, S. H. & Borman, W. C. (1989). Examination of race and sex effects on performance ratings. *Journal of Applied Psychology*, *74*, 770–780.
26 Greenhaus, J. H., Parasuraman, S. & Wormley, W. M. (1990). Effects of race on organizational experiences, job performance evaluations, and career outcomes. *Academy of Management Journal*, *33*, 64–86; Sinangil, H. K. & Ones, D. S. (2003). Gender differences in expatriate job performance. *Applied Psychology: An International Review*, *52*, 461–475.
27 Rodríguez-Ruiz, O., Rodríguez-Duarte, A. & Gómez-Martínez, L. (2016). Does a balanced gender ratio improve performance? The case of Spanish banks (1999–2010). *Personnel Review*, *45*, 103–120.
28 Hernandez, M., Avery, D. R., Tonidandel, S., Hebl, M. R., Smith, A. N. & McKay, P.F. (2016). The role of proximal social contexts: Assessing stigma-by-association effects on leader appraisals. *Journal of Applied Psychology*, *101*, 68–85; Kraiger, K. & Ford, J. K. (1985). A meta-analysis of ratee race effects in performance ratings. *Journal of Applied Psychology*, *70*, 56–65; McKay, P. F. & McDaniel, M. A. (2006). A reexamination of black–white mean differences in work performance: More data, more moderators. *Journal of Applied Psychology*, *91*, 538–554; Roth, P. L., Huffcutt, A. I. & Bobko, P. (2003). Ethnic group differences in measures of job performance: A new meta-analysis. *Journal of Applied Psychology*, *88*, 694–706; Wingfield, A. H. & Wingfield, J. H. (2014). When visibility hurts and helps: How intersections of race and gender shape black professional men's experiences with tokenization. *Cultural Diversity and Ethnic Minority Psychology*, *20*, 483–490.
29 Baxter (2012); Greenhaus et al. (1990); Pulakos et al. (1989).
30 McKay & McDaniel (2006); Roth et al. (2003) reported smaller job performance differences between Hispanics and whites than between blacks and whites.
31 Kraiger & Ford (1985). Note that several subsequent studies found either no evidence that raters give higher performance ratings to same-race subordinates (Waldman, D. A. & Avolio, B. J. (1991). Race effects in performance evaluations: Controlling for ability, education, and experience. *Journal of Applied Psychology*, *76*, 897–901), or only a very small tendency to give higher ratings to same-race subordinates (Pulakos et al., 1989).
32 Holder et al. (2015); Johnson, C. & Eby, L. T. (2011). Evaluating career success of African American males: It's what you know and who you are that matters. *Journal of Vocational Behavior*, *79*, 699–709; Wingfield & Wingfield (2014).
33 Greenhaus, J. H. & Parasuraman, S. (1993). Job performance attributions and career advancement prospects: An examination of gender and race effects. *Organizational Behavior and Human Decision Processes*, *55*, 273–297.
34 Yap & Konrad (2009).
35 Ilgen, D. R. & Youtz, M. A. (1986). Factors affecting the evaluation and development of minorities in organizations. In Rowland, K. & Ferris, G. (Eds.), *Research in personnel and human resource management: A research annual* (pp. 307–337). Greenwich, CT: JAI Press.
36 Block, C. J. (2006). Stereotyping of workers. In Greenhaus, J. H. & Callanan, G. A. (Eds.), *Encyclopedia of career development* (pp. 766–767). Thousand Oaks, CA: Sage.
37 Ashburn-Nardo, L., Morris, K. A. & Goodwin, S. A. (2008). The Confronting Prejudiced Responses (CPR) model: Applying CPR in organizations. *Academy of Management Learning & Education*, *7*, 332–342; Holder et al. (2015); Lyness (2006); Wingfield & Wingfield (2014).
38 Bell, E. E. & Nkomo, S. M. (2003). *Our separate ways: Black and white women and the struggle for professional identity*. Boston, MA: Harvard Business School Press Books; Jones, E. (1986). Black managers: The dream deferred. *Harvard Business Review*, *64*, 84–93.
39 Catalyst. (2005). Retrieved from www.catalyst.org/publication/94/women-take-care-men-take-charge-stereotyping-of-us-business-leaders-exposed; Eagly, A. H. (2007). Female leadership advantage and disadvantage: Resolving the conflict. *Psychology of Women Quarterly*, *31*, 1–12; Eddleston, K. A., Veiga, J. F. & Powell, G. N. (2006). Explaining sex differences in managerial career satisfier preferences: The role of gender self-schema. *Journal of Applied Psychology*, *91*, 437–445; Heilman, M. E. & Eagly, A. (2008). Gender stereotypes are alive, well, and busy producing workplace discrimination. *Industrial & Organizational Psychology*, *1*, 393–398.
40 Gutek (2006).
41 Heilman, M. E. (2001). Description and prescription: How gender stereotypes prevent women's ascent up the organizational ladder. *Journal of Social Issues*, *57*, 657–674.

42 Catalyst. (2014). Retrieved from www.catalyst.org/zing/how-new-discrimination-holding-women-back.

43 Finkelstein, L. M., Allen, T. D. & Rhoton, L. (2003). Examining the role of age in mentoring relationships. *Group and Organization Management*, *28*, 249–281; Green, S. G., Anderson, S. E. & Shivers, S. L. (1996). Demographic and organizational influences on leader-member exchange and related work attitudes. *Organizational Behavior and Human Decision Processes*, *66*, 203–214; Tsui, A. S., Egan, T. D. & Xin, K. R. (1995). Diversity in organizations: Lessons from demography research. In Chemers, M. M., Oskamp, S. & Costanzo, M. A. (Eds.), *Diversity in organizations: New perspectives for a changing workplace* (pp. 191–219). Thousand Oaks, CA: Sage.

44 Almeida, S. & Bertone, S. (2016). The role of contextual factors in employer recruitment decision making: Evidence from regional Australia. *New Zealand Journal of Employment Relations*, *41*, 22–40; Korman, A. K. (1988). *The outsiders: Jews and corporate America*. Lexington, MA: Lexington Books.

45 Tubergen, F., Maas, I. & Flap, H. (2004). The economic incorporation of immigrants in 18 Western societies: Origin, destination, and community effects. *American Sociological Review*, *69*, 704–727. Quotation is on p. 709.

46 Holder et al. (2015); Ilgen & Youtz (1986); Johnson & Eby (2011); Kanter, R. M. (1989). Differential access to opportunity and power. In Alvarez, A. (Ed.), *Discrimination in organizations* (pp. 52–68). San Francisco: Jossey-Bass; Wingfield & Wingfield (2014).

47 Holder et al. (2015); Lyness, K. S. & Thompson, D. E. (1997). Above the glass ceiling? A comparison of matched samples of female and male executives. *Journal of Applied Psychology*, *82*, 359–375; Wingfield & Wingfield (2014); Kanter (1989); Martin (1991).

48 Fernandez, J. P. (1988). Human resources and the extraordinary problems minorities face. In London, M. & Mone, E. M. (Eds.), *Career growth and human resource strategies* (pp. 227–239). New York: Quorum Books; Greenhaus et al. (1990); Ibarra, H. (1995). Race, opportunity, and diversity of social circles in managerial networks. *Academy of Management Journal*, *38*, 673–703; Kanter (1989).

49 Blake-Beard, S. D., Murrell, A. & Thomas, D. (2007). Unfinished business: The impact of race on understanding mentoring relationships. In Ragins, B. R. & Kram, K. E. (Eds.), *The handbook of mentoring at work: Theory, research, and practice* (pp. 223–247). Thousand Oaks, CA: Sage; Holder et al. (2015); Johnson & Eby (2011); McKeen, C. & Bujaki, M. (2007). Gender and mentoring. In Ragins, B. R. & Kram, K. E. (Eds.), *The handbook of mentoring at work: Theory, research, and practice* (pp. 197–222). Thousand Oaks, CA: Sage.

50 Allen, T. D. (2006). Mentoring. In Greenhaus, J. H. & Callanan, G. A. (Eds.), *Encyclopedia of career development* (pp. 486–493). Thousand Oaks, CA: Sage; Dreher, G. F. & Cox, T. H. (1996). Race, gender, and opportunity: A study of compensation attainment and the establishment of mentoring relationships. *Journal of Applied Psychology*, *81*, 297–308; Ragins, B. R. (1997). Diversified mentoring relationships in organizations: A power perspective. *Academy of Management Review*, *22*, 482–521.

51 Bell & Nkomo (2003); Holder et al. (2015); Johnson & Eby (2011).

52 Allen (2006); Ortiz-Walters, R. & Gilson, L. L. (2005). Mentoring in academia: An examination of the experiences of protégés of color. *Journal of Vocational Behavior*, *67*, 459–475.

53 Blake-Beard et al. (2007).

54 Allen (2006); Lyons, B. D. & Oppler, E. S. (2004). The effects of structural attributes and demographic characteristics on protégé satisfaction in mentoring programs. *Journal of Career Development*, *30*, 215–229; Ragins (1997); Ragins, B. R. & McFarlin, D. B. (1990). Perceptions of mentor roles in cross-gender mentor relationships. *Journal of Vocational Behavior*, *37*, 321–339.

55 McKeen & Pujaki (2007); Morgan, L. M. & Davidson, M. J. (2008). Sexual dynamics in mentoring relationships: A critical review. *British Journal of Management*, *19*, S120–S129.

56 Ortiz-Walters, R., Eddleston, K. A. & Simione, K. (2010). Satisfaction with mentoring relationships: Does gender identity matter? *Career Development International*, *15*, 100–120.

57 Morgan & Davidson (2008).

58 Jenkins, M. (2005). Why you need a mentor: Mentors are the most important resource for success on the job. Finding them can be a task: Positioning yourself to be selected as a mentee is another. Here's how to accomplish both. *Black Enterprise*, March, 1–5.

59 Charleston, L. J. (2012). A qualitative investigation of African Americans' decision to pursue computing science degrees: Implications for cultivating career choice and aspiration. *Journal of Diversity in Higher Education*, *5*, 222–243; Charleston, L. J., Gilbert, J. E., Escobar, B. &

Jackson, J. F. L. (2014). Creating a pipeline for African American computing science faculty: An innovative faculty /research mentoring program model. *Journal of Faculty Development*, *28*(1), 85–92. Retrieved from http://mentornet.org/organization/index.html.

60 Kanter, R. M. (1977). *Men and women of the corporation*. New York: Basic Books; Yoder, J. D. (2006). Tokenism. In Greenhaus, J. H. & Callanan, G. A. (Eds.), *Encyclopedia of career development* (pp. 810–811). Thousand Oaks, CA: Sage.

61 Holder et al. (2015); Kanter (1977); Wingfield & Wingfield (2014).

62 Holder et al. (2015); Wingfield & Wingfield (2014).

63 Holder et al. (2015); Yoder (2006).

64 Joplin, J. R. W. & Daus, C. S. (1997). Challenges of leading a diverse workforce. *Academy of Management Executive*, *11*, 32–47; Meghna, S. (2014). Is diversity management sufficient? Organizational inclusion to further performance. *Public Personnel Management*, *43*, 197–217; Robinson & Dechant (1997).

65 Rosener, J. B. (1990). Ways women lead. *Harvard Business Review*, November–December, 119–125; Heilman (2001); Heilman & Eagly (2008).

66 Grant, J. (1988). Women as managers: What they can offer to organizations. *Organizational Dynamics*, Winter, 56–63; Nanton, C. R. (2015). Shaping leadership culture to sustain future generations of women leaders. *Journal of Leadership, Accountability and Ethics*, *12*, 92–112.

67 Cox & Blake-Beard (1991); Holder et al. (2015); Wingfield & Wingfield (2014).

68 Carter, S. L. (1991). *Reflections of an affirmative action baby*. New York: Basic Books. Quotation is on p. 32.

69 Horwitz, S. K. & Horwitz, I. B. (2007). The effects of team diversity on team outcomes: A meta-analytic review of team demography. *Journal of Management*, *33*, 987–1015; McMahon, A. M. (2010). Does workplace diversity matter? A survey of empirical studies on diversity and firm performance, 2000–09. *Journal of Diversity Management*, *5*, 37–48. Bell, S. T., Villado, A. J., Lukasik, M. A., Belau, L. & Briggs, A. L. (2011). Getting specific about demographic diversity variable and team performance relationships: A meta-analysis. *Journal of Management, 37*, 709–743.

70 Thomas (1991). Quotation is on pp. 171–172.

71 Blake-Beard, S. (2006). Multicultural organization. In Greenhaus, J. H. & Callanan, G. A. (Eds.), *Encyclopedia of career development* (pp. 518–519). Thousand Oaks, CA: Sage. Quotation is on p. 518.

72 Cox, T. H. (1991). The multicultural organization. *Academy of Management Executive*, *5*, 34–47; also see Cox, T. H. (1993). *Cultural diversity in organizations: Theory, research & practice*. San Francisco: Berrett-Koehler.

73 Bell et al. (2013).

74 Cox (1991).

75 Ibid. Quotation is on p. 46.

76 Nishii, L. H. (2013). The benefits of climate for inclusion for gender-diverse groups. *Academy of Management Journal*, *56*, 1754–1774.

77 De Dreu, C. K. W. & Weingart, L. R. (2003). Task versus relationship conflict, team performance, and team member satisfaction: A meta-analysis. *Journal of Applied Psychology*, *88*, 741–749.

78 Cox, T. H. (2001). *Creating the multicultural organization: A strategy for capturing the power of diversity*. San Francisco, CA: Jossey-Bass; DeNisco, A. (2016, September 28). Does your company need a chief diversity officer? Retrieved from www.techrepublic.com/article/does-your-company-need-a-chief-diversity-officer; Fujimoto, Y., Härtel, C. E. J. & Azmat, F. (2013). Towards a diversity justice management model: Integrating organizational justice and diversity management. *Social Responsibility Journal*, *9*, 148–166; Linnehan, F. (2006). Affirmative action. In Greenhaus, J. H. & Callanan, G. A. (Eds.), *Encyclopedia of career development* (pp. 6–10). Thousand Oaks, CA: Sage; Pitts, D. (2009). Diversity management, job satisfaction, and performance: Evidence from U.S. federal agencies. *Public Administration Review*, *69*, 328–338; Thomas (2006); Thomas, R. R., Jr. (1990). From affirmative action to affirming diversity. *Harvard Business Review*, March–April, 107–117; Thomas (1991).

79 Linnehan (2006). Quotation is on p. 6.

80 Kellough, J. E. & Naff, K. C. (2004). Responding to a wake-up call: An examination of Federal Agency Diversity Management programs. *Administration & Society*, *36*, 62–90.

81 Thomas (1990).

82 Thomas (1991).

83 Konrad, A. M. & Linnehan, F. (1999). Affirmative action: History, effects and attitudes. In Powell, G. N. (Ed.), *Handbook of gender in organizations* (pp. 429–452). Thousand Oaks, CA: Sage; Linnehan (2006).

84 Pitts (2009).
85 Thomas (1991). Quotation is on p. 24.
86 Ibid.
87 Ibid. Quotation is on p. 167.
88 Ibid. Quotation is on p. 26.
89 Fujimoto et al. (2013).
90 Kossek, E. E. & Zonia, S. C. (1993). Assessing diversity climate: A field study of reactions to employer efforts to promote diversity. *Journal of Organizational Behavior*, *14*, 61–80; Cox & Blake-Beard (1991); Thomas (1991).
91 Raver, J. L. & Nishii, L. H. (2010). Once, twice, or three times as harmful? Ethnic harassment, gender harassment, and generalized workplace harassment. *Journal of Applied Psychology*, *95*, 236–254.
92 Thomas (2006). Quotation is on p. 242.
93 Kulik, C. T. & Roberson, L. (2008). Common goals and golden opportunities: Evaluations of diversity education in academic and organizational settings. *Academy of Management Learning & Education*, *7*, 309–331.
94 The discussion of Sodexo's diversity learning program is based on material presented in Anand, R. & Winters, M. (2008). A retrospective view of corporate diversity training from 1964 to the present. *Academy of Management Learning & Education*, *7*, 356–372.
95 Thomas (1991). Quotation is on p. 174.
96 Retrieved from www.mcdonalds.com/us/en-us/careers/training-and-education.html.
97 Retrieved from www.eeoc.gov/eeoc/publications/fs-sex.cfm.
98 Bose-Sperry, L. (2006). Sexual harassment. In Greenhaus, J. H. & Callanan, G. A. (Eds.), *Encyclopedia of career development* (pp. 734–738). Thousand Oaks, CA: Sage; Dionisi, A. M., Barling, J. & Dupré, K. E. (2012). Revisiting the comparative outcomes of workplace aggression and sexual harassment. *Journal of Occupational Health Psychology*, *17*, 398–408; Fitzgerald, L. F., Drasgow, F., Hulin, C. L., Gelfand, M. J. & Magley, V. J. (1997). Antecedents and consequences of sexual harassment in organizations: A test of an integrated model. *Journal of Applied Psychology*, *82*, 578–589; Settles, I. H., Buchanan, N. T., Yap, S. C. Y. & Harrell, Z. A. T. (2014). Sex differences in outcomes and harasser characteristics associated with frightening sexual harassment appraisals. *Journal of Occupational Health Psychology*, *19*, 133–142.
99 Benavides-Espinoza, C. & Cunningham, G. B. (2010). Bystanders' reactions to sexual harassment. *Sex Roles*, *63*, 201–213; Vijayasiri, G. (2008). Reporting sexual harassment: The importance of organizational culture and trust. *Gender Issues*, *25*, 43–61.
100 Thomas (1991). Quotation is on p. 10.
101 Thomas (2006); Martin (1991).
102 Cox & Blake-Beard (1991). Quotation is on pp. 52–53; Blake-Beard, S., Finley-Hervey, J. & Harquail, C. V. (2008). Journey to a different place: Reflections on Taylor Cox, Jr.'s career and research as a catalyst for diversity education and training. *Academy of Management Learning & Education*, *7*, 394–405.
103 Kalev, A., Dobbin, F. & Kelly, E. (2006). Best practices or best guesses? Assessing the efficacy of corporate affirmative action and diversity policies. *American Sociological Review*, *71*, 589–617; O'Brien, K. R., Scheffer, M., Nes, E. H. & van der Lee, R. (2015). How to break the cycle of low workforce diversity: A model for change. *PLoS One*, *10*, 1–15.
104 Retrieved from www.nfbpa.org/i4a/pages/index.cfm?pageid=3292 on February 9, 2017.
105 Avery (2006).
106 Rabenu, E. & Tziner, A. (2016). Selection of employees with disabilities—has the burden on the employer become too heavy? *Amfiteatru Economic*, *18*, 423–431.
107 Thomas (1991). Quotation is on p. 180.
108 Maddux, W. W., Bivolaru, E., Hafenbrack, A. C., Tadmor, C. T. & Galinsky, A. D. (2014). Expanding opportunities by opening your mind: Multicultural engagement predicts job market success through longitudinal increases in integrative complexity. *Social Psychological and Personality Science*, *5*, 608–615.

12 Entrepreneurial Careers

Just about everyone has, at one time or another, fantasized about owning his or her own business. A great many people actually make the fantasy a reality by becoming an entrepreneur. Indeed, interest in entrepreneurial careers and the establishment of new business ventures on a worldwide basis have grown steadily since the end of the Great Recession in 2009, and people all over the world see entrepreneurship as a high status and desirable career alternative.[1] According to data from the United States Bureau of Labor Statistics, the number of new business establishments in the U.S. increased by more than 20 percent during the period 2010 to 2015, rising from 560,000 new firm establishments in 2010 to nearly 700,000 by mid-decade.[2] In addition, entrepreneurial firms are the growth engine for new jobs. Newly established firms (less than one year old) created more than three million new jobs in the U.S. in 2015,[3] and each new firm that is established adds about six employees to total employment in the U.S.[4]

Entrepreneurs are agents of change.[5] They play an important role in the overall welfare of society by spurring economic growth and development, creating new jobs, and serving as role models for future generations of entrepreneurs.[6] Over the past three decades as the payrolls of Fortune 500 companies have declined significantly, entrepreneurial organizations have created tens of millions of jobs. As of 2015, it is estimated that 27 million working age adults in the U.S. are starting or running businesses, accounting for 14 percent of the total workforce.[7] Globally, entrepreneurship is viewed as the primary source of commercial development and the main tool to alleviate poverty and malnutrition.[8] In developing and underdeveloped sectors of the world, small and medium-sized enterprises generate economic growth, create jobs, and allow for technological innovation.[9]

Part of the allure and fantasy of being an entrepreneur is the potential for the wealth that can be attained through business success. It has been estimated that entrepreneurs own nearly one-third of all household wealth in the United States, and their median net worth is more than four times that of non-entrepreneur households.[10] *Forbes Magazine*'s annual list of the 400 Richest People in America reports that a great majority are entirely self-made. Clearly, entrepreneurship can be a rewarding career choice if the venture is successful.

Why the ongoing interest in entrepreneurial careers? Answering this question is not an easy task—the reasons are almost as varied as the number of entrepreneurs. They can range from seeking freedom from the corporate rat race to inheriting a business from a long-lost relative; from having a passion for a certain product or activity to taking advantage of favorable economic conditions. Whatever the factors involved, the decision to become an entrepreneur represents an appealing career choice to many people, and the interest in entrepreneurship continues to grow. In this chapter, we present an in-depth examination of the unique aspects of the entrepreneurial career. First, we define entrepreneurship and consider the various factors that lead individuals to seek entrepreneurial careers. Next, we review the social and educational support available to current and aspiring entrepreneurs. We then review the career experiences and the challenges faced by women and minority entrepreneurs. We conclude the chapter with suggestions for managing the entrepreneurial career that are linked with the career management model presented in this book.

Entrepreneurship: An Overview

There exist in the literature a variety of definitions for the terms entrepreneur and entrepreneurship, each reflecting a distinct perspective on the topic.[11] The 19th-century economist John Stuart Mill identified "risk bearing," or the ability to accept and take risks, as the characteristic that distinguishes an entrepreneur from an organizational manager.[12] Another economist, Joseph Schumpeter, saw entrepreneurship as simply the "creative activity of an innovator."[13] From his perspective, innovation is the distinguishing characteristic. A significant stream of research sees entrepreneurs as having unique "psychological characteristics," including the values, attitudes, and needs that drive them to be in charge of a firm and to exhibit persistence in an entrepreneurial endeavor.[14] Several additional views of entrepreneurship have emerged linked to certain behaviors and competencies such as creative opportunism, taking advantage of favorable technological or economic conditions, and insight into market conditions.[15] The consistent themes in these views are creativity, innovation, and risk-taking propensity.

Taking all of these notions into account, we define entrepreneurship as *managing a business of one's own that requires personal sacrifice, creativity, and risk-taking, to create something of value*. This definition combines the relevant aspects of prior characterizations covering ownership, innovation, novelty, risk-taking, and creative opportunism—themes that the literature consistently applies to the term entrepreneurship.

Choosing an Entrepreneurial Career

There are a number of factors that make an entrepreneurial career distinct from the more traditional career where one is employed by an organization.[16] First, entrepreneurial careers are marked by a substantially higher degree of personal commitment to the success of the firm because the career and the business are intertwined. In this sense, the career is the business and the business is the career. Success or failure in one domain is directly tied to success or failure in the other. Thus, as we've indicated, the entrepreneurial career involves a substantially higher degree of risk—of personal failure, monetary loss, and career turbulence. Indeed, the failure rates of new U.S. business ventures are significant, with an average of about 10 percent per year for the first several years after establishment.[17] For example, for firms in the U.S. started in 1994, about 20 percent were still surviving two decades later, while for firms begun in 2005, only about a third were still surviving a decade later.[18] While these statistics indicate that entrepreneurial efforts are risky, the positive aspects continue to make business ownership an attractive career option, especially in comparison with ongoing limitations with a standard organizational career.

Another factor that makes the entrepreneurial career unique is the lower degree of structure, predictability, and support as compared to what an employer would provide. Of course, for some, structure and predictability are the exact reasons to avoid an organizational career. But for others who are unprepared, the lack of corporate infrastructure and support systems can be discomfiting.

A third distinguishing factor is that those in entrepreneurial careers must possess a greater tendency toward action and innovation. Specifically, the nature of entrepreneurial firms is that decisive actions are required to respond to uncertain market conditions. By extension, the entrepreneur, as the person in charge, must show the ability to respond quickly to environmental change. In contrast, life in an organizational career is slower-paced. In many large organizations, entrenched bureaucracies with risk-averse layers of management normally do not allow, nor do they necessarily reward, quick and innovative decision-making.

A fourth distinctive element of the entrepreneurial career is that the business owner performs a number of functional roles simultaneously. More precisely, the entrepreneur can be involved with operations, marketing, accounting, human resources, and planning functions all at the same time. Conversely, those in an organizational career typically play one functional role at a time, and the chance for organizational managers to have multi-functional influence is limited.

With the comparatively higher risk for personal and financial failure, the more extensive demands, and the lack of structure and support, one could ask why so many individuals would throw caution to the winds and embark on an entrepreneurial career. Research points to several general factors that can influence the choice of an entrepreneurial career.[19] These factors include seeking autonomy and independence, specific personality characteristics and psychological conditions that predispose one to an entrepreneurial career, environmental conditions, a passion for a specific product or activity, and the presence of role models. We will explore each of these factors in depth.

Need for Autonomy and Independence

One could argue that all employees value a certain degree of autonomy and independence in their work. Autonomy and independence imply that the individual experiences a substantial amount of freedom in his or her job—freedom of choice in decision-making, freedom of expression in work, freedom from close supervision, and freedom from the bureaucratic process. As we discussed in Chapter 5, in his research on career anchors, Edgar Schein identified *autonomy/independence* as a primary category in describing a person's possible occupational self-concept. Individuals who have an autonomy/independence anchor are mainly concerned with being free from organizational rules and restrictions, and tend to favor a career in which the person can decide when to work, on what to work, and how hard to work.[20] Reflecting the need for autonomy, early research on entrepreneurs also indicated that they often have trouble responding to authority figures, showing an unwillingness to submit to authority, feeling uncomfortable working under it, and consequently needing to escape from it.

Pursuing an entrepreneurial career is one of the primary ways that individuals can find an outlet for their autonomy and independence needs and their unwillingness to submit to authority and supervision.[21] Indeed, many entrepreneurs who drop out of traditional corporate jobs do so because of a need for freedom in decision-making and to avoid meddling from more senior managers or executives. It is clear that the desire for autonomy, independence, and freedom is a significant motivator for many entrepreneurs. Being one's own person by owning and managing a business is an alluring proposition, one that more and more aspiring entrepreneurs worldwide are acknowledging.

Personal Characteristics

A vast amount of research has examined whether entrepreneurs possess certain personality and psychological characteristics, traits, and attitudes that predispose them to undertaking business ventures of their own.[22] In this sense, it is believed that current and future entrepreneurs have common personalities and background factors that allow them to embark more easily on, and be successful in, an entrepreneurial career.

Need for Achievement

David McClelland first proposed that need for achievement is an important psychological characteristic of entrepreneurs. According to McClelland, those high in need for achievement exhibit three main behavioral traits: they take personal responsibility for finding solutions to problems; they set moderate performance goals and take moderate, calculated risks; and they desire specific feedback concerning performance.[23] Several studies have investigated the link between need for achievement (or achievement motivation) and entrepreneurship, with most of this research finding that achievement motivation does serve as a prevalent predictor of entrepreneurship.[24] Of course, a high need for achievement is characteristic of many successful leaders, not just entrepreneurs, but there is enough evidence to suggest that a high need for achievement can influence an individual's decision to become an entrepreneur.

Internal Locus of Control

Individuals with an internal locus of control believe they can largely manage their environment and their fate through their own actions and behaviors. In theory, those who believe they alone can control their destiny may be more likely to become, and be successful as, entrepreneurs than those who do not. However, locus of control has shown an inconsistent relationship with entrepreneurial behavior. Similar to need for achievement, an internal locus of control is generally associated with successful people, not just entrepreneurs. Still, research has concluded that a comparatively higher internal locus of control may differentiate entrepreneurs from the larger population.[25] Thus, an internal locus of control may serve as another underlying factor that influences the undertaking of and success in an entrepreneurial career.

Tolerance for Ambiguity

Research has shown that the ability to accept and deal with conflicting and uncertain situations, and to handle multiple, ambiguous assignments appear to distinguish the entrepreneurial personality from non-entrepreneurs.[26] Given the multiple demands of business ownership, it should not be surprising that entrepreneurs have a greater capacity to tolerate uncertainty in their lives than do organizational managers.

Risk-Taking Propensity

In discussing the definition of entrepreneurship, we noted that a willingness to take risks is a common element in describing entrepreneurs. While several studies have found entrepreneurs to be more likely to take risks than organizational managers, a few have found mixed results regarding risk-taking propensity as a personality trait of entrepreneurs.[27] However, some management scholars now suggest that while entrepreneurs are more aggressive and risk-oriented in their decision-making than managers in large organizations, this may not be self-evident to entrepreneurs because they often perceive comparatively lower risk in a given situation.[28] Specific cognitive biases, such as overconfidence, an illusion of control, and the use of limited (but positive) information, tend to influence the entrepreneur's perception of risk.[29] In addition, many entrepreneurs have such a strong belief in their ability to influence business outcomes that the possibility of failure is perceived as relatively low. Therefore, given similar situations, the entrepreneur is likely to perceive lower levels of risk than the non-entrepreneur. It may be more insightful to view entrepreneurs as capable risk managers whose natural abilities tend to defuse what non-entrepreneurs might view as high-risk situations.

Entrepreneurial Self-Concept

As we discussed in Chapter 5, individuals can have certain orientations toward work that reflect their personal motives, values, and talents. These orientations, known as career anchors, are the manifestation of the individual's self-concept or image in his or her career choice.[30] Another one of the career anchors described by Edgar Schein is entrepreneurial, where the individual's primary concern is to create something new and the desire for personal prominence in whatever is accomplished. The entrepreneurial anchor also reflects a desire to have freedom and autonomy to build the organization and create the business into the entrepreneur's own self-image. In effect, the entrepreneurial career anchor takes into account the prior personality traits discussed thus far—need for achievement, an internal locus of control, a tolerance for ambiguity, the willingness to bear risks, and desire for autonomy and control. The entrepreneurial anchor also suggests an individual's belief in his or her own abilities, a drive toward innovativeness, a tolerance for stress, and a proactive (take-charge) personality.[31]

In addition to Schein's career anchors, management scholars have studied the construct "entrepreneurial orientation," which conceptually represents a composite of entrepreneurial characteristics derived from self-exploration. Indeed, entrepreneurial orientation is defined as a "higher order" construct that reflects a number of underlying variables found to influence entrepreneurial behavior and success, including need for autonomy, innovativeness, proactivity, risk-taking, and competitive aggressiveness.[32]

Demographic and Background Factors

Studies have been conducted to see whether entrepreneurs could be differentiated from non-entrepreneurs based on a variety of demographic characteristics including the influence of one's parents. As with virtually any career choice, one's parents can play an important role in influencing the decision. But with the selection of an entrepreneurial career, influence from one's parents can be especially salient. The mother or father may play a powerful role in establishing the desirability and credibility of an entrepreneurial career for the offspring.

As this section has shown, trying to get a handle on what constitutes a typical entrepreneur in terms of personality traits and background characteristics is a difficult, if not impossible, task. There is a high degree of diversity in the backgrounds of entrepreneurs and their impetus for starting a business. Indeed, entrepreneurs are innovative and idiosyncratic, and tend to be so unique that they cannot easily be categorized. Nonetheless, prior research has given us insights into what makes the entrepreneur tick, at least in a general sense. We can conclude that entrepreneurs generally show a need for autonomy and independence, have a high achievement motivation, view themselves as being quite capable and able to determine their own destiny, have the ability to handle multiple assignments and ambiguous situations effectively, are willing to take risks, and may have been favorably influenced by their parents and others in their social network.

While these same characteristics are commonplace among many successful people, entrepreneurs and non-entrepreneurs alike, it is apparent that entrepreneurs as a group consistently possess this combination of traits. An entrepreneurial orientation (or self-concept), which includes such individual characteristics as innovativeness, a need for autonomy and independence, risk-bearing ability, creativity, proactivity, and a strong goal focus can predispose certain individuals to embark on an entrepreneurial career.[33]

Environmental Conditions

Becoming an entrepreneur can also be influenced by a number of environmental conditions and experiences.[34] We will consider three prominent environmental factors: job loss, work dissatisfaction, and favorable business conditions.

Job Loss

As we discussed in Chapter 1, the virtual demise of the relational psychological contract, technological advancements, economic uncertainty, globalization, and waves of corporate downsizings and mergers have combined to cause millions of workers to experience job loss (or to undergo multiple episodes of job loss). For many displaced employees, starting (or acquiring) their own firm represents a worthwhile career option. It should not be surprising that employees who are the unwitting victims of downsizings and restructurings, and who still have unique competencies and a motivation to achieve, start their own companies. Being discharged from an organization may provide the final impetus for aspiring entrepreneurs. Also, individuals who are terminated may vow never again to become a pawn in a large organization's chess game. Of course, deciding to become an entrepreneur after being discharged from an organization should be done only after a thorough analysis of all available options. Given the uncertainties, the sacrifices, and the risks involved, the entrepreneurial career is not for everyone. It is possible that entering into a business venture without proper planning and insight can only compound the personal toll that might have commenced with the loss of one's job.

Work Dissatisfaction

Work or occupational dissatisfaction, independent of or in conjunction with job loss or the unavailability of regular employment options, can be a driving force for the consideration of an entrepreneurial career.[35] Dissatisfaction with a job or an employer can also serve to convince an individual that no other form of employment represents an acceptable alternative. As was the case with job loss, using work dissatisfaction as the primary (or sole) reason for becoming an entrepreneur may lead to difficulties. Based on the career management model we have discussed throughout this book, aspiring entrepreneurs need to explore their interests, values, talents, and lifestyle preferences and then examine whether having their own business will satisfy these personal needs. If the decision to become an entrepreneur is not based on a thorough self-evaluation, but instead represents a knee-jerk reaction to an onerous work situation, then the individual is likely destined for personal unhappiness and further disappointment. Work dissatisfaction may contribute to the choice of an entrepreneurial career, but it should never be the sole deciding factor.

Favorable Business Conditions

Entrepreneurship as a career is obviously influenced by business conditions and opportunities. Although for the past three decades business conditions have been mostly favorable, the Great Recession and its after-effects did slow down the pace of new business establishments in the U.S.[36] However, as we move through the early part of the 21st century, several favorable trends continue to drive new business ventures on a worldwide basis. First, the steady increase in international trade has changed the structure of the world's economy, opening up both new consumer markets and previously untapped productive capacity. Globalization has thus created vast opportunities for new business. Second, the revolution in information and communications technology has "shrunk the world" and enabled entrepreneurs to create new businesses and to reach suppliers and customers worldwide, with little upfront capital. Today's reality is that the capabilities afforded by personal computers, mobile devices, instantaneous communication, and other technology products give the entrepreneur working at home or anywhere in the world the power of a big business.

It is apparent that a number of environmental, economic, and technological factors have combined to provide fertile ground for undertaking ownership of a business of one's own. Nonetheless, it is still important to recognize that the decision to become an entrepreneur should be the product of thorough analysis, covering personal desires, as well as conditions in the business environment.

Other Factors that Encourage Entrepreneurial Careers

Beyond the various individual characteristics and environmental elements that we have highlighted, there are several other well-known reasons why individuals are prompted to pursue an entrepreneurial career. Three of the most widely recognized reasons include a passion for a product or service, the presence of an entrepreneurial role model (or models), and the potential for a bridge career to maintain involvement in the workforce.

Passion for a Product or Service

Some people embark on an entrepreneurial career because of a personal zeal for a specific type of product or activity. Thus, someone with a passion for cooking may decide to open a restaurant or perhaps start a catering business. There are many examples of people who turned their passion into successful businesses. Often, the product or service represents an extension of the individual's self-concept, wherein the individual identifies so closely with the product or service that the provision of such becomes a natural career choice. Consider the following example:

When Al was employed in corporate finance he would often find himself daydreaming about woodworking—he could almost smell the scent of freshly sawed oak in his office. On other occasions, Al would be penciling sketches of a new dresser he could make, or maybe a coffee table. On nights and weekends, you could always find Al working away in his woodworking shop (which doubled as his garage), turning out carefully crafted wood products. He never made a profit on his creations, charging his friends and family only the cost of the raw materials he used. Al loved woodworking so much that the creation itself, and the admiration of his customers, was satisfaction enough.

Al liked working for the corporation. He had majored in accounting as an undergraduate, and had gotten his MBA in finance. Solving complex financial questions and preparing business plans were stimulating to him. But woodworking continued to be his first love—it was in his blood. His father was a carpenter and he passed on to Al a passion for creativity with wood. Al had never seen woodworking as a vocation, only as a hobby to relieve the stress of the corporate world.

After ten years in corporate finance, Al began seeing woodworking in a new light. The demand for his creations was more than he could fulfill. Comparable wood products at commercial establishments were selling for double and triple what Al charged. Also, Al's corporation was the subject of takeover rumors—the grapevine said that Al's department would be one of the first to go if a merger did take place. Al began talking seriously to his wife about starting his own woodworking business. They concluded that her job as head of corporate research for an investment banking firm would cover them financially and with needed health insurance while the business was getting started. They spent time looking for commercial real estate properties to rent to set up the shop. Once they found the proper location, they spent $20,000 on equipment and tools. The merger finally occurred at Al's company, and he was happy to resign, take his severance package, and become a full-fledged entrepreneur. Al and his wife took out advertisements in upscale magazines, approached local interior designers for referrals, and used their friends and families to spread the word of their nascent business to other potential customers. They took orders by mail, by phone, and over their website. After three months in business, the demand for Al's wood products was exceeding his capacity and he was now thinking about hiring an assistant. Personally, Al is happier than he has ever been. The time pressure and demands are intense, but he is doing what he loves. He is wondering why he did not start the business sooner.

This vignette, while fictional, identifies the process many fledgling entrepreneurs go through as they begin their new ventures. There are literally hundreds of real stories about entrepreneurs who have become successful following their passion for a product or service.

Presence of Role Models

In Chapter 7 we discussed the influence of social forces on the selection of an occupation. Specifically, we advanced the view that parents, other family members, and friends can serve as important role models and mentors in making career decisions. With regard to entrepreneurship, the value of social networks and social capital as instrumental in the undertaking of, and progress in, an entrepreneurial career is well-recognized.[37] It has long been established that the presence of an entrepreneurial role model or models can have a positive effect not only on intentions to embark on an entrepreneurial career, but also the degree of persistence once the venture has been started.[38] Specifically, when entrepreneurial role models engage potential entrepreneurs in various professional activities (such as an employment relationship or discussions about business ventures) the potential entrepreneur's desire to own a business is increased.[39] Perhaps the most important role models for budding entrepreneurs are parents. As we stated previously, either a father or mother or both can provide support and encouragement to influence the establishment of an entrepreneurial career as a desirable and credible alternative for their children.[40]

A special case of parental influence on the undertaking of the entrepreneurial career concerns the encouragement of the children of entrepreneurs to enter the family business. Indeed, prior exposure to a family business is a key motivator for the intention to pursue an entrepreneurial career.[41] Often, entrepreneurial parents see their children as the future standard-bearers of the company, the ones who can carry the business on for future generations. For many children of entrepreneurs, the decision to enter the family company is uneventful and free of stress, due to a desire to carry on the family legacy and build upon the efforts of one's parents. In this case, the children feel unthreatened, free to choose the career goals they desire. But for others, the decision to join and help run the family business can be a stressful experience, as the need to assert independence from the family unit clashes with parental pressure to enter the family enterprise. The pressure to be employed by the family firm would likely be highest when the individual is emerging from the school years and his or her formal education is complete. But at this time, the individual is in the process of entering the adult world, confronting the psychological conflict that results from the need to be one's own person versus the pull of the safety and security of the family.

Regardless of the level of pressure one feels from family, the process of considering whether to enter the family business should follow the career management model presented earlier. The individual should thoroughly assess personal values, interests, talents, and lifestyle preferences and assess the work environment (both within and outside the family firm) to have sufficient knowledge to determine the most appropriate career goals. One's decision to enter the family firm should be made only if it is consistent with personal desires and fits with conditions in the internal and external work environments.

In summary, it does appear that parents can play an influential role in encouraging their children to pursue entrepreneurial careers. Once one becomes an entrepreneur, the role of parents, mentors, and other alliances may diminish considerably. The nature of the entrepreneurial career is such that decisive individual action is paramount. While social support may aid in the decision to become an entrepreneur, advice and intrusion from the social network may actually inhibit the established entrepreneur from taking required actions.

Entrepreneurial Bridge Careers

In Chapter 9 we discussed how bridge employment allows workers who have retired from a career-oriented job to move to a transitional work position that provides a bridge or link between one's long-term career and the entry into total retirement from all work. With millions of baby boomers leaving their full-time careers over the next 20 years, it is likely that many will see an entrepreneurial career as a viable form of bridge employment. These new entrepreneurs may hire other retirees to work for them, thus establishing "gray businesses" made up of older workers. Depending on the business and industry one is in, entrepreneurial careers can offer a flexible work environment that would be appealing to retirees and potential retirees who are looking at bridge employment opportunities.[42]

Support for the Entrepreneurial Career

Coincident with the increase in interest in entrepreneurial careers is the emergence of a variety of support mechanisms. These mechanisms include social networks and alliances, training and education programs, publications, and websites. In addition, governments at all levels have initiatives designed specifically to support the undertaking and managing of an entrepreneurial venture. For example, the U.S. Small Business Administration has a number of programs intended to provide support for entrepreneurs.[43] Each type of support is discussed briefly below.

Social Networks, Alliances, and Support Groups

Entrepreneurs can be helped by a variety of different social groups and mutual-benefit organizations. Social networks operate at two different levels. Informal alliances include business support from friends and relatives. Formal assistance can come from such larger organizations as community groups, state or local governmental agencies, ethnic institutions, religious associations, fraternal organizations, and other small business associations. Supportive alliances, such as those providing for cooperative buying arrangements, trade groups, joint venture capital-raising activities, and community professional advice, provide help for potential entrepreneurs. Alliances increase the entrepreneur's likelihood of making contact with other entrepreneurs, getting necessary advice, and most importantly, enabling contact with potential venture capital providers. An entrepreneur can easily access supportive alliance resources through the Internet. Venture capital clubs meet regularly across the country and a city's Chamber of Commerce can also help entrepreneurs and their businesses. Practically every major city or metropolitan region has a Chamber of Commerce.[44]

Training and Education Programs

Colleges and universities recognize the importance of, and student demand for, educational programs in entrepreneurship, and these programs have grown in numbers and in scope of coverage.[45] On a worldwide basis, university-based entrepreneurship education programs and courses number in the thousands, with hundreds of endowed professorships and funded centers devoted to entrepreneurial education.[46] Many entrepreneurship programs and centers were started when successful entrepreneurial alumni-funded initiatives focused specifically on helping students learn about starting and running businesses.

Courses in entrepreneurship are extremely popular among students and are designed to meet career and training needs of essentially two groups: traditional undergraduate and graduate students interested in an entrepreneurial career, and nontraditional students such as practicing and potential entrepreneurs who may pursue a graduate education. Content of the courses and programs can vary somewhat from school to school, but in general they cover traditional business subjects (for example, marketing, finance, accounting, management), combined with a specific focus on the competencies needed in an entrepreneurial venture.[47] Entrepreneurship coursework can enhance important capabilities, including the abilities to recognize and assess business opportunities, find capital sources and funding, develop new products, manage risk, write a business plan, and build entrepreneurial networks.[48] In addition, these educational programs play an important role in the career exploration process because individuals can gain self-insight as to whether an entrepreneurial career represents a "fit" with their personality and background.[49]

Publications and Websites

Recognizing the interest in entrepreneurial careers and in new business formations, the publishing industry has moved forcefully to supply related literature. Indeed, there exists a variety of periodicals, journals, magazines, books, and websites that cover such topics as owning your own firm and being successful once you become an entrepreneur. These publications play an important role in advancing the understanding of entrepreneurship by providing advice on starting and managing a business venture and giving realistic previews of what one will encounter in an entrepreneurial career. Entrepreneurial-based websites have also proliferated over the past two decades. As one example, Entrepreneur Media, which owns the website Entrepreneur.com and *Entrepreneur* magazine, traces its history to the 1970s. It focuses its products on individuals who are looking to own a small business as well as those who are already entrepreneurs. It offers practical advice and information on entrepreneurship through its website and also offers a monthly magazine, books, and related events.[50]

Characteristics and Experiences of Female and Minority Entrepreneurs

In earlier sections of this chapter we discussed two different views of entrepreneurial career selection—as a product of certain personality and psychological characteristics and as a function of environmental influences. Much has been written over the past few decades concerning whether female and minority entrepreneurs possess the typical entrepreneurial personality profile and have similar social learning experiences as men and non-minorities.[51] In addition, given the economic and sociological benefits of entrepreneurship, attention has also been paid to the unique hurdles that women and minorities face in achieving and surviving with business ownership. The following sections will discuss the entrepreneurial experiences of women and minorities.

Female Entrepreneurs

Since the end of the Great Recession, while overall growth in new business formations in the U.S. has been nearly flat, the increase in female-owned businesses has been impressive, with a growth of more than 25 percent from 2009 through the middle of the next decade.[52] In the U.S., more than ten million firms are owned by women, employing roughly eight million people, and generating nearly $1.5 trillion in sales; and these women-owned companies account for one-third of all privately held firms.[53] As the number of female-owned businesses has grown over the past half-century, so too has research into women entrepreneurs.[54] Several questions emerge from a review of this literature.

Are women entrepreneurs characteristically different from either their male counterparts or female managers in organizations? In general, research has found few differences between women entrepreneurs and either their male counterparts or female organizational managers in terms of the standard personality-based and environmental variables associated with entrepreneurial careers, including the need for achievement, proactivity, desire for autonomy, risk-taking propensity, innovativeness, level of education, degree of prior work experience, and the degree of planning conducted.[55] Further, the management practices of men and women entrepreneurs are largely similar, with comparable strategies and related organizational actions.[56]

In contrast, other studies have found differences. For example, on a worldwide basis, women are less likely than men to be engaged in entrepreneurial activity or to show an interest in an entrepreneurial career.[57] In addition, businesses headed by women tend to be financed at a comparatively lower level and tend to perform at a lower level financially as compared to those firms headed by men.[58] These differences are the result of a variety of factors, including gender stereotyping of entrepreneurship as a "masculine-based" or male endeavor, which can negatively influence such factors as access to financing and capital; family demands that disproportionately affect the strategies and the time commitments to the business of women entrepreneurs; the lack of entrepreneurial role models for women; and the fact that women entrepreneurs pursue goals for their business that go beyond mere economic performance.[59]

What are the underlying reasons why women enter an entrepreneurial career? Given that female entrepreneurs do not appear to display any major differences in personality or psychological characteristics compared to either their male counterparts or female organizational managers, a question arises as to whether there are other special factors or circumstances that underlie the entrepreneurial career selection of women. Three factors seem to dominate women's selection of entrepreneurial careers: allowing more freedom and flexibility in time management and the balancing of work and family responsibilities, escaping the restrictions of the corporate world and the limitations of the "glass ceiling," and achieving economic success and independence.[60]

A primary factor influencing the choice of an entrepreneurial career for women is the embeddedness of entrepreneurial activity in family systems, where there is a desire to combine entrepreneurial career aspirations with family roles and other relationships.[61] Many women entrepreneurs tend to work fewer hours and invest less time in the development of their businesses than men, primarily in an attempt to achieve the dual goals of supporting themselves and their families financially while managing other nonwork demands such as caring for children, parents, and the household. In contrast, men may work more hours because their goal is usually to earn money and because they face fewer competing demands for their time. Consistent with this view, a significant motivator for many women's choice of an entrepreneurial career is to escape the double shift of being primarily responsible for the home and children while managing a full corporate workload where there is comparatively less flexibility in handling time commitments as compared to an entrepreneurial career.[62] In this sense, the less restrictive entrepreneurial career offers a greater opportunity for freedom in scheduling work hours, work location, and ease in making time adjustments for family demands. Of course, combining entrepreneurship with extensive family time can have a downside in that the time demands arising from family responsibilities may diminish the success of the enterprise. Indeed, work–family conflict, a real concern for the female entrepreneur, can be particularly troublesome and detrimental to the economic success of an enterprise especially in the initial years of the firm.

Thus, the relationship between entrepreneurship and family obligations is paradoxical. On the one hand, the generally greater personal freedom offered by entrepreneurship can allow individuals flexibility in allotting time to family commitments. But on the other hand, an entrepreneurial pursuit usually carries with it escalating demands and strong psychological involvement in the business that can interfere with family responsibilities and produce work–family conflict.[63] Accordingly, a significant challenge for many female entrepreneurs is to successfully resolve the conflict between entrepreneurial and family commitments, which requires seeking support from family and others to relieve some of the demands at home, as well as making well-informed choices regarding time commitments to business and family based on the relative importance of these two spheres of their lives.

Beyond the desire for greater time flexibility, it is well-documented that women choose to pursue entrepreneurial careers in response to dissatisfaction over limited mobility options and potential discrimination related to the glass ceiling that takes place in the corporate world.[64] In this sense, an entrepreneurial career is a way for high-achieving women to escape mobility blockages that occur within traditional organizational careers. Women who wish to reach the executive ranks often realize either that the "old boys' network" still prevails or that the extensive time and effort put into an organizational career does not produce the intended results in terms of upward mobility. Recognizing this slow or nonexistent progress to the top, many achievement-oriented women opt out of corporations to run their own firms, where success is more a matter of one's own abilities and hard work.

Much evidence also exists that women around the world launch entrepreneurial ventures as a way to achieve economic success and independence.[65] Under this view, individuals are "pushed" into an entrepreneurial career out of economic necessity stemming from a family's financial situation or other contextual factors. On a global scale, women are more likely than men to be pushed into entrepreneurial careers due to a lack of other viable alternatives for the attainment of financial independence.[66]

Are there factors that limit the choice of entrepreneurship as a career for women? As was discussed earlier in this chapter, there are few if any major differences between male and female entrepreneurs in terms of personality factors and environmental influences. However, it has been found that women tend to have a lower overall preference for entrepreneurship than men, and women entrepreneurs tend to be concentrated in specific industries such as health care, social assistance, and educational services.[67] The reduced preference for an entrepreneurial career is reflective of a host of factors. It has been suggested that cultural conditioning, social learning, a lack of encouragement and role models, and comparatively lower entrepreneurial self-efficacy can channel women away from an entrepreneurial career.[68] As was stated earlier, on many fronts, entrepreneurship is portrayed as "masculine" activity that is more suitable for men than for women. This stereotype can help explain why women indicate a lower self-confidence in entrepreneurship as a career and express lower intentions to pursue an entrepreneurial career.[69]

Beyond reduced entrepreneurial intentions, women start businesses that are, on average, smaller than those started by men, reflective of the influence of lower self-efficacy, the lack of access to larger-scale business opportunities, and lower access to the financial resources necessary to start or increase the size of a firm. Women are also more likely to set limits beyond which they do not want to expand their businesses to ensure that they do not adversely affect their family and personal lives. In addition, the greater degree of household commitments faced by women can lead many female entrepreneurs to confront comparatively more start-up problems, with the most consistently noted difficulties involving access to credit and conflicts between work and family lives.

Regardless of the potentially limiting factors that they face, there are a number of positive qualities generally possessed by female entrepreneurs. These qualities include high energy levels, skill in influencing others and gaining consensus, and a high degree of pragmatism in their business decisions. Many women find the challenge and the opportunity for self-determination as important reasons for pursuing entrepreneurial careers. Further, women draw personal and professional satisfaction from running their own businesses and achieving hybrid business goals that place emphasis not only on economic outcomes but also on non-economic objectives associated with personal growth, product quality, societal impact, establishing positive relationships in their workplaces, and achieving balance between work and family lives.[70]

As this chapter has discussed, all current and aspiring entrepreneurs face a variety of challenges, limitations, and difficulties in launching and operating their businesses. However, it appears that female entrepreneurs must confront a unique set of hurdles primarily because of societal influences and cultural conditioning. Recognizing the importance of supporting women-owned businesses, societal institutions, educational bodies, and government agencies have developed training and education programs and other resources to support female entrepreneurship.[71] As just one example, the U.S. Small Business Administration offers extensive online resources in support of women entrepreneurs, including guidance on how to start, grow, finance, and maintain a business.[72] As more and more women become successful entrepreneurs, we hope that the identified limitations and barriers will diminish all over the world.

Minority Entrepreneurs

Even with the ongoing interest in entrepreneurial activity overall, only a limited amount of research attention has been given to the characteristics and experiences of minority entrepreneurs. This fact is surprising given the significant growth in minority-owned businesses overall and as a percentage of all companies. According to data from the U.S. Census Bureau, there are more than eight million minority-owned firms nationally (as of 2012), up from fewer than six million five years earlier, representing a growth rate of more than 38 percent. Receipts for minority-owned firms in the U.S totaled nearly $1.5 trillion in 2012, and climbed nearly 35 percent in the period from 2007 to 2012. Minority-owned firms accounted for nearly 30 percent of all U.S. firms in 2012, with Hispanic Americans, African Americans, and Asian Americans owning 12.2 percent, 9.5 percent, and 7.1 percent, respectively, of all U.S. businesses as of 2012.[73]

Research into the career experiences of minority entrepreneurs, while less extensive, tends to follow the same paths as that for women entrepreneurs. This includes an evaluation of whether minority entrepreneurs show differences when compared with all entrepreneurs or managers in organizations and whether factors exist that limit minorities from entering or succeeding in entrepreneurial careers.[74] As with women entrepreneurs, researchers have found no major differences in personal characteristics or other individual background factors when comparing minority and non-minority entrepreneurs. However, there are environmental barriers encountered by minority entrepreneurs that can either negatively affect the ability to enter an entrepreneurial career or can limit advancement of the business and the career.[75] Consistent with women entrepreneurs, these barriers include access to credit, more limited opportunities to access social and economic networks, and discrimination.[76]

In terms of background and environmental factors, as with all entrepreneurs, role models and family members are influential for minorities when starting a business and gaining access to key markets.[77] For many minority entrepreneurs, extensive support can come from mutual benefit associations that are centered on racial or ethnic ties. Strong ethnic networks can provide aid in the form of venture capital, lines of credit, market and product information, a ready customer base, training opportunities, and the regulation of competition. Many groups have followed this model of strong ethnic solidarity and assistance to achieve entrepreneurial success.[78]

As with female entrepreneurs, one of the most important factors that lead minorities into entrepreneurial careers is treatment discrimination and bias in the corporate business environment. Indeed, real and perceived closure of upper-level management positions to minority employees can cause frustration and a reduced level of commitment to the corporation. Thus, the lack of access in the corporate world can be a motivator in undertaking an entrepreneurial career. Consider the following example:

Roberta has been a top real estate executive at a large fast food franchiser for the past 15 years. Starting at the lowest levels of the managerial hierarchy after college, she rose to her current level through her talent and a great deal of hard work. In fact, Roberta has been so involved in her job that she has had little personal life.

Roberta's personnel evaluations are always excellent, and she has been told that the next high-level job to open up will be hers. However, Roberta realizes that she has been in her current job for the past two years, and recently one of her white male counterparts received the promotion to chief operating officer that she was expecting to receive. When she inquired as to why she was not even offered an interview for the job, Roberta was told that her counterpart had more experience and had a better working relationship with the CEO. Roberta was angered by these comments. She had been the one to put this fast food chain literally "on the map" by expanding operations on the East Coast over the past ten years. And while she was rewarded financially for her efforts, she wanted to receive the position for which she had worked so hard.

Roberta began to think that her talents might be better suited to running her own company. There are many discount drug chains, food stores, and other retail outlets that need to negotiate real estate deals throughout the East Coast. Roberta knew the territory, and had contacts in every state. She had been a contract negotiator many times, and she enjoyed the thrill those negotiations entailed. Roberta began considering a career as a "freelance" real estate negotiator, and looking for the opportunity to pursue such a career as an entrepreneur.

In total, minority entrepreneurs possess personality characteristics and face demands and concerns that are similar to those of entrepreneurs in general. Unfortunately, minority entrepreneurs also face additional challenges that must be overcome, including built-in racism and bias, possibly a singular focus on their own ethnic customer base, an inability to attract a larger customer base, possibly less business experience and availability of financing, and other barriers to business establishment and success. As with female entrepreneurs, the elimination of these barriers can be accelerated through greater self-determination among current and future minority entrepreneurs, combined with increased social and educational support for minority enterprises. A variety of governmental and nongovernmental programs exist to support the establishment and ongoing viability of minority-owned enterprises. As one example, the U.S. Small Business Administration offers a variety of initiatives that can help qualifying minority-owned firms develop and grow their businesses through one-on-one counseling, training workshops, management and technical guidance, and access to government contracting opportunities.[79]

It must be recognized that minority entrepreneurs not only play a growing and increasingly important role in the economic vitality of the world's economy as a whole, but also are crucial to the economic development of many growing communities across the industrialized world. Accordingly, it is important for governments around the world to support entrepreneurship of all people and to better understand the motivations, barriers, and factors that drive entrepreneurial success.[80]

Selecting and Managing the Entrepreneurial Career

Throughout this book we have underscored the need for a systematic and informed approach to career management. Selection of an entrepreneurial career, while admittedly somewhat different from the choice of an organizational career, should still be based on a thorough analysis of personal desires and characteristics as well as a detailed review of conditions and expectations in the work environment. Management scholars have termed the desire to become an entrepreneur as *entrepreneurial intention*. Entrepreneurial intention is defined as an interest in, and a personal conviction to, pursuing an entrepreneurial career, and reflects the confluence of the personal and environmental influences discussed earlier in the chapter.[81] As would be expected, a strong entrepreneurial intention has a substantial influence on the act of becoming an entrepreneur given its linkage to the motivational elements of goal-setting and strategy development.[82] Accordingly, entrepreneurial intention, or the goal to become an entrepreneur, should be the result of a thorough and systematic process of self- and environmental career exploration. And that exploration should lead to a greater awareness as to whether an entrepreneurial career represents a wise choice. In addition, throughout one's entrepreneurial career, regular reappraisal should occur regarding whether key expectations and goals are being fulfilled and whether exiting a business venture is an appropriate action. Let us consider each of these steps and elements in more detail.

Self-Assessment

In Chapter 5 we discussed the view that self-awareness is critical in choosing career goals that are compatible with one's interests, values, and lifestyle preferences. Previously discussed assessment instruments, such as the Strong Interest Inventory, have separate categories that indicate whether an entrepreneurial self-concept or theme is present.

In addition to gaining insight into personal interests and psychological characteristics, aspiring entrepreneurs also need to ask themselves more fundamental questions concerning business success. The following lists a number of these questions:[83]

- Is my business idea good enough?
- Do I have the management skills needed to succeed?
- How important is money to me?
- Can I live with the risk of owning my own business?
- What will be my family's reaction to my becoming an entrepreneur?

The interlocking nature of the entrepreneur's career and the business itself dictates that the individual's assessment of interests, needs, and chances for success becomes an assessment of the business's interests, needs, and chances for success.

Assessment of the Work Environment

As with the gathering of self-information, the accumulation of knowledge about the work environment takes on a broader meaning for the entrepreneur. Thus, a personal analysis of conditions in the business environment becomes a wider assessment of expected conditions that one's potential company would face. In this sense, the individual's assessment of the work environment can represent an environmental analysis for the company, covering expectations on financing and economic conditions, changes in demographics, market preferences, legal and regulatory issues, technological advancements, and a host of other factors. The choice of an entrepreneurial career, and the selection of the type of business to pursue, should take into account the knowledge gained through this environmental review.

Setting Career Goals

Individuals who see themselves in an entrepreneurial career (that is, display a strong entrepreneurial intention) should set career goals that reflect this aspiration. Operational goals for an entrepreneurial career would likely indicate objectives for personal success and achievement of the firm. In this way, personal career goals and business objectives intersect. But entrepreneurial career goals can also be conceptual, reflecting one's significant values and the intrinsic enjoyment gained from the entrepreneurial experience.

Many times, entrepreneurs take a circuitous route to business ownership. As with any career selection, it may take a relatively long period of time to fully understand one's likes and dislikes, special talents, and aspirations. Also, the realities of the business environment may change rapidly, or may become apparent only after several years of experience. The experiences of many successful businesspeople often reflect the "trial-and-error" approach. One well known example of the trial-and-error route to an entrepreneurial career is John Paul Jones DeJoria:

As the co-founder and CEO of the John Paul Mitchell Systems company, Mr. DeJoria is a highly successful entrepreneur. But his route to the leadership of the Beverly Hills-based maker of hair care products and beauty aids was certainly not routine. From 1964, when he got out of the Navy, to 1980, when he cofounded the John Paul Mitchell Systems company, Mr. DeJoria held (and then was fired from or quit) a long list of sales jobs. He began his career working for such large corporations as Savin and Time, but did not last in either job because he did not see eye-to-eye with either company's management. Indeed, he quit Savin because he disliked wearing neckties on his sales calls. After his time with the large corporations, Mr. DeJoria became a door-to-door salesperson, selling such products as life insurance, encyclopedias, and medical linens. In 1971, Mr. DeJoria landed a job with Redken Laboratories, selling shampoo through hair salons, but left after a short period. He held additional jobs in the beauty business but did not last in any of them. At one organization, his commission schedule had him making more money than the person who owned the company. Finally, in 1980, Mr. DeJoria came to the conclusion that the only boss for whom he could work was himself. That year he teamed with a Scottish hairdresser named Paul Mitchell to found the John Paul Mitchell Systems company. Working in a more free-wheeling environment of self-determination, he flourished. His company experienced many consecutive years of sales increases. The privately held John Paul Mitchell Systems sells a variety of hair care products through distributors within North America to more than 100,000 hair salons. Its products are also sold internationally in 86 countries that supply thousands of hair salons. In addition, the company operates its own salons in the U.S. Even though he has received lucrative offers from public corporations to buy John Paul Mitchell Systems, Mr. DeJoria refuses to sell. He has also branched out into other successful entrepreneurial ventures, including nightclubs, liquor, energy, a motorcycle dealership, and grooming products for pets. Mr. DeJoria revels in his celebrity status and enjoys the lifestyle that successful entrepreneurship allows. After years of struggle and floundering, John Paul Jones DeJoria was able to achieve success, satisfaction, and worldwide recognition in an entrepreneurial career.[84]

Development of Career Strategies

Some of the career strategies that we discussed in Chapter 6 do not necessarily have direct relevance to the entrepreneurial career. For example, such strategies as image-building and organizational politics would most likely be less useful or unnecessary for the entrepreneur. More appropriately, the entrepreneur's career strategies would reflect the strategies of the company, such as an expansion of the product line or perhaps a move into another geographic market. Other strategies that we discussed are appropriate for the entrepreneur. Competency in one's job (in this case as a business owner), extended work involvement, skill development, and opportunity development would all be relevant career strategies for the entrepreneur.[85] Moreover, the importance of seeking support from family members cannot be overemphasized because a supportive family can enable an individual to pursue an entrepreneurial career, facilitate the success of the venture, and promote feelings of work–family balance.[86] Additional strategies that could have instrumental value include the development of business relationships with other firms, locating access to capital and financing sources, and tapping into and utilizing social networks and support groups.[87]

Career Appraisal

Once an entrepreneurial career is undertaken, regular reappraisal should occur.[88] Assessing one's career accomplishments in light of established goals and strategies could lead to the conclusion that no changes are necessary, or that some fine-tuning is required, or that wholesale alterations in career goals and strategies are mandatory. For the entrepreneur, feedback on career progress can be immediate and crystal clear, because progress in the business venture should track closely with the success of the entrepreneur's career. Often, but not always, failure of the business portends a lack of achievement in meeting the entrepreneur's career goals, especially if the career goals are focused on the financial success and accomplishment of the enterprise. Of course, if one's career goals or strategies are centered on gaining hands-on business experience or learning about financing options, then the time in the entrepreneurial career is well spent, regardless of the success of the firm. Further, the entrepreneur should assess the effect that business ownership has (either positively or negatively) on other parts of life, such as family, community, and personal life commitments. In any case, the entrepreneur should periodically reappraise his or her career to see whether important needs are being met. If they are not, then changes may be warranted—perhaps even leaving the world of entrepreneurship.

At some point in the career appraisal process, an entrepreneur might make a decision to exit the business or the entrepreneurial career entirely. Entrepreneurial exit means that the entrepreneur chooses to leave the firm that he or she helped to create and manage, reflecting a removal from ownership and the decision-making processes within the company.[89] An exit from an entrepreneurial career can take many different paths, including an initial public offering (IPO) of the stock, an acquisition of the business, family succession, employee buyout, independent sale, or business failure and liquidation.[90] As these exit choices show, an entrepreneur's decision to leave the business after going through the career appraisal process could be reflective of many outcomes, including a failure of the business, the opportunity to grow the business, such as through an IPO of stock or acquisition, or a conscious, intentional decision to leave the business and pursue other career alternatives.[91] Regardless of the form of exit, the exiting entrepreneur normally has to decide on a new career path. This decision will likely be a function of the form of the exit as well as the information and learning gained through the appraisal process.

In total, we believe that the process of managing the entrepreneurial career is essentially the same as that for an organizational career. The aspiring (and current) entrepreneur needs to attain a thorough understanding of self and the work environment, set realistic and informed career goals, develop career strategies to fulfill these goals, and regularly reappraise progress and personal fulfillment.

Summary

The past several decades have seen a worldwide expansion of interest in entrepreneurial careers. Political changes, economic turbulence, corporate restructuring and downsizing, employee discontent with life in a large corporation or with non-permanent "gig" jobs, and a host of other factors all influence the interest in entrepreneurial careers.

This chapter explored several topics relevant to the entrepreneurial career. Prior definitions of entrepreneurship focused on the themes of creativity, innovation, and risk-taking propensity. Taking these themes into account, we defined entrepreneurship as managing a business of one's own that requires personal sacrifice, creativity, and risk-taking, to create something of value.

Becoming an entrepreneur means experiencing a career that is quite different from the traditional organization-based notion. The entrepreneurial career is marked by extensive personal commitment to the success of the firm, acceptance of lower degrees of structure and predictability, an orientation toward action and decisiveness, the simultaneous performance of multiple roles, and a willingness to accept risk. Because of these distinctive features, entrepreneurs find substantial challenge and stimulation in their work, but also must confront the precarious nature of business ownership.

Past research has questioned whether the selection of an entrepreneurial career is more a function of personal traits and characteristics, or a product of environmental influence and opportunities, or perhaps a combination of both. Such personal factors as the need for autonomy and independence, the need for achievement, an internal locus of control, a tolerance for ambiguity, a risk-taking propensity, an entrepreneurial self-concept, and various demographic and background factors have been found to have a positive influence on the choice of an entrepreneurial career. Of course, these same characteristics are present among many successful people, entrepreneurs and non-entrepreneurs alike. But they do give a fairly distinct picture of the common traits that constitute a "typical" profile of the entrepreneur.

In addition to personality characteristics, a number of environmental conditions can work to direct people toward an entrepreneurial career. In this chapter, we concentrated on three such factors—job loss, work dissatisfaction, and favorable business conditions. We discussed how a passion for a particular product or service or the need for bridge employment could be strong motivators in undertaking business ownership. We also reviewed how the presence of role models and mentors has been shown to positively influence the pursuit of entrepreneurship. Having a successful entrepreneurial role model, whether it is parents, relatives, or friends in the community, can often encourage entrepreneurial effort.

The national and worldwide interest in entrepreneurial activity has brought with it the establishment of social networks and alliances, training and education programs, websites, publications, and governmental and educational programs that are all designed to assist aspiring and current entrepreneurs to deal with the challenges of business ownership and provide a realistic preview of what can be expected from an entrepreneurial career.

In line with the general trend of interest in business ownership, entrepreneurial activity among females and minorities has grown considerably during the past three decades. While the personal motivations and background factors of female and minority entrepreneurs are consistent with entrepreneurs in general, they must also confront and overcome a variety of unique challenges. These include built-in discrimination and bias, social learning restrictions, cultural conditioning, lack of financial capital that may discourage entrepreneurial activity, lower self-efficacy regarding entrepreneurship, and in the case of many women, additional role demands regarding family commitments.

As with any career choice, the decision to become an entrepreneur should follow the career management model as outlined in this book. Specifically, entrepreneurial career goals should be based on a thorough understanding of individual interests, talents, values, and preferences, as well as information on the work environment. The entrepreneur should then set career strategies that will help achieve the established career and business goals. Finally, career reappraisal should be conducted regularly to ensure that relevant needs and expectations are being met.

Career Management *for Life*: Work–Life Implications from Chapter 12

- The generally greater flexibility provided by an entrepreneurial career can allow individuals control in allotting time to family and other nonwork commitments.
- This is a powerful motive for many women (and some men) to become entrepreneurs.
- However, an entrepreneurial career usually carries with it extensive demands that can diminish the amount of time the entrepreneur can spend on family and personal life activities.
- Therefore, an important concern for entrepreneurs (women and men) is the successful resolution of the conflict between entrepreneurial and nonwork commitments, which requires seeking support from different parts of life, and making informed choices regarding the relative emphasis on these two spheres of their life.
- An important aim of career exploration for aspiring and current entrepreneurs is to understand the impact of entrepreneurial activities on their family and personal life as well as the effects of family and personal commitments on the pursuit of an entrepreneurial career.
- An entrepreneur's career goals and career strategies should be geared toward achieving the success of the venture in the context of one's whole life, which can include commitments to family, community, and self-development.
- As part of the career appraisal process, entrepreneurs should regularly consider whether the entrepreneurial lifestyle is helping or harming other parts of their life.

Assignment

Interview someone who owns his or her own business. Determine the factors that led this person into an entrepreneurial career. How successful is the person's enterprise? To what factors does he or she attribute business success or failure? What are the rewards and stresses the person experiences in his/her entrepreneurial career? If the individual is a woman or person of color, what hurdles did he or she experience in the startup of the business?

Discussion Questions

1. Do you think you would be successful and happy as an entrepreneur? Why or why not?
2. Do you believe that there is a "typical" entrepreneurial personality? Why or why not?
3. How does an entrepreneurial career differ from an organizational career? How do these differences influence the setting of career strategies among entrepreneurs?
4. How can social learning and cultural conditioning influence the choice of an entrepreneurial career? What role do one's parents play in the choice?
5. What special career challenges do women and minority entrepreneurs face in launching and operating their businesses? What actions can women and people of color take to overcome these challenges?
6. What types of social support are available to current and aspiring entrepreneurs? How do colleges and universities contribute to the level of entrepreneurship across the country?

Chapter 12 Case: Dave the Aspiring Executive (Part B)

At the conclusion of Chapter 11 we provided Part A of this case. If you haven't done so already, please read Part A of this case before reading Part B. At the end of Part A, Dave had just met with the vice-president of human resources of the Xtel Corporation concerning his chances for future advancement with the company. The clear message he received was that his career at Xtel was in a holding pattern. Dave concluded it was time for a change. (Remember, Xtel is a fictitious name and should not be confused with any real company.)

While in graduate school, Dave had become friendly with a fellow student who was interested in developing and marketing software that could be used to help control production operations. Dave had been intrigued with the prospects for the software, especially because he saw its potential application at Xtel Corporation. Dave decided to give his friend a call to see what progress she had made. Dave also sought the advice of one of his neighbors who had experience in financing business start-ups. Working part-time on nights and weekends, Dave and his partners were able to finalize the software and put together a realistic business plan. They sought and received financing for their venture from a local commercial bank. Once they lined up their first client, Dave felt confident enough to resign from his position at Xtel Corporation. The resignation was tendered with mixed emotions. He felt a sense of gratitude and loyalty to Xtel for the financial and educational support they had given him, but he was also disturbed by the treatment he received during the latter part of his career.

In any event, Dave is enthusiastic about his prospects as an entrepreneur. He is confident that he and his partners have tapped into a potentially lucrative market. He is strongly motivated to make the venture succeed and achieve financial security for his family.

Case Analysis Questions

1. Given his many years in an organizational career with a large corporation, do you think that Dave will be in for a rude awakening now that he has become an entrepreneur? Why or why not? What differences in experiences do you think he will encounter in his entrepreneurial career as opposed to his organizational career?
2. What qualities does Dave have that will help him in his entrepreneurial venture? Does Dave have any shortcomings that might limit his success as an entrepreneur?
3. Now that Dave has embarked on an entrepreneurial career, to whom should he turn for personal and professional support, advice, and assistance?

Notes

1 Kelley, D., Singer, S. & Herrington, M. (2016). Global Entrepreneurship Monitor, 2015/2016 Report. Available at www.gemconsortium.org/report.

2 United States Department of Labor, Bureau of Labor Statistics. (2016). *Business Employment Dynamics*. Available at www.bls.gov/bdm/entrepreneurship/entrepreneurship.htm.

3 Ibid.
4 Hathaway, I., Schweitzer, M. E. & Shane, S. (2014). The shifting source of new business establishments and new jobs. *Federal Reserve Bank of Cleveland Economic Commentary*, August 21.
5 Rindova, V., Barry, D. & Ketchen, D. J. (2009). Entrepreneuring as emancipation. *Academy of Management Review*, *34*, 477–491.
6 Bjørnskov, C. & Foss, N. J. (2016). Institutions, entrepreneurship, and economic growth: What do we know and what we still need to know? *Academy of Management Perspectives*, *30*, 292–315; Toma, S., Grigore, A. & Marinescu, P. (2014). Economic development and entrepreneurship. *Procedia Economics and Finance*, *8*, 436–443; Hitt, M. A., Ireland, R. D., Sirmon, D. G. & Trahms, C. A. (2011). Strategic entrepreneurship: Creating value for individuals, organizations, and society. *Academy of Management Perspectives*, *25*, 57–75.
7 Buchanan, L. (2015). The U.S. now has 27 million entrepreneurs. *Inc. Magazine*, September 5.
8 Koveos, P. (2016). Global importance of entrepreneurship. *Journal of Developmental Entrepreneurship*, *21*, 1–2; Gasiorowski-Denis, E. (2015). The big business of small companies. *ISO focus*, March. Available at www.iso.org; Bruton, G. D., Ketchen, D. J. & Ireland, R. D. (2013). Entrepreneurship as a solution to poverty. *Journal of Business Venturing*, *28*, 683–689.
9 Gasiorowski-Denis (2015).
10 De Nardi, M., Doctor, P. & Krane, S. D. (2007). Evidence on entrepreneurs in the United States: Data from the 1989–2004 *Survey of Consumer Finances. Economic Perspectives*, *31*, 18–36.
11 DeCarolis, D. M. & Litzky, B. E. (2006). Entrepreneurship. In Greenhaus, J. H. & Callanan, G. A. (Eds.), *Encyclopedia of career development* (pp. 284–288). Thousand Oaks, CA: Sage.
12 Mill, J. S. (1848). *Principles of political economy with some applications to social philosophy.* London, UK: John W. Parker.
13 Schumpeter, J. A. (1934). *The theory of economic development.* Cambridge, MA: Harvard University Press.
14 Callanan, G. A. & Zimmerman, M. (2016). To be or not to be an entrepreneur: Applying a normative model to career decision making. *Journal of Career Development*, *43*, 447–461; Frese, M. & Gielnik, M. M. (2014). The psychology of entrepreneurship. *Annual Review of Organizational Psychology and Organizational Behavior*, *1*, 413–438; Patel, P. C. & Thatcher, S. M. B. (2014). Sticking it out: Individual attributes and persistence in self-employment. *Journal of Management*, *40*, 1932–1979; Hirschi, A. & Fischer, S. (2013). Work values as predictors of entrepreneurial intentions. *Career Development International*, *18*, 216–231.
15 Kyndt, E. & Baert, H. (2015). Entrepreneurial competencies: Assessment and predictive value for entrepreneurship. *Journal of Vocational Behavior*, *90*, 13–25.
16 Callanan & Zimmerman (2016).
17 United States Department of Labor, Bureau of Labor Statistics (2016).
18 Ibid.
19 Callanan & Zimmerman (2016). DeCarolis & Litzky (2006).
20 Schein, E. H. (2006). Career anchors. In Greenhaus, J. H. & Callanan, G. A. (Eds.), *Encyclopedia of career development* (pp. 63–69). Thousand Oaks, CA: Sage.
21 Patel & Thatcher (2014).
22 Callanan & Zimmerman (2016); Patel & Thatcher (2014).
23 McClelland, D. C. (1967). *The achieving society.* New York: The Free Press.
24 Carsrud, A. & Brännback, M. (2011). Entrepreneurial motivations: What do we still need to know? *Journal of Small Business Management*, *49*, 9–26; Rauch, A. & Frese, M. (2007). Let's put the person back into entrepreneurship research: A meta-analysis on the relationship between business owners' personality traits, business creation, and success. *European Journal of Work and Organizational Psychology*, *16*, 353–370; Stewart, W. H. & Roth, P. L. (2007). A meta-analysis of achievement motivation differences between entrepreneurs and managers. *Journal of Small Business Management*, *45*, 401–421.
25 Diaz, F. & Rodriguez, A. (2003). Locus of control, nAch and values of community entrepreneurs. *Social Behavior and Personality*, *38*, 739–748; Hansemark, O. C. (2003). Need for achievement, locus of control and the prediction of business start-ups: A longitudinal study. *Journal of Economic Psychology*, *24*, 301–319.
26 De Pellis, E. & Reardon, K. K. (2007). The influence of personality traits and persuasive messages on entrepreneurial intention: A cross-cultural comparison. *Career Development International*, *12*, 382–396.
27 Zhao, H., Seibert, S. E. & Lumpkin, G. T. (2010). The relationship of personality to entrepreneurial intentions and performance: A meta-analytic review. *Journal of Management*, *36*, 381–404; Stewart & Roth (2007).

28 Busenitz, L. W. (1999). Entrepreneurial risk and strategic decision making: It's a matter of perspective. *Journal of Applied Behavioral Science, 35*, 325–340.
29 DeCarolis & Litzky (2006).
30 Schein (2006).
31 Rauch & Frese (2007).
32 Anderson, B. S., Kreiser, P. M., Kuratko, D. F., Hornsby, J. H. & Eshima, Y. (2014). Reconceptualizing entrepreneurial orientation. *Strategic Management Journal, 36*, 1579–1596; Saeed, S., Yousafzai, S. Y. & Engelen, A. (2014). On cultural and macroeconomic contingencies of the entrepreneurial orientation-performance relationship. *Entrepreneurship Theory and Practice, 38*, 255–290; Covin, J. G. & Wales, W. J. (2011). The measurement of entrepreneurial orientation. *Entrepreneurship Theory and Practice, 36*, 677–702; George, B. A. & Marino, A. (2011). The epistemology of entrepreneurial orientation: Conceptual formation, modeling, and operationalization. *Entrepreneurship Theory and Practice, 35*, 989–1024.
33 Schein (2006); Covin & Wales (2011); George & Marino (2011).
34 Alvarez, S. A. & Barney, J. B. (2010). Entrepreneurship and epistemology. *Academy of Management Annals, 4*, 557–583; Jain, R. K. (2011). Entrepreneurial competencies: Conceptualizations for future research. *Journal of Business Perspectives, 15*, 127–152.
35 Schjoedt, L. & Shaver, K. G. (2007). Deciding on an entrepreneurial career: A test of the pull and push hypotheses using the panel study of entrepreneurial dynamics data. *Entrepreneurship Theory and Practice, 31*, 733–752.
36 United States Department of Labor, Bureau of Labor Statistics, *Business Employment Dynamics* (2016).
37 DeCarolis, D. M. & Saparito, P. (2006). Social capital, cognition, and entrepreneurial opportunities: A theoretical framework. *Entrepreneurship Theory and Practice, 30*, 41–56; Terjesen, S. (2005). Senior women managers' transition to entrepreneurship: Leveraging embedded career capital. *Career Development International, 10*, 246–259.
38 Austin, M. J. & Nauta, M. M. (2016). Entrepreneurial role-model exposure, self-efficacy, and women's entrepreneurial intentions. *Journal of Career Development, 43*, 260–272; BarNir, A., Watson, W. E. & Hutchins, H. M. (2011). Mediation and moderated mediation in the relationship among role models, self-efficacy, entrepreneurial career intention, and gender. *Journal of Applied Social Psychology, 41*, 270–297; Burke, A. E., FitzRoy, F. R. & Nolan, M. A. (2008). What makes a die-hard entrepreneur? Beyond the "employee or entrepreneur" dichotomy. *Small Business Economics, 31*, 93–115; Van Auken, H., Fry, F. L. & Stephens, P. (2006). The influence of role models on entrepreneurial intentions. *Journal of Developmental Entrepreneurship, 11*, 157–167.
39 Van Auken et al. (2006).
40 Schoon, I. & Duckworth, K. (2012). Who becomes an entrepreneur? Early life experiences as predictors of entrepreneurship. *Developmental Psychology, 48*, 1719–1726.
41 Tolentino, L. R., Sedoglavich, V., Lu, V. N., Garcia, P. R. J. M. & Restubog, S. L. D. (2014). The role of adaptability in predicting entrepreneurial intentions: A moderated mediation model. *Journal of Vocational Behavior, 85*, 403–412.
42 Singh, G. & DeNoble, A. (2003). Early retirees as the next generation of entrepreneurs. *Entrepreneurship Theory and Practice, 27*, 207–226.
43 See the website www.sba.gov/smallbusinessplanner/plan/index.html.
44 Local Chambers of Commerce are listed at www.chamberofcommerce.com.
45 Duval-Couetil, N. (2013). Assessing the impact of entrepreneurship education programs: Challenges and approaches. *Journal of Small Business Management, 51*, 394–409.
46 Morris, M. H. & Kuratko, D. F. (2014). Building university 21st century entrepreneurship programs that empower and transform. In Hoskinson, S. & Kuratko, D. F. (Eds.), *Innovative pathways for university entrepreneurship in the 21st century (Advances in the Study of Entrepreneurship, Innovation & Economic Growth, Volume 24)* (pp. 1–24). Bingley, UK: Emerald Group Publishing; Kuratko, D. F. (2005). The emergence of entrepreneurship education: Development, trends, and challenges. *Entrepreneurship Theory and Practice, 29*, 577–597.
47 Morris, M. H., Webb, J. W., Fu, J. & Singhal, S. (2013). A competency-based perspective on entrepreneurship education: Conceptual and empirical insights. *Journal of Small Business Management, 51*, 352–369.
48 Morris et al. (2013); Kuratko (2005); Solomon, G. T., Duffy, S. & Tarabishy, A. (2002). The state of entrepreneurship education in the United States: A nationwide survey and analysis. *International Journal of Entrepreneurship Education, 1*, 65–86.

49 von Graevenitz, G., Dietmar, H. & Weber, R. (2010). The effects of entrepreneurship education. *Journal of Economic Behavior and Organization, 76*, 90–112.
50 Maneshwari, S. (2016). A publisher joins an industry it covers, blurring lines. *The New York Times*, September 4, www.nytimes.com.
51 Edelman, L. F., Brush, C. G., Manolova, T. S. & Greene, P. G. (2010). Start-up motivations and growth intentions of minority nascent entrepreneurs. *Journal of Small Business Management, 48*, 174–196; Cardon, M. S., Shinnar, R. S., Eisenman, M. & Rogoff, E. G. (2008). Segmenting the population of entrepreneurs: A cluster analysis study. *Journal of Developmental Entrepreneurship, 13*, 293–314; Malach-Pines, A. & Schwartz, D. (2008). Now you see them, now you don't: Gender differences in entrepreneurship. *Journal of Managerial Psychology, 23*, 811–832; Mueller, S. L. & Dato-on, M. C. (2008). Gender-role orientation as a determinant of entrepreneurial self-efficacy. *Journal of Developmental Entrepreneurship, 13*, 3–20; Heilman, M. E. & Chen, J. J. (2003). Entrepreneurship as a solution: The allure of self-employment for women and minorities. *Human Resource Management Review, 13*, 347–364.
52 Becker-Medina, E. H. (2016). Women-owned businesses on the rise. *Random Samplings, Official Blog of the U.S. Census Bureau.* Posted March 23 and available at http://blogs.census.gov/2016/03/23/women-owned-businesses-on-the-rise.
53 Becker-Medina (2016); U.S. Census Bureau. (2014). Measuring America: An overview of women-owned business and related statistics. Available at www.census.gov.
54 For a thorough review and discussion of research on women entrepreneurs, see: Jennings, J. E. & Brush, C. G. (2013). Research on women entrepreneurs: Challenges to (and from) the broader entrepreneurship literature? *Academy of Management Annals, 7*, 663–715.
55 Malach-Pines & Schwartz (2008).
56 Jennings & Brush (2013).
57 Ibid.
58 Ibid.
59 Jennings & Brush (2013); Austin & Nauta (2016); Thébaud, S. (2015). Business as plan B? Institutional foundations of gender inequality in entrepreneurship across 24 industrialized countries. *Administrative Science Quarterly, 60*, 671–711; Davis, A. E. & Shaver, K. G. (2012). Understanding gendered variations in business growth intentions across the life course. *Entrepreneurship Theory and Practice, 36*, 495–512.
60 Jennings & Brush (2013).
61 Ibid.
62 For a review of the impact of family factors on the decision to start one's own business, see Powell, G. N. & Greenhaus, J. H. (2010). Sex, gender, and decisions at the family–work interface. *Journal of Management, 36*, 1011–1039.
63 Parasuraman, S. & Simmers, C. A. (2001). Type of employment, work–family conflict and well-being: A comparative study. *Journal of Organizational Behavior, 22*, 551–568; Beutell, N. J., O'Hare, M. M., Schneer, J. A. & Alstete, J. W. (2016). Is self-employment a viable work–family strategy for married women? Paper presented at the 2016 Annual Meeting of the Eastern Academy of Management.
64 Mattis, M. C. (2004). Women entrepreneurs: Out from under the glass ceiling. *Women in Management Review, 19*, 154–163; Heilman & Chen (2003); Moore, D. P. & Buttner, E. H. (1997). *Women entrepreneurs: Moving beyond the glass ceiling.* Thousand Oaks, CA: Sage.
65 Jennings & Brush (2013).
66 Kelley et al. (2016); Coleman, S. & Robb, A. (2012). Gender-based firm performance differences in the United States: Examining the roles of financial capital and motivations. In Hughes, K. D. & Jennings, J. E. (Eds.), *Global women's entrepreneurship research: Diverse settings, questions and approaches* (pp. 75–94). Cheltenham, UK: Edward Elgar.
67 United States Census Bureau. (2015). Number of minority- and women-owned firms each increase by more than 2 million nationally. Released on December 15, 2015. Available at www.census.gov/newsroom/press-releases/2015/; Jennings & Brush (2013).
68 Austin & Nauta (2016).
69 Ibid.
70 Ibid.
71 Frese, M., Gielnik, M. M. & Mensmann, M. (2016). Psychological training for entrepreneurs to take action: Contributing to poverty reduction in developing countries. *Current Directions in Psychological Science, 25*, 196–202; Bullough, A., De Luque, M. S., Abdelzaher, D. & Heim, W.

(2015). Developing women leaders through entrepreneurship education and training. *Academy of Management Perspectives*, *29*, 250–270.
72 See the SBA website: www.sba.gov/starting-business/how-start-business/business-types/women-owned-businesses.
73 McManus, M. (2016). Minority business ownership: Data from the 2012 Survey of Business Owners. *Issue Brief of the U.S. Small Business Administration*, *12*, 1–13.
74 Edelman et al. (2010); Cardon et al. (2008); Köllinger, P. & Minniti, M. (2006). Not for lack of trying: American entrepreneurship in black and white. *Small Business Economics*, *27*, 59–79.
75 Shelton, L. M. (2010). Fighting an uphill battle: Expansion barriers, intra-industry social stratification, and minority firm growth. *Entrepreneurship Theory and Practice*, *34*, 379–398.
76 Bates, T. & Robb. A. (2013). Greater access to capital is needed to unleash the local economic development potential of minority-owned businesses. *Economic Development Quarterly*, *27*, 250–259. Park, Y. & Coleman, S. (2009). Credit rationing and black-owned firms: Is there evidence of discrimination? *Journal of Developmental Entrepreneurship*, *14*, 255–271.
77 Rhodes, C. & Butler, J. S. (2004). Understanding self-perceptions of business performance: An examination of black American entrepreneurs. *Journal of Developmental Entrepreneurship*, *9*, 55–71.
78 Liu, C. Y. (2012). The causes and dynamics of minority entrepreneurial entry. *Journal of Developmental Entrepreneurship*, *17*, 1–23.
79 See the SBA website: www.sba.gov/starting-business/how-start-business/business-types/minority-owned-businesses.
80 Terjesen, S., Hessels, J. & Li, D. (2016). Comparative international entrepreneurship: A review and research agenda. *Journal of Management*, *42*, 299–344; Edelman et al. (2010).
81 Schlaegel, C. & Koenig, M. (2013). Determinants of entrepreneurial intent: A meta-analytic test and integration of competing models. *Entrepreneurship Theory and Practice*, *38*, 291–332; De Clerq, D., Honig, B. & Martin, B. (2013). The roles of learning orientation and passion for work in the formation of entrepreneurial intention. *International Small Business Journal*, *22*, 652–676; Lee, L., Wong, P. K., Foo, M. D. & Leung, A. (2011). Entrepreneurial intentions: The influence of organizational and individual factors. *Journal of Business Venturing*, *26*, 124–136; Zhao, H., Seibert, S. E. & Hills, G. (2005). The mediating role of self-efficacy in the development of entrepreneurial intentions. *Journal of Applied Psychology*, *90*, 1265–1272.
82 Schlaegel & Koenig (2013); Fini, R., Grimaldi, R., Marzocchi, G. L. & Sobrero, M. (2012). The determinants of corporate entrepreneurial intention within small and newly established firms. *Entrepreneurship Theory and Practice*, *36*, 387–414.
83 For a more in-depth discussion of these questions, see Hyatt, J. (1992). Should you start a business? *INC.*, February, 48–58.
84 The description of the entrepreneur John Paul Jones DeJoria was taken from several sources including Palmeri, C. (1991). Often down but never out. *Forbes*, March 4; also from the company website www.paulmitchell.com and from Bloomberg Research at www.bloomberg.com/research.
85 Miller, D. & Sardais, C. (2015). Bifurcating time: How entrepreneurs reconcile the paradoxical demands of the job. *Entrepreneurship Theory and Practice*, *39*, 489–512; De Clerq, D., Menzies, T. V., Diochon, M. & Gasse, Y. (2009). Explaining nascent entrepreneurs' goal commitment: An exploratory study. *Journal of Small Business and Entrepreneurship*, *22*, 123–140; Alvarez & Barney (2010).
86 Powell & Greenhaus (2010); Powell, G. N. & Eddleston, K. A. (2016). Family involvement in the firm, family-to-business support, and entrepreneurial outcomes: An exploration. *Journal of Small Business Management*, *55*, 614-631; Eddleston, K. A. & Powell, G. N. (2012). Nurturing entrepreneurs' work–family balance: A gendered perspective. *Entrepreneurship Theory and Practice*, *36*, 513–541.
87 Terjesen, S. & Sullivan, S. E. (2011). The role of developmental relationships in the transition to entrepreneurship: A qualitative study and agenda for future research. *Career Development International*, *16*, 482–506; DeCarolis & Saparito (2006).
88 Callanan & Zimmerman (2016).
89 DeTienne, D. R. (2010). Entrepreneurial exit as a critical component of the entrepreneurial process: Theoretical development. *Journal of Business Venturing*, *25*, 203–215.
90 DeTienne, D. R. & Cardon, M. S. (2012). Impact of founder experience on exit intentions. *Small Business Economics*, *38*, 351–374.
91 Wennberg, K. & DeTienne, D. R. (2014). What do we really mean when we talk about "exit"? A critical review of research on entrepreneurial exit. *International Small Business Journal*, *32*, 4–16.

13 International Careers

In Chapter 1 we discussed how globalization has radically changed worldwide commerce and fundamentally altered business patterns and relationships. Indeed, beginning in the latter part of the 20th century and continuing into the 21st, the volume and value of international trade in goods and services have grown rapidly. In 1994, global trade, representing the collective value of exported merchandise and services, totaled $5.2 trillion. Twenty years later the value had risen to $23.4 trillion, a more than fourfold increase.[1] Large and small companies throughout the industrialized world now have commercial interests and dealings that span the globe. This explosive growth in trade and cross-border business activity has commensurately reshaped career patterns and influenced individual approaches to career management and decision-making.[2]

In the contemporary business environment, individuals must be prepared to consider undertaking an international assignment, a decision that should be informed by an understanding of the potential positive and negative consequences of such an endeavor. From the organizational side, companies with international operations must be aware of the consequences for their employees who are engaged in international careers and also need to establish related programs that facilitate individual and organizational success.

This chapter examines international careers from multiple perspectives. First, we provide a definition of an international career. Next, we describe the different types of international careers and the challenges that each presents. We then look more closely at the expatriation and repatriation processes, giving extensive consideration to the different phases of each activity along with the individual actions that help ensure successful transitions. We also discuss organizational responsibilities associated with managing those employees who are involved in expatriation assignments. The chapter concludes with a discussion of how the career management model can be used in navigating an international career and how the human resource management programs of an organization can support international careers.

Definition of an International Career

An *international career* is defined as one in which the individual employee performs work that unfolds over and across the boundaries of countries and geographic regions, and which takes place over an extended period of time.[3] An international career by its very nature means that the individual is dealing with a much wider spectrum of work interactions on a regular basis. These interactions can take a variety of forms, ranging from regular Internet or phone communication with customers or other stakeholders from around the world to physically relocating to work in a foreign country. With the rapid acceleration in globalization, it is a near certainty that today's younger millennial workers will be involved in an international career at some point during their work lives.

Much attention has been given to positive outcomes, both personal and professional, that can result from being immersed in an international career. As will be discussed in more detail later in this chapter, these favorable results include an improved understanding of global business practices, an enhanced level of professional development and advancement potential, a higher level of objective and subjective career success, and personal growth and development through exposure to peoples and cultures throughout the world. To attain these outcomes, it is important for an individual to properly manage all aspects of an international career and to use the steps in the career management model to ensure that career decisions are made consistent with personal values, interests, abilities, aspirations, and a preferred lifestyle.

Types of International Careers

As shown in Table 13.1, international careers can take several different forms.[4] First, standard expatriate career assignments involve the physical relocation of the individual from the parent company in his or her home (or base) country to an operation in a host (or foreign) country, usually for some set period of time.[5] Two forms of standard expatriation exist. *Corporate expatriations* are overseas assignments that are initiated by the employing organization, usually involving assignment to one particular country and lasting more than one year.[6] In contrast, a *self-initiated expatriation* is, as the name implies, orchestrated and normally financed by an individual who, through his or her own volition, relocates to and works in a particular foreign country.[7] Self-initiated expatriation can be undertaken for various reasons—to take a work position in a foreign country, to bolster individual development, to gain exposure to another culture, or to build relationships with host country nationals.[8] Because it is self-initiated, this type of expatriation experience can vary in length and in scope depending on individual preferences. When an expatriate returns to the home country, the process is referred to as *repatriation*.[9]

In some cases, the expatriate (possibly with the support of his or her organization) chooses to establish a more permanent legal residence in the host country, thus becoming an *immigrant worker*. The immigrant expatriate normally would remain in the host country on a longer-lasting basis, but could stay for a more temporary period of time.[10] A *virtual expatriate* is an employee of a parent company who uses various forms of technology to manage and coordinate the work of employees who work at operations or subsidiaries in other parts of the world. In this case, the virtual expatriate does not physically relocate out of the home country, but uses Skype, email, online video conferencing, and smartphones to communicate regularly with the foreign operation or operations.[11] Thus, the virtual expatriate continues to live and be deployed in a home country and culture, but works primarily with individuals from other cultures.[12]

Another form of an international career is known as *flexpatriation*.[13] Flexpatriates travel to and live in multiple host countries on a regular basis on assignments that usually last one or two months. Flexpatriation is often associated with project-based or problem-solving work that requires the application of expertise for a specific period of time. An additional category of an international career involves short-term *international work assignments*. In

Table 13.1 Types of International Careers*

Category	*Definition*	*Duration*	*Location(s)*
Corporation-Sponsored Expatriation	Employee relocates to and works in a foreign country at behest of parent company	1 to 3 years	Normally one host country
Self-Initiated Expatriation	Individual chooses to relocate to and work in a foreign country	Variable, but normally more than one year	Normally one host country
Immigrant Worker	Expatriate who chooses to more permanently relocate to and work in a foreign country	Longer-term, likely several years	Normally one host country
Virtual Expatriation	Employee works and stays in home country, but manages workers in a foreign country	Variable	Home country
Flexpatriation	Employee travels to, works in, and lives in host countries for short-term assignments	Usually 1 to 2 months per assignment	Multiple countries
International Work Assignments and Business Travel	Periodic project-based work and business trips to foreign countries.	Usually 1 to 3 weeks at a time	Multiple countries
Employee in home country working for organization headquartered in another country	Employee does not necessarily need to travel to foreign country	Variable	Home country

* Adapted from multiple sources, including: Baruch, Y., Dickmann, M., Altman, Y. & Bournois, F. (2013). Exploring international work: Types and dimensions of global careers. *International Journal of Human Resource Management*, *24*, 2369–2393; Shaffer, M. A., Kraimer, M. L., Chen, Y. & Bolino, M. C. (2012). Choices, challenges, and career consequences of global work experiences: A review and future agenda. *Journal of Management*, *38*, 1282–1327; Tharenou, P. (2006). International careers. In Greenhaus, J. H. & Callanan, G. A. (Eds.), *Encyclopedia of career development* (pp. 398–404). Thousand Oaks, CA: Sage.

this case, the individual is periodically required to travel to, and work in, one or more foreign countries, although the individual primarily works from the parent company's domestic base. These international work assignments can take the form of overseas business trips that last a few days up to short-term assignments that could be a month or more in duration. The final category of international careers occurs when an individual in a home or base country is *employed by an organization that is headquartered in another country*. In this case the individual's work does not necessarily necessitate international travel, but typically requires an adaptation to the foreign organization's management style, culture, and performance expectations.[14]

All of these types of international careers can have positive and negative consequences for the individual in terms of their careers and their work–life balance. Indeed, all types of foreign assignments can have a positive impact on one's career, but they can also potentially cause career disruptions and can pose challenges to employees' family and personal lives. In addition, as will be discussed later in this chapter, all international assignments require that the individual develop distinct "global" or "cross-cultural" competencies that facilitate the adaptation to other cultures and business practices and the formation of social and business relationships in the host country. The development of these competencies can help ensure success in the global arena.[15]

Career Issues Related to Expatriation

Given that corporation-initiated expatriation involves longer-term physical relocation to a host country, the majority of the research on international careers has focused on the implications of this type of expatriation. Several individual and organizational perspectives can be used to examine the expatriation process, but the primary focus is ultimately on the factors associated with the success (or failure) of the expatriation assignment for the individual employee and the parent company.[16] More precisely, research on international careers has investigated the individual and organizational actions and environmental issues that influence the expatriation assignment. Included as part of this assessment are the effects of expatriation on family relationships, the potential career outcomes of expatriation, and the organizational programs that produce a successful expatriation experience.[17]

An individual's willingness to undertake an expatriation assignment can be based on several possible positive outcomes, but is most often seen as a boost to longer-term career advancement prospects.[18] This perspective is based on the view that the acceleration in globalized commerce has commensurately driven organizations to hire, develop, and promote individuals with global business experience. Indeed, one of the compelling reasons for the expanding popularity of expatriation is that it serves as a developmental tool for those rising to the ranks of middle and senior management. However, while the positive outcomes of expatriation are well recognized, there is also a high potential for failure.

Expatriation failure can involve an inability to properly adjust to the foreign assignment and the culture, language(s), and business practices of the host country; opting out of the assignment prior to the expected completion date; not performing well in the assignment; and choosing to sever the employment relationship with the parent organization while the assignment is ongoing. For the individual and the employing organization, the costs of failure can be high. For the employee, the costs can manifest in a disrupted career, a sub-optimization in compensation progression, and negative implications for his or her family. For the organization, expatriate failure can affect financial performance, because it is estimated that the cost of an expatriate assignment can total two to three times the base salary of the expatriated employee.[19] Therefore, it is incumbent on the employee and the corporation to take the necessary steps to ensure success of the appointment. We now discuss in more detail the individual and organizational perspectives on expatriation.

Individual Actions during an Expatriation Assignment

An individual perspective on expatriation can be viewed as a series of phases,[20] starting with the preparation stage, moving to the period of adaptation, and concluding with the contribution (or performance) phase. The next step, repatriation to the home country, will be discussed in a separate section of this chapter.

The Preparation Phase

In order to avoid the negative personal and career consequences resulting from a failed expatriation, it is critical for the individual to be properly prepared prior to the commencement of the assignment. Further, if family or other nonwork considerations were relevant to the expatriation initiative, then those factors would need to be addressed previous to and during the assignment. As with any career move, in order to ensure fit with the overseas assignment, the individual should ensure that it is consistent with individual interests, values, and talents, and is capable of fulfilling career goals.[21] In terms of preparation, it is imperative that the individual be fully equipped to function in the foreign country and culture. Several dimensions of the expatriate assignment will guide the level of preparation.[22] These dimensions include the length of time that will be spent in the host country, the level of intensity and breadth of interaction in the relationship between the expatriate and the host country nationals, and the extent of the "gap" between the expatriate's home country culture and the culture of the host country.[23] In addition, other related dimensions that should be taken into account prior to the actual assignment include the degree of language differences, variations in remuneration methods, whether there are alternative approaches for performance evaluation, and any legal considerations that govern employment in the foreign country.

Perhaps the most important consideration in the preparation phase is the extent to which family considerations come into play. Of course, if the individual has little or no family obligations, then the overseas appointment can be undertaken without undue concern for family matters. But in many cases, expatriation has an impact on family relationships, and in fact, the magnitude of the effect on family relationships and commitments will often dictate whether the expatriation assignment is actually undertaken.[24] If the assignment is accepted, prior to the move, a determination is needed as to whether the family will accompany the expatriate, and if it does, the conditions under which the family members will go through preparations for the transfer. If the family will not accompany the expatriate, then accommodations regarding visits home for the expatriate would need to be negotiated.

In total, an individual contemplating or undertaking an expatriate appointment has a variety of factors to consider, both from a career management vantage point and from a work–life perspective. An awareness of these factors, and whether the individual takes preparatory steps to properly address them, will determine whether the expatriate is likely to have a positive experience.

The Adaptation Phase

Once the expatriation assignment has been initiated, the next stage involves the adaptation to the foreign operation, its employees, the host country, and the culture (or cultures) of the country and the geographic region. Much attention in the scholarly and popular press has been devoted to the factors that influence successful (or unsuccessful) adaptation.[25] This focus is understandable given the potential costs to the individual, his or her family, and the company should the assignment end in failure. Indeed, there are a number of stakeholders who have an interest in a successful adaptation, including the expatriate, the expatriate's family or social network, the home-based parent company, and the host-based operation.[26]

Clearly, the programs and policies of both the parent and the foreign unit will have a significant influence on whether the expatriate and his or her family will be able to make a successful adjustment to the foreign assignment. Nonetheless, a number of individual and environmental factors come into play in the adjustment process. The most important factor related to a successful adjustment is the level of motivation that the individual exhibits toward the assignment, both in terms of performing well on the job as well as assimilating into the host culture.[27] A strong desire to be successful in the foreign assignment by adjusting effectively to the new work environment and to a substantially different culture will go a long way in determining whether the employee will successfully complete the expatriate appointment.[28]

In addition to motivation, expatriate adjustment is enhanced when the individual feels empowered to exercise personal control over the work that is being performed.[29] In this sense, if the individual has the freedom to control the direction of the work and has latitude in deciding how and when the work is performed, there is a greater likelihood of successful adaptation. A number of other individual factors have been linked with a higher degree of work and cultural adjustment, including personality factors such as conscientiousness, extraversion, emotional stability, openness to experience, and a people orientation, as well as a lower level of ethnocentrism.[30] Of course, these individual characteristics are linked with success in all types of assignments, not just international ones. But they do seem to have predictive value in determining whether the individual will have a higher chance for success in the expatriation assignment.

Another critical element in expatriate adjustment is the interaction and relationships with the individual's family once the assignment has been undertaken.[31] As noted earlier, a major determination with any expatriate assignment is whether the family stays in the home country or accompanies the individual to the host country. Both cases can positively or negatively affect expatriate adjustment. If the family remains in the home country, the expatriate does not need to deal with his or her family's adjustment in the host country, but must be concerned with whether the family can properly manage day-to-day activities in the absence of the expatriate. In addition, the individual may have trouble functioning in the work role because his or her family is not present in the host country. If the family accompanies the expatriate, the family's difficulties in becoming accustomed to the foreign country could jeopardize the expatriate's adjustment to the assignment. In this case, the stresses resulting from the family's difficulties in adjusting to the new environment can spill over into the expatriate's work role, thereby causing negative performance consequences for the expatriate.

In reality, family relationships and interactions can have dual influences on expatriate assignments. On one hand, a family's adjustment difficulties can be a primary factor in causing the ultimate failure of the expatriate assignment. On the other hand, the supporting presence of a partner and a family can facilitate a more positive adjustment to the assignment for the employee.[32] In these ways, the expatriate and his or her family affect one another through a "crossover process" that could produce both positive and negative synergy and thereby produce positive and negative career outcomes related to the expatriation assignment.[33]

The Contribution Phase

Once an expatriate has made a successful adjustment to the foreign operation and becomes established in the assignment, the next stage involves making work contributions and fulfilling responsibilities in line with the expectations of the parent company. As with any task, the capacity of an individual to perform well throughout the expatriation assignment is a function of work motivation, ability, and behaviors and actions on the job. Another factor critical to success in this phase is the degree to which the person is able to function effectively with host country nationals. The establishment of network ties with individuals in the host country can bring important supportive resources to the expatriate that allow improved functioning on the job.[34] Specifically, networking with host country nationals can provide both informational and emotional support to the expatriate that can facilitate heightened performance.[35] In addition, the presence of mentors and other supportive alliances at the foreign operation or within the host country can enhance the performance of the expatriate through the provision of cultural guidance and psychosocial support.[36]

In an idealized sense, the successful conclusion of the expatriate experience should have a positive effect on the individual's overall career path by facilitating the accomplishment of career goals and by contributing to longer-term career success. Research on whether the expatriate experience is beneficial to an individual's career shows somewhat inconclusive results.[37] On one side, expatriation, both corporate sponsored and self-initiated, can lead to a broader understanding of a company's operations, improved career competencies, and a personal perception of increased career prospects, at least as compared to non-expatriates. On the other side, an expatriation appointment can be disruptive to the career because the employee is away from the parent company for an extended period of time and likely loses direct access to key corporate decision-makers. In addition, when brought back to the parent company and the home country, there might be difficulties in re-assimilation as well as a lack of a viable career path. While difficulties in the repatriation process will be discussed in a later section of this chapter, it is clear that the international experience gained through an expatriation appointment does not always lead to career progress or satisfaction.

Organizational Issues and Actions Related to Expatriation

Company-initiated expatriation has grown substantially over the past three decades.[38] This growth is fueled by a number of corporate objectives.[39] First, an organization could send an expatriate from the parent to the host country as a means to exercise command, coordination, and control over the activities of the foreign operation. Second, expatriation could be a mechanism to transfer knowledge and expertise from the parent to the foreign unit. Third, the expatriation assignment is a way to develop and groom employees for more senior roles in the hierarchy of the parent. Fourth, expatriation and the resulting step of repatriation is a way for the parent corporation to import knowledge and expertise from the foreign operation. Finally, expatriation can be a mechanism to raise cultural sensitivity and awareness regarding a particular country or geographic region, which could be a necessary step for future global expansion. For all of these reasons, it is important for the parent to take an active role in managing expatriation assignments.[40]

In order to help ensure successful expatriation assignments, several organizational actions are necessary and are in line with the stages of expatriation as outlined earlier. These steps include employee selection, pre-deployment training and preparation, mentoring of the expatriate, performance monitoring, appraisal, and feedback, career management assistance, and ultimately, repatriation.[41]

Selection

Depending on the overall objective of the expatriation appointment, the company's first step is to choose employees who have a high chance of success in a foreign appointment. As indicated earlier, certain personality traits, a comparatively low level of ethnocentrism, and a high degree of motivation to succeed in a foreign culture can all have a positive influence on expatriation success. In addition, the selected employees should benefit from the developmental aspects of the assignment. In this sense, organizations should establish a baseline set of global competencies that they wish to develop within those chosen for an expatriation assignment.[42] Finally, selected expatriates should have the capacity to constructively influence the foreign-based operation by effectively interacting with host country nationals and by adapting to the culture and business practices of the foreign operation.

Pre-Deployment Training and Preparation

Without question, the most important action that an organization can take to ensure a successful deployment is to fully prepare expatriates for the foreign appointment. There are a number of programs that the parent company could use in this phase.[43] Among the more well-known of these programs are: cross-cultural training; language immersion courses; the appointment of a parent-company-based mentor or coach; a review of the legal, regulatory, and business practice standards of the host country; a discussion of any political or safety concerns that could arise within the host country; a delineation of performance standards and expectations; and plans for career paths once the assignment is completed.

In addition to these steps, it is also critical to ensure that the family considerations of the expatriate are addressed. If the family is to accompany the expatriate on the assignment, then a variety of preparations are necessary, ranging from cultural training to living arrangements and the coverage of household expenses to educational options if children are involved in the relocation.[44] If the family remains in the home country, accommodations need to be established for regular contact between the expatriate and the family. In both cases, if the expatriate's partner is employed or wishes to become employed, the parent company should provide career support, meaning that the partner is offered assistance in the job search process and in negotiating employment.[45]

To the extent possible, the responsibilities of the parent company and the expatriate should be put in writing during the pre-deployment process. In this way both parties would understand clearly the requirements of the expatriation appointment and the standards by which the assignment will take place. Further, other factors related to the assignment should be stipulated in writing, such as the number of visits home while the expatriation is ongoing and how fluctuations in currency valuations will be handled in terms of total compensation for the expatriate.

Ongoing Mentoring and Coaching

Support from the host country operation and its employees plays a substantial role in facilitating adjustment to the expatriate assignment. The formal appointment of a host country mentor and coach for the expatriate can ease the transition to the new country and culture, can help build positive relationships with host country personnel, and can assist in knowledge transfer related to the assignment and the workings of the foreign operation.[46] As in a domestic relationship, the mentor also provides valuable feedback on job performance and offers advice on where changes might be warranted.[47]

Performance Monitoring, Appraisal, and Feedback

Expatriation success for the individual and the parent organization is enhanced when performance goals and standards are stated clearly and when those norms are used to monitor and appraise accomplishments.[48] Indeed, a failure to communicate standards or not regularly gauge performance is an important reason why an expatriation assignment ends in failure. At a minimum, the parent company should establish regular performance reviews with the expatriate and his or her home and host country supervisors to ensure that expectations are being met. In this regard, the host supervisor plays a critical role in the performance evaluation process because physical proximity allows for a higher degree of interaction with the expatriate and the ability to provide support and offer advice on any corrective actions that might be needed.[49]

Career Management Assistance

For many if not most expatriates the willingness to take on a foreign assignment is based on the expectation that it will result in positive career outcomes in terms of hierarchical advancement and compensation progression. However, the repatriation of the expatriate to the parent organization and the home country often occurs with limited regard for the career aspirations of the individual and with little or no guarantee of upward mobility.[50] Accordingly, it is recommended that no later than six months prior to the end of the assignment the parent company provide to the expatriate a career orientation review that maps out possible future positions with the parent company once the foreign deployment has ended.[51]

In summary, there are many steps that can be taken by the parent organization to ensure a successful expatriation experience, where both the employee and the organization reap rewards from the endeavor. Clearly, a company's human resource management function has a significant role to play in the selection, preparation, performance monitoring, and career management assistance related to the assignment. Once an expatriation assignment has ended, the next step is repatriation, or the return of the expatriate to the home country. In the next section, we discuss the repatriation process from an individual perspective and we identify steps to be taken by the parent organization in the management of the process.

Career Issues and Actions Related to Repatriation

Like expatriation, the repatriation process has been studied extensively.[52] Several factors, both individual and organizational, have been examined for their influence on the success of the repatriation initiative. These factors include the appropriateness of the plans and preparations for the employee's return home; the potential for "reverse" culture shock once the employee and his or her family arrives back in the home country and culture; whether the employee can be placed in a work position that is appropriate to his or her career goals and aspirations; the ability to craft a longer-term career development plan and career path; and the degree of difficulty for the employee's family in becoming reestablished in the home country. In addition, from the organizational perspective, there is much interest in the mechanisms that could be utilized to increase the retention rate of expatriates once they return from the foreign assignment.[53] Voluntary turnover rates for returning expatriates can be significant, ranging up to and beyond 50 percent within three months after the beginning of repatriation.[54] This turnover can have competitive implications because those returning expatriates leaving the company would typically take positions with competitor firms.[55] We now consider these individual and organizational factors in more detail.

The Repatriation Process

Research on international career management has extensively examined the implications of the readjustment process for the expatriate (and his or her family) upon arrival back at the parent company and the home country.[56] The act of readjustment can be both professional (becoming re-acclimated to job and work processes) and personal (the employee and his or her family becoming reestablished in the community).[57] These transitions can be stressful because there are a number of simultaneous demands on the returning expatriate, and he or she might be reentering a company and a culture that has changed substantially since the origination of the expatriate assignment.[58] In addition, the repatriation process has clear career implications because the primary goal for the organization and the employee is for the employee to be re-assimilated successfully into the culture and work processes of the parent company. In addition, depending on the nature of the expatriate assignment, the parent organization and the individual can use the knowledge and the skills gained through the assignment to improve individual functioning and organizational performance.[59]

A number of steps can be taken to ensure a proper and successful repatriation.[60] First, the parent organization and the employee should proactively plan for the repatriation, including having a dialogue on the timing and the logistics required to complete the transfer back to the parent as well as a general discourse on career-related details.[61] This first step should happen well in advance of the actual date of the transfer, typically no later than six months prior to the end of the expatriation assignment.[62] Second, unless it is stipulated ahead of time, the organization and the employee should discuss and come to a conclusion on the specific position into which the employee will be placed once he or she returns from the foreign assignment. While conditions might change within the parent that could obviate the plans for an intended position upon return, at least the expatriate would have a solid idea for continued employment with the parent company. Third, and consistent with the prior step, the organization and the employee should have a more in-depth review of longer-term career plans and the paths that the employee could reasonably follow. This dialogue would give the returning employee a realistic preview of longer-term career and job opportunities and could clear up any uncertainties about the employee's career prospects once the repatriation process begins.[63]

While the readjustment of the expatriate is the most important element of the repatriation process, it is also vital that the expatriate's family successfully navigate the move back to the home country.[64] If the expatriate's family had accompanied him or her to the host country, then there are a number of necessary tasks that must be accomplished for the family to become reestablished in the home country. To cite a few requirements, plans for household and living arrangements, schooling and care options for the children (if necessary), and job and career plans for the expatriate's partner would all need to be made as part of the repatriation process. If the transfer back to the parent involves relocation to another city within the home country, then the stresses of repatriation for the family could be magnified even further.

Just as an expatriation assignment can fail, so too can repatriation if the process is not handled properly. Repatriation failure occurs when the returning expatriate performs poorly on the job, experiences dissatisfaction with the work environment, and at the extreme, chooses to leave the parent company either immediately upon return or soon thereafter.[65] Dissatisfaction and the resulting voluntary turnover among returning expatriates is a major strategic concern for multinational corporations because it represents a loss of human capital and the accumulated knowledge gained through the foreign assignment or assignments.[66] Accordingly, organizational approaches to repatriation become strategically important given the stakes involved. One important step is to validate and show appreciation for the international experiences of the repatriated employee. This can be accomplished by having repatriated employees participate in debriefing sessions with more senior managers, involving them in strategy sessions dealing with international operations, and having them serve as training resources or mentors for current or future expatriates.[67]

In addition to the steps outlined above, the parent company should also, to the extent possible, provide rewards for the returning employees. At a basic level, the reward could be a credentialing for the international experience or a monetary stipend or bonus for the successful completion of the expatriation assignment.[68] Of course, promotions to a higher level in the organization could be a more significant form of reward for the returning employee.[69]

Ultimately, organizations must recognize that after an extended time away from the home country many changes could have taken place through expatriation—in the employee, with his or family, and within the parent company.[70] These changes can certainly have an influence on the readjustment process and the employee's ability to fit back into the parent company.[71] Therefore, organizations need to strategically manage the repatriation process to ensure logistical and emotional support for the repatriated employee and his or her family as a way to improve employee satisfaction and reduce the voluntary turnover of valuable human resources.[72]

Applying the Career Management Model to International Careers

Since the latter part of the 20th century there has been a consistent and discernible expansion in all forms of international careers. This growth has meant that many employees, regardless of the size of their employer, must be prepared to consider an international assignment at any moment. Given this reality, an individual should be prepared to systematically make decisions regarding whether an international assignment represents a correct fit within his or her overall career plans. Although the nature of the international assignment will dictate the career management practices to be used by the individual, it is appropriate that any decision be made by employing the steps in the career management model as described earlier in this book in Chapters 4, 5, and 6. In this sense, several questions can be asked. First, is the international assignment (or assignments) consistent with my interests, values, abilities, and lifestyle preferences? Second, is the host country (or countries) a good fit for my personal aspirations and/or do I have reservations about going to this particular country or region of the world? Third, does an international component to my career align with my conceptual and operational goals? Fourth, what career strategies would work best or be most beneficial to my career if an international assignment is undertaken? Fifth, how will an international career affect my family and personal life? And finally, will an international assignment help my career over the long run? We now address each of these questions.

Is the International Assignment Consistent with my Interests, Values, Abilities, and Lifestyle Preferences?

One of the themes of this book is that all career decisions, to the extent possible, should be made with the goal of achieving a fit with personal characteristics and lifestyle preferences. The need for consistency between the person and a career decision is especially important when considering an international assignment or a broader global direction in one's career. International assignments normally carry with them a high degree of change, including differences in physical location, culture, language, interpersonal and social connections, and work responsibilities. In addition, embarking on an international career can produce alterations and disruptions in one's family and personal lives. Because all of these changes bring with them stress and a risk of disappointment, the individual must do a thorough job of considering whether his or her personal qualities and lifestyle preferences are in sync with an international opportunity.

For some people, the desire for an international career can be part of their personal make-up. Specifically, it is possible that certain people can have an internationalism orientation that predisposes them to the pursuit of an international career.[73] In this sense, an individual's interests, values, personality, and desired lifestyle coalesce to form a personal profile where there is a strong push to pursue an international career.

Is the Host Country a Good Fit for my Personal Aspirations?

If the international career opportunity involves a physical relocation for an extended period of time, the individual has to decide whether the country (or region) of destination represents a good fit. One consideration in making this decision is the degree of cultural gap; that is, the difference between the culture of the person's home country and that of the host country.[74] If the difference is substantial, the individual (and possibly his or her family) might have a difficult time adapting to, or gaining acceptance in, the foreign operation and/or the host country. For example, depending on the country and region of the world, lesbian, gay, bisexual, and transgendered expatriates can experience discrimination and stereotyping in the host country, as well as limited organizational and host-country support.[75]

Beyond a cultural gap, other considerations can come into play when deciding on an international assignment. Certain parts of the world pose obvious safety risks due to geopolitical turmoil, civil war, threat of kidnapping, and terrorism. A person contemplating an international career would need to weigh the benefits of a foreign appointment versus the risks inherent in the assignment. In addition, from a career advancement perspective, an assignment to certain parts of the world might be more or less helpful in achieving future career goals than a movement to other parts. To give one example, an assignment to Antarctica, where one is truly "out of sight and out of mind," might not be an advantageous move in terms of longer-term career mobility.

Does an International Component Align with my Career Goals?

The pursuit of an international career is often undertaken to satisfy career goals. For example, many individuals who choose to become self-initiated expatriates do so in a desire to improve skill sets and to become more aware of cultures and business practices in other parts of the world.[76] These experiences can satisfy both conceptual and operational career goals. On the conceptual side, global experiences can fulfill the desire to "see the world" and be exposed to, and enriched by, other cultures. On the operational side, an international assignment can be focused on a future outcome that a person wishes to attain. It is well-recognized that globalization has shrunk the world and presented new job opportunities that cross borders and continents. Thus, while permanent jobs and career prospects can be limited within industrialized countries, greater opportunities might exist in developing and underdeveloped sectors of the world. Further, upward mobility in many multinational corporations is predicated on international experience, meaning that those striving for hierarchical advancement would want to incorporate attaining international proficiency into their career goals.

What Career Strategies would be Most Beneficial in an International Career?

In Chapter 6 we outlined a number of career strategies that could be utilized in career management. Many of these strategies can be applied to the management of international careers. In terms of timing, the strategies can be segregated into two categories—those that are useful prior to deployment into an international career or assignment and those that are beneficial during the assignment. Younger individuals, such as college students who are interested in pursuing an international career, could invest in *skill development*. For example, the person could consider majoring or minoring in international business or taking related coursework. Learning an additional language could also be beneficial because those who are fluent or conversational in another language could have an advantage in gaining international employment.

Once employed, individuals could *develop and pursue new mobility opportunities* by using self-nomination or "signaling" to indicate to senior management a willingness to take on an international appointment or to travel internationally. In addition, researching the culture and business practices of different parts of the world where the parent company has subsidiaries or operations would be another useful technique to learn more about the demands and challenges of a possible foreign deployment. Once in a foreign assignment, additional career strategies become prominent. As was discussed earlier in this chapter, two important international career strategies are to *seek out networking opportunities* with host country nationals and to *find a mentor* within or outside of the foreign operation. These two actions could help build social capital, with both the network connections and the mentor serving as valuable sources of advice and guidance on the foreign operations and culture and as providers of feedback on performance.[77] Another strategy useful in an international career is for the individual to *build his or her image and reputation*. In using this strategy, the individual makes sure that accomplishments that occur while in a foreign assignment are relayed back to the parent company and are publicized to the supervisors overseeing the assignment.

How Will an International Career Affect my Family and Personal Life?

The effects of an international career on an individual's family and personal life are heavily dependent on the circumstances of the family and the conditions under which the international career is conducted.[78] For short-term foreign assignments and periodic overseas travel, the negative effects on work–life balance primarily involve the stresses that result when one or both partners in the relationship are away from the family unit and unable to perform routine family duties and functions. The length of time devoted to foreign travel, when it occurs, and the destination could all have an effect on work–family balance.[79] Of course, short-term assignments and foreign business travel could also have an enriching effect if the travel can periodically involve the family accompanying the employee on the trip. In addition, business travel can, at times, serve as a needed respite from the day-to-day chores and personal interactions on the home front, thus allowing for a "recharging of the batteries" and reducing the overall stresses felt by the employee.[80]

If a longer-term international assignment is undertaken, typically through expatriation or flexpatriation, then the impact on the individual's nonwork life will be comparatively greater than if short-term, periodic international trips are taken. When a foreign assignment is longer-term, a defining factor would be whether the family accompanies the expatriate on the assignment to the host country or maintains residency in the home country. As was stated earlier in this chapter, the presence of the expatriate's family in the host country could be positive or negative. If difficulties in adaptation to the host country are encountered, then the presence of the family could be detrimental to the work performance of the expatriate and harmful to the psychological well-being of the family. In contrast, if the adjustment is relatively problem free, then both the expatriate and the family will likely experience more favorable outcomes.

Will an International Assignment Help my Career over the Long Run?

A great deal of research has examined the intrinsic and extrinsic outcomes of international assignments.[81] In the most fundamental sense, international career assignments can work to build the career capital and the competencies of the individual and improve opportunities for mobility and advancement.[82] As was discussed earlier in this book, Michael Arthur and his colleagues proposed three primary competencies that facilitate success in modern careers, including looking outside the organization for identity (knowing-why), expanding one's transferable skill set (knowing-how), and establishing networks of information and influence (knowing-whom).[83] Participation in an international career, where the individual typically crosses the boundaries from one's home country to others, can lead to an enhancement of all of these competencies and can be a precursor to success in multiple global contexts.[84]

As noted earlier, international activities, if conducted properly, can lead to improved skill sets, a better understanding of the culture and work contexts in other parts of the world, and the building of global social networks. Multinational corporations see the development of these individual skills as an important outcome of international assignments and as a way to develop managers and leaders who are capable of being promoted to more senior leadership positions with expanded global responsibilities. For the individual, global experience, especially through expatriation, can enhance marketability and improve chances of finding positions in the external job market.[85] Thus, if a parent company does not appreciate the accomplishments and the enhanced skill set of a returning expatriate, then he or she could in effect become a "proactive repatriate" by seeking out other employers that will recognize and reward his or her international experiences.[86]

Organizational Actions and Responsibilities with International Assignments

The rapid globalization of business has led multinational corporations to search for ways to develop human resources to fill executive and middle management positions that have international responsibilities. In this regard, a company's strategic human resource management function plays the major role in ensuring the development, deployment, and repatriation of global human resources.[87] While Chapter 14 will discuss strategic human resource management and career management programs in greater detail, it is clear that a company's competitive strength in a global marketplace is tied directly to its strategic human resource initiatives and how well it develops and deploys its global workforce.

Many of the basic functions of human resource management are linked with global talent management. First, the recruitment, selection, and hiring of individuals for present and future international assignments are critical initial steps to ensure that a pipeline of talent exists for international assignments. In addition, in line with the goal of broadening diversity and inclusion within multinational corporations, there is a need for organizational attention to greater employee diversity in expatriation in terms of gender, race, disability status, sexual orientation, and age.[88] Second, a multinational company needs to invest in training, education, development, and career planning activities to properly prepare individuals for international business careers. Third, as discussed earlier in this chapter, mentoring of employees engaged in foreign assignments, by both home and host country personnel, can help ensure that expatriates and flexpatriates are given the support, guidance, and helpful performance feedback they need while deployed in a foreign country. Fourth, the performance appraisal system should be designed to evaluate the most critical effectiveness factors related to the foreign assignment and also provide timely feedback so that corrective actions can be taken if necessary. In addition, performance evaluations should take into account the fact that employees in different cultures view job performance and career success in different ways.[89] Fifth, compensation and benefits systems should reflect the differences in reward approaches that exist between and among different countries or regions of the world. For example, in comparison with the United States, the governments of certain countries offer employees a much wider array of time-off and other benefits. These differences could require adjustments in reward programs to create parity for employees assigned to different countries. Also, fluctuations in currency values could force multinational companies to make adjustments in compensation amounts to keep an employee on a foreign assignment from "losing ground" depending on the movement in comparative values of host versus home country currencies. Finally, as was discussed previously, attention should be given to the repatriation process to make sure that those returning from foreign deployments are treated fairly and are given career opportunities commensurate with their enhanced inter-cultural competency.

Summary

Globalization of commerce over the past several decades has led to a significant increase in the number of people engaged in international careers as well as an expansion of individual interest in pursuing an international career. Because most types of international careers involve travel or relocation to foreign countries, there is a great risk of professional and personal dissatisfaction if the international career is not managed properly. For organizations, competitive advantage on a global scale depends on properly coordinating the international assignments of their employees as well as leveraging the skills and insights gained through international experience to achieve greater success. If international assignments are not managed properly, organizations risk the loss of talented resources with embedded knowledge and cross-cultural competencies.

This chapter explored several topics relevant to international careers. We defined an international career as one in which the individual employee performs work that unfolds over and across the boundaries of countries and geographic regions, and that takes place over an extended period of time. A number of positive outcomes can result from an international career, including an improved understanding of global business practices, an enhanced level of professional development and advancement potential, a higher level of objective and subjective career success, and personal growth and development through exposure to peoples and cultures throughout the world.

Research has identified several categories of international careers. A corporate expatriation is an overseas assignment that is initiated by the employing organization, while the self-initiated form is undertaken and financed by an individual. A virtual expatriate is an employee of a parent company who uses technology to manage and coordinate the work of employees who work at foreign operations. When an expatriate chooses to establish a permanent legal residence in a host country, he or she then becomes an immigrant worker. Flexpatriation is a type of an international career where the individual travels to and lives in multiple host countries on a regular basis. Short-term international work assignments involve an individual periodically traveling to and working in one or more foreign countries, but the individual primarily works from the parent company's domestic base. A final category of international careers occurs when an individual in a home or base country is employed by an organization that is headquartered in another country.

The majority of the research on international careers has focused on the implications of corporate-initiated expatriation, especially the factors associated with the success of the assignment for the individual employee and for the parent company. For the individual, an expatriation assignment can be looked at as a series of stages, starting with the preparation stage, moving to the period of adaptation, and concluding with the contribution (or performance) phase. Each stage carries with it a set of challenges for the employee. For an organization, the management of expatriate assignments is an important task. To ensure successful assignments, several organizational actions are necessary, including employee selection, pre-deployment training and preparation, mentoring of the expatriate, performance monitoring, appraisal and feedback, and career management assistance.

Repatriation is the process by which an expatriate returns from the foreign assignment to the parent company and the home country. Several factors can influence the success of the repatriation initiative, including the appropriateness of the plans and preparations for the employee's return home, the potential for "reverse" culture shock, the placement of the employee in an appropriate work position, the ability to craft a longer-term career development plan, and the level of difficulty the employee's family experiences in becoming reestablished in the home country. Because voluntary turnover rates for returning expatriates can be significant and costly, organizations need to pay special attention to mechanisms that increase the retention rate of expatriates once they return from the foreign assignment.

Growth in international business means that many employees must be prepared to consider whether they want to accept an international assignment. Therefore, individuals need to systematically evaluate international opportunities and make career decisions regarding whether the opportunity represents a correct fit with career goals and objectives. In this regard, decisions on an international career should be made using the steps in the career management model. Several questions can be asked in evaluating an international opportunity —whether the international assignment is consistent with interests, values, abilities, and lifestyle preferences, whether the host country is a good fit with personal aspirations, whether an international component aligns with career goals, what career strategies work best in an international career, how an international career affects family and personal life, and whether an international assignment can help the career over the long run.

A company's strategic human resource management function ensures that the development and deployment of global human resources are managed effectively. Nearly all of the functions of human resource management are linked with global talent management, including recruitment and selection, training and development, career planning, performance appraisal and feedback, compensation and benefits, and the expatriation and repatriation processes. Ultimately, a company's strength in the global marketplace is directly linked to the effectiveness of these activities.

Career Management *for Life*: Work–Life Implications from Chapter 13

- International assignments can pose challenges to employees' family and personal life.
- Therefore, in consultation with their family, employees must consider the positive and negative impact of an international assignment on their family and personal life in deciding whether to seek or accept an assignment.
- Prior to expatriation, a determination is needed as to whether the family will accompany the expatriate to the host country or remain in the home country. Each option has advantages and challenges.
- If the family accompanies the expatriate, a variety of preparations are necessary, ranging from cultural training to living arrangements and the coverage of household expenses to educational options if children are involved in the relocation.

- If the family remains in the home country, accommodations need to be established for regular contact between the expatriate and the family.
- In either case, a family's adjustment is critical to the success of the employee and the international assignment.
- Successful repatriation involves assuring that the expatriate's family navigates the move back to the home country satisfactorily. Plans for living arrangements, children's education and care, and job and career opportunities for the expatriate's partner all need to be made as part of the repatriation process.

Assignment

Interview someone who has spent time in an international career. It could be someone who has been on an expatriation assignment or someone who has regularly traveled to foreign countries on business trips. Ask this person what career-related issues or concerns he or she confronted in deciding to embark on an international career. Find out what are (or were) the most positive aspects of being in an international career. Similarly, did the person have any negative or unfavorable experiences? Finally, ask the person about the level of support that was provided by his or her parent company. What kind of organizational support was offered? And did the person see this support as being effective before, during, and after the international experience(s)? Why or why not?

Discussion Questions

1. Why do you think that it is a near certainty that younger workers in today's globalized economy will experience an international job assignment during their careers? From your *personal* perspective, what do you see as the positives and negatives of an "internationalized" career?
2. Why do you think that international assignments can have a negative or disruptive influence on a person's career? Do you think that it is possible that an international career could lead to simultaneous feelings of objective career success but subjective dissatisfaction? Why or why not? When a person is in an international career, do you think that there are inevitable trade-offs that occur between the person's professional life and his or her personal/family life?
3. Why is cultural awareness such an important competency in the contemporary globalized business environment? In what ways could an individual increase his or her cultural awareness prior to an international assignment? How can cultural awareness and adaptation be achieved once a person is deployed in a foreign assignment?
4. Do you think employers should make a guarantee to an expatriate that he or she will be placed in a higher-level position upon a return to the parent company at the conclusion of a successful expatriation assignment? What do you see as the positives of this type of guarantee for the employer? What would be the possible negatives?

Chapter 13 Case: Jessa the Headhunted Consultant

Jessa was deep in thought as she sipped her iced tea. She has so little time and has such a difficult decision to make! About a month ago, a high-profile international recruiting firm (a headhunter) contacted Jessa. The recruiting firm's client, a world-renowned U.S.-based hospital system, was preparing to open a state-of-the-art medical center in Doha, Qatar. When completed, the new facility was expected to be the most "technologically advanced" hospital in the world. As a health care consultant with international experience, Jessa was being targeted by the recruiting firm. They wanted her to interview for the position of director of information technology for the medical center. While flattered at being considered, Jessa was reluctant, at least at first, to seriously consider the offer to interview. After all, she was young and still establishing herself as a consultant. But Jessa was intrigued by the idea of living and working in a foreign country and this sounded like a tremendous career opportunity.

With some trepidation, Jessa decided to interview for the position. She flew to Doha and over a two-day span met with most of the senior executives of the medical center and also had a complete tour of the nearly completed facility. Jessa thought the interviews went well, but she did detect some hesitation from a couple of the senior officers over how young she was. When she returned home, Jessa was surprised at how quickly an offer was made. The headhunter called within a couple of hours of her plane landing. The medical center wanted her, and they were willing to make her a lucrative offer. The offer came the next day, and it was indeed lucrative. Now Jessa has just two more days to decide whether to accept the position and become a self-initiated expatriate in the far away land of Qatar.

Jessa's Background and Initial Job Search

Jessa has always been an overachiever. She graduated at the top of her high school class and completed her undergraduate studies as quickly as she could. In fact, by taking coursework during the summers, she was able to get her bachelor's degree in management by the age of 20. During her college years she always saw herself as more driven, focused, and mature than her classmates. It wasn't that she did not have fun in college, but she knew that she wanted to make a name for herself, and college was just a stepping stone to get to bigger things.

In her last year of college Jessa began taking on-campus interviews. She really thought that a job in consulting would be a perfect fit for her based on her personality, interests, abilities, and desire to travel. Unfortunately, her university did not have any consulting firms recruiting on campus. On a whim, she accompanied a friend to a job fair at another university. To her surprise, there were several consulting firms at the job fair and Jessa met with representatives from most of them. Jessa secured an interview with the one firm in which she was most interested. The company flew her to their headquarters for a full day of interviews. Afterward, she thought she had secured the position, but was bitterly disappointed when she received a rejection letter. Undeterred, Jessa continued to pursue job leads in the consulting industry. Through a friend of her father, Jessa landed a meeting with the CEO of a mid-sized consulting company. After some intensive interviews, she was offered the job of an associate consultant. The compensation was highly competitive, but the benefits were only so-so. She would be traveling nearly 100 percent of the time, mostly domestically within the United States, but with some international assignments as well. Jessa accepted the offer and her career was well on its way.

Jessa's Early Career

Jessa's first two years with the consulting company were a whirlwind of travel, meetings, consulting interviews, report deadlines, and crafting management recommendations. In her initial assignments, Jessa's role was mainly that of a supporting analyst. But after about a year she began taking on the role of lead consultant. Jessa clearly was thriving as a consultant and the company was putting its faith in her. Her assignments typically involved spending anywhere from three weeks to three months with a client getting to know its business, industry, and competitive advantages and weaknesses. Her company specialized in information technology (IT) solutions to business problems and opportunities, and Jessa's background in and comfort with IT, helped her gain the trust of the clients. In fact, a couple of her clients actually made offers of full-time employment to her, but Jessa wished to remain a consultant and continue to gain more multi-industry experience. She did not mind the travel and living out of her suitcase too much. The biggest plus was that she could survive on her expense account and meal allowance and "bank" her paycheck. Besides, with the long hours of a consultant, it really did not matter what city she was in. Her "residence-du-jour" was her hotel room and she became an expert at ordering room service. Hotel food wasn't that bad if matched with a nice glass of wine.

After four years as a consultant Jessa started doing some career reappraisal. She was doing well as a consultant and wanted to stay the course, but she also realized that she needed to invest in her skill sets if she wanted to continue to progress. Jessa began investigating top-ten business schools in the U.S. to see if she could find an MBA program that would fit with her travel and work schedule and would have the right elements to advance her career. She also began talking to her company about tuition reimbursement, knowing full well that an MBA from a top school would cost well into the six-figures. To her surprise, her company told Jessa that it was not willing to support her MBA efforts financially. However, they were willing to give her scheduling flexibility to attend in-person and residency classes, but only if it all could be worked out with limited disruptions to her work commitments. Jessa was disappointed at the lack of financial support, but she went ahead with the graduate degree anyway. She was accepted and enrolled in an elite business school, working on an MBA in cross-cultural management. The MBA program had a substantial online component, with the in-person classes mainly concentrated on weekends. While the pursuit of the MBA caused her stress levels to skyrocket, Jessa loved the coursework and the give-and-take with her professors and her classmates. Fortunately, she had banked enough of her salary over the years that she was able to pay for the degree out of her own pocket.

Six years into her career, Jessa had extensive consulting experience and an MBA from a top-tier program. Through her work and her graduate program, she had been to 11 different countries. About six months earlier, her company had made a strategic decision to specialize in health care consulting, given the growth in that industry and regulatory changes that required creative IT solutions. Jessa was in agreement with the company's move and she quickly ramped up her knowledge of the health care industry. Eight years into her career, she was the top consultant for her company when it came to health care clients, and her name was becoming well-known in the industry.

Jessa's Family and Personal Life

Jessa's nearly all-consuming focus on her career and her graduate coursework left little time for leisure or for socializing. One of the known occupational hazards of consulting is the lack of time for anything other than the job itself and the traveling. Living on the road, and often on consulting assignments by herself, meant that she spent a considerable amount of time alone. She dared not socialize with employees of clients, thinking that could jeopardize her work and her objectivity. Jessa was close with her family. She communicated regularly with her parents and her siblings while on the road, using Skype, email, and texting to stay in touch. Jessa owned a condo that served as her home base when she did get off the road. Fortunately, her house was close to where her parents lived and she visited them as often as she could.

Jessa recognized that she needed to socialize more, but she just did not have the time. She had career goals that needed to be accomplished. She rationalized that her career could come first now, and then later she could think about marriage and starting a family. But she vowed to herself to leave more time for leisure and to try to establish closer personal relationships. When she did fantasize about the future she often thought about going back to school to get a Ph.D. and become a college professor. Her father was a professor and Jessa saw that it gave him great flexibility to have a nice balance between work and family commitments. She was sure she could handle the academic side of the doctorate, but the thought of devoting five or more years of schooling to get the Ph.D. gave her pause. But in the back of her mind it was something to contemplate.

The Doha Offer and the Dilemma

Jessa continued to nurse her iced tea. She was waiting for her former professor to arrive at the restaurant. She had contacted him to get his advice on her impending career choices. She had always trusted her professor's guidance and she really hoped that he could give her insight. Her professor had been the one who encouraged her to pursue consulting as a career. When he arrived, Jessa quickly described the offer and how conflicted she was over it. The details were pretty straightforward and had been laid out in a formal offer sheet. She would have a substantial salary that would be adjusted based on the movement in the exchange rate between the U.S. dollar and the Qatari riyal. In addition, she would have allowances for living expenses, clothing, and food. She would also be allotted three expense-paid trips back to the U.S. annually. Jessa liked the idea that everything was in writing; it gave her confidence that the offer and the commitment to her were solid. Jessa also reasoned that if the expatriation move to Qatar did not work out, she could always repatriate back to the U.S. Of course, a premature exit from the position at the medical center might not be a wise move from a career perspective.

Jessa then described the dilemma to her professor. First, her family members, especially her father, were dead set against the move. There were multiple reasons why her family was pressuring her to reject the offer. She would be much further away from home; she would be traveling to a country with a typically patriarchal culture and with societal restrictions on the dress and behaviors of women; and although Qatar is relatively safe and open, it sits in the Middle East with the attendant geopolitical uncertainty and terrorism threats. Second, Jessa was herself not certain that leaving consulting would be the best career move. She was obviously successful as a consultant, with a proven track record and a loyal set of clients. Although there were no promises from the consulting company, Jessa thought she might be able to become a partner sometime in the next five to ten years. If she took the job in Doha, the consulting career and future promotions would be curtailed. Third, Jessa was concerned that a move to the Middle East might further hamper her ability to establish a more meaningful social life. She knew that Qatar had a vast expatriate population, but it was transitory with most expatriates spending only two or three years in the country. Finally, in the back of Jessa's mind was the possibility of pursuing a Ph.D. and becoming a college professor. A self-initiated expatriation move to a Middle Eastern country would delay that possibility or even remove it from consideration.

After hearing Jessa's story, her professor knew they had quite a bit to discuss. He suggested they order dinner and then talk this through.

Case Questions

1. Based on the definition and description of expatriation in this chapter, do you think Jessa has the background and the personal make-up to be successful as a self-initiated expatriate? Why or why not?
2. Do you think Jessa is too "career focused?" Why or why not? Should she be more attuned to achieving greater balance in her life by increasing her involvement in nonwork interests and activities?
3. What family and personal life factors are influencing Jessa's career decision-making? How big a role should her parents' opinions play in her career decisions? At her age and level of experience, should they play a role at all?
4. If Jessa were to accept the position with the medical center in Doha, what potential cultural challenges, issues, or risks do you think she would encounter? Do you think these factors should give Jessa pause or hesitation in considering the offer? Why or why not?
5. If Jessa sought your help, what advice would you give her in terms of the management of her career? If you had to make a prediction, do you think that Jessa will accept the Doha offer? Why or why not?

Notes

1 World Trade Statistical Review 2016. (2016). Available from the World Trade Organization: www.wto.org/statistics.
2 Baruch, Y., Dickmann, M., Altman, Y. & Bournois, F. (2013). Exploring international work: Types and dimensions of global careers. *International Journal of Human Resource Management*, *24*, 2369–2393; Baruch, Y., Altman, Y. & Adler, N. J. (2009). Guest editors' note: Introduction to the special issue. *Human Resource Management*, *48*, 1–4.
3 Shaffer, M. A., Kraimer, M. L., Chen, Y. & Bolino, M. C. (2012). Choices, challenges, and career consequences of global work experiences: A review and future agenda. *Journal of Management*, *38*, 1282–1327; Tams, S. & Arthur, M. (2007). Studying careers across cultures: Distinguishing international, cross-cultural, and globalization perspectives. *Career Development International*, *12*, 86–98; Tharenou, P. (2006). International careers. In Greenhaus, J. H. & Callanan, G. A. (Eds.), *Encyclopedia of career development* (pp. 398–404). Thousand Oaks, CA: Sage.
4 For an extensive review of the different types of international careers and assignments, see Baruch et al. (2013); Shaffer et al. (2012); Tharenou (2006).
5 Selmer, J. (2006). Expatriate experience. In Greenhaus, J. H. & Callanan, G. A. (Eds.), *Encyclopedia of career development* (pp. 306–307). Thousand Oaks, CA: Sage.
6 Baruch et al. (2013); Shaffer et al. (2012).
7 Ibid.
8 Ibid.
9 Baruch, Y., Altman, Y. & Tung, R. S. (2016). Career mobility in a global era: Advances in managing expatriation and repatriation. *Academy of Management Annals*, *10*, 841–889.
10 Baruch et al. (2013).
11 Baugh, S. G., Sullivan, S. E. & Carraher, S. M. (2013). Global careers in the United States. In Reis, C. & Baruch, Y. (Eds.), *Careers without borders* (pp. 297–322). New York: Routledge.
12 Holtbrügge, D. & Schillo, K. (2008). Intercultural training requirements for virtual assignments: Results of an explorative empirical study. *Human Resource Development International*, *11*, 271–286.
13 Mayerhofer, H., Hartmann, L. C., Michelitsch-Riedl, G. & Kollinger, I. (2004). Flexpatriate assignments: A neglected issue in global staffing. *International Journal of Human Resource Management*, *15*, 1371–1389.
14 Tharenou (2006).
15 Tams & Arthur (2007).
16 Baruch et al. (2016).
17 Greenhaus, J. H. & Callanan, G. A. (2012). Career dynamics. In Wiener, I., Schmitt, N. W. & Highhouse, S. (Eds.), *Comprehensive handbook of psychology, volume 12: Industrial and organizational psychology*, 2nd ed. (pp. 593–614). Hoboken, NJ: Wiley.
18 Ramaswami, A., Carter, N. M. & Dreher, G. F. (2016). Expatriation and career success: A human capital perspective. *Human Relations*, *69*, 1959–1987.
19 Baruch et al. (2016).
20 Ibid.
21 Cerdin, J. L. & Le Pargneux, M. (2009). Career and international assignment fit: Toward an integrative model of success. *Human Resource Management*, *48*, 5–25.
22 Baruch et al. (2013).
23 Ibid.
24 Richardson, J. (2006). Self-directed expatriation: Family matters. *Personnel Review*, *35*, 469–486.
25 Firth, B. M., Chen, G., Kirkman, B. L. & Kim, K. (2014). Newcomers abroad: Expatriate adaptation during early phases of international assignments. *Academy of Management Journal*, *57*, 280–300; Takeuchi, R. (2010). A critical review of expatriate adjustment research through a multiple stakeholder view: Progress, emerging trends, and prospects. *Journal of Management*, *36*, 1040–1064.
26 Takeuchi (2010).
27 Firth et al. (2014); Chen, G., Kirkman, B. L., Kim, K., Farh, C. I. C. & Tangirala, S. (2010). When does cross-cultural motivation enhance expatriate effectiveness? A multilevel investigation of the moderating roles of subsidiary support and cultural distance. *Academy of Management Journal*, *53*, 1110–1130.
28 Firth et al. (2014).
29 Ibid.

30 Chen et al. (2010); Shaffer, M. A., Harrison, D. A., Gregersen, H., Black, J. S. & Ferzandi, L. A. (2006). You can take it with you: Individual differences and expatriate effectiveness. *Journal of Applied Psychology, 91*, 109–125; Stahl, G. K. & Caligiuri, P. (2005). An examination of crossover and spillover effects of spousal and expatriate cross-cultural adjustment on expatriate outcomes. *Journal of Applied Psychology, 90*, 603–615.
31 Lazarova, M. B., Westman, M. & Shaffer, M. A. (2010). Elucidating the positive side of the work–family interface on international assignments: A model of expatriate work and family performance. *Academy of Management Review, 35*, 93–117.
32 Greenhaus, J. H. & Kossek, E. E. (2014). The contemporary career: A work–home perspective. *Annual Review of Organizational Psychology and Organizational Behavior, 1*, 361–388; Richardson (2006).
33 Lazarova et al. (2010); Takeuchi (2010).
34 Farh, C. I. C., Bartol, K. M., Shapiro, D. L. & Shin, J. (2010). Networking abroad: A process model of how expatriates support ties to facilitate adjustment. *Academy of Management Review, 35*, 434–454.
35 Ibid.
36 Shen, Y. & Kram, K. E. (2011). Expatriates' developmental networks: Network diversity, base, and support functions. *Career Development International, 16*, 528–552.
37 Ramaswami et al. (2016); Biemann, T. & Braakmann, N. (2013). The impact of international experience on objective and subjective career success in early careers. *International Journal of Human Resource Management, 24*, 3438–3456.
38 Firth et al. (2014).
39 Baruch et al. (2016).
40 Collings, D. G., Doherty, N., Luethy, M. & Osborn, D. (2011). Understanding and supporting the career implications of international assignments. *Journal of Vocational Behavior, 78*, 361–371.
41 Baruch et al. (2016); Collings et al. (2011).
42 Conger, J. A. (2014). Addressing the organizational barriers to developing global leadership talent. *Organizational Dynamics, 43*, 198–204.
43 Ibid.
44 Collings et al. (2011).
45 Ibid.
46 Conger (2014).
47 Shen & Kram (2011).
48 Pattie, M. W., Benson, G., Casper, W. & McMahan, G. C. (2013). Goal congruence: Fitting international assignment into employee careers. *International Journal of Human Resource Management, 24*, 2554–2570.
49 Benson, G. S. & Pattie, M. (2009). The comparative roles of home and host supervisors in the expatriate experience. *Human Resource Management, 48*, 49–68.
50 Pattie, M., White, M. M. & Tansky, J. (2010). The homecoming: A review of support practices for repatriates. *Career Development International, 15*, 359–377.
51 Collings et al. (2011).
52 Ren, H., Bolino, M. C., Shaffer, M. A. & Kraimer, M. L. (2013). The influence of job demands and resources on repatriate career satisfaction: A relative deprivation perspective. *Journal of World Business, 48*, 149–159; Oddou, G., Szkudlarek, B., Osland, J. S., Deller, J., Blakeney, R. & Furuya, N. (2013). Repatriates as a source of competitive advantage: How to manage knowledge transfer. *Organizational Dynamics, 42*, 257–266; Kraimer, M. L., Shaffer, M. A., Harrison, D. A. & Ren, H. (2012). No place like home: An identity strain perspective on repatriate turnover. *Academy of Management Journal, 55*, 399–420; Tharenou, P. & Caulfield, N. (2010). Will I stay or will I go? Explaining repatriation by self-initiated expatriates. *Academy of Management Journal, 53*, 1009–1028; Kraimer, M. L., Shaffer, M. A. & Bolino, M. C. (2009). The influence of expatriate and repatriate experiences on career advancement and repatriate retention. *Human Resource Management, 48*, 27–47; Stahl, G. K., Chua, C. H., Caligiuri, P., Cerdin, J. L. & Taniguchi, M. (2009). Predictors of turnover intentions in learning-driven and demand-driven international assignments: The role of repatriation concerns, satisfaction with company support, and perceived career advancement opportunities. *Human Resource Management, 48*, 89–110.
53 Stahl et al. (2009).
54 Pattie et al. (2010).
55 Kraimer et al. (2012).

56 Osman-Gani, A. & Hyder, A. S. (2008). Repatriation readjustment of international managers: An empirical analysis of HRD interventions. *Career Development International*, *13*, 456–475; Shen, Y. & Hall, D. T. (2009). When expatriates explore other options: Retaining talent through greater job embeddedness and repatriation adjustment. *Human Resource Management*, *48*, 793–816; Hyder, A. S. & Lövblad, M. (2007). The repatriation process—a realistic approach. *Career Development International*, *12*, 264–281.
57 Greenhaus & Callanan (2012).
58 Ren et al. (2013).
59 Oddou et al. (2013).
60 Pattie et al. (2010); MacDonald, S. & Arthur, N. (2005). Connecting career management to repatriation adjustment. *Career Development International*, *10*, 145–159.
61 Wittig-Berman, U. & Beutell, N. J. (2009). International assignments and the career management of repatriates: The boundaryless career concept. *International Journal of Management*, *26*, 77–88.
62 Collings et al. (2011).
63 Osman-Gani & Hyder (2008).
64 Herman, J. L. & Tetrick, L. E. (2009). Problem-focused versus emotion-focused coping strategies and repatriation adjustment. *Human Resource Management*, *48*, 69–88.
65 Kraimer et al. (2012).
66 Pattie et al. (2010).
67 Kraimer et al. (2012).
68 Ibid.
69 Kraimer et al. (2009).
70 Baruch et al. (2016).
71 Kraimer et al. (2012).
72 Pattie et al. (2010).
73 Lazarova, M., Cerdin, J. & Liao, Y. (2014). The internationalism career anchor: A validation study. *International Studies of Management and Organizations*, *44*, 9–33.
74 Baruch et al. (2013).
75 McPhail, R., McNulty, Y. & Hutchings, K. (2016). Lesbian and gay expatriation: Opportunities, barriers and challenges for global mobility. *International Journal of Human Resource Management*, *27*, 382–406; Paisley, V. & Tayar, M. (2016). Lesbian, gay, bisexual and transgender (LGBT) expatriates: An intersectionality perspective. *International Journal of Human Resource Management*, *27*, 766–780.
76 Altman, Y. & Baruch, Y. (2012). Global self-initiated corporate expatriate careers: A new era in international assignments. *Personnel Review*, *41*, 233–255; Tharenou & Caulfield (2010).
77 Shen & Kram (2011); Farh et al. (2010).
78 Greenhaus & Kossek (2014).
79 Mäkelä, L., Kinnunen, U. & Suutari, V. (2015). Work-to-life conflict and enrichment among international business travelers: The role of international career orientation. *Human Resource Management*, *54*, 517–531.
80 Westman, M., Etzion, D. & Gattenio, E. (2008). International business travels and the work–family interface: A longitudinal study. *Journal of Occupational and Organizational Psychology*, *81*, 459–480; Westman, M., Etzion, D. & Chen, S. (2008). Crossover of positive experiences from business travelers to their spouses. *Journal of Managerial Psychology*, *24*, 269–284.
81 Shaffer et al. (2012); Biemann & Braakmann (2013).
82 Dickmann, M. & Doherty, N. (2010). Exploring the career capital impact of international assignments within distinct organizational contexts. *British Journal of Management*, *19*, 145–161; Haslberger, A. & Brewster, C. (2009). Capital gains: Expatriate adjustment and the psychological contract in international careers. *Human Resource Management*, *48*, 379–397; Suutari, V. & Makela, K. (2007). The career capital of managers with global careers. *Journal of Managerial Psychology*, *22*, 628–648.
83 Tams, S. & Arthur, M. B. (2006). Boundaryless career. In Greenhaus, J. H. & Callanan, G. A. (Eds.), *Encyclopedia of career development* (pp. 44–49). Thousand Oaks, CA: Sage; Arthur, M. B., Khapova, S. N. & Wilderom, C. P. M. (2005). Career success in a boundaryless career world. *Journal of Organizational Behavior*, *26*, 177–202.
84 Ramaswami et al. (2016); Shaffer et al. (2012); Suutari & Makela (2007).
85 Biemann & Braakmann (2013); Collings et al. (2011).

86 Lazarova, M. & Cerdin, J. (2007). Revisiting repatriation concerns: Organizational support versus career and contextual influence. *Journal of International Business Studies*, *38*, 404–429.
87 Takeuchi (2010).
88 McNulty, Y. & Hutchings, K. (2016). Looking for global talent in all the right places: A critical literature review of non-traditional expatriates. *International Journal of Human Resource Management*, *27*, 699–728.
89 Mayrhofer, W., Briscoe, J. P., Hall, D. T., Dickmann, M., Dries, N., Dysvik, A., Kaše, R., Parry, E. & Unite, J. (2016). Career success across the globe: Insights from the 5C project. *Organizational Dynamics*, *45*, 197–205.

Part IV

Career Management in Work Organizations

14 The Role of Strategic Human Resource Management Systems in Career Management

With the highly competitive business environments that exist all over the world, organizations need to be flexible and innovative to ensure their success and survival. In this context, businesses that employ, develop, and retain the most talented and committed workforce will, undoubtedly, be more successful than ones that do not. While the early focus of human resource management (HRM) was concentrated primarily on functional activities such as recruiting, training, and compensation and benefits, today the role of HRM within an organization is much more strategic in nature. Indeed, the plans and initiatives involving workforce deployment and development are tied directly to the organization's strategic plans as a means to gain competitive advantage.[1] As would be expected, the fit and consistency between a firm's HRM strategies and its business strategies is associated with that firm's overall success.[2] More precisely, several worldwide studies have found that when organizations align their HRM systems with their corporate strategies, the results are increased levels of productivity, organizational commitment, job satisfaction, and organizational citizenship behavior among their employees and, not surprisingly, the achievement of improved organizational financial performance.[3]

As this discussion indicates, HRM systems, such as workforce planning and staffing procedures, performance management and reward systems, and training and development efforts, need to be consistent with the strategic plans of the organization. For example, a company with strong growth objectives requires a steady supply of qualified, motivated, and talented human resources to support the business expansion, and its human resource and career management systems should reflect this corporate strategy. In the case of a firm whose strategic direction includes downsizing and the divestiture of businesses, the HRM system and related career programs may be more concerned with outplacement or retraining, helping employees identify their interests and career goals, and assisting them with the process of finding a new job.

In this chapter, we discuss a model of an integrated strategic HRM system that depicts how career management and individual development are embedded in this system to improve overall organizational effectiveness. We describe the key functional human resource areas and how career management is rooted in these activities; we provide examples of corporate programs that position their human resource systems to supplement individual development; and we discuss how a firm's HRM systems can support its strategic plans.

Integration of Career Management within Strategic HRM Systems

HRM systems represent an organization's mechanisms for forecasting its human resource needs and for recruiting, selecting, training, developing, appraising, promoting, and rewarding its employees. Career management and human resource systems are linked or integrated to the extent to which they help each other meet individual and organizational needs. To be most effective, career management programs need to be consistent with all human resource functions and be incorporated into the overall corporate human resource strategies of the company.[4]

Ralph Christensen, a former vice-president of human resources at Hallmark Cards, developed a comprehensive and strategic HRM system that weaves various activities of career management throughout five basic components of employee talent management. These five fundamental components are: workforce planning and staffing, learning and development, performance management, employee relations, and organization development.[5] Christensen notes that diversity is an important function that cuts across all others, and hence is viewed as a building block of the five principal functions, along with the various strategic and tactical actions that are necessary components of the work of the human resource professional.

These fundamental HRM components dovetail with the broader strategies undertaken by an organization. The strategic view of human resources includes the notion that talent is the engine that creates organizational value. Given that perspective, human resources need to be directly connected to the business strategy so that customer needs can be met.[6] Therefore, the firm's human resources need to be linked to the firm's core competencies, its vision, mission, values, strategies, and goals. Similarly, the firm's vision and strategies are informed by the business environment (e.g., customers, industry competitors, governmental regulations, and local and global economies) within which it operates. The relationship among these components is influenced by factors both within and outside the firm, and the HR professional needs to understand and act within this framework to supply appropriate personnel who can help optimize organizational performance. It is important that a company's human resource plans not be developed in a vacuum to ensure that during the development of human resource strategies there is an emphasis on the needs of the customer and other stakeholders. Thus, customer needs should be a determining factor in whom the firm employs and how these human resources are developed. As Christensen states, "Everything that the HR organization does should be focused on leveraging those human competencies to create capabilities that allow the organization to win with its strategy in the marketplace."[7] In this sense, Christensen's model focuses on leveraging the firm's human talent for competitive advantage.

Strategic Human Resource Processes

In the following sections, we consider four of the main functions of Christensen's model of strategic human resource management that are directly associated with individual and organizational career management: workforce planning and staffing, learning and development, performance management, and employee relations. Next, we discuss each of these four strategic HR functions as well as the related activities that are associated with human resource development and career management, and we provide examples of corporate human resource systems that support individual career development.

1. *Workforce Planning and Staffing*

This activity focuses on fulfilling the staffing needs of the organization and projecting future requirements. Both current and future assessments are based on the strategic needs of the firm. Workforce planning and staffing also includes processes whereby the firm attracts, integrates, and retains talent. We will discuss several processes important to workforce planning and staffing, specifically forecasting future workplace demands, staffing and transition plans, recruiting, and college relations and anticipatory socialization programs.

Forecasting Future Workplace Demands

Once a firm has determined its strategic direction, it must assess the level and type of human resources needed to fulfill corporate goals. As Dianna Peterson and Tina Krieger suggest, forecasting future workplace needs is a bit like a gap analysis. "Estimates of the organization's future demand for talent are compared to the projected internal supply of talent to identify surpluses and shortages."[8] Because the talent of the workforce is a driving factor in value creation, the identification and hiring of the right person for the right job is the essence of strategic human resource management.

A number of factors are relevant to human resource forecasting, including an external environmental forecast (industry trends, demographics, and external workforce supply), an internal capabilities analysis (are the necessary skill sets available with the company?), and finally a future workforce forecast. The workforce *forecast* includes an analysis of the number and types of jobs available, the skills required, and a gap analysis that indicates how the firm would move from the current workforce to a future workforce.[9] Once the supply of workers is identified, the level of required training and development is specified.

In determining the types of resources needed, organizations have a basic choice of selecting (or "buying") their personnel from the external labor market or developing (or "making") their personnel from the internal labor market. The "buy or make" decision is one that virtually all organizations face. The organizational decision as to whether selection or development is the appropriate strategy depends on the availability of people with the right skills in the external labor market compared to the feasibility of developing current employees.[10] It must be stressed that depending exclusively on either the external or the internal labor pool can create problems. Hiring solely from external labor markets reduces advancement opportunities for existing employees and thus weakens their commitment to the organization, whereas staffing exclusively from within may limit the number of fresh ideas brought into the organization and restrict an organization's ability to move rapidly in a different strategic direction.[11] While some experts have suggested a specific ratio (for example, four to one) of internal to external hiring, Peter Cappelli has provided a number of questions that organizations must answer (e.g., For how long will the organization need the talent? How essential is it for the organization to maintain its existing culture?) to determine the appropriate mix of buying and making talent.[12]

Organizational Staffing

If a firm has determined that the internal system cannot fully supply the required talent, then selection from the external labor market is necessary. Staffing is a critical management function because the quality of the people hired by the organization is, in most cases, the single greatest determinant of the firm's effectiveness. In a broad sense, *staffing* allows a company to buy its needed competencies from outside the organization.[13]

In Chapter 7, we discussed organizational selection and staffing from the individual's perspective, covering such topics as interviewing, recruitment, and choice of job and organization. When organizations go through the staffing process many of the steps are the same, albeit from a different perspective. As a first step, the organization determines, through the human resource forecasting process, the number and types of employees it needs to hire.

The number of required employees is dictated by expected expansion and related resource needs, as well as actual and expected turnover (including retirement) among existing staff at all levels and in all functions within the company. The types of employees needed are related to the skill level, professional experience, and abilities required by the jobs to be filled. It is obvious that openings in entry-level positions would require a different set of skills and experiences than senior-level positions.

Once the number and type of resources are determined, or as open positions arise through turnover and internal transfer, the organization then has several options in terms of the actual hiring approach to be used. College recruiting, internal staffing/placement, postings on the company's or external websites, advertisements, executive search firms, and personal recommendations or nominations are various ways for job candidates to become known to a hiring company.

After a pool of candidates is identified, the next step in the staffing process normally is the interview. Usually, the interviewee will first meet with a representative of the firm's human resource department who will conduct a general screening. Normally, this first round of inquiry and interest is assessed via email, or telephone or videoconference interview. Telephone interviewing can be difficult as few visual clues are present. Candidates need to project confidence and enthusiasm verbally. Or when videoconferencing, candidates need to project a professional appearance just as if they are face-to-face, although they may be located in a dorm room or home office. Next, the candidate will be interviewed by one or more members of the hiring department. Once the interviewing phase is complete, the hiring area assesses all the candidates, rank orders them from most to least qualified, determines its recommendations to management, and then makes its offers. These basic steps would typically be followed regardless of the level of the position that is being filled.

David Ulrich and Dave Lake offer a number of key factors to consider in the external sourcing of job candidates.[14] A primary consideration is the degree of professional experience that is required. In particular, the organization must review the trade-off between hiring at the entry level, where candidates usually lack extensive experience but are more malleable in terms of new work ideas and approaches, versus hiring at a higher level, where candidates usually have more experience but could be less flexible or adaptive in reaction to new methods. Of course, less experienced candidates are often less expensive to hire, when compared to more experienced candidates. Ulrich and Lake suggest that companies expand the pool of talent that is considered. Companies should pay particular attention to achieving diversity in their hiring to meet the challenge of the global marketplace. Serious consideration of multiple candidates and the use of multiple interviews for each candidate will allow hiring managers to receive information from a variety of sources when evaluating job candidates.

In addition to the influence of the firm's strategic plan, environmental trends and general business conditions also affect staffing from the external market. Factors such as the make-up of the local labor market, population demographics, social trends, economic conditions, government regulations, and legislative actions may all influence the type and quality of potential employees who are available to the corporation. Corporate downsizings, the use of outsourcing, and the trend toward non-permanent work arrangements have all affected the availability of labor, in most cases creating a greater pool from which to attract and hire workers. Yet at the same time, these transitioned workers may not have the necessary skills for the new jobs made available by changing business trends and technological innovations. Hence, honest self-appraisal and "re-skilling" may be necessary for these workers to find their way back into more permanent employment.[15]

Transition Plans

One of the great tests of the human resource function, and the leadership of the firm, is to determine how employees should be transitioned into different jobs, or out of the company entirely, when corporate strategies require changes in the composition of the workforce. Factors such as a weak economy, the search for less expensive labor options, or an excess of human resources may necessitate the need for downsizing. Changes in technology or business strategy may also require different skills to be exhibited by the workforce.

Transitions may take the form of redeploying human resources.[16] *Redeployment* is an option that may be used for two basic reasons: to improve the skill levels and broaden the experiences of certain personnel and to respond strategically to changing business conditions. In the former case, the movement of employees is a planned developmental technique to gain more seasoned staff. For example, a company with extensive international interests may want its fast-track employees to take one or more tours of duty in overseas operations so that they gain a multinational perspective. In the latter case, redeployment is used as a strategic response to shifting business conditions resulting from internal or external factors. Also, the closing of a plant in one geographic location to take advantage of a better business climate (and lower expenses) in another geographic area is a strategic decision that may necessitate the redistribution (and relocation) of key staff.

When business conditions call for drastic action, organizations may need to eliminate individual positions or whole units to improve competitiveness. From the organization's view, displacing staff is normally a difficult decision, one that some companies try to avoid at all costs.

To help displaced employees with the transition and to find reemployment, many companies provide outplacement services or retraining to affected staff. The reputation of an organization is often on the line when conducting mass layoffs and downsizings; thus, it is in the best interest of the company to do all it can to help displaced employees cope with the job loss and to assist them in finding new employment. In this regard, all organizations must recognize the disruptions to human life and the threat to self-esteem that redeployment and displacements can cause. To state the obvious, unnecessary or poorly planned transitions are not only counterproductive, but can lead to alienated, unproductive workers and a loss of the company's positive reputation.

Recruiting

Chapter 7 discussed the tendency of many employers to present themselves in an overly favorable light during the recruitment process. It was noted that job candidates who develop unrealistic expectations are likely to experience "reality shock" upon entering the organization. This can contribute to employee dissatisfaction and turnover. Realistic recruitment, where candidates receive a balanced, accurate view of the prospective job and the organization, is designed to reduce levels of reality shock, dissatisfaction, and turnover.[17] Several companies, like the Vanguard Group and PricewaterhouseCoopers (doing business as PwC), have established realistic college recruitment efforts.[18] The following is a description of Vanguard's EXPLORE program, which uses the principles of anticipatory socialization (discussed in Chapter 8) to foster a culture of realistic recruitment with college students before they even apply to Vanguard:

> The Vanguard Group, one of the world's largest investment management companies, faces a challenge of maintaining a staff of employees who understand their jobs,

the company and its culture, and the fast paced market within which the company works. While the company understands that most external job candidates are entertaining multiple job offers, it expects the management team to accurately portray job opportunities within the organization.

Vanguard's key to recruiting success is to offer realistic recruitment techniques early in the college students' experience. The EXPLORE program invites freshmen and sophomores to the Vanguard campus and is considered an early talent identification strategy. Students are welcomed to participate in a day-long experiential learning session where the company shares different job opportunities and requirements for those jobs. Students get to see the culture live and in action and get to "try on the corporation." It is important to Vanguard that students feel connected to the mission of the corporation, and come away from the day with a sense of whether the company is the right one for them. Similarly, Vanguard gets a sense of those students who might be prospective interns. The EXPLORE program concludes with professional development and networking opportunities, as well as résumé writing and interview tips. Students can then progress to apply for internship opportunities, as well as Vanguard's leadership development programs which are available to college graduates.

Vanguard believes this process to be efficient and allows for the hiring of the best recruits, giving them a step ahead of the competition. In preparation for interviewing, candidates are offered a wealth of information about the company, its top executive team, the Vanguard culture, the supportive workplace, and how the company is focused on providing exceptional client support via its website.[19]

Case interviews and behavioral event interviews are two methods that attempt to create a realistic situation in which the candidate's responses can be evaluated. In a case interview, applicants are presented with a business issue facing a company and are required to analyze the situation and propose a solution to the problem. In a behavioral event interview, applicants are asked to think back to a particular challenge they faced in a prior job and describe how they handled the situation. The content, creativity, deductive reasoning, and common-sense nature of the responses can indicate to recruiters the candidate's ability to perform in a given work environment. Many companies, including Google, JP Morgan Chase, and Microsoft, have also become well-known for asking "wacky" questions during the interview process. These questions may be interspersed with questions based on work-related, situational scenarios that inquire about the recruit's behavior in a given situation. While questions might be specific to the position for which the person is being hired, others are intended to get a sense of the candidate's composure and reasoning skills. Here are a few examples from these companies:[20]

- How many people enter London every day for work?
- How many trees are there in Central Park?
- Why are manholes round?
- How much should you charge to wash all the windows in Seattle?
- How many golf balls can fit in a school bus?

Interview techniques such as these may appear at first to provide the interviewer with more information than the interviewee. However, these techniques, particularly behavioral event interviews, provide recruits with the opportunity to present their values and also give them the ability to learn more about the values and culture of the organization. The recruit can ask questions about the type of customers with whom the position would interface, how the company maintains customer satisfaction, and finally about the overlap between departments that serve a particular customer (e.g., customer service, sales, accounting, research and development). This information can help to clarify the relationships the company has with its clientele, how departments interact to serve the customer, and can provide the candidate with a framework to decide if this is the type of company for which he or she could work.

In addition, organizations can encourage employees to refer friends, family members, and acquaintances for upcoming job postings. Employee referrals can be a particularly successful way to realistically recruit new employees because the employees are often knowledgeable about the job, work group, and company, and individuals are likely to trust and understand what their friends and colleagues tell them about potential job opportunities. Employees who refer might be encouraged to do so through monetary benefits. Companies also benefit because employee referrals tend to yield motivated workers who fit well in the work environment, and are often retained longer. The company might gain access to someone who might not otherwise apply. The downside of using employee referrals is that these sources may limit diversity, if the referrals tend to reach few members of minority groups. Also, a referred employee may cause tension in the workplace if the new employee does not work out, or there could be a risk of alienating other staff if a referred hire is seen as getting preferential treatment.[21]

While there are a variety of techniques that may be used for offering candidates realistic recruitment, the overarching purpose is to give accurate information about the company and the posted job. Research suggests that realistic recruiting can aid in decreasing turnover and increasing job satisfaction and commitment.[22] The presentation of realistic information on jobs and careers to candidates and employees remains a positive approach to integrating individual and organizational needs.

College Relations and Anticipatory Socialization

Chapters 7 and 8 described the process by which individuals enter work organizations and become socialized into their new work roles. It was noted that anticipatory socialization begins even before the newcomer joins the organization on a full-time basis. During this stage, values and talents are clarified and expectations are formed. One of the major tasks of this stage is the development of accurate, realistic expectations about one's chosen career field, and, more generally, about the world of work. In addition, anticipatory socialization practices can help companies gain a positive recruiting image and ensure an available pool of talented newcomers. The most well-known of the anticipatory socialization programs, internships and cooperative educational experiences, allow companies to establish relationships with colleges and universities and provide prospective employees with the chance to test out the prospective employer.

A number of large companies, including Aetna Life Insurance Co., Allstate Insurance Co., Boeing Co., Boston Consulting Group, Kohl's, and Procter & Gamble have used internships to achieve more efficiency in the recruitment and staffing activities.[23] Internships, both paid and unpaid, allow college students and job-seekers the opportunity to gain relevant work experience and acquire real-life knowledge of particular occupations and work organizations.

Cooperative education programs (co-ops) are another vehicle that can be used to facilitate the transition from school to work. *Co-ops* differ from internships in that they are paid assignments, usually longer in length, and are normally a required part of the student's academic program. Many universities across the U.S. have well-established co-op programs, including Butler University, Creighton University, and Northeastern University.[24]

The following briefly describes the cooperative education program at Drexel University, one of the largest and most successful programs in the United States:

> At Drexel University, cooperative education provides an opportunity for the student to integrate classroom theory and practical work experience. Drexel has been operating the co-op program since 1919. Students work at their co-op jobs for a three to six-month period, alternating with six months of classroom study. Cooperative education at Drexel is a degree requirement for most majors, and students receive academic credit for these experiences. Co-ops are paid employment experiences.[25]
>
> Drexel graduates enter the workforce having had as many as three different positions within their field of study, which allows them to be familiar with job interviews, and have practical experience, often resulting in higher paying starting salaries. Students at Drexel work for more than 1,600 companies in 32 states and 51 countries. Each year, 91% or over 5,000 undergraduate students are enrolled in the cooperative education program. The professional staff of the Steinbright Career Development Center (SCDC) effectively assists students with placements into co-op work experiences each year. Employers of Drexel business school co-ops include Comcast Corporation, GlaxoSmithKline, Johnson & Johnson, KPMG, and SAP America.[26]

Like internships, cooperative education programs are designed to help students develop a greater sense of responsibility, maturity, and self-confidence, as well as a better understanding of other people, a more serious appreciation of their academic studies, and a more practical, realistic orientation to the world of work. The experience gained through cooperative work assignments can either reinforce students' original occupational choices or convince them to consider other fields of study. Many students return to a former cooperative education organization for full-time employment upon graduation.

Anticipatory socialization programs represent a win-win proposition in that they provide an avenue for individuals to test out prospective employers while allowing employers to have access to job candidates who have already been indoctrinated into the organization. Internships and cooperative education initiatives provide a flexible supply of human resources where, through on-the-job assessments, a determination can be made whether the person should be a candidate for full-time employment. Those individuals engaged in anticipatory socialization activities have already been exposed to the company's culture, have familiarity with the firm's facilities and equipment, and have been trained in specific functional areas. Anticipatory socialization programs also benefit the neophyte. Soon-to-be or newly minted graduates are provided with an opportunity to learn about themselves, their chosen career field, and working in general. Specific skills, both technical (e.g., marketing research) and interpersonal (communicating as a member of a group), can be learned, practiced, and reinforced by internship and co-op experiences. In all, anticipatory socialization programs help to advance participants toward their desired career goals.

2. *Learning and Development*

HR professionals spend a significant amount of time delivering learning and development programs to employees. Normally, the talent needs of a company change as it grows and transforms. Christensen suggests that the shelf life for many professional skills is approximately three to five years.[27] Therefore, organizations have a critical need to build their learning and development processes so that they can continually upgrade their workforce. Several important processes are part of learning and development, including employee development, orientation programs, succession planning, competency development, and leadership coaching. Employee development differs from competency development in that the former is a joint effort on the part of an employee and organization to enhance the employee's knowledge, skills, and abilities. Successful employee development requires a balance between an individual's career needs and goals, and the organization's need to get work done. *Competency* development is the systematic collection and analysis of data to determine what characteristics differentiate outstanding from average performers in an organizational job or role.[28] Competency development has broader implications for organizational hiring processes, while employee development is more focused on enhancing the skill set of the individual and thus has important career advancement implications.

Employee Development

Organizations support their business strategies by developing their human resources to achieve greater levels of proficiency. In this sense, the company's current staff is viewed as a critical resource, one that is necessary to sustain organizational growth. An organization needs to invest in the development of all of its employees so that it gains the talent and skill sets necessary to achieve its goals.

Developmental activities can be grouped into two basic categories: education/training and on-the-job experiences. Education and training programs are generally formal activities that can take place either in the work setting or at an outside organization. To supplement the skills that employees bring to the job, corporate "universities" are often called upon to increase the organization's human capacities.[29] Another model of university training occurs when firms offer tuition reimbursement. Employees must be accepted by the college of their choice and complete required credits to graduate with either a baccalaureate or post-baccalaureate degree, or with a professional or vocational certification. In some cases, the employee's coursework is pursued via distance education technologies that may include the use of the Internet, interactive simulations, and videos. Distance education allows greater flexibility for employees to learn, and may occur wherever and whenever the employee is able to engage in learning.[30]

A number of larger organizations have established a corporate "university" approach to the training and education of employees. These companies work with traditional universities or training organizations to provide courses through an education portal (or intranet site). The company may create its own campus, either real brick-and-mortar or virtual, complete with a company's logo and related information. Corporate universities can develop and provide training that is tailored to address specific learning objectives and to fulfill the company's needs regarding skill development. Organizations can also use the continuing education programs and standard curriculums of traditional universities as a way to offer a complete academic program to their employees. The popularity of corporate universities continues to grow, with more than 4,000 companies around the world now having in-house universities.[31]

The following are examples of corporate university initiatives at Boeing and at McDonald's:

The Boeing Company's technical university is called MyBoeingTraining. At this corporate university, employees gain knowledge regarding the maintenance of various jets, and video-based and other courses on cockpits for flight crews. Also, a developmental program for pilots is offered so that employees can earn an Airline Transport Pilot License (ATPL).[32] Boeing also provides education to other employees through its Leadership Center, located in St. Louis, Missouri. Leaders at Boeing have the opportunity to respond to different work challenges, discuss best management practices, and share experiences with contemporaries from across the company. Thousands of current and future leaders have travelled to the Leadership Center from around the world. The company's goal is to grow leadership capabilities from within at all levels of the firm. Boeing has invested more than $1 billion on employee development through these programs. Boeing also has Engineering Career Development Centers, which are designed to target and develop talent in various engineering disciplines throughout the company. The Engineering Centers are intended to foster the career growth and development of its employees.[33]

McDonald's Center of Training Excellence, also known as Hamburger University, emphasizes training in consistent restaurant operations, the provision of high quality service, and restaurant cleanliness. Hamburger University also serves as McDonald's global center of excellence for operations training and leadership development. Its curriculum uses a combination of classroom instruction, hands-on lab activities, and computer-based distance learning modules. The curriculum covers the full range of employees, with learning paths offered for crew members, restaurant managers, and middle managers, along with executive development activities.[34]

In addition to raising the skill levels of their employees, corporations can also use their universities as recruiting tools and as a way to retain the top graduates of their programs. Although the investment in a corporate university can be expensive and the absolute return on investment difficult to calculate, the benefits in employee attraction, development, and retention and organizational success can mean that it is usually money well spent.[35]

A second way that organizations can develop their employees is through on-the-job (OTJ) learning. Even with the heavy corporate investment in formal programs, most development and learning occurs through OTJ experiences. Research suggests that if learning is going to be absorbed and if work-related competencies are to be developed fully, training needs to be continuous and provide opportunities for practice and reinforcement.[36] On-the-job learning is a critical method for organizations to prepare their employees for the future. Through the use of different assignments and multifunctional experiences, companies can ensure a steady supply of trained staff who understands the business and key strategic imperatives. Effective organizations integrate learning opportunities into all business functions and work experiences and make the assurance of OTJ learning part of every manager's job.[37]

There are many different projects, assignments, and other activities that can serve as OTJ developmental experiences. To cite an old maxim, there is no substitute for experience. During the early career years, employees can benefit from job challenge and the opportunity to experience a number of different OTJ assignments. Through job challenge and rotational opportunities, employees build a base of experience and develop a wider range of competencies that can lead to career success in later years. One part of Boeing's learning and development strategy is its business rotation program. In this program, junior employees work with experts to solve a variety of challenges, gaining hands-on experience while participating in large-scale assignments.[38] Another example, Air Products and Chemicals, Inc., uses an innovative approach to encourage rotational work assignments during the early years of employment. Many past and current leaders of Air Products joined the company through the Career Development Program.[39] As described below, new employees are placed in a number of challenging assignments as a way to stimulate their personal and professional development:

Since its inception, Air Products and Chemicals has encouraged recent college graduates to take an active role in the planning and development of their careers. This philosophy was formalized in 1959 with the establishment of the Career Development Program (or CDP), which allows individuals with finance, marketing, supply chain management, engineering, or information technology undergraduate or graduate degrees to fulfill their immediate, individual career objectives while preparing for and defining the challenges and opportunities that lie ahead. The CDP is characterized by movement and flexibility, while providing an environment where the individual has a real influence on the direction of his or her career from the very beginning. The long-term goal of the program is to help participants identify and begin to cultivate professional skills, interests, and potential to the best benefit of the individual and Air Products.

The CDP is not a structured training program. Instead, it challenges new employees with actual work experience and gives them a broad perspective on the company's operations and objectives. Participants develop their skills and interests through a rotation of three different assignments, lasting 8 to 12 months each, during the first several years of employment. Every participant takes an active role in influencing his or her own career path. Positions are designed to give each person exposure to a variety of company activities and to provide a high degree of visibility among all levels of management. Individuals develop their CDP with the help of their assigned mentor, ultimately resulting in a career path that optimally matches the individual's longer-term career plans and opportunities within the company.[40]

Orientation Programs

Even if an organization practices realistic recruitment, employees still have to adjust to a new environment when they enter the organization. Orientation programs not only help new employees become integrated into the work environment and organization's culture in a general sense, but can also address specific information needs and attend to any problems experienced by newcomers in the organization. Presented below is a description of the well-known orientation program used by Walt Disney World in Orlando, Florida:[41]

For a company like Disney, with extensive contact between customers and employees, it is imperative that its staff be knowledgeable, courteous, and always willing to meet the needs of the guests. To ensure that new recruits are properly integrated into this culture, Disney employs a three-day orientation program it calls "Traditions." The first days of employment at Disney World involve attendance at a full-day session that describes the history of the organization. The session emphasizes the four key values of the Disney culture:[42] keeping close attention to detail (ensuring safety in the workplace, displaying courtesy to all customers, and making sure the customer comes first); walking the talk (recognizing that all employees are here to help our guests and showing a commitment to quality); offering encouragement and feedback (advocate for patients and families, reward, recognize, and celebrate employees, and provide constant feedback to employees); and making a difference (teamwork is critical to success and live the Disney philosophy so all may recognize it).

During orientation, all Disney employees are taught that they have a role in serving the guests and that they should observe how experienced employees perform this role during a tour of the facilities. Service standards are explained and demonstrated. These standards help them make the day-to-day decisions without having to refer questions to management.On the second day of the orientation, the employees hear about the support systems, policies, and procedures within the company, with the primary focus on safety and benefits. The third day involves on-the-job training. The recruit is assigned to an experienced co-worker who, during the next two days to two weeks, provides the new employee with a series of experiences specific to his or her work role. These peer trainers are role models who work with supervisors to provide the coaching, feedback, and reinforcement needed to help the newcomer learn the job and acquire the Disney spirit. The whole point of this training is to have new employees understand their part as "cast members" in their work shift (often referred to as the "performance"). The goal is to create a strong bond between cast member and the company. Disney's orientation might seem extensive, with attention to such details as specifying clothing, hair style, and nail neatness, but the program has been clearly successful in keeping Disney's attrition rate at low levels in comparison to other organizations in the hospitality industry.[43]

Firms with more specific employee learning needs can also benefit from well-designed orientation programs. Aramark Corporation, headquartered in Philadelphia, PA, is one of the world's leading providers of food, facilities, and uniform services and has more than 270,000 employees worldwide who serve clients in 19 countries.[44] Aramark's orientation program for recent hires provides an example of how new professionals are integrated into all areas of the company's operation. Aramark's orientation program is described below:

Program participants, generally the most promising college graduates, are selected to join the Accelerate to Leadership (A2L) Program. A2L is designed to provide new hires with the resources they need to reach their full potential and prepare for an accelerated career path to a leadership role within the organization. During the program, participants receive career guidance, real hands-on training, and functional management experiences at client sites. By managing these day-to-day operations with one of Aramark's many business units, recent graduates develop real business and leadership know-how. New hires are able to network with peers and grow both personally and professionally, all while experiencing the diverse cultures in the various A2L market centers.[45]

The initial task in developing a successful orientation program is to identify the detailed information, skills, and support required by new employees. The major strengths of the Disney and Aramark programs are accurate identification and articulation of a need—describing the corporate values (outstanding customer service at Disney) or job function (at Aramark), as well as a determination of how best to get the message across. These orientation approaches demonstrate how custom-made programs can be used to improve newcomers' understanding of the organization's core values and modes of operation.

Succession Planning

All organizations must recognize that they regularly need to replace executives and managers throughout the life cycle of the firm. Voluntary and involuntary turnover, retirements, health issues, disability, or death mean that organizations need to be prepared to fill open positions with qualified personnel. Succession planning refers to the efforts of the firm to select and develop future leaders who, in time, will replace current leaders.[46]

Finding high-potential employees who are prepared to take on greater responsibilities is a complex process. While a variety of succession planning approaches have been observed, HR professionals typically use four models, either individually or in combination with one another. The primary goal of these programs is generally to assess preparedness for executive leadership. First, firms may offer *job rotation* as an opportunity for a high-potential employee to learn skills across a variety of positions or assignments. Air Products' CDP program referenced earlier in this chapter is a good example of job rotation. Employees may be transferred to different functional areas (e.g., manufacturing, finance, supply chain management) so that they learn how each functional area works and interacts with other functions within the company. Job rotations in sales and marketing give the high-potential employee experiences working with customers as well. Using job rotation as a developmental experience allows the high-potential employee to see the firm from a broader perspective.

A second succession model that HR professionals use is to identify a specific *talent pool* from which to draw future leaders. This approach encourages the high-potential employee to develop his or her skills more broadly, including assignments on cross-functional teams, undertaking difficult jobs, using cutting-edge technology, and taking advantage of key networking opportunities.[47] While the strength of the talent pool model is dependent on the recruitment and development of high-potential employees, the "wait until the management job becomes available" approach to advancement can be problematic for the upwardly mobile employee. High potential employees may leave for jobs in other companies, or other companies may try to raid the talent pool. Nonetheless, companies like Lockheed Martin have developed leadership training programs (in communications, engineering, finance, operations and security) to encourage high potential employees to become a more permanent or stable part of their resource base.[48]

A third method for succession planning is to *buy talent* from the external labor market when replacements are needed. This model is beneficial because the entire labor market can be sourced for the desirable skill set. It may be difficult to find just the right person from within a firm, especially when the corporate strategy requires a move to a new business arena. Buying talent is most effective when a firm needs to keep pace with the competition and needs to acquire specialized skills.[49] However, there are risks associated with hiring from outside the organization. First, high-potential employees may believe that they are never good enough for high-level positions if the company always buys outside talent. Also, companies need to take a "buyer beware" approach to bringing in talent from the external market. Often when new, high-potential employees are hired from outside, they need to overcome a steep learning curve that might delay their full contribution to the organization, especially when the company's culture and work ethic do not mesh with expectations of the newcomer. Sometimes new hires do not meet the expectations of the position, and after extraordinary investment, companies realize that they have not hired the person they thought they had.[50] Even with these potential pitfalls, it can make good sense to "buy talent" as a succession strategy, but only when a thorough interviewing process has screened potential employees.

The final succession planning model is what Jon Briscoe and Brooklyn Derr call the "*smaller is better*" method. "Smaller is better" emphasizes the job rotation and talent pool approaches mentioned above, but shrinks the size of the pool considerably to make it more selective.[51] This model stresses that only those high-potential employees who have the talent, desire, and interest in staying with the company long enough to make a leadership contribution are considered for future advancement. Laura Chalkley has suggested a similar approach, where high-potential employees who enter middle management then enter a leader challenge program where their continuing progression can be observed and measured through a variety of more challenging assignments.[52] Obviously, the potential for greater responsibility can be discovered only after thorough analysis of individual performance and through conversations with the high potential employees themselves. While this method runs the risk of "putting all of one's eggs in one basket," the level of employee commitment this model engenders can be significant.

Overall, succession planning is a vital responsibility of the HR function. By maintaining a full "depth chart" of high-potential employees, the firm is ready to position these employees in leadership positions as they become available. Investment by the organization in succession planning is crucial for long-term sustainability and growth.

Competency Development

Chapter 6 discussed how the development of new competencies is an important career strategy for most individuals because it facilitates improved performance and sets the stage for career growth. Organizations can assist employees in the attainment of enhanced competencies by becoming "knowledge creators"; that is, by actively developing their employees through the provision of opportunities for learning and knowledge creation. Indeed, talent management strategies that focus on competency development can help the organization in recruiting the best talent (including internal talent), can lessen the attrition of key performers, and can allow firms to fill key positions through succession planning.[53] Both the University of British Columbia (UBC) in Canada and the Massachusetts Institute of Technology (MIT) are examples of organizations using competency development initiatives to increase the skill portfolio of their personnel.[54]

At UBC's Information Technology (IT) department, competencies have been identified both for specific jobs, as well as broader capabilities that are essential for all employees. UBC believes that such competencies as being able to communicate results effectively, solve problems, and collaborate with others are essential to success for all employees. They have also identified other functional competencies for certain job classifications as displayed in Table 14.1.[55] In Table 14.1, the columns represent examples of career ladder and/or job opportunities available within the department. The rows represent the specific competencies that are necessary for each given job opportunity. Employees then are able to have conversations with management about needed competencies for future jobs, or increased responsibilities in current jobs, they are interested in pursuing.

MIT's program identifies essential competencies that are specifically expected for managers and leaders. One example, *communicating and building relationships*, is seen as an essential capability. This skill is described as being able to build productive work relationships, being cooperative, working well with others to solve challenges, and seeking opportunities to collaborate with others. Other key competencies include relationship-building, creating opportunities for teamwork, and effectively managing conflict.[56]

Table 14.1 Career Framework Competencies at the University of British Columbia's Information Technology Department

Competencies	Career Ladders/Job Opportunities within the Department												
	Application Development	*AV Support*	*Business Analysis*	*Client Services*	*Database Administration*	*Enterprise Architecture*	*IT Leadership & Management*	*Network Analysis*	*Project Management*	*Quality Assurance*	*Support Analysis*	*Systems Administration*	*Systems Analysis*
Accountability	X	X			X				X	X	X	X	X
Analytical Thinking		X	X			X		X	X	X	X		
Building Relationships				X									
Business Enterprise Knowledge				X		X			X				
Business Process Knowledge	X		X										X
Change Advocate				X									
Collaboration	X	X	X	X	X	X	X	X	X	X	X	X	X
Communicating for Results	X	X	X	X	X	X	X	X	X	X	X	X	X
Information Systems Knowledge	X							X			X	X	X
Initiative		X	X									X	
Leading Others							X						
Leading the Organization							X						
Leading Self							X						
Problem Solving	X	X	X	X	X	X	X	X	X	X	X	X	X
Strategic Technology Planning					X	X							
Thoroughness					X			X		X			

These examples of competency development programs illustrate the processes organizations pursue to continually develop their workforces. Organizations can identify and enhance both essential and functional competencies in their workforce, which improves job performance by placing the right employee in the right job, and aids in long-term employee career goal attainment. Additionally, companies that create and articulate competency classifications can also use these classifications for selection, placement, skill assessment, and training for their key personnel.

Leadership Coaching

In order to facilitate more individualized development, many companies use professional coaches to help their leaders function more effectively and to assist in the refinement of skills that will allow for further advancement. In their interactions with leaders, coaches tend to focus on three factors—the personal qualities and behavioral traits of the leader and how well those qualities and traits fit the work setting; the interpersonal interactions of the leader with his or her staff and whether those interaction have positive or negative consequences; and the efficacy of the relationship between the leader and his or her company in terms of fit between the goals and culture of the organization and the personal qualities and career aspirations of the leader.[57] Ultimately, the goal of coaching is to help people successfully achieve their performance goals and their professional objectives. Effective coaching should cover assessment and goal-setting (for both performance and career management), action planning and implementation, and improvement processes.

Coaching can be an important developmental tool not only for executives or senior managers but also for supervisors and middle managers.[58] In addition to improving leader performance, a case can be made that coaching can enhance leader sustainability and preparedness for more demanding assignments.[59] Optimal coaching is designed to provide employees with the skills, resources, support, and most importantly, the self-awareness needed so they can continue to do their best work. Key experiences gained from coaching include building trusting relationships, openness to diverse experiences and people, moral understanding, developing as future supervisors, increased work motivation, and recognition for the need for change.[60] Given these noted positive outcomes, leadership coaching will continue to be a central developmental activity as organizations need to provide greater career opportunities to retain high-performing employees.

In sum, organizations promote the learning and development of their human resources in a variety of ways—employee development, orientation programs, succession planning, competency development, and leadership coaching—so that their financial investment in their employees is realized and organizational performance is optimized.

3. Performance Management and Rewards

After organizations identify, recruit, and develop their employees it is necessary to establish an effective process to manage employee performance. Performance management is essential to ensure that organizational goals and outcomes are met. While performance management has its roots in compensation and formal recognition systems, it also includes the assessment of individual performance in light of strategic organizational goals. Christensen's approach to performance management includes three components—performance objectives and measures, benefits programs, and human resource information systems (HRIS)—each of which is discussed below.

Performance Objectives and Measures

The human resources function plays an important and strategic organizational role by assisting in the assessment of individual performance and by linking (or comparing) that performance to desired individual and organizational outcomes.[61] Performance objectives and measures are established so that (a) individual and organizational goals are aligned, (b) individual and organizational performance is consistent, (c) insight is provided into needed adjustments in goals and performance, and (d) critical input is provided for individual development planning.[62] To further describe the actions at the corporate, group, and individual levels, Christensen provides a framework for understanding the steps in establishing performance objectives and measures as discussed below.

Christensen's approach to performance objectives and measures involves three steps, each of which is carried out at the level of the individual employee, the group or team, and the organization as a whole. The *first step* is setting expectations for performance. Mutually agreed-upon performance expectations must be established so that individuals understand the level of performance for which they will be held accountable, the consequences of meeting these expectations, and the developmental plans that can help them accomplish their objectives. The performance expectations must be aligned with the performance expectations at the group and corporate levels. In the *second step*, performance must be monitored, feedback provided, and coaching offered so that adjustments can be made when necessary. In the *third step*, effective performance must be recognized at all levels—individual, group, and organizational—through a variety of incentives that are intended to maintain high levels of performance.

Because performance feedback is critical to performance management systems, we highlight one particular feedback mechanism that we introduced earlier in the book, 360-degree feedback. As a developmental tool, 360-degree feedback allows for the gathering of performance information from multiple sources "in a circle" around the individual, including co-workers, customers, subordinates, supervisors, and peers on a work team. If conducted properly, 360-degree feedback systems provide a full assessment of critical competencies, specific behaviors and skills, overall performance, and areas that require further development.[63]

Companies such as BP Amoco, Honeywell, Intel, and Proctor & Gamble have used 360-degree feedback systems to help achieve strategic goals and carry out organizational change efforts.[64] Multisource feedback systems support organizational performance in several ways. First, feedback helps the company reinforce the skills and competencies needed to meet business goals. Second, feedback received from those individuals who work most closely with the employee allows the employee to understand his or her strengths and weaknesses from various perspectives. Finally, assessment, training, and developmental opportunities can be offered so the employee can develop the needed skills and track his or her progress in applying those skills on the job.[65]

Such 360-degree feedback systems can improve leaders' performance and enhance their subordinates' work engagement, satisfaction, and leadership capabilities, as well as reduce their subordinates' intentions to quit. Additionally, these feedback systems improve communication on the topic between leaders and subordinates.[66] It would be difficult to develop realistic career goals in the absence of useful performance feedback on one's current job. Periodic performance management sessions that focus on specific job behaviors, in conjunction with more broad-based indicators of accomplishments provided by 360-degree feedback, are most likely to improve current performance and build a solid foundation for future career growth.

Benefits Programs

Benefits programs are also an essential component of a total performance measurement and reward system. Employee benefits are various forms of compensation provided in addition to normal wages or salaries to increase employees' security and well-being. Fringe benefits can include but are not limited to employer-provided (or employer-paid) housing, group insurance (e.g., health, dental, vision, life, pet), prescription plans, disability income protection, retirement benefits, childcare benefits, tuition reimbursement, sick leave, vacation (paid and nonpaid), and profit-sharing. Other specialized benefits may include relocation reimbursement, adoption assistance, transportation benefits, pre-retirement counseling, and wellness programs.

Human Resource Information Systems (HRIS)

HRIS enable an organization to acquire, store, manipulate, analyze, retrieve, and distribute information relevant to human resources to aid organizational decision-makers.[67] They have grown in popularity since the 1960s, and are used not only for routine, personnel-related tasks, but also for strategic and business decision-making purposes. Well-designed HRIS have many benefits to organizations, including the provision of analytics on human resources that aid management in making personnel decisions, enabling employees to view, verify, and self-correct personal information in the system by providing interactive functionality, the ability to perform succession planning, and the facilitating of equal employment opportunity and affirmative action monitoring and reporting.[68] Clearly, as firms move toward a more strategic approach to human resource management, HRIS will continue to play a vital role in the growth of their HR management capabilities.

4. Employee Relations

Employee relations is the fourth strategic human resource function, along with workforce planning and staffing, learning and development, and performance management and rewards. Employee relations covers a variety of programs that an organization offers so that employees can work more effectively, can better integrate work and nonwork lives, and can sustain their work efforts over time.[69] Three efforts related to career management—work–life programs, employee morale initiatives, and attention to employee diversity—are discussed briefly below.

Work–Life Programs

As we discussed in Chapter 3, organizations invest in work–life programs largely to attract and retain employees who are juggling their multiple commitments to work, family, community, leisure, and self-development. We noted that a blend of formal programs (e.g., parental leave, flexible work schedules), informal support from supervisors and co-workers, and a supportive culture that recognizes employees' lives outside of work can help employees to balance their work with these other important parts of their lives. In this chapter, we highlight and reinforce the important steps that employers can take in this important area:[70]

- Provide formal programs of the type shown in Table 3.3. These programs provide employees with resources (e.g., flexibility control, time, financial assistance) that enable employees to manage their responsibilities in different parts of life, and signals the organization's commitment to their employees' well-being.

- Encourage the use of formal programs. Providing a particular work–life program, such as parental leave or telecommuting, and then punishing employees who use them is self-defeating. Employees are understandably reluctant to use a program when they believe that their manager will stereotype them as uncommitted to their work and will withhold career-related opportunities and resources to those who take advantage of work–life programs. Organizations should encourage employees to use available programs and work with them to assure that they meet their responsibilities at work *and* in other parts of their lives.
- Provide informal support to supplement formal programs. Supportive supervisors and co-workers provide flexibility (e.g., leaving work early to take care of a sick child, working at home occasionally), tangible assistance (e.g., redistributing work, covering for an overloaded colleague), and advice (e.g., childcare options, suggestions on how to telecommute productively) to employees who are trying to achieve more balance in life.
- Provide work teams with control over how their work gets accomplished to eliminate unnecessary work, streamline procedures, meet the team's performance goals, and enable team members to balance work with their personal life.
- Respect the needs of *all* employers. Employees who are not married, or who don't have children, have a life outside of work that is important to them. Limiting work–life support to parents, and restricting assistance only to those with extensive family responsibilities, is likely to cause other employees to feel that they are being treated unfairly. All employees should receive formal and informal support to meet their responsibilities at work while also pursuing a life outside of work.

Employee Morale

The essence of employee relations is the building of a strong relationship between employer and employee, a relationship maintained by a corporate culture that is conducive to helping employees stay motivated, loyal, and performing at a high level. *Morale* can be defined as the general outlook that employees display toward their work organization or unit.[71] High morale is associated with positive employee attitudes, heightened energy levels, reduced stress levels, and an overall sense of esprit de corps among the employees. Additionally, organizations can reduce productivity losses within a downsizing environment by heightening management's consideration for employees' morale and welfare.[72]

To create or maintain a workforce with high morale, organizations should communicate honestly with employees on business conditions and the direction the company is taking. In addition, organizations should listen to their employees by asking for employee input and advice, which can yield creative solutions and provide employees with a much-desired sense of control in uncertain times. The organization should also focus on positive results by celebrating and using positive reinforcement on a regular basis. Finally, organizations should offer a comprehensive benefits package that attends to the needs of employees and their family. By creating a work environment that helps employees meet their long-term career goals, employees experience improved morale and build lasting loyalty both to the company and fellow employees.[73]

Attention to Employee Diversity

Diversity within an organization is not just a specific program (like a diversity awareness activity), but rather should be an integral part of all organizational functions, including human resources. HRM plays an important role in ensuring that attention to diversity is treated in a comprehensive manner throughout the organization. As discussed in

Chapter 11, a comprehensive approach should: (a) communicate the importance of diversity throughout the organization; (b) identify critical diversity issues within the organization; (c) eliminate discrimination not only in hiring but also in the progression of employees throughout their career; (d) develop appropriate policies and programs regarding sexual harassment, the use of different languages in the workplace, and work–life challenges; and (e) hold the leadership of the organization accountable for managing diversity effectively.

Summary

An important consideration for all organizations is the implementation of human resource management systems that have a focus on individual development and career management. This chapter discussed a model of an integrated strategic human resource system that depicts how career management can help improve overall effectiveness. We described the key functional human resource areas (workforce planning and staffing, learning and development, performance management and rewards, and employee relations), and showed how career management is rooted in these activities. We also provided examples of corporate programs where human resource systems support individual careers and career management. We discussed how a firm's HRM systems can support its strategic business plans as well as individual employee development. Organizations can offer an array of programs that help their employees manage their careers throughout the life cycle. Recognizing that individuals at different career stages have varying career needs and challenges, companies can and should tailor their career management programs to meet the requirements of all their employees. In order to gather and synthesize all this data, HR professionals can use data analytics to manage the vast amount of information that is generated and to better inform HRM and business strategies.

Career Management *for Life*: Work–Life Implications from Chapter 14

- Organizations should provide formal work–life programs, such as maternity and paternity support, dependent care assistance, flexibility, and informational and social support as shown in Table 3.3.
- Organizations should encourage employees to use formal work–life programs and assist them in meeting their responsibilities at work and other parts of their lives. Employees are unlikely to use work–life programs if their managers stigmatize them as being uncommitted to their work and withhold career resources and rewards from them for using the programs.
- Supervisors and co-workers should be encouraged to provide informal support to employees to supplement formal work–life programs or to compensate for the absence of formal programs.
- Work teams should be given the autonomy to decide how their work gets accomplished to meet the team's performance goals *and* the team members' commitments outside of work.
- Work–life support should be provided to *all* employees who require it rather than limiting the support to employees with extensive family responsibilities. All employees can benefit from opportunities to balance their work responsibilities with other parts of life that are important to them.

Assignment

Choose an organization for which you have worked or one you can investigate. Identify the company's unique culture and describe the human resource management programs that it provides. Explain how the organization's culture has either helped or hindered the development of an effective HRM system and describe the type of culture that is ideally suited for an effective HRM system. How has the firm's HRM systems positively impacted its career management systems?

Discussion Questions

1. What techniques can organizations use to ensure that their strategic direction and business plans are reflected in their human resource systems and career management programs?
2. To what extent should organizations be committed to developing and promoting their resources from within? Are organizations better off just hiring their resources from the external labor market? Which situations might warrant the internal development approach and which might warrant the external selection approach?
3. Do you think that the waves of employee layoffs that have occurred over the past three decades indicate a general lack of loyalty toward employees on the part of most organizations? How does the lack of job security affect organizational philosophies regarding the strategic human resource programs they should provide? What are the implications of your answers in terms of the management of your own career?
4. Do you believe that employers have a moral obligation to assist their employees in managing their careers? Why or why not?

Chapter 14 Case: The Corporate Policy Change

Located in the beautiful Adirondack Mountains of upstate New York, Be Our Guest Family Resort (BOGFR) was recently sold to a French international hotel chain. Previously, BOGFR (fictitious name) had been a family-owned business, and the owners treated all employees like an extended family. BOGFR is well-known for its friendly, top-notch accommodations. In the summer and fall, BOGFR offers families a variety of outdoor activities, including six tennis courts, an 18-hole golf course, a lake for boating and fishing, an indoor/outdoor pool, and horseback riding. During the winter and spring, downhill and cross-country skiing are the outdoor activities of choice at BOGFR. Other activities available throughout the year include bowling, shopping, and an onsite movie theater. BOGFR also has four restaurants and a tavern.

Because BOGFR provides many amenities, it has a large year-round staff, many of whom have worked for the company for 15 years or more. In fact, BOGFR often hired members from multiple generations of the same family. BOGFR has a focused mission that is made clear to all its employees—to provide a premium vacation experience to all who come to BOGFR. This means that the customer comes first. Employees are asked to do all they can to keep customer satisfaction high and fulfill BOGFR's mission. This focus encourages customers to schedule return visits to BOGFR, and also to tell their friends about their vacations at BOGFR. Upon check-out, employees always ask guests to use social media and tell others about their positive experiences.

BOGFR employees know that their town relies almost exclusively on the tourism generated by the resort, because few other substantial businesses are located in the immediate area.

BOGFR has a "home-grown" mentality regarding the advancement of its human resources. Many of the hotel and restaurant managers grew up working summers as valets, house cleaners, and wait staff. This human resource policy reflected the "small town" and family atmosphere of the BOGFR. This policy also allowed the employees to have a variety of work experiences, and to learn first-hand what customers expect from a top-of-the-line resort. Many children of BOGFR employees attend a local university that has a hotel administration major. This education allows the young adults to come back to their hometown to work. Yet, the acquisition of BOGFR by an international concern will soon cause its human resource policies to change.

The Mansion Corporation (fictitious name), a well-known hotel and restaurant corporation, has recently purchased BOGFR. The Mansion's human resource strategies are dramatically different from those of BOGFR. The Mansion attracts "star" quality employees from other hotels around the world and provides them with high-level administrative positions. These positions may be offered at any one of a number of the Mansion's resort holdings. The Mansion is generous with offers of relocation packages to lure potential employees away from their current employer.

The Mansion's policy regarding human resource selection is more of the "buy" than the "make" approach. The Mansion fills its skill gaps by hiring needed personnel from outside the company. In fact, the Mansion has recently hired a CFO and chief technologist from competitors. Both employees and their families moved from the United States to the Mansion's European headquarters in Paris, France. Many of the hotel's general managers are from either top hotels or premier restaurant chains. The general premise under which Mansion operates is that it is more cost-efficient to bring in the "best and the brightest." This allows the Mansion to hire the skills it needs when and where it may need those skills. The Mansion plans to make this policy known to BOGFR's personnel as part of their Introduction to the Mansion's Human Resources Policies package. The Mansion corporate policies become effective in a few weeks. The Mansion does not intend to discuss the effect of this policy with BOGFR's employees unless asked.

Case Questions

1. What effect, if any, will the Mansion's policies have on current BOGFR personnel?
2. What effect, if any, will the Mansion's policies have on the business strategies of BOGFR?
3. How should the Mansion implement this new policy change at BOGFR? How might the Mansion communicate this policy change? What types of career management systems are most compatible with the Mansion's human resource strategy?
4. If you were an employee of the BOGFR community, what might you do in light of this human resource policy change? What effect would the international nature of Mansion have on you?

Notes

1 Bartlett, C. A. & Ghoshal, S. (2002, Winter). Building competitive advantage through people. *MIT Sloan Management Review*, 34–41; Colarelli, S. M., Hemingway, M. & Monnot, M. (2006). Strategic human resource management (SHRM). In Greenhaus, J. H. & Callanan, G. A. (Eds.), *Encyclopedia of career development* (pp. 767–771). Thousand Oaks, CA: Sage; Ward, D. L., Tripp, R. & Maki, B. (2013). *Positioned: Strategic workforce planning that gets the right person in the right job*. New York: AMACOM.

2 Wang, D. S. & Shyu, C. L. (2008). Will the strategic fit between business and HRM strategy influence HRM effectiveness and organizational performance? *International Journal of Manpower*, *29*, 92–110.

3 Akong'o Dimba, B. (2010). Strategic human resource management practices: Effect on performance. *African Journal of Economic and Management Studies*, *1*, 128–137; Fabi, B., Lacoursière, R. & Raymond, L. (2015). Impact of high-performance work systems on job satisfaction, organizational commitment, and intention to quit in Canadian organizations. *International Journal of Manpower*, *36*, 772–790; García-Chas, R., Neira-Fontela, E. & Varela-Neira, C. (2016). High-performance work systems and job satisfaction: A multilevel model. *Journal of Managerial Psychology*, *31*, 451–466; Green, K. W., Wu, C., Whitten, D. & Medlin, B. (2006). The impact of strategic human resource management on firm performance and HR professionals' work attitude and work performance. *The International Journal of Human Resource Management*, *17*, 559–570; Gupta, M. (2016). An empirical study on fit between strategic human resource management and business strategy. *International Journal of Management Research and Reviews*, *6*, 102; Huselid, M. A. (1995). The impact of human resource practices on turnover, productivity, and corporate financial performance. *Academy of Management Journal*, *38*, 635–672; Jiang, K., Lepak, D. P., Hu, J. & Baer, J. C. (2012). How does human resource management influence organizational outcomes? A meta-analytic investigation of mediating mechanisms. *Academy of Management Journal*, *55*, 1264–1294; Mansour, M. (2015). The practice of strategic human resource management in a developing country. *European Online Journal of Natural and Social Sciences*, *4*, 500–517; Nigam, A. K., Nongmaithem, S., Sharma, S. & Tripathi, N. (2011). The impact of strategic human resource management on the performance of firms in India. *Journal of Indian Business Research*, *3*, 148–167; Renaud, S., Morin, L., Saulquin, J. & Abraham, J. (2015). What are the best HRM practices for retaining experts? A longitudinal study in the Canadian information technology sector. *International Journal of Manpower*, *36*, 416–432; SamGnanakkan, S. (2010). Mediating role of organizational commitment on HR practices and turnover intention among ICT professionals. *Journal of Management Research*, *10*, 39–61; Sattar, T., Ahmad, K. & Hassan, S. M. (2015). Role of human resource practices in employee performance and job satisfaction with mediating effect of employee engagement. *Pakistan Economic and Social Review*, *53*, 81–96; Sun, L. Y., Aryee, S. & Law, K. S. (2007). High performance human resource practices, citizenship behavior, and organizational performance: A relational perspective. *Academy of Management Journal*, *50*, 558–577; Thanigaivel, R., Liew, S. A. & Koon, V. Y. (2017). The effect of human resource management (HRM) practices in service-oriented organizational citizenship behaviour (OCB): Case of telecommunications and internet service providers in Malaysia. *Asian Social Science*, *13*, 67–81; Ugheoke, S. O., Isa, M. F. M. & Noor, W. S. W. M. (2014). Assessing the impact of strategic human resource management on tangible performance: Evidence from Nigerian SMEs. *International Review of Management and Business Research*, *3*, 1163–1173; Wang & Shyu (2008).

4 Appelbaum, S. H., Ayre, H. & Shapiro, B. T. (2002). Career management in information technology: A case study. *Career Development International*, *7*, 142–158; Baruch, Y. (2003). Career systems in transition: A normative model for organizational career practices. *Personnel Review*, *32*, 231–251; Baruch, Y. (2004). Transforming careers from linear to multidirectional career paths: Organizational and individual perspectives. *Career Development International*, *9*, 58–73; Baruch, Y. & Peiperl, M. (2000). Career management practices: An empirical survey and implications. *Human Resource Management*, *39*, 347–366; Delery, J. E. & Roumpi, D. (2017). Strategic human resource management, human capital and competitive advantage: Is the field going in circles? *Human Resource Management Journal*, *27*, 1–21; Egan, T. M., Upton, M. G. & Lynham, S. A. (2006). Career development: Load-bearing wall or window dressing? Exploring definitions, theories, and prospects for HRD-related theory building. *Human Resource Development Review*, *5*, 442–477; McDonald, K. S. & Hite, L. M. (2005). Reviving the relevance of career development in human resource development. *Human Resource Development Review*, *4*, 418–439; Morgan, R. (2006). Making the most of performance management systems. *Compensation and Benefits Review*, *38*, 22–27; Ward et al. (2013).

5 Christensen, R. (2006). *Roadmap to strategic HR: Turning a great idea into a business reality.* New York: AMACOM.
6 Christensen (2006); Delery, J. E. & Gupta, N. (2016). Human resource management practices and organizational effectiveness: Internal fit matters. *Journal of Organizational Effectiveness: People and Performance*, *3*, 139–163; Delery & Roumpi (2017).
7 Christensen (2006). Quotation is on p. 53.
8 Peterson, D. & Krieger, T. (2013). Strategic workforce planning at Boeing. In Ward, D. L., Tripp, R. & Maki, B. (Eds.), *Positioned: Strategic workforce planning that gets the right person in the right job* (pp. 42–50). New York: AMACOM. Quotation is on p. 43.
9 Christensen (2006); Peterson & Krieger (2013).
10 Dunn, J. (2006). Strategic human resources and strategic organization development: An alliance for the future? *Organization Development Journal*, *24*, 69–76; Greer, C., Youngblood, S. A. & Gray, D. A. (1999). Human resource management outsourcing: The make or buy decision. *Academy of Management Executive*, *13*, 85–96; McCowan, R. A., Bowen, U., Huselid, M. A. & Becker, B. E. (1999). Strategic human resource management at Herman Miller. *Human Resource Management*, *38*, 303–308; Savino, D. M. (2016). Assessing the effectiveness of outsourcing human resources recruiting. *American Journal of Management*, *16*, 17–22; Wang, G. & Spitzer, D. (2005). Human resource development. *Advances in Developing Human Resources*, *7*, 5–15.
11 Capelli, P. (2008). Talent management for the twenty-first century. *Harvard Business Review*, March, 74–81; Ulrich, D. & Lake, D. (1990). *Organizational capability*. New York: John Wiley.
12 Capelli (2008).
13 Bonder, A., Bouchard, C. & Bellemare, G. (2011). Competency-based management: An integrated approach to human resource management in the Canadian public sector. *Public Personnel Management*, *40*, 1–10; Ulrich & Lake (1990).
14 Ulrich & Lake (1990).
15 Nicholson, N. (1996). Career systems in crisis: Change and opportunity in the information age. *Academy of Management Executive*, *10*, 40–51.
16 Holt, D. J. (2006). Redeployment. In Greenhaus, J. H. & Callanan, G. A. (Eds.), *Encyclopedia of career development* (pp. 679–681). Thousand Oaks, CA: Sage.
17 Wanous, J. P. (2006). Realistic recruitment. In Greenhaus, J. H. & Callanan, G. A. (Eds.), *Encyclopedia of career development* (pp. 672–675). Thousand Oaks, CA: Sage.
18 Retrieved from www.pwc.com/us/en/careers/campus/programs-events/explore.html; www.vanguardjobs.com/students-recent-graduates/explore/.
19 Retrieved from www.vanguardjobs.com/students-recent-graduates/explore/; www.vanguardjobs.com/students-recent-graduates/internships/; www.vanguardjobs.com/students-recent-graduates/leadership-development-programs-2/.
20 Retrieved from http://news.efinancialcareers.com/us-en/222184/j-p-morgan-interview-questions-the-definitive-list/, www.businessinsider.com/microsoft-interview-questions-2015-10/#why-are-manholes-round-software-development-engineer-candidate-7,www.businessinsider.com/15-google-interview-questions-that-used-to-make-geniuses-feel-dumb-2012–11#how-much-should-you-charge-to-wash-all-the-windows-in-seattle-2.
21 Deveney, G. (2015, January 28). The pros and cons of employee referrals. Retrieved from www.beyond.com/articles/the-pros-and-cons-of-employee-referrals-16593-article.; Papandrea, D. (2015, January 8). The pros and cons of employee referrals. Retrieved from www.findtherightjob.com/employer/pros-cons-employee-referrals.; Reddy, K. (2015, April 23). 10 Advantages and disadvantages of employee referrals. Retrieved from http://content.wisestep.com/advantages-and-disadvantages-of-employee-referrals.
22 Baur, J. E., Buckley, M. R., Bagdasarov, Z. & Dharmasiri, A. S. (2014). A historical approach to realistic job previews. *Journal of Management History*, *20*, 200–223; Billsberry, J. (2007). *Experiencing recruitment and selection*. Hoboken, NJ: Wiley & Sons; Ganzach, Y., Pazy, A., Ohayun, Y. & Brainin, E. (2002). Social exchange and organizational commitment: Decision-making training for the job choice as an alternative to the realistic job preview. *Personnel Psychology*, *55*, 613–637; Thorsteinson, T. J., Palmer, E. M., Wulff, C. & Anderson, A. (2004). Too good to be true? Using realism to enhance applicant attraction. *Journal of Business and Psychology*, *19*, 125–137.
23 Strauss, K. (2016, February 24). The 12 best internships for 2016. Retrieved from www.forbes.com/sites/karstenstrauss/2016/02/24/the-12-best-internships-for-2016/3/#361e21952ccc.; Retrieved from www.aetna.com/about-us/student-programs/undergraduate-summer-internships.html, www.allstate.com/careers/students-and-new-grads.aspx, www.boeing.com/careers/college/business-internships.page, http://us.pgcareers.com/students/internships-co-ops/, www.bcg.com/en-us/careers/path/internships/default1.aspx, and https://corporate.kohls.com/internship-program-2016.

24 Retrieved from www.usnews.com/education/best-colleges/articles/2015/03/31/understand-the-differences-between-a-co-op-internship.
25 Retrieved from http://drexel.edu/scdc/co-op/undergraduate.
26 Retrieved from http://drexel.edu/undergrad/co-op/overview/, http://drexel.edu/difference/co-op/, http://drexel.edu/scdc/co-op/undergraduate/fastfacts.
27 Christensen (2006).
28 Paré, G. & Tremblay, M. (2007). The influence of high-involvement human resources practices, procedural justice, organizational commitment, and citizenship behaviors on information technology professionals' turnover intentions. *Group & Organization Management*, *32*, 326–357; Yang, Y. C. (2012). High-involvement human resource practices, affective commitment, and organizational citizenship. *The Service Industries Journal*, *32*, 1209–1227.
29 Retrieved from http://elearningmind.com/the-corporate-university-shift.
30 Retrieved from www.iadl.org.uk/Article30.htm.
31 Keeping it on the company campus (2015, May 16). Retrieved from www.economist.com/news/business/21651217-more-firms-have-set-up-their-own-corporate-universities-they-have-become-less-willing-pay.
32 Retrieved from www.myboeingtraining.com/, www.myboeingtraining.com/PilotDevelopment-Program.aspx#, and www.boeing.com/careers/life-at-boeing.
33 Retrieved from www.eleapsoftware.com/spotlight-on-boeing-employee-training/, www.3m.com/3M/en_US/sustainability-report/global-challenges/education-and-development.
34 Retrieved from http://corporate.mcdonalds.com/mcd/corporate_careers/training_and_development/hamburger_university.html, and http://corporate.mcdonalds.com/mcd/corporate_careers/training_and_development/hamburger_university/our_curriculum.
35 Rhéaume, L. & Gardoni, M. (2015). The challenges facing corporate universities in dealing with open innovation. *Journal of Workplace Learning*, *27*, 315–328.
36 Fender, C. M. (2006). On-the-job training. In Greenhaus, J. H. & Callanan, G. A. (Eds.), *Encyclopedia of career development* (pp. 571–572). Thousand Oaks, CA: Sage; Rowold, J. & Kauffeld, S. (2009). Effects of career-related continuous learning on competencies. *Personnel Review*, *38*, 90–101.
37 Bernthal, P. & Wellins, R. (2006). Trends in leader development and succession. *Human Resource Planning*, *29*, 31–41.
38 Retrieved from www.eleapsoftware.com/spotlight-on-boeing-employee-training.
39 The Career Development Program. Air Products and Chemicals, Inc. Retrieved from www.airproducts.com/Careers/NorthAmerica/UniversityRecruiting/Welcome.; Retrieved from www.airproducts.com/Careers/students-and-recent-university-graduates/us-region/career-development-program.aspx.
40 Retrieved from www.airproducts.com/Careers/career-paths/career-development-program.aspx.
41 Connellan, T. (2007). *Inside the Magic Kingdom: Seven keys to Disney's success*. Austin, TX: Bard Press; Heise, S. (1994). Disney approach to managing. *Executive Excellence*, *11*, 18–20; Retrieved from http://cp.disneycareers.com/en/onboarding/fl/working-here/disney-traditions.
42 Middaugh, D. J., Grissom, N. & Satkowski, T. (2008). Goofy management: Taking the magic to the workplace. *Medsurg Nursing*, *17*, 131–132.
43 Cirilo, R. & Kleiner, B. H. (2003). How to orient employees into new positions successfully. *Management Research News*, *26*, 16–26.
44 Retrieved from www.aramark.com/about-us/our-people.
45 Retrieved from www.aramark.com/students.
46 Derr, C. B. (2006). Succession planning. In Greenhaus, J. H. & Callanan, G. A. (Eds.), *Encyclopedia of career development* (pp. 785–789). Thousand Oaks, CA: Sage.
47 Ibid.
48 Retrieved from www.lockheedmartinjobs.com/leadership-development-program.aspx.
49 Hills, A. (2009). Succession planning—or smart talent management? *Industrial and Commercial Training*, *41*, 3–8.
50 Groysberg, B., Nanda, A. & Nohria, N. (2004). The risky business of hiring stars. *Harvard Business Review*, *82*, 92–100; Hills (2009).
51 Briscoe, J. R. & Derr, C. B. (2003). *The roundabout model: A flexible approach to managing leadership development*. Paper presented at the Academy of Management meeting, August, Seattle, WA.
52 Chalkley, L. (2013). Do as I say, not as I do! In Ward, D. L., Tripp, R. & Maki, B. (Eds.), *Positioned: Strategic workforce planning that gets the right person in the right job* (pp. 128–134). New York: AMACO.
53 Abby, S. K., Schumacher, E. J., Dellifraine, J., Clement, D., Hall, R., O'Connor, S., Haiyan, Q., Shewchuk, R. & Stefl, M. (2016). Competency development and validation: An update of the collaborative leadership model. *The Journal of Health Administration Education*, *33*, 73–93; Bird, A. (1994). Careers as repositories of knowledge: A new perspective on boundaryless careers.

Journal of Organizational Behavior, *15*, 325–344; Hills (2009); Sharma, R. & Bhatnagar, J. (2009). Talent management—competency development: Key to global leadership. *Industrial and Commercial Training*, *41*, 118–132.
54 Retrieved from http://careerframework.ubc.ca/competencies/competency-development-guide/ and http://hrweb.mit.edu/performance/pdr/competencies.
55 Retrieved from http://careerframework.ubc.ca/competencies/competency-development-guide.
56 Retrieved from http://hrweb.mit.edu/performance/pdr/competencies.
57 Arnone, M. (2006). Executive coaching. In Greenhaus, J. H. & Callanan, G. A. (Eds.), *Encyclopedia of career development* (pp. 302–304). Thousand Oaks, CA: Sage.
58 Ellinger, A. D., Ellinger, A. E. & Keller, S. B. (2003). Supervisory coaching behavior, employee satisfaction, and warehouse employee performance: A dyadic perspective in the distribution industry. *Human Resource Development Quarterly*, *14*, 435–458.
59 Boyatzis, R. E., Smith, M. L. & Blaize, N. (2006). Developing sustainable leaders through coaching and compassion. *Academy of Management Learning & Education*, *5*, 8–24.
60 Murthy, S., Dingman, M. E. & Mensch, K. G. (2011). Experiential leader development at the United States Marine Corps Intelligence: A pilot study evaluation. *Organization Development Journal*, *29*, 23–38.
61 Christensen (2006); Lawler, E. E., III & Boudreau, J. W. (2012). *Effective human resource management: A global analysis*. Stanford, CA: Stanford University Press.
62 Christensen (2006).
63 O'Boyle, I. (2013). Traditional performance appraisal versus 360-degree feedback. *Training & Management Development Methods*, *27*, 201–207; Panda, S. & Sahoo, C. K. (2015). Larsen & Toubro strides out strategically on talent management. *Human Resource Management International Digest*, *23*(6), 5–8; Prochaska, S. (2006). Three-Hundred-Sixty-Degree (360°) Evaluation. In Greenhaus, J. H. & Callanan, G. A. (Eds.), *Encyclopedia of career development* (pp. 507–572). Thousand Oaks, CA: Sage.
64 Levy, P. E. (2010). *Industrial/Organizational psychology: Understanding the workplace*. New York: Worth Publishers.
65 Atwater, L. E., Brett, J. F. & Charles, A. C. (2007). Multisource feedback: Lessons learned and implications for practice. *Human Resource Management*, *46*, 285–307; Levy (2010); Newbold, C. (2008). 360-degree appraisals are now a classic: Good preparation and execution are the keys to success. *Human Resource Management International Digest*, *16*, 38–40.
66 Atwater, L. E. & Brett, J. F. (2006). 360-Degree feedback to leaders: Does it relate to changes in employee attitudes? *Group & Organization Management*, *31*, 578–600; Atwater et al. (2007); O'Boyle (2013); Panda & Sahoo (2015).
67 Lengnick-Hall, M. L. (2006). Human resource information systems (HRIS). In Greenhaus, J. H. & Callanan, G. A. (Eds.), *Encyclopedia of career development* (pp. 362–366). Thousand Oaks, CA: Sage.
68 Beckers, A. M. & Bsat, M. Z. (2002). A DSS classification model for research in human resource information systems. *Information Systems Management*, *19*, 41–50; Dery, K., Grant, D. & Wiblen, S. (2009). Human resource information systems: Replacing or enhancing HRM, 15th World Congress of the International Industrial Relations Association (IIRA): 'The New World of Work, Organisations and Employment', Sydney, Australia, August 27; Shiri, S. (2012). Effectiveness of human resource information system on HR functions of the organization—a cross sectional study. *US-China Education Review*, *9*, 830–839; Wiblen, S. L., Grant, D. & Dery, K. (2010). Transitioning to a new HRIS: The reshaping of human resources and information technology talent. *Journal of Electronic Commerce Research*, *11*, 251–267.
69 Christensen (2006).
70 This discussion is based on material from Greenhaus, J. H. & Powell, G. N. (2017). *Making work and family work: From hard choices to smart choices*. New York: Routledge.
71 Perri, D. (2006). Morale. In Greenhaus, J. H. & Callanan, G. A. (Eds.), *Encyclopedia of career development* (pp. 510–511). Thousand Oaks, CA: Sage.
72 Iverson, R. D. & Zatzick, C. D. (2011). The effects of downsizing on labor productivity: The value of showing consideration for employees' morale and welfare in high-performance work systems. *Human Resource Management*, *50*, 29–44.
73 Perri (2006).

15 Closing Thoughts on Career Management

In this book, we have shown how individuals face constant change as they move through the course of their careers. These changes come from a variety of sources. From the personal side, there are a number of factors that influence our careers. Just the process of aging produces changes in our perspectives regarding our careers. For example, the concerns of a 25-year-old are vastly different from those of a 65-year-old. In addition, our interests, values, and lifestyle preferences can, and oftentimes do, go through modifications as we encounter various life experiences and events. Beyond aging, behavioral scientists point to a number of changes in individual attitudes, behaviors, and coping mechanisms that have occurred over the past several decades. Some of these changes reflect cultural shifts in beliefs, whereas others are reactions to social forces. Other changes are underscored by the globalization of our world, and our ability to communicate across it at practically any time and place due to advances in technology. One of the most significant cultural changes affecting individuals is the heightened challenge of managing commitments to work *and* other important parts of life. Many dual-earner couples face dilemmas in juggling work and nonwork responsibilities, and by necessity, members of these relationships must learn to balance two careers as well as extensive family responsibilities.

Individuals also must continue to adapt to the new work environment. Significant changes have occurred both in the way people are employed and in the types of jobs they hold.[1] The rise of the "gig" economy and nonpermanent work arrangements throughout much of the industrialized world has altered the relationship between employer and employee for large numbers of workers, which has, in turn, created greater uncertainty in career management.[2] In this new environment, standard jobs, with traditionally higher degrees of stability and predictability, have been replaced on a broad scale by evolving work engagements that require flexibility and adaptability on the part of the employee.

The alterations in work organizations and in their approaches to staffing directly challenge the career competencies of affected workers. The result has been that the playing field for the individual managing his or her career has changed. As we discussed in Chapter 2 and throughout this book, this ever-changing work environment has dictated that individuals be "boundaryless" and "protean" in the way they manage their careers. Individuals need to be proactive in the acquisition of the career competencies of knowing-why (self-identity), knowing-how (portable job-related skills and career-related knowledge), and knowing-whom (broad networks of relationships). These competencies should help individuals navigate their increasingly uncertain careers to achieve personally meaningful goals and values.[3]

While organizations have been shifting their levels of and approaches to staffing, the workforce itself has seen dramatic changes over the past several decades. For example, the workforce is becoming more diverse and globally focused, and well-run organizations recognize the need to manage this diversity effectively. Workforce diversity and globalization also challenge employees to understand and appreciate the similarities and differences between themselves and their co-workers and to work cooperatively with others who may have different perspectives. Future career achievements could well depend on an employee's ability to thrive in a multicultural environment.

Looking to the Future

It is difficult to predict with any certainty how the process of career management will evolve in the future. As we have discussed throughout this book, the shifting landscape of work and the constant increases in nonwork pressures bring greater uncertainty into the process. Several environmental factors that are influencing career management currently will also present challenges in the future. For example, advancements in technology will affect the types and number of jobs that need to be filled. The application of new technology has the power to wipe out certain occupations while creating new ones. In addition, continuing upgrades in communications technology will make it easier for many workers to be "untethered" to a physical work location, but also will put pressure on them to become electronically tethered to their jobs seven days a week, 24 hours a day in response to extensive organizational demands, both domestic and global.

Demographic shifts, primarily the aging and retirement of the baby boom generation, will have a profound impact on the future supply of labor. As a consequence, younger workers are likely to have greater career opportunities over the next three decades as organizations look for ways to fill open positions. At the same time, older workers will need to assess their career options regarding alternative work situations, part-time employment, and retirement.

Responding to economic conditions and increased global competition, organizations will continue to make changes in their structures and staffing approaches, including the increased use of team-based structures, the deployment of a higher proportion of contract and contingent workers, and a willingness to empower all employees to make data-based decisions in response to work demands. The further globalization of business will create new career opportunities on a worldwide basis, with increased prospects either for an expatriation assignment or a permanent relocation to a host country. All forms of international careers will require employees to be more aware of, and adaptable to, foreign cultures and expectations.

Finally, it is likely that nonwork demands will continue at a high level for the majority of workers. Family commitments, community involvement, and the likelihood of being part of a dual-earner relationship will challenge workers to balance different parts of their lives. As we discussed throughout this book, individuals need to stay vigilant in their career management approaches to respond to these future opportunities, challenges, and demands. Presented below are our recommendations for effective career management, both in the present and in the future.

Effective Career Management

Regardless of the current and future challenges and uncertainties, career management as a problem-solving process does not really change in fundamental form. Information, insight, goals, plans, and feedback are essential at all career stages and for all generations of employees. Reflecting this view, we offer below our thoughts on several career issues that transcend a particular time or place.

First, effective career management requires individual initiative—an active, probing approach to work and life. It requires inquisitiveness about oneself and the world and a willingness to take action and appropriate risks. Career management is based on the belief that people can exert control over significant portions of their lives. Although total control is impossible, the willingness to explore, set goals, and develop and implement plans can make a difference in the quality of one's career and one's life. In this sense, it is critically important that one establish a clear self-identity. Indeed, the primary building block for career success and fulfillment is the need for one's work to be consistent with one's self-identity. This maxim is even more relevant in the current environment of job instability, where one's personal needs can easily be overlooked. Establishment of a clear self-identity normally involves a process of self-exploration where individuals use standard assessment tools in conjunction with introspection, experimentation, and feedback from trusted others in their professional and social networks to understand better their interests, talents, and lifestyle preferences.

Second, people must appreciate the relationship between their work and nonwork lives. Career management efforts should be based on an awareness of life goals, not just career goals. Career goals and achievements affect (and are affected by) participation in family, community, leisure, and self-development spheres of life. Even if people cannot "have it all," they can decide what they want and what trade-offs they are willing to make. Understanding the interplay between work and nonwork roles and managing this delicate balance with the assistance of other people are essential ingredients of career and life management.

Third, people must avoid succumbing to other people's definition of success for their lives. Many people pursue a specific career path to satisfy other people—parents, professors, friends, bosses, spouses, or perhaps some general notion of what one "should" do. Happiness and fulfillment, however, depend on satisfying one's own values and aspirations, not other people's. Much of the recent popularity of entrepreneurial careers can be traced to individuals pursuing their own career interests, that is, being one's own man or woman. Nonetheless, this book has not advocated a hedonistic "me" attitude toward career management. Sacrifices and compromises are necessary if people are to live in a global world, share their lives with other people, and become committed to a cause, a relationship, a community, or an organization. Taking other people's or institutions' needs into account and trying to achieve mutually acceptable and beneficial solutions to career dilemmas are healthy actions. However, continually trying to please others at the expense of oneself can be destructive to one's sense of well-being.

Fourth, employees are responsible for attaining (and maintaining) a portfolio of skills that is transferable to various work situations and employers. Individuals should ensure that they have the competitive skills to improve their chances of finding a new position when it is needed. In this sense, the individual should possess a set of portable competencies that can be applied in any number of organizations or work settings.

Related to the idea of a portable set of skills is the recommendation that individuals invest in lifelong learning to keep their skills relevant and thereby transferable to other jobs and organizations.[4] Continuous learning can take many forms, and can positively affect future performance. One category would involve pursuing additional schooling; another could include seeking out assignments that allow new competencies to be learned. A commitment to learning might also involve staying abreast of developments within one's current organization as well as other firms in the industry.

Finally, career management is not the exclusive domain of the elite. It does not belong only to the top executive, the upwardly mobile, the affluent, or the entrepreneur. Career management is for everyone who wants to enhance the quality of his or her life. Career management is not always easy, but, to paraphrase an old saying, nothing important ever is. Hopefully, this book has shown that effective career management is possible for people who are ready to take on the challenge.

At its core, career management is a personal process. Although organizational programs and practices can aid it immeasurably, only individuals, with the help of family members, friends, and colleagues, can develop insight into themselves and their environment, become committed to career goals and strategies, and accurately appraise the course of their careers and make necessary adjustments. Nothing can ever replace the commitment of the individual to the active management of his or her own career.

Career Management *for Life*: Work–Life Implications from Chapter 15

- One of the most significant challenges facing contemporary employees is managing their commitment to work *and* to other important parts of their life.
- Advanced communications technology that electronically tethers employees to their jobs 24/7 requires individuals to control the extent to which they allow work to intrude into other parts of their life.
- Career management efforts should be based on an awareness of life goals, not just career goals, and individuals must decide what they want in different parts of life and what trade-offs, if any, they are willing to make.
- Career management is an ongoing process that is relevant at all stages of life.

Assignment

It is difficult to predict what the future holds for career management. While recognizing the uncertainties, in this assignment you are asked to try to predict the future challenges that you will face as you go through the process of career management. Specifically, write a scenario of the future that depicts your view of how the work world will look in a decade. You should describe the related implications for your career and your organization. Your narrative could address such issues as the new career competencies you will need for achieving career success in the future, the role new technologies might play in helping you manage your career, the techniques that might be available to achieve better balance between your work and other parts of life, the effects on your career of continued international integration of work organizations and cultures, the career assistance strategies that organizations will use to help you grow in your career, and the degree to which you and your employers will see loyalty as playing a role in your respective decisions. Try to be as creative as possible in making your predictions about the future.

Notes

1 Greenhaus, J. H., Callanan, G. A. & DiRenzo, M. S. (2008). A boundaryless perspective on careers. In Barling, J. & Cooper, C. L. (Eds.), *The Sage handbook of organizational behavior*, Volume 1 (pp. 277–299). Thousand Oaks, CA: Sage.

2 Callanan, G. A., Perri, D. F. & Tomkowicz, S. M. (2017). Career management in uncertain times: Challenges and opportunities. *Career Development Quarterly*, *65*, 353–365.

3 Eby, L. T., Butts, M. & Lockwood, A. (2003). Predictors of success in the era of the boundaryless career. *Journal of Organizational Behavior*, *24*, 689–708; Jokinen, T., Brewster, C. & Suutari, V. (2008). Career capital during international work experiences: Contrasting self-initiated expatriate experiences and assigned expatriation. *The International Journal of Human Resource Management*, *19*, 979–998; Tams, S. & Arthur, M. B. (2006). Boundaryless career. In Greenhaus, J. H. & Callanan, G. A. (Eds.), *Encyclopedia of career development* (pp. 44–49). Thousand Oaks, CA: Sage.

4 Bierema, L. L. (2006). Lifelong learning. In Greenhaus, J. H. & Callanan, G. A. (Eds.), *Encyclopedia of career development* (pp. 473–475). Thousand Oaks, CA: Sage; Rowold, J., Hochholdinger, S. & Schilling, J. (2008). Effects of career-related continuous learning: A case study. *The Learning Organization*, *15*, 45–57; Rowold, J. & Kauffeld, S. (2008). Effects of career-related continuous learning on competencies. *Personnel Review*, *38*, 90–101.

Name Index

Subject Index